Praise for Beyo

"*Beyond Physicalism* articulates a co the distorted 'all or nothing' dichotomy between narrow-minded religious fundamentalisms and an equally dogmatic and rigid scientism."

—**G. William Barnard**, professor of Religious Studies, Southern Methodist University

"*Beyond Physicalism* lays several stones for the foundation of a new world-view. No book has gone further toward reconciling science and spirituality."

—**William Eastman**, former Director of SUNY Press

"This book offers a third way, reconciling science and spirituality without diluting either. Robust and evidence based, this work by highly respected scholars and scientists demolishes orthodoxies right and left, allowing the reader a way forward past the Scylla and Charybdis of religious and scientific fundamentalisms."

—**David J. Hufford**, professor emeritus, Penn State College of Medicine

"*Beyond Physicalism* is much more than a book. It is the intimate expression of a decade and a half of critical but collegial conversations between established scientists and professional humanists around some of the most important but still unsettled questions facing humanity: those involving the nature of mind or consciousness—that is, the nature of *us*."

—**Jeffrey J. Kripal**, J. Newton Rayzor Professor of Religious Studies, Rice University

"Some of the philosophical problems that occupied William James longest and deepest, along with solutions he thought most promising, have literally been written out of history. This volume presents the first serious collective attempt since James' death to revive his project. Its chapters are characterized by an intellectual ethos reminiscent of the 'father' of modern American psychology himself: sympathetic open-mindedness made fruitful through disciplined, calm and penetrating rigor."

—**Andreas Sommer**, junior research fellow in History and Philosophy of Science, Churchill College, University of Cambridge

"Kelly and colleagues' first book, *Irreducible Mind*, carefully documented research supporting the notion that consciousness is not simply a product of neural activity. This second book, *Beyond Physicalism*, brings together key scholars in the areas of quantum physics, psychology, Asian philosophy and mysticism to thoughtfully explore how mystical and psi experiences can fit into an expanded scientific worldview."

—**Marjorie Woollacott**, professor, Department of Human Physiology and Institute of Neuroscience, University of Oregon

BEYOND PHYSICALISM

BEYOND PHYSICALISM

Toward Reconciliation of Science and Spirituality

Edited by Edward F. Kelly, Adam Crabtree, and Paul Marshall

ROWMAN & LITTLEFIELD
Lanham • Boulder • New York • London

Published by Rowman & Littlefield
A wholly owned subsidiary of The Rowman & Littlefield Publishing Group, Inc.
4501 Forbes Boulevard, Suite 200, Lanham, Maryland 20706
www.rowman.com

Unit A, Whitacre Mews, 26-34 Stannary Street, London SE11 4AB

British Library Cataloguing in Publication Information Available

Library of Congress Cataloging-in-Publication Data

Beyond physicalism : toward reconciliation of science and spirituality / edited by Edward F. Kelly,
Adam Crabtree, and Paul Marshall.
pages cm
Includes bibliographical references and index.
ISBN 978-1-4422-3238-9 (cloth : alk. paper)—ISBN 978-1-5381-2596-0 (paperback)—ISBN 978-1-
4422-3240-2 (electronic)
1. Religion and science. I. Kelly, Edward F., editor. II. Crabtree, Adam, editor. III. Marshall, Paul
(Paul David), editor.
BL241.B445 2015
201'.65—dc23
2014039921

♾™ The paper used in this publication meets the minimum requirements of
American National Standard for Information Sciences Permanence of Paper for
Printed Library Materials, ANSI/NISO Z39.48-1992.

Printed in the United States of America

CONTENTS

PREFACE AND ACKNOWLEDGMENTS

The rise of modern science has brought with it increasing acceptance among intellectual elites of a picture of reality that conflicts sharply both with everyday human experience and with beliefs widely shared among the world's great cultural traditions. A particularly stark but influential early statement of the emerging picture came from philosopher Bertrand Russell:

> That Man is the product of causes which had no prevision of the end they were achieving; that his origin, his growth, his hopes and fears, his loves and his beliefs, are but the outcome of accidental collocations of atoms; that no fire, no heroism, no intensity of thought and feeling, can preserve an individual life beyond the grave; that all the labours of the ages, all the devotion, all the inspiration, all the noonday brightness of human genius, are destined to extinction in the vast death of the solar system, and that the whole temple of Man's achievement must inevitably be buried beneath the débris of a universe in ruins—all these things, if not quite beyond dispute, are yet so nearly certain, that no philosophy which rejects them can hope to stand. Only within the scaffolding of these truths, only on the firm foundation of unyielding despair, can the soul's habitation henceforth be safely built. ("The Free Man's Worship," 1903)

There can be no doubt that this bleak vision continues to dominate mainstream scientific thinking and has contributed to the "disenchantment" of the modern world with its multifarious attendant ills. Prominent recent spokesmen include, for example, Nobel prize winners such as theoretical

physicist Steven Weinberg, for whom "the more the universe seems comprehensible, the more it also seems pointless," and physicist-turned-
neurobiologist Francis Crick, whose "astonishing hypothesis" declares
that " 'You,' your joys and your sorrows, your memories and your ambi-
tions, your sense of personal identity and free will, are in fact no more
than the behavior of a vast assembly of nerve cells and their associated
molecules. As Lewis Carroll's Alice might have phrased it: 'You're nothing but a pack of neurons.' "

Overt conflict between science and religion has erupted sporadically
since the first stirrings of science centuries ago, and recent years have
witnessed a series of heavily publicized attacks on nearly all things religious by well-meaning defenders of Enlightenment-style rationalism. Such
persons clearly regard themselves, and current mainstream science itself,
as reliably marshaling the intellectual virtues of reason and objectivity
against retreating forces of irrational authority and superstition. For them
the truth of the picture sketched above has been demonstrated beyond
reasonable doubt, and to think anything different is necessarily to abandon centuries of scientific progress, release the black flood of occultism,
and revert to primitive supernaturalist beliefs characteristic of bygone
times.

Contributors to the present volume share a very different view. We
believe it takes astonishing hubris to dismiss en masse the collective
experience and wisdom of a large proportion of our forebears, including
persons widely recognized as pillars of all human civilization, and we are
united in believing that the single most important task confronting all of
modernity is that of *meaningful* reconciliation of science and religion. We
emphatically reject, moreover, the idea of simply exiling these humanly
vital subjects to independent "magisteria" where they can go their separate ways as a means to uneasy truce, as originally decreed by Descartes
and recently suggested again by Stephen Jay Gould.

Rather, we believe that emerging developments within science itself
are leading inexorably in the direction of an expanded scientific understanding of nature, one that can accommodate realities of a "spiritual"
sort while also rejecting rationally untenable "overbeliefs" of the sorts
targeted by critics of the world's institutional religions. We advocate no
specific religious ideology, and we aspire to remain anchored in science
while expanding its horizons. As explained in greater detail in the pages
that follow, we are attempting in this way to find a middle path between

the excessively polarized fundamentalisms—religious *and* scientific—
that have so far dominated public discourse.

Our book itself is the latest product of a fifteen-year collaboration
involving an uncommonly diverse group of participants including scientists, scholars of religion, philosophers, and historians, among others.
Brought together under the auspices of Esalen Institute's Center for Theory and Research (CTR) by its guiding spirit, Michael Murphy, we are in
many ways representative of the sorts of people we view as our primary
target audience—scientifically minded, intelligent adults with broad
interests, who regard themselves as "spiritual" but not "religious" in any
conventional sense, and who are skeptical of the mainstream scientific
vision sketched above but equally wary of uncritical embrace of any of
the world's major religious systems with their often conflicting beliefs
and decidedly mixed historical records.

It took a long time and a lot of hard work for us to overcome sufficiently for practical purposes the deep stylistic and ideological differences that typically impede communication between scientific and humanistic scholars—the "two cultures," in the terminology of C. P.
Snow—and we have sometimes joked about our task being rather like
that of building the transcontinental railroad. Nonetheless, we think it will
be evident to most readers that the resulting book is more compound than
mixture and manifests a surprising degree of coherence given the extreme
diversity of its subject matter. We believe it can provide sustenance to
those who, like ourselves, hunger for a more uplifting and intellectually
satisfying worldview that draws upon the best in both science *and* religion.

Many persons have contributed to our discussions over the years, and
our membership has changed as we adapted to our evolving challenges by
recruiting relevant sorts of targeted professional expertise. Our current
core group includes, in addition to the chapter authors identified below,
Bill Barnard, Deb Frost, Bruce Greyson, David Hufford, Emily Kelly,
Jeff Kripal, Gary Owens, Bob Rosenberg, Charles Tart, Jim Tucker, and
Sam Yau. We thank all those who have read and commented on some or
all of the chapters: these include Eben Alexander, Ross Dunseath, Bill
Eastman, Jim Gilchrist, James Keaten, Fritz Klein, Jim Lenz, Jared Lin-
dahl, Rafael Locke, Ohkado Masayuki, Binita Mehta, Andreas Sommer,
and Vik Vad. Special thanks to John Cleese, Deb Frost, Gary Owens, and
the Institute of Noetic Sciences for financial support of the project at

various critical times, and to Steve Dinan and Frank Poletti for efficient organization and administration of our many meetings. Most of those meetings took place, appropriately, in the unique ambience provided by Esalen's CTR community, operating as it does outside conventional academic boundaries, perched on a cliff overlooking the Pacific Ocean in Big Sur.

We would also like to thank Stanley Plotnick, Jon Sisk, and their staff at Rowman & Littlefield for their continued interest in our project, which began with the publication of *Irreducible Mind*, to which the present book is a companion volume. Rowman & Littlefield also kindly granted permission for substantial excerpts from *Irreducible Mind* to be made available on Esalen Institute's CTR website, as part of a collection of supplemental materials for the present book (we thank Bob Rosenberg for setting up this facility, and also for compiling the index). We are also grateful to the Alister Hardy Trust and the Alister Hardy Religious Experience Research Centre, University of Wales Trinity Saint David, Lampeter, UK, for permission to quote from their archive of spiritual accounts in Chapter 2. We thank Imprint Academic for permission to reproduce in Chapter 6 some parts of Harald Atmanspacher's article "Dual-aspect monism à la Pauli and Jung," published in 2012 in the *Journal of Consciousness Studies*, *19*(9–10), 96–120. The two figures in Chapter 11 are based on diagrams originally published in 2005 in Paul Marshall, *Mystical Encounters with the Natural World*, modified and included in the present volume by permission of Oxford University Press. Michael Murphy's "The Emergence of Evolutionary Panentheism" was published in 2014 in Loriliai Biernacki and Philip Clayton (Eds.), *Panentheism across the World's Traditions* (Chapter 9, pp. 177–199), and a modified version is included here by permission of Oxford University Press, USA.

Above all, we again thank Michael Murphy for initially conceiving this project, for bringing us together in the spectacularly stimulating environment of Esalen, and for his apparently limitless reserves of comradeship, wit, and wisdom.

INTRODUCTION

Science and Spirituality at a Crossroads

Edward F. Kelly

Round about the accredited and orderly facts of every science there ever floats a sort of dust-cloud of exceptional observations, of occurrences minute and irregular and seldom met with, which it always proves more easy to ignore than to attend to. . . . Any one will renovate his science who will steadily look after the irregular phenomena. And when the science is renewed, its new formulas often have more of the voice of the exceptions in them than of what were supposed to be the rules.

—William James, "What Psychical Research Has Accomplished"[1]

The rejection of any source of evidence is always treason to that ultimate rationalism which urges forward science and philosophy alike.

—A. N. Whitehead, *The Function of Reason*[2]

The unusual character of this book should already be evident from its title, our preface, and the epigraphs above. The purpose of this introduction is to explain in greater detail what the book is all about, and to provide a brief description of its content.

Our point of departure is the currently prevailing scientific worldview, especially in its bearing on brain/mind relations. Most contemporary psychologists, neuroscientists, and philosophers of mind, as well as scientists in general, subscribe explicitly or implicitly to some version of ontological "physicalism," the modern philosophical descendant of the "materialism" of previous centuries. Physicalist conceptions of human mind and personality vary significantly in nuance and detail but are fundamentally alike insofar as they conflict sharply with traditional and common-sense notions and run instead along roughly the following lines:

In the end all facts are determined by physical facts alone, and we human beings are thus nothing more than extremely complicated biological machines. Everything we are and do is explainable, at least in principle, in terms of our physics, chemistry, and biology—ultimately, that is, in terms of local interactions among self-existent bits of matter moving in accordance with mathematical laws under the influence of fields of force. Some of what we know, and the substrate of our general capacities to learn more, are built in genetically as complex resultants of biological evolution. Everything else comes to us directly or indirectly by way of our sensory surfaces, through energetic exchanges with the environment of types already largely understood. All aspects of mind and consciousness are generated by, or supervenient upon, or in some mysterious way identical with, neurophysiological processes occurring in the brain. We are "meat computers" in Marvin Minsky's chilling phrase, or "moist robots" in its Dilbert parody. Mental causation, free will, and the self are mere illusions, by-products of the grinding of our neural machinery. And of course since mind and personality are entirely products of our bodily machinery, they are necessarily extinguished, totally and finally, by the demise and dissolution of the body.

Views of this sort hold sway over a great majority of contemporary scientists, and mass-media science reporters routinely pass them along without question or hesitation to the public at large. They seem to most observers to be supported by mountains of evidence. Nevertheless, the authors of this book are united in the conviction that such pictures are not only seriously incomplete—which few if any would deny—but at a number of critical points demonstrably *incorrect*.

First some history: our group came into being in 1998 under the auspices of Esalen Institute's Center for Theory and Research, focused initially on the considerable but still little-known empirical evidence for the possibility of postmortem survival (see following chapter; parenthetically, this gave rise to our nickname—"Sursem," from "survival seminar"). We spent our first two meetings presenting and discussing the existing evidence for survival and surveying some possible alternatives to physicalism, and by the end of the second meeting a concrete plan of action had emerged. We saw clearly that our work needed to proceed in two overlapping stages: first, to assemble in one place the main lines of evidence demonstrating the empirical inadequacy of conventional physicalism; second, and even more challenging, to try to find some better conceptual framework to take its place.

An ideal vehicle for the first stage was available in the form of the extraordinary magnum opus of F. W. H. Myers, entitled *Human Personality and Its Survival of Bodily Death*, published in 1903. Myers, one of the founders in 1882 of the Society for Psychical Research, had systematically collected evidence of human capacities that resist explanation in conventional materialist terms, and on that basis had advanced an expanded model of human mind and consciousness that was greatly admired by many leading contemporaries including William James. We were also aware that James himself had explicitly applied this model to his psychological studies of *The Varieties of Religious Experience* (1902), and that he had gone on to explore possible further extensions in his late metaphysical work *A Pluralistic Universe* (1909). We therefore decided to take advantage of the impending centennial of Myers's landmark contribution by revisiting and reevaluating it in the context of the subsequent century of relevant psychological and neurobiological research.

This turned out to be a mammoth project—far larger than we imagined at the outset—but it resulted in the publication in 2007 of *Irreducible Mind: Toward a Psychology for the 21st Century* (Kelly, Kelly, Crabtree, Gauld, Grosso, & Greyson, henceforth *IM*), an 800-page behemoth that also included on CD a complete copy of Myers's *Human Personality* itself (1,400 pages in two volumes) plus its five most significant contemporary reviews. Parenthetically, *IM* has subsequently been released in paperback without the CD, but all of that supplemental material and several other relevant scholarly resources are now freely available on the Esalen website at http://www.esalen.org/ctr. Topics addressed include (in addition to everyday phenomena such as autobiographical and semantic memory, intentionality, the qualitative features of consciousness, and indeed consciousness itself) phenomena of extreme psychophysiological influence such as stigmata and hypnotically induced blisters, prodigious forms of memory and calculation, psychological automatisms and secondary centers of consciousness, near-death and out-of-body experiences including experiences occurring under extreme physiological conditions

such as deep general anesthesia and/or cardiac arrest, genius-level creativity, and mystical-type experiences whether spontaneous, pharmacolog-
ically induced, or induced by transformative practices such as intense
meditative disciplines of one or another sort (see the following chapter
for more details).

In contrast with the prevailing *production* model of the brain/mind
relation, as described above, these "rogue" data collectively support an
alternative class of models which view the brain not as the generator of
mind and consciousness but as an organ of adaptation to the everyday
environment, selecting, focusing, channeling, and constraining the operations of a mind and consciousness inherently far greater in capacities and
scope. As Myers (1903) himself expressed it:

> There exists a more comprehensive consciousness, a profounder facul-
> ty, which for the most part remains potential only . . . but from which
> the consciousness and the faculty of earth-life are mere selections. . . .
> [N]o Self of which we can here have cognisance is in reality more than
> a fragment of a larger Self,—revealed in a fashion at once shifting and
> limited through an organism not so framed as to afford it full manifes-
> tation. (Vol. 1, pp. 12, 15)

The primary purpose of the present book is to develop this central concept in greater depth and detail.

Before moving on it is also worth pointing out that *IM* added a rich
empirical dimension to what appears to be a rising chorus of *theoretical*
dissatisfaction with physicalism as a philosophical position (for example,
Chalmers, 1996, 2002; Koons & Bealer, 2010; Nagel, 2012; Velmans,
2009), coupled with resurgent interest in formerly "deviant" philosophical views including not only interactive dualism (Baker & Goetz, 2011),
but panpsychism or panexperientialism (for example, Griffin, 1998;
Seager & Allen-Hermanson, 2013; Skrbina, 2005; Strawson et al., 2006),
neutral and dual-aspect monisms (Velmans & Nagasawa, 2012), and even
absolute idealism (Sprigge, 1983). Our cumulative sense of the philosophical situation is that we are at or very near a major inflection point in
modern intellectual history.

Physicalism in its current forms seems clearly inadequate, but what
should take its place? This is by far the harder task, and the focus of the
present theory-oriented sequel to *IM*. I emphasize again that we intend to
remain anchored in science, and that what we are trying to do is not to

overthrow science but to *expand* it to dimensions more fully commensurate with the complexity of our subject matter: in the words of Francis Bacon (1620/1960), at the dawn of modern science, "[T]he world is not to be narrowed till it will go into the understanding . . . but the understanding to be expanded and opened till it can take in the image of the world as it is in fact" (p. 276).[3] Descartes' conceptual bifurcation of reality into physical and mental parts enabled science to get on efficiently with its analysis of the physical side for several centuries, with undeniably spectacular theoretical and practical results, but now it's time to get on too, and better than we have thus far, with the humanly more vital psychological side.

A critical and unique feature of our approach to this daunting task lies in our willingness to take into consideration *all* relevant classes of data. One of our central contentions is that precisely because of its physicalist presuppositions, the currently dominant mainstream scientific approach to brain/mind issues has been seriously compromised by virtue of systematically and deliberately excluding from consideration some of the *most* important and theoretically significant categories of mental phenomena, including in particular (1) paranormal, psychic, or "psi" phenomena, and (2) "higher" or "mystical" altered states of consciousness.

With regard to psi phenomena, here I will simply say that in our collective judgment the thousands of field and laboratory studies carried out by competent scientists over the 130-plus years since the founding of the Society for Psychical Research cumulatively provide an overwhelming body of evidence—*for those who will take the trouble to study it with an open mind*—that these phenomena really do exist as facts of nature. The italicized qualifications are important, however, because public discussion is being systematically distorted at present by a small cadre of highly vocal, entrenched professional skeptics—*deniers*, really—who conspicuously lack those credentials.

The theoretical significance of psi phenomena arises from the fact that they are so unexpected—perhaps even *impossible*, although this is not entirely clear—in the context of classical physicalism. This fact by itself accounts for much of the skepticism about psi among mainstream scientists, who typically have little or no time to devote to firsthand study of the relevant literature and must depend on others for their information. It is also evident that one major obstacle if not *the* major obstacle to wider acceptance of psi is the absence at present of a conceptual framework or theory in terms of which these phenomena make sense and do not conflict with other parts of our scientific understanding of nature. For readers who wish to pursue this subject further we recommend *IM* itself, which deals fairly briefly with psi but provides many pointers into the literature via an annotated bibliography, and other recent books which focus more specifically on this topic and the debates surrounding it (for example, Carter, 2012; Radin, 2006; Tart, 2009).

The public controversy regarding psychical research is in principle mainly a *scientific* controversy, although workers professionally engaged in such research routinely suffer accusations of heresy and/or incompetence from persons for whom current scientific opinion constitutes a set of fixed beliefs to be defended at any cost. But our other scientifically "taboo" topic, mystical experience, and higher states of consciousness, is even more contentious, because it draws us into the far larger and more superheated cultural arena occupied by the ongoing public hostilities, alluded to in our Preface, between science and *religion*.[4]

Viewed from a sufficiently high altitude, the current science–religion debate here in the United States resembles a Tolkien-like mythic clash of armies, one consisting mainly of secular humanists claiming for themselves the mantle of science, and the other made up of vocal adherents of warring traditional faiths including in particular radical Islam and evangelical forms of Christianity who seem determined to cling to received religious doctrine no matter what science has to say. Both camps, interestingly, appear mostly hostile to psychical research while knowing little if anything about it.

This cartoon-style description obviously caricatures a much more complex reality, particularly in ignoring the millions of serious and open-minded persons who quietly continue practicing their faiths of origin while struggling to resolve apparent conflicts with contemporary science, but it will serve for present purposes. The point is that one enters the treacherous no-man's land between these powerful and highly polarized cultural forces, shrouded as it is with the smoke and debris of ongoing combat, only at one's peril and with considerable trepidation. More must therefore be said about why and how we are doing this, as background for the chapters to follow.

Most fundamentally, our view is that both sides are mistaken in thinking that they represent the only possible alternatives. What we are attempting to do here is to open up a third way—a tertium quid—that somehow combines an expanded science with the recognition of genuine empirical realities underlying traditional forms of religion.[5]

Turning now to the religion side itself, one striking difference between the modal Asian and Western approaches to a comprehensive description of nature lies in the Asian traditions' more overt reliance upon direct experience of powerful altered states of consciousness as the primary background for a millennia-long evolution and mutual contesting of mystically informed philosophical theologies. Our concern here is with these sorts of experiences and the associated philosophies, not with religions as social institutions characterized by discordant doctrinal particularities, and it is essential to recognize here at the outset that contemporary attacks on religion such as those noted in our Preface have been directed primarily at the latter.

We believe that a vital task of scientific modernity is to try to extract from the great mass of religious experience and philosophy whatever may be valid and useful both for theory construction and for soteriological purposes. As a working scientist I further believe, again with F. W. H. Myers, that "such an inquiry must be in the first instance a scientific, and only in the second instance a religious one. Religion, in its most permanent sense, is the adjustment of our emotions to the structure of the Universe; and what we now most need is to discover what that cosmic structure is" (1893/1961, p. 37).

The information we are looking for, however, is unlikely to be found at the level of overt religious forms or institutional histories. The public critics of religion are certainly correct in pointing out that numerous and sometimes profound doctrinal differences divide the world's major faiths. I personally cannot help but think of traditional religions in terms of the familiar parable of the blind men and the elephant, each in touch with aspects of a tremendous and objectively existent reality, but all suffering from characteristically human limitations of perspective and none in position to claim exclusive possession of the truth in its entirety. I believe what we need to do is to look beyond these differences at the level of surface forms in an effort to get at whatever truth or truths may underlie them, and that the most effective way to accomplish this is through comparative studies of mystical experience—studies carried out, moreover, in direct and deep conversation with emerging science.

Before proceeding further in this direction, however, let me briefly note certain kinds of resistance we have already encountered (leaving aside scientistic critics who see nothing whatsoever worth preserving in religion). The first comes from persons who remain strongly anchored in their faiths of origin, and who may be inclined to experience such comparative efforts as attacks upon themselves and/or their personal religious commitments. We wish to assure such readers that we harbor no intention to dislodge them from their existing beliefs, although we do of course hope they will be open-minded enough to be interested in possible commonalities with the beliefs of others.

Other resistances, less expected, have emerged from within the various academic fields of religious study. The American Academy of Religion, for example, includes a sizeable faction who have apparently embraced current physicalist orthodoxy more or less wholesale and who seem intent upon explaining away most or all religious experiences, including any apparently supernormal aspects, in reductive terms grounded in social dynamics, power relations, psychological theories (often psychoanalytic), or speculative biology (the so-called neurotheology). More insidiously, the relevant humanistic disciplines currently seem deeply afflicted by the prevailing postmodern aversion to universal narratives of any kind, and excessively preoccupied with the sorts of doctrinal and textual differences that feed academic specialization and territorialism but obscure the empirical realities and commonalities we're after. Many scholars of religion also seem terrified of being perceived as having lost scholarly objectivity and having become mere "insiders" should they express support for any truth-claims of the traditions they study.

To put the point more bluntly, contemporary studies in comparative religion sometimes seem, from the viewpoint of an outside scientific observer such as myself, in danger of missing the forest for the trees. I should emphasize here that we do not mean to deprive anyone of a perfectly legitimate academic livelihood, but are simply approaching the available comparative material from a different direction and with different purposes in mind. We take seriously the possibility that the world's mystical traditions disclose genuine empirical truths about the nature of reality, and we are looking for the guidance potentially afforded to our theory-building efforts by certain experiential and philosophic highpoints of those traditions.

Philosopher Michael Grosso and I made some headway, I think, in Chapter 8 of *IM*, by pointing out a way of resolving or at least sharply attenuating the decades-long conflict between observers such as Aldous

Huxley, Huston Smith, and Walter Stace, who argue for the reality of a core *introvertive* mystical experience of pure, undifferentiated, effulgent consciousness, and radical "constructivists," including in particular Steven Katz, Wayne Proudfoot, and their allies, who argue that there can be no such thing as unmediated or unconditioned experience and that all mystical experiences are necessarily and entirely shaped by the traditions, doctrinal contexts, or situations in which they occur.

Our proposal recognizes merit in both positions. What is needed now, we believe, is neither an easy "perennialism" based on preoccupation with the supposed sameness of all mystical traditions, nor a radical constructivism based on overemphasis of their undeniable differences, but a more sophisticated comparativism that affirms *both* sameness and difference, as appropriate, while recognizing deeper properties of our shared human nature (Kripal, 2014). In our view the mystical domain is best conceived as *stratified in depth*, with constructivist-type influences predominating at the "shallow" end but diminishing in importance as we progress toward a "deep" end populated increasingly by experiences approaching Stace's introvertive type. We also believe that experiences of the latter type are highly relevant to theory construction, and that they are validated at least in part by common (but not invariable) accompaniments such as influxes of creative and psi capacities and radically uplifting transformations of personality.

I continue to think that this picture is basically correct, but wish to add here some further observations relevant to carrying it forward in the context of the present book. One major development post-*IM* is that I have become convinced, thanks mainly to the excellent book by Paul Marshall (2005), that Michael Grosso and I—like Stace in particular—seriously underestimated the importance and value of mystical experiences of the *extrovertive* type. In his book Paul first reviews in unusual detail the rich and variegated phenomenology of such experiences, and then traces the entire modern history of attempts to explain them. In this context he clearly demonstrates the superiority of a Myers–James–*IM*-type psychological theory to conventional reductionist alternatives. He also makes numerous provocative and interesting suggestions as to how such a theory might be fleshed out and embedded within a realist-idealist ontology compatible with leading-edge physics and cosmology, and he argues effectively for the view (which I share) that in these rare and exalted states mystics are directly encountering real properties of the natural world that remain hidden from us in ordinary states of consciousness.

This upgrading of extrovertive forms of mystical experience also brought with it a clearer sense of the relationship between experience and doctrine in the mystical realm. The mystical traditions themselves, with their practical emphasis on personal liberation, tend to value experience over doctrine and theory. Such experience is universally characterized, moreover, as both *ineffable*—beyond ordinary forms of reason, understanding, and verbal expression—and yet profoundly *noetic*—somehow directly revealing the nature of deeper realities and answering our questions about them. Systems of religious philosophy can attempt to rationalize such experiences and to provide a kind of intellectual scaffolding that may assist others to rise to the same experiential heights, but these systems cannot substitute for the experiences themselves.

The world's mystically informed philosophical systems themselves, moreover, are not equally cogent on their own terms. One immediate consequence of this picture is that it makes sense to pay particularly close attention to those rare historical figures who have combined high philosophic acumen with direct personal experience of deep mystical states— notably, persons such as Plotinus, Śaṅkara, Abhinavagupta, and in modern times Sri Aurobindo. As noted already by William James in the *Varieties,* the views of such persons tend at least roughly toward the sorts of philosophy that also dominated Western metaphysical thinking from German idealists such as Fichte, Schelling, and Hegel up through the early twentieth century, and it is important to recognize that such views were never decisively refuted, but simply brushed aside by the advancing tide of modern physicalism.

Myers's psychological theory has been substantially rehabilitated by *IM*, and we surmise that a companion metaphysics of some broadly idealist type can also be rehabilitated, and may in fact prove *necessary*, especially in light of the empirical phenomena of psi and mystical experience. It is noteworthy for example that idealism's central philosophical problem of relations between the Many and the One—the main focus of James's *A Pluralistic Universe*—has been revisited in an important modern defense of absolute idealism by Sprigge (1983), who explicitly recognizes the striking correspondence between his philosophic views and those of certain monistic Indian schools. It is also encouraging to us that all of the great mystically informed religious philosophies explicitly accept the reality of phenomena such as psi, postmortem survival, and inspirations of genius flowing in from higher realms of consciousness, although it remains to be seen to what degree such philosophies may really help us to understand or explain these "rogue" phenomena.

We had already taken a first stab at theory in the concluding chapter of *IM*, where we sketched possibilities ranging from post-Cartesian forms of interactive dualism to some sort of idealism or perhaps a neutral or dual-aspect monism, leaning slightly toward the latter. We also attempted there to show how theories of these types might fit together with leading-edge developments in physics and neuroscience. As our discussions have continued to evolve, commonalities across a wide range of conceptual frameworks have begun to emerge more clearly, with the psychological theories of Myers and James at the empirical center, flanked by quantum theory and Whiteheadian-type process metaphysics on one side and the various mystically informed religious philosophies on the other.

Our current net sense of the situation is that the empirical phenomena surveyed in *IM*, including in particular the deeply correlated phenomena of psi and mystical experience, collectively point the way to an expanded science, one that penetrates deep into territory traditionally occupied by the great world religions and that accommodates the central notion of something God-like at the heart of individual human beings and of nature itself. A pathway seems to be opening up toward some sort of fundamentally spiritual worldview that is compatible with science, one that would appeal to the large number of discontented modern persons who hunger for such a worldview but experience difficulties with scientifically problematic "overbeliefs" associated with the traditional faiths.

A common figure thus seems to be emerging, though still partially hidden, from the fog and mist. To expedite its emergence we have gradually reinforced our membership, adding two physicists and a cosmologist, a historian of science, a basic neuroscientist, a Whiteheadian philosopher, a folklorist/anthropologist, and Paul Marshall himself plus several other scholars of religion representing various branches of the mystical tradition including Neoplatonism, Hinduism, and Tantric outgrowths of Hinduism such as the nondual mystical philosophies of Abhinavagupta and Sri Aurobindo. The resulting group is extremely unusual in terms of its capacity to bring to bear high-level professional expertise on *both* of the theoretically crucial but scientifically "taboo" topics identified above, individually and jointly: many of our scientific members have devoted large parts of their careers to investigation of paranormal phenomena and altered states of consciousness in laboratory and/or field settings, and our scholars of religion, similarly, are internationally recognized experts on the mystical tradition generally as well as specialists regarding some of its historically most significant and philosophically able exemplars.

In general terms, then, our goal is to find or construct a conceptual framework potentially capable of accommodating psi phenomena (provisionally including postmortem survival), mystical experiences, and all of the other "rogue" phenomena documented in *IM*, as well as phenomena of more everyday sorts, and we are pursuing that goal by bringing together the diverse and normally non-interactive perspectives of empirical science, metaphysical philosophy, and the great mystical traditions with their broadly similar but far-from-identical views. In effect, we are attempting to drive as far and as quickly as possible toward an empirically justified, theoretically satisfying, and humanly useful "big picture" of how things really are and how we humans fit in. We have no interest in fighting rearguard actions against entrenched psi-deniers and scientific fundamentalists and the like, important though such efforts undoubtedly are, and we are not apologetic about prospecting in the literature of mystical experience and mystically informed religious philosophies for clues about how best to advance our theoretical purposes.

Although a common picture of some sort seems to be emerging, it has not yet fully emerged, and we remain short of full agreement on the form(s) it may ultimately take. The present book therefore amounts to a kind of progress report based on an initial reconnaissance of what we now collectively view, borrowing our guiding metaphor from the Lewis and Clark Expedition, as a crucial "undiscovered country" of science. We believe our efforts to be headed in the right general direction, although sure to be flawed in many details.

Part I, consisting of two chapters, provides essential background. Chapter 1, by myself, summarizes the central arguments of *IM* and the synoptic empiricism that we regard as the obligatory foundation for adequate theorizing. Its primary task is to identify the principal empirical issues and data that candidate conceptual frameworks or theories must address in useful fashion if they are to be of serious long-term interest to us.

Chapter 2, by Paul Marshall, goes on to flesh out in detail the special theoretical challenges and opportunities associated with mystical experience. As indicated above, a unique aspect of this book in the context of contemporary scientific and scholarly work concerns its strong emphasis on comparative study of mystical experience and mystically informed philosophical systems in service of theory development. Paul's chapter further justifies that emphasis, focusing mainly but not exclusively on experiences of the extrovertive type. Discussion centers on key features of these experiences such as unitive feeling, special luminosities, altered temporality, and expansive knowing—that is, "gnosis" as a special way of knowing, different from sense and reason, which may sometimes provide access to normally hidden aspects of reality.

Part II provides a sampling of theoretical perspectives that currently seem in various respects promising to us, including indications of how each deals with at least some of the relevant empirical phenomena. Our sample is not exhaustive of relevant possibilities, having been constrained by the interests and skills available within our current core group. Furthermore, all of these perspectives are viewed individually as works in progress, and none makes any pretense of being complete or correct in all respects. Note that we have arranged these chapters roughly in order from more scientific or "grounded" frameworks to more metaphysical or "grand" ones. The chapters themselves have been deliberately limited in length, but many also contain pointers to supplemental materials available through a special section of the Esalen website devoted to this book (see http://www.esalen.org/ctr-archive/bp).

Chapter 3, by Michael Grosso, sets the stage by providing a first-ever large-scale historical inventory of relevant thinkers. This chapter, which could easily become a book in itself (and probably will), traces the long and illustrious pedigree of the movement central to our book—that is, the movement away from physicalist "production" models and toward some sort of generalized or expanded "permission" or "filter" model of the Myers–James–*IM* type. Models of this sort picture everyday conscious life as emerging in the context of what James described as a "something more," something mental like our everyday conscious selves but of greater scope and power, to which most of us gain access only fitfully at best, under conditions which at present are very poorly understood but which are definitely amenable to systematic research. The central message of Mike's chapter is that against this common background of world intellectual history, current physicalist brain/mind orthodoxy stands out as an aberration, a pathologically contracted and impoverished vision of our human possibilities.

Chapter 4, by myself and David Presti, presents the basics of the Myers–James–*IM* picture as an alternative to the currently standard production model, emphasizing possible neurobiological and psychophysiological approaches to deeper analysis of its central "permission" metaphor and identifying numerous possibilities for further empirical research, research which can be expected with confidence to lead both to improved understanding and to fruitful applications in real human lives.

Chapter 5, by Henry Stapp, presents a summary of his "orthodox" and "quasi-orthodox" ontological interpretations of quantum theory (building upon its original formalization by John von Neumann), and outlines their applications to brain/mind theory in general and to many of the critical phenomena targeted in Chapter 1. Particularly noteworthy, I believe, is Henry's cautiously worded judgment that all of our targeted phenomena, even extreme ones such as postmortem survival and rebirth, are in principle potentially compatible with—and certainly not ruled out by—this most fundamental of current basic-science theories.

Chapter 6, by Harald Atmanspacher and Wolfgang Fach, provides an introduction to the dual-aspect monism conceived by physicist Wolfgang Pauli in collaboration with psychologist Carl Gustav Jung, according to which the physical and mental aspects of the experienced world are complementary, and arise through transformation of an underlying psychophysically neutral holistic reality to which they cannot be reduced. They further show that this picture leads naturally to a conceptual typology of exceptional experiences which closely mirrors the forms of such experiences actually occurring in a large sample of human adults.

Chapter 7, by Bernard Carr, first briefly summarizes the main features of previous hyperdimensional or hyperspace theories as conceived by persons such as philosopher C. D. Broad, neuroscientist John Smythies, and others, and then provides a compact exposition of his own updated and generalized version of such a theory plus a discussion of its connections with emerging physics and cosmology, and its possible applications to many of our targeted phenomena.

Chapter 8, by Greg Shaw, provides an introduction to the mystically informed metaphysics of Plotinus, which profoundly influenced all of our Western monotheistic faiths, and its subsequent "applied" developments in the theurgical mysticism of Iamblichus and later Neoplatonists. This

Neoplatonic school represents an important historical, geographic, and conceptual bridge between Asian and Western threads of the mystical tradition.

Chapter 9, by myself and Ian Whicher, presents the dualistic Sāṃkhya–Yoga strand of the central Indian philosophical tradition, which combines a sophisticated experience-based metaphysical theory with an applied psychology having much in common with the Myers–James–*IM* model. We emphasize Patañjali's account of the *siddhis* or attainments (including psychic powers) in terms of the "knowledge by identity" which arises in deep meditative states, and point out some deep connections between his views and various modern developments.

Chapter 10, by Loriliai Biernacki, goes on to introduce the medieval Indian spiritual genius Abhinavagupta and his nondual Kashmiri Śaivism, an experience-based metaphysics similar to that of Advaita Vedānta, but one which takes a Tantric or panentheistic turn that more explicitly embraces the everyday world as fully real and the *siddhis* as an important part of that world, not to be belittled or ignored. Loriliai also points out the broad compatibility of this system with core parts of modern science, especially quantum theory as represented in Chapters 5 and 6.

Chapter 11, by Paul Marshall, presents his own neo-Leibnizian realist-idealist theory, emphasizing its close connections with psychological "filter" or "permission" theories of the sort outlined in Chapter 4, its compatibility with modern physical science, and its ability to make sense of the conceptually difficult aspects of ordinary experience as well as various supernormal forms of "rogue" data targeted in Chapter 1.

Chapter 12, by Adam Crabtree, examines the works of Charles Sanders Peirce to draw out the implications of his philosophical framework, with a view to providing explanations for targeted phenomena including postmortem survival. Emphasizing that Peirce's philosophy is both scientifically oriented and thoroughly evolutionary in character, Adam elaborates the implications of Peirce's "objective idealism," which sees all reality as mind, but with no overarching absolute God who determines beforehand the outcome of the evolutionary trajectory of the universe. He finds that Peirce the empiricist was friendly to the possibility that paranormal phenomena including survival actually exist, and that Peirce the theorist offered explanations in terms of what he called a "synechistic metaphysics"—what today would be called a panentheistic evolutionary philosophy—which envisions all existing things as part of one continuum.

Chapter 13, by Eric Weiss, provides a concise introduction to "transphysical process philosophy," his extension of Alfred North Whitehead's process metaphysics in light of the mystical philosophy of the modern Indian Tantric sage Sri Aurobindo, and shows how it can potentially accommodate most of our targeted phenomena. Important context for this chapter is provided by the comfort that many theoretical physicists have with the use of Whitehead's system, updated as necessary in light of more recent developments in physics, as a possible way of rounding out the ontological side of quantum theory.

Part III, consisting of two chapters, summarizes the overall progress of our project and our collective judgment as to where things now stand, theoretically.

Chapter 14 draws upon the entire history of Sursem and the materials of Parts I and II in an effort to synthesize a first rough sketch of the undiscovered country of the mind, one that conveys our emerging sense of its overall structure and character. Although I am identified as this chapter's nominal author, I have had help from the entire Sursem group, and the views expressed represent majority views even at points where we have failed to reach full consensus.

We are essentially unanimous in thinking that expanded *psychological* models of the general sort advanced by Myers and James are scientifically viable and that many opportunities exist for their further empirical development. We are less sure about what specific form(s) of such models will ultimately prove most useful, but feel confident that this can be sorted out in normal scientific fashion, particularly as science becomes increasingly proficient in dealing with the subjective or "first-person" aspects of human experience, and as empirical research advances along the many relevant lines that are certainly available, as indicated in this chapter itself and elsewhere in the book.

Most significantly in terms of the largest-scale purposes of this book, we have gradually come to recognize that emerging developments in science and comparative religion, viewed in relation to centuries of philosophical theology, point toward some form of idealist or dual-aspect panentheism as our current best guess about the metaphysically ultimate nature of things. This family of interrelated positions attempts in various ways to overcome the historical polarization between pantheisms and classical theisms in their various forms, and although a great deal remains to be done both theoretically and empirically to narrow the class to its most viable member(s), we at least now have an overall sense of direction.

Chapter 15, by Michael Murphy, articulates the worldview that has implicitly guided Esalen Institute for the past fifty years. In this wide-ranging, provocative, and long-gestating essay, which has served as a navigational aid for our other chapters and a destination for the book as a whole, Mike portrays evolutionary panentheism as an emerging metaphysical vision which integrates the great but neglected modern philosophical tradition of German idealism (Fichte, Schelling, Hegel, et al.) with the common deliverances of the world's great mystical traditions more generally (as represented within Vedāntic, Tantric and Kashmiri Śaivite, Buddhist, Jewish, Christian, Islamic, and Neoplatonic perspectives), *and* with the incipient expansion of science itself as previewed in Mike's *Future of the Body* (1992) and our own *Irreducible Mind*. This synoptic vision not only appears broadly compatible with the more specific conceptual frameworks set forth in Part II but has tremendous practical implications—its "cash value"—in terms of providing humanity with an expanded worldview that is fundamentally life-affirming and optimistic, profoundly spiritual and ecumenical in character, and defensible in light of our most fundamental traditions including that of leading-edge modern science.

NOTES

1. James (1890–1896/1910, pp. 299–300).
2. Whitehead (1929/1958, p. 61).
3. Bacon himself unfortunately did not apply his own principle without restriction, but took the view that in regard to fundamental matters such as survival of bodily death we should refrain from empirical investigation. Myers (1903), however, consciously and deliberately removed that restriction: "The realm of 'Divine things' he [Bacon] left to Authority and Faith. I here urge that that great exemption need be no longer made" (Vol. 2, p. 279).
4. European readers in particular may be surprised by the amount of space devoted to this topic, which for them is probably less contentious than that of paranormal phenomena, but we assure any such readers that the situation here in the United States really exists at present as described in the text.

5. It is worth pointing out here that modern popular claims as to the supposed intrinsic incompatibility of science and religion are largely false, a product of crude nineteenth-century scientistic attacks on evangelical Christianity. See for example Dixon, Cantor, and Pumfrey (2010), and Sommer (2013). I thank Andreas Sommer for this information.

REFERENCES

Bacon, F. (1960). *The New Organon and Related Writings* (F. H. Anderson, Ed.). New York: Liberal Arts Press. (Original work published 1620)

Baker, M. C., & Goetz, S. (Eds.). (2011). *The Soul Hypothesis: Investigations into the Existence of the Soul.* New York: Continuum.

Carter, C. (2012). *Science and Psychic Phenomena: The Fall of the House of Skeptics.* Rochester, VT: Inner Traditions/Bear & Co.

Chalmers, D. J. (1996). *The Conscious Mind: In Search of a Fundamental Theory.* New York: Oxford University Press.

Chalmers, D. J. (2002). Consciousness and its place in nature. In D. J. Chalmers (Ed.), *Philosophy of Mind: Classical and Contemporary Readings* (pp. 247–272). New York: Oxford University Press.

Dixon, T., Cantor, G., & Pumfrey, S. (Eds.). (2010). *Science and Religion: New Historical Perspectives.* Cambridge: Cambridge University Press.

Griffin, D. R. (1998). *Unsnarling the World-Knot: Consciousness, Freedom, and the Mind–Body Problem.* Berkeley and Los Angeles: University of California Press.

James, W. (1902). *The Varieties of Religious Experience: A Study in Human Nature.* New York: Longmans, Green.

James, W. (1910). What psychical research has accomplished. In *The Will to Believe and Other Essays in Popular Philosophy* (pp. 299–327). London: Longmans, Green. (Composed of segments originally published 1890, 1892, and 1896)

James, W. (1971). *A Pluralistic Universe.* In *Essays in Radical Empiricism and A Pluralistic Universe* (pp. 121–284). New York: E. P. Dutton. (Original work published 1909)

Kelly, E. F., Kelly, E. W., Crabtree, A., Gauld, A., Grosso, M., & Greyson, B. (2007). *Irreducible Mind: Toward a Psychology for the 21st Century.* Lanham, MD: Rowman & Littlefield.

Koons, R. C., & Bealer, G. (2010). *The Waning of Materialism.* New York: Oxford University Press.

Kripal, J. J. (with Anzali, A., Jain, A. R., & Prophet, E.). (2014). *Comparing Religions: Coming to Terms.* Chichester, England: Wiley Blackwell.

Marshall, P. (2005). *Mystical Encounters with the Natural World: Experiences and Explanations.* Oxford: Oxford University Press.

Murphy, M. (1992). *The Future of the Body: Explorations into the Further Evolution of Human Nature.* New York: Jeremy P. Tarcher/Putnam.

Myers, F. W. H. (1903). *Human Personality and Its Survival of Bodily Death* (Vols. 1–2). London: Longmans, Green. (Available on CTR website, http://www.esalen.org/ctr/scholarly-resources)

Myers, F. W. H. (1961). *Fragments of Inner Life: An Autobiographical Sketch.* London: Society for Psychical Research. (Original work published privately 1893)

Nagel, T. (2012). *Mind and Cosmos: Why the Materialist Neo-Darwinian Conception of Nature Is Almost Certainly False.* New York: Oxford University Press.

Radin, D. (2006). *Entangled Minds: Extrasensory Experiences in a Quantum Reality.* New York: Simon & Schuster.

Seager, W., & Allen-Hermanson, S. (2013). Panpsychism. In E. N. Zalta (Ed.), *The Stanford Encyclopedia of Philosophy* (Fall 2013 ed.). Retrieved from http://plato.stanford.edu/archives/fall2013/entries/panpsychism/

Skrbina, D. (2005). *Panpsychism in the West.* Cambridge, MA: MIT Press.

Sommer, A. (2013). Crossing the boundaries of mind and body: Psychical research and the origins of modern psychology (Unpublished doctoral thesis). UCL Center for the History of Psychological Disciplines, University College London.

Sprigge, T. L. S. (1983). *The Vindication of Absolute Idealism.* Edinburgh: Edinburgh University Press.

Strawson, G. et al. (2006). *Consciousness and Its Place in Nature: Does Physicalism Entail Panpsychism?* (A. Freeman, Ed.). Charlottesville, VA: Imprint Academic.

Tart, C. T. (2009). *The End of Materialism: How Evidence of the Paranormal Is Bringing Science and Spirit Together.* Oakland, CA: New Harbinger Publications.

Velmans, M. (2009). *Understanding Consciousness* (2nd ed.). Hove, England: Routledge.

Velmans, M., & Nagasawa, Y. (Eds.). (2012). Monist alternatives to physicalism [Special section]. *Journal of Consciousness Studies, 19*(9–10), 4–165.

Whitehead, A. N. (1958). *The Function of Reason.* Princeton, NJ: Princeton University Press. (Original work published 1929)

I

The Essential Background:
"Rogue" Phenomena in Search of a Theory

I

EMPIRICAL CHALLENGES TO THEORY CONSTRUCTION

Edward F. Kelly

In the Introduction I briefly described our 2007 book *Irreducible Mind* (*IM*), which forms the principal background and baseline for Sursem's ongoing theoretical efforts. I believe *IM* accomplished its central objective of demonstrating—*empirically*—the inadequacy of conventional mainstream physicalist conceptions of the brain/mind connection. Not everybody has sufficient time or interest, of course, to work through that mountain of material in detail, and we have therefore decided to summarize here in condensed outline form its central arguments, emphasizing some points of special relevance to subsequent chapters. I will do this under ten major headings representing the main types of empirical phenomena we regard as difficult or impossible to explain in conventional physicalist terms. Much more detailed presentations and discussions of relevant evidence, and abundant supporting references, can of course be found in *IM* itself, which provides the real authority for most of the views expressed here.

PSI PHENOMENA

Here I'm referring to experimental and field observations systematically adduced in the course of over 130 years of scientific effort by workers in psychical research and its narrower modern descendent, experimental parapsychology. The basic phenomena in question involve, by definition, correlations occurring across physical barriers that should be sufficient, on presently accepted physicalist principles, to prevent their formation ("basic limiting principles" as formulated by Broad, 1962, and refined by Braude, 2002). Popular terms for the main classes of relevant phenomena are "extrasensory perception" (ESP) and "mind-over-matter" or "psycho-kinesis" (PK). ESP itself is sometimes broken down into subtypes such as "telepathy" (unmediated awareness of the mental state or mental activity of another person), "clairvoyance" (of distant or hidden events or objects), and "precognition/retrocognition" (of future/past events). It is widely recognized by researchers that these popular terms are unduly theory-laden and probably do not correspond to real differences in underlying process, and many therefore prefer the more theory-neutral terminology introduced by Thouless and Wiesner (1947)—"psi" for paranormal phenomena in general, occasionally divided into "psi gamma" for the input (ESP) side and "psi kappa" for the output (PK) side.

As already indicated in the Introduction, a large amount of peer-reviewed research involving experimental, quasi-experimental, and case studies of various kinds has produced cumulative results more than sufficient to demonstrate beyond reasonable doubt to open-minded persons who take the trouble to study it that the sheer existence of the basic input/output phenomena is a fact of nature with which we must somehow come to scientific terms (Radin, 2006; Tart, 2009). Indeed, we predict with high confidence that future generations of historians, sociologists, and philosophers of science will make a good living trying to explain why it took so long for scientists in general to accept this conclusion.

All psi phenomena are theoretically important by virtue of providing examples of human behavioral capacities that appear impossible to account for in terms of presently recognized psychological, biological, or classical-physics principles. Two special subcategories stand out, however, in terms of the magnitude of the challenges they represent for theoreticians.

First is "macro-PK," psychokinesis involving human-scale physical objects. There are many sources of evidence for such occurrences, including individual spontaneous PK events, often associated with extreme emotions of one or another sort; recurrent spontaneous PK (RSPK or "poltergeist" cases), typically involving disturbed adolescents; and various kinds of physical manifestations associated with trance mediums such as D. D. Home and Eusapia Palladino (Braude, 1986). I will illustrate the subject here with a single case that exemplifies the theoretical challenges in particularly stark form.

Levitation, a phenomenon reported of mystics from many traditions, was a principal feature in the case of Joseph of Copertino, a seventeenth-century Franciscan monk for whom "ecstatic flight" was a literal reality. Joseph was observed levitating in broad daylight on hundreds of occasions that cumulatively involved thousands of witnesses of varied types including skeptical and even hostile witnesses. Sworn testimony was obtained within a few years from scores of these and exhaustively reviewed in connection with the formal investigatory processes leading to Joseph's canonization. His flights occurred both indoors and outdoors, covered distances and altitudes ranging from a few feet to thirty yards or more, and went on for periods ranging from a few seconds to many minutes at a time. The reported phenomena, in short, were anything but subtle, and not glibly dismissible in terms of global allegations about "inattentional blindness" (Simons & Chabris, 1999), "mass hypnosis," or other possible errors of observation and/or memory. Of special interest is the fact that during his canonization proceedings, the *promotor fidei*—the "Devil's Advocate" or defender of the faith—was none other than the great humanist (and acquaintance of Voltaire) Prospero Lambertini, later Pope Benedict XIV, who was also the principal codifier of the Church's rules of procedure and evidence for canonization. Lambertini himself was initially hostile to Joseph's cause, but upon thorough and searching examination of all details of the case, including the sworn depositions, he concluded that the ecstatic flights must have occurred essentially as reported. Subsequently, as Pope, he published the decree of Joseph's Beatification.

Further details and supporting references are provided in Chapter 8 of *IM*, but a definitive treatment of this extraordinary case is available in the form of a book by our colleague Mike Grosso (2015), who not only provides a thorough and detailed account of Joseph's own well-documented phenomena but situates them in the larger history of macro-PK and related psychic phenomena. Meanwhile, we have placed on the Center for Theory and Research (CTR) website as supplemental material for this chapter a summary prepared by Mike of the main features of the case (http://www.esalen.org/ctr-archive/bp).

Second and in some ways even more disturbing is "true precognition"—direct or unmediated apprehension of future events. Such phenomena would seem on the surface to suggest that the future is fully determined, and hence to undermine any possibility of free will. This greatly troubled F. W. H. Myers (1895), who was therefore relieved to discover cases in which future accidents seemed to have been anticipated clearly and in detail, but were then averted by appropriate interventions.

The conceptual issues related to precognition are complex and deeply entangled. I will not attempt to unravel them here but rather will simply address the state of the evidence itself. We have devoted special attention to this subject in the context of previous Sursem meetings, and our collective sense is that true precognition too is a genuine phenomenon. The large amount of apparently supportive evidence from forced-choice precognition experiments is rendered somewhat uncertain in its bearings by the possibility that it might have been produced or contaminated by PK (Morris, 1982), but precognitive "remote viewing" experiments in which the possible targets are not even known to the subjects in advance and have not been picked at the time of the viewing seem less subject to alternative explanations of this sort. Most significant, in our view, are the many well-documented spontaneous cases involving multiple low-level factual details that are recorded at the time of the original experience (which often takes the form of an unusually vivid or intense dream), and then verifiably occur at a distant point in the future. Bob Rosenberg, who has led our investigation of this subject, has placed on the CTR website an annotated bibliography of case studies covering 130 years of serious precognition literature, including summaries of a few cases and discussions of the various authors' interpretations and conclusions.

Still more important for our theoretical purposes is the large further body of evidence directly suggestive of postmortem survival, the persistence of elements of mind and personality following bodily death. It is simply *false* to declare, as does physicalist philosopher Paul Churchland (1988, p. 10), that we possess no such evidence. We in fact possess a great deal of such evidence, much of it of very high quality, but unfortunately this work remains practically unknown outside the small circle of persons professionally involved with it. Here I can provide only the barest glimpses into a literature consisting of literally hundreds of thousands of pages of heavily documented case studies—anything but mere "anecdotes," as would-be critics often allege. Three main lines of survival research are of special interest for our purposes here.

The first concerns trance mediumship, a principal focus of the Society for Psychical Research (SPR) during the first several decades of its work. "Mediums" here are persons who seem able, usually when in some sort of trance-like altered state of consciousness, to make contact with the dead (Gauld, 1982). A large proportion of the most important research revolves around a half-dozen or so such persons who proved especially good at providing, under well-controlled conditions, detailed and accurate information seeming to derive from specific deceased persons about whom they could not have learned in any normal way. There is a difficult issue here related to proper interpretation of such evidence, which we will get to shortly, but let me first indicate the character of the evidence itself.

One of the first and best of the great trance mediums was Leonora Piper, discovered by William James in 1885, and the most important phase of her mediumship involved a communicator named GP (George Pellew), ostensibly the surviving personality of a young man who had recently died unexpectedly in a fall. Over several years her principal investigator, Australian lawyer Richard Hodgson, arranged for some 150 "sitters," exactly thirty of whom had been known to GP during his lifetime, to be introduced to sessions anonymously after Mrs. Piper had entered her trance state. The GP communicator recognized all and only those thirty sitters, and for most of them provided numerous and appropriate details of events and memories they shared, often with compelling verisimilitude in terms of GP's own characteristic vocabulary, diction, sense of humor, and so on. Hodgson himself, initially a skeptic, became convinced of the reality of survival largely on the strength of this one series of sittings (Hodgson, 1898).

Speaking more generally, all of the main properties of minds or personalities as we customarily understand these terms are sometimes evident in high-grade mediumistic communications. In the formulation of Pols (1998), for example, building on that of Descartes in Book II of the *Meditations*: "mind knows, makes (that is, forms, produces, creates), understands, thinks, conceives, perceives, remembers, anticipates, believes, doubts, attends, intends, affirms, denies, wills, refuses, imagines, values, judges, and feels" (p. 98). Summarizing a very large literature, it is fair to say that all of these properties are exemplified individually in many cases, and most or all of them jointly in the best cases such as that of GP. Not only are previously existing semantic, autobiographical, and procedural memories apparently in considerable degree preserved, but new memories can also be formed, mediated at least in part by continuing and presumably psi-based interactions with the world of the living, whether directly or by way of the medium. Less verifiably, the communicating personalities also seem to experience themselves as continuous with their prior selves, and as conscious selves who inhabit some sort of body and are able to interact with other deceased persons in some sort of shared phenomenal world.

The full picture regarding trance mediumship is of course far more complicated and hazy than this brief summary suggests. A large proportion of garden-variety mediumistic (and "channeled") communications are pure twaddle, and even the best cases sometimes display surprising weaknesses and limitations. Some of these limitations seem to derive from the medium, some from the communicators, and some perhaps from the still largely unknown nature of the connection between them. The GP persona for example exhibited certain curious lacunae, such as a determined unwillingness to discuss philosophic and scientific matters that had been of burning interest to the living GP, and he vouched for the authenticity of other Piper "controls" who were transparently bogus, such as the *soi-disant* "Walter Scott" and "Julius Caezar" (*sic*) personae. As in many other cases GP's awareness of ongoing events in this world was also very limited and imperfect, often extending even to uncertainty as to whether his attempted communications had gotten through Mrs. Piper to the sitters. For further information about Mrs. Piper and other great mediumistic cases see for example Balfour (1935), Braude (2003), Broad (1962), Gauld (1982), Hart (1959), Murphy (1961), Salter (1950), and Sidgwick (1915).

A second large area of survival research concerns what we call "cases of the reincarnation type" (CORT), in which small children—typically ages two to five—begin to speak and act as though they are remembering events from a previous, usually very recent, lifetime. The children often give detailed information about people and places they had known, or talk about the circumstances in which they died, and with this information the parents, or sometimes an independent investigator, can identify a deceased person whose life and death corresponds to what the child was saying. In the best cases, detailed records of the child's statements have been made by independent investigators before the child visits the home and family of the ostensible previous personality (PP). The children also frequently show strong and unusual behaviors that seem appropriate for the PP—such as an extreme fear of water when that person had died by drowning—and in a sizeable subset of cases the child has an unusual birthmark or birth defect corresponding to fatal injuries of the PP.

The originator and principal architect of this line of work was our colleague Ian Stevenson, and between 1961 and the present, he and others including Jim Tucker and Emily Kelly of our Sursem group have directly investigated over 2,500 such cases, many in great detail (see for example Kelly, 2013; Stevenson, 1975–1983, 1997, 2001; Tucker, 2005, 2013). Although the great majority of cases to date have come from countries where belief in reincarnation is strong, such as India and Burma, good cases have also been found in most other parts of the world including the countries of Europe and North America. An important further development now nearing completion is the entry of all cases into a cumulative database according to a detailed coding system. Work has already been reported using subsets of cases, and completion of the database opens a path toward development of statistical models and testing of hypotheses about factors that govern the phenomena—for example, predictors of the number and accuracy of remembered details, or the length of the "intermission" between death and rebirth.

Although the latter work in particular is still at an early stage, a number of points have already emerged that should command the attention of theorists. First and foremost is the possibility that rebirth may at least sometimes occur. Second, although it is easy to imagine more complex scenarios in which personalities split or merge—that is, one-to-many or many-to-one relations between PPs and the corresponding children—the data available so far strongly support one-to-one correspondence as the predominant pattern. *Something seems to encourage continuity of personality both within and between lives.* This picture has been reinforced, moreover, by results from the database indicating strong tendencies toward conservation of gender and of some basic personality characteristics between successive lifetimes. Another striking fact is the high incidence of violent or unnatural death among PPs (around two-thirds of the cases), which may be related somehow to these children's unusual capacity or impulse to recall (Stevenson, 1997). Little evidence has yet emerged of anything like moral improvement or punishment for past misdeeds, such as might be expected from Hindu theories of *karma* and the like, but this is conceivably due to limitations of the available sample, biased as it is toward unusual conditions of death in the PPs. If all or most of us in fact reincarnate, and we could discover means for reliably accessing past-life memories in adults, a fuller picture might conceivably emerge; however, although there is some relevant meditative lore and a bare handful of interesting hypnotic-regression and psychedelic cases suggestive of such possibilities, no meaningful conclusions can be drawn about such things at the present time. A final point concerning birthmark/birth-defect cases is that in most such cases the dying and perhaps surviving PP seems likely to have been aware of the fatal injury, and hence is plausibly suspected of being the source of the subsequent marks or defects. A surviving PP might similarly be the source in the important subclass of "experimental birthmark" cases in which the child's marks correspond to marks deliberately placed on the deceased person's body after the death by grieving relatives in hopes of identifying the successor. However, there are other cases, for example cases involving wounds to visually inaccessible or even interior parts of the PP's body, in which such interpretations seem less plausible.

The third main area of survival research concerns what we call crisis apparitions, in which a "percipient," person A, may see an actual visual apparition, hear a voice, have a dream, or simply feel the presence of a loved one, person B, at or near the time that B, the "agent," is undergoing serious or fatal injury at some physically remote location. The early SPR took a special interest in such events, carefully collecting and documenting large numbers of cases, and produced as its first major work the landmark two-volume study *Phantasms of the Living* (Gurney, Myers, & Podmore, 1886), which is also freely available (thanks to Bob Rosenberg) on the CTR website. This remarkable study includes not only detailed reports of over 700 individual cases (many including detailed documentation such as supporting testimony from witnesses or interlocutors, and medical and legal records), but also an elaborate and sophisticated discussion of methodological issues regarding eyewitness testimony and means for dealing with them. Subsequent case collections, mostly carried out with far less concern for detailed documentation, have shown generally similar patterns, as revealed especially by initial trailblazing attempts to encode their features in standardized fashion for computer modeling and analysis (Schouten, 1979, 1983).

A number of general features of crisis-apparition cases stand out in terms of theoretical relevance and interest. First is the apparent importance of strong emotional ties as a driver of these unique events, somehow overriding normally existing barriers. Also striking is their apparent association with altered states of consciousness in the percipients, especially dreaming and hypnagogic/hypnopompic states—the "twilight zone" between waking and sleeping. In many cases the event begins with a vague feeling of distress or disturbance, sometimes accompanied by a vivid sense that the injured person is present at a particular location nearby, and progresses into a full-fledged apparition only later on when the percipient enters a more receptive state. Third, as argued by Myers (1903), the timing of the events relative to verified times of death is sharply asymmetrical, rising steeply just before death and declining slowly thereafter (Vol. 2, p. 14). Percipients also typically have only a single such experience in their entire lifetime and remember it vividly for decades afterward as something uniquely significant (and note that Gurney and colleagues took pains to show that when questioned repeatedly over long intervals of time percipients reported *fewer* rather than *more* details as time passed).

Many crisis apparitions seem potentially interpretable as hallucinations generated by percipients alerted at some level to their loved ones' circumstances by a psi process, as argued in particular by Louisa Rhine (1977). Others, however, seem to locate agency and purpose squarely in the dying or deceased, as for example in the case of a long-dead husband who seems to have come for his newly deceased wife but is seen by her tenant, a total stranger. Many apparitions also display what are aptly described as "quasi-physical" properties, as discussed by Tyrrell (1953, pp. 77–80). For example, they sometimes obscure the background, cast shadows, and can be seen in mirrors, like ordinary physical objects. They may also be detected by pet animals, and if more than one human is present all or most may observe it, with differences of perspective appropriate to their differing locations in the communal space. On the other hand, apparitions sometimes enter and exit through walls or floors, become transparent and disappear, and in sundry other respects behave very *unlike* normal physical objects. Thus, they both resemble and differ from ordinary embodied persons, approximating them in widely varying degree, from marionette-like to so lifelike as to be mistaken temporarily for the corresponding person. (Similar properties apply, parenthetically, to "haunting" cases in which the apparitional form is recurrently associated with some particular *place.*) Complicating the picture further, there are also a number of well-documented "reciprocal" and "experimental" cases

of out-of-body experiences in which one living person more or less deliberately "projects" to a distant location, observes verifiable circumstances
there, and is observed at the corresponding location in the form of an
apparition by one or more persons present (Hart & Hart, 1933; Myers,
1903, Vol. 1, pp. 682–685).

The bulk of the available evidence concerning apparitions thus seems
consistent with a picture in which some part or aspect of a given person
departs from one place and appears in another in a form which is somehow intermediate between genuinely physical and purely hallucinatory.
Further confirmation lies in the fact that certain kinds of crisis apparitions
which might be expected on the telepathy-plus-hallucination model seem
not in fact to occur—in particular, what might be called "disseminated"
apparitions, in which a dying person appears simultaneously to loved
ones in widely separated locations. This is essentially the picture originally arrived at by Myers (in debate with Gurney), which has also been
endorsed reluctantly and after lengthy consideration by our *IM* co-author
Alan Gauld (1982).

What shall we make of this survival evidence? Ironically, the primary
threat to survivalist interpretations usually arises not from considerations
of evidential *quality*—problems of fraud, credulity, errors of observation
or memory, and the like—but from the difficulty of excluding alternative
explanations based upon psi interactions involving only living persons.
For example, a trance medium who appears to be delivering veridical
information from your deceased uncle might actually be acquiring that
information by means of a psi-type process from you as the sitter, or from
other living persons who knew him, or from physical records of some
relevant sort, rather than from your deceased uncle himself, and in general it proves difficult to determine with certainty which sort of explanation
is correct. This is the infamous "survival vs. superpsi" debate, discussed
at some length in the concluding chapter of *IM* (pp. 595–599), and for
convenience we have added those pages to the supplemental material for
this chapter.

Either horn of this interpretive dilemma—survival or psi—seriously
threatens the prevailing physicalist brain/mind orthodoxy, and this undoubtedly helps explain the hostility of dogmatic physicalists to both. It
should also be evident that compelling evidence for postmortem survival,
an element of belief common in some form to all of the world's great
religious traditions, would demonstrate especially clearly the inadequacy

of present-day mainstream physicalism. In our collective Sursem judgment we are at or very close to that point—close enough, certainly, to justify rational belief in the *possibility* if not indeed the *likelihood* of one's own personal survival. For the theoretical purposes of this volume we will therefore assume the empirical reality of both survival and rebirth without further discussion or argument.

Evidence for the occurrence of psi phenomena in general and postmortem survival in particular played an important though largely tacit role in the overall argument of *IM*, and my exertions here will be rewarded if they lead scientifically minded readers to take these subjects more seriously than they otherwise might. It is crucial to recognize, however, that psi cannot be isolated and quarantined as though it were the *only* serious threat to contemporary physicalism. The many other kinds of evidence surveyed in following sections point in the same general direction.

EXTREME PSYCHOPHYSIOLOGICAL INFLUENCE

Under this heading comes a variety of phenomena especially suggestive of direct mental agency in the production of physiological or even physical effects (for a comprehensive review see *IM*, Chapter 3).

Placebo effects and related kinds of psychosomatic phenomena, to begin with, have long been informally recognized and are now widely accepted, but they were accepted by modern biomedical science only grudgingly, as new mechanisms of brain/body interaction came to light that seemed potentially capable of explaining them. In particular, psychoneuroimmunology has demonstrated the existence, previously unsuspected, of interactions between the central nervous system and the immune system. Nevertheless, the adequacy of such explanations even for some kinds of placebo effects remains in question, and there are many kindred phenomena that pose progressively greater challenges to explanation in such terms. The following examples will serve to capture their flavor.

Both Sigmund Freud and F. W. H. Myers were impressed by hysterical "glove anesthesias," in which a patient loses sensation from the skin of a hand in the absence of identifiable organic lesion. In such cases the anesthetic skin region typically corresponds only to a *psychological* entity, the patient's idea, in complete disregard of the underlying anatomical organization. At the same time, curiously, something in the patient remains aware of the afflicted region and protects it from injury.

Related phenomena have often been reported in the context of deep hypnosis. Highly suggestible persons who can vividly imagine undergoing an injurious circumstance such as receiving a burn to the skin sometimes suffer physiological effects closely analogous to those that the physical injury itself would produce, such as a blister. More rarely, the correspondence between the hypnotic blister and its imagined source extends even to minute details of geometric shape, details too specific to account for in terms of known mechanisms of brain/body interaction. Similarly dramatic phenomena have occasionally been documented in psychiatric patients in connection with exceptionally vivid recall of prior physical trauma (see *IM*, pp. 156–158). A closely related and well-documented phenomenon is that of "stigmata," in which fervently devout or pious believers in Christ develop wounds analogous to those inflicted during his crucifixion. The injuries are again localized and specific in form, vary in locus and character in accordance with their subjects' differing conceptions of Christ's own injuries, and appear and disappear, often suddenly and regularly, and also in accordance with subjects' expectations.

The conventional hope, of course, is that even the most extreme phenomena of the sorts just mentioned might ultimately prove explainable in terms of physiological processes alone. Continuing allegiance to this hope, despite the indicated explanatory difficulties, is undoubtedly encouraged by the fact that the phenomena described so far all involve effects of a person's mental state on that person's *own* body. Still more drastic explanatory challenges are posed, however, by phenomena in which one person's mental state seems to have directly influenced *another* person's body. These include "maternal impressions" (unusual birthmarks or birth defects on a newborn that correspond to an unusual and intense experience of the mother during the pregnancy), distant healing (including studies of effects of prayer on healing), experimental studies of distant mental influence on living systems, and cases in which a child who claims to have memories of the life of a deceased person also displays unusual birthmarks or birth defects corresponding closely with marks (usually fatal wounds) on the body of that person (Stevenson, 1997). In addition, there has been a considerable accumulation of spontaneous cases and experimental evidence demonstrating the reality of psychokinesis (PK), which by definition involves direct mental influence on the physical environment.

INFORMATIONAL CAPACITY, PRECISION, AND DEPTH

A number of well-documented psychological phenomena involve levels of detail, precision, or logical depth that are difficult to reconcile with what can be achieved by a brain which must operate in statistical fashion with neural components of low intrinsic precision and reliability. I will give just three examples from a very large class.

The first involves a case of "automatic writing" observed by William James (1889). The subject wrote with his extended right arm on large sheets of paper, his face meanwhile buried in the crook of his left elbow. For him to see what he was doing was "a physical impossibility." "Nevertheless," James continues, "two or three times in my presence on one evening, after covering a sheet with writing (the pencil never being raised, so that the words ran into each other), he returned to the top of the sheet and proceeded downwards, dotting each *i* and crossing each *t* with absolute precision and great rapidity" (pp. 554–555).

This remarkable episode illustrates two features that have often appeared together in the large but neglected scientific literature dealing with automatic writing (Stevenson, 1978): the subject is in an altered state of consciousness, and the motor performance, itself remarkable, is apparently guided by an extremely detailed memory record, an essentially photographic representation of the uncompleted page.

The latter property relates to the phenomenon of eidetic imagery, my second example, the most dramatic demonstration of which has been provided by Charles Stromeyer using Julesz stereograms (Stromeyer, 1970; Stromeyer & Psotka, 1970). These are essentially pairs of computer-generated pictures, each of which by itself looks like a matrix of randomly placed dots, but constructed in such a way that when viewed simultaneously (by presentation to the two eyes separately) a visual form emerges in depth. Stromeyer presented pictures of this type to the eyes of his single subject, a gifted female eidetiker, at different *times*, ultimately as much as three days apart. Under these conditions, the subject could extract the hidden form only if she could somehow fuse current input to one eye with an extremely detailed memory image of previous input to the other eye. Remarkably, she was able to succeed under a wide variety of increasingly demanding conditions: the original stereograms, for example, were 100×100 arrays, but she eventually succeeded under double-blind conditions with arrays as large as $1,000 \times 1,000$, or a million "bits," viewed up to four hours apart. These results were understandably shocking to many psychologists, who sought to escape their force by pointing to the dependence on a single subject and the absence of replications. At least one successful replication has subsequently occurred, however: specifically, Crawford, Wallace, Nomura, and Slater (1986) demonstrated that their highly hypnotizable subjects were able to succeed with the small stereograms, but only when hypnotized.

The literature already contains many additional examples of prodigious memory. Stromeyer and Psotka themselves mention the famous mnemonist studied by Luria (1968) and the case of the "Shass Pollak," who memorized all twelve volumes of the Babylonian Talmud, and Oliver Sacks (1987, Chapter 22) has reported a similar case of a person who among other things knew by heart all nine volumes and 6,000 pages of Grove's *Dictionary of Music and Musicians*. Other examples could easily be cited. Prodigious memory of this sort is a real psychological phenomenon.

My third example comes from the family of "calculating prodigies." Of special interest here is the "savant syndrome," often associated with autistic disorders, in which islands of spectacular ability appear in the midst of generalized mental disability (Treffert, 2010). The abilities are of many types, but almost invariably involve prodigious memory. The depth of the problems they pose for brain theory is exemplified by the case of "The Twins," also described by Sacks (1987). These profoundly impaired individuals, unable to perform even single-digit additions and subtractions with any accuracy, nonetheless proved able to generate and test prime numbers "in their heads." Sacks was able to verify the primacy up to ten digits, but only by means of published tables, while the twins themselves went on happily exchanging numbers of progressively greater length, eventually reaching twenty digits. Sacks makes the intriguing suggestion that they cannot literally be *calculating* these enormous numbers, but may instead be *discovering* them by navigating through some vast inner imaginal landscape in which the relevant numerical relations are somehow represented pictorially. The twins themselves of course cannot say how they do it.

Phenomena of these sorts look hard to explain in terms of brain processes. The most serious attempt to do so known to me (Snyder & Mitchell, 1999) is in fact devoid of specific neural mechanisms. Its central argument is rather that early-stage brain processes like those subserving visual perception, for example, must also be savant-like in terms of their speed, precision, complexity, and informational capacity. What is unusual about savants, therefore, might consist merely in their access to these mechanisms. This "explanation" of course presupposes a positive answer to the fundamental question at issue, whether the brain alone can accomplish *any* of these things including ordinary perceptual synthesis itself, and in a later section I will explain my doubts about that.

As proved long ago by mathematician John von Neumann, the only practical way to get increased arithmetical precision out of individually unreliable computing elements is to use more of them. This biocomputational perspective clearly implies that calculating prodigies must use large portions of their brains in very abnormal ways to achieve the observed effects, but the few neuroimaging studies currently available provide little if any support for that expectation. Furthermore, although the cognitive deficits that typically accompany autistic-savant skills could conceivably reflect such substitutions, we must remember that comparable skills have sometimes occurred in geniuses such as the mathematicians Gauss, Ampère, and Ramanujan, as well as von Neumann himself.

MEMORY

The previous section focused on phenomena such as high-precision calculations and prodigious memory that appear incompatible with the physical properties of the brain considered as a kind of computing device. Problems also arise, however, in regard to memory in its more familiar and everyday forms.

Memory is increasingly recognized as central to all human cognitive and perceptual functions, yet we remain largely ignorant of where and in what forms our past experience is stored and by what means it is brought to bear upon the present. Generations of psychologists and neurobiologists have taken it as axiomatic that all memories must exist in the form of "traces," physical changes produced in the brain by experience and carried forward more or less reliably in time, but there has been little real progress toward scientific consensus on the details of these mechanisms despite many decades of intensive research.

Significant progress *has* been made, to be sure, in regard to "learning" and "memory" in simple creatures such as the sea slug, and more generally in regard to what might be called "habit memory" (Bergson, 1908/ 1991), the automatic adjustments of organisms to their environments. But these discoveries fall far short of providing satisfactory explanations of the most central and important characteristics of the human memory system, including in particular our supplies of general knowledge (semantic memory) and our ability to recall voluntarily and explicitly our own past experience (autobiographical or episodic memory). Furthermore, recent functional neuroimaging studies, although generating vast amounts of data, have yielded little if any progress toward a comprehensive and coherent account of memory based on trace theory.

Meanwhile, deep conceptual problems have been identified in trace theory itself (Braude, 2002; Bursen, 1978; *IM*, Chapter 4). For example, autobiographical memory clearly involves something more than mere revival of traces of experiences past, something that allows us to interpret what we experience now as a representation of our own past rather than a contemporary perception, dream, or hallucination. Traces as such, that is, provide only memory aids rather than memories per se, and it has proven extremely difficult to specify in conventional physicalist terms what that extra something is, without falling into regressive forms of explanation that presuppose and hence cannot explain the phenomenon of memory itself. Similarly, the content of a concept or semantic memory typically transcends any finite set of experienced circumstances that can plausibly be imagined as having deposited corresponding "traces" in a form capable of explaining its future deployment in an unlimited variety of novel but semantically appropriate contexts, including metaphorical contexts.

Most challenging of all to mainstream views is the large body of evidence directly suggesting that autobiographical, semantic, and procedural (skill) memories sometimes survive bodily death. If this is the case, memory in living persons presumably exists at least in part outside the brain and body as conventionally understood.

These conceptual problems regarding trace theories of memory have deep connections with issues raised below in regard to central and unexplained properties of everyday conscious mentation, and as shown in Chapter 4 of *IM*, similar issues arise in relation to allied components of current cognitive theory such as "information" and "representation."

PSYCHOLOGICAL AUTOMATISMS AND SECONDARY CENTERS OF CONSCIOUSNESS

Phenomena catalogued under this heading involve what looks like multiple concurrent engagement, in potentially incompatible ways, of major cognitive skills (linguistic skills, for example) and the corresponding brain systems. I will next explain in more detail what this means, and provide relevant examples.

Current cognitive neuroscience pictures the mind or "cognitive system" as a hierarchically ordered network of subprocessors or "modules," each specialized for some particular task and corresponding (it is hoped) to some particular brain region or regions. Leaving aside major issues regarding the details of its specification, this picture seems broadly consistent with the overall manner in which our minds seem *ordinarily* to operate. Our basic way of consciously doing things, that is, is essentially one at a time in serial fashion. Although psychologists recognize that with suitable training people can do more things simultaneously than they customarily suppose, this generalization applies mainly to relatively divergent things, and conspicuously fails as the simultaneous tasks become more complex and more similar.

Nevertheless, a large body of credible evidence, some dating back to the late nineteenth century, demonstrates that additional "cognitive systems," dissociated psychological entities indistinguishable from full-fledged conscious minds or personalities as we normally understand these terms, can sometimes occupy the same organism—not in *alternation,* moreover, but *concurrently*—carrying on their varied existences as it were in parallel and largely outside the awareness of the primary, everyday consciousness. In essence, the structure that cognitive neuroscience conventionally pictures as *unitary*, as instantiated within and identified with a particular organization of brain systems, can be functionally divided—divided, moreover, not "side-to-side," leading to isolation of the normal cognitive capacities from each other, but "top-to-bottom," leading to the appearance of what seem to be two or more complete cognitive systems each of which includes all of the relevant capacities. Emergent "multiple" or "alter" personalities also can differ widely, not only in demeanor and knowledge but even in regard to deep involuntary physiological characteristics such as visual defects and susceptibilities to allergies. Secondary personalities are also sometimes markedly superior to the primary personality in knowledge, skills, and creativity, as in the cases of Victor Race, "Hélène Smith," and Patience Worth described in *IM* (pp. 447–450). More challenging still, it sometimes happens that one of these personalities has direct access to the conscious experience of one or more others, but not vice versa (Braude, 1995; *IM*, Chapter 5).

Two brief examples drawn from an enormous literature will help convey a more concrete sense of the character of these phenomena. The first comes from a report by Oxford philosopher F. C. S. Schiller on automatic writing produced by his brother (Myers, 1903, Vol. 2, pp. 418–422). As is characteristic of this genre of automatisms, the writer was typically unaware of the content of his writing, which went on continuously while he was fully and consciously engaged in some other activity such as reading a book or telling a story. Of particular relevance here, however, were occasions on which he wrote simultaneously with both hands and on completely different subjects, one or the other of these streams of writing also sometimes taking mirror-image form.

Second is the case of Anna Winsor, described by William James in his report on automatic writing. This case was protracted and bizarre, and only superficially resembles the neurological "alien hand" (Dr. Strangelove) syndrome. Its central feature is that the patient, Anna, at a certain point lost voluntary control of her right arm, which was taken over by a distinctive secondary personality. This personality, whom Anna herself named "Old Stump," was benign, often protecting Anna from her pronounced tendencies toward self-injury. As in the case of Schiller's brother, Stump typically wrote or drew while Anna was occupied with other matters. But Stump also continued writing and drawing even when Anna was asleep, and sometimes in total darkness. This secondary personality also remained calm and rational during periods when Anna was feverish and delusional, and it manifested knowledge and skills—such as knowledge of Latin—which Anna herself did not possess.

THE UNITY OF CONSCIOUS EXPERIENCE

Under this heading I will briefly address two interrelated problems. The first and narrower is the so-called binding problem, which emerged as a consequence of the success of contemporary neuroscientists in analyzing sensory mechanisms, particularly in the visual system. It turns out that different properties of a visual object such as its form, color, and motion in depth are handled individually by largely separate regions or mechanisms within the brain. But once the stimulus has been thus dismembered, so to speak, how does it get back together again as a unit of visual experience?

Only one thing is certain: the unification of experience is *not* achieved anatomically. There are no privileged places or structures in the brain where everything comes together, either for the visual system itself or for the sensory systems altogether. Some early theorists such as James and McDougall had argued that the evident disparity between the multiplicity of physiological processes in the brain and the felt unity of conscious experience could only be resolved in materialist terms by anatomical convergence, and since there is no such convergence, materialism must be false. This argument, although ingenious, relied upon the faulty premise that the only possible physical means of unification must be *anatomical* in nature. All current neurophysiological proposals for solving the binding problem are instead *functional* in nature: the essential concept common to all of them is that oscillatory electrical activity in widely distributed neural populations can be rapidly and reversibly synchronized, particularly in the "gamma" band of EEG frequencies (roughly 30–80 Hz), thereby providing a possible mechanistic solution.

A great deal of sophisticated experimental and theoretical work over the past thirty years has demonstrated that such mechanisms do in fact exist in the nervous system, and that they are active in conjunction with normal perceptual synthesis. Indeed, contemporary physicalism has crystallized neurophysiologically in the form of a family of "global neuronal workspace" theories, all of which make the central claim that conscious experience occurs specifically—and only—in conjunction with large-scale patterns of oscillatory neuroelectric activity capable of linking widely separated areas of the brain at frequencies extending into the gamma band (e.g., Crick, 1994; Dehaene & Naccache, 2001; Edelman,

Gally, & Baars, 2011; Engel, Fries, & Singer, 2001; Laureys & Tononi, 2009; Singer, 2007; Varela, Lachaux, Rodriguez, & Martinerie, 2001).

The neurophysiological global workspace, however, cannot be the whole story, because a large body of recent research on "near-death experiences" (NDEs) demonstrates that elaborate, vivid, and life-transforming conscious experience sometimes occurs under extreme physiological conditions—including conditions such as deep general anesthesia, cardiac arrest, and coma—that *preclude* normal workspace operation (Laureys & Tononi, 2009). Moreover, and especially relevant to the concerns of the present book, the more extreme transformations of consciousness associated with NDEs sometimes extend deep into the mystical realm, include veridical psi elements, and more commonly occur when the subjects are in fact physiologically closer to death (see *IM*, Chapter 6; Alexander, 2012; Holden, Greyson, & James, 2009; Owens, Cook [Kelly], & Stevenson, 1990; van Lommel, 2010, 2013).

In short, it appears that McDougall and James were right after all, albeit for the wrong reason. In effect, I believe, recent progress in biomedical science has provided new means for the falsification of mainstream physicalist theories of brain/mind relations. We can also expect to see more and better cases of this sort as our technical capacity to retrieve human beings from the borderlands of death continues to improve (Parnia, 2013).

Availability of this emerging evidence emboldens me to make some further and more contentious remarks regarding the second and larger problem of ordinary perceptual synthesis, and the direction in which things seem to me to be moving.

It is a historical fact that mainstream psychology has always tended on the whole to try to solve its problems in minimalist fashion and with as little reference as possible to what all of us experience every day as central features of our conscious mental life. The early workers in "mechanical translation," for example, imagined that they could do a decent job simply by constructing a large dictionary that would enable substitution of words in one language for words in the other. This approach failed miserably, and we were slowly driven, failed step by failed step, to the recognition that truly adequate translation presupposes *understanding,* or in short a full command of the capacities underlying the human use of language.

A similar evolution is underway in regard to perceptual theory. Following the lead of Marr (1982), most of the work to date has taken a strongly "bottom-up" approach, which views perceptual synthesis as a kind of exhaustive calculation from the totality of input currently present at our sensory surfaces. Machine vision and robotics, for example, necessarily took this approach, and even in neuroscience it seemed to make sense to start with the most accessible parts of the perceptual systems— the end organs and their peripheral connections—and work our way inward. The great sensory systems themselves—vision, audition, somatosensation, and so on—were also presumed to operate more or less independently, and were in fact typically studied in isolation.

A separate tradition dating back at least to Kant and the early Gestalt theorists, and carried forward into the modern era by psychologists such as Ulric Neisser and Jerome Bruner, has been sensitive to the presence of "top-down" influences, both within and between sensory modalities. Although a few perceptual subsystems (such as those that engender incorrigible visual illusions) may be truly autonomous or "cognitively impenetrable," these seem to be isolated and special cases. A very different overall picture of perceptual synthesis is currently emerging in which top-down influences predominate. On this view perceptual synthesis is achieved not *from* the input, but *with its aid*. This is necessarily the case for example in regard to ambiguous figures such as the Necker cube, where the stimulus information itself is insufficient to determine a uniquely "correct" interpretation. More generally, we routinely ignore information that is present in the input and supply information that is not, speed-reading providing a characteristic example. Recall here too that crisis apparitions partly or wholly *override* current physical stimulus input. Something within us, a sort of cosmogenic, world-generating, or virtual-reality system, is continuously updating and projecting an overall model of the perceptual environment and our position within it, guided by very selective samplings of the available information (Simons & Chabris, 1999; Tart, 1993).

As in the case of understanding spoken or written language, an enormous amount of general knowledge is constantly mobilized in service of this projective activity, which freely but selectively samples the information potentially available to it. Top-down and cross-modal sensory interactions have recently been recognized as the rule rather than the exception in perception, and neuroscientist Rodolfo Llinás and his coworkers have even advanced the view, which I believe is profoundly correct, that *dreaming*, far from being an odd and incidental part of our mental life, also reflects the workings of this projective activity. *Ordinary perceptual synthesis, on this inverted view of things, amounts to oneiric (dreamlike) activity constrained by sensory input* (Llinás & Ribary, 1994). Psychoanalyst Ernest Hartmann (1975) has proposed similar ideas in regard to hallucinatory activity more generally, with dreaming included: on his view such activity is again a ubiquitous and fundamental feature of our mental life, and the critical question is not "why do we sometimes hallucinate?" but rather "what keeps us from hallucinating most of the time?" The answer, he suggests, lies in inhibitory influences exerted by the brain activity that accompanies ongoing perceptual and cognitive functions of the ordinary waking sorts. Similar arguments for the primacy and importance of this sort of cosmogenic imaginative capacity have been advanced by persons as diverse as Brann (1991), Corbin (1997), and Globus (1987).

So far so good, but where exactly is the "top," the ultimate source of this top-down projective activity? The mainstream scientists who have already recognized its existence invariably presume that it arises entirely within the brain itself, in accordance with conventional production models of the brain/mind relation. However, evidence such as that of near-death experiences occurring under extreme physiological conditions, and the more direct evidence of postmortem survival, indicates that it actually originates *outside* the brain as conventionally understood, in accordance with the alternative Myers–James "permission" model advanced in *IM* and the present book.

GENIUS-LEVEL CREATIVITY

Any scientific theory of mind and personality truly worthy of the name surely must help us to understand this humanly vital topic, but by this standard we have so far made distressingly little progress. The main reason for this failure, in my opinion, is that for the most part we have tried to understand the exceptional—real genius, in its fullest expressions—as an amplification of the commonplace—"creativity," or even "talent," as found in convenience samples of undergraduates and the like.

Consider for example some recent work on the closely allied topic of "intuition." Several recent treatments by mainstream psychologists and neuroscientists essentially ignore the vast historical literature on this subject and seek instead to reduce it without residue to "unconscious cerebration"—the automatic, fast, parallel, cheap, and often reliable but sometimes error-prone out-of-sight operations of a nervous system tuned to its normal environment by factors such as genetics, learning and conditioning, priming, and so on (Eagleman, 2011; Kahneman, 2011; D. G. Myers, 2002).

There is undoubtedly much truth in this picture, especially in the context of everyday life and ordinary cognitive function, but it does not by any means exhaust the subject matter. Indeed, as reviewed in Chapter 5 of *IM*, we've had this conversation before! Specifically, at the end of the nineteenth century F. W. H. Myers and William James found the unconscious cerebration doctrine then being advanced by W. B. Carpenter, T. H. Huxley, and others specifically unable to account for well-documented empirical phenomena such as the highly developed secondary personalities that sometimes also displayed paranormally acquired knowledge in the context of automatic writing. Many social psychologists in particular appear to have forgotten James's (1890) counsel that postulation of unconscious mental states "is the sovereign means for believing what one likes in psychology, and of turning what might become a science into a tumbling-ground for whimsies" (Vol. 1, p. 163). It also does not help that a number of recent experiments previously thought to support the concept of elaborate and intelligent unconscious cerebration have turned out to be difficult to replicate or in some cases outright fabrications.

Psi phenomena, of course, pose another kind of threat to the unvarnished automaticity story. To his credit D. G. Myers (2002) recognizes this, and for that reason provides in his book a chapter which seeks to dismiss all of the accumulated evidence for psi. That chapter makes practically no contact with the real scientific literature of the field, however, relying for the most part on the opinions of professional psi-deniers and on anecdotes from the popular press, and the threat remains.

The farther reaches of intuition and creativity include much more than psi phenomena, too, as recognized clearly by more traditional authors such as Wild (1938), who surveys the long philosophical history of the subject and its deep association with unusual states of consciousness and unusual forms of cognition. Her work complements that of Myers and James, who similarly invert the modern "deflationary" approach by consciously and deliberately focusing on extreme examples of genius that point in the direction of the enlarged conception of human personality they were struggling to articulate. Myers (1903) himself specifically targeted what "the highest minds have bequeathed to us as the heritage of their highest hours" (Vol. 1, p. 120). Responding to the cultural levelers of his own era, he encapsulated the main features of his picture of genius as follows:

> Genius . . . should rather be regarded as a power of utilising a wider range than other men can utilise of faculties in some degree innate in all;—a power of appropriating the results of subliminal mentation to subserve the supraliminal stream of thought;—so that an "inspiration of Genius" will be in truth a *subliminal uprush*, an emergence into the current of ideas which the man is consciously manipulating of other ideas which he has not consciously originated, but which have shaped themselves beyond his will, in profounder regions of his being. I shall urge that there is here no real departure from normality; no abnormality, at least in the sense of degeneration; but rather a fulfilment of the true norm of man, with suggestions, it may be, of something *supernormal;*—of something which transcends existing normality as an advanced stage of evolutionary progress transcends an earlier stage. (Vol. 1, p. 71)

The deeper forms of subliminal uprush, moreover, are notable both for their typically involuntary character and for their "incommensurability" with the subject's characteristic everyday forms of mentation. Myers saw both of these properties as present in germ in the case of calculating prodigies, but he also pointed to the existence of a "mythopoeic" realm of heightened imagination potentially available to all of us. In this he echoed the views of Romantic poets such as Blake, Wordsworth, and especially Coleridge, who distinguished between the imaginal and the imaginary— between Imagination, which he regarded as a higher faculty of the mind, and mere Fancy or fantasy (*IM*, pp. 454–457)—and anticipated the views of contemporary scholars such as Brann (1991), Corbin (1997), and Globus (1987), noted in the previous section.

All of the challenging phenomena surveyed in this chapter—including extreme psychophysiological influence, psychological automatisms and secondary centers of consciousness, flashes of inspiration involving unusual forms of thinking and symbolism, prodigious memory, spontaneous psi phenomena, and altered states of consciousness sometimes overlapping the mystical realm—are inescapably bound up with genius in its fullest development, but these connections go virtually unmentioned in contemporary mainstream discussions (see *IM*, Chapter 7).

A particularly dramatic case in point is that of the Indian mathematician Ramanujan, rated by his distinguished British sponsor G. H. Hardy as standing alone at 100 atop a scale of mathematical ability on which most of us lie at or near 0, Hardy himself only at 25, and the magnificent David Hilbert, Ramanujan's nearest rival, at 80. Replete with demonstrations of prodigious memory, psychological automatisms, mathematical discoveries presented in the form of dreams, and profound and beautiful intuitions of hidden but ultimately verifiable properties of the physical world, this astonishing case fairly beggars the theoretical apparatus currently available to cognitive science and could well serve as a kind of reality check and navigational aid for this important field of study (Eysenck, 1995; Kanigel, 1991).

To put the central point of this section in more general terms, the speed, precision, complexity, novelty, and truth-bearing character of these "subliminal uprushes" reveal the presence within human beings of something that radically transcends ordinary cognitive capabilities and forms, and something moreover that is rooted more deeply than ordinary experience in the world in which we find ourselves embedded. This leads directly to our next topic, with which genius is profoundly connected both psychologically and historically.

MYSTICAL EXPERIENCE

Experiences of this type have deeply influenced the world's major religious traditions and civilizations and have occurred throughout history and across cultures. Their existence as a distinctive and important class of psychological phenomena can scarcely be denied. Nevertheless, they have largely been ignored by modern mainstream science, and the few previous commentators from the viewpoints of clinical psychology, psychiatry, and neuroscience have almost invariably sought to devalue and pathologize them. Even when acknowledging that such experiences are typically life-transforming and self-validating for those who have them, the historically standard epistemological approaches in psychology and philosophy treat them as purely subjective events having authority only for those who experience them, and thus deny their objective significance and the testability of the associated truth claims.

However, a large though scattered literature testifies to the common occurrence in such experiences, or in individuals who have them, of genius-level creativity, spontaneous psi-type events, and many other un-usual empirical phenomena of the sorts catalogued in this chapter. Mysti-cal-type states of consciousness are also now known to be at least partial-ly reproducible by psychedelics ("entheogens") such as LSD and psilocy-bin, and they can be induced by protracted self-discipline involving trans-formative practices such as the various forms of meditation. A more objective, informed, and sympathetic appraisal of mystical experience thus finds within it much additional support for an enlarged conception of human personality, and many new opportunities for empirical research (see *IM,* Chapter 8, and Marshall, 2005). Furthermore, as already indicat-ed in the Introduction, and as brought out more fully by Paul Marshall in the following chapter, this region of human experience appears especially germane to our ongoing efforts to identify a conceptual framework more comprehensive and satisfying than that of contemporary physicalism.

THE HEART OF THE MIND

In this section I will comment briefly on a hornet's nest of issues lying at the core of human mental life as all of us routinely experience it, every day of our lives. These issues have been the focus of extensive recent debates, especially in the philosophical literature, precisely because of their resistance to understanding in conventional physicalist terms. The issues are deep, individually complex, and densely interconnected, and what I can say here will necessarily amount to little more than a summary of my own opinions. The crucial point I want to make, especially to my fellow psychologists, is this: our a priori commitment to conventional physicalist accounts of the mind has rendered us systematically incapable of dealing adequately with the mind's most central properties. We need to rethink that commitment.

Consider first the issue of semantic content, the "meanings" of words and other forms of representation. Throughout our history, we have tried unsuccessfully to deal with this by "naturalizing" it, reducing it to some-thing else that seems potentially more tractable. An old favorite among psychologists and philosophers, traceable at least as far back as Locke and Hume, was the idea that representations work by *resembling* what they represent, by virtue of some sort of built-in similarity or structural isomorphism, but any hope along these lines was long ago exploded (see e.g., Goodman, 1972; McClendon, 1955). The central move subsequently made by classical cognitive psychology is essentially the semantic counterpart of the prevailing "functionalist" doctrine in philosophy of mind. Thus, meanings are not to be conceived as intrinsic to words or concepts, but rather as deriving from and defined by the functional role those words or concepts play in the overall linguistic system. Similarly, there is currently great interest in "externalist" causal accounts of meaning. In connectionism, dynamic systems theory, and neuroscience, for example, the "meaning" of a given observed response (such as the settling of a neural network into one of its attractors, or the firing off of a volley of spikes by a neuron in the visual cortex) is identified with whatever in the organism's environment provoked that response. But this simply cannot be right: how can such an account possibly deal with abstract things, for example, or nonexistent things? Responses do not qualify ipso facto as representations, nor signs as symbols. Something essential is being left out. That something, as John Searle (1992) so effectively argued, is precisely what matters, the semantic or mental content.

Closely related to this is the more general and abstract philosophical problem of "intentionality," the ability of representational forms to be *about* things, events, and states of affairs in the world. Mainstream psychologists and philosophers have struggled to find ways of making intentionality intrinsic to the representations themselves, but again it just does not and cannot work, because something essential is left out. That something is the *user* of the representations. Intentionality is inherently a three-way relation involving users, symbols, and things symbolized, and the user cannot be eliminated. As Searle puts it in various places, the intentionality of language is secondary and derives from the intrinsic intentionality of the mind. Searle thus agrees in part with Brentano (1874/1995), for whom intentionality was the primary distinguishing mark of the mental, but he ignores the other and more fundamental part of Brentano's thesis, which is that intentionality cannot be obtained from *any* kind of physical system, including brains (but see, for example, Dupuy, 2000, for an opposing point of view).

Talk of "users" and the like raises for many contemporary psychologists and philosophers the terrifying specter of the self as a homunculus, a little being within who embodies all the capacities we sought to explain in the first place. Such a result would be disastrous, because that being would evidently need a similar though yet smaller being within itself, and so on without end. Cognitive modelers seeking to provide strictly physicalist accounts of mental functions must therefore do so without invoking a homunculus, but in this they routinely fail. Often the homuncular aspect is hidden, slipped into a model by its designers or builders by covertly enlisting the semantic and intentional capacities of its users or observers. Much contemporary work on computational modeling of memory, metaphor, and semantics harbors subtle problems of this sort (for examples, see *IM*, Chapters 4 and 7). Sometimes, however, the homunculus is more brazenly evident. Searle (1992) uses as an example the influential account of vision by David Marr (1982), which applies computations to the two-dimensional array of retinal input in order to generate a "description" of the three-dimensional world that produced it, but then needs something else to read and interpret the description. Another is Stephen Kosslyn's model of visual imagery, which essentially puts up an image on a sort of internal TV screen, but then needs somebody else to view the image.

Particularly in its more blatant forms the homunculus has attracted the attention of physicalist philosophers such as Daniel Dennett (1978), who have attempted to remove its philosophic sting. Dennett's solution is to "discharge" the homunculus by a process of "recursive decomposition." His basic idea is that the "smart" homunculus appearing at the top of a model can be replaced by progressively larger numbers of less smart homunculi at lower levels until we get to a vast bottom layer corresponding to the "hardware" level of computer flip-flops or neuron firings. But as Searle (1992) pointed out, this maneuver fails, because even at the bottom level there has to be something outside the decomposition, a homunculus in effect, that knows what those lowest-level operations *mean*.

Cognitive models cannot function without a homunculus, I believe, precisely because they lack what we have—*conscious minds*, with their capacities for semantics, intentionality, and all the rest built in. No homunculus problem, moreover, is posed by the structure of our conscious experience itself. The efforts of Dennett and others to claim that there *is* such a problem, and to use that to ridicule any residue of dualism, rely upon their deeply flawed metaphor of the "Cartesian theater," a place where mental contents get displayed and we then supposedly pop in separately to view them. But we and our experience cannot be separated in that way. Descartes himself, James, and Searle, among others, all have this right: conscious experience comes to us whole and undivided, with the qualitative feels, phenomenal content, unity, and subjective point of view all built-in, intrinsic features.

Finally, I wish simply to record, without argument, my own deepest intuition as to where these issues lead. All of the great unsolved mysteries of the mind—semantics, intentionality, volition, the self, and conscious-ness—seem to me inextricably interconnected, with *consciousness* some-how at the root of all.

The consciousness I have in mind, however, is emphatically not that of people like David Chalmers (1996), a consciousness that is irreducible but ineffectual, consisting merely of phenomenal properties or "qualia" arbitrarily tacked on to some sort of computational intelligence that sup-posedly does all the cognitive work. Ordinary perception and action are saturated with conceptual understanding, and conceptual understanding is saturated with phenomenal content. Volition too has an intentionality aspect, for one cannot just *will*, one must will *something*. And as William James so forcibly argued at the dawn of our science, all of this perceptual, cognitive, and volitional activity somehow emanates from a mysterious and elusive "spiritual self," which we often sense at the innermost subjec-tive pole of everyday conscious experience—the "something more" that James himself traced in his later years into the depths of Myers's sublimi-nal consciousness as revealed in mystical experience (*IM*, Chapter 8; Leary, 1990).

Consciousness, in short, far from being a passive epiphenomenon, seems to me to play an essential role—indeed *the* essential role—in all of our most basic cognitive capacities. I applaud the trenchant conclusion of philosopher E. J. Lowe (1998), which encapsulates my own views: "re-ductive physicalism, far from being equipped to solve the so-called 'easy' problems of consciousness, has in fact nothing useful to say about *any* aspect of consciousness" (pp. 121–122). I find it astonishing, and predict that it will be found so as well by our intellectual descendants, that so much of contemporary science and philosophy has sought—conscious-ly!—to slight or ignore these first-person realities of the mind, and some-times even to deny that they exist. There is perhaps no better example of the power of preexisting theoretical commitments to blind us to counter-vailing facts.

QUANTUM MECHANICS AND ITS IMPLICATIONS

It cannot be emphasized too strongly that these unresolved explanatory problems concerning consciousness, the heart of the mind, and all the other empirical phenomena surveyed above have a common source in the narrow physicalist consensus that undergirds practically everything now going on in mainstream psychology, neuroscience, and philosophy of mind. But that consensus itself rests upon an outdated conception of nature, deriving from Galileo, Descartes, Newton, and Laplace, that be-gan its career by deliberately banishing conscious human minds from its purview! And as I will next briefly explain, *that* sort of physicalism is itself incompatible with the deepest of our current physical sciences.

William James, like Newton and Leibniz before him, clearly recog-nized the impossibility of explaining consciousness and allied phenomena within the framework of classical physics. James himself cautioned that its underlying physical-science concepts were "provisional and revisable things," but he had no good alternatives in sight. As he clearly and cor-rectly anticipated, however, that classical conception of nature was soon to be undermined by a tectonic shift in the foundations of physics itself—specifically, the shift driven by the rise of quantum mechanics early in the twentieth century.

The founders of quantum mechanics discovered to their horror that in application to the subatomic world the fundamental ideas of classical physics were not just limited but wrong, leading repeatedly to predictions that were falsified by experiment. The theory they were ultimately driven to in response, quantum theory, is a more fundamental and more compre-hensive physical theory that explains everything explainable in classical terms and a host of additional things as well, often to extraordinary levels of accuracy. No prediction made by it has ever been experimentally fal-sified.

Furthermore, the rise of quantum theory demonstrates that the undeni-able experimental and practical triumphs of classical mainstream science were insufficient to validate its associated physicalist ontology. It may in the past have been appropriate to say, as did Burtt (1932) just prior to the advent of quantum theory, that "It has, no doubt, been worth the meta-physical barbarism of a few centuries to possess modern science" (p. 303), but the situation now is radically different. Despite many remaining uncertainties regarding its proper interpretation, quantum theory clearly impacts our most fundamental ideas about the nature of reality and opens the door to new and very different conceptions (Rosenblum & Kuttner, 2011). Conventional physical realism has been radically undermined, and "matter" as classically conceived shown not to exist. Quantum theory essentially inverts the priority of the mental and physical aspects of nature by shifting the focus of physics itself to regularities in the connections between *psychologically* described events—i.e., conscious experiences of human observers. For example, mathematical physicist Henry Stapp (2007; see also Chapter 5) has proposed an interpretation in which the conscious human mind with its powers of attention and decision making plays a critical role in completing the quantum dynamics. As a corollary, the classical doctrine of causal closure or completeness of the physical, which underwrites contemporary physicalist denials of free will, collapses. It also appears likely, as discussed later in this book, that many of the "rogue" empirical phenomena cited above, from stigmata and hypnotic blisters to psi phenomena and even postmortem survival, are potentially accommodated within broader conceptual frameworks of this sort.

In sum, the empirical challenges systematically marshaled in *IM* and sketched above seem sufficient in themselves to compel, and to some extent foreshadow, a radical reworking of conventional production models of brain/mind relations along the alternative lines envisioned by Myers and James, among numerous others (see Chapter 3). But it is also vital to recognize that a scientific psychology enlarged in these ways will likely prove not *less* but *more* compatible than current mainstream doctrine both with everyday human experience and with our most fundamental physical science!

Let me now close this chapter with a telegraphic summary of the principal mental and psychophysical phenomena that we regard as firmly established or probable, and beyond the reach of explanation in conventional physicalist terms:

1. Psi phenomena of all currently recognized types, including in particular true precognition and macro-PK.

2. Postmortem survival, where what survives at least sometimes approximates a full-fledged mind or personality that preserves previous semantic, autobiographical, and procedural memories, forms new memories in conjunction with continuing interactions with the world of living persons, and displays other features of mind such as thinking, planning, imagination, volition, and a continued sense of embodied selfhood. Under this heading I also include the possibility of rebirth and the quasi-physical properties of apparitions as described above.

3. Phenomena of extreme psychophysiological influence such as stigmata, hypnotic blisters, or other skin markings of specific shapes and at specific locations induced by suggestion or vivid imagination; maternal impressions; distant mental influence on living systems; and unusual birthmarks and birth defects in cases of the reincarnation type.

4. Prodigious memory and calculation abilities, as seen in the savant syndrome, eidetic imagery, and related phenomena.

5. Phenomena of dissociation and superior forms of secondary personality, including not only concurrent streams of consciousness but overlapping and sometimes asymmetrical relationships between them.

6. Deep, life-transforming NDEs, especially those occurring under extreme physiological conditions such as deep general anesthesia, cardiac arrest, and coma, in which cerebral conditions regarded by contemporary neuroscience as necessary for consciousness have been grossly degraded or abolished altogether.

7. Extreme cognitive phenomena associated with the inspirations of true genius, including novel and complex forms of imagination and veridical intuition of previously unrecognized properties of the natural world.

8. Life-transforming mystical experiences of both extrovertive and introvertive forms, and their connections with genius-level creativity, psi phenomena, and NDEs occurring under extreme physiological conditions.

9. The central phenomena of our everyday conscious mental life including meaning, intentionality, and consciousness itself with its built-in features of unity, qualitative or phenomenal content, and subjective point of view.

Our central goal henceforth is to find or construct some sort of enlarged conceptual framework that can potentially accommodate or explain (in some sense yet to be determined) some or all of these challenging empirical phenomena. I should perhaps also add in closing that the second item on this list—postmortem survival—seems especially critical in the sense that a theory capable of handling *that* group of phenomena in satisfactory fashion would likely handle most or all of the rest as well.

REFERENCES

Alexander, E. (2012). *Proof of Heaven: A Neurosurgeon's Journey into the Afterlife.* New York: Simon & Schuster.

Balfour, G. W., Earl of (1935). A study of the psychological aspects of Mrs. Willett's mediumship, and of the statements of the communicators concerning process. *Proceedings of the Society for Psychical Research, 43,* 41–318.

Bergson, H. (1991). *Matter and Memory* (N. M. Paul & W. S. Palmer, Trans.). New York: Zone Books. (Original 5th ed. published 1908)

Brann, E. T. H. (1991). *The World of the Imagination: Sum and Substance.* Lanham, MD: Rowman & Littlefield.

Braude, S. E. (1986). *The Limits of Influence: Psychokinesis and the Philosophy of Science.* London: Routledge & Kegan Paul.

Braude, S. E. (1995). *First Person Plural: Multiple Personality and the Philosophy of Mind* (Rev. ed.). Lanham, MD: Rowman & Littlefield.

Braude, S. E. (2002). *ESP and Psychokinesis: A Philosophical Examination* (Rev. ed.). Parkland, FL: Brown Walker Press.

Braude, S. E. (2003). *Immortal Remains: The Evidence for Life after Death.* Lanham, MD: Rowman & Littlefield.

Brentano, F. (1995). *Psychology from an Empirical Standpoint* (A. C. Rancurello, D. B. Terrell, & L. L. McAlister, Trans.). London: Routledge. (Original work published 1874)

Broad, C. D. (1962). *Lectures on Psychical Research.* London: Routledge & Kegan Paul.

Bursen, H. A. (1978). *Dismantling the Memory Machine.* Dordrecht, The Netherlands: Reidel.

Burtt, E. A. (1932). *The Metaphysical Foundations of Modern Physical Science: A Historical and Critical Essay* (Rev. ed.). London: Routledge & Kegan Paul.

Chalmers, D. (1996). *The Conscious Mind: In Search of a Fundamental Theory.* New York: Oxford University Press.

Churchland, P. M. (1988). *Matter and Consciousness* (Rev. ed.). Cambridge, MA: MIT Press.

Corbin, H. (1997). *Alone with the Alone: Creative Imagination in the Sūfism of Ibn ʿArabī* (R. Manheim, Trans.). Princeton, NJ: Princeton University Press. (Original work published 1969)

Crawford, H. J., Wallace, B., Nomura, K., & Slater, H. (1986). Eidetic-like imagery in hypnosis: Rare but there. *American Journal of Psychology, 99,* 527–546.

Crick, F. (1994). *The Astonishing Hypothesis: The Scientific Search for the Soul.* New York: Simon & Schuster.

Dehaene, S., & Naccache, L. (2001). Towards a cognitive neuroscience of consciousness: Basic evidence and a workspace framework. *Cognition, 79,* 1–37.

Dennett, D. (1978). *Brainstorms: Philosophical Essays on Mind and Psychology.* Cambridge, MA: MIT Press.

Dupuy, J.-P. (2000). *The Mechanization of the Mind: On the Origins of Cognitive Science.* (M. B. DeBevoise, Trans.). Princeton, NJ: Princeton University Press.

Eagleman, D. (2011). *Incognito: The Secret Lives of the Brain.* New York: Pantheon Books.

Edelman, G. M., Gally, J. A., & Baars, B. J. (2011). Biology of consciousness. *Frontiers in Psychology, 2*, article 4. doi:10.3389/fpsyg.2011.00004

Engel, A. K., Fries, P., & Singer, W. (2001). Dynamic predictions: Oscillations and synchrony in top-down processing. *Nature Reviews: Neuroscience, 2*, 704–716. doi:10.1038/35094565

Eysenck, H. J. (1995). *Genius: The Natural History of Creativity.* New York: Cambridge University Press.

Gauld, A. (1982). *Mediumship and Survival: A Century of Investigations.* London: Heinemann. (Available on CTR website, http://www.esalen.org/ctr/scholarly-resources)

Globus, G. (1987). *Dream Life, Wake Life: The Human Condition Through Dreams.* Albany: State University of New York Press.

Goodman, N. (1972). Seven strictures on similarity. In N. Goodman (Ed.), *Problems and Projects* (pp. 437–446). New York: Bobbs-Merrill.

Grosso, M. (2015). *The Man Who Could Fly: St. Joseph of Copertino and the Mystery of Levitation.* Lanham, MD: Rowman Littlefield.

Gurney, E., Myers, F. W. H., & Podmore, F. (1886). *Phantasms of the Living* (Vols. 1–2). London: Trübner. (Available on CTR website, http://www.esalen.org/ctr/scholarly-resources)

Hart, H. (1959). *The Enigma of Survival.* Springfield, IL: Charles C. Thomas.

Hart, H., & Hart, E. B. (1933). Visions and apparitions collectively and reciprocally perceived. *Proceedings of the Society for Psychical Research, 41*, 205–249.

Hartmann, E. (1975). Dreams and other hallucinations: An approach to the underlying mechanism. In R. K. Siegel & L. J. West (Eds.), *Hallucinations: Behavior, Experience, and Theory* (pp. 71–79). New York: Wiley.

Hodgson, R. (1898). A further record of observations of certain phenomena of trance. *Proceedings of the Society for Psychical Research, 13*, 284–582.

Holden, J. M., Greyson, B., & James, D. (Eds.). (2009). *The Handbook of Near-Death Experiences: Thirty Years of Investigation.* Santa Barbara, CA: Praeger.

James, W. (1889). Notes on automatic writing. *Proceedings of the American Society for Psychical Research, 1*, 548–564.

James, W. (1890). *The Principles of Psychology* (Vols. 1–2). New York: Henry Holt.

James, W. (1986). *Essays in Psychical Research* (F. H. Burkhardt, Ed.). Cambridge, MA: Harvard University Press.

Kahneman, D. (2011). *Thinking, Fast and Slow.* New York: Farrar, Strauss and Giroux.

Kanigel, R. (1991). *The Man Who Knew Infinity: A Life of the Genius Ramanujan.* New York: Scribners.

Kelly, E. F., Kelly, E. W., Crabtree, A., Gauld, A., Grosso, M., & Greyson, B. (2007). *Irreducible Mind: Toward a Psychology for the 21st Century.* Lanham, MD: Rowman & Littlefield.

Kelly, E. W. (Ed.). (2013). *Science, the Self, and Survival After Death: Selected Writings of Ian Stevenson.* Lanham, MD: Rowman & Littlefield.

Laureys, S., & Tononi, G. (Eds.). (2009). *The Neurology of Consciousness: Cognitive Neuroscience and Neuropathology.* London: Elsevier, Academic Press.

Leary, D. E. (1990). William James on the self and personality: Clearing the ground for subsequent theorists, researchers, and practitioners. In M. G. Johnson & T. B. Henley (Eds.), *Reflections on* The Principles of Psychology*: William James After a Century* (pp. 101–137). Hillsdale, NJ: Lawrence Erlbaum.

Llinás, R., & Ribary, U. (1994). Perception as an oneiric-like state modulated by the senses. In C. Koch & J. L. Davis (Eds.), *Large-Scale Neuronal Theories of the Brain* (pp. 111–124). Cambridge, MA: MIT Press.

Lowe, E. J. (1998). There are no easy problems of consciousness. In J. Shear (Ed.), *Explaining Consciousness—The "Hard Problem"* (pp. 117–123). Cambridge, MA: MIT Press.

Luria, A. R. (1968). *The Mind of a Mnemonist* (L. Solotaroff, Trans.). New York: Avon Books.

Marr, D. (1982). *Vision: A Computational Investigation into the Human Representation and Processing of Visual Information.* San Francisco: W. H. Freeman.

Marshall, P. (2005). *Mystical Encounters with the Natural World: Experiences and Explanations.* Oxford: Oxford University Press.

McClendon, H. J. (1955). Uses of similarity of structure in contemporary philosophy. *Mind, 64,* 79–95.

Morris, R. L. (1982). Assessing experimental support for true precognition. *Journal of Parapsychology, 46,* 321–336.

Murphy, G. (with Dale, L. A.). (1961). *Challenge of Psychical Research.* New York: Harper.

Myers, D. G. (2002). *Intuition: Its Powers and Perils.* New Haven, CT: Yale University Press.

Myers, F. W. H. (1895). The subliminal self. Chapter 9: The relation of supernormal phenomena to time;— Precognition. *Proceedings of the Society for Psychical Research, 11,* 408–593.

Myers, F. W. H. (1903). *Human Personality and Its Survival of Bodily Death* (Vols. 1–2). London: Longmans, Green. (Available on CTR website, http://www.esalen.org/ctr/scholarly-resources)

Owens, J. E., Cook [Kelly], E. W., & Stevenson, I. (1990). Features of "near-death experience" in relation to whether or not patients were near death. *Lancet, 336,* 1175–1177.

Parnia, S. (2013). *Erasing Death: The Science That Is Rewriting the Boundaries Between Life and Death.* New York: Harper One.

Pols, E. (1998). *Mind Regained.* Ithaca, NY: Cornell University Press.

Radin, D. (2006). *Entangled Minds: Extrasensory Experiences in a Quantum Reality.* New York: Simon & Schuster.

Rhine, L. E. (1977). Research methods with spontaneous cases. In B. B. Wolman (Ed.), *Handbook of Parapsychology* (pp. 59–80). New York: Van Nostrand Reinhold.

Rosenblum, B., & Kuttner, F. (2011). *Quantum Enigma: Physics Encounters Consciousness* (2nd ed.). New York: Oxford University Press.

Sacks, O. (1987). *The Man Who Mistook His Wife for a Hat.* New York: Simon & Schuster.

Salter, W. (1950). *Trance Mediumship: An Introductory Study of Mrs. Piper and Mrs. Leonard.* London: Society for Psychical Research.

Schouten, S. (1979). Analysis of spontaneous case as reported in "Phantasms of the Living." *European Journal of Parapsychology, 2,* 408–455.

Schouten, S. (1983). A different approach for analyzing spontaneous cases: With particular reference to the study of Louisa E. Rhine's case collection. *Journal of Parapsychology, 47,* 323–340.

Searle, J. R. (1992). *The Rediscovery of the Mind.* Cambridge, MA: MIT Press.

Sidgwick, E. (1915). A contribution to the study of the psychology of Mrs. Piper's trance phenomena. *Proceedings of the Society for Psychical Research, 28,* 1–657.

Simons, D. J., & Chabris, C. F. (1999). Gorillas in our midst: Sustained inattentional blindness for dynamic events. *Perception, 28,* 1059–1074.

Singer, W. (2007). Large-scale temporal coordination of cortical activity as a prerequisite for conscious experience. In M. Velmans & S. Schneider (Eds.), *The Blackwell Companion to Consciousness* (pp. 605–615). Malden, MA: Blackwell.

Snyder, A. W., & Mitchell, D. J. (1999). Is integer arithmetic fundamental to mental processing?: The mind's secret arithmetic. *Proceedings of the Royal Society of London—B, 266,* 587–592.

Stapp, H. P. (2007). *Mindful Universe: Quantum Mechanics and the Participating Observer.* Berlin: Springer.

Stevenson, I. (1975–1983). *Cases of the Reincarnation Type* (Vols. 1–4). Charlottesville: University of Virginia Press.

Stevenson, I. (1978). Some comments on automatic writing. *Journal of the American Society for Psychical Research, 72,* 315–332.

Stevenson, I. (1997). *Reincarnation and Biology: A Contribution to the Etiology of Birthmarks and Birth Defects* (Vols. 1–2). Westport, CT: Praeger.

Stevenson, I. (2001). *Children Who Remember Previous Lives: A Question of Reincarnation* (Rev. ed.). Jefferson, NC: McFarland.

Stromeyer, C. F., III (1970). Eidetekers. *Psychology Today, 4,* 76–80.

Stromeyer, C. F., III, & Psotka, J. (1970). The detailed texture of eidetic images. *Nature, 225,* 346–349.

Tart, C. T. (1993). Mind embodied: Computer-generated virtual reality as a new, dualistic-interactive model for transpersonal psychology. In K. R. Rao (Ed.), *Cultivating Conscious-*

ness: Enhancing Human Potential, Wellness, and Healing (pp. 123–137). Westport, CT: Praeger.

Tart, C. T. (2009). *The End of Materialism: How Evidence of the Paranormal is Bringing Science and Spirit Together.* Oakland, CA: New Harbinger Publications.

Thouless, R. H., & Wiesner, B. P. (1947). The psi process in normal and "paranormal" psychology. *Proceedings of the Society for Psychical Research, 32,* 177–196.

Treffert, D. (2010). *Islands of Genius: The Bountiful Mind of the Autistic, Acquired, and Sudden Savant.* Philadelphia: Jessica Kingsley.

Tucker, J. B. (2005). *Life Before Life: A Scientific Investigation of Children's Memories of Previous Lives.* New York: St. Martin's Press.

Tucker, J. B. (2013). *Return to Life: Extraordinary Cases of Children Who Remember Past Lives.* New York: St. Martin's Press.

Tyrrell, G. N. M. (1953). *Apparitions* (Rev. ed.). London: Society for Psychical Research. (Original edition published 1943)

Van Lommel, P. (2010). *Consciousness Beyond Life: The Science of the Near-Death Experience.* New York: Harper Collins.

Van Lommel, P. (2013). Non-local consciousness: A concept based on scientific research on near-death experiences during cardiac arrest. *Journal of Consciousness Studies, 20*(1–2), 7–48.

Varela, F., Lachaux, J.-P., Rodriguez, E., & Martinerie, J. (2001). The brainweb: Phase synchronization and large-scale integration. *Nature Reviews: Neuroscience, 2,* 229–239. doi:10.1038/35067550

Wild, K. W. (1938). *Intuition.* Cambridge: Cambridge University Press.

2

MYSTICAL EXPERIENCES AS WINDOWS ON REALITY

Paul Marshall

St. Benedict of Nursia was once deep in prayer at the monastery of Monte Cassino when an extraordinary light appeared to him. It was nighttime, and the monks were sound asleep. Only Benedict was awake, keeping vigil high in the tower that he used as his quarters. As Benedict stood by a window and prayed to God, a great light flashed out from above and dispelled the darkness. But this was no ordinary radiance: it was brighter than the light of day and brought together the created world in its entirety, both heaven and earth. The cosmic vision, which nowadays would attract the label "mystical," was joined by a more specific, "clairvoyant" perception. Gazing intently into the light, Benedict discerned what he took to be the soul of his friend Germanus, Bishop of Capua, carried aloft in a fiery sphere by angels. Benedict had a messenger sent to Capua, and it was found that at the time of the vision the Bishop had passed away.

The story is told in Book II of *The Dialogues of Gregory the Great*, composed by Pope Gregory around 593, over 40 years after the death of Benedict. Gregory helpfully provides an explanation of the mysterious occurrence, for the deacon Peter, Gregory's interlocutor in the dialogues, asks in wonderment how it is possible for one man to see the entire world. Gregory explains that when a soul is raised up in the light of God, everything below becomes visible to it and appears small. But heaven and earth have not shrunk. Rather, the mind has expanded in God, opened up by the divine light and lifted above the world.

Even if the story is a hagiographical concoction indebted to Greco-Roman sources for some of its details, the combination of unifying mystical vision and psychical perception in conjunction with Gregory's attempt at explanation provides an appropriate entrée to the guiding idea behind the present chapter: *if deep connections exist between mystical experience and other types of extraordinary phenomena, such as the psychical range of perceptions, then the study of mystical experience is likely to contribute significantly to the explanation of these other phenomena.* It will do so in the first instance by expanding the range of data to be taken into account when formulating and evaluating explanations. But it will contribute in a more radical fashion too *if* mystical states are windows on reality, "windows through which the mind looks out upon a more extensive and inclusive world," as William James (1902, p. 428) put it.[1] Moreover, the story of Benedict's vision introduces a feature of mystical experience that will be important here, namely a special luminosity associated with what appear to be heightened powers of perception and knowing that can even be cosmic in reach.

There is good reason to think that mystical and psi phenomena are related. Elsewhere I have described several points of contact (Marshall, 2011):

1. They both appear to bring perceptual and cognitive enhancements of a "paranormal" kind, not possible according to present-day, mainstream science, or more generally, to the often unquestioned, culture-specific, period-specific assumptions about the nature of the world and how it can be known, assumptions that Broad (1949, 1962) called "Basic Limiting Principles."
2. Certain personality traits, including high transliminality, thin boundaries, and high absorptive capacity, predispose individuals to both kinds of experiences.
3. They share many triggers, including meditation, sensory deprivation, psychological distress, illness, near-death trauma, dreams, and psychedelics.
4. They can both feature in the same near-death experience (NDE).
5. Psychical experiences can develop into mystical ones: for example, clairvoyant perceptions and out-of-body experiences (OBEs) sometimes take a mystical turn.

In addition, mystical experiences are sometimes preceded or followed by events of a psychical or synchronistic character, giving rise to temporal clusters of unusual experiences. It is also noteworthy that some systems of spiritual cultivation bring together psi and mystical phenomena. These include the yoga of Patañjali, discussed by Kelly and Whicher in Chapter 9, and the yogic-tantric systems that seek to raise a power (*kuṇḍalinī*) said to be latent in the body through a series of wheels or knots (*cakras*), bringing at first psychical abilities and then mystical realizations (Biernacki, Chapter 10). Consciousness, which is ordinarily constricted by the somatic knots, is progressively released by yogic practice. In modern parlance, these systems can be construed as early examples of "filter theory," according to which consciousness is not generated by the body but constrained by it, with the senses, nervous system, and brain acting as "reducing valves" in some way (Grosso, Chapter 3). Another example of great interest is to be found in Jainism. Here omniscience (*kevalajñāna*) is said to be the intrinsic possession of the soul, but it is ordinarily obscured by various kinds of karmic matter that are attracted to the soul and which bind to it. Stage-by-stage removal of the obscuring karmas yields first the clairvoyant and clairaudient perceptions of bodily things, then the subtler telepathic knowledge of mental things, and finally unlimited knowledge, perception, bliss, and power. Again, the scheme may qualify as filter theory, one in which various kinds of karmic matter act as the reducing valves.

Scholars of mysticism have often neglected psi phenomena despite the occurrence of these and other so-called miraculous or accidental phenomena on the mystical path, and parapsychologists have been similarly neglectful, paying little attention to mystical experience (Carr, 2007; Marshall, 2011).[2] However, the connections highlighted above do require explanation, and, if they are as significant as they appear to be, it would be remiss to treat mystical, psychical, and related phenomena (such as near-death and out-of-body experiences) in isolation. Theories of telepathy, clairvoyance, precognition, and psychokinesis that might seem plausible within their own field of application could be found lacking when called upon to accommodate mystical cognitions. Similarly, theories of mystical experience may show their limitations when asked to find a place for veridical psi perceptions. A theory of NDE that dwells on the neuropsychology of the "dying brain" will be unsatisfactory if it is unable to account for very similar experiences of a mystical character in circumstances that are not at all life-threatening, such as appreciation of music and the beauty of nature. Clearly, theorists of psi and NDE will have to include the mystical range of experiences in their considerations, and theorists of mysticism cannot afford to neglect psi and the other secondary phenomena associated with the mystical path. Indeed, a unifying theoretical framework is called for, one that subsumes the related phenomena, attentive to differences as well as similarities. It is to be hoped that the framework would surpass single-phenomenon approaches in the way that unified theories in the sciences are richer and deeper than theories of individual phenomena.

Of the various kinds of rogue phenomena to be brought together in such a framework, mystical experience may be the one that holds the key to the "big picture." This is because mystical experience seems to reach into the deeper nature of things, to disclose reality behind its outward appearances, as some definitions have emphasized. For example, Carmody and Carmody (1996) define mystical experience succinctly as "direct experience of ultimate reality" (p. 10). For present purposes a slightly more elaborate definition will be useful: *experiences are "mystical" if they bring a sense of deepened contact with reality, the contact consisting of unity or at least intimate connection or presence, and often an intuitive type of knowing*. In this more inclusive definition, contact is not limited to ultimate reality, variously understood as God, "the ground of being," pure consciousness, "the Absolute," and so forth, but can involve facets, levels, or contents of reality that may not be ultimate yet have a claim to objective existence, to be "real," such as the natural world, fellow human beings, otherworldly realms, and various spiritual entities. A narrow understanding of reality is thereby avoided, and so too a concomitantly narrow definition of mystical experience.

Perhaps more so than any other kind of experience, mystical experience invites us to question received assumptions about the nature of reality, the ways in which it can be known, and our relation to it. Mystics can feel as though they have looked behind the veil of appearances and caught sight of the nature of self, world, consciousness, time, and even the meaning of it all. While the traditional branch of philosophy called "metaphysics" has approached a similar set of concerns through discursive reasoning, mystical experience is said to involve a direct intuition, a special way of knowing or "gnosis" independent of the senses and rational analysis. In the modern period, philosophers have not generally acknowledged the possibility of an "intellectual intuition" that grasps its object directly, but if there is such a form of knowing, the study of mystical experience may offer special insights into the nature of reality and so help elucidate psi and other extraordinary experiences, and indeed the nature of consciousness itself.

PRELIMINARIES: THEORETICAL AND PRACTICAL CHALLENGES

The proposal that mystical experiences offer insights into the deeper nature of things faces significant challenges. On the theoretical side, many have denied that the experiences do bring contact with objective reality. Indeed, it is often claimed that they merely reflect the subjective religious/cultural contexts of those who have them or are simply products of a disordered brain. However, these viewpoints, which can be called *radical contextualism* and *neuroscientific reductionism*, respectively, are beset by serious difficulties, which have been detailed elsewhere (e.g., Forman, 1990, 1999; Kelly & Grosso, 2007b; Marshall, 2005; Studstill, 2005). This is not to say that religious conditioning, neurobiology, or a combination of the two are irrelevant, for there can be little doubt that they do contribute to some features, as I observe below in connection with time and luminosity. Moreover, filter theory alerts us to the possibility that psychology and biology have important roles to play in the occurrence of mystical experience because they regulate the contents of consciousness.

How, then, might one go about ascertaining whether mystical experiences do what they seem to do, which is to bring deepened contact with reality? One approach is to appeal to the "realness" of the experiences, for the experiences feel very real indeed. The feeling of realness presumably derives from their clarity, vividness, intensity, and knowing quality. In comparison with the crystal-clear awareness and profound knowing of mystical experience, everyday experience can feel dreamlike, shadowy, lifeless, limited, superficial. For those personally acquainted with the contrast, the appeal to realness carries great weight, but it is unlikely to impress critics, who will counter with the observation that psychotic episodes can feel very real, and that a sense of "realness" is not a reliable guide to what is "real" (Deikman, 1966, pp. 332–333). Nevertheless, the clarity, wakefulness, and intensity of mystical experiences are by all accounts truly astonishing and should not be dismissed lightly. The feeling of realness certainly requires explanation, whether in neuropsychological terms or by reference to the nature of the realities disclosed by mystical experience. If deeper reality is characterized by clear, wakeful consciousness, then contact with it will bring clarity and wakefulness and therefore a sense of realness.

Next there is the appeal to unanimity. At first sight, the common occurrence of certain features, such as unity, knowing, luminosity, and timelessness, across the mystical experiences of many different persons might be thought to testify to their objectivity, as if a shared reality beyond personal subjectivities and varied cultural contexts had given rise to the experiential commonalities. But as James (1902) observed, the appeal to consensus is just an appeal to numbers and is at best suggestive (p. 424). Neuroscientific reductionists will put the commonalities down to biology and psychology shared by all human beings, not to shared deeper realities. However, if reductionists are unable to give an adequate account of the common features in terms of shared neuropsychology, then the appeal to unanimity becomes stronger.

Finding the argument from unanimity incomplete, the philosopher W. T. Stace (1960) raised a logical argument to show that a mystical core exists that transcends individual mystics. He could do so because he took the essence of genuine mystical experiences to be a pure consciousness empty of all sensations, images, and concepts. Having no distinguishing features, this consciousness must be one and the same for everyone and is therefore "transsubjective." The merit of Stace's purely logical argument, which invokes the principle of the identity of indiscernibles, has been debated (e.g., Kelly & Grosso, 2007b, pp. 519–521; Price, 1962), and is not applicable to the many mystical experiences that are rich in content.

Another approach is to appeal to the morally and therapeutically transformative consequences of mystical experiences. Although the experiences can initially bring confusion, it seems that in the short term they can also help individuals through crises and in the longer term encourage growth. The appeal to positive consequences is to adopt a traditional way of evaluating religious experiences ("by their fruits ye shall know them") or an updated, pragmatic, Jamesian version that takes results to be a criterion of truth, on the assumption that the positive influences exerted by experiences attest to their genuineness (Barnard, 1997, pp. 281–293). The argument assumes that mystical experiences do foster ethical attitudes and promote psychological well-being, and there is evidence that they do (e.g., Wulff, 2000), although there is also room for debate (e.g., Barnard & Kripal, 2002). For example, it can be asked whether mystical experience in itself is sufficient to encourage positive transformation or whether it needs reinforcement from spiritual teachings that provide interpretation and guidance. It can also be asked why those who have the experiences sometimes go on to indulge in unedifying behaviors: are their actions due to or in spite of their experiences? Mystical traditions have long recognized the dangers of the path, including ego-inflation and misdirected eros.

There may, however, be more convincing ways of establishing objectivity. First, given the intimate connections between mystical and psi phenomena outlined above, good-quality evidence for the veridicality of psi cognitions points to the genuineness of mystical ones. The veridicality of psi is open to relatively straightforward investigation, and there is indeed good evidence for psi (Kelly et al., 2007; Radin, 2006), even if it is not widely recognized in the mainstream. It follows that there is indirect support for the objectivity of mystical experience. Second, mystical experiences sometimes appear to furnish insights into the natural world, such as the coexistence of past, present, and future, and the existence of holistic interconnections between things. There is a body of literature, mostly of a popular bent, that sets out parallels between mysticism and physics in order to suggest that the mystics of old anticipated modern scientific discoveries through their special insights into physical reality (e.g., Capra, 1975). If it were established that mystical experiences have furnished such insights, there would be compelling evidence for their objectivity. Although scholars have been quick to highlight the many deficiencies of the popular mysticism–physics literature, there has been little constructive work of a philosophical nature on the topic, as Jones (2010, pp. iii–iv) has observed, and the possibility remains that mystical experiences afford genuine insights into the natural world (Marshall, 1997, 2005, pp. 276–277).

But if mystics do make contact with deeper realities, including ordinarily hidden aspects of nature, why are there significant differences between the metaphysical teachings of the various mystical traditions? I address this concern in a supplemental article ("Mystical Experience and Metaphysics") on Esalen Institute's CTR website,[3] but, very briefly, even if mystical experiences do provide deepened contact with reality, there can still be a diversity of metaphysical teachings across the mystical traditions. In the first place, such teachings do not derive from mystical experiences alone but draw upon religious and philosophical ideas too, which can vary considerably across traditions. Moreover, if reality is multifaceted or stratified, containing domains or levels, then mystics in different traditions may latch onto different aspects of reality, emphasizing and valuing mystical contact with some more than others, in accordance with their religious backgrounds.

There are practical challenges too. Mystical experience is not an everyday occurrence and not usually inducible at will. When it does occur, it may be hard to comprehend, and subsequently forgetfulness and difficulty of expression can intervene. It is a common regret of mystics that they are unable to bring back to mind their discoveries or give adequate expression to them. Fortunately, mystics do grasp and recall their experiences up to a point, and they do report specific details, general characteristics, and stages of development, and so the situation is not as bleak as it might first appear. There is, however, another difficulty relevant to a study of the present kind. Choices have to be made about the types and specific examples of mystical experiences on which to draw, and also the kinds of mystical texts, traditions, and thinkers. These choices can reflect the presuppositions of the researcher and so introduce "selection bias." My preference is to use predominantly modern-day reports of mystical experiences that occur "spontaneously" and are relatively "unattached" or "unchurched," that is, not deeply entrenched within traditions of belief and practice. In the main, these reports are more descriptive, less metaphorical, and less doctrinally loaded than the reports furnished by mystics situated within traditions. To use Smart's (1962) term, the modern accounts tend not to be so laden with *ramified* language, with expressions and concepts that derive their meanings from the belief systems in which they are embedded. It is true that the testimonies of mystical virtuosi in the religious traditions, whose long-term training may have led them on several occasions to profound mystical states, could be very informative indeed, more so than those of untrained moderns, who may report just one or two experiences, and lack the contemplative techniques and interpretative resources that immersion in a tradition can give. However, if their mystical writings are appreciably ramified, it will be difficult or impossible to gauge the extent to which the writings express mystical experience or indeed whether they have a basis in experience at all. For example, in the absence of autobiographical evidence, it has been debated whether Meister Eckhart's mystical writings derive from learning alone or draw on personal mystical experience too (e.g., Tobin, 1984).

As a methodological strategy, it will therefore pay to give primary attention, at least in the early stages of inquiry, to the more descriptive, less obviously ramified reports, whether located in traditions of practice and belief, or more likely, spontaneous and unattached. With some basic phenomenological details established from these unadorned reports, recourse can then be made to the religious traditions for testimonies, formal schematizations of contemplative experiences, and metaphysical doctrines. My use of these traditions here is necessarily restricted, but more detailed consideration of three examples is given in Part II (Shaw, Chapter 8; Kelly & Whicher, Chapter 9; Biernacki, Chapter 10).

A consequence of this approach is that one particular type of mystical experience will be emphasized in the following, for it is common among the spontaneous cases and can be rich in descriptive detail, namely the "extrovertive" (Stace, 1960) or "natural" (Zaehner, 1957) mystical type. In these, experience of the world is transformed by some combination of *unity, reality, knowledge, heightened perception, self-transcendence, altered time-experience, luminosity, love, joy,* and *peace*, to mention the more commonly reported features, although most experiences exhibit just a selection (Marshall, 2005, pp. 26–27, 59–81). A bias toward the extrovertive type is in fact advantageous in the present context, for this mystical type is closest to the psi perceptions, both seeming to afford "paranormal" cognitions of the world, cognitions that should not be possible according to present-day, mainstream science and epistemology (Marshall, 2011, pp. 5–7).

It might be objected that extrovertive experience is an inferior, undeveloped type of mystical experience, as some have asserted, and is therefore of limited metaphysical interest. While extrovertive experiences can involve fairly modest extensions of consciousness, with transformed perceptions largely confined to the immediate surroundings, some have a much greater reach, appearing to confer knowledge and perception on a vast, even cosmic scale. Stace assumed that extrovertive experiences always take place through the bodily senses, but they also occur when the senses are off duty, when the "eyes are closed," as in sleep, near-death crises, meditative withdrawals, and anesthesia. In fact, loss of sensory contact with the world can precipitate the more expansive, cosmic experiences, as if the loss of sensory input brings into the open a mode of perception more penetrating and inclusive than the everyday kind. If I give emphasis to the cosmic type of mystical experience here and neglect less inclusive ones, it is because of its potential significance. If truly what it seems to be, this type of experience will have far-reaching implications for the philosophy of perception and for epistemology and metaphysics more generally.

Although it is no easy matter to establish the objectivity of mystical experience, we can still pose and attempt to answer "what if" questions: what do mystical experiences, including mystical NDEs, tell us if they are indeed revelatory of reality? Here I shall focus on the implications of some mystical characteristics directly relevant to psi: altered time-experience, knowing, unity, self-transcendence, and luminosity.

NO TIME/ALL TIME

Mystical experiences often begin suddenly and can be of a duration that is hard to judge, but are generally brief, often lasting no more than a few seconds or minutes of clock time. It can feel as if time is unimportant or no longer relevant, or even that it has stopped. Indeed, one of the more intriguing time-related characteristics is *temporal cessation*. Time or the sense of it seems to stop: "Eventually, the sense of time passing stopped entirely. It is difficult to describe this feeling, but perhaps it would be better to say that there was no time, or no sense of time. Only the present moment existed" (Smith & Tart, 1998, p. 100). It is not surprising that mystical transformations of time-experience should be hard to describe. Even in ordinary circumstances, the temporal qualities of experience are difficult to pin down, and the language of time is unhelpfully abstract and metaphorical, based as it often is on the questionable reification of time into a thing that flows or passes, as if it were a river rather than a quality of experience. Those who try to describe the changes to time-experience often resort to such phrases as "time stopped," "out of time," "it was eternal," "a timeless moment," which certainly indicate that something curious happened but are not very informative. Recollecting a childhood experience, Yvonne Lubbock (1961) strove to express the change thus:

> I was in the garden, muddling about alone. A cuckoo flew over, call-
> ing. Suddenly I experienced a sensation that I can only describe as an
> effect that might follow the rotating of a mental kaleidoscope. It was a
> feeling of timelessness, not only that time stood still, that duration had
> ceased, but that I was myself outside time altogether. Somehow I knew
> that I was part of eternity. And there was also a feeling of spaceless-
> ness. I lost all awareness of my surroundings. With this detachment I
> felt the intensest joy I had ever known, and yet with so great a long-
> ing—for what I did not know—that it was scarcely distinguishable
> from suffering. (p. 21)

When applied to various kinds of mystical experiences, "timeless" or
"eternal" may indicate that the "fleeting" or "transient" quality was absent, or, as in the above example, that time was completely left behind, as
if a condition entirely beyond time and space had been reached. Nevertheless, a "timeless" experience may have some kind of time-related quality, such as the sense of living in the "now."

Some descriptions indicate more concretely how the timelessness was
experienced. It can involve a cessation of motion and sound. Objects in
the visual field stop moving, and a silence or "hush" descends: "Suddenly, everything stopped. I stopped. The birds were no longer singing. The
distant traffic sounds from the village ceased. Nothing moved. Utter silence, utter stillness. The May sunlight was transformed into a white
radiance" (RERC No. 004415,[4] in Maxwell & Tschudin, 1996, p. 53).
Yet timelessness does not preclude a dynamic or rhythmic quality. The
above account continues: "When first trying to describe the experience I
said it was as if I were hearing music and *knew* I was one of the notes" (p.
54). Despite the cessation, this description perhaps suggests a sense of
unity with, of being part of, a harmonious flow. Timelessness can be
vibrant, pulsating with "suspended animation":

> I was walking, alone, downhill, and the prospect before me was a wide
> expanse of sky and sea shimmering under the afternoon sun. Again, all
> sensation of time disappeared—or rather I felt that time had become
> frozen. There was also a feeling of the cessation of all sound. The
> shimmering of the water was extended to a quivering and throbbing of
> the whole physical universe, but this quivering seemed to be frozen in
> the sense of not taking part in time. (RERC No. 003401, in Maxwell &
> Tschudin, 1996, p. 135)

Changes to time-experience occur in a variety of situations, ranging from the commonplace, such as the "dragging of time" due to boredom and clock watching, to the dramatic transformations in mystical states (e.g., Flaherty, 1999; Taylor, 2007). It is well known that some psychoactive drugs alter time-experience, bringing slowing-down, speeding-up, and standing-still effects, and more bizarre ones too, such as reversal, repetition, and disjointedness (e.g., Shanon, 2001). Pahnke and Richards (1966) were of the opinion that while slowing down and speeding up may precede or follow the mystical phases of psychedelic experiences they should not be considered mystical in themselves. Certainly, it would be hasty to assume that all transformations of time-experience have great metaphysical significance. The underestimation and overestimation of elapsed time have received plausible neurological and psychological explanations (Grondin, 2010), such as the cognitive, information-processing approaches that emphasize the role of attention and changes to the perceptual registration of contents, more registration in a given period leading to overestimation, less leading to underestimation. While "time estimation" explanations may be applicable to speeding-up and slowing-down effects in a variety of circumstances, it is debatable whether they could be extended to the complete temporal cessation in mystical experience, except perhaps for those states that are empty of discriminable contents or involve absorptive concentration on a static object. In these cases, there is no registered change of contents and therefore nothing on which to base estimates of elapsed time. But it is not obvious why experiences rich in transforming contents, such as those that occur in a natural environment, should "freeze."

Perhaps time-effects such as cessation may be explicable if ordinary experience is dependent on the construction of the so-called specious, psychological, sensible, or phenomenal present, to note just a few of its many names. As William James (1890) famously pointed out, there is reason to think that moments of experience are not pure instants but durations or intervals that encapsulate a temporal range of contents with different degrees of prominence (Vol. 1, pp. 605–610), as exemplified by the after-image trails of moving objects. The phenomenal present was termed "specious" by E. Robert Kelly (James's "E. R. Clay") because its temporal span of perceptual contents derives from the immediate past, and so it has to be distinguished from the instantaneous "real" present of clock time (Andersen & Grush, 2009).[5] This extended, phenomenal present is sometimes thought to make perception of motion possible. It can be conjectured that the sense of transience and the time direction of ordinary experience derive from the composite contents of these "drops of experience," and that dramatic transformations such as stoppage and reversal follow from changes to the composition of these moments, including changes to the ordering and relative prominence of "past," "present," and "future" contents (Marshall, 2006, pp. 110–112, 139–142). For example, if the phenomenal present is narrowed, shorn of much of its receding ("past") and leading ("future") contents, or if all the contents have the same prominence, then the sense of transience may vanish. That the phenomenal present is affected in psychedelic states is suggested by the dramatic intensification there of after-image trails or "tracers."

However, this is not to say that altered time-experience is always a purely neuropsychological affair and lacks metaphysical significance. There are experiences in which time and space seem to be left behind entirely, sometimes in connection with a pure luminosity that is felt to be the ultimate reality. Also of considerable metaphysical interest are experiences in which time and space still have meaning but are fundamentally transformed. This condition is sometimes called "eternity," but perhaps *temporal inclusiveness* would be less ambiguous and more descriptive. Although a mystical experience may seem to pass in a flash, it is nevertheless felt to transcend ordinary time and space by encompassing a very great span of time and space, as if the field of experience has expanded enormously to embrace not only the concurrent states of things but their successive states too, in an expanded field of awareness. It appears that the "life reviews" and "life previews" of near-death experience can have this quality too, "so that past, present and future all seem to be happening at once" (Grey, 1985, p. 118), although life reviews that show everything together in "panoramic" fashion are less frequent than those that proceed in forward time sequence (Stevenson & Cook [Kelly], 1995, pp. 454–455). The precognized events, whether personal or on the world stage, are sometimes reported as alterable, conditional on choices to be made, or sometimes as "already there," as fully existent as the present from which they are viewed.

The "timeless moment" of mystical experience seems to disclose a vast span of sequential states, being inclusive not just of the immediate past and anticipated future of the specious present but of great stretches of the actual past and actual future. The span of contents, if truly what it seems to be, is so great that psychological processes as ordinarily understood could not possibly be responsible for putting it together. In extreme cases of cosmic consciousness, the neuropsychologically constructed phenomenal present seems to have given way to a present that is temporally and spatially all-inclusive, one that could be called the "noumenal present" if it discloses the intuitively apprehended universe-in-itself.

The following mystical account illustrates temporal inclusiveness. Past and future ceased to have meaning outside the present moment, for everything that had been or would be was contained in the moment:

> I cannot recall that I was thinking of anything in particular, when all of a sudden I was in a new dimension of experience. I can only attempt to explain this by saying that at one moment I was rigid, and the next I had become fluid and merged with all there is. There was no sense of individual identity, yet personal awareness and appreciation remained. There was no past and no future, only awareness of living in an eternal moment that encompassed all that has been, that is, and that will be. I felt that I knew all, and nothing seemed to be unnecessary or out of place. There was perfect harmony and perfect blending of all into an indescribable expression of joy, peace, beauty, and love. (Johnson, 1984, pp. 111–112)

In another case, a girl felt her "head" increase in size until it contained the world, the heavens, and all of time: "Everything that had ever happened or would happen was within myself" (Johnson, 1959, p. 71). Recalling in adulthood this expansion of consciousness, she claimed to have seen then many events of which she later came to learn. Applied to experiences such as these, "eternal" and "timeless" may again refer to a felt lack of transience but additionally indicate their inclusiveness, the coexistence of many temporal states of things in the one experience. Once again, it would be a mistake to think that the experience is a lifeless stasis in which nothing happens: rather, it would appear that it is a vibrant everywhere and everywhen in which everything is happening.

The expanded spatial character of temporal inclusiveness is conveyed by one of the most interesting premodern depictions. Long before physicists found reason to spatialize time into the block universe of spacetime (see Carr, Chapter 7 below), the seventeenth-century mystic, poet, and Anglican priest Thomas Traherne explained that all places and times, all "Kingdoms and Ages," are present in a great space. While it is conceivable that Traherne arrived at the idea through theological reflection alone, his autobiographical remarks confirm that he was personally familiar with mystical expansions. Traherne (1908) observed that infinite space is made even more infinite because it exists in a greater space "wherein all moments are infinitely exhibited" and in which "all ages appear together, all occurrences stand up at once," visible to "all comprehensors and enjoyers" (pp. 323–324). It is an eternal moment, an "immovable duration" that contains all "moving durations" (p. 324), a space that contains all spaces and times.

It is difficult to imagine how purely neuroscientific theories would go about explaining the experience of far-reaching spatial and temporal inclusiveness, other than to dismiss the claims of mystics as misinterpretations of their experiences. Zaehner supposed that when mystics believe they are conscious of the entire universe they are merely experiencing the ordinarily unconscious contents of their own minds and misinterpret the expansion of awareness as genuine experience of the universe (Marshall, 2005, pp. 213–216). But it is not obvious that an experience of the contents of one's own mind that are normally below the threshold of awareness, understood as a rather limited, psychological image of the world in the way that Zaehner does, would be at all like the cosmic inclusiveness reported by mystics, or indeed would exhibit the order, harmony, luminosity, bliss, and intellectual clarity that mystical experiences do, an inclusiveness not just of past states but, it would seem, of future ones too. Experience of the normally subconscious contents of one's own mind, understood in a limited way as purely personal in extent or enlarged by inherited collective contents, might well be a rather patchy, murky, chaotic, and backward-looking affair, very much focused on the past.

There is, then, reason to entertain the possibility that the mystic's eternal moment is metaphysically significant and to make the following two-part conjecture: (1) the universe exists as a spatiotemporal whole in which all concurrent and successive states of things exist together; (2) the full spatiotemporal range of contents is open to inspection in certain mystical states, and information about specific contents can be accessed in retrocognitive, clairvoyant, and precognitive psi. Furthermore, the mystical data suggest that this spatiotemporal whole is not some lifeless repository of events but is vibrant with animation.

The first part of the conjecture is not without independent support, given developments in twentieth-century physics, although the physicist's concept of spacetime is open to a variety of interpretations, some of which reject the idea of a block universe in which all events are laid out. The second part needs further attention: it is not enough to posit the existence of a spatiotemporal substratum that contains all events, for it remains to be explained how something so vast and full of detail can be known in mystical states, and how very specific items of information about events can be extracted from it and find their way into psi cognitions. It is therefore appropriate to turn now to the question of mystical knowing.

KNOWING, UNITY, SELF-TRANSCENDENCE

As James (1902) observed, "noetic quality" is a key feature of mystical experiences: they are "states of knowledge . . . states of insight into depths of truth unplumbed by the discursive intellect" (p. 380). They bring what seems to be an immediate, effortless kind of knowing very different from everyday cognition, with its indirect, piecemeal ways. One man, finding himself surrounded by light, realized that he possessed an intrinsic power of knowing that was different from the usual kind: "There was also an amazing 'knowingness' rather than knowledgeableness, that is, I knew, not by application to study, but because it was in my mind from the beginning and had so existed as an attribute, a primary possession" (RERC No. 000189, in Beardsworth, 1977, pp. 15–16). The observation that the "knowingness" is an original possession echoes the oft-reported feeling that mystical experience is not a completely novel condition but a "coming home." The condition had been known before but was lost, or it has been there all along but was concealed. R. H. Ward (1957) expressed it thus, recounting an episode of progressively deepening consciousness under the dentist's nitrous oxide:

> I had no impression of suddenly receiving new knowledge, understanding and being. Rather I felt that I was rediscovering these things, which had once been mine, but which I had lost many years before. While it was altogether strange, this new condition was also familiar; it was even in some sense my rightful condition. (p. 27)

Mystical intuition can be a comprehensive knowing of the world, an omniscience that is "simultaneous knowledge of the universe and all it

contains," as Ward put it (p. 28). The experiences can also bring understanding and meaning, including insights into the puzzle of existence, the
true nature of self, the meaning of suffering, the ultimate "all-rightness"
of the world, the impossibility of absolute death, and the supreme importance of love. There can be specific insights too. Some are personal,
involving reappraisal of one's conduct and priorities. Others relate to the
natural world, to structures and processes of nature, from the microphysical to the cosmic. It can seem as if any question posed instantly receives
an answer, a phenomenon also described in accounts of near-death experience: "I was my own questioner and answerer, and fast as the questions
came, out trundled the answer, so easy to comprehend and always, always
right, the only possible answer" (RERC No. 000189, in Beardsworth,
1977, p. 16).

While specific details are sometimes brought back into ordinary consciousness, the knowledge gained often fades as the experience comes to
an end, leaving only the impression that everything was known and
understood. That this should happen in the case of all-encompassing
knowing is not surprising, for it is unlikely that a vast field of knowledge
could be taken in and stored for later recall by the limited discriminative
abilities and memory capacity of the human brain/mind in its ordinary
state. However, the fact that specific understandings and insights are
possible during the experiences suggests that the comprehensive knowing
has an intrinsic discriminative capability of its own attuned to details, and
it can be speculated that this capability supports the psi cognitions (see
below).

There appears to be a link between mystical knowing and *unity*. Poet
and scholar Kathleen Raine (1975) was gazing at a hyacinth on her writing desk when the following occurred:

> I found that I was no longer looking *at* it, but *was* it; a distinct, inde-
> scribable, but in no way vague, still less emotional, shift of conscious-
> ness into the plant itself. Or rather I and the plant were one and indis-
> tinguishable; as if the plant were a part of my consciousness. I dared
> scarcely to breathe, held in a kind of fine attention in which I could
> sense the very flow of life in the cells. I was not perceiving the flower
> but living it. I was aware of the life of the plant as a slow flow or
> circulation of a vital current of liquid light of the utmost purity. (p.
> 119)

Although reminiscent of some clairvoyant perceptions, the experience has a mystical feel as a result of its unitive quality, and, interestingly, the insights into structure and process are associated with the unity, the plant being a "part" of Raine's consciousness. Raine has a special awareness of the plant by being or living it, not by perceiving it as an external observer. It is mystical *knowledge by identity* (Forman, 1999, pp. 109–127). Special knowledge by virtue of unity is explicitly recognized in the teachings of Patañjali's *Yoga Sūtras* and associated texts, as discussed by Kelly and Whicher in Chapter 9 below.

Several kinds of unity are described in reports of extrovertive mystical experience (Marshall, 2005, pp. 60–64). For example, things normally understood to exist in isolation are now felt to be parts of the whole (*integral unity*). One aspect of this integrality can be the "solidification" of space: the gaps that ordinarily seem to keep things apart are now experienced as filled, and so the world presents itself as a continuum. Other common unities are those in which one seems part of the world (*immersive unity*), identified with the world (*identificatory unity*), or inclusive of the world (*incorporative unity*). All three are mentioned in the following account, which describes a progression through the unities:

> I suddenly realized that I was conscious of everything that is, and that I was part of it all. Then I became aware of it from a different aspect. I was everything that is. It seemed curious at first, but then turned into a feeling of being very much alone. I thought surely there must be something or somebody outside of me, but I searched and searched and could find nothing that was not a part of me. (RERC No. 004764, in Maxwell & Tschudin, 1996, p. 171)

Conscious of everything, one is united with everything, as a part of the whole, as the whole itself, and as inclusive of all that the whole contains.

It is no surprise to find that feelings of unity with objects, plants, animals, human beings, or the entire universe, are accompanied by a transformed sense of *self*, for the unity brings a redefinition of self-boundaries. In fact, mystical experiences are sometimes triggered when the everyday, tightly focused sense of self is relaxed or destabilized, for example through a peaceful state of mind, love, compassion, absorption in beauty, or suffering. Relaxation of the habitual self-focus and return to one's "home" condition can be quite a relief, as the medium Mrs. Willett nicely observed: "Don't you ever walk out of yourself? Aren't you tired of being always yourself? It's so heavenly to be out of myself—when I am everything, and everything else is me" (Tyrrell, 1947, p. 160).

The conventional self-concept is undermined by mystical experience, but this is not to say that there is a complete annihilation of self or that distinctions between things vanish, at least not in extrovertive mystical experience, for here the multiplicity remains but is now unified as a "multiplicity-in-unity." Warner Allen (1946) was absorbed in Reality but "without ceasing to be one and myself, merged like a drop of quicksilver in the Whole, yet still separate as a grain of sand in the desert" (p. 33). The self persists but is put in its place, seen for what it is in the greater scheme of things, which can be humbling but also liberating. Unity with others can bring inclusive feelings of love and the realization that all beings are equal and joined in kinship (*communal unity*). It may even seem that love is integral to the deeper reality.

With the everyday self no longer foremost, it can seem as if a higher dimension of self has emerged. It can be asked whether this greater self has a reality of its own or merely consists of self-identifications projected upon the newly discovered realities. The former alternative is suggested by Allen's case: he found that he was not the "I" he had thought he was but an immortal Self, a truth he had always known but had forgotten (p. 31). Allen was drawn to the idea of the "twofold self" expressed by the philosopher and mystic Plotinus (ca. 205–270 CE), founder of Neoplatonism, who located a higher self at the level of Intellect, the penultimate reality of his metaphysics. But there is no unanimity among the mystical traditions on whether a higher self truly exists or how deeply selfhood is rooted in reality, with attitudes ranging from early Buddhism, which steered clear of the idea of an essential self, to nondual Kashmir Śaivism, which takes even the everyday ego-sense to be rooted in the selfhood of God.

Mystical unity can also be an awareness of connections between things (*interconnective unity*). The most remarkable kind is mentioned only rarely in modern-day accounts, perhaps because it is encountered at a depth of experience that is difficult to reach or comprehend. This form of interconnection depends on each basic unit of reality being in a sense the whole of reality. If these units are understood to be living beings, the interconnective unity is a form of communal unity too. It is a feature of Neoplatonic metaphysics, having been portrayed by Plotinus in his discussions of the realm of Intellect, which is populated by beings who mutually contain one another. They contain one another because each is a complete whole, the total expression of a common source, the One, and so a totality in itself. An approximate parallel is found in the Indian Buddhist *Avataṃsaka Sūtra* and the Chinese Hua-yen philosophy that built on it. The sutra contains lengthy descriptions of the universe as Buddhas and advanced practitioners experience it. In this endlessly inter-reflecting "realm of reality," the tiniest particles are found to contain the whole. It has sometimes been claimed that the insights of mystics into interconnectedness and holistic relations anticipated the discoveries of physics, particularly the interconnectedness revealed by quantum physics, but also Mach's Principle, which links the inertial mass of a body to the universe as a whole. The claim has not been popular with those who maintain that mysticism and physics are non-overlapping magisteria, concerned with the separate domains of spirit and matter respectively (Jones, 1986; Wilber, 1982). However, the compartmentalization of reality into sharply distinct domains brings difficulties, as the dualist separation of mind and matter has long demonstrated, and so it would be unwise to rule out the possibility that mystics do have genuine insights into the structure of the world (Marshall, 1997).

A number of conjectures follow from the above. First, if mystical experiences truly are metaphysical windows, they suggest that knowing is more deeply a feature of reality than is commonly supposed. In conventional views, it is inconceivable that everything can be perceived and known. The world is knowable only by way of sense organs and cognitive processing in the neuropsychological "wetware," and so perception and knowledge must be limited. Omniscience and direct knowing are impossible. However, the special cognitions of mystical, near-death, and psi experiences suggest that the standard view is incorrect. In fact, the ordinary capacity to know and think may depend on a greater knowing that is intrinsic to the world and which, in mystical experience, presents itself as a natural but forgotten condition to which the mystic has come home. Several types of mind–matter metaphysics can support this possibility, such as idealisms that view mind or consciousness as more fundamental than matter and dual-aspect monisms that take the material universe to be inseparable from a mental aspect.

Second, we can understand psi cognitions to be dependent on the hypothesized greater knowing, drawing directly upon it or on a discriminative capacity intrinsic to the greater knowing itself. The latter alternative seems the more likely, for it is not at all obvious how our unaided human brains/minds could identify and extract the specific, often relevant information that appears in psi cognitions from so vast a field of knowledge as the universe presents. It is more likely that psi cognitions depend on a discriminative ability that belongs to the greater knowing itself, an ability to home in on details within the total field of knowing.

Third, the unitive characteristics of extrovertive mystical experience suggest, at the very least, that our customary perceptual, cognitive, and affective habits of breaking up the world into radically separate bits and pieces may be out of step with the way things are. Extrovertive experiences suggest that the universe is an undivided whole, that we are united with it in profound ways, and that its parts are deeply interconnected, perhaps by virtue of each part encapsulating the spatiotemporal whole.

Fourth, intuitive knowing is possible because the object of knowledge is not separate from the knower. It is likely that knowledge by identity will have to be understood in a strong, metaphysical sense, not merely as unity in the phenomenal stream of sense perception, but in the world at large too, in the noumenal background to phenomena. For the entire world to be open to intuitive knowing, it must exist as the known of a knower, or, expressed otherwise, it must exist as the contents of mind, experience, or consciousness. Such a metaphysical understanding of knowledge by identity is important in Plotinus' philosophy. At the level of the Intellect (*nous*) and its intelligible cosmos (*kosmos noētos*), knower and known are united (but it should be noted that this cosmos, as usually understood, is not our everyday world but ontologically prior to it). All things are known there, and known intuitively, because they are all the thinking activity of the Intellect. Souls are able to know that universe because in their depths they are the Intellect. When purified, they see themselves as Intellect and its "intelligible universe full of light" (*Ennead* IV.7.10; Armstrong, 1966–1988, Vol. 4, p. 383). Light as well as unity characterizes the higher knowing.

Finally, if psi cognitions are ultimately traceable to knowledge by identity, then psi actions (psychokinesis) may have a similar origin, deriving from unity or "at-oneness," as Fodor (1963) suggested, drawing on Yoga philosophy. Unity with an object may confer not only knowledge of it but also control over it: one can act on something directly because one is it. *Action by identity* complements knowledge by identity. Psychokinetic phenomena are well-known accompaniments on the mystical path, as for example documented in the lives of the Catholic saints (Kelly & Whicher, present volume; Murphy, 1992, pp. 478–526; Thurston, 1952). However, they do not seem to be common in spontaneous cases of mystical experience, perhaps because these do not arise from focused prayer or concentrative practice intentionally directed toward particular objects, spiritual figures, ideas, or outcomes. Rather, the experiences overwhelm the ordinary self and any impulses it may have to act: the experiences are ones of "passivity," as James (1902) observed, with the mystic feeling "as if his own will were in abeyance" (p. 381). However, passivity of the ordinary self will be supplemented by all-inclusive activity if the mystic finds a center of identity that has the universe as its field of activity. In theistic mysticism, assimilation to the divinity can be understood to bring participation not only in the divine knowledge and love but also in the divine will, power, and cosmic body.

MYSTICAL LUMINOSITIES

It would be difficult to overstate the prominence of light in the mystical literature (Arbman, 1963; Eliade, 1965; Fox, 2008; Kapstein, 2004). Although references to light can be metaphorical, there is no doubt that special luminosities are a common feature of mystical experiences, including those that occur in near-death circumstances, and they are met elsewhere too, for example, in meditative, out-of-body, psychedelic, and apparitional experiences. In the case of extrovertive mystical experiences, luminous phenomena include a bright light that completely obscures perception of the surroundings but brings special intuitions of the world, or which first obscures and then subsides to leave enhanced perceptions (Marshall, 2005, pp. 68–71). The environment may look clear but unusually bright, or there can be a hazy brightness. Objects may appear to glow from the inside, and vision may seem to reach into them, as if they have become luminously transparent. In extreme cases, it can seem as if the universe has become translucent and open to view. The light may seem interior to the experiencer, exterior, or both, and it is sometimes associated with a "presence" or "being." The light is very often white or golden, but other colors are reported too, especially in the early stages. Rainbow hues are occasionally experienced, and there can be sparkling effects.

Although blackness and darkness are rarely mentioned in reports of extrovertive mystical experience, they do have a place in the mystical literature, and are described in some accounts of inward experience, mystical, meditative, psychedelic, and near-death. The language of darkness entered Christian mystical literature with "apophatic" or "negative" theology, which puts the divine beyond positive description and resorts to statements about what it is not. The "dazzling darkness" (and the "black light" of Sufism too) can therefore have a metaphorical sense, expressive of the inaccessibility of the divine essence and the limitations of affirmative language, and is not necessarily indicative of a mystic's experience (e.g., Sells, 1994). In modern accounts, references to "dazzling darkness" and the like can be intended literally, as for example the "shining darkness" that followed John Wren-Lewis's (1988) near-death experience, an "aliveness" that "seemed to contain everything that ever was or could be, all space and all time," but without division (p. 112), James Austin's (1998) infinite, glistening void of "crystalline, jet blackness" during Zen meditation (p. 479), and Eben Alexander's (2012) mystical "Core" in near-death coma, which was infinite and "pitch black" but "brimming over with light" (pp. 47–48).

Luminosity and knowing are frequently mentioned together in mystical testimonies, which can suggest that the two have a basic connection and are not really distinct:

> I lost all normal consciousness and became engulfed as it were in a great cloud of light and an ecstasy of knowing and understanding all the secrets of the Universe, and a sense of the utmost bliss in the absolute certainty of the perfection and piercing purity of goodness in the Being in whom it seemed all were finally enclosed, and yet in that enclosure utterly liberated. (RERC No. 000514, in Beardsworth, 1977, p. 32)

The connection can be made explicitly too. Irina Starr (1991) experienced a light in the objects around her, a light that was "intelligent" in some way:

> There was the luminous quality—a light which contained color in the way that a brilliant diamond refracts color, only this color seemed an integral part of the essential substance and not a form of refracted light. The one thing which was, above all, significant was that every-

thing was literally *alive*; the light was living, pulsating, and in some way I could not quite grasp, *intelligent*. The true substance of all I could see was this living light, beautiful beyond words. (p. 9)

It is not just knowing that is inseparable from the light. There can be a fusion of qualities in which light, knowing, love, bliss, life, and timelessness come together. A mystical experience in natural surroundings brought a luminosity that united everything within itself: "we flowed into, became, the great Golden Light—the rocks, trees, etc. and this 'I' were no longer just kindred separatenesses. We disappeared. We became the Light which is Love, Bliss. This Light was neither hot nor cold; but Love, Consciousness, Eternity, It" (J. P. W., in Johnson, 1959, p. 66). It seems that luminosity, knowing, love, and bliss are so integral to the mystical consciousness that they are inseparable from it and one another.

What observations can be made on the above? If mystical experiences truly are metaphysical windows, then the reports suggest that luminous quality is fundamental to reality, an intrinsic characteristic of the world at large and of consciousness at its deeper levels. Some mystical accounts indicate that the world was not only flooded with luminosity but seemed to be *made* of it. While the ascription of experiential light qualities to the external world goes against common scientific and philosophical opinion, there is good reason to suppose that luminosity is no mere epiphenomenal "glow" generated by and confined to brain activity. Ever since early modern thinkers revived ancient atomism and banished "secondary qualities" from the universe, including color qualities, it has become a great mystery how the brain can support experience. However, if the brain is itself an intrinsically luminous structure, part of a luminous world, there is no puzzling mind–body gap between visual experience and the brain, and the problematic dualist split of mind and matter is eased in this regard.

Although contemporary philosophers have asked whether objects in the external world are colored, they do not usually mean to ask if external objects really have color qualia, except those philosophers who subscribe to some form of "Primitivism," such as the view that objects have the colors we take them to have (Byrne & Hilbert, 2007). Rather, they typically debate whether the physical properties of external objects can rightly be called "color," or whether colors are the "dispositions" of the subjects who view the objects. Mystical experiences, if windows on reality, suggest that color qualia are indeed intrinsic to objects, filling in their extended geometries. However, unlike Primitivists, we should not expect the intrinsic color qualia of objects to correspond closely or indeed at all to those experienced in sensory vision (Marshall, 2001). For one thing, visionary and mystical experiences can bring translucency, with objects divested of their opacity and the world now crystalline or gem-like in appearance. This phenomenon inspired Aldous Huxley (1999) to inquire "Why are precious stones precious?" in his talks on visionary experience (pp. 190–209). Translucency is to be expected if objects are known directly, for there would be no obstruction to vision and no opaque surfaces. It follows that opaque colors will be absent, and hues, if present, will have a transparent quality, like colored crystals and beams of spectral light. As Starr (1991) observed, the luminosity out of which objects were made "contained color in the way that a brilliant diamond refracts color" (p. 9).

However, it should not be assumed that all mystical experiences of the natural world provide direct access to objects as they are in themselves. For example, when a mystic perceives a tree as luminously transfigured, it is possible that the transfigured object is not the tree itself but a sensory representation of the tree. In philosophy of perception, a distinction is traditionally made between direct and indirect theories: *direct realists* naively assume or openly conjecture that we perceive objects directly, while *indirect realists* suppose that we perceive them indirectly through mental representations, through the so-called sense-data with which we are directly acquainted. For direct realists, ordinary perceptions of a tree show the tree itself; for indirect realists, perceptions of the tree are mediated through sensory representations of it. What happens, then, when a tree is luminously transfigured in a mystical experience? The direct realist will suppose that the tree itself has been transfigured, while the indirect realist will say that the perceptual representations of the tree have been transfigured, not the tree itself. In the first case, nature itself is transfigured; in the second, the sensory representations. It is the burden of the direct realist to explain how nature itself has been transfigured and why only the mystic perceives the change. The indirect realist need only explain the changes to the mystic's representations.

But extrovertive mystical experiences can go beyond perceptions of the immediate environment, reaching through the surfaces of things, and bringing unifying vision of the world at large, even of the entire universe.

How might direct and indirect realists account for such perceptual expansions, assuming them to be genuine? The direct realist can call upon filter theory and suppose that the universe of objects consists of unperceived percepts ("unsensed sensa," "sensibilia"). Our ordinary percepts are selections from this universal reservoir of percepts. In normal circumstances, only those of immediate relevance are selected for inclusion in consciousness, but psi and mystical experiences occur when more extensive selection from the subliminal reservoir takes place. However, direct theories of perception, whether conventional or extended to accommodate psi, have significant difficulties. For one thing, direct perception should be infallible because it presents its objects directly. But ordinary perception is known for its illusions, and psi perception for its errors and disguises. Indirect theories have an advantage here because they take perception to be mediated via representations, and the process of representation can be held responsible for introducing illusions, errors, and disguises. Indirect realism is advantageous in this regard, but can it be adapted to accommodate the direct perceptions that the deeper mystical experiences seem to bring? I believe it can, as I explain in Chapter 11.

TOWARD THE LIGHT: ALTERED STATES AND MYSTICAL TYPES

Mystical experiences are sometimes preceded by stages that are not themselves mystical or only incipiently so, and it is these earlier stages that are most likely to have mediated contents and show evidence of biological, psychological, and religious/cultural contributions. The stages can bring psychical and visionary experiences, but at their most basic they consist of simple lights and patterns of varying complexity. Some meditative traditions have at their disposal techniques that encourage a succession of light experiences, such as the death-transition practices of Tibetan Buddhism (e.g., Wangyal, 1993). Modern-day accounts of near-death experience also describe stages of visual phenomena. These include out-of-body experience with psi perceptions, passage toward a light through darkness (or through a tunnel or scenery of some kind), meetings with deceased relatives and other beings in paradise-like locales, and mystical luminosities. For example, Reinee Pasarow (1981) described a near-death experience, brought on by an allergic reaction, in which mystical unity with the light occurred at the end of several stages: (1) a state of darkness and peace; (2) out-of-body experience, with keener sight and hearing than usual, and ability to read the thoughts and feelings of bystanders; (3) upward flight; (4) a sea of light, love, and music, and the presence of a deceased relative; (5) a vast, loving light into which she was drawn and with which she became united. The vast light's knowledge now her own, she had insights into her life and the "direction of the whole of mankind" (p. 11). The descent from the light again involved stages, including passage through a rainbow-hued tunnel, and further out-of-body experience.

It is not just NDEs that can develop through stages toward a mystical light. Warner Allen's (1946) experience, noted previously, is reminiscent of multistage NDEs but occurred without any real or apparent threat to life. At the time, Allen was in a relaxed state, listening to Beethoven's Seventh Symphony in a concert hall (p. 30). Closing his eyes, he first experienced simple luminosities: "a silver glow which shaped itself into a circle with a central focus brighter than the rest" (p. 33). The circle transformed into a tunnel along which Allen felt himself drawn into a golden luminosity, accompanied by feelings of power and peace, and a brightening of the light. When the sense of "time and motion" stopped, a "dream scene" appeared, consisting of a flat-topped rock surrounded by sea, with a sandy pool at its base. The scene vanished and gave way to mystical experience proper, with Allen "absorbed in the Light of the Universe," in "Reality glowing like fire with the knowledge of itself" (p. 33).

The stages of Allen's experience prior to its mystical finale are reminiscent of those observed in the development of *altered states of consciousness* (ASC), experiences that bring "a qualitative shift" in one's "pattern of mental functioning" as Tart (1969, p. 2) put it, a departure in felt quality and psychological functioning from the normal waking state. For example, the hypnagogic transition from the waking state to sleep can at first bring diffuse luminosities and simple geometric patterns of an *entoptic* nature, defined broadly as light experience originating anywhere in the optic system, from eye to cortex. Allen (1946) recognized that his own experience had begun with such a light and observed that Plotinus (*Ennead* V.5.7) was familiar with the phenomenon too (pp. 186–187). More complex images such as landscapes and faces may appear next, and then yet more elaborate images, such as entire scenes played out like movie trailers (Mavromatis, 1987, pp. 14–33, 78–80). A similar progression has long been observed in psychedelic experiences (e.g., Knauer & Maloney, 1913). Siegel (1977) described two broad stages. In the first, luminous forms evolve into more complicated geometrical patterns, and colors change from black and white to blue, and then to red, orange, and yellow when the predominant form becomes the "lattice-tunnel," a tunnel with crosshatch markings. After some time, the second stage begins, with the tunnels supplemented by complex images and scenes, informed by memories and environmental cues. Drawing on Louis Jolyon West's "perceptual release theory," Siegel proposed a filter theory of hallucinatory images: a "gate" mechanism ordinarily keeps suppressed memories out of consciousness but allows them to enter when normal perceptual input is decreased or impaired, as in sensory deprivation. A slightly more elaborate version of Siegel's model, with three stages instead of two, was proposed by Lewis-Williams and Dowson (1988) in their controversial theory of the origins of Upper Paleolithic art in shamanic altered states of consciousness. The stages and associated luminous phenomena described in the two models are summarized in Figure 2.1, but with additional, mystical stages included that the models fail to address.

Neuropsychological models of altered states, such as those devised by Siegel, and Lewis-Williams and Dowson, bring together universal biological factors (entoptics) with personal and cultural ones (hallucinatory images), and so are both neuroscientific and contextual. But while they

LIGHT PHENOMENA	ASC STAGES		CATEGORY OF EXPERIENCE	
	Lewis-Williams & Dowson (1988)	Siegel (1977)		
supreme light luminous cosmos	stages not recognized		MYSTICAL	
complex imagery & unfolding scenes simple imagery	stage 3 _vortex tunnel_ stage 2	stage 2 _tunnel_	IMAGINAL visionary psychical dream/lucid	hypnagogic — / hypnopompic —
luminous patches, dots, & patterns	stage 1	stage 1	ENTOPTIC	
visual percepts	waking consciousness		SENSORY	

Figure 2.1.   Light phenomena and stages of ASC.

serve to remind us that biological, psychological, and religious/cultural factors contribute to altered states of consciousness, they ignore the possibility that transpersonal contributions may inform some or all of the stages. Siegel (1980) later applied his hallucination theory to NDEs, but because the theory was again purely biological and psychological, with no recognition that transpersonal contents might find their way through the gate, the NDE was reduced to entoptics and hallucination.

However, it should not be assumed that all geometric forms and imagery encountered in altered states are simply expressions of brain architecture and psychological construction. With regard to entoptics, Luke (2010) has questioned whether neurological structures, as commonly understood, can really produce the startlingly complex and seemingly "multidimensional" geometries encountered in psychedelic states. As for the later stages, in which entoptics are said to be elaborated into imagery informed by personal and cultural material, application of the term "hallucination" is likely to obstruct unprejudiced evaluation of what they involve. Just as dreams can be venues for inspirations, meaningful revelations, numinous encounters, and psi cognitions, so too the complex visual experiences of altered states in general, for all their personal and cultural specificity, may sometimes be informed by transpersonal factors and involve contact, if only mediated, with objective realities. The ontological status of the strange entities and fabulous realms of visionary experiences, such as the little folk of "Lilliputian hallucinations," remains open to debate (Luke, 2011), many rejecting the entities and realms as hallucinatory, some taking them to be symbolic and meaningful in the manner of dreams, and others understanding them to be as real as ourselves and the world we inhabit (e.g., Weiss, 2012, and present volume). Certainly, it would be premature to reject them as mere hallucinations constructed by the imagination from biological and contextual sources alone, for visionary beings and realms encountered in the more exotic dreams, lucid dreams/OBEs, NDEs, and psychedelic experiences can seem in their intelligence, autonomy, beauty, horror, peculiarity, and complexity to go beyond anything that memory and imagination, as understood by present-day, mainstream psychology, would be able to conjure up.

It is apposite here to mention Henry Corbin's (1972) distinction between "imaginary" and "imaginal": the former term all too easily implies that the objects of imagination are unreal fabrications, whereas the latter allows them to be very real indeed but apprehended by a special faculty

of "imaginative perception" rather than by the senses.[6] The Islamic texts
studied by Corbin interpose a realm of imagination between the realms of
the senses and intellectual intuition, a *mundus imaginalis* as existent as
the sensory and intellectual worlds (see Shaw, Chapter 8 below). Many
centuries later, among Romantics such as Blake, Wordsworth, Coleridge,
and Shelley, the imagination was valued as a creative, transformative,
visionary faculty that goes beyond sensory appearances and habitual
ways of perceiving things. Far more than the empiricist's associative
linking and combining of sense-derived images, the imagination of the
Romantics was a higher power of the mind and a pathway to reality (e.g.,
Kelly & Grosso, 2007a). While imagination is sometimes shallow or
delusory "fancy," it can be informed by genuine sources of knowledge
beyond the sensory given.

But even more seriously, the neuropsychological models noted above
fail to recognize a mystical denouement as altered states of consciousness
achieve greater depth. Warner Allen's experience developed from a simple luminosity (silver light) and geometric form (circle), through a more
complicated form (tunnel), to complex visual imagery (the coastal scene),
but became a full-blown, cosmic mystical experience that was of a different order from the stages that preceded it. The lesson seems to be that the
unfolding of altered states and their luminous phenomena, whether in
hypnagogia, psychedelic intoxication, out-of-body jaunts/lucid dreams,
and near-death trauma, can end in profound mystical experiences and so
bring a metaphysical depth that purely neuropsychological models of
altered states are ill-equipped to handle.

Mystical experiences themselves can develop through stages. For example, Ward's (1957) upward flight under nitrous oxide brought him to a
"region of ideas" in which everything in the universe was found to be
interconnected and known directly, and to exist within himself. But the
flight culminated in a luminosity of "utterly indescribable purity and
lucency," a "final and perfect unity" that was the "still centre of the
universal unity" (p. 30). The "region of ideas" stage appears to have been
a mystical experience of cosmic reach, while the subsequent stage is
difficult to categorize with any confidence. It may have been a yet deeper
level of cosmic experience, for it had what appear to be discriminable
contents. Ward says that everything there was alive but motionless, yet he
puts the experience beyond eternity as well as time. It does not seem to
have been the pure, undifferentiated consciousness that Stace took to be

the ultimate. However, Stace's pure consciousness, which constitutes his introvertive type of mystical experience, is obscure to say the least, for he thought it was beyond logic and could be expressed only in paradox, by asserting a paradoxical identity of creative source and created world, and of an ultimate with and without qualities (Marshall, 2005, pp. 162–163).

The extrovertive type has been prominent in my discussion because it is the type of mystical experience most obviously related to psi cognitions, but a more ambitious project would look further afield to a variety of mystical types and attempt a more extensive cartography of reality, including the ultimate reality that Stace tried to capture in his paradoxes. According to some thinkers, including naturalists and pantheists, there is no ultimate reality beyond the universe—the universe is all there is. For others, including classical theists and panentheists, there are realities that transcend the universe, even though they may be immanent too. If there are indeed such transcendent realities, then study of mystical accounts may provide some clues, and recourse can also be made to the mystical traditions. For example, Christian theology has recognized, in addition to Benedict's *visio mundi* or vision of the entire created world, a *visio mundi archetypi* or vision of the archetypal ideas in the divine mind, and the unclouded *visio dei*, the unmediated vision of God's essential nature (Bell, 1977). Plotinus has "the One" as his ultimate, the supreme reality that is encountered at the apex of the mystical ascent but which is ineffable in itself, although describable up to a point in relation to its luminous products (Bussanich, 1996; Shaw, present volume). Nondual Kashmir Śaivism has a pulsating, self-reflexive light of consciousness, *prakāśa-vimarśa*, as its primordial reality (Biernacki, present volume; Muller-Ortega, 2004) and sets out a number of derivative levels of cosmic experience. While it may be unnecessary to explore the farthest reaches of mystical experience in order to understand psi perception, they cannot be ignored if reality is to be mapped out in full, and they will be important for understanding some experiences, such as NDEs that go all the way into the light, and perhaps synchronistic "meaningful coincidences" between inner states and the outer world, if these are informed by archetypes rooted at a deep level of reality (Atmanspacher & Fach, present volume).

CONCLUDING REMARKS

In the above, I followed up the idea that the study of mystical experience has much to contribute to the understanding of psi, NDE, and other extraordinary experiences, in the first place by expanding the range of data that theorists need to take into account, and more speculatively by furnishing insights into the nature of reality. Several characteristics of mystical experience were identified, primarily in connection with the extrovertive type:

- temporal cessation and inclusiveness
- intuitive knowing, both comprehensive and specific, seemingly one's natural possession ("coming home") but ordinarily concealed
- various kinds of unity, from integral to interconnective and communal, including all-embracing love
- shift away from the centrality of the usual sense of self, sometimes to what appears to be a higher self
- special luminosities in mystical experience and the stages that precede and follow it
- intimate association of light, consciousness, knowing, love, bliss

Given the close connections between psi and mystical experience, theorists of psi will have to address these and other mystical characteristics. There was the hope that such theoretical efforts would be considerably aided if mystical experiences, as "windows on reality," furnish metaphysical pointers, and some tentative conjectures were put forward:

- The universe exists as a spatiotemporal whole, vibrant with animation.
- The universe is knowable in mystical states, psi cognitions, and ordinary experience because knowing is intrinsic to the constitution of universe and ourselves in some profound way.
- More specifically, mystical intuitions are possible by virtue of "knowledge by identity": the object of knowledge, whether the entire universe, the immediate environment, or some domain in between, is knowable directly because it exists as the known of a knower.
- The knower at its most inclusive constitutes a "higher self."

- Psi cognitions, which are very specific, depend on a discriminative capacity intrinsic to the all-inclusive knowing.
- Psi actions are rooted in "action by identity": through unity with the object, the object becomes part of one's field of activity.
- The universe is thoroughly unified: it is a seamless whole, and its parts are deeply interconnected.
- Luminosity is intrinsic to reality, and so it is a mistake to think that color qualia are absent from the world at large.
- Luminosity and intuitive knowing are inseparable from each other, constituting luminous cognition or "intelligent light."

If brought to bear on filter theory, these conjectures sketch out a subliminal consciousness of cosmic reach, a global consciousness with an inbuilt discriminative capacity that supports the psi cognitions. James (1909/ 1986), in his final thoughts on psychical research, concluded that there is a "continuum of cosmic consciousness, against which our individuality builds but accidental fences, and into which our several minds plunge as into a mother-sea or reservoir" (p. 374). While some phenomena, abnormal, normal, and supernormal, throw light on the shallower regions of the reservoir, on its personal and collective contents, the deeper extrovertive mystical experiences would appear to confirm that the reservoir in its fullness is indeed a consciousness of cosmic extent, temporally as well as spatially, and even to suggest that a "Subliminal Self" (upper case) of the kind postulated by F. W. H. Myers is best understood as cosmically inclusive (see Kelly et al., 2007; Kelly, Chapter 14 below). I have speculated that consciousness can have such a reach because the universe exists as the known of the knower, or, expressed otherwise, as the contents of mind, experience, or consciousness. The speculation requires elaboration, of course, for in this bare form it is not yet a full-grown theory, and can be taken in various directions. There are suggestions too that the subliminal reality has a dimension transcendent to the universe, accessible in the deepest mystical experiences, a dimension that is the source of the cosmic multiplicity and its holistic unity, although I have only touched on the matter here. If this transcendent reality is understood to be "in" the world in some sense, and the world "in" it, then a panentheistic vision is in the making (Murphy, Chapter 15 below).

Also relevant to filter theory are questions about the directness or indirectness of various kinds of perceptions, ordinary, psychical, and

mystical. The "filter" and related metaphors may incline theorists to regard all types of percepts as direct "selections" or "extracts" from a
subliminal reservoir. But there are reasons to think that ordinary perception is indirect, and that psi perception is mediated, given its errors and
disguises. Less-developed mystical perceptions may also be mediated, if
these consist of transfigured sensory impressions or contain imagery derived from specific cultures and religious traditions, while the deeper
mystical perceptions may be direct intuitions. There is, then, reason to
seek a theory of perception that takes ordinary perception to be indirect,
mediated through direct acquaintance with sensory representations of objects, but which also has a place for direct acquaintance with the objects
themselves, as suggested by some mystical experiences. I shall outline
such a theory in Chapter 11.

It has not been my intention in this chapter to construct or justify a
particular metaphysical system. Rather I set out to describe some mystical
characteristics and raise a few conjectures that may stimulate full-scale
theoretical work. But in selecting the data, making the conjectures, and
expressing them in the way I have, it is likely that I have been influenced
by my own philosophical inclinations, which tend toward a form of idealism (Marshall, 2001, 2005). It is therefore important that others with
different outlooks familiarize themselves with the mystical evidence and
reach their own conclusions. In addition to personal testimonies, there is a
wealth of material in the religious traditions that will be of value in such
an undertaking, as my all-too-brief excursions into religious doctrines
have hopefully indicated. There is no metaphysical consensus to be found
among these traditions, but there are many interesting points of contact in
both doctrine and technique, and there is much that can be learned from
comparative study of the similarities and differences.

Investigation of the metaphysical implications of mystical experience
undoubtedly has its challenges, theoretical and practical, and there is
reason to think that some experiential characteristics and stages involve
contributions from biology, psychology, and religion/culture, as highlighted in the sections above on time-experience and the luminosities of
altered states. A well-rounded theory will attempt to incorporate several
possible contributions, biological, psychological, cultural, and transpersonal. Commonly it is the transpersonal dimension that is overlooked in
present-day theorizing, but care must be taken not to go to the other
extreme and emphasize metaphysics to the exclusion of other factors. The

intersection of biology, psychology, and metaphysics in mystical and other altered states affords opportunities for fruitful research. Filter theories are of great interest in this respect because they are situated at the intersection, bringing together neuropsychology in the shape of the filter with a subconscious that in its farther reaches has metaphysical depths, as the data of mystical experience strongly suggest.

NOTES

1. The "window" metaphor conveys the idea that mystical experiences are openings to reality but is not entirely satisfactory because it implies a separation of experiencer and experienced, a separation typically overcome during mystical states.

2. Exceptions include Hollenback (1996), Hood (2008), and Kripal (2010, 2011) from the mystical side, and Crookall (1969), Fodor (1963), Johnson (1953), Kelly and Grosso (2007b), and Kelly and Locke (1981/2009) from the parapsychological.

3. Esalen Center for Theory & Research, http://www.esalen.org/ctr-archive/bp

4. Accounts from the Alister Hardy Religious Experience Research Centre, University of Wales Trinity Saint David, Lampeter, UK, are designated "RERC" followed by the official archive number and the publication reference.

5. Sprigge (1993) provides a detailed discussion of James's understanding of time and the specious present (pp. 198–214).

6. Note Price's (1953/1965) comparable distinction between *imagining* and *imaging*. The latter consists in having mental images, without any suggestion that they are unreal: "there is nothing imaginary about a mental image. It is an actual entity, as real as anything can be" (p. 5). Imaging is the type of perception that Price suggests may take over from sense perception after death, in a dreamlike otherworld. It follows that the postmortem realm is an "imagy" world, not an "imaginary" one.

REFERENCES

Alexander, E. (2012). *Proof of Heaven: A Neurosurgeon's Journey into the Afterlife*. London: Piatkus.

Allen, W. (1946). *The Timeless Moment*. London: Faber and Faber.

Andersen, H. K., & Grush, R. (2009). A brief history of time-consciousness: Historical precursors to James and Husserl. *Journal of the History of Philosophy, 47*, 277–307. doi:10.1353/hph.0.0118

Arbman, E. (1963). *Ecstasy or Religious Trance: Vol. 1. Vision and Ecstasy*. Stockholm: Svenska Bokförlaget.
Armstrong, A. H. (Trans.). (1966–1988). *Plotinus: Enneads I–VI* (Vols. 1–7). Loeb Classical Library. Cambridge, MA: Harvard University Press.
Austin, J. H. (1998). *Zen and the Brain: Toward an Understanding of Meditation and Consciousness*. Cambridge, MA: MIT Press.
Barnard, G. W. (1997). *Exploring Unseen Worlds: William James and the Philosophy of Mysticism*. Albany: State University of New York Press.
Barnard, G. W., & Kripal, J. J. (Eds.). (2002). *Crossing Boundaries: Essays on the Ethical Status of Mysticism*. New York: Seven Bridges Press.
Beardsworth, T. (1977). *A Sense of Presence: The Phenomenology of Certain Kinds of Visionary and Ecstatic Experience*. Oxford: Religious Experience Research Unit.
Bell, D. N. (1977). The vision of the world and of the archetypes in the Latin spirituality of the Middle Ages. *Archives d'Histoire Doctrinale et Littéraire du Moyen Âge, 44*, 7–31.
Broad, C. D. (1949). The relevance of psychical research to philosophy. *Philosophy, 24*, 291–309.
Broad, C. D. (1962). *Lectures on Psychical Research*. London: Routledge & Kegan Paul.
Bussanich, J. (1996). Plotinus's metaphysics of the One. In L. P. Gerson (Ed.), *The Cambridge Companion to Plotinus* (pp. 38–65). Cambridge: Cambridge University Press.
Byrne, A., & Hilbert, D. R. (2007). Color primitivism. *Erkenntnis, 66*, 73–105. doi:10.1007/s10670-006-9028-8
Capra, F. (1975). *The Tao of Physics: An Exploration of the Parallels between Modern Physics and Eastern Mysticism*. London: Wildwood House.
Carmody, D. L., & Carmody, J. T. (1996). *Mysticism: Holiness East and West*. Oxford: Oxford University Press.
Carr, B. (2007). Parapsychology as a bridge between science and religion. *Christian Parapsychologist, 18*, 134–148.
Corbin, H. (1972). *Mundus imaginalis* or the imaginary and the imaginal. *Spring* (1972), 1–19.
Crookall, R. (1969). *The Interpretation of Cosmic and Mystical Experiences*. Cambridge: James Clarke.
Deikman, A. J. (1966). De-automatization and the mystic experience. *Psychiatry, 29*, 324–338.
Eliade, M. (1965). Experiences of the mystic light. In *The Two and the One* (pp. 19–77). London: Harvill Press.
Flaherty, M. G. (1999). *A Watched Pot: How We Experience Time*. New York: New York University Press.
Fodor, N. (1963). At-oneness: A new phenomenon for parapsychology. *Research Journal of Philosophy and Social Sciences, 1*, 57–64.
Forman, R. K. C. (1999). *Mysticism, Mind, Consciousness*. Albany: State University of New York Press.
Forman, R. K. C. (Ed.). (1990). *The Problem of Pure Consciousness: Mysticism and Philosophy*. New York: Oxford University Press.
Fox, M. (2008). *Spiritual Encounters with Unusual Light Phenomena: Lightforms*. Cardiff: University of Wales Press.
Grey, M. (1985). *Return from Death: An Exploration of the Near-Death Experience*. London: Arkana.
Grondin, S. (2010). Timing and time perception: A review of recent behavioral and neuroscience findings and theoretical directions. *Attention, Perception, & Psychophysics, 72*, 561–582. doi:10.3758/APP.72.3.561
Hollenback, J. B. (1996). *Mysticism: Experience, Response, and Empowerment*. University Park: Pennsylvania State University Press.
Hood, R. W., Jr. (2008). Mysticism and the paranormal. In J. H. Ellens (Ed.), *Miracles: God, Science, and Psychology in the Paranormal: Vol. 3. Parapsychological Perspectives* (pp. 16–37). Westport, CT: Praeger.
Huxley, A. (1999). *Moksha: Aldous Huxley's Classic Writings on Psychedelics and the Visionary Experience* (M. Horowitz & C. Palmer, Eds.). Rochester, VT: Park Street Press.
James, W. (1890). *The Principles of Psychology* (Vols. 1–2). New York: Henry Holt.

James, W. (1902). *The Varieties of Religious Experience: A Study in Human Nature*. New York: Longmans, Green.

James, W. (1986). The confidences of a "psychical researcher." In F. H. Burkhardt (Ed.), *Essays in Psychical Research* (pp. 361–375). Cambridge, MA: Harvard University Press. (Original work published 1909)

Johnson, R. C. (1953). *The Imprisoned Splendour*. London: Hodder & Stoughton.

Johnson, R. C. (1959). *Watcher on the Hills*. London: Hodder & Stoughton.

Johnson, R. C. (1984). *Light of All Life*. Tasburgh, England: Pilgrims Book Services.

Jones, R. H. (1986). *Science and Mysticism: A Comparative Study of Western Natural Science, Theravāda Buddhism, and Advaita Vedānta*. Lewisburg, PA: Bucknell University Press.

Jones, R. H. (2010). *Piercing the Veil: Comparing Science and Mysticism as Ways of Knowing Reality*. New York: Jackson Square Books.

Kapstein, M. T. (Ed.). (2004). *The Presence of Light: Divine Radiance and Religious Experience*. Chicago: University of Chicago Press.

Kelly, E. F., & Grosso, M. (2007a). Genius. In E. F. Kelly, E. W. Kelly, A. Crabtree, A. Gauld, M. Grosso, & B. Greyson, *Irreducible Mind: Toward a Psychology for the 21st Century* (pp. 423–493). Lanham, MD: Rowman & Littlefield.

Kelly, E. F., & Grosso, M. (2007b). Mystical Experience. In E. F. Kelly, E. W. Kelly, A. Crabtree, A. Gauld, M. Grosso, & B. Greyson, *Irreducible Mind: Toward a Psychology for the 21st Century* (pp. 495–575). Lanham, MD: Rowman & Littlefield.

Kelly, E. F., Kelly, E. W., Crabtree, A., Gauld, A., Grosso, M., & Greyson, B. (2007). *Irreducible Mind: Toward a Psychology for the 21st Century*. Lanham, MD: Rowman & Littlefield.

Kelly, E. F., & Locke, R. G. (2009). *Altered States of Consciousness and Psi: An Historical Survey and Research Prospectus* (2nd ed.). New York: Parapsychology Foundation. (1st ed. published 1981)

Knauer, A., & Maloney, W. J. M. A. (1913). A preliminary note on the psychic action of mescalin, with special reference to the mechanism of visual hallucinations. *Journal of Nervous and Mental Disease, 40*, 425–436.

Kripal, J. J. (2010). *Authors of the Impossible: The Paranormal and the Sacred*. Chicago: University of Chicago Press.

Kripal, J. J. (2011). *Mutants and Mystics: Science Fiction, Superhero Comics, and the Paranormal*. Chicago: University of Chicago Press.

Lewis-Williams, J. D., & Dowson, T. A. (1988). The signs of all times: Entoptic phenomena in Upper Palaeolithic art. *Current Anthropology, 29*, 201–245. doi:10.1086/203629

Lubbock, Y. (1961). *Return to Belief*. London: Collins.

Luke, D. P. (2010). Rock art or Rorschach: Is there more to entoptics than meets the eye? *Time and Mind, 3*, 9–28. doi:10.2752/175169710X12549020810371

Luke, D. P. (2011). Discarnate entities and dimethyltryptamine (DMT): Psychopharmacology, phenomenology and ontology. *Journal of the Society for Psychical Research, 75*, 26–42.

Marshall, P. (1997). *Mysticism and Physics* (Unpublished master's thesis). Lancaster University, Lancaster, England.

Marshall, P. (2001). Transforming the world into experience: An idealist experiment. *Journal of Consciousness Studies, 8*(1), 59–76. Available at http://www.esalen.org/ctr-archive/bp

Marshall, P. (2005). *Mystical Encounters with the Natural World: Experiences and Explanations*. Oxford: Oxford University Press.

Marshall, P. (2006). *The Living Mirror: Images of Reality in Science and Mysticism* (Rev. ed.). London: Samphire Press.

Marshall, P. (2011). The psychical and the mystical: Boundaries, connections, common origins. *Journal of the Society for Psychical Research, 75*, 1–13.

Mavromatis, A. (1987). *Hypnagogia: The Unique State of Consciousness between Wakefulness and Sleep*. London: Routledge.

Maxwell, M., & Tschudin, V. (Eds.). (1996). *Seeing the Invisible: Modern Religious and Other Transcendent Experiences*. Oxford: Religious Experience Research Centre.

Muller-Ortega, P. E. (2004). Luminous consciousness: Light in the tantric mysticism of Abhinavagupta. In M. T. Kapstein (Ed.), *The Presence of Light: Divine Radiance and Religious Experience* (pp. 45–79). Chicago: University of Chicago Press.

Murphy, M. (1992). *The Future of the Body: Explorations into the Further Evolution of Human Nature*. New York: Jeremy P. Tarcher/Putnam.

Pahnke, W. N., & Richards, W. A. (1966). Implications of LSD and experimental research. *Journal of Religion and Health, 5*, 175–208.

Pasarow, R. (1981). A personal account of an NDE. *Vital Signs, 1*(3), 11, 14.

Price, H. H. (1962). W. T. Stace's *Mysticism and Philosophy. Proceedings of the Society for Psychical Research, 41*, 299–312.

Price, H. H. (1965). Survival and the idea of "another world." In J. R. Smythies (Ed.), *Brain and Mind: Modern Concepts of the Nature of Mind* (pp. 1–24). London: Routledge & Kegan Paul. (Original work published 1953)

Radin, D. (2006). *Entangled Minds*. New York: Paraview.

Raine, K. (1975). *The Land Unknown*. London: Hamish Hamilton.

Sells, M. A. (1994). *Mystical Languages of Unsaying*. Chicago: University of Chicago Press.

Shanon, B. (2001). Altered Temporality. *Journal of Consciousness Studies, 8*(1), 35–58.

Siegel, R. K. (1977). Hallucinations. *Scientific American, 237*(4), 132–140.

Siegel, R. K. (1980). The psychology of life after death. *American Psychologist, 35*, 911–931.

Smart, N. (1962). Mystical experience. *Sophia, 1*(1), 19–26.

Smith, A. L., & Tart, C. T. (1998). Cosmic consciousness experience and psychedelic experiences: A first person comparison. *Journal of Consciousness Studies, 5*(1), 97–107.

Sprigge, T. L. S. (1993). *James and Bradley: American Truth and British Reality*. Chicago: Open Court.

Stace, W. T. (1960). *Mysticism and Philosophy*. Philadelphia: Lippincott.

Starr, I. (1991). *The Sound of Light: Experiencing the Transcendental* (3rd ed.). Ojai, CA: Pilgrim's Path.

Stevenson, I., & Cook [Kelly], E. W. (1995). Involuntary memories during severe physical illness or injury. *Journal of Nervous and Mental Disease, 183*, 452–458.

Studstill, R. (2005). *The Unity of Mystical Traditions: The Transformation of Consciousness in Tibetan and German Mysticism*. Leiden, The Netherlands: Brill.

Tart, C. T. (Ed.). (1969). *Altered States of Consciousness: A Book of Readings*. New York: Wiley.

Taylor, S. (2007). *Making Time: Why Time Seems to Pass at Different Speeds and How to Control It*. Cambridge: Icon Books.

Thurston, H. (1952). *The Physical Phenomena of Mysticism*. London: Burns Oates.

Tobin, F. (1984). Mysticism and Meister Eckhart. *Mystics Quarterly, 10*, 17–24.

Traherne, T. (1908). *Centuries of Meditations* (B. Dobell, Ed.). London: Bertram Dobell.

Tyrrell, G. N. M. (1947). *The Personality of Man: New Facts and Their Significance*. Harmondsworth, England: Penguin.

Wangyal, T. (1993). *Wonders of the Natural Mind: The Essence of Dzogchen in the Native Bon Tradition of Tibet*. Barrytown, NY: Station Hill Press.

Ward, R. H. (1957). *A Drug-Taker's Notes*. London: Victor Gollancz.

Weiss, Eric M. (2012). *The Long Trajectory: The Metaphysics of Reincarnation and Life After Death*. Bloomington, IN: iUniverse.

Wilber, K. (Ed.). (1982). *The Holographic Paradigm and Other Paradoxes*. Boston: New Science Library.

Wren-Lewis, J. (1988). The darkness of God: A personal report on consciousness transformation through an encounter with death. *Journal of Humanistic Psychology, 28*(2), 105–122.

Wulff, D. M. (2000). Mystical experience. In E. Cardeña, S. J. Lynn, & S. Krippner (Eds.), *Varieties of Anomalous Experience: Examining the Scientific Evidence* (pp. 397–440). Washington, DC: American Psychological Association.

Zaehner, R. C. (1957). *Mysticism Sacred and Profane: An Inquiry into Some Varieties of Præternatural Experience*. Oxford: Clarendon Press.

II

Old and New Worldviews That Accommodate the Targeted Phenomena

3

THE "TRANSMISSION" MODEL OF MIND AND BODY

A Brief History

Michael Grosso

> The phenomena under discussion are, at least from the philosophical standpoint, of all facts presented to us by the whole of experience, without comparison the most important; it is, therefore, the duty of every learned man to make himself thoroughly acquainted with them.
>
> —Arthur Schopenhauer, *Essay on Spirit Seeing*[1]

The "phenomena" referred to in the epigraph are the supernormal ones associated with mesmerism (Crabtree, 1993), used by Schopenhauer in his discussion of the mind–body problem. The mind–body problem is perhaps the greatest of philosophical riddles, which he famously called the "world-knot." It was a knot he would try to untie in the *Essay on Spirit Seeing*. Where to begin?

We know that we have minds, and we know that we have brains and central nervous systems; what is problematic is how the two relate to each other. Mental and brain events certainly seem to differ in kind, although it's clear that they are somehow related. The question is whether mind or matter is basic in nature, the other derivative, illusory, a shadow of the more basic reality.

Scientists and philosophers have long disagreed on these questions. The rift that concerns us is between physicalists and mentalists: people who believe everything at bottom is material or physical, and people who believe in the irreducible character of mental life. The different viewpoints have different consequences and implications. The differences are no doubt conditioned, but not determined, by education and cultural locale, by personal experience, and by biases, temperaments, and dispositions. In my view, the physicalist camp exerts an influence disproportionate to the merits of its position; it should moreover be noted that physicalism is *metaphysics,* not science; an interpretation of matters of fact, not itself a matter of fact.

TERMINOLOGY

This chapter will focus on a particular account of mind and body, one that is viewed with sympathy by people who have studied puzzling types of psychophysical experience. Often referred to as the "filter" or "transmission" model, it allows for a concept of mind that is consistent with, and begins to make intelligible, the "rogue" phenomena that mainline materialism cannot accommodate.

Terms like "transmission" or "filter," meant to describe the function of the brain, are inevitably metaphorical. The brain or nervous system is understood as the "filter" or the "organ of transmission"; what is filtered, transmitted, etc., are the mental forms of our conscious experience. There is no option but to use metaphors taken from our experience of tangible reality, and they are bound to mislead us if we take them too literally.

William James's term *transmission* suits our needs; the Latin etymon signifies a "sending across." For the transmissionist, the brain doesn't produce anything; it permits movement across boundaries and thresholds, i.e., from the subliminal to the supraliminal mind, from subconscious to conscious states and back. In more common use is the term *filter,* a variant of Aldous Huxley's "reducing valve" (see below). Other figures of speech are possible, such as "permit," "release," "open up to," "unveil," "disclose," "reveal," and "resonate." They all have their uses, some yet to be discovered. In the end, the exact relationship between mind and brain is likely to remain irreducibly obscure, a mystery, as Colin McGinn the mysterian argues and quantum mechanics seems to illustrate. Nietzsche once characterized truth as a "mobile army of metaphors." In trying to describe, no less explain, the mystery of the mind, we might well have to rely on a mobile army of metaphors and perspectives. But whether like

Menelaus wrestling with Proteus we can induce this god to yield its secrets remains to be seen.

This must be an abbreviated history: beginning with a small group of philosophers and psychologists (James, Myers, Bergson, Schiller) who were the first to articulate it in the modern context, we will fan out backward and forward in time to other accounts of efforts to frame this view. What emerges is a picture, deeply embedded in the historical psyche, of an intuition of mind as primordial and transcendent, mind interactively interwoven with and essentially pervading physical nature. It is an intuition at odds with currently prevailing outlooks that lean en masse toward physicalism.

There are, however, many outstanding exceptions. Neuroscientist John Eccles (1965) wrote:

> Contrary to the physicalist creed, I believe that the prime reality of my experiencing self cannot with propriety be *identified* with . . . brains and neurones and nerve impulses and even complex spatio-temporal patterns of impulses. . . . I cannot believe that this wonderful divine gift of a conscious existence has no further future, no possibility of another existence under some other unimaginable conditions. At least I would maintain that this possibility of a future existence cannot be denied on scientific grounds. (pp. 42–43)

Still, compared with most workers in the field, Eccles and others of like mind remain a minority of outliers. One aim of this chapter is to indicate the longevity and recurrent appeal of the intuition of mind as transcendent.

JAMES, TRANSMISSION, IMMORTALITY

In 1897, William James (1842–1910) gave the Ingersoll Lecture at Harvard University, titled *Human Immortality: Two Supposed Objections to the Doctrine*. We pass over the second objection, which addresses the inability of the imagination to cope with the supposed "overpopulation" problem of immortality, for example, when it applies to our social and biological inferiors; the problem, James argues, is caused by a deficiency in imaginative power. Our concern is with the first objection, which is logical, and concerns the mind–brain problem.

James was speaking to an educated Harvard University audience, people very much aware of the growing triumphs of the physical sciences. Educated people were beginning to find it difficult to imagine life after death, and James needed a theory that could handle the data collected by psychical researchers, especially the data produced by mental mediums, which did suggest human survival. Conscious of the emotional and metaphysical needs of his audience, he used philosophy as therapy to mentally uncramp and lead his listeners toward a wider view of the possibilities. James was temperamentally opposed to ideas that suggest the premature closure of human experience. Arguing for the possibility of immortality, he said: "My words ought consequently already to exert a releasing function on your hopes" (James, 1898/1961, p. 293).

His task was to furnish a theory that would at least permit his audience to rationally entertain the hypothesis of some form of afterlife. He begins by fully granting that minds are indeed a *function* of brains. But the notion of function is ambiguous, and mind can be a function of brain in two very different ways, (1) as a *product* of the brain, something that has somehow *emerged from the physical structures* of the brain, its causal root clearly physical, or (2) in a different sense of function, the brain would *not produce* mind, but would serve as a vehicle that detects, deflects, screens, filters, transduces, or, to use James's terms, *transmits* or *permits* expressions of mind, consciousness, feelings, willings, imaginings, and so forth. In the second sense of function, mind interacts with the material brain but in a way that preserves its separate reality. According to this model, the mental factor, as James wrote, "preexists" the brain that it operates upon and through.

Positing the preexistence of mind is a metaphysical game changer. It may at first seem like an extreme position, but the idea that mind "emerges" from brain is really no less extreme and fantastic. This question about the *emergence* of consciousness with all its qualitative properties is the famous "hard problem"; science is clueless about how to get consciousness out of physical reality. Thus, in a recent book by Alva Noë (2009), praised by Oliver Sacks and Daniel Dennett, we read in the Preface: "After decades of concerted effort on the part of neuroscientists, psychologists, and philosophers, only one proposition about how the brain makes us conscious—how it gives rise to sensation, feeling, subjectivity—has emerged unchallenged: we don't have a clue" (p. xi). If so, I would then say we are as entitled to take mind as our basic starting point as we are to assume that physical science will someday explain the origins of mind; after a prolonged period of fruitless promissory materialism, the nonemergent option seems perfectly valid.

But it's more than logically valid; it has explanatory and experimental potential, completely lacking in the rival view. The transmission model has the advantage of being consistent with, and may serve to explain, a host of vitally interesting phenomena of human experience. Writes James (1898/1961):

> The transmission theory also puts itself in touch with a whole class of experiences that are with difficulty explained by the production theory. I refer to those obscure and exceptional phenomena reported at all times throughout human history, which the "psychical researchers," with Mr. Frederic Myers at their head, are doing so much to rehabilitate; such phenomena, namely, as religious conversions, providential leadings in answer to prayer, instantaneous healings, premonitions, apparitions at time of death, clairvoyant visions or impressions, and the whole range of mediumistic capacities, to say nothing of still more exceptional and incomprehensible things. (p. 298)

None of these things would be remotely intelligible if the productive-materialistic view of consciousness were true. Suppose you saw the ghostly phantom of a person you knew who at that moment was dying miles away. Such a so-called crisis apparition would be unthinkable on the productive view because there would be no known way the dying brain could produce the correct, information-bearing apparition and transmit it across space. But on James's model, the brain does not have to "produce" anything. The information is "ready-made in the transcendental world, and all that is needed is an abnormal lowering of the brain-threshold to let them through" (James, 1898/1961, p. 299). In other words, the person dying at a distance is clairvoyantly present to the subliminal mind of the percipient; in a vision you might have of this sort, the subliminal perception you already own becomes supraliminal—the shutter, as it were, is opened, and you can glimpse what is present.

Two ideas are crucial to James's model. The first concerns the "transcendental world." Myers would call it the metetherial environment or World-Soul; Emerson, the Over-Soul; Aldous Huxley, Mind at Large; Carl du Prel, the Transcendental Ego, etc. Our individual minds are surface growths that appear separate and distinct but whose roots lie in a deeper psychic underground; there we are mutually entangled and part of a more extended mental system.

The second idea is one that James owes to Gustav Fechner, concerning the notion of a *psychophysical threshold* (see James, 1898/1961, pp. 295–298, long footnote). It is the mobility of this threshold upon which turns the explanatory and the experimental potential of the transmission model. Lower the threshold and the contents of the subliminal mind become more accessible; this can come about by deliberate shamanic or mystical practice or by chance, blows to the head, or near-death experiences. In the normal struggle to adapt to the physical world, consciousness is confined and colored by contingent, body-mediated experience; we therefore mostly live our lives oblivious to any hint of our deep interior selves.

Technically, James's move in this work is to posit substance dualism, a step beyond property dualism. According to the latter, mind is an irreducible property of living brains but is causally inert and supervenes on brain activity. Hence property dualism is not strong enough to carry the burden of survival or of any paranormal or mystical phenomena. It is a feckless philosophical position deeply at odds with human experience. According to the transmission model, however, mind is not a property of the brain but a user of the brain, indeed a person who enjoys autonomous self-existence. Few academically trained people are prepared to entertain substance dualism nowadays;[2] but few of them pay much attention to experiences characterized as supernormal, mystical, and the like, experiences that challenge mainline views of mind and body.

Summarizing the main points of James's theory:

1. The brain *transmits*—it does not *produce*—consciousness.
2. Consciousness preexists the brain; it does not emerge from the brain.
3. There is a *transpersonal* mind, i.e., a mind at large, a cosmic consciousness, James's "mother-sea" of consciousness. The first and second view strongly suggest the third: the notion of a *trans*personal mind, the existence of which is an intuition had or entertained by many (if not most) cultures in one form or another throughout history. As we'll see, it often appears in the guise of different religious metaphors—God, Brahman, Nirvana, etc.

4. James, drawing on Fechner, stresses as crucial the ever-fluctuating threshold that separates subliminal from supraliminal mental life. The notion of a threshold serves as an explanatory principle and as a broad framework for pursuing various experimental procedures, often discovered and described by native peoples, yogis, shamans, saints, and mystics of the great traditions. James says that his idea helps to explain experiences like telepathy or clairvoyance, for in the "mother-sea" of consciousness the boundaries between our minds are more permeable.

James's model has applications. In light of it, we can understand why yogis, mystics, and shamans sometimes harshly discipline their minds and bodies, striving to subdue distractions that screen or "filter" the influx of potentially higher perceptions. To gain receptivity to the transpersonal realities of consciousness, blocked by normal brain activity, is often likened to a "death" in shamanism and mysticism. In the *Phaedo* (81a), Plato said that a *meletē thanatou* ("practice of death") was the way to enlightenment; in short, methods of freeing the soul from bodily influence. Also implicit in the general model is the suggestion that at death we may be overwhelmed by consciousness, as described in *The Tibetan Book of the Dead,* which offers instruction on how to prepare for the experience. The model takes on added value in light of the near-death experience, especially during cardiac arrest when brain function is suspended, and consciousness reportedly expands dramatically (Van Lommel, 2010, p. 20).

James (1898/1961) quotes from Emerson's essay "Self-Reliance," linking his model with Transcendentalism:[3] "We lie in the lap of immense intelligence, which makes us receivers of its truth and organs of its activity" (p. 295). Our full cognitive and motor capacities reside in something deeper than our apparent selves. James holds back from identifying the "immense intelligence" with the "Absolute Mind of transcendental Idealism," which he regarded as too rigid a construction. "All that the transmission theory absolutely requires," he states, "is that they [the higher truths] should transcend *our* minds,—which thus come from *something* mental that pre-exists, and is larger than themselves" (p. 295).

There are two other essays by Emerson (1883) full of statements that bear witness to the intuition of the greater mind, "The Over-Soul" and "Circles." From "The Over-Soul": "Man is a stream whose source is hidden. Our being is descending into us from we know not whence" (p. 252). Or, "I am constrained every moment to acknowledge a higher origin for events than the will I call mine" (p. 252). Emerson's intuition extends to everybody, as in this remark that reframes the idea of conversation with our neighbors: "We do not yet possess ourselves, and we know at the same time that we are much more. I feel the same truth how often in my trivial conversation with my neighbors, that somewhat higher in each of us overlooks this by-play, and Jove nods to Jove from behind each of us" (p. 261).

Or consider the essay "Circles," crowded with images designed to illustrate the inexhaustible power of self-transcendent consciousness: "There are no fixtures to men, if we appeal to consciousness" (p. 286). It makes all the difference to how we live. "The life of man is a self-evolving circle, which, from a ring imperceptibly small, rushes on all sides outwards to new and larger circles, *and that without end*" (p. 284, italics added). The preexistent entity we have hypothesized is Heraclitean—boundless, nonlocal. From this "circular" reasoning, Emerson concludes that we may look upon endings as beginnings, for the movement of nature is toward continual conscious expansion and comprehension of whatever we experience: "The one thing which we seek with insatiable desire is to forget ourselves, to be surprised out of our propriety, to lose our sempiternal memory and to do something without knowing how or why; in short to draw a new circle" (p. 300). But now to another key formulator of the theory.

FREDERIC MYERS

Like William James, F. W. H. Myers (1843–1901) rejected the mainstream materialism of his day because it failed to account for phenomena he spent a good part of his life investigating. James (1898/1961) wrote that Myers's "theory of the whole range of phenomena is, that our normal consciousness is in continuous connection with a greater consciousness of which we do not know the extent, and to which he gives, in its relation to the particular person, the name . . . of his or her 'subliminal' self" (p. 298). Myers too uses the idea of a psychophysical threshold when he states that the contents of the subliminal mind are more likely to emerge into consciousness when supraliminal awareness is in abeyance. The "abeyance of the supraliminal" is another way of talking about lowering the psychophysical threshold, becoming less prone to "filter out" what experience is poised to offer.

Myers was interested in automatic writing as a method of exploring the subliminal self. The so-called method of distraction, used to facilitate automatic writing, shows the transmission model in action: by distracting one's attention, for example by reading the newspaper, the subliminal mind is less impeded from expressing itself through the motor activity of writing, provided one prepares with pencil in hand. The focus on automatic writing anticipates postmodern suspicions about the problematic entity known as "the author," but it also moves in directions undreamed of by most postmodernists. In light of the importance he attached to ecstatic self-oblivion, Myers (1903) raises questions about the ambiguities of authorship (Vol. 2, Chapter 10). Who or what is writing the various scripts of the automatic writer? The importance of the automatisms, however, lay in their significance for a comprehensive theory of human personality. Unlike the postmodern deflationary temper, Myers the Romantic poet and evolutionary idealist was interested in expanding the scope of human capacity.

Another metaphoric equivalent of "filter" was *gate*. Reflecting on how a medium's mind may open up to the subliminal influx of ideas, Myers (1903) wrote, "these sensitives have but to sink into a deep *recueillement*, a guarded slumber, and the gate stands manifestly ajar" (Vol. 2, p. 251). The "gate ajar" is equivalent to Fechner's lowered threshold. Something opens to an existent presence, a reality about to manifest, hidden from one's surface consciousness.

Myers's (1903) discussion of Mrs. Piper's trance mediumship links the transmission model to the evolution of consciousness. At first she went through violent spasms before becoming entranced, but she eventually learned to enter the desired state more smoothly. Hodgson thought that Piper's interaction with the spirits had a salutary effect, producing in her a new "stability" and "serenity" (Vol. 2, p. 251). Myers reflects on the evolutionary potential of the medium's development:

> If we look, in fact, at the flesh-and-blood side of this strange converse, we seem to watch a process of natural evolution opening upon us with unexpected ease; so that our main duty is carefully to search for and train such other favoured individuals as already show this form of

capacity—always latent, perhaps, and now gradually emergent in the human race. (Vol. 2, p. 251)

Myers had a vision of a new normality, which he defined in terms of a more perfect integration of subliminal and supraliminal mental life. This marriage of the two spheres of our mental life was his conception of genius, a conception perhaps anticipated by William Blake when he wrote more paradoxically of the "Marriage of Heaven and Hell." As with many of the writers touched on here who have so much to say about our theme, we have to move on.

HENRI BERGSON

Around the same time as James and Myers, the younger Henri Bergson (1859–1941) was giving shape to his own version of the theory. For Bergson the key to understanding the spiritual dimension of human experience was memory, a phenomenon he regarded as irreducible to any brain substrate. In 1913, he gave the Presidential Address to the English Society for Psychical Research; in discussing the possibility of surviving death, he produced his version of the transmission theory. Study of aphasia led him to infer the resilience and irreducibility of mind. Aphasia, he observed, is an effect of cerebral lesion, but the lesion does not destroy the memory of the word. What is lost is the capacity to evoke the memories; the memories themselves remain intact.

Consider the common experience of feeling something on the "tip of your tongue"; you know but can't recall it to full awareness. There is a barrier preventing the recall—the specter of Fechner's threshold. You try but fail to recall the name of the author of a book you read so you quit trying and think about something else. Then, in a flash, the memory comes back. This is a common experience. The effort of trying to remember gets in the way of recall; once you cease making an effort, the memory pops into consciousness. The brain doesn't create the memory; it creates "the frame," Bergson says, that allows the memory to slip into awareness. Nothing is added; something is removed.

In a recently reported phenomenon, sufferers from Alzheimer's, stroke, or other brain lesion are reported to regain their lost memories just before death. In such cases of *terminal lucidity*, nearing death apparently restores access to memories (Grosso, 2004, pp. 41–43; Nahm & Greyson, 2009, pp. 942–944). This seems to confirm Bergson's argument that memories are not destroyed by brain lesions, but rendered inaccessible. Terminal lucidity deserves careful study; as it appears, in dying, consciousness begins to disengage from the damaged brain and regains memories that had become inaccessible. We might expect terminal lucidity to occur, if the transmission model were correct; the phenomena are unintelligible on the production theory.

Like James, Bergson rejected emergentism, the doctrine that consciousness is a brain creation; his views, expressed in *Matter and Memory* (1896), complement the basics of James's transmission theory. "The truth is that my nervous system, interposed between the objects which affect my body and those which I can influence, is a mere conductor, transmitting, sending back, or inhibiting movement" (Bergson, 1908/1911, p. 40).

Far from identifying consciousness with the brain or any brain derivative, he says, "Speaking generally, the psychical state seems to us to be, in most cases, immensely wider than the cerebral state. I mean that the brain state indicates only a very small part of the mental state, that part which is capable of translating itself into movements" (p. xiii). Brains "store" patterns of motor behavior, but memory images, cognitions, and the sense of self are not brain-localized. If so, there is no reason to suppose that brain death automatically implies memory-and-consciousness death.

Bergson's formulation is dynamic. In the struggle for existence, our attention is riveted to the "plane of life." But sometimes the "whole personality, which, normally narrowed down by action, expands with the unscrewing of the vice in which it has allowed itself to be squeezed" (p. xiv). This corresponds to what James calls the "obstruction" that we erect against lowering our psychic defenses, lest we be swamped by waves from the "mother-sea." Once we take note of this obstruction—the natural tendency to "screw ourselves down"—we can see why it is natural to recoil from the possibly disorienting excesses of consciousness.

Like James, Bergson strikes a therapeutic chord when he encourages readers to be aware of how mental activity continually seems to "overflow" the boundaries of our brains and bodies: feelings, memory images, intendings, reasonings, judgments of various sorts, none of which seem strictly localized in the brain. More dramatic yet are supernormal mental functions like ESP and PK that overflow the neural substrate by definition. The more we reflect on the fact that our mental life overflows our bodily life, Bergson wrote, the easier and more natural to entertain the idea of life after death.

According to this French thinker, all our memories are intact, despite the apparent blanket of oblivion that covers us most of the time; hard-wired to focus on the steady onrush of our local future, it is difficult to project consciousness backward in time. But freed from fixation on the plane of life, whatever the proximate cause, we may see and feel every-thing quite differently.[4]

Anticipating Bergson's idea of "duration," Boethius was in prison in Pavia in 524 CE when he wrote *The Consolation of Philosophy* (see Boethius, 1962, p. 15). He describes an experience he calls the *nunc stans* or eternal now, the *totum simul* or simultaneity of everything. For the Roman thinker this rare experience was "the whole, perfect, and simulta-neous possession of endless life" (V.6). Boethius tells of a visitation on death row of the goddess of philosophy who instructs him to dwell on the idea of eternity. Bergson's theory of brain-liberated mind renders such strange talk somewhat more intelligible. According to Boethius, one's mind may be "in full possession of itself, always present to itself, and [able to] hold the infinity of moving time present before itself" (V.6). If there is a greater consciousness and we can under certain conditions experience it more fully, our ordinary sense of time is bound to be drasti-cally altered.

F. C. S. SCHILLER

The English philosopher F. C. S. Schiller (1864–1937) was an early for-mulator of the transmission theory. James recalled Schiller (1891/1910), who argued that "our ordinary selves are neither our whole selves nor our true selves" (p. 278). Describing how he did philosophy, he wrote, "The fatal flaw in almost all these metaphysics of the past was their abstract-ness, their inability to come down to concrete fact" (p. 157).

Philosophers who discuss the mind–body problem often focus on itches, pains, and afterimages as examples of mental life. Far less atten-tion is given to features of mental life that express the depths and origi-nality of human personality, such as reason, morality, dreams, imagina-tion, creative inspiration, mystical and paranormal events, and so forth.

Doing philosophy of mind without recourse to the latter would be like claiming to study English literature but systematically excluding Shakespeare, Blake, and Yeats. Schiller is true to his word and deals with the concrete facts of psychical research.

In *Riddles of the Sphinx* (1891), he describes his own progressive theory of evolution that includes the possibility of immortality and the evolutionary perfection of humanity. Human and divine reality gradually merge, according to Schiller, who forms his theory from various empirical observations and phenomenologies. In particular, he contends, Darwin failed to account for the rise of consciousness in nature. More recently, Thomas Nagel (2012) made the same point, seriously upsetting some devoted physicalists.

Schiller's concept of evolution has several points in common with the writers so far discussed: (1) unlike materialists, transmissionists are prepared to extend and expand the concept of mind, if the empirical data demand it; (2) the extended concept is based on a large database of psychophysical phenomena; (3) the extended concept represents latent though largely ignored potentials of normal human beings. The distinction crucial to our discussion "may be marked by calling the self as it appears, the *phenomenal self*, and the self as the ultimate reality, the *Transcendental Ego*. By the latter name it is intended to suggest its extension beyond the limits of our ordinary consciousness . . . and yet to emphasize its fundamental kinship with our normal self" (Schiller, 1891/1910, pp. 274–275).

In Schiller's discussion, the brain is a labor-saving device; suppose we had to learn to use knife and fork or to drive our car every time, without having stored the necessary motor routines. In one sense, the brain is the enemy of consciousness; for its main job is to negotiate the business of mundane survival, which too often becomes all-consuming and mind-narrowing. Signs of the wider reality—Schiller's Transcendental Ego—show up in extraordinary experience. "These curious phenomena forcibly bring home to us what a partial and imperfect thing our ordinary consciousness is, how much goes on within us of which we know nothing, how far the phenomenal falls short of being co-extensive with our whole nature" (p. 277).

According to Schiller, the brain enables us to use our bodies efficiently and automatically; but in fact much greater control over the body is possible: "it may perhaps be suspected that our direct control of our bodily organism, though an obscured, is not an extinct power, that under favorable circumstances we possess what appears to be a supernatural and is certainly a supernormal power over our bodies, and this is the true source of the perennial accounts of miracles of healing and extraordinary faculties" (pp. 286–287). The model helps us understand the "favorable circumstances" conducive to heightened psychophysical causality; as noted, they seem to be whatever lowers Fechner's psychophysical threshold.

When we look at the relationship between our apparent self and our "Transcendental Ego," Schiller writes, "we shall perceive that matter is an admirably calculated machinery for regulating, limiting, and restraining the consciousness which it encases" (p. 287). Further on he says:

> Herein lies the final answer to Materialism: it consists in showing in detail what was asserted at the outset, viz., that Materialism is a hysteron proteron, a putting of the cart before the horse, which may be rectified by just *inverting* the connexion between Matter and consciousness. Matter is not that which *produces* consciousness, but that which *limits* it and confines its intensity within certain limits: material organization does not construct consciousness out of arrangements of atoms, but contracts its manifestation within the sphere which it permits. (p. 289)

Schiller's ideas are often striking and deserve more attention; he was one of the earliest modern formulators of the transmission model.

James, Myers, Bergson, and Schiller were roughly contemporary; they read and influenced each other, each phrasing the core ideas slightly differently. They formed this theoretical redoubt in reaction to Darwinism and the growth of nineteenth-century materialism; and their resistance to materialism was motivated by experience: encounters with the superordinary, or with reports, narratives, and biographies detailing the superordinary. Allied to these four we may now turn to a selection of some more recent writers who formulated the model in related terms from their own perspective.

ALDOUS HUXLEY, MESCALINE, AND "REDUCING VALVES"

In attempting to make sense of his mescaline experience, novelist and essayist Aldous Huxley (1894–1963) deserves a place in this narrative. Huxley (1954/1990, p. 22) found himself agreeing with philosopher C. D. Broad (1949), who had written that we should take more seriously the kind of theory that Bergson had raised for normal memory and sense perception:

> The suggestion is that the function of the brain and nervous system and sense organs is in the main *eliminative* and not productive. Each person is at each moment capable of remembering all that has ever happened to him and of perceiving everything that is happening everywhere in the universe. (p. 306; italics in the original; see Chapter 4 below for Broad's words in full)

Huxley introduced a term several writers have taken up: "According to such a theory, each one of us is potentially Mind at Large." He adds: "To make biological survival possible, Mind at Large has to be funneled through the reducing valve of the brain and nervous system. What comes out at the other end is a measly trickle of the kind of consciousness which will help us to stay alive on the surface of this particular planet" (p. 23). An expanded conception of mind is invoked to explain extraordinary phenomena, like the effects of ingesting a psychoactive chemical. Creative disruptions of brain function vary in kind and intensity, and range from drug-induced and near-death episodes to ascetic practices like fasting, prolonged meditation, and sleep deprivation.

CYRIL BURT AND CURT DUCASSE

Two other accomplished modern writers count as exponents, each with their own emphases, of the model under discussion. The British psychologist Sir Cyril Burt (1883–1971) wrote:

> Why should we assume that consciousness needs a material brain to produce it? . . . a closer scrutiny of the actual facts makes it far more probable that the brain is an organ for selecting and transmitting con-

sciousness rather than for generating it. Even without a brain, I should hold, a mind by its very nature could cognize events; but it would do so by a process akin to clairvoyance or telepathy. . . . But for life on this terrestrial planet . . . these cognitive and creative powers would be a handicap rather than a help. The brain and its associated organs must restrict our information and activity to what is both relevant and indispensable for our bodily survival. (1975, p. 9)

For Burt, ordinary perception reveals a problem, a mystery: "And conscious awareness is a fact which itself admits of no physical explanation. It is unique and irreducible. Ordinary sensory perception, as it seems to me, is just as miraculous as extrasensory perception" (1975, p. 79). Burt goes on to quote the eminent neuroscientist Sherrington: "it is a far cry from an electrical reaction in the brain to suddenly seeing the world around me with all its colour and chiaroscuro. We ought to feel startled; but we are too accustomed to the fact to feel even surprised" (pp. 79–80). An additional point comes from Lord Adrian (also cited by Burt), another eminent neuroscientist: the same kind of electrical action, occurring in another part of the brain, permits the variety of auditory experiences. The point is that the physical part of hearing has nothing to do with the quality of what it is like to hear the music of Bach or the sounds of a spring morning. Burt affirms the present model when he writes:

it becomes far easier to regard the brain, as Kant, Bergson, James, and several others have suggested, not as an organ which generates consciousness, but rather as an instrument evolved to transmit and limit the process of consciousness and of conscious attention so as to restrict them to those aspects of the material environment which at any moment are crucial for the terrestrial survival of the individual. In that case such phenomena as telepathy and clairvoyance would be merely instances in which some of the usual limitations were removed. (p. 80)

Burt thought this general view of consciousness increased the plausibility of postmortem survival.

In 1961 the philosopher Curt Ducasse (1881–1969) published a book on the belief in a life after death. In theoretical discussion, he refutes the doctrine of epiphenomenalism, according to which our mental life is a causally vacuous process that supervenes on brain activity. Some claim that drugs like mescaline and LSD produce experiences that are mere byproducts of chemical agency, but Ducasse (1961) remarks:

what needs to be accounted for is not only *that* hallucinations then occur, but also *what* specifically their content—which in fact varies greatly—happens to be. That is, do these drugs cause *what* they cause one to see in a sense comparable to that in which a painter's action causes *the picture* he paints and sees; or, on the contrary, do they cause one only *to see* what one then sees, in a manner analogous to that in which the raising of the blind of a window on a train causes a passenger in the train to see the landscape which happens to be outside at the time? (p. 80)

Clearly, it is the latter for Ducasse: the brain is like a window blind on a moving train, opening and shutting, enabling glimpses of what is out there. The brain doesn't create the passing scenery; it makes it possible to see what is there.

In Chapter XI, Ducasse lays out his counter-reductionistic theory, titled "Hypophenomenalism: The Life of the Organism as Product of Mind." The term and the concept, *hypophenomenalism*, are meant to upend epiphenomenalism, the doctrine that mental and psychic things are ontologically derivative, causally nugatory, and so on. Then, as now, hypophenomenalism would rank as pure heresy for it holds that biological and physical reality are the epiphenomena, the outward manifestations of more primary, more causally potent mental factors at work in nature.

Ducasse cites two canonical philosophers he thought were hypophenomenalists, Plotinus and Schopenhauer. Like James and other transmissionists, they posit a fundamental, nonemergent mind (or "will"), conceived as the creative agency of the manifest physical world. For Plotinus, the body is an emanation of mind; for Schopenhauer, objectified will. Ducasse's argument is based on the purposive, goal-oriented nature of life. From that angle, the body would be a tool of the mind, and the brain would be the epiphenomenon, a necessary by-product of the mind's evolutionary nisus. Ducasse (1961) was deeply acquainted with psychical research, and claims to have witnessed extraordinary materialization phenomena (pp. 164–170). Anyone, I would guess, who had actually witnessed (and believed in) something as striking as the materialization of a physical entity, living or dead, might well be tempted to place mind at the center of his scheme of nature. Passing over the various arguments Ducasse uses to make his case, enough to say that he arrived at a philosophy of mind resembling transmission theory, with a large emphasis on the creativity and the teleology of mental life.

SOME GERMAN TRANSMISSIONISTS

I want now to turn back in time and consider several German writers who
anticipated the transmission model. In James's Ingersoll Lecture, for example, we find a related reference to Kant's *Critique of Pure Reason*.
Kant's motive is not to prove that the soul survives death but to show how
we may conceive it *as possible*. This, as James did, offers therapy for
those suffering spiritual malaise caused by the rising tide of materialism.
According to Kant, we cannot *know* the truth about God, freedom, and
immortality; but we can believe and act *as if* our beliefs were grounded in
such truth. Kant is at pains to prove that the belief in immortality is
neither impossible nor self-contradictory.

We may admit that our mental powers are affected by the "diverse
modifications of our organs," but this would not imply that the body is
"the cause of thought, but merely a restrictive condition of it" (Kant,
1781/1956, p. 618). The body would merely be a "hindrance to the pure
and spiritual life" (pp. 618–19). This may be argued as a theoretical
possibility, Kant believed, but not as in any way empirically verifiable. It
is a "concept *devised* merely for the purposes of self-defence" against
dogmatic materialism (p. 619).

The move is similar to the one James made in his Ingersoll Lecture.
There is, however, a difference. *Immortality* for Kant was merely think-
able (*noumenal*); he thought it cannot be proved by any conceivable
experience, and he was probably right about that. James used the word
immortality too but meant something more modest like *survival*. The
empirical researchers were not as sweeping as Kant; they collected factual evidence supporting the modest claim that some people survive death
for some time. Not exactly the Good News, but neither entirely bad news.
Kant was like most philosophers, who rarely bother to ask if there is
anything factual to all the lore about ghosts, mediumship, reincarnation
memories, and the like.

Now consider a philosopher who admired Kant greatly, but who did
bother to study the real data and in fact wrote an early classic on psychical research (see the epigraph for this chapter). Arthur Schopenhauer
(1788–1860) published a treatise with the ungainly title "Essay on Spirit
Seeing and Everything Connected Therewith" (1851/1974, pp. 227–309).
The empirical data that he relied on to make his case against materialism
came from the records of mesmerism and spiritualism, and from classical

literature. Lacking the terminology and history of modern research, he invented his own terminology.

Schopenhauer forged a model of mind and body in tune with the intuition we're tracking; I will discuss his "transmission" affinities, but must pass over a wealth of his ideas worthy of study. The raw materials he focused on were dreams, visions, apparitions, ghostly phantoms, and hallucinations. "For the notion of a spirit or spectre really consists in its presence becoming known to us in a way quite different from that in which we know the presence of a body" (p. 227).

Schopenhauer discussed the facts that struck him as important; that such *were* facts he treated as given. "Whoever at the present time doubts the facts of animal magnetism and its clairvoyance should be called not a sceptic but an ignoramus" (1851/1974, p. 229). He was impressed by the creativity of the dream, which nightly produces alternate phenomenologies, simulations of physical worlds, new forms of time and space. "[W]hile dreaming everyone is a Shakespeare," he wrote (p. 231). Every dreamer creates dramas, whole casts of personae on makeshift mental stages. Like the external world, the dream forces itself on our consciousness, appearing as something totally unexpected, as we can verify by observing our own hypnagogic imagery.

Schopenhauer posits a "dream organ," his name for the faculty of intuition. During dreamlike altered states, consciousness extends beyond its normal sensory-rational range:

> It is incontestable that, when the state of somnambulism is complete, the external senses have entirely suspended their functions; for even the most subjective of these, namely bodily feeling, has so completely disappeared that the most painful surgical operations have been performed during magnetic sleep without the patient's having betrayed any sensation of them. Here the brain appears to be in a state of the deepest sleep and thus of complete inactivity. (p. 242)

Normal brain activity contracts consciousness; the inactive somnambulist brain may facilitate episodes of clairvoyance, visionary, or mystical experience. Schopenhauer held that "the objective world is a mere phenomenon of the brain. For the order and conformity to law thereof which are based on space, time, and causality . . . are to some extent set aside in somnambulist clairvoyance" (p. 263).

Schopenhauer would grant the human mind a certain godlike potential, thanks to "that mysterious faculty of knowledge which is concealed within us and is not restricted by relations of space and time" (p. 279). This faculty, which he supposes is virtually "omniscient," is normally veiled by ordinary consciousness. It can, however, cast "off its veil in magnetic clairvoyance." *Veil* here refers to the brain understood as "filter," "gate," or "reducing valve." The brains of the multitude are devoted to the needs of their bellies and their genitals, Schopenhauer believed; the artist or somnambulist breaks free and opens his mental shutters to new sights, forms, and modes of consciousness.

The writings of Kant and Schopenhauer bore fruit in another German philosopher, who likewise drew on the phenomena of somnambulism, dreams, and memory, in the resistance to autocratic materialism. Carl du Prel (1839–1899) developed a theory of human personality that rivaled Myers's in scope, and which is also permeated by transmission ideas.[5] Du Prel (1889) wrote:

> Because the mind acts through its organ, Materialism says that it is developed from the organ. Mental activity is normal with the healthy brain, and morbid in brain diseases; from which Materialism infers the identity of mind and brain activity. But if the violin player plays well or ill according to the character of his instrument, the identity of artist and instrument is not thence to be inferred. Psychology has therefore never found a better expression for the relation between mind and cerebral-system, senses and brain, than that of Plato [*Theaetetus* 185]: "We know *through* the senses *with* the soul." (Vol. 1, p. 170)

Like James, du Prel deployed Fechner's psychophysical threshold to explain and systematize a range of phenomena, and to suggest various experimental procedures conducive to psi occurrences. For example, the traditional methods, techniques, and disciplines of yoga, mysticism, shamanism, etc., are ways of interfering with the brain's normal functions, thus attempting to force open the barriers that normally clog the flow of consciousness and block access to the subliminal mind.

Du Prel distinguished ordinary consciousness from the greater entity he called the Transcendental Ego, a term and notion Schiller adopted. Du Prel also believed in irreducible, nonemergent mind, and thought it was possible to experiment with the "veil" that screens the everyday from the transcendental. As with all the rest, experimentation was based on Fechner's mobile threshold of sensibility. Apply the requisite stimulus, said William James, and new worlds of consciousness spring forth. Not unlike Myers, du Prel believed it should be possible to accelerate mental evolution by experimenting with one's psychophysical threshold.

According to du Prel, "two persons" inhabit the whole or complete self; the everyday conscious personality and the relatively unknown transcendental self whose ways are obscure. Each of us then is rooted in a much larger mental reality than what is known to our waking, rational perspective. Du Prel and Schopenhauer were struck by the unpredictability and incommensurability of dream life in relationship to waking life. The images that come while falling asleep are typically discontinuous with our last waking thoughts, although hidden connections may later emerge. For du Prel the unexpected uprushes of hypnagogia were portents of the Transcendental Ego.

Two other features of dream life struck him as important. The first is the amazing creativity of dreams, a fact we take for granted because it is so common. It is hard to elucidate how the material brain nightly creates scenes, worlds, dramas, which to the dreamer can be totally absorbing and convincing in their phenomenal reality. Not only are dreams partial replicas of the sensory world, they are sometimes more vivid, more awe-inspiring and beautiful, more packed with meaning—and sometimes more prescient—than our waking states. The creativity of dreams is cause for philosophical wonder. I wonder about that old conceit that each of our minds is, or has, a spark of divinity—if by divinity we mean something like super-creativity. Dreams are a serious challenge to reductive views of mind.

The other big point about dreams: they demonstrate the power of "self-sundering," a tendency to create secondary personalities, to im-personate and trans-personate; to personify "controls"; and to generate spirit guides, daimons, fairies, guardian angels, and probably diabolic adversaries. Myers embraced the "multiplex" human personality as a potential benefit, as well, of course, as a force not to trifle with. In dreams we encounter beings, lower or perhaps higher aspects of our transcendental personality. Some rare souls extend their "dream organ" into lofty transcendental domains; for example, Socrates and Joan of Arc (Myers, 1889). Du Prel moves on to visionary experience, somnambulism, inspired states, from detail to detail, arguing for a much expanded conception of human personality.

GREEK PRECURSORS

From our sampling of German thinkers, I want now to go back further in time and provide some examples from the ancient Greek thinkers. While we cannot pursue this in the detail it calls for, the intuition we're tracing is beginning to take on the trappings of a recurrent or archetypal idea, an idea rooted deeply in human experience or (as we might say) in the human psyche. We seem in fact to be led back to the notion of an "unbounded" psyche, to a place at the historical antipodes of reductive physicalism. "You would not find out the boundaries of soul (*psuchēs peirata*)," said Heraclitus (fl. ca. 500 BCE), "even by travelling along every path: so deep a measure does it have" (Kirk & Raven, 1957, p. 205). Heraclitus, like William James, refers to this unbounded soul by indirection and suggestion, using metaphors and other figures of speech. In a somewhat different sense, Anaxagoras of Clazomenae (ca. 500–428 BCE) argued that the first principle of the cosmos was a certain *nous apeiron*, "unbounded mind or intellect."

Part of the core intuition we're tracing is the Platonic idea of the body as organ *through which* soul operates. Plato sharply distinguished soul from body, pretty much creating the mind–body problem. Conversion to an enlightened state, according to the famous (and probably authentic) Seventh Epistle, was based on an experience of sudden (*exaiphnēs*) illumination. In the *Phaedrus*, Socrates praises the powers of extreme states of consciousness, especially the manic and maniacal prophets, artists, healers, and lovers. Among the generally cautious lot of philosophers, Plato was an epistemic extremist, making Socrates argue in the *Phaedo* that only *after death*, completely free from the body, is ultimate knowledge possible.

Plotinus (ca. 205–270 CE) seems to have advanced *in actual experience* toward the Platonic ideal during his *ecstatic* episodes. In cultures everywhere, ecstatic transport (leaving the body) is reported. According to his biographer Porphyry, Plotinus was ashamed of being in his body; he is said to have had at least four ascents to the One, but many ascents to Intellect (*nous*), as Plotinus himself reports. These experiences no doubt informed his theorizing. We may represent his thought in the figure of a circle, in the image of the uroboros, the serpent that feeds on its tail. In the beginning the One differentiated, pouring itself forth in emanations— a timeless origin, not a beginning in time, in which the One remains undiminished. It did and does so in a descending ontological hierarchy through intellect and soul that terminates in the material world. Moving somewhere on this eternal circle, the soul, emanation of the One, gets lost in the cosmos. The divine game is to return to one's point of origin, back to the bosom of the One, and complete the circular journey.

From the beginning, help was available, love and beauty were the means of divine rescue; they orient the soul on the long journey home. In the ideal circle of destiny, according to Plotinus, the soul is an active player that uses its body to travel "home." The body, in this perennial vision, is the instrument of the soul.

It's hard to do justice to the thought of Plotinus, informed by so much of Greek philosophy, enriched with personal introspection and inspired by self-authenticating mystical experience (see Shaw, Chapter 8 below). A few quotes will illustrate the transmission motif. He says, for example, that "discursive reason is not in the brain as in a place" (Clark, 1940, p. 232). The brain doesn't create discursive reason, but discursive reason "participates" in the brain, uses it to speak and act out its intentions; reason employs the brain to direct the body's motor output, as Bergson argued in *Matter and Memory*. Plotinus talks about immortality and thinks of body and soul. Our material part is not immortal. "But the chief part, that is the man himself, is either related to body as form to matter or as a user to his instrument. Either way, it is the soul which is the man himself" (p. 235). The brain then is not the "man" but the means whereby persons play the divine game and navigate the mighty circle of their destinies.

Plotinus writes as if he would induce in his disciples an experience of union with the One. In the supreme experiment, the soul makes every effort to purify itself and be "as far as possible without commerce with the body." He is probably describing his own experiences. "Investigate, then, by setting aside the additions," by which he means, all the extraneous accretions and attachments of psychic life, "or rather, let the one who sets aside see himself, and he will believe that he is immortal when he beholds himself in the intelligible and pure state" (p. 237). Here he's urging readers to know themselves as a way of perceiving the fact of their immortality, a gnosis that in form would differ from evidence taken to support belief in survival by inference.

Plotinus offers a different experiment, a way to lower the threshold, and enter a stratum of consciousness adjacent (so to speak) to postmortem

disembodied reality. If we survive death, it will be a change of consciousness, not a change of physical location. Direct encounters with the "next"
world seems to be what mystics and near-death experiencers have had.

This emphasis on direct experience provides a model for research.
There is also research based on evidence that permits us to infer, with
some measure of probability, that there is an afterlife. The direct encounters are more powerful and transformative. But also the slow, cumulative,
inference-based approach may lead to momentous conclusions. The two
kinds of evidence are compatible and complementary. I believe there is
enough knowledge by inference to encourage the more dramatic, transformative model of research.

Porphyry (ca. 232–305 CE) studied with Plotinus and edited and published his teacher's writings; he was also an author in his own right. One
work we have of his, *On Abstinence from Animal Food*, clearly suggests
an account of the mind–brain relationship consistent with our model. The
idea of a diet or way of life that purifies consciousness by fasting fits the
model. One breaks the fetters of what Bergson called the "plane of life"
and thus may experience "the One." Porphyry rings many changes on this
theme in the four books of his treatise on abstinence; it not only clarifies
the model but shows how it may be applied. Porphyry (1823) writes:

> it is necessary, if we intend to return to things which are truly our own,
> that we should divest ourselves of every thing of a mortal nature which
> we have assumed, together with an adhering affection towards it, . . .
> and that we should excite our recollection of that blessed and eternal
> essence, . . . which is without colour and without quality. . . . (p. 22)

The goal is to divest ourselves of all the "adhering" contents of our
minds so we can "return" to our "eternal essence," our pure preexisting
consciousness. A telltale sign of the transmission model is the emphasis
on *subtraction* as the key to spiritual method. One seeks to divest, not to
invest; to subtract and simplify, not to add or complicate.

In passing, and still on the theme of fasting (an idea inherently hateful
to a consumer society), we should note that the Greek Eleusinian mystery
rites were a two-thousand-year-old repeatable experiment that, with the
help of a nine-day fast plus a psychoactive *kukeōn* (brew), induced experiences in celebrants that convinced them of the reality of another world
and of their own immortality (Wasson, Hofmann, & Ruck, 1978). It is
possible to imagine experimental procedures that in ways yet to be de-

vised will be the psychospiritual equivalent of the Eleusinian mysteries. We have the entheogenic technology; what's missing is a living mythology and viable protocols.

According to the Hellenistic philosopher, Philo Judaeus (ca. 20 BCE–ca. 50 CE), God is the mind of the universe just as each of us is the god of our bodies. A wonderful piece of analogical thinking! Philo interpreted the Biblical statement that man is made in the image and likeness of God as a figurative way of talking about our personal minds being parts of a greater mind, an entity we could intelligibly call subliminal or superconscious, transpersonal or transcendent. There is a striking passage marking the process of return to the divine mind by means of introspection: "for the mind which exists in each individual has been created after the likeness of that one mind which is in the universe as its primitive model" (Clark, 1940, p. 171). The individual mind, like the divine mind, is "invisible, though it sees everything itself; and it has an essence which is undiscernible, though it can discern the essences of all other things, and making for itself by art and science all sorts of roads . . . investigating everything" (p. 171). The individual mind by degrees expands in its quest to explore the universe until it

> yields to enthusiasm, becoming filled with another desire, and a more excellent longing, by which it is conducted onwards to the very summit . . . till it appears to be reaching the great King himself. And while it is eagerly longing to behold him pure and unmingled, rays of divine light are poured forth upon it like a torrent, so as to bewilder the eyes of its intelligence by their splendor. (p. 171)

Or, for the "transmissive" coloring of Hellenistic philosophy, consider some remarks from Sallustius' *Concerning the Gods and the Universe*, written during the last quarter of the fourth century CE. Our interest is with Section 8, "Concerning mind and soul," where we read that the rational soul "despises human affairs as not affecting itself" (Sallustius, 1926, p. 17). This is not narcissism, just practical metaphysics. Thus we learn that "every good soul has employed mind, and mind is created by no body; how indeed could things lacking in mind create mind?" (p. 17).

Yes, how indeed! This remains an unanswerable question, posed by William James and company and more recently by philosophers such as Jerry Fodor, Thomas Nagel, Colin McGinn, and many others. Sallustius (1926) grasped transmission theory: "The soul uses the body as an instrument, but is not within it, just as the engineer is not within the engine" (p. 17). Nowadays, instead of an engine, we make the analogy with a TV set or a radio; the image is coming through the TV set, and the voice is not in the radio. Neoplatonists, like other transmissionists, claim extraordinary experience they prefer not to dismiss on ideological grounds.

Neoplatonic transmissionism, a climax of many trends of classical Greek philosophy, strongly influenced Western thought. Neoplatonic motifs shaped the ideas of St. Augustine, Dionysius the Areopagite, Meister Eckhart, St. Bonaventure, and—as I can attest—the thought of St. Joseph of Copertino, a seventeenth-century mystic noted for his abundant charisms (Grosso, 2015). With appropriate variations in metaphor, symbol, and existential crisis, the intuition of body as instrumental to spirit is an archetypal idea.

For example, in a short work by Bonaventure (1221–1274), *Retracing the Arts to Theology*, the central image is "light," a term by which he clearly means *consciousness*. The opening sentence is from the epistle of St. James: "Every good gift and every perfect gift is from above, coming down from the Father of Lights." All the riches of consciousness are "gifts from above" that must "come down" or, in Myers's metaphor, "uprush." In Bonaventure's Neoplatonic project, the universe is a process of different modes of being, all pursuing the root of their true being, all converging toward the ineffable One. In this work that retraces not only the arts but all human faculties to a single unifying source, Bonaventure offers a phenomenology of consciousness: the different functions of the soul—sensory, imaginative, intellectual (*intuitive*, we say)—all embody a form of "light," a mode of consciousness that converges toward the One, the "simultaneous endless life" that consoled Boethius on death row.

ON THE THRESHOLD OF THE MODERN WORLD: RENAISSANCE NEOPLATONISM

The Neoplatonic spirit was reborn during the Renaissance when Marsilio Ficino translated Plato, Plotinus, Hermes Trismegistus, Porphyry, and other Neoplatonic writings into Latin, and a humanistic Christian Neoplatonism became a powerful creative influence, the intellectual inspiration of new art, music, and ways of thought (Panofsky, 1972, p. 9). Ficino, Pico della Mirandola, and others created a scholarly dialogue between

Neoplatonic philosophy, Kabbala, and Arabian, Egyptian, and Christian thought and imagination. The great assumption: the Supreme Reality dispensed its insights universally; philosophy was to blaze a dialectical trail to the unifying, harmonizing core of all the traditions.

The Renaissance humanists forged a conception of human personality as free, mobile, multiple (Pico) and transcendent (Ficino), concerned with defending the rights of *human* potential against the dogmas of the Church. Overall, Renaissance thinkers sought, in the words of Charles Trinkaus (1970), "ways in which a new and more positive evaluation of human experience and human capacity . . . was assimilated into the religious preconceptions and practices of the age" (Vol. 2, p. 461). Trinkaus's study of Renaissance thought is entitled *In Our Image and Likeness*. The title is a phrase from a passage in the Book of Genesis (1:26) stating that man is made in the image and likeness of God—*Et Deus dixit: "Faciamus Hominem ad imaginem et similitudinem nostram."*

The title is clue to the book's main theme: Renaissance thinkers and artists used this Biblical passage to justify the liberation of human potential. Instead of directing spiritual energies toward mystical introversion, the Genesis statement was construed as license for launching a renaissance of the arts, science, biography, history, and letters. The extraordinary statement of the Hebrew Bible was taken as an invitation to perfect our divine potentials *here on earth*.

As part of this raising up of humanity, Giovanni Pico della Mirandola (1463–1494), an exponent of what Leibniz called *philosophia perennis*, sought to harmonize Christian, Pagan, Jewish, and Arabic traditions. The *Oration on the Dignity of Man*, published in 1486, portrays the human being as a "creature of indeterminate image," one who is the "free and proud shaper of his own being" (Pico della Mirandola, 1956). In Pico's image of multipotential man, whatever seeds of possibility we cultivate we become; we can "descend to the lower, brutish forms of life" or "rise again to the superior orders whose life is divine" (p. 8).

Invoking the *Phaedrus*, he exhorts his scholarly audience: "Let us be driven, Oh Fathers, by those Socratic frenzies which lift us to such ecstasy that our intellects and our very selves are united to God" (p. 26). This is a most unusual way to address a convention of scholars. Rephrasing the point more like Plotinus, he speaks of love that takes us "outside ourselves, filled with godhead, we shall be, no longer ourselves, but the very One who made us" (p. 27). Pico's Plotinian philosophy of mind is based on the assumption that an altered state of consciousness—frenzy, ecstasy, possession—is a negotiable path to experience the transcendent One.

Marsilio Ficino (1433–1499), James Hillman (1975) believed, was a pioneer of archetypal psychology. Ficino's conception of the soul was in the Neoplatonic "transmission" mode. In his philosophy of human immortality (see Trinkaus, 1970, Vol. 2, pp. 461–504), the first step is to recognize that the soul cannot know itself when attention is identified with anything sensory and mundane. We must go, Ficino declares, "Where no spatial limits are imposed. . . . Therefore seek yourself outside the material world. But in order to seek and find yourself beyond the world, fly beyond, indeed look beyond; for you are outside the world when you regard the entire world" (Trinkaus, 1970, Vol. 2, p. 470).

If immersed in the sensory, we identify ourselves with material things; if in spiritual ideas, we feel our spirituality. Philosophers, Ficino wrote, should become so immersed in corporeal experience that they end by fully identifying themselves with their corporeal existence. However, it is open to them to "learn that the unique way not only of attaining but of possessing the incorporeal is to render themselves incorporeal, that is to withdraw the mind from movement, sense, affect, and corporeal imagination as far as they are able" (pp. 472–473).

Ficino as physician needed to demonstrate the soul's immortality (once again) for therapeutic reasons. His method was pluralistic, using rational demonstration, analogy, metaphor, intuition, and mystical practice. His theory of immortality shades into a theory of mystical experience, for the mystic seeks to demonstrate the reality of the immortal One, not by argument but by experience.

Nevertheless, his approach to experiment was not exclusively otherworldly. In the *Theologia Platonica*, he argues for immortality by describing "the greatness of human nature as manifested in its this-worldly capacities and achievements" (p. 476). "Psychic dominance" of the lower mental and physical functions is a step in his argument for immortality; the soul is no mere epiphenomenon; it can dominate the body, and it creates its own world and culture; this proves it is godlike and therefore immortal. The exploration of the "afterlife" should begin with a renaissance of *this* life. Ficino said: "In these industrial arts it may be observed how man everywhere utilizes all the materials of the universe as though all were subject to man" (p. 483). Power over nature was part of a many-sided argument that the human soul, not reducible to anything material, can master physical and biological reality; and by extension, possess the power to survive bodily death.

Parallel to Myers, who thought the plays of Aeschylus were verbal icons of transcendent genius, Ficino took speech itself as a sign of the most sublime spiritual power: "Hence speech is granted to us for a certain more excellent task, namely as the interpreter of the mind, and herald and messenger of infinite discoveries" (Trinkaus, Vol. 2, p. 485). We need to stop here, but like many of the German writers cited above, Ficino and other Renaissance thinkers used concepts consonant with the model whose history we are narrating.

Space forbids further discussion of where the transmission model seems operative. We have scarcely touched on the Asian exponents of the present view; but see Chapter 9 (Sāṃkhya and Yoga) and Chapter 10 (Tantra) in the present book. There is space for two further points of discussion, meant to show the lively presence of the transmission idea throughout history.

THE AXIAL AGE

The intuition of the brain or body as a filter or transmission apparatus for mind and consciousness—terminology aside—was first expressed during the so-called Axial Age. The philosopher Karl Jaspers identified a unique period in history that he named the Axial Age (800–200 BCE), during which he said that human consciousness attained major breakthroughs in self-understanding. Why this miracle took place when it did, Jaspers discusses at some length, but apart from the general instability of the times, he found no obvious explanation of why such a transformation of consciousness took place. In India, China, and the West, figures like Buddha, Lao-tzu, Plato; sages, prophets, schools, and writings appeared, forming the basis of the world's great wisdom traditions. Jaspers (1953), a philosopher preoccupied with authenticity, wrote:

> Human beings dared to rely on themselves as individuals. Hermits and wandering thinkers in China, ascetics in India, philosophers in Greece and prophets in Israel all belong together, however much they may differ from each other in their beliefs, the contents of their thought and their inner dispositions. Man proved capable of contrasting himself

inwardly with the entire universe. He discovered within himself the
origin from which to raise himself above himself and the world. (p. 3)

The great advance of the Axial Age, according to Jaspers, was to
discover that human beings possessed internal resources for transcending
their limitations—reason, speculation, intuition, observation, voluntary
intelligence, imagination—all functions of mind and consciousness. During this Axial revolution of consciousness, the prophets, mystics, and
philosophers of East and West discovered the mystery of transcendent
consciousness.

Jaspers speaks of the "miracle" of the Axial Period, the miracle, he
believed, being the simultaneous discovery of all this that occurred at the
same time in three different places, China, India, and the West. The Axial
Age witnessed a flowering of consciousness that would establish patterns
of belief and models of spiritual experience for millennia—forever, some
believers would contend. In the main, Axial systems of salvation worked
with metaphysical assumptions that resembled the transmission model;
they were aware of a transpersonal reality, variously named God, Dao,
Brahman, Nirvana, etc. From the standpoint of modern physicalism, the
transcendent emphasis of the Axial Age was of necessity a "delusion."
But most Axial thinkers adopted "transmission" metaphors because they
corresponded to, and seemed to make sense of, their deepest experiences.

The modern "filter" or "transmission" model as described above was
the product of a late nineteenth-century metaphysical crisis, for many a
spiritual emergency, in which Darwinism and other advances in the material sciences seemed to menace whole epochs of traditional belief. The
creation of psychical research was one reaction to this crisis. In the modern period, German, English, French, and American thinkers resisted the
all-consuming materialist ideology of nineteenth-century science. Myers,
James, Bergson, Schiller, du Prel, and others promoted a revivified conception of mind and human personality. With Emerson's philosophy of
circles in mind we may plausibly expect periodic "axial" ages.

CONCLUDING THOUGHTS

Most of the writers we discussed were alert to the evolutionary potential
of the model. If our daily life is made of "measly trickles" of conscious-

ness, it leaves room for tinkering with the various filters and transmitters; we might be able to learn how to "open the valve" or "raise the shutter" onto novel landscapes of experience. The theory provides a naturalistic framework for modeling our mental evolution and for making sense of the extraordinary experiences regularly reported in the context of religious, spiritual, and magical experience.

The stunning achievements of modern technology have created in many the illusion that materialism must be true. On the other hand, the alternate conception has deep roots in the history of thought. And the core intuition endures, I believe, because it is experience-driven. Whatever the reigning metaphysical dogmas of the day, a significant minority always seem to come out with reports of some form of transcendent experience. These individuals will continue to find themselves at odds with the established view on fundamental issues. The transmission model has a perennial attraction precisely because people keep having the kinds of experiences that demand a model of its open type. Physicalism will continue to fail to account for the full spectrum of human experience; for this reason it is grossly inadequate, and should once and for all be tossed on the ash heap of history.

The transmission model has explanatory value. This is clear from our review of the various exponents of the idea. In almost every instance, the expansion of the concept of mind was driven by the need to account for some anomalous experience. James had afterlife phenomena worthy of consideration that forced him to posit his enlarged conception of mind. Bergson kept noticing how mental life spills over the boundaries of the body (e.g., in telepathy), from which he, like James, inferred the existence of a wider mental environment. Myers likewise was immersed in whole spectra of extended mental performance, which drove him to enlarge his theoretical apparatus, and led him to posit concepts like the "subliminal self" and the "World-Soul."

Contrary to most reductive, i.e., destructive, approaches to supernormal phenomena, the transmission view helps us understand how individual experience can arise from a subliminal mental matrix, thus permitting a spectrum of extraordinary phenomena. With a nonemergent, subliminal mental dimension as a starting point, we can begin to make sense of certain extraordinary experiences recurrently reported in history.

The explanatory wedge also provides an experimental wedge. There are various ways the model can be tried, tested, and used experimentally.

One is the traditional way, using established spiritual practices like prayer, fasting, meditation, and so on, all widely employed to induce experiences associated with spiritual enlightenment and creative inspiration. Many of the techniques are designed to reduce resistance to the subliminal influx; they lower Fechner's threshold, allowing what is present to present itself with minimal impediment. Many ascetic practices and extreme beliefs refer at the bottom to procedures designed to remove the inner and outer obstructions to transcendent experience.

A second way of experimentation, unlike the traditional, is more varied, ad hoc, improvisational. The outcomes here are typically unpredictable and perhaps difficult even to identify as what they are. At all times, and probably to an intensified degree today, there are large classes of spiritual loners and outliers; a motley world, a cultural underground, so to speak, of unclassifiable seekers. There are people, in short, whom fate has forced to feel the need to break through their ordinary lives to new modes of existence; however, their idiosyncratic stories may more readily be found in literature than in science. An iconic example of anarchic psychospiritual experimentation is brilliantly evident in the case of the poet Arthur Rimbaud (1954, pp. 269–273).

The third type of experimentation is the conventionally scientific, using controls, suitable technology, and statistics. There are different ways of translating the model into something that works according to the rules of quantitative science. Take one example: Charles Honorton (1977) reported that evidence linking psi performance with altered states of consciousness supported Bergson's filter theory. Honorton meta-analyzed eighty experimental studies that establish the connection. Results proved that during internal attention states like hypnosis or meditation subjects *detect* psi impressions more readily.

Experiments are built around reducing sensori-somatic noise, with the key idea of *deafferentation*: cutting off sensory input by using techniques of meditation, hypnosis, sensory deprivation, progressive muscular relaxation, induced hypnagogia, and Ganzfeld (uniform sensory input). Experimental strategies are designed to lower the psychosomatic noise level. With consciousness detached from external reality, one becomes more aware of internal states such as images, feelings, and intuitions. The rule: lower the internal barriers, and remove the obstructions to subliminal agency.

Kelly and Locke's monograph (1981/2009) on psi and altered states looks at this more broadly in light of historical and anthropological evidence, underscoring the need for new, richer participatory epistemologies. Here we find a wealth of untrod paths for exploration, especially where experimenters learn to partake of the reality they're investigating. Such an emphasis on direct experience would constitute a paradigm shift in the methodology of the human sciences.

In general, whether by methods of shamans, vision questors, Indian yogis, Sufis, Christian, Kabbalistic, or Eleusinian mystics, or by stories of the lightning-struck, the brain-injured, the cardiac arrested, or the psychoactively altered, we invariably find there is a disruption of the "filtering" brain mechanisms. Attention is more or less violently diverted from its usual functions, consciousness from its habitual interests and obsessions. The model offers a basis for exploring life-changing experimental approaches to the evolution of consciousness. The next chapter will further explore the psychobiology of this type of experimentation.

Finally, I believe the mind–brain model we have looked at is compatible with panentheism (see Murphy, Chapter 15 below), and I can imagine science and spirituality coming together in a creative coincidence of opposites—probably a tertium quid that is neither like religion nor like science as we normally think of them today. It may come in the guise of new art forms of the spirit, works of para-science fiction, collective adventures of active imagination. Another Axial Age may be in the offing, clarified by science and accelerated by technology: new forms of experience, perhaps of life itself, may arise from our perennial mystical urges.

NOTES

1. Cited in du Prel (1889, Vol. 1, p. 189).
2. "Substance dualism" need not be the final way of describing the relationship between mind and matter; for the moment it will serve to mark the contrast with epiphenomenalism. Later, we will briefly consider *panentheism* as a possible label for this position.
3. See Frothingham (1972).
4. For a fresh and more detailed account of Bergson's thought, see Barnard (2011).
5. Sommer (2009) provides an overview of du Prel's life and thought.

REFERENCES

Barnard, G. W. (2011). *Living Consciousness: The Metaphysical Vision of Henri Bergson.* Albany: State University of New York Press.

Bergson, H. (1913). Presidential address (H. W. Carr, Trans.). *Proceedings of the Society for Psychical Research, 27,* 157–175.

Bergson, H. (1911). *Matter and Memory* (N. M. Paul & W. S. Palmer, Trans.). New York: Macmillan. (Original 5th ed. published 1908)

Boethius (1962). *The Consolation of Philosophy* (R. Green, Trans.). New York: Bobbs-Merrill.

Broad, C. D. (1949). The relevance of psychical research to philosophy. *Philosophy, 24,* 291–309.

Burt, C. (1975). *ESP and Psychology* (A. Gregory, Ed.). London: Weidenfeld and Nicolson.

Clark, G. H. (Ed.). (1940). *Selections from Hellenistic Philosophy.* New York: Appleton-Century-Crofts.

Crabtree, A. (1993). *From Mesmer to Freud: Magnetic Sleep and the Roots of Psychological Healing.* New Haven, CT: Yale University Press.

Ducasse, C. J. (1961). *A Critical Examination of the Belief in a Life After Death.* Springfield, IL: Charles C. Thomas.

Du Prel, C. (1889). *The Philosophy of Mysticism* (C. C. Massey, Trans., Vols. 1–2). London: George Redway. (Original work in German published 1885)

Emerson, R. W. (1883). *Essays: First and Second Series.* Boston: Houghton Mifflin.

Eccles, J. (1965). *The Brain and the Unity of Conscious Experience.* Cambridge: Cambridge University Press.

Frothingham, O. B. (1972). *Transcendentalism in New England: A History.* Philadelphia: University of Pennsylvania Press. (Original work published 1876)

Grosso, M. (2004). *Experiencing the Next World Now.* New York: Simon & Schuster.

Grosso, M. (2015). *The Man Who Could Fly: St. Joseph of Copertino and the Mystery of Levitation.* Lanham, MD: Rowman Littlefield.

Hillman, J. (1975). *Re-Visioning Psychology.* New York: Harper & Row.

Honorton, C. (1977). Psi and internal attention states. In B. B. Wolman (Ed.), *Handbook of Parapsychology* (pp. 435–472). New York: Van Nostrand Reinhold.

Huxley, A. (1990). *The Doors of Perception.* In *The Doors of Perception, and, Heaven and Hell* (pp. 7–79). New York: Perennial Library, Harper & Row. (Original work published 1954)

James, W. (1961). Human immortality: Two supposed objections to the doctrine. In G. Murphy & R. O. Ballou (Eds.), *William James on Psychical Research* (pp. 279–308). London: Chatto and Windus. (Original work published 1898)

Jaspers, K. (1953). *The Origin and Goal of History* (M. Bullock, Trans.). London: Routledge & Kegan Paul. (Original work in German published 1949)

Kant, I. (1956). *Critique of Pure Reason* (N. K. Smith, Trans.). London: Macmillan. (Original work published 1781)

Kelly, E. F., & Locke, R. G. (2009). *Altered States of Consciousness and Psi: An Historical Survey and Research Prospectus* (2nd ed.). New York: Parapsychology Foundation. (1st ed. published 1981)

Kirk, G. S., & Raven, J. E. (1957). *The Presocratic Philosophers.* Cambridge: Cambridge University Press.

Myers, F. W. H. (1889). Automatic writing—IV. The daemon of Socrates. *Proceedings of the Society for Psychical Research, 5,* 522–547.

Myers, F. W. H. (1903). *Human Personality and Its Survival of Bodily Death* (Vols. 1–2). London: Longmans, Green. (Available on CTR website, http://www.esalen.org/ctr/scholarly-resources)

Nagel, T. (2012). *Mind and Cosmos: Why the Materialist Neo-Darwinian Conception of Nature Is Almost Certainly False.* New York: Oxford University Press.

Nahm, M., & Greyson, B. (2009). Terminal lucidity in patients with chronic schizophrenia and dementia: A survey of the literature. *Journal of Nervous and Mental Disease, 197,* 942–944. doi:10.1097/NMD.0b013e3181c22583

Noë, A. (2009). *Out of Our Heads: Why You Are Not Your Brain, and Other Lessons from the Biology of Consciousness*. New York: Hill and Wang.

Panofsky, E. (1972). *Studies in Iconology: Humanistic Themes in the Art of the Renaissance*. New York: Harper & Row. (Original work published 1939)

Pico della Mirandola, G. (1956). *Oration on the Dignity of Man* (A. R. Caponigri, Trans.). Chicago: Henry Regnery.

Porphyry (1823). *Abstinence from Animal Food*. In T. Taylor (Trans.), *Select Works of Porphyry* (pp. 1–170). London: Thomas Rodd.

Rimbaud, A. (1954). *Oeuvres Complètes*. Bibliothèque de la Pléiade. Paris: Gallimard.

Sallustius (1926). *Concerning the Gods and the Universe* (A. D. Nock, Trans.). Cambridge: Cambridge University Press.

Schiller, F. C. S. (1910). *Riddles of the Sphinx: A Study in the Philosophy of Humanism* (3rd ed.). New York: Macmillan. (1st ed. published 1891)

Schopenhauer, A. (1974). *Parerga and Paralipomena: Short Philosophical Essays* (E. F. G. Payne, Trans., Vols. 1–2). Oxford: Clarendon Press. (Original work published 1851)

Sommer, A. (2009). From astronomy to transcendental Darwinism: Carl du Prel (1839–1899). *Journal of Scientific Exploration, 23*, 59–68. Retrieved from http://www.scientific-exploration.org/journal/jse_23_1_sommer.pdf

Trinkaus, C. (1970). *In Our Image and Likeness: Humanity and Divinity in Italian Humanist Thought* (Vols. 1–2). Chicago: University of Chicago Press.

Van Lommel, P. (2010). *Consciousness Beyond Life: The Science of the Near-Death Experience*. New York: HarperCollins.

Wasson, R. G., Hofmann, A., & Ruck, C. A. P. (1978). *The Road to Eleusis: Unveiling the Secret of the Mysteries*. New York: Harcourt Brace Jovanovich.

4

A PSYCHOBIOLOGICAL PERSPECTIVE ON "TRANSMISSION" MODELS

Edward F. Kelly and David E. Presti

> There exists a more comprehensive consciousness, a profounder faculty, which for the most part remains potential only . . . but from which the consciousness and the faculty of earth-life are mere selections. . . . [N]o Self of which we can here have cognisance is in reality more than a fragment of a larger Self,—revealed in a fashion at once shifting and limited through an organism not so framed as to afford it full manifestation.
>
> —F. W. H. Myers, *Human Personality and Its Survival of Bodily Death*[1]

In the previous chapter Mike Grosso sketched the long and distinguished history of models of the general sort under consideration. To recapitulate, this includes Western historical figures such as Plato and some pre-Socratic philosophers, Plotinus and the Neoplatonic school, Ficino and other Renaissance thinkers, Romantic poets like Blake, Wordsworth, Coleridge, and Tennyson, the German idealists Fichte, Schelling, and Hegel, and the American "transcendentalists" Emerson and Thoreau, along with Asian representatives such as Patañjali, Śaṅkara, and Abhinavagupta, and more recently Sri Aurobindo and the philosopher and statesman Sarvepalli Radhakrishnan.

The Western stream crystallized around the end of the nineteenth century in the psychological and philosophical work of Myers, James, Bergson, and Schiller, and in more recent times similar models have been advanced somewhat independently by persons such as Aldous Huxley

and Albert Hofmann, inspired chiefly by their experiences with psychedelics. They have also been taken seriously by the eminent modern philosophers C. J. Ducasse, H. H. Price, and C. D. Broad, as well as physi-
cist/engineer G. N. M. Tyrrell and psychologist Cyril Burt. The latter two
individuals, significantly, were steeped in both psychical research and
physical science, with Burt (1968) in particular pointing out affinities
with twentieth-century developments in physics. Our Sursem group is
attempting to carry this modern lineage forward while remaining anchored in science.

In identifying all these persons as members of a family, we certainly
do not mean to suggest that they held identical views, for in fact they
represent a broad spectrum of related but distinctive visions of human
nature and our place in the world. What they do all have in common,
however, is an insistence—in stark contrast with current physicalist orthodoxy—that there is far more to us human beings than just our biology,
our bodies. In the concluding chapter of *Irreducible Mind* (*IM*, pp.
603–643), we tentatively bracketed a range of theoretical positions which
maps reasonably well onto this historical diversity, extending from some
sort of post-Cartesian interactive dualism at one end to metaphysically
more radical neutral or dual-aspect monisms or perhaps even some form
of idealism at the other, and we attempted to show in some detail how
such views might be reconcilable with modern developments in neuroscience and physics. That material forms useful background for the present
theory-oriented book, and we encourage readers who have not already
done so to familiarize themselves with it (for convenience, we have
placed that entire section of *IM* on the Center for Theory and Research
(CTR) website as supplemental material for this chapter). [2]

We will next begin to explore this theoretical territory in greater depth,
drawing upon a wide variety of modern and historical sources in hopes of
identifying recurring themes and eliciting potentially useful theoretical
ideas. In the current chapter we intend to focus mainly at the point closest
to current mainstream science, taking the views of F. W. H. Myers and
the early William James as representative of post-Cartesian interactive
dualism.

Everyone recognizes that mental states and brain states are somehow
intimately related: we see this for example in evolution, in human development, in everyday life, and in the consequences of brain injury and
disease. All of the traditional philosophical positions on the mind–body

problem arise from different ways of interpreting this undisputed fact of correlation. The current mainstream consensus, of course, is that brain processes *generate* or *constitute* mind and consciousness, but that is not the only way of viewing the matter. Even if the correlation were perfect—which it manifestly is not, as sketched in Chapter 1 and detailed in *IM*—this would not *entail* the production model. It remains conceivable that minds and brains are ontologically distinct, however closely linked they may be functionally.

This logical possibility was explored with particular clarity by William James in his 1897 Ingersoll Lecture on Human Immortality, as already indicated by Mike Grosso in Chapter 3. Especially in his foreword to the second edition of *Human Immortality*, James (1899) makes clear that one can think of the mental side as a finite mind or personality or soul in some way functionally coupled to the brain but different from it. This is essentially the same position James (1890) had sketched a few years earlier, in *The Principles of Psychology*:

> If there be such entities [souls] . . . they may possibly be affected by the manifold occurrences that go on in the nervous centres. To the state of the entire brain at a given moment they may respond by inward modifications of their own. These changes of state may be pulses of consciousness, cognitive of objects few or many, simple or complex. . . . I confess, therefore, that to posit a soul influenced in some mysterious way by the brain-states and responding to them by conscious affections of its own, seems to me the line of least logical resistance, so far as we yet have attained. (Vol. 1, p. 181)

The basic picture here is that of a conscious mind which normally operates in close conjunction with its associated brain in a manner strongly dependent on that brain's functional state. This would be illustrated, for example, by ordinary perceptual synthesis conceived in the "inverted" manner suggested in the section on the unity of consciousness in Chapter 1 above. On such a view the mind is in part a sort of virtual-reality system, constantly updating its conscious experience of the surroundings by somehow taking into account the brain's momentary global state in response to current input. Dreaming can be reimagined in parallel fashion, with its characteristic phenomenal properties resulting from the fact that the overall pattern of brain activity during sleep periodically approaches but does not quite attain its functional proficiency in waking life, and is less constrained by cross-modal consistencies of ongoing sensory input. We believe that all known neuropsychological phenomena can in principle be interpreted in similar inverted fashion—i.e., as disturbances, due to loss of function on the brain side, of the normal construction and shaping of conscious experience by cooperative interactions between a conscious mind and its associated brain. More generally, there seems to us no insuperable conceptual barrier to conceiving of the normal brain/mind connection in dualistic terms (and see *IM*, Chapter 9, or the supplemental material for numerous further details).

Before proceeding further we pause to take note of a relevant development within mainstream neuroscience itself. In his autobiographical book on *Consciousness*, neuroscientist Christof Koch (2012) confesses that after a protracted struggle he has given up on the idea that consciousness is somehow manufactured by brain processes:

> I used to be a proponent of the idea of consciousness emerging out of complex nervous networks. Just read my earlier *Quest*. But over the years, my thinking has changed. Subjectivity is too radically different from anything physical for it to be an emergent phenomenon. . . . The phenomenal hails from a different kingdom than the physical and is subject to different laws. I see no way for the divide between unconscious and conscious creatures to be bridged by more neurons. (p. 119)

Koch goes on to embrace tentatively a panpsychist view deriving from Leibniz, and links that to the widely heralded "integrated information" theory of his colleague and friend Giulio Tononi (2012), who has said that "consciousness is a fundamental part of the universe—just as fundamental as mass, charge, and so forth" (Rothman, 2012), associated with but not produced by material structures and processes.

These are significant defections from the orthodox production model, on the part of leading representatives of the lineages of contemporary neurobiology deriving from Francis Crick and Gerald Edelman respectively. Koch and Tononi have moved a crucial step closer to pictures like those advanced in *IM* and the present book, and their view of ordinary perceptual synthesis in particular now comes within a hair's breadth of the quantum-theoretic account offered by Henry Stapp in the following chapter.

The Myers–James picture itself, however, goes much further. The central concept of Myers's dynamic psychology is that of the Subliminal

Self—briefly, the totality of the psyche, soul, or Individuality, a wider consciousness encompassing both supraliminal and subliminal contents and capacities. The supraliminal or everyday self represents only that small portion of the psyche adapted by biological evolution to addressing the demands of the everyday world, with the brain as its "organ of attention to life" in the terminology of Bergson (1913). One or more "subliminal selves" (lower case) may sometimes also be associated with a given organism, displacing the supraliminal or primary self under special conditions such as cases of multiple personality or dissociative identity disorder. But the Subliminal Self—the underlying, more comprehensive Self—is the centerpiece of Myers's theoretical construct, for it is at this level that he sought to reconcile the then prevailing "colonial" (Ribot) vs. "unitary" (Reid) accounts of human personality in terms of a unity more profound than that of the everyday self or ego (see *IM*, Chapters 2, 5, and 9, for further details and analysis, plus Braude, 1995, who independently arrives at a similar picture).

James was thoroughly familiar with Myers's model, and deliberately and approvingly applied it to his later studies of religious experience and metaphysics (James, 1902, 1909/1971). That influence is already apparent in the Ingersoll lecture, where he suggests that the mental reality behind the brain might conceivably take a wide variety of forms, from that of a finite mind or personality to some sort of "World Soul" or mother-sea of consciousness. Within this basic framework James goes on to describe the brain variously as straining, sifting, canalizing, limiting, and perhaps individualizing that larger mental reality existing behind the scenes, whatever it may ultimately be. He also quotes approvingly Schiller's (1891, pp. 293, 295) characterization of matter as "an admirably calculated machinery for regulating, limiting, and restraining the consciousness which it encases. . . . Matter is not that which *produces* Consciousness, but that which *limits* it, and confines its intensity within certain limits" (James, 1899, pp. 66–67; italics in the original). James also explicitly portrays the brain as exerting these effects in a manner dependent on its own functional status, and links this idea to Gustav Fechner's conception of a fluctuating psychophysical threshold (pp. 24, 59–66). The parallels are clear with Myers's purely psychological conception of a subliminal region of the mind which includes capacities inherently greater than those normally accessible to us, plus an intrapsychic barrier of some sort which constrains and shapes their supraliminal expression.

James's later work demonstrated that Myers's model of human personality can extend naturally in the overall direction suggested by the
mystical traditions, and we will pursue that theoretical possibility further
in Chapter 14. In the present chapter, however, we wish to focus more
narrowly on the original Myers–James interactive-dualist "transmission,"
"permission," or "filter" picture itself, in its neurobiological aspects.

Like any other scientific model or theory, the Myers–James interactive-dualist picture must ultimately stand or fall on its empirical merits,
and so far its prospects look good. Having established the bare logical
possibility of "transmission" or "permission" interpretations of brain/
mind correlation as alternatives to the standard "production" view, James
(1899) himself went on to argue in their favor. In the first place they are
in principle compatible with all of the facts conventionally interpreted in
terms of the production model (as also indicated above), and however
metaphorical and incomprehensible they may at first seem, they are in
reality no worse off in that respect than their physicalist rivals (as now
grudgingly admitted by neuroscientist Christof Koch, philosopher Galen
Strawson, and a number of other prominent contemporary physicalists).
In addition, they appeared to James to have definite positive *superior-
ities*—in particular, the potential to explain aspects of religious experience and the various kinds of facts being unearthed by Myers and his
colleagues in psychical research.

IM has already reinforced the Myers–James empirical argument at
numerous points, and Paul Marshall (2005) has pointed out several further potential advantages in the specific context of his studies of extrovertive mystical experience: for example, not only can such models provide
a role for neurophysiological processes (without making them causally
productive of the experiences), they may help us explain why wildly
diverse circumstances or "triggers" can lead to strikingly similar experiences, they may prove useful in explaining the various types and stages of
mystical experiences, and they provide possible means for integrating all
of the various sorts of neurological, psychological, sociological, and doctrinal or situational factors currently recognized as contributory (pp.
274–275, and Chapter 2 above). Much further work remains to be done,
of course, to flesh out more details of this general picture and its metaphysical requirements or implications, and that is the central purpose of
the present book.

We must next comment briefly on terminology.[3] None of the metaphors currently in circulation for the sort of picture we are advancing is very satisfactory. James's "transmission" idea connotes faithful conveyance from one place to another, which does not fully capture what Myers had in mind. The "filter" metaphor also seems to us inadequate, although it has gained considerable historical currency and is by now the one most commonly encountered. For one thing it shares with "transmission" the notion of something entering the filter on one side and coming out faithfully on the other (albeit disentangled from other components of the input), and for both metaphors this engenders a homunculus problem (see *IM*, pp. 606–607). More contemporary technological metaphors picturing the brain as an antenna, a TV set, or radio receiver, or a laptop or smart phone connected to the Internet or the Cloud have similar issues. Most importantly, all are too rigidly mechanical in connoting a system somehow designed in advance to let through specific types of subliminal materials or capacities, without transformation or distortion. Myers's picture is much more fluid and dynamic than that. He conceives the subliminal region itself as *stratified in depth*, but the "strata" are not quasi-geological entities, static, immobile, or rigidly separated by impassable barriers: "They are strata (so to say) not of immovable rock, but of imperfectly miscible fluids of various densities, and subject to currents and ebullitions which often bring to the surface a stream or bubble from a stratum far below" (Myers, 1892, p. 307). Note in passing that such a picture potentially explains, at least metaphorically, why material from the depths of the subliminal region often emerges in disguised or distorted form, cloaked in accretions deriving from more superficial layers.

What ultimately gains access to supraliminal consciousness is also determined by something much more complicated than simple movement up or down of a mechanical "threshold" or "barrier," or the opening and closing of a Huxley-type "reducing valve," something more akin to an overall change in "permeability" or "tuning," which provides entryway or access to these normally inaccessible subliminal capacities and contents. *These "openings" clearly must be tied, in ways we presently do not understand, to functional states of the brain*. James's alternative "permission" metaphor really comes closest to what we have in mind: the brain-based perspective of the early James and the more purely psychological perspective of Myers can be reconciled by thinking of dynamic alterations of brain function as somehow permitting various sorts of incursions into supraliminal conscious life from these deeper layers of the psyche, through some as yet ill-defined process of cooperation or resonance between psyche and brain. The broad consistency of such a picture with empirical realities such as psi phenomena, genius, and mystical experience should already be evident, and we will be developing it further throughout the remainder of this volume.

We will next go on to explore possibilities for deeper psychobiological analysis of the nature and operations of the brain now reconceived as a system which somehow limits, constrains, and conditions the supraliminal conscious expression of these normally inaccessible subliminal resources.

GENERAL NEUROBIOLOGICAL BACKGROUND

Many kinds of selective, permissive, or filtering operations can easily be identified in everyday life. For example, it is by now a scientific commonplace that our organisms themselves drastically select among the physical stimuli impinging upon us, simply by virtue of the physical properties of our sensory transducers. We respond visually to just a tiny segment of the electromagnetic spectrum, and we hear a range of acoustic frequencies that can only be described as impoverished relative to the hearing of our dogs and cats. Our chemosensory capacities, taste and smell, are even more radically impoverished relative to those of many other creatures. In effect, we have been adapted by biological evolution in such fashion that under everyday circumstances we inhabit an experienced world that represents but a tiny fraction of what actually exists. As Cyril Burt (1968) put it:

> [M]an is concerned biologically neither with the very, very huge—the distant stars or galaxies rushing away at incredible speeds—nor yet with the very, very minute—atoms, electrons and other elementary particles obeying quantum principles. From all this it follows that man's natural conception of the universe, or rather of the restricted portion of it with which he has to cope, is that of a world of tangible objects of moderate size, moving about with moderate speeds in a visible three-dimensional container under the impact of contact forces (the push and pull of simple mechanical interactions), all in accor-

dance with fairly simple laws. Until quite recently this has also been the conception of the universe adopted by the scientist. (p. 58)

In this light it is perhaps not surprising that despite all of our genuine scientific knowledge and technical expertise, patiently accumulated over centuries of systematic and disciplined effort, we had apparently overlooked until the past decade or so something like 95% of the *physical* content of the universe—its so-called dark matter and energy. This chastening discovery should certainly encourage humility, and perhaps a sense of excitement as well, regarding what may remain to be discovered about the human mind!

As many previous authors have noted, everyday forms of attention, memory, thinking, and speech—as characteristically informed by culturally deposited expectations as well as our abiding intellectual interests, likes and dislikes, motivations, and so on—clearly involve additional layers of selective or filtering action that are constantly at work in service of our supraliminal conscious purposes, shaping what we experience. What we are really searching for in this chapter, however, is something quite different—specifically, physiological conditions which permit or encourage emergence of capacities and materials originating in deeper subliminal regions of the mind. These threads are clearly interconnected, however. Indeed, an important clue guiding our search resides in the fact that one bedrock component of the world's transformational or spiritual practices—meditation in its various forms—aims specifically at silencing the everyday "mental chatter" that for most of us seems to go on incessantly within our heads, even when we are sitting alone in a dark and quiet room. More generally, the conditions we are looking for—conditions which remove or circumvent mental limitations associated with ordinary conscious states and/or create conditions conducive to expression of extraordinary ones—seem to involve various ways of undoing or replacing those that typically accompany ordinary wakeful embodiment: in the terminology of Myers, the subliminal appears to manifest roughly in proportion to abeyance of the supraliminal. What sorts of conditions might these be, physiologically speaking?

To begin, they seem likely in general to involve large-scale patterns of brain activity. Myers himself, for example, spoke of altered patterns of "dynamogeny and inhibition" among multiple interacting brain regions as the likely correlate of deep hypnosis, based on its phenomenology, and recent neuroimaging research appears to be confirming that expectation (Jamieson, 2007). The human sleep–waking cycle provides another example, in that hypnagogic ("twilight zone") and dreaming states, which are physiologically distinctive on a global scale, are also known to be more conducive to psi effects than the waking state (Gurney, Myers, & Podmore, 1886; Rhine, 1962a, 1962b). Even in cases of "paradoxical functional facilitation" caused by localized brain injury or degeneration, such as the emergence of artistic skills in elderly patients suffering from fronto-temporal dementia, the facilitation appears to involve plastic reorganization of large-scale patterns of brain activity rather than release of area-specific capacities previously dammed up by inhibition (Kapur, 2011). Small changes in attentional set have also recently been shown to alter systematically the global pattern of brain response to identical film stimuli (Çukur, Nishimoto, Huth, & Gallant, 2013), again confirming the holism embraced in Chapter 9 of *IM* as against strong forms of modularity (see the supplemental material for this chapter on the CTR website).

In the abstract at least, the modern conception of the brain as a gigantic network of coupled oscillators already at some level naturally accommodates or even entails filter-like properties, and the possibilities for dynamic readjustment of its operating characteristics are almost inconceivably vast. A useful conceptual framework is that provided by physicist and brain researcher Paul Nunez (2010), who portrays the brain as a complex adaptive system made up of subunits operating at multiple spatial and temporal scales, with nonlinear dynamics emerging from circular causal interactions including bottom-up, top-down, and even resonant interactions among nonoverlapping neural networks embedded in global synaptic fields. The sorts of resonant interactions Nunez portrays as definitely capable of occurring *within* the brain could also conceivably link brains somehow to the wider environment, and Nunez himself playfully advances, without explicitly adopting it, the possibility that we might be immersed in an ocean of "Ultra-Information" to which we gain selective access by virtue of some sort of resonance between that source and our changing brain-states (see Davies & Gregersen, 2010, and Jahn & Dunne, 2011, for related ideas).

As of today, unfortunately, there really is no solid basis either in brain theory itself or in a theory of what might be "out there," for firm expectations about what form(s) the relevant brain conditions might take. We must look to actual data instead. Some mild "tuning" of our exceedingly complicated brain/mind system certainly occurs during the waking state through influences exerted by circadian rhythms, global fluctuations in activation level or arousal, nonspecific modulatory neurotransmission, and the like, together with the ongoing operations of normal everyday consciousness, but these kinds of excursions from the normal baseline are generally insufficient to produce "openings" of the sort that interest us here. Current mainstream consciousness research, unfortunately, doesn't help very much either, because most of this work too revolves around mind–brain correlations occurring under ordinary or everyday conditions. As already indicated in Chapter 1, the key result of this decades-long effort has been the emergence of "global neuronal workspace" theories according to which everyday human conscious experience *requires* a brain capable of producing synchronous neuroelectric activity reciprocally linking large parts of a spatially extended thalamocortical network across a spectrum of frequencies extending into the gamma range (30–80 Hz). Much additional work currently focuses on systematic *degradations* of mind and consciousness that occur as a result of functional disruption of the global workspace, whether spontaneously in connection with brain injury or disease, or deliberately in conjunction with general anesthesia (Laureys & Tononi, 2009). Very little of the current research effort— except for that on "twilight" states plus sleep and dreaming, as indicated above—involves physiological conditions and states of consciousness associated with psi, creativity, and/or mystical experience.

Our intention here, by contrast, is to focus particularly on phenomena of these latter, more extreme sorts, which we believe take us much closer to the heart of our theoretical problems as described in the Introduction to this book. Previous attempts to conceive altered states of consciousness and associated supernormal phenomena in systematic relation to changing conditions in the brain, body, and psychosocial environment include Kelly and Locke (1981/2009), Tart (1975), and Winkelman (2010), all of which go beyond the more conventional approaches by deliberately taking into account a wider-than-customary range of altered states and associated supernormal phenomena, but here we will try to push this approach still further.

Two main lines of research are available which can potentially yield neurobiological insight, both presently underdeveloped but lending themselves to systematic further elaboration: first, *between-subject* studies, which try to identify the relevant characteristics of persons who conspicuously and consistently display targeted forms of supernormal functioning; and second, *within-subject* studies, which try to correlate manifestations of such functioning with changing psychophysiological conditions and corresponding states of consciousness in the individual persons under study. These are not entirely independent, of course, since there can be interactions between trait-like predispositions and the states that result from precipitating practices or circumstances of sorts we will identify below. For each of the three main groups of targeted phenomena we will next briefly and selectively survey existing studies of both kinds, but we must warn readers in advance that at present there is a considerable disparity of available information in favor of the within-subject type, and not nearly enough information even there.

PSYCHOBIOLOGICAL STUDIES OF PSI, CREATIVITY, AND MYSTICAL-TYPE EXPERIENCES

We will begin by pointing out that there has already been considerable work on development of self-report scales that connect more or less directly with Myers's central concept of "permeability" in whatever barrier exists between supraliminal and subliminal strata of the mind, a psychological characteristic presumed to be deeply implicated in all three groups of phenomena. This includes research on "positive schizotypy" (Claridge, 1997), "boundary thinness" (Hartmann, 1991), "absorption" (Tellegen & Atkinson, 1974), "fantasy-prone personality" (Wilson & Barber, 1983), hypnotic susceptibility as measured in various ways, and paranormal experiences and beliefs. Although unaware of Myers, apparently, psychologist Michael Thalbourne produced a 29-item "transliminality" scale which appears to tap into Myers's original construct rather well and which correlates strongly and positively with all of these other instruments and with a single underlying factor common to all. This scale has also undergone purification using Rasch scaling techniques, and in its revised form, the RTS (Houran, Thalbourne, & Lange, 2003; Lange, Thalbourne, Houran, & Storm, 2000), it provides an interval-level measurement that is free of age and gender bias and displays excellent reliability and validity. A useful recent summary of most of these interconnections, with abundant references, can be found in Kelley (2010).

Some preliminary work has also been carried out to explore possible physiological correlates of transliminality itself. Thalbourne, Houran, Alias, and Brugger (2001) reported two studies in which they found significant positive correlations between transliminality and experiences of synesthesia, interpreting this as support for their hypothesis that high transliminality must involve some sort of "hyperconnectivity" (or perhaps defects of normal inhibition) in the brain. Something more complicated, however, is suggested by a preliminary study from Fleck et al. (2008), who compared resting electroencephalographic (EEG) patterns of persons high vs. low on the RTS. In brief, they found that these groups differed significantly, but did so in different ways in different scalp regions and frequency bands, indicating that high transliminality involves altered *patterning* of cortical behavior rather than some simple global shift. More work along these lines is surely warranted, and it would likely profit from a wider range of RTS scores, better control over what subjects do while "resting," and more appropriate EEG analysis techniques. Meanwhile, deployment of the RTS itself to further studies of all three main topics of this section seems highly desirable.

Psychobiology of Psi

Between-Subject Studies

Exceptional psi subjects have produced a disproportionate share of the field's best results (sometimes no doubt in the role of experimenters), but there have so far been few meaningful psychobiologically oriented studies, and practically nothing is currently known about possible sources of their abilities. Personality theorist Cyril Burt (1968) long ago issued a call for gifted subjects to be "put through the whole routine of ability and personality tests, with a thorough clinical, physiological, and neurological examination, and a case-history" (p. 32), but his advice has yet to be taken seriously. We still need a standardized special-subject protocol along these lines, one that could be applied in studies of genius and mystical experience as well!

There has, however, been substantial work on personality correlates of performance by (mostly) unselected subjects in controlled psi tasks, good recent summaries of which can be found in Carpenter (2012). One point of interest concerns the possible role of extraversion, which Eysenck has connected with high alpha density in resting EEG. This tends to go with the nothing-doing or "default-mode" condition, and increased alpha density was associated with enhanced scoring in several early psi/EEG studies, notably that of Morris, Roll, Klein, and Wheeler (1972) with the high-scoring subject Sean Harribance, in whom alpha rhythms were uncommonly abundant even at rest and became more so in high-scoring runs. The results obtained to date seem generally in line with the notion that lower levels of chronic "noise" or mental chatter go with better psi performance.

Another underresearched topic of relevance here concerns Recurrent Spontaneous PK (RSPK or "poltergeist") cases, which tend strongly to revolve around disturbed adolescents who harbor high levels of unconscious rage and who sometimes display possible signs of neurobiological involvement such as temporal lobe epilepsy as well (Parker, 2010; Roll, 1977; Roll & Joines, 2013). Roll emphasized certain systematic features of these cases—such as their long duration, their association with identifiable persons, and the tendency for the PK effects to focus on particular objects, types of objects, and locations—which create significant opportunities for further research. In particular, in addition to applying the sort of special-subject protocol noted above, it would now be technically feasible to monitor RSPK agents' EEGs while they freely move about, and to correlate changes in EEG with concurrent recordings of object movements. Finally, note that RSPK phenomena connect with crisis apparitions (Chapter 1) in showing that material originating within the subliminal region and cut off from supraliminal consciousness can sometimes have sufficient emotional force or "energy" to break through whatever barrier is normally in place, in accord with Myers's more general conception of the "nunciatory" or message-bearing character of sensory and motor automatisms (see *IM*, Chapters 2 and 5).

Within-Subject Studies

Large amounts of evidence from both laboratory and field studies point to deep linkages between psi and altered states of consciousness (e.g., Kelly & Locke, 1981/2009; Luke, 2012; Parker, 1975). An important landmark in this area is the review by Rhea White (1964), who sought to identify psychological conditions associated with unusual levels of success in some older "free-response" ESP experiments involving special subjects (these used complex target materials such as physical objects and drawings rather than ESP cards or the like). Her resulting "recipe" for psi success proved strikingly parallel to the traditional four-stage model of the creative process: specifically, it prescribes an initial period of sensory isolation and relaxation ending in a deliberate demand for the sought-after information ("preparation"); release of effort and quiet waiting ("incubation"); spontaneous emergence of information into consciousness ("inspiration," usually in the form of involuntary visual or auditory imagery); and evaluation or elaboration of the information so received ("verification"). White's analysis was one of the main influences leading to Honorton's (1977) model of psi and internal attention states, and to a subsequent large body of successful psi experiments using relaxation and "Ganzfeld" procedures even with unselected subjects (Braud, 1978; Radin, 2013). Also consistent with the Myers–James picture is the general tendency of persons rated high on various measures of creativity to score better on such tasks (see Carpenter, 2012, pp. 163–185, for a comprehensive survey).

Twilight states between waking and dreaming, and dreaming itself, are also known to be fertile sources of strong psi effects. Gurney, Myers, and Podmore (1886) pointed out that far more spontaneous experiences occur in twilight states than would be expected based on the proportion of time we typically spend in them, and Louisa Rhine (1962a, 1962b) confirmed and extended these observations in her very large series of spontaneous cases occurring at different points in the sleep–waking cycle. Ullman and Krippner (1973) subsequently pioneered experimental studies of free-response ESP during vivid dreaming episodes signaled by the rapid eye movements (REM) that often accompany them, and Child (1985) systematically dismantled methodological criticisms of these experiments subsequently published by psychologists. From a psychological point of view, the obvious common feature of these psi-conducive conditions is again reduction of external sensory input and increased relative contributions of internal processes—a physiologically enforced "abeyance of the supraliminal," if you will.

Subsequent functional neuroimaging studies of sleep and dreaming using PET and fMRI have also revealed much of the relevant neurophysiology, with interesting results: in particular, REM sleep has been shown to differ sharply from both slow-wave sleep and the waking state in levels and patterns of brain activation (e.g., Braun et al., 1997; Macquet et al., 2005). The main differences from the waking state revolve around decreased dorsolateral prefrontal activation, perhaps implying degradation of associated cognitive functions such as executive control, planning and decision making, working memory and the like, and increased activity in medial prefrontal cortex and associated limbic structures, perhaps implying heightened involvement of emotion.

Mainstream cognitive neuroscientists committed to the "modularity" thesis of strong connections between cognitive processes and activity in specific neural structures were quick in attempting to map the phenomenological properties of dreaming directly onto these and other observed changes in neural activation, but things are certainly not that tidy: in particular, the association between dreaming and REM sleep is not nearly so precise and exclusive as once thought, and more detailed characterization of the cognitive properties of dreaming reveals that normal functional capacities of the waking mind are much more in evidence than previously recognized (Dawson & Conduit, 2011; Kahan & LaBerge, 2011). We would not go so far as to say that this situation amounts to a compelling further argument *against* conventional production models and *for* the Myers–James view of brain/mind relations, but it definitely seems headed in that direction. The basic idea of studying cognitive changes in relation to changes in patterns of brain activation of course remains sound, but working it out in the context of dreaming is going to take a lot more scientific effort, and better integration of its first-person ("subjective," or view-from-within) and third-person ("objective," or view-from-without) aspects. Precisely what aspects of the physiological changes that accompany dreaming are relevant to its psi-conducive character remain for now unclear, but the subject is definitely researchable.

Hypnosis has also long been known to be psi-conducive—somewhat so even in unselected subjects—and deep hypnotic states in susceptible persons clearly merit special attention in regard both to the states themselves and to the unusual capacities of various sorts that sometimes accompany them (Honorton, 1977; Kelly & Locke, 1981/2009; *IM*, Chapter 3). The neurophysiology of hypnosis is even more complicated and confusing than that of sleep and dreaming, unfortunately, and the whole subject remains somewhat mired in a long-standing debate as to whether any such thing as a "hypnotic state" even exists. That debate goes on even now, mainly between behaviorist social psychologists who prefer to work with convenience samples of unselected or mildly selected subjects and undemanding tasks, and who insist that hypnosis involves nothing but role-playing and conformance behavior, and those who pay greater attention to individual differences and subjective reports, and who work with more extreme phenomena such as hypnotic control of experimental or surgical pain.

Until recently there was little direct evidence of unusual physiological accompaniments of hypnosis, and indeed the absence of such evidence was one of the principal factors permitting the debate to continue. In early EEG studies, for example, one typically saw under hypnosis more or less the same patterns that would be expected to occur in conjunction with the same task in the ordinary waking state. Kelly and Locke (1981/2009), relying mainly on behavioral and phenomenological evidence, argued in favor of a qualified altered-state view which pictures hypnosis not as a single, homogeneous state that is likely to have a unique physiological correlate but as a family of related altered states extending beyond the normal range and stratified in depth. More recent functional neuroimaging research, especially research using appropriate tasks and individuals selected for high or extreme hypnotizability, has in our opinion strongly confirmed this picture (see, e.g., Jamieson, 2007; Nash & Barnier, 2008, Chapters 13 and 14). There still does not appear to be any *single* physiological condition or marker that is unique to hypnosis and common to all of its manifestations, but there have been numerous demonstrations of unusual physiological patterns that appear only in highly susceptible subjects, and only when they are hypnotized. These findings are far too complicated to go into here in any detail, but they generally revolve around altered patterns of large-scale functional connectivity among the brain areas normally involved in the tasks under study, possibly mediated by altered top-down influence of executive-type monitoring and control functions conventionally associated with prefrontal cortex (Fuster, 2008). The altered patterns of prefrontal control seem likely to be closely connected with the vivid imagery and narrowed attention in response to suggestions that seem to mediate many hypnotic effects psychologically, but precisely what sorts of hypnotic instructions and associated physiological conditions are optimally psi-conducive—and why—remains to be elucidated. These again are clearly researchable questions.

Large amounts of historical and cross-cultural testimony also affirm the psi-conduciveness of *meditation* in various forms, and modern experimental results supporting the existence of such a connection have gradually accumulated (Honorton, 1977; Kelly & Locke, 1981/2009; Radin,

2013). The physiological picture, however, remains cloudy, despite the explosion of meditation research that has occurred in recent decades, fueled by its marriage with behavioral medicine and public health and hence access to conventional funding mechanisms. A valuable resource here is the searchable online bibliography maintained by the Institute of Noetic Sciences, based on that of Murphy and Donovan (1997), which now contains upward of 6,000 entries.

Research to date has remained for the most part at a very superficial level, unfortunately, relying upon brief practice with meditation techniques of diverse and often questionable sorts to demonstrate modest albeit clinically significant improvements in various behavioral, psychological, and/or physiological indices of well-being. Most obviously relevant to the concerns of this chapter is the fact that progress in meditation involves, by definition, stilling of the chattering supraliminal mind, which requires mastery of partly dissociable neurophysiological mechanisms of selective and sustained attention, controlled primarily by "executive" prefrontal cortex (Fuster, 2008), that have been extensively studied in recent years. Lutz, Slagter, Dunne, and Davidson (2008) have provided a useful framework for ongoing research by showing how two principal forms of Buddhist meditation—focused attention and open monitoring—engage these mechanisms in differing ways, leading to a variety of testable behavioral and neurobiological predictions that have already been partly confirmed.

Especially important from our point of view, however, are the few existing physiologically oriented studies involving advanced meditation practitioners of various sorts. Important context for such work is provided by the modern demonstration of plasticity in the adult brain, which has made clear that it is premature and unwise to attempt to understand what goes on in advanced meditators by loosely extrapolating from neuropsychological and neurophysiological data obtained from ordinary persons operating under more or less ordinary conditions. The brains of advanced meditators are likely to differ from those of ordinary persons and novice meditators in surprising ways, both in anatomical structure and in functional organization, and we need to investigate these differences *directly*, with minimal presuppositions regarding their possible form. Things seem now to be slowly moving in this direction: for example, Lutz, Greischar, Rawlings, Ricard, and Davidson (2004), in their work with highly experienced Buddhist meditators, have confirmed and extended the startling early findings of Das and Gastaut (1955) pointing to high-frequency (gamma) EEG rhythms as a possible marker of deeply focused meditative states, and additional work is underway in various places along similar lines (see the online bibliography noted above). It is already clear that in advanced meditators, as in hypnotic virtuosos, physiologically unusual things happen that we do not otherwise see. We do not yet have anything like a solid cartography of deep meditative states and their associated physiological profiles, or a good understanding of how they facilitate psi, but we certainly know how to work in these directions (see also *IM*, pp. 567–573, and Chapter 9 below).

Mediumistic "trances" constitute another family of psi-conducive states with wide historical and cross-cultural distribution, and as already indicated in Chapter 1 the early history of psychical research was dominated by studies of great mediums such as Mrs. Piper, Mrs. Leonard, and Mrs. Willett, who produced much of the best evidence we have for post-mortem survival. Regrettably, essentially nothing is presently known about these or any other such persons that casts any light on possible psychobiological underpinnings of their unusual abilities. Good contemporary mediums would certainly be prime candidates for application of the special-subjects protocol called for above, if they can be found.

The situation is hardly any better at present regarding physiological correlates of the trance states themselves, but there are good reasons for thinking that research along these lines would be productive. We should point out first that the relevant states are again somewhat heterogeneous in type, both within and among mediums: good material was sometimes produced in relaxed states of reverie within or near the normal range (as in contemporary "channelers"), but the most significant results emerged in conjunction with a variety of states characterized by deepening dissociation—that is, by increasing control of the medium's body from sites lying outside normal awareness. At the most superficial level this might involve the appearance of automatic writing or other automatisms in the context of more or less full ordinary consciousness, as in Mrs. Willett's "lone scripts." Mrs. Willett in particular also manifested progressively a range of states characterized by increasing sensory automatism, from the nonsensory awareness of her "daylight impressions" through a deeper kind of trance in which she experienced full-fledged hallucinatory figures of the ostensible communicators. Even in the case of her deep trances, however, Mrs. Willett remained in control of her body, although she was generally amnesic after the event. Mrs. Piper and Mrs. Leonard, on the other hand, generally underwent much deeper dissociations, with the normal supraliminal consciousness entirely displaced during periods in which "spirit guides," or sometimes ostensible communicators such as "GP" (Chapter 1), appeared to gain more or less complete control of the body. In some particularly spectacular cases, further dissociations of control appeared, permitting the medium to interact with multiple sitters concurrently, speaking with one and simultaneously writing to others about different matters with one or both hands. Entry into trance, like transitions between "alters" in dissociative identity ("multiple personality") cases, is typically well-marked and often dramatic, with drastic changes of posture, demeanor, physiognomy, voice, diction, and so on accompanying the appearance of successive communicators. Although some of these features could certainly be faked, others cannot: Mrs. Piper, for example, became profoundly isolated from her sensory environment and did not respond to intense stimuli such as pinpricks and open bottles of ammonia held under her nose (Gauld, 1968, p. 256).

In sum, this topic again seems eminently researchable, mainly requiring identification of suitable participants, and could quickly lead to better physiological characterization of these poorly understood but basically benign and psi-conducive states and their differences from pathological relatives such as multiple personality disorder. Trance mediumship is alive and well in many parts of the world including for example Brazil, and intimations of what may be possible can be found in a neuroimaging study of automatic writing by Peres, Moreira-Almeida, Caixeta, Leao, and Newberg (2012), who report reductions of activity (relative to similar but voluntary writing) in several cortical areas specifically associated with the task, including cortex belonging to the frontal attention system. This could well be a reflection of the dissociative aspect of the performance, which clearly must involve some sort of altered behavior of that system.

Altered states of consciousness and psi also come together in the worldwide complex of *shamanism*, found in varying forms in a large proportion of preliterate societies (Kelly & Locke, 1981/2009; Walsh, 2007; Winkelman, 2010). The essential point here is that literally thousands of such societies have discovered, often independently, procedures for inducing special states of consciousness including trance and possession trance that are expected to provide access to socially desirable skills such as divination, prophecy, and healing. Indeed, a significant measure of the value attached to such states is the extremity of the psychological and physiological measures routinely employed to produce them! Although currently providing little in the way of hard evidence of psi, the anthropological literature harbors a vast amount of information related to the altered states themselves and especially to means of inducing them. Of special interest here are the recurrent features of such recipes (Locke & Kelly, 1985): these include, for example, psychoactive agents of numerous kinds (see below); self-flagellation, body piercing, and related austerities; deprivation of food, water, and sleep; and "driving procedures" such as drumming, dancing, chanting, and clapping, often carried out with great intensity over protracted periods of time. Persons undergoing such hardships sometimes physically collapse and only then enter the targeted state, illustrating the pattern of extreme ergotropic arousal followed by collapse and trophotropic rebound described by Davidson (1976). Note that there are also strong parallels here with phenomena such as the spontaneous emergence of altered states and psi in connection with extreme sports situations (Murphy & White, 1995), and the role of physical austerities in the lives of late medieval mystics (Kroll & Bachrach, 2005).

Physiological study of such scenarios directly, in field settings, is difficult but increasingly possible (Oohashi et al., 2002). An indirect approach, advocated by Kelly and Locke (1981/2009) but still to be pursued in depth, would attempt to distill the physiologically essential principles of altered-state induction from the available anthropological material, with the expectation that if we can learn to produce the relevant states in the laboratory we could efficiently study all of their properties including their hypothesized association with psi. This would be a further stage in what we see as a key methodological development in modern parapsychology—specifically, learning to adapt experimental methods better to the "natural history" of the phenomena.

Psychobiology of Creativity

Between-Subject Studies

Many decades of work have produced a fairly good understanding of the nature of creative personality, and much of that literature is summarized in Chapter 7 of *IM*. Until recently, however, it made little contact with neurobiology, except for some loose talk about a possible special role for the right hemisphere and some connectionist-type speculations about how brains might implement the uncommon and distant associations or "divergent thinking" long thought to be crucial to the creative process. This has now changed for the better. We find especially helpful the theoretical work of psychologist Arne Dietrich (2004, 2007), who has made a serious effort to integrate the cumulative results of creativity research with modern knowledge of brain organization and function. In brief, Dietrich views creativity as utilizing all of the normal information-processing resources of the brain, but utilizing them in unusual ways. Those information-processing resources are organized in a hierarchical and reciprocally interactive fashion, with information deriving from sensory and memory systems located mainly in the back of the brain (in temporal, occipital, and parietal cortex) flowing generally toward the front in two great streams, roughly divided functionally into "cognitive" and "affective" streams. Both streams terminate in prefrontal cortex (PFC), our highest, most distinctive, and most recent acquisition through biological evolution—the cognitive stream mostly associated with dorsolateral PFC, and the emotional stream, including anterior cingulate cortex and associated limbic structures, with ventromedial PFC. The PFC as a whole collects, evaluates, integrates, and regulates information received from the lower levels, and provides for associated functions such as working memory, sustained and directed attention, and planning and scheduling of actions (Fuster, 2008).

Dietrich conceives of these resources as being flexibly deployed to creative tasks in two main processing modes, which he terms "deliberate" vs. "spontaneous." Following orthodox lines, he suggests that massive amounts of parallel processing are constantly going on in the background, not subject to the limitations that apply to voluntary conscious processing, and that when the deliberate system goes off-line for any of a variety of reasons, novel products generated in this way by the spontaneous system can gain access to working memory, where the occurrent or momentary contents of consciousness are maintained. This picture seems to him sufficient to account in full for the phenomenology of creative inspiration—its automatism and incommensurability, in Myers's terms—and he specifically identifies his spontaneous system with the traditional concept of intuition. Note that this provides another example of the modern impulse to reduce intuition without residue to "unconscious cerebration," as discussed in Chapter 1.

Dietrich's general picture is neurobiologically more sophisticated than anything we've seen before, and in many respects it is certainly on target. Creativity is a hugely complicated business in which many parts of the brain are involved at all times, *not* some single monolithic process operating out of a dedicated module or "creativity spot" located in the right hemisphere or anywhere else. But what might be different about brains that are unusually proficient at producing creative products? Shelley Carson (2011) addresses this issue in the context of the recognized partially heritable linkage between high levels of creativity and certain forms of psychopathology (especially schizophrenia, bipolar disorder, and alcoholism). Her analysis of this overlap strongly confirms the general picture originally expressed by Myers (1903) and expanded in *IM* (pp. 470–476), but she also attempts to identify specific aspects of brain function in these groups that could potentially explain their "shared vulnerability" of unusual access to subliminal products and capacities. One is a phenomenon of "latent inhibition" (LI), widely present among mammalian species, which amounts to an automatic tendency to ignore repeated inconsequential stimuli. Carson, Peterson, and Higgins (2003) showed that reduced LI, known to be characteristic of highly schizotypal or psychosis-prone persons and the acute phase of schizophrenia, is also associated with creative achievement and the personality trait of openness to experience (which correlates with both transliminality and psi performance). Both creative and psychosis-prone individuals have also been shown to habituate more slowly than normal to various kinds of repetitive stimulation. The general picture thus seems to be that automatic inhibitory or filtering mechanisms of various sorts which for most of us improve the efficiency of our dealings with the everyday world are somehow weakened in these groups, rendering them more open to information coming at them from whatever direction.

Carson also points to the possible existence of *hyperconnectivity*, both anatomical and functional, as characteristic of creative and psychosis-prone brains. Unusual patterns of anatomical hyperconnectivity, thought to result from failures of the synaptic pruning that normally occurs during development, have long been suspected of contributing to the unusual associations and metaphors produced by such persons. They may also play a role in synesthesia, which runs in families and is far more preva-

lent among creative persons than in the general population (Ramachandran & Hubbard, 2001). Recent neuroimaging research has also revealed
the presence of abnormal functional connectivity within the default or
resting-mode network of early-stage schizophrenics and their first-degree
relatives (Whitfield-Gabrieli et al., 2009).

There seem to be many possible genetic contributors to these mechanisms of cognitive disinhibition, the far-reaching effects of which remain
to be sorted out, and additional such contributors undoubtedly remain to
be discovered (Carson, 2011). Intriguingly, several of the current candidates are involved with regulation of serotonin neurotransmission, which
also figures prominently in altered states induced by psychedelics such as
LSD and psilocybin (on psychedelics, see below). One especially promising candidate seems to be a variant of the Neuregulin 1 gene, which is
definitely associated both with creativity and with increased risk of
psychosis, and which is thought to exert these effects through reduction
of inhibitory actions normally originating in the frontal lobes (Kéri,
2009).

Within-Subject Studies

The central question here is whether modern functional neuroimaging
methods have yielded insight into what is going on in the brain in connection with moments of creative inspiration, or "subliminal uprush" in
Myers's terms. The answer, unfortunately, is "not much" (Dietrich &
Kanso, 2010; Sawyer, 2011). The reasons for this are apparent: to do such
studies effectively, one needs to create conditions in which significant
creative insights repeatedly and detectably occur, with temporal and spatial properties well matched to those of the imaging methods in use, and
these enormous experimental challenges have rarely been met in even the
most approximate fashion. Instead one mostly finds convenience samples
of undergraduates, whose "creativity" is measured in a wide variety of
ways, performing low-level cognitive tasks thought to require "insight"
for their solution, with imaging results derived from a profusion of modalities and analysis methods and averaged over most or all of the task
performance. Dietrich and Kanso (2010) conclude from their exhaustive
review of existing neuroimaging studies, appropriately in our judgment,
that "not a single currently circulating notion on the possible neural
mechanisms underlying creative thinking survives close scrutiny" (p.
845).

A possible additional slant on this subject concerns bipolar disorder and its cyclic within-subject connections with genius. In this case, mentation produced during the hypomanic phase of the illness cycle often conspicuously displays properties of the sort used by Myers to describe subliminal uprushes, such as extreme fluency, speed, and flexibility as well as automaticity and incommensurabilty. It should be possible, using appropriate physiological and neuroimaging methods, to determine what sorts of brain conditions transiently accompany its cyclic emergence, but to our knowledge this important possibility remains to be pursued in depth (see *IM*, pp. 472–476).

Psychobiology of Mystical Experience

Between-Subject Studies

It is essentially unknown at present whether there are physiologically grounded predispositions to mystical experience, including those that occur in connection with deep near-death experiences (NDEs). We normally only discover such persons after their experiences have occurred, and this makes it difficult to disentangle predispositions from consequences. It would still be highly desirable, of course, to systematically collect new cases and apply special-subject protocols of the sort called for above. Previous neurobiological speculations have mainly revolved around claims of a special linkage between mystical experiences and epilepsy, especially temporal-lobe or temporo-limbic epilepsy (TLE), but these claims were carefully reviewed in *IM* (pp. 531–534) and found to be unwarranted. A new study led by our Sursem colleague Bruce Greyson confirms that conclusion: among ninety-eight epilepsy patients, fifty-five of whom recalled one or more experiences surrounding their (typically recurrent) seizures, not one reported anything resembling a genuine mystical experience (Greyson, Broshek, Derr, & Fountain, 2014).

Within-Subject Studies

From a physiological point of view, the single most striking fact about spontaneously occurring mystical experiences and NDEs is the extreme diversity of circumstances under which they occur. To make this more concrete, a composite listing would include at least the following: experiences of great beauty in nature, art, music, poetry, etc.; feelings of concern, compassion, or love for other beings; solitude, quiet, and peaceful inwardly directed states of mind; meditative or spiritual practices of various kinds; success in creative tasks; sexual orgasm; protracted exercise and extreme sports situations; altered-state induction measures of the sorts found in preliterate societies; confinements, as in illness, childbirth, jail, or shipwreck; states of depression, suffering, despair, bereavement; high fevers, systemic infections, loss of blood, dehydration, hypothermia, sleep deprivation; life-threatening situations such as near-accidents and mountaineering falls that do not in fact result in physical injury; actual life-threatening injuries including direct damage to the brain; lightning strike, and electrocution; surgical procedures involving general anesthesia; and cardiac arrest and coma resulting from diverse circumstances. The fact that similar types of experiences can result from situations varying this widely suggests to us that their common underpinning involves some sort of overall alteration of the normal brain/mind relationship, achievable in many ways, rather than engagement of specific neural structures or mechanisms of the sorts typically studied in cognitive neuroscience.

If we could bring the relevant states and phenomena into the laboratory, of course, we could study them using all the psychobiological tools at our disposal, and that would undoubtedly provide the most efficient way forward. Two such approaches stand out as the current best prospects. The first, already discussed above (and see also *IM*, pp. 563–573, and Chapter 9 below), would focus primarily on advanced practitioners of meditation.

The other, which we will emphasize here, focuses on classical psychedelic or "mind-manifesting" agents.[4] In their plant and fungal forms, and under the guidance of shamans, such agents have been used for millennia to evoke mystical-type connections with nature and to access associated capacities such as healing and divination. Shamanic practices have included ritual use of *Psilocybe* mushrooms, peyote and San Pedro cacti, African iboga, Amazonian snuffs, ayahuasca preparations, and *Salvia divinorum*, to name just a few. Both William James and F. W. H. Myers had powerful experiences with nitrous oxide, and both recognized the potential of such substances to support empirical investigations of mystical experience. However, it was perhaps Aldous Huxley who first forged the link between psychedelics and mysticism in Western popular culture. His encounter with mescaline led to his writing *The Doors of Perception* in 1954, a little book that became one of the primary ways by which knowledge of these powerful substances reached the general populace. In that book Huxley advanced the idea that psychedelics may work in large part by impacting a filtering capacity of the brain: "According to such a theory, each one of us is potentially Mind at Large. But in so far as we are animals, our business is at all costs to survive. To make biological survival possible, Mind at Large has to be funneled through the reducing valve of the brain and nervous system. What comes out at the other end is a measly trickle of the kind of consciousness which will help us to stay alive on the surface of this particular planet" (Huxley, 1954, p. 23). The discoverer of LSD, Albert Hofmann (1988), proposed a similar picture, driven by his own experiences with that powerful agent.

Philosopher C. D. Broad (1949), on whom Huxley relied, had already come to a similar picture based more generally upon the results of psychical research:

> I have the impression that we should do well to consider much more seriously than we have hitherto been inclined to do the type of theory which Bergson put forward in connection with *normal* memory and sense-perception. The suggestion is that the function of the brain and nervous system and sense-organs is in the main *eliminative* and not productive. Each person is at each moment potentially capable of remembering all that has ever happened to him and of perceiving everything that is happening anywhere in the universe. The function of the brain and nervous system is to protect us from being overwhelmed and confused by this mass of largely useless and irrelevant knowledge, by shutting out most of what we should otherwise perceive or remember at any moment, and leaving only that very small and special selection which is likely to be practically useful. An extension or modification of this type of theory seems to offer better hopes of a coherent synthesis of normal and paranormal cognition than is offered by attempts to tinker with the orthodox notion of events in the brain and nervous system *generating sense-data*. (p. 306; italics in the original)

Substances that have such powerful potential to open up the psyche also inevitably carry with them great complexity. During the 1950s and 1960s literally millions of people experienced their powerful effects, and the impact of psychedelics on the history of that era is enormous—on music, on art, on political thought and action, on innovation and technology. Many stories are yet to be told. But the complexity of these substances proved to be too much for science and society to handle at that time. The first laws against LSD and other psychedelics began to appear in the late 1960s, and in 1970 the new United States Federal Controlled Substances Act declared all the classical psychedelics to be prohibited from human use and without medical utility. What had been a highly regarded experimental and clinical research agenda, filled with great potential, was rapidly closed down and marginalized. Only twenty years later, through the heroic efforts of a small number of individuals, did psychedelics research with humans slowly begin to reenter the scientific mainstream.

A compact summary of the early work on psychedelics and mystical experience can be found in *IM* (pp. 542–553). One of the main results of that early work on the psychological side was to show that genuine mystical experiences can definitely be triggered by the classical psychedelics, especially with proper attention to set and setting, and more recent studies have reinforced that conclusion. A major project at Johns Hopkins Medical School, for example, has focused on giving psychedelics to healthy people in order to foster psychological flourishing. These studies began as a replication and extension of the classic Good Friday experiment with psilocybin, but now without the specific religious context and with an improved experimental protocol. The initial studies found that 30 mg of psilocybin, administered orally to individual subjects in a supportive environment, produced mystical-type experiences with sustained benefits on subjects' lives (Griffiths, Richards, McCann, & Jesse, 2006). Enhanced personal well-being and perceived spiritual significance of these experiences were robustly sustained more than a year later (Griffiths, Richards, Johnson, McCann, & Jesse, 2008). Additionally, quantitative assessment of personality traits indicated a sustained increase in the domain of "openness to experience," a measure of receptivity to new ideas and experience, intellectual engagement, and sensitivity to feelings in oneself and others (MacLean, Johnson, & Griffiths, 2011). This project is now expanding to address the impact of psychedelic experience on many aspects of spirituality.

Even more significant for purposes of this chapter are recent studies in humans of the basic neurobiology of psychedelics, using modern functional neuroimaging methods. Starting in the 1990s, psychiatrist Franz Vollenweider and colleagues in Switzerland carried out a series of positron emission tomography (PET) studies of changes in regional glucose metabolism (reflecting neural activity) following moderate oral doses of agents including psilocybin and ketamine. Despite their very different primary actions on cortical neurotransmission, these agents were found to produce substantially overlapping although distinctive altered states of consciousness (see Vollenweider & Kometer, 2010, Box 1) and strikingly similar global effects on neural activity. The neural effects consisted primarily of marked activation of prefrontal areas including anterior cingulate cortex (ACC) and the insula, with lesser activation of temporal and parietal areas and the thalamus (*IM*, pp. 546–547). Vollenweider and collaborators have themselves interpreted these imaging results as consistent with top-down disruption of a filtering action normally exerted at the level of the thalamus, and with the conventional expectation that intensified experience would likely be associated with some sort of intensified neural activity (*IM*, pp. 546–547).

This picture has been called into question, however, by more recent work on psilocybin using very different experimental and neuroimaging methods. Specifically, Carhart-Harris et al. (2012) combined intravenous injection of psilocybin with two different fMRI techniques—arterial spin labeling for measurement of blood flow, and BOLD for measurement of blood oxygenation. Each method was applied to a separate sample of fifteen volunteers, using it to contrast responses to the drug vs. a saline placebo. The main results were very similar in both samples and startlingly different from those of the Vollenweider group: specifically, under these conditions, no *increases* in activation were observed anywhere in the brain. Instead, the short-lasting psychedelic state was accompanied by large *reductions* in neural activity in many of those same "hub" regions, including in particular medial prefrontal cortex (mPFC), anterior and posterior cingulate cortex (ACC and PCC), and the thalamus. Furthermore, the intensity of the psychedelic experience was significantly correlated with the magnitude of these decreases, especially in the ACC, PCC, and thalamus, and the normal positive coupling between mPFC and PCC was also sharply reduced by the drug. A subsequent study from the same group using the same drug protocol in conjunction with magnetoencephalographic (MEG) neuroimaging revealed sharp decreases in oscillatory power across a wide range of frequencies in the same cortical regions (Muthukumaraswamy et al., 2013).

These results, unlike the earlier PET results, appear potentially consistent with the "transient hypofrontality" hypothesis of Dietrich (2003), and more importantly with the sort of "filter" models advanced in this book. The apparent conflict with those earlier results remains to be resolved in detail, but to us the Carhart-Harris picture seems likely to be closer to the physiological truth of the matter, in that the temporal and spatial resolution of fMRI is far better than that of PET, and the fMRI scans were carried out in close temporal coordination with the span of the intense but short-lasting psychedelic states produced by venous injection of the drug.

The bottom line here is that it is now possible to conduct carefully controlled human studies with psychedelics in laboratory settings, bringing to bear all the sophisticated tools of contemporary functional neuro-imaging and phenomenological inquiry in order to find out what is going on as these agents "open the filter" by modifying the activity of the brain. As the pioneer psychedelic researcher and therapist Stanislav Grof wrote in the reissue of his classic book on *LSD Psychotherapy*: "it does not seem to be an exaggeration to say that psychedelics, used responsibly and with proper caution, would be for psychiatry what the microscope is for biology and medicine or the telescope is for astronomy. These tools make it possible to study important processes that under normal circumstances are not available for direct observation" (Grof, 2001, p. 12).

GENERAL DISCUSSION

Having now briefly sketched the current very patchy state of research on neurobiological conditions associated with our targeted phenomena, we must try to make sense of it all. One way of approaching this task was set forth by Kelly and Locke (1981/2009) in their "Research Prospectus," which we have placed on the CTR website as additional supplemental material for this chapter. Their basic plan was threefold: (1) try to create a principled cartography of the altered states of consciousness that are specifically known to facilitate expression of subliminal resources including high-grade psi, uprushes of genius, and mystical experiences, together with various pathological and nonpathological relatives; (2) identify and characterize more precisely the main phenomenological features or dimensions underlying this array of altered states; and then (3) interpret these dimensions individually and neurobiologically in the context of a Myers–James filter-type model. After discussing various general features of the problem space, such as the interesting family resemblances linking various classes of phenomena, Kelly and Locke (1981/2009) recorded their fundamental intuition:

> [T]he true diversity of these ASC phenomena may actually be substantially less than appears on the surface; that is, we have the distinct impression that the great diversity of observed phenomena is generated by socially conditioned processes playing upon a relatively small number of underlying psychobiological themes. Identification of the critical dimensions of these basic themes, if they exist, could lead ultimately to an elegant conceptual and practical reorganization of the entire domain. (p. 45)

Kelly and Locke could get no further at that time and not much of relevance has happened since. Most other theoretical approaches to ASCs have taken a similar phenomenology-driven path, and in addition most of the resulting cartographies or models have been impoverished by failing to take into account a sufficiently comprehensive range of states and/or up-to-date neurophysiology. The range issue applies for example to the well-known Activation/Input/Modulation (AIM) model of Alan Hobson (2007), which deals mostly with conventional topics such as the sleep–waking cycle, plus hallucinations, and which has also been criticized even within its narrow sphere of intended application by Dawson and Conduit (2011). This limitation also applies with somewhat lesser force to the four-dimensional descriptive system of Vaitl et al. (2005), and similar comments apply to the textbook by Farthing (1992) and to Clark's (1983) "map of mental states," which specifically attempts to include mystical states but provides nothing in the way of biological insight.

A rather different situation is presented by the work of anthropologist Michael Winkelman (2010), who shares the fundamental intuition stated above but thinks he has already solved the problem. Specifically, Winkelman claims to have discovered and physiologically characterized what he calls an "Integrative Mode of Consciousness" (IMC), embracing not only "shamanic flight" but OBEs and NDEs, possession trance, hypnosis, meditation, and mystical experience, all of which he claims rest on an archaic neurobiological foundation that we share to a considerable extent with lower species. His central claim is that shamanic rituals and the various other relevant circumstances all lead to states of parasympathetic dominance in which high-amplitude slow-wave neuroelectric activity originating in limbic and subcortical structures propagates into frontal cortex, disrupting normal patterns of executive control. Quite apart from the perversity of assimilating all of these highly diverse ASCs to a single meta-state and attempting to interpret even the highest flights of human consciousness in regressive terms, his largely speculative account relies heavily on antiquated neuroscience and is replete with dubious factual assertions not supported by evidence based on direct observation of the relevant states. Note also that it rests squarely on the production model and therefore collapses completely under the weight of phenomena such as NDEs occurring under extreme physiological conditions (Chapter 1).

The value of Winkelman's book lies more in his descriptions of shamanism than his speculative neurobiology, but in one important respect, as we will now explain, we think he may be on target. An alternative approach to analysis of ASCs that now seems more promising parallels our earlier move to an "inverted" interpretation of the brain/mind correlation: that is, instead of viewing the problem as one of identifying distinctive physiological conditions that are associated individually with distinctive phenomenological dimensions of these altered states of consciousness—*and that produce those qualities, in accord with physicalist orthodoxy*—we should instead think of the various precipitating circumstances as different ways of reducing or eliminating some more general normal barrier to expression of the relevant states and capacities.

The main common ingredient here, psychologically, amounts to "abeyance of the supraliminal" in Myers's terms, or withdrawal of the mind/brain system from its customary "attention to life," in those of Bergson (1913). From this point of view it seems natural to start by taking deep mystical-type NDEs occurring under extreme physiological conditions as the limiting case, and viewing various other conditions as approaching that limit from different directions. A recurring element from our survey above which seems to make sense in this light is the feature of variously altering, disabling, or intensifying executive functions normally associated with frontal cortex, which appears common to psi performance, creative activity, and mystical experiences induced by psychedelics, along with sleep and dreams, hypnosis, meditation, mediumistic trance, the acute phases of psychosis, and altered states induced by shamanic rituals. Note that this alternative conceptualization also potentially helps us understand the diversity of "triggers" for the ASCs of interest, for as pointed out by Paul Marshall (2005), doors can be opened by sledgehammers as well as keys, with results that are both similar and different in various ways (p. 275), and to vary the metaphor a bit, one can perhaps open a given door a little or lot depending on the amount one applies of whatever is opening it.

Here we also make contact with a major modern development in systems neuroscience. Specifically, it has only recently become clear that overall patterns of brain activity typically reflect the operation of not one but two, anti-correlated, large-scale functional systems. Most previous functional neuroimaging research has ignored intrinsic activity, focusing instead on how the brain responds to various stimuli or tasks. However, it was eventually noticed that when a "resting" state was used as the control condition for the targeted tasks, the small and widely distributed *activations* that had long been the primary focus (Raichle, 2006; Raichle et al., 2001) were consistently accompanied by *de-activations* of a network of midline regions including in particular medial portions of prefrontal cortex, parts of temporal and parietal cortex, and posterior cingulate cortex (PCC). Further work has shown that these and a few additional "hub" areas, now collectively known as the default-mode network (DMN), are strongly linked both anatomically and functionally. The DMN accounts for nearly all of the brain's ongoing energy consumption under all conditions, matures and then declines with chronological age, and under waking conditions is involved especially in self-related activities such as autobiographical memory, imagining possible futures, engaging neural resources needed for performing stimulus-processing and other external tasks, and "mind-wandering" from such tasks (Buckner, Andrews-Hanna, & Schacter, 2008; Raichle, 2009; Raichle et al., 2001; Raichle & Snyder, 2007). Note that this is the same system the major nodes of which have recently been shown by Carhart-Harris et al. (2012) to be deactivated and decoupled by psilocybin.

Building on the emerging picture of the DMN, Carhart-Harris and Friston (2010) have pointed out that it theoretically opens a path toward explaining in contemporary neurobiological terms Freud's fundamental contrast between "primary" and "secondary" process. Secondary process here means, roughly, the sorts of mental activity that go on in normal everyday conscious life, while primary process, conceived as originating in the Freudian unconscious, drives the unusual forms of mentation found in dreams, psychedelic experiences, and the early or acute stages of psychosis. Carhart-Harris and Friston attempt to show how this phenomenological distinction can be mapped neurophysiologically and computationally onto the operations of the DMN conceived as a hierarchically organized Helmholtzian inference machine. Their basic move is to equate the normally functioning DMN with the Freudian ego and secondary process, while primary-process material emerges when cortical nodes of the DMN lose control of limbic and subcortical nodes the activity of which they can normally predict and hence control. In making these proposals they specifically characterize themselves as "addressing topics which have hitherto been considered incompatible with the cognitive paradigm" (2010, p. 1275; see also Carhart-Harris et al., 2014).

We genuinely applaud these important efforts, but with caveats: First, it is unfortunate that these authors pathologize primary process throughout their paper as something inevitably *degrading* ordinary waking consciousness, which for them apparently represents the highest possible form of consciousness. They do not even mention the important role that primary process has long been recognized to play in the creative process, for example, and for them the only value of psychedelics is apparently to provide models of psychotic states. Second, they do not fully come to grips with the difficulties of accounting in their terms for the striking qualitative differences between primary-process mentation and everyday forms of thought—the "incommensurability" of subliminal uprushes, as conceived by Myers in his account of genius (see *IM*, pp. 451–470).

Most fundamentally, for Carhart-Harris and Friston as for all other reductive physicalists it is simply axiomatic that anything unusual that enters the mind during these altered states of consciousness *must* come from somewhere else in the brain. But that axiom is falsified, we submit, by the existence of psi phenomena and mystical-type NDEs occurring under physiologically extreme conditions, among other things (Chapter 1). Our alternative view is therefore that at least some of the relevant properties and capacities actually must come from somewhere else—Myers's subliminal or James's B-region of the mind—and that what Carhart-Harris and Friston and other mainstream workers are really doing is to help to elucidate the brain conditions under which these openings occur. It is interesting in this respect that their model comes close to those of Dietrich (2003, 2004) and Carson (2011) for creativity and altered states, in pointing to the DMN and especially its termination zone in medial prefrontal cortex as playing a crucial role in these phenomena.

In sum, converging evidence suggests that the DMN plays a special role in creating or sustaining our ordinary sense of embodied selfhood anchored in the here and now—our "attention to life"—and that disruption of its normal functioning can provide increased access to the Myers–James subliminal or a Huxleyan Mind at Large. The DMN, that is, may constitute a major part of the neurological basis for the brain's hypothesized "filtering" action. This of course is merely a speculative hypothesis of our own, requiring investigation through further research. Recently emerging technologies such as transcranial magnetic stimulation (TMS) and transcranial direct current stimulation (tDCS) permit reasonably selective, reversible, and safe activation (or deactivation and disruption) of targeted cortical regions (Wasserman et al., 2008), and they could be deployed in conjunction with the still emerging picture of DMN structure and operations to explore directly the role of these prefrontal (and other) cortical regions in relevant states or task situations. A small amount of existing research suggests there may be value in this approach (Freedman, 2010; Snyder, 2009).

Summing up now more generally where things seem to us to stand, we do not claim to have established anything conclusive in this chapter with regard to the psychobiology of the Myers–James picture, but we *have* shown, we believe, that progress in this direction is definitely possible. To date there has been altogether too much premature theorizing founded on a very slender basis of reliable facts, but some parts of the picture are already visible, and many pathways lie open for further empirical research.

This is our main message: what we need is intensified work of relevant sorts that we know how to do, such as studies of gifted subjects of various sorts, studies of relevant altered states including in particular experimentally controllable deep meditative states and psychedelic states, and expanded studies with contemporary individuals who have undergone mystical-type experiences. A great deal of ground-breaking research of these sorts cries out to be done, and much of it could be done without a priori commitment to the more radical theoretical perspectives under consideration in this book. Further empirical progress is clearly possible on numerous fronts!

One last theoretical point deserves mention before we close. Most of what we have talked about above has to do with "disruptive forces," in the terminology of Charles Tart (1975)—that is, with procedures or conditions that destabilize ordinary modes of functioning of the brain/mind system. But another aspect, equally important and even less well understood, has to do with "patterning forces" that guide and stabilize the altered states of consciousness that emerge. Much of this undoubtedly has to do with ordinary factors such as "set and setting," prior instruction, socioculturally based expectations, and so on, but we think it likely that some also originates in the subliminal region itself, the source of at least some of what emerges—in effect, something akin to "grace," as recognized throughout the mystical traditions. This too constitutes an important subject for future research.

Success in research of the sorts sketched above could obviously lead not only to deepened basic understanding of these unusual states of consciousness but in addition to improved access to the humanly valuable potentials associated with them. This sort of systematic exploration of inner space will ultimately require resources on the scale of those society has previously marshaled for exploration of outer space, and can certainly have comparably enormous and mostly benevolent practical implications. What could be more exciting and challenging than that?

NOTES

1. Myers (1903, Vol. 1, pp. 12, 15).
2. See http://www.esalen.org/ctr-archive/bp
3. Here we wish to thank our *IM* colleague Alan Gauld in particular for sustained and insightful commentary on these difficult conceptual and terminological issues. We will make a new terminological suggestion of our own in Chapter 14.
4. The word "psychedelic" (Greek *psychē* = mind; *dēlos* = manifest) was coined in 1956 by psychiatrist Humphry Osmond in correspondence with author Aldous Huxley. "Classical psychedelic" is used to refer to the chemicals LSD (lysergic acid diethylamide), DMT (dimethyltryptamine), psilocin (as well as its pro-drug psilocybin), and mescaline. These drugs are all appreciated as having agonist actions at serotonin-type-2A (5-HT2A) receptors as an essential feature of their neurochemical action (Nichols, 2004). This term may also sometimes be applied to other psychedelic molecules, including some of the newer synthetic substances—such as DOI (2,5-dimethoxy-4-iodoamphetamine) and DOB (2,5-dimethoxy-4-bromoamphetamine)—that have substantial agonist activity at the 5-HT2A receptor. Methylenedioxymethamphetamine (MDMA), nitrous oxide,

carbogen, salvinorin A, delta-9-tetrahydrocannabinol (THC), and ketamine are examples of chemicals that can be called psychedelic, but are definitely not considered "classical psychedelics." Although these substances also have "mind-manifesting" characteristics, the experiences they produce are qualitatively different from those of the classical psychedelics, and their known interactions with the nervous system also differ from 5-HT2A receptor agonism.

REFERENCES

Bergson, H. (1913). Presidential address (H. W. Carr, Trans.). *Proceedings of the Society for Psychical Research, 27,* 157–175.

Braud, W. G. (1978). Psi conducive conditions: Explorations and interpretations. In B. Shapin & L. Coly (Eds.), *Psi and States of Awareness* (pp. 1–41). New York: Parapsychology Foundation.

Braude, S. E. (1995). *First Person Plural: Multiple Personality and the Philosophy of Mind* (Rev. ed.). Lanham, MD: Rowman & Littlefield.

Braun, A. R., Balkin, T. J., Wesensten, N. J., Carson, R. E., Varga, M., Baldwin, P., . . . Herscovitch, P. (1997). Regional cerebral blood flow throughout the sleep–wake cycle: An $H_2^{15}O$ PET study. *Brain, 120,* 1173–1197. doi:10.1093/brain/120.7.1173

Broad, C. D. (1949). The relevance of psychical research to philosophy. *Philosophy, 24,* 291–309.

Buckner, R. L., Andrews-Hanna, J. R., & Schacter, D. L. (2008). The brain's default network: Anatomy, function, and relevance to disease. *Annals of the New York Academy of Sciences, 1124,* 1–38. doi:10.1196/annals.1440.011

Burt, C. (1968). *Psychology and Psychical Research.* London: Society for Psychical Research.

Carhart-Harris, R. L., Erritzoe, D., Williams, T., Stone, J. M., Reed, L. J., Colasanti, A., . . . Nutt, D. J. (2012). Neural correlates of the psychedelic state as determined by fMRI studies with psilocybin. *Proceedings of the National Academy of Sciences USA, 109,* 2138–2143. doi:10.1073/pnas.1119598109

Carhart-Harris, R. L., & Friston, K. J. (2010). The default-mode, ego-functions and free-energy: A neurobiological account of Freudian ideas. *Brain, 133,* 1265–1283. doi:10.1093/brain/awq010

Carhart-Harris R. L., Leech, R., Hellyer, P. J., Shanahan, M., Feilding, A., Tagliazucchi, E., . . . Nutt, D. (2014). The entropic brain: A theory of conscious states informed by neuroimaging research with psychedelic drugs. *Frontiers in Human Neuroscience, 8,* article 20. doi:10.3389/fnhum.2014.00020

Carpenter, J. C. (2012). *First Sight: ESP and Parapsychology in Everyday Life.* Lanham, MD: Rowman & Littlefield.

Carson, S. H. (2011). Creativity and psychopathology: A shared vulnerability model. *La Revue canadienne de psychiatrie, 56,* 144–153.

Carson, S. H., Peterson, J. B., & Higgins, D. M. (2003). Decreased latent inhibition is associated with increased creative achievement in high-functioning individuals. *Journal of Personality and Social Psychology, 85,* 499–506. doi:10.1037/0022-3514.85.3.499

Child, I. L. (1985). Psychology and anomalous observations: The question of ESP in dreams. *American Psychologist, 40,* 1219–1230.

Claridge, G. (Ed.). (1997). *Schizotypy: Implications for Illness and Health.* Oxford: Oxford University Press.

Clark, J. H. (1983). *A Map of Mental States.* London: Routledge & Kegan Paul.

Çukur, T., Nishimoto, S., Huth, A. G., & Gallant, J. L. (2013). Attention during natural vision warps semantic representation across the human brain. *Nature Neuroscience, 16,* 763–770.

Das, N. N., & Gastaut, H. (1955). Variations de l'activité électrique du cerveau, du coeur et des muscles squelletiques au cours de la meditation et de l'extase yogique. *Electroencephalography and Clinical Neurophysiology*, Suppl. 6, 211–219.

Davidson, J. (1976). The physiology of meditation and mystical states of consciousness. *Perspectives in Biology and Medicine*, 19, 345–379.

Davies, P., & Gregersen, N. H. (Eds.). (2010). *Information and the Nature of Reality: From Physics to Metaphysics*. Cambridge: Cambridge University Press.

Dawson, J. L., & Conduit, R. (2011). The substrate that dreams are made on: An evaluation of current neurobiological theories of dreaming. In D. Cvetkovic & I. Cosic (Eds.), *States of Consciousness: Experimental Insights into Meditation, Waking, Sleep and Dreams* (pp. 133–156). Berlin: Springer.

Dietrich, A. (2003). Functional neuroanatomy of altered states of consciousness: The transient hypofrontality hypothesis. *Consciousness and Cognition*, 12, 231–256.

Dietrich, A. (2004). The cognitive neuroscience of creativity. *Psychonomic Bulletin & Review*, 11, 1011–1026.

Dietrich, A. (2007). Who's afraid of a cognitive neuroscience of creativity? *Methods*, 42, 22–27. doi:10.1016/j.ymeth.2006.12.009

Dietrich, A., & Kanso, R. (2010). A review of EEG, ERP, and neuroimaging studies of creativity and insight. *Psychological Bulletin*, 136, 822–848. doi:10.1037/a0019749

Farthing, G. W. (1992). *The Psychology of Consciousness*. Englewood Cliffs, NJ: Prentice Hall.

Fleck, J. I., Green, D. L., Stevenson, J. L., Payne, L., Bowden, E. M., Jung-Beeman, M., & Kounios, J. (2008). The transliminal brain at rest: Baseline EEG, unusual experiences, and access to unconscious mental activity. *Cortex*, 44, 1353–1363.

Freedman, M. (2010). Psi and the brain. In S. Krippner & H. L. Friedman (Eds.), *Mysterious Minds: The Neurobiology of Psychics, Mediums, and Other Extraordinary People* (pp. 151–161). Santa Barbara, CA: ABC-CLIO.

Fuster, J. M. (2008). *The Prefrontal Cortex* (4th ed.). London: Academic Press.

Gauld, A. (1968). *The Founders of Psychical Research*. London: Routledge & Kegan Paul.

Greyson, B., Broshek, D. K., Derr, L. L., & Fountain, N. B. (2014). Mystical experiences associated with seizures. *Religion, Brain & Behavior*. Advance online publication. doi:10.1080/2153599X.2014.895775

Griffiths, R. R., Richards, W. A., Johnson, M. W., McCann, U. D., & Jesse, R. (2008). Mystical-type experiences occasioned by psilocybin mediate the attribution of personal meaning and spiritual significance 14 months later. *Journal of Psychopharmacology*, 22, 621–632. doi:10.1177/0269881108094300

Griffiths, R. R., Richards, W. A., McCann, U., & Jesse, R. (2006). Psilocybin can occasion mystical-type experiences having substantial and sustained personal meaning and spiritual significance. *Psychopharmacology*, 187, 268–283. doi:10.1007/s00213-006-0457-5

Grof, S. (2001). *LSD Psychotherapy* (3rd ed.). Sarasota, FL: Multidisciplinary Association for Psychedelic Studies. (1st ed. published 1980)

Gurney, E., Myers, F. W. H., & Podmore, F. (1886). *Phantasms of the Living* (Vols. 1–2). London: Trübner. (Available on CTR website, http://www.esalen.org/ctr/scholarly-resources)

Hartmann, E. (1991). *Boundaries in the Mind: A New Psychology of Personality*. New York: Basic Books.

Hobson, J. A. (2007). States of consciousness: Normal and abnormal variation. In P. D. Zelazo, M. Moscovitch, & E. Thompson (Eds.), *The Cambridge Handbook of Consciousness* (pp. 435–444). Cambridge: Cambridge University Press.

Hofmann, A. (1988). The transmitter-receiver concept of reality. *ReVision*, 10(4), 5–11.

Honorton, C. (1977). Psi and internal attention states. In B. B. Wolman (Ed.), *Handbook of Parapsychology* (pp. 435–472). New York: Van Nostrand Reinhold.

Houran, J., Thalbourne, M. A., & Lange, R. (2003). Methodological note: Erratum and comment on the use of the Revised Transliminality Scale. *Consciousness and Cognition*, 12, 140–144. doi:10.1016/S1053-8100(02)00025-9

Huxley, A. (1954). *The Doors of Perception*. New York: Harper & Brothers.

Jahn, R. G., & Dunne, B. J. (2011). *Consciousness and the Source of Reality: The PEAR Odyssey*. Princeton, NJ: ICRL Press.

James, W. (1890). *The Principles of Psychology* (Vols. 1–2). New York: Henry Holt.

James, W. (1899). *Human Immortality: Two Supposed Objections to the Doctrine* (2nd ed.). Boston and New York: Houghton, Mifflin. (1st ed. published 1898)

James, W. (1902). *The Varieties of Religious Experience: A Study in Human Nature*. New York: Longmans, Green.

James, W. (1971). *A Pluralistic Universe*. In *Essays in Radical Empiricism and a Pluralistic Universe* (pp. 121–284). New York: E. P. Dutton. (Original work published 1909)

Jamieson, G. A. (Ed.). (2007). *Hypnosis and Conscious States: The Cognitive Neuroscience Perspective*. Oxford: Oxford University Press.

Kahan, T. L., & LaBerge, S. P. (2011). Dreaming and waking: Similarities and differences revisited. *Consciousness and Cognition, 20*, 494–514. doi:10.1016/j.concog.2010.09.002

Kapur, N. (Ed.). (2011). *The Paradoxical Brain*. Cambridge: Cambridge University Press.

Kelley, M. P. (2010). The evolution of beliefs in God, spirit, and the paranormal. II. Transliminality as the mediating factor. *Journal of Parapsychology, 74*, 359–381.

Kelly, E. F., & Locke, R. G. (2009). *Altered States of Consciousness and Psi: An Historical Survey and Research Prospectus* (2nd ed.). New York: Parapsychology Foundation. (1st ed. published 1981)

Kéri, S. (2009). Genes for psychosis and creativity: A promoter polymorphism of the *Neuregulin 1* gene is related to creativity in people with high intellectual achievement. *Psychological Science, 20*, 1070–1073. doi:10.1111/j.1467-9280.2009.02398.x

Koch, C. (2012). *Consciousness: Confessions of a Romantic Reductionist*. Cambridge, MA: MIT Press.

Kroll, J., & Bachrach, B. (2005). *The Mystic Mind: The Psychology of Medieval Mystics and Ascetics*. New York: Routledge.

Lange, R., Thalbourne, M. A., Houran, J., & Storm, L. (2000). The Revised Transliminality Scale: Reliability and validity data from a Rasch top-down purification procedure. *Consciousness and Cognition, 9*, 591–617. doi:10.1006/ccog.2000.0472

Laureys, S., & Tononi, G. (Eds.). (2009). *The Neurology of Consciousness: Cognitive Neuroscience and Neuropathology*. London: Academic Press.

Locke, R. L., & Kelly, E. F. (1985). A preliminary model for the cross-cultural analysis of altered states of consciousness. *Ethos, 13*, 3–55.

Luke, D. P. (2012). Psychoactive substances and paranormal phenomena: A comprehensive review. *International Journal of Transpersonal Studies, 31*, 97–156.

Lutz, A., Greischar, L. L., Rawlings, N. B., Ricard, M., & Davidson, R. J. (2004). Long-term meditators self-induce high-amplitude gamma synchrony during mental practice. *Proceedings of the National Academy of Sciences USA, 101*, 16369–16373. doi:10.1073/pnas.0407401101

Lutz, A., Slagter, H. A., Dunne, J. D., & Davidson, R. J. (2008). Attention regulation and monitoring in meditation. *Trends in Cognitive Sciences, 12*, 163–169. doi:10.1016/j.tics.2008.01.005

MacLean, K. A., Johnson, M. W., & Griffiths, R. R. (2011). Mystical experiences occasioned by the hallucinogen psilocybin lead to increases in the personality domain of openness. *Journal of Psychopharmacology, 25*, 1453–1461. doi:10.1177/0269881111420188

Maquet, P., Ruby, P., Maudoux, A., Albouy, G., Sterpenich, V., Dang-Vu, T., . . . Laureys, S. (2005). Human cognition during REM sleep and the activity profile within frontal and parietal cortices: A reappraisal of functional neuroimaging data. *Progress in Brain Research, 150*, 219–228. doi:10.1016/S0079-6123(05)50016-5

Marshall, P. (2005). *Mystical Encounters with the Natural World: Experiences and Explanations*. Oxford: Oxford University Press.

Morris, R. L., Roll, W. G., Klein, J., & Wheeler, G. (1972). EEG patterns and ESP results in forced-choice experiments with Lalsingh Harribance. *Journal of the American Society for Psychical Research, 66*, 253–268.

Murphy, M., & Donovan, S. (1997). *The Physical and Psychological Effects of Meditation: A Review of Contemporary Research with a Comprehensive Bibliography, 1931–1996* (2nd ed.). Sausalito, CA: Institute of Noetic Sciences.

Murphy, M., & White, R. A. (1995). *In the Zone: Transcendent Experience in Sports*. New York: Penguin, Arkana.

Muthukumaraswamy, S. D., Carhart-Harris, R. L., Moran, R. J., Brookes, M. J., Williams, T. M., Errtizoe, D., . . . Nutt, D. J. (2013). Broadband cortical desynchronization underlies the human psychedelic state. *Journal of Neuroscience, 33*, 15171–15183. doi:10.1523/jneurosci.2063-13.2013

Myers, F. W. H. (1892). The subliminal consciousness. Chapter 1: General characteristics and subliminal messages. *Proceedings of the Society for Psychical Research, 7*, 298–327.

Myers, F. W. H. (1903). *Human Personality and Its Survival of Bodily Death* (Vols. 1–2). London: Longmans, Green. (Available on CTR website, http://www.esalen.org/ctr/scholarly-resources)

Nash, M. R., & Barnier, A. J. (Eds.). (2008). *The Oxford Handbook of Hypnosis: Theory, Research, and Practice*. New York: Oxford University Press.

Nichols, D. E. (2004). Hallucinogens. *Pharmacology & Therapeutics, 101*, 131–181.

Nunez, P. L. (2010). *Brain, Mind, and the Structure of Reality*. New York: Oxford University Press.

Oohashi, T., Kawai, N., Honda, M., Nakamura, S., Morimoto, M., Nishina, E., & Maekawa, T. (2002). Electroencephalographic measurement of possession trance in the field. *Clinical Neurophysiology, 113*, 435–445.

Parker, A. (1975). *States of Mind: ESP and Altered States of Consciousness*. New York: Taplinger.

Parker, A. (2010). The mind–body problem and the issue of psychokinesis. In S. Krippner & H. L. Friedman (Eds.), *Mysterious Minds: The Neurobiology of Psychics, Mediums, and Other Extraordinary People* (pp. 65–83). Santa Barbara, CA: ABC-CLIO.

Peres, J. F., Moreira-Almeida, A., Caixeta, L., Leao, F., & Newberg, A. (2012). Neuroimaging during trance state: A contribution to the study of dissociation. *PLoS ONE, 7*(11): e49360. doi:10.1371/journal.pone.0049360

Radin, D. (2013). *Supernormal: Science, Yoga, and the Evidence for Extraordinary Psychic Abilities*. New York: Random House, Deepak Chopra Books.

Raichle, M. E. (2006). The brain's dark energy. *Science, 314*, 1249–1250.

Raichle, M. E. (2009). A paradigm shift in functional brain imaging. *Journal of Neuroscience, 29*, 12729–12734. doi:10.1523/jneurosci.4366-09.2009

Raichle, M. E., MacLeod, A. M., Snyder, A. Z., Powers, W. J., Gusnard, D. A., & Shulman, G. L. (2001). A default mode of brain function. *Proceedings of the National Academy of Sciences USA, 98*, 676–682. doi:10.1073/pnas.98.2.676

Raichle, M. E., & Snyder, A. Z. (2007). A default mode of brain function: A brief history of an evolving idea. *NeuroImage, 37*, 1083–1090.

Ramachandran, V. S., & Hubbard, E. M. (2001). Synaesthesia—A window into perception, thought and language. *Journal of Consciousness Studies, 8*(12), 3–34.

Rhine, L. E. (1962a). Psychological processes in ESP experiences. Part I. Waking experiences. *Journal of Parapsychology, 26*, 88–111.

Rhine, L. E. (1962b). Psychological processes in ESP experiences. Part II. Dreams. *Journal of Parapsychology, 26*, 172–199.

Roll, W. G. (1977). Poltergeists. In B. B. Wolman (Ed.), *Handbook of Parapsychology* (pp. 382–413). New York: Van Nostrand Reinhold.

Roll, W. G., & Joines, W. T. (2013). RSPK and consciousness. *Journal of Parapsychology, 77*, 192–211.

Rothman, J. (2012, August 19). How to measure consciousness [Interview with Giulio Tononi]. *The Boston Globe*. Retrieved from http://www.bostonglobe.com

Sawyer, K. (2011). The cognitive neuroscience of creativity: A critical review. *Creativity Research Journal, 23*, 137–154. doi:10.1080/10400419.2011.571191

[Schiller, F. C. S.] (1891). *Riddles of the Sphinx: A Study in the Philosophy of Evolution*, by A. Troglodyte. London: Swan Sonnenschein.

Snyder, A. (2009). Explaining and inducing savant skills: Privileged access to lower level, less-processed information. *Philosophical Transactions of the Royal Society B, 364*, 1399–1405. doi:10.1098/rstb.2008.0290

Tart, C. T. (1975). *States of Consciousness*. New York: E. P. Dutton.

Tellegen, A., & Atkinson, G. (1974). Openness to absorbing and self-altering experiences ("absorption"), a trait related to hypnotic susceptibility. *Journal of Abnormal Psychology, 83*, 268–277.

Thalbourne, M. A., Houran, J., Alias, A. G., & Brugger, P. (2001). Transliminality, brain function, and synesthesia. *Journal of Nervous and Mental Disease, 189*, 190–192.

Tononi, G. (2012). *PHI: A Voyage from the Brain to the Soul*. New York: Pantheon Books.

Ullman, M., & Krippner, S. (with Vaughan, A.). (1973). *Dream Telepathy: Scientific Experiments in Telepathy*. New York: Macmillan.

Vaitl, D., Birbaumer, N., Gruzelier, J., Jamieson, G. A., Kotchoubey, B., Kübler, A., . . . Weiss, T. (2005). Psychobiology of altered states of consciousness. *Psychological Bulletin, 131*, 98–127. doi:10.1037/0033-2909.131.1.98

Vollenweider, F. X., & Kometer, M. (2010). The neurobiology of psychedelic drugs: Implications for the treatment of mood disorders. *Nature Reviews Neuroscience, 11*, 642–651. doi:10.1038/nrn2884

Walsh, R. (2007). *The World of Shamanism: New Views of an Ancient Tradition*. Woodbury, MN: Llewellyn Publications.

Wasserman, E. M., Epstein, C. M., Ziemann, U., Walsh, V., Paus, T., & Lisanby S. H. (2008). *The Oxford Handbook of Transcranial Stimulation*. Oxford: Oxford University Press.

White, R. A. (1964). A comparison of old and new methods of response to targets in ESP experiments. *Journal of the American Society for Psychical Research, 58*, 21–56.

Whitfield-Gabrieli, S., Thermenos, H. W., Milanovic, S., Tsuang, M. T., Faraone, S. V., McCarley, R. W., . . . Seidman, L. J. (2009). Hyperactivity and hyperconnectivity of the default network in schizophrenia and in first-degree relatives of persons with schizophrenia. *Proceedings of the National Academy of Sciences USA, 106*, 1279–1284. doi:10.1073/pnas.0809141106

Wilson, S. C., & Barber, T. X. (1983). The fantasy-prone personality: Implications for understanding imagery, hypnosis, and parapsychological phenomena. In A. A. Sheikh (Ed.), *Imagery: Current Theory, Research, and Application* (pp. 340–390). New York: Wiley.

Winkelman, M. (2010). *Shamanism: A Biopsychosocial Paradigm of Consciousness and Healing* (2nd ed.). Santa Barbara, CA: ABC-CLIO.

5

A QUANTUM-MECHANICAL THEORY OF THE MIND/BRAIN CONNECTION

Henry P. Stapp

The phenomena targeted in Chapter 1 are "anomalous" in the sense that they are incompatible with the principles of classical physics that prevailed in science during the eighteenth and nineteenth centuries. Those precepts are now known to conflict with many empirical findings of mainstream physics. They have been replaced at the foundational level by the principles of a new physics called quantum mechanics (QM). The question thus naturally arises whether these anomalies can be accommodated by the new physics, and if so, then "how."

The answer is that these phenomena *can* be covered within the general mathematical framework of quantum mechanics, provided certain elaborations are given regarding two types of "choices" that enter crucially into the basic quantum dynamics. A choice of the first kind is what Heisenberg called "a choice on the part of the observer," while a choice of the second kind is what Dirac called "a choice on the part of nature." Choices of these two types enter in a fundamental way into standard quantum dynamics, but their causal origins and the scope of their physical consequences are not fully spelled out in the current form of the theory. However, certain stipulations allow the elaborated theory to explain the anomalies in question, which, in line with the aims of this book, are accepted as science-based givens. The question at issue in this chapter is whether, given the postulated existence of these anomalous happenings, they can be comprehended within an appropriately elaborated version of contemporary quantum mechanics; and if so, then what are these elaborations, and how are the anomalies then explained.

A core feature of quantum mechanics, as set forth by its founders, is an essential distinction between the observation-based and the atom-based descriptions of the physically described world. We describe our perceptions of the world, to ourselves, and to each other, in terms of the everyday idea that the physical world consists of objects each of which occupies a definite location in space at each instant in time. Large objects are imagined to be made of tiny invisible objects, called "particles," which move continuously about with the passage of time. Those "classical" ideas are the foundation of classical physics, but they are unable to account for the detailed structure of our conscious experiences. Those earlier ideas have been replaced by new ones in which the imagined particles of classical physics are replaced by the atomic particles of quantum physics. These atomic particles are described in the mathematical language of quantum mechanics, and have properties profoundly different from those of the classical particles. The standard quantum theory accounts for the scientifically established data, apart from the aforementioned anomalies, and beautifully reconciles the classical character of our experienced observations with the quantum-mechanical character of the underlying atom-based physical structure.

Quantum mechanics rests, then, on a fundamental distinction between the observation-based and atom-based features of the theory. The boundary between the part expressed in classical terms and the part expressed in quantum terms was often considered to lie at external measuring devices. However, both the quantum and the classical descriptions can be pushed toward the observer, and eventually to the limit where the transition from the atom-based to the observation-based description lies at the interface between the brain and the mind of the observer. The problem of reconciling these two disparate aspects of our understanding of the world thereby gets shifted to the place where it naturally belongs: the mind–brain interface.

THE MIND/BRAIN PROBLEM IN CLASSICAL PHYSICS

The great nineteenth-century physicist John Tyndall (1874) eloquently described the problem of understanding the mind–brain connection within the framework of nineteenth-century physics:

> We can trace the development of a nervous system, and correlate with it the parallel phenomena of sensation and thought. We see with undoubting certainty that they go hand in hand. But we try to soar in a vacuum the moment we seek to comprehend the connexion between them. . . . Man the *object* is separated by an impassable gulf from man the *subject*. There is no motor energy in intellect to carry it without logical rupture from the one to the other. (p. 59)

The problem here is simply that classical mechanics makes no mention of mind, and is logically and dynamically complete without containing either any hint of the existence of mind, or of any logical toehold for a rational passage from the physically described world to the disparate realm of our psychologically described mental processes.

In spite of this irresolvable conceptual difficulty, mainline neuroscience has adopted what Sir Karl Popper described as "Promissory Materialism"—the "promise" being that dogged adherence to the precepts of classical physics will eventually lead to an understanding of consciousness.

Such a promise is irrational! It is irrational to accept as the basis for the connection between the conscious and physical aspects of nature a theory that is known to be fundamentally false, that makes no mention of consciousness, and that provides, in principle, no way of generating from its consciousness-free premises our known-to-exist conscious experiences. That classical-physics-based approach is particularly unreasonable when its hugely successful and scientifically accepted replacement is a theory of unprecedented accuracy that is concordant with all established empirical findings, that is fundamentally about the connection of our conscious experiences to the atom-based properties of the physical world, and that, in direct conflict with a central premise of classical physics, elevates our conscious intentions from causally inert bystanders to critical elements of the basic dynamical process.

COPENHAGEN QUANTUM MECHANICS

Early in the twentieth century a series of theoretical and experimental findings showed that the classical principles that work so well for astronomical and large terrestrial objects fail to work for their atomic constituents. A new set of laws was found to hold at the level of atoms. These laws apply, in principle, not merely to individual atoms, but also to systems consisting of arbitrarily large numbers of atoms.

If, however, we try to apply these atomic laws directly to a system consisting of the atomic constituents of both an observing person and also a system that he or she is observing, then we find that the experiences of observers are different from what the atomic theory predicts. Specifically, the orthodox atomic laws entail—due to dynamical effects of the quantum uncertainty principle, which prevent the position and velocity of any particle from being simultaneously well defined—that the brain of the observer evolves into a continuous mixture of many different quantum states, each of which corresponds to a different perception. Yet only one of these different possible perceptions occurs in any actual empirical instance. Thus the atomic theory, if understood in the simple and direct way, fails to agree with experience.

The founders of quantum mechanics dealt with this and other conflicts between the raw atomic theory and the character of human experience by abandoning the conceptual framework that Isaac Newton had created in the seventeenth century. That "classical" way of thinking had, for more than two centuries, been accepted by scientists as the proper foundation of science. But that classical approach excluded, as a matter of basic principle, any irreducible causal participation of our conscious intentions in the unfolding of the physically described reality. Every mental property was asserted by the classical precepts to be completely determined by prior physical properties alone. The connection between our conscious observations and physically described reality was thus asserted to be "bottom up": perceptual realities were claimed to be—just as in astronomy—consequences of stand-alone physical properties.

Standard quantum theory rejects that idea. It elevates our conscious experiences from passive witnesses to active participants in the creation of the future. The mind–brain connection is converted from bottom-up to top-down: the conscious mind probes and thereby influences the brain, rather than being controlled by it.

To understand this profound transformation in science's conception of our own human role in the creation of the future, it is helpful to review how this radical change came about.

To cope with the glaring inability of classical concepts to account for puzzling twentieth-century findings, the founders of quantum theory accepted the empiricist doctrine that science must be anchored in what we know. But everything we know resides in our experiences. The founders therefore backed away from the idea that the aim of science was to comprehend the reality that lies *behind* our experiences. They focused instead on the structure of these experiences themselves. In the words of Niels Bohr (1934): "in our description of nature the purpose is not to disclose the real essence of the phenomena but only to track down, as far as it is possible, relations between the manifold aspects of our experience" (p. 18).

Quantum mechanics was, therefore, originally viewed not as a theory of "reality," as defined in some abstract classical sense. It was offered, rather, as a practical tool for making testable and useful predictions about our future experiences on the basis of information gleaned from our past experiences. Our human experiences thereby became the basic realities of the new theory, with the physical concepts relegated to the role of conceptual tools that our species has invented to aid our comprehension of the structure of our experience.

Classical physical theory grew out of our astronomical observations of the motions of the planets. Those motions were empirically found to be independent of anyone's acts of observation: the findings of astronomers everywhere and at various times all fitted together into a single universal conception of planets moving in space in a way conceived to be unaffected by our observations of them. That property of the motions of the planets was extrapolated by classical mechanics to the motions of the atomic particles in the bodies and brains of us observers, even though the motions of such particles are, of course, strongly correlated with the observer's physical and mental acts of making observations.

That potential contradiction was resolved in classical mechanics by assuming, in effect, that a person's observations—and all other mental properties as well—are simply aspects of the motions of the atomic constituents of that person's body and brain, and that, moreover, the motions of these atomic constituents, just like the motions of the planets, are determined by prior physical properties alone. In short, the mind–brain connection was assumed to be strictly bottom-up, with the "bottom" made essentially of planet-like atomic particles.

Quantum mechanics avoids this confounding of atoms and planets! According to the quantum ideas, the atomic particles in our brains, unlike the heavenly bodies, are strongly influenced by our "free choices" of which probing action to initiate.

These causally efficacious "Heisenberg" choices made by observers are key elements of the orthodox quantum dynamics. They are called "free choices" because they are not determined by the local deterministic laws that control the evolution of the quantum states in the absence of observations. These "free choices" seem to us, on the empirical basis of our everyday life experiences, to arise from a mental realm of felt values and sufficient reasons.

This understanding is in line with the basic quantum idea that the known realities are our thoughts, ideas, and feelings, including our perceptions, which are ontologically distinct from the atom-based physically described reality. This ontological separateness of our human mental qualities from the atom-based aspects of reality is also an essential part of John von Neumann's logically and mathematically rigorous formulation of quantum mechanics, both as spelled out by his words, and also as deduced from his analysis of the process of measurement. That proof of ontological separateness will be discussed presently.

These "free choices" were originally introduced into quantum mechanics as the experimenter's choices of which actions to perform. Each such choice picks out, in a way not determined by the quantum dynamical rules, some particular *possible* experience from a smeared-out continuum of potential future experiences. These *potential* experiences are generated from the prior actual quantum state of the world by the Schrödinger equation, which is the quantum analog of the classical equations of motion that generate the *actual* future. This creation of the future potentialities is called "Process 2" in von Neumann's rigorous reformulation of the earlier original "Copenhagen" descriptions of quantum mechanics. Von Neumann's formulation has the virtue of being realistically interpretable, while the earlier formulation eschews such an interpretation, claiming to be merely a useful set of rules that work in practice, and hence are claimed to be "true" only in the pragmatic sense of practically useful.

VON NEUMANN'S ORTHODOX QUANTUM MECHANICS

The distinguished Nobel Laureate Hans Bethe described John von Neumann by saying: "I have sometimes wondered whether a brain like von Neumann's does not indicate a species superior to that of man" (Blair, 1957, p. 90). Another expression of the same idea was a (joking) suggestion that von Neumann was actually an outer space alien who had trained himself to perfectly imitate a human being in every way.

Nobel Laureate Eugene Wigner (1963), in a paper entitled "The Problem of Measurement," used the term "orthodox interpretation" to identify the interpretation spelled out in mathematical detail by von Neumann (1932/1955) in his book *Mathematische Grundlagen der Quantenmechanik*. In Chapter 6, "The Measuring Process" (pp. 417–445), von Neumann showed how to expand the quantum-mechanical description of a system to include the physical variables of the measuring device, or, more generally, the physical variables of any system that interacts with an original system of interest. He then provided a detailed analysis of the process of measurement.

As just mentioned, von Neumann gave the name "Process 2" to the continuous evolution of the quantum state (or wave function) generated by what is called the Schrödinger equation. This Process 2 is the quantum-mechanical generalization of the classical mechanical process that generates evolution in time. Process 2, like its classical counterpart, is locally deterministic: the physical universe at each instant of time is defined by attaching to each point in three-dimensional space at that instant a set of mathematical properties, and demanding that all the physical properties at any later spacetime point "p" are, under the action of Process 2 (in the relativistic formulation of the theory), completely determined by those physical properties at the earlier instant that can be transferred to "p" without traveling faster than light. This locality condition prevents Process 2 from producing any faster-than-light action at a distance.

But, according to orthodox quantum mechanics, this Process 2 is not the whole story. The Process-2 evolution is interrupted by observational processes involving two kinds of choices: a Process-1 choice of a probing question on the part of an observing agent, and for each such probing question, a Process-3 response from nature.

The general logical form of the quantum-mechanical process of observation is this: an observing agent chooses and performs a probing question that inquires of nature whether the physical world has, or does not have, a certain physical property. This choice of a probing question was called by Heisenberg "a choice on the part of the observer." Nature immediately responds by choosing either the positive ("Yes") answer or the negative ("No") answer. This choice was called by Dirac "a choice on the part of nature." If the positive ("Yes") response is selected by nature, then two things happen: (1) at the experiential level, the observer experiences the response associated in his mind with the existence of the physical property about which he is inquiring; (2) at the level of atom-based physical descriptions, the quantum state of the universe "collapses" to the part of itself that is compatible with the existence of that physical property. A negative response is accompanied by a reduction of the physically described state of the universe to the part of itself that definitely does not have the property in question, but with no associated experience. (This final condition allows a sequence of yes–no queries to be strung together to form one single multiple-choice question.)

The choice made by the observing agent is called "Process 1," and the associated choice on the part of nature is called "Process 3." Although Process 1 *logically* precedes the associated Process 3, all of the physical changes associated with an observation occur, in von Neumann's original non-relativistic formulation, at the same instant of time. (The generalization to the relativistic version will be described later.)

An essential feature of this process of observation is that the observer-chosen property is something that the system being observed definitely possesses *after* a positive response, but may not have possessed *before* the process was initiated. For example, the quantum state of an observed system before the observation might be represented by a physical system that is spread out over a large spatial region, like a wave, whereas after the positive response the state might be confined to a tiny atom-sized region. Such a "collapse of the quantum state" provides a resolution of the famous "wave–particle duality" problem. But it does so at the expense of requiring an instantaneous change over a large region of space at a single instant of time: most of the large region occupied by the "wave" that represents the system being studied suddenly becomes no longer occupied by that system. Thus if one tries to go beyond mere practical utility, puzzles arise pertaining to these sudden instantaneous collapses.

Are they really happening in some objectively existing sense, or are they mere artifacts of our own theoretical invention?

This "collapse" idea resolves—by official edict—the wave–particle duality problem. Indeed, when coupled to a certain specified statistical rule, it accounts for all relevant data. But these collapses raise the above-mentioned "locality" puzzles. The founders dodged them by claiming to be providing only a practical tool that works in actual practice, and refusing to be drawn into debates about "reality" that go beyond practical utility.

John von Neumann faced the puzzles head-on, and, following the logic, produced a rigorous formulation of quantum mechanics that is widely used by physicists, and by others who need a mathematically precise version of the theory. Von Neumann's version can be interpreted as describing a psychophysical reality that evolves only forward in time, and in which each of us human beings exists as a psychophysical agent that can make "free and causally efficacious choices," and in which the nonlocal aspects do not disappear, but are brought under rational control in a way eventually made compatible with the empirical demands of the theory of relativity. This reconciliation with the special theory of relativity will be described below. But the bottom line is that the quantum rules then make a vast set of predictions about the structure of our experiences that are, leaving aside for the moment our targeted anomalies, concordant with all relevant empirical facts. In this theory, the connection between the psychologically and physically described aspects of the putative reality is basically top-down, with mental actions probing the physical, rather than bottom-up, with the physical properties controlling our streams of conscious experience.

How did von Neumann achieve this rational reconciliation of the mental and physical aspects of the theory?

The original "Copenhagen" way of describing this collapse process was tied to a mysterious thing called the "Heisenberg cut." Everything lying "below" this cut was supposed to be described in the mathematical language of quantum mechanics, whereas everything lying "above" the cut was to be described either in the language of classical physics—which we use to describe to ourselves and to others "what we have done and what we have learned"—or in psychological terms. The experiential aspects are described in mental and classical-physics terms, whereas their atomic underpinnings are described in terms of the quantum mathematics.

A practical account, in order to be useful to us, must accommodate our mental intentions. It must allow them to be "freely chosen," not predetermined at the birth of the universe, and it must support the capacity of our "freely chosen" mental intentions to influence our future experiences. This Heisenberg cut was "movable": its placement depended on what practical use was to be made of the theory. But that "movability" meant that the same physical thing could be described in two logically incompatible ways—either classically or quantum mechanically—depending on the practical application. Such an inconsistency might be all right for a purely pragmatic theory, but it is not acceptable for a putative description of reality itself.

A principal move made by von Neumann was to show that the Heisenberg cut could be moved all the way up, so that reality is unambiguously separated into a mental part, and a part described in terms of the mathematical language of quantum mechanics. The external measuring devices then become parts of that latter world, while the "classical descriptions" of these devices become identified as aspects of the perceptions of observers—a status often emphasized by Bohr.

The Heisenberg cut is shifted up, step by step, until all atomically constituted things, including our physical bodies and brains, lie below the cut, and hence are described in the mathematical language of quantum mechanics. The observer's mental aspects are *held fixed* during these shifts of the cut, and they are eventually pushed completely out of the physically described universe.

These preserved mental aspects were called "abstract egos" by von Neumann. They are mental in character because they are the parts of the psychophysical structure that represent what the theory is supposed to explain, namely the structure of our conscious experiences, and they are, by virtue of von Neumann's argument, ontologically distinct from the atomically constituted physical world. Yet each such ego retains, in the orthodox theory, a quantum dynamical linkage to its associated physical brain.

Thus Tyndall's "impassable gulf" between "man the *object*" and "man the *subject*" was bridged by rigorous quantum mathematics. Von Neumann converted what had originally been offered as a mere practical tool into a rationally coherent putative description of a dynamically integrated psychophysical reality.

Von Neumann's formulation eliminates the notion that things become classical merely by being "big"—that mere "bigness" can somehow cause the quantum-to-classical transition. But how big is big? Von Neumann's formulation ties the collapse not to something as nebulous as "big," but to something that, according to the theory, is separate and distinct from the atomically constituted physical world—namely our conscious experiences! And his theory specifies the physical place where a person's conscious actions act. They act, via nature's choice, on that person's physically described brain, which is linked via mathematically described physical connections to the rest of the physically described universe.

Thus quantum mechanics, in its orthodox form, is not simply a theory of a world made of atomic constituents. It is basically a theory of *"the manifold aspects of our experience"* and their connections to each other via atomically constituted, physically described brains—which are, in turn, connected to each other via other parts of the atomically described world. An important aspect of the new theory is a revised "quantum neuroscience" that contradicts "promissory materialism" by allowing our ontologically non-physical minds, or egos, to inject logically required and causally effective inputs into quantum mechanically described brain dynamics.

THE CAUSAL EFFECTIVENESS OF MENTAL INTENT

It might seem that a mere capacity to pose questions and register answers would leave our conscious egos just as helpless and impotent as before. But the quantum-mechanical process of posing questions and receiving responses is not like the classical mechanical process, in which our observations have no physical effects. In QM, the observer's "free choice" of which question to ask plays a critical role in determining which potential physical properties will become actualized.

In QM, the observer asks nature a yes/no question about the state of an observed system. If nature's response is "Yes," then, after this response is delivered, the observed system will definitely have the property that the observer inquired about.

Normally, this dependence of the post-observation properties of the system being probed upon the observer's choice of question does not give the observer any effective control over the observed system. That is because nature's response can be "No."

However, there is an important situation in which, according to the quantum rules, the "No" answers will be strongly suppressed. In that case, the free choices made by the observer *can* exert effective control over the system being probed—which, in von Neumann's theory, is the brain of the observer.

Suppressions of the "No" responses occur if an initial "Yes" response is followed by a sufficiently rapid sequence of posings of the same question. In that case the observer becomes empowered, by his own free choices of what property to probe, *and when to probe it*, to hold stably in place a brain activity that otherwise would quickly fade away. This effect is the celebrated Quantum Zeno Effect (QZE), which was conceptually linked by Misra and Sudarshan (1977) to the paradox of the "arrow in flight" posed by the Greek philosopher Zeno of Elea: at every instant the arrow is motionless, so how can it move?

Advances in mathematical concepts have made this "paradox" no longer puzzling to us. But the quantum dynamics brings it back into play, by virtue of the mathematical fact that if the quantum observations—which do affect the system being observed—become increasingly rapid, then in the limit of an infinitely rapid sequence of observations the observed system becomes "frozen" in place—much like Zeno's arrow.

In Zeno's case, which rests upon an essentially classical-type worldview, the argument is invalid. However, the quantum dynamics renders it valid, in the particular sense that each successive answer "Yes" in a sequence of all "Yes" responses returns the quantum state back to its initial state, which is the state that corresponds to the answer "Yes." As long as the answers keep coming up "Yes," the quantum state of the system being probed will, after each probing action, be returned to what it was at the beginning of the sequence. If the interval between successive probing actions tends to zero then the probability that *all of the answers in any fixed time interval* will be "Yes" tends to unity (one) in the limit, and hence the state of the system being probed becomes effectively frozen at the initial starting point.

The cause of this result is that quantum rules specify that, for small t, the probability for the individual answer to be "Yes" is approximately $(1-(vt)^2/2)$, where t is the time interval between successive probing actions and v is a certain finite velocity that depends on the physical situation. Due to the *t squared*, the probability for the answer to be "Yes" *for every probing action in a given finite time interval* tends quickly to unity as *t* tends to zero.

But how can this abstruse mathematical result be exploited to convert our conscious intentions from powerless side effects to the rationally coherent psychophysical underpinnings of purposeful, meaningful lives?

A coordinated action of a human being requires that a precisely timed sequence of neural impulses be sent to appropriate muscles. This evidently demands that a relatively stable neural state be created, and persist, and release the accurately timed sequence of motor commands. Let us call such a persisting neural state a "template for action."

The simplest QZE-based effect of mind upon a bodily action involves holding the external boundary conditions for a template for action "frozen" in place, due to the rapid repetition of essentially identical probing action, thereby allowing the internal dynamics of the template to generate the required accurately timed motor commands. However, the same mathematics covers also the case in which the rapid sequence of probing actions advances step by step along an observer-conceived continuous path in a physical-property space. If the mind-controlled rapidity of the probing actions can be made sufficiently great, then instead of the probed property of the brain being frozen in place, it will be dragged along the path specified by the evolving sequence of physical probing actions. This effect allows a strong control of the person's physical behavior to be exercised, via his or her quantum brain, by that person's mental "ego."

It is, of course, Process 3—nature's choice—that actualizes the physical realities associated with the ego's "free (not physically determined) choices." Nature does the real work of changing the physical state of the universe—by its action of changing that state to one concordant with its answer to the ego's probing query.

The profound change in the dynamical role of us observers was repeatedly emphasized by Bohr and the other founders, in statements such as: "in the drama of existence we are ourselves both actors and spectators" (Bohr, 1949, p. 236). This change also vindicates William James's (1890/1950) judgment: "It is to my mind quite inconceivable that consciousness should have *nothing to do* with a business which it so faithfully attends" (Vol. 1, p. 136).

THE ADVANCING GLOBAL RELATIVISTIC INSTANTS "NOW"

Von Neumann's orthodox quantum mechanics was non-relativistic. In his version, each individual "collapse event" occurs over all of three-dimensional space at a fixed instant of time; and an ordered sequence of such global events, each occurring at a time in an ordered sequence of times. This simple structure is, as mentioned above—and as von Neumann himself emphasized—incompatible with the concepts of Einstein's special theory of relativity.

This defect was removed by the works of Tomonaga (1946) and Schwinger (1951). They created the foundation for a mathematically consistent relativistic quantum (field) theory by replacing the advancing-in-time sequence of constant-time 3-dimensional surfaces in 4-dimensional spacetime by a well-ordered sequence of advancing-in-time 3-dimensional *space-like surfaces* "now," each of which separates the full 4-dimensional spacetime into an associated "past" and "future."

In the non-relativistic version each instant "now" is a "flat" constant-time surface. But in the relativistic case the "present global *instants* now" need not be flat: they can be curvy. Thus each new "present instant now" can coincide with the preceding instant over almost all of space, and be later in time only over a small region in space. Thus each new event can be associated with a finite region in space, such as the region occupied by some person's brain.

Each instant "now" is "spacelike" in the sense that no pair of distinct points on that 3D surface can be connected by a continuous path without moving, at some point on that path, faster than the speed of light—i.e., in a "spacelike" direction. Thus information located at one point on the surface cannot get to any other point on that surface without, at some point, traveling faster than the speed of light.

Although the observer's choice *logically* precedes nature's response to it, this response is assumed to be "instantaneous": the posed question and the associated collapse are assumed to refer to physical properties specified on the same instant "now." Thus the unfolding of our common future can be conceived to be marked off by a well-ordered temporal sequence of present instants "now," each associated with an increase in our common collective knowledge.

CLASSICAL DESCRIPTION IN THE QUANTUM UNIVERSE

The representation in the mind of the observer of the property that he or she is inquiring about is, as noted above, expressed in terms of the intuitive concepts of the classical worldview. This means, *logically*, that the quantum-mechanical states of the brain that are the correlates of our conscious experiences must be able to be *identified* in terms of the concepts of classical physics even though these states obey the dynamical laws of quantum mechanics. That is, our minds use classical concepts to specify the states of the brain that are associated with conscious experiences, even though these states are strictly quantum-mechanical structures that evolve in accordance with the quantum laws. On the other hand, it has been discovered, *empirically*, that our conscious experiences are correlated to spatiotemporally structured activities in the brain that are sparsely distributed over the brain, but with all parts of the structure seeming to behave like parts of a single classical simple harmonic oscillator (SHO).

Those coupled facts pertaining to the mind–brain connection lead naturally to the proposal about the mind–brain connection originally described in Stapp (1988). The suggestion is that the quantum states of the brain associated with conscious experiences are the well-studied kind of quantum states called "Quantum Coherent States" of the electromagnetic field. Each such quantum-mechanical state is the quantum analog of a corresponding state of a classical simple harmonic oscillator (SHO). In the mind–brain dynamics the pertinent strictly quantum state is unambiguously *identified* by specifying the state of the corresponding classical SHO, but the correspondence breaks down at the instants at which a Process-3 collapse associated with a conscious experience occurs. At each such instant, nature's choice actualizes the brain state that represents nature's response to the ego's probing action. The puzzle of the observer's classical description of the fundamentally quantum-mechanical brain state is thereby resolved by exploiting the tight correspondence between the consciousness-related quantum coherent state and its classical analog.

The frequency of such a quantum state is the frequency that would be measured by EEG and MEG devices that are detecting, for example, a 40 Hz signal in a pertinent network in the brain. This pertinent part of the brain can be considered to be divided into many tiny spatial regions, each containing a strictly quantum-mechanical state of the electromagnetic field, which is, however, completely identified by specifying the corresponding state of a classical electromagnetic field. This relationship allows the quantum state (i.e., density matrix) that is associated with a conscious experience to be *identified* or *specified* in the language of classical physics, even though it is dynamically connected to conscious experience by means of the three-part quantum dynamics.

The empirical frequency recorded by an EEG or MEG is not the frequency of the Process-1 probing actions. Nor is this measured frequency the quantum frequency that is directly proportional to the energy via Planck's famous quantum rule "Energy equals frequency times Planck's constant." The frequency of a quantum SHO is, like the frequency of a classical SHO, independent of its energy, and of the frequency at which we are probing it. It is, rather, the directly measured frequency of the electromagnetic oscillations.

This model is spelled out in more detail in my article "Physicalism versus Quantum Mechanics" in Stapp (2009), which is mainly a critique of Jaegwon Kim's (2005) book *Physicalism, or Something Near Enough*. It allows the part of the behavior of the quantum-mechanically described brain that is directly associated with a person's conscious thoughts to be *talked about* partially in terms of the concepts of classical physics, while being, however, dynamically connected to our streams of consciousness by the states and laws of quantum mechanics (see also Stapp, 2008).

A basic problem related to classical description is this: how does an essentially top-down probing process account for what contemporary neuroscience and common sense explain in bottom-up classical terms? For example, ingestion of alcohol, or a blow to the head, disrupts normal brain function, which alters the normal flow of consciousness. The causal connection is evidently *from* the physical event *to* the altered mental events, not vice versa: The disruption of the later thinking did not bring about the earlier blow to the head! The causal flow is seemingly bottom-up, from brain to mind—and we are thus apparently reduced to mechanical automata.

How does that argument fail? The answer given by orthodox quantum mechanics is the essential core of that theory!

According to von Neumann's dynamics the person in question, drunk or sober, bopped on the head or not, will, if conscious, have a sequence of experiences, each initiated by a Process-1 probing action that is not determined by the known laws of quantum physics. But that choice feels to that person's "ego"—to his felt psychologically described aspect—as if it is being posed by itself, in response to the exigencies of the situation in which it finds itself.

To account for the ego's needed awareness of its physical situation it is reasonable to assume that this ego is scanning the potentialities represented by its brain, which has been responding to features of its environment via its various sense organs. The probing questions that the ego poses can then be determined jointly by its own felt values and the current state of its brain.

The physical execution of the intended bodily actions will then be generated by the Schrödinger-equation-directed evolution of the state of the ego's brain—and of the physical universe of which it is a part. The pertinent state is the reduced (collapsed) physical state that is generated in conjunction with nature's choice of response to the ego's Process-1 probing action.

This model accounts in principle for the blatant physical facts and injects the ego's Process-1 choices into the determination of a person's bodily actions.

The role of the observer is thus to choose, on the basis of his or her mentally felt reasons and values, what to attend to, and how effortfully to attend to it. These choices effectively select from the huge mass of existing potentialities a sequence of classically describable observations that, to the extent that quantum effects are unimportant, will conform to the predictions of classical physics. If it is assumed that the intensity of the effort is positively correlated to the rapidity of the probing actions, then the physical effectiveness of the mental intentions will, by virtue of the Quantum Zeno Effect, be positively correlated to the intensity of the mental effort. One's mental self thereby acquires responsibility for one's bodily actions.

Notice that the original idea of the function of the Process-1 choices was that it merely selects what properties of the environment the observer/experimenter wishes to find out about. In ordinary perception the Process-1 choices account for the aspects of our focus of attention that stem from our conscious intentions.

But the function of Process 1 is automatically expanded within the orthodox theory, in which the probing actions act directly on the brain of the observer, to include influences upon large-scale bodily actions. These Process-1 choices thus become the general vehicle by means of which the ego cannot only find out things about the physical world around him, but also harness the power of nature in order to help bring to pass what that ego consciously values.

QUANTUM MECHANICS AND PHILOSOPHY OF MIND

Quantum mechanics began by justifying itself by its practical utility. Von Neumann converted this pragmatic offering into a rationally coherent psychophysical ontology that combined the psychologically and physically described aspects of our theoretical understanding of nature into a unified conception of reality that retains its practical utility by allowing a person's freely chosen mental intentions to influence his or her physical behavior. It explains how this influencing comes about, while being mathematically consistent, logically coherent, and empirically concordant with all "well-established" data.

But that achievement is precisely what philosophy of mind, moral philosophy, and philosophy in general have forever been seeking: a rationally coherent conception of reality that is inclusive—that encompasses both the mental and physical sides of nature, and the connection between them—and that allows science to move beyond the dead end of promissory materialism, by describing the workings of a purely science-based, top-down, and hence potentially useful, understanding of our dynamical role in the unfolding of the physically describable aspects of our experience.

Some physicists have tried to remove consciousness from the quantum-mechanical description and thereby return to the seventeenth-century classical idea of man as an essentially mindless machine. But that move defeats the whole purpose of science, which is to provide an empirical-evidence-based, hence conscious-experience-based, understanding of the world in which we find ourselves in order to help us bring to pass what we consciously value.

It is not possible to understand the world in which we find ourselves in terms of a theory that systematically leaves out everything we know, and know exists, namely our conscious thoughts, ideas, and feelings. And a theory cannot be useful to us in creating a future that conforms to what we consciously value if that theory has been stripped of the consciousness in which those values inhere, and moreover ordains a physical world whose entire history was computable in principle before anyone was born.

The task of science is not to cast the known-to-exist mental realities out of science. It is rather to understand how these realities are connected to the rest of nature. It is about reconciling "man the *object*" with "man the *subject*." Orthodox quantum mechanics provides an understanding of this kind.

APPEARANCES ARE DECEIVING

The question naturally arises why most psychologists, neuroscientists, and philosophers interested in the mind–brain connection continue to ignore the quantum-mechanical understanding of this relationship.

One reason, of course, is the power of inertia. Another is the unfamiliar mathematics and logic of quantum mechanics. More important is the fact that physics textbooks follow the pragmatic Copenhagen tack, in which the quantum collapses are imagined to occur at external measuring devices, rather than in our brains—coupled to the authoritative pronouncements of some influential scientists who proclaim that the classical ideas that work in astronomy will eventually work also in psychology (Crick, 1994; Koch & Hepp, 2006).

But probably the most important inhibitor is the fact that the orthodox von Neumann theory entails that the seeming validity of classical ideas at the level of visible-sized properties is illusory: according to orthodox quantum mechanics, "Appearances are profoundly deceiving!"

According to realistically interpreted orthodox quantum theory, the world of tables and chairs and other atomically constituted macroscopic objects is considered to be fully quantum mechanical. But that means that, in spite of its classical material appearance, the macroscopic physical world is "really" a bundle of potentialities pertaining to what will appear to observers if someone *actually looks. Perceivable properties* become actual properties only insofar as perceptions actualize them.

The normally observed "classical" appearance of the visible world is, according to the orthodox theory, created by all of the observations that have been made over the entire course of the history of the universe. Those conditions are very restrictive, but they still allow a lot of quantum-mechanical uncertainty for the status of perceivable-sized things that are not actually perceived.

Our brains, for example, are highly quantum mechanical. Large amounts of quantum uncertainty are introduced by the passages of ions through ion channels. The small spatial diameters of these channels entail large uncertainties in the velocities of the ions emerging from them. A living person's brain is therefore a generator of huge amounts of quantum uncertainty. This uncertainty can percolate up to the macroscopic level without being perceived either by the person himself or by anyone else. Brains *must* therefore be treated quantum mechanically: that is what permits the behavior of a person's brain to be strongly influenced by nature's responses to the free choices made by that person's conscious mind.

Weird as this quantum feature might seem to scientists and others steeped in Newtonian physics, it is where quantum mechanics rationally leads. Still leaving aside the targeted anomalies, it provides a broad science-based understanding of ourselves. And it is in line with a certain idea of parsimony that would not allow nature to encumber itself with highly developed conscious aspects that can make no difference in what actually happens.

THE NONLOCAL AND NON-MATERIAL CHARACTER OF NATURE

It may seem hard to believe that perceivable properties that have not been fixed by actual perceptions do not have definite values. Indeed, one of the first things that we all learn about the world is the evident existence of perceivable but not currently perceived properties. Why should a sensible scientist believe the radical quantum idea that what exists depends on what is perceived?

A fundamental feature of quantum mechanics is its inescapable need for faster-than-light (FTL) transfer of information. Relativistic classical physics has the following "No FTL" property: if two spacetime regions are situated such that no information located in either region can get to the other region without traveling faster than light, then the outcomes of experiments in either region cannot depend upon which of two alternative possible experiments is locally chosen in the other region.

The manifest workings of quantum theory involve sudden quantum "collapses" of the quantum states that seem to imperil this "No FTL" property. Einstein believed this feature of quantum theory to be merely a property of the quantum statistical formalism, and not a property of a yet-to-be-discovered underlying reality. However, I have rigorously proved, by arguments that make no reference at all to any microscopic or atomic property, that any world such as ours that conforms to a certain four empirically validated macroscopic predictions of quantum mechanics cannot forbid essentially instantaneous transfer of information about the local free choices of experiments: thus, Einstein notwithstanding, the "No FTL" property is not satisfied in the quantum world (Stapp, 1977, 1979; 2011, pp. 197–200; 2012, 2013).

We live in a world where long-range, near-instantaneous transfers of information cannot be forbidden. Mainstream physicists have universally embraced a theory that explicitly exhibits such transfers yet accommodates all "empirically established" facts. This theory also violates the classical worldview by allowing our psychological acts of perceiving, *which are not determined by the atomically constituted physically described world*, to influence that world. Thus contemporary physics violates two key principles of the worldview upon which the classical metaphysical doctrine of "physicalism" is based.

These non-classical properties of quantum mechanics are closely connected to the fact that according to classical mechanics the world is built essentially out of material stuff that cannot move faster than the speed of light, whereas according to realistically interpreted quantum mechanics the world is made of knowledge, and physically described potentialities for actual events connected to increments in knowledge. Nature's choices about what will become actual depend on "our knowledge," which is a *global* reality.

This quantum view is akin to Berkeley's classical statement of idealism, "To be is to be perceived," which, at the time it was made, seemed to many to be utterly contrary to the findings of science, as well as everyday experience. But today's most basic science, quantum mechanics, if realistically interpreted, is not only in general concordance with Berkeley's statement, but is far more detailed. It explains *how* that statement is reconciled with the local, dynamical, no-faster-than-light aspect of reality represented by the quantum-mechanical Schrödinger equation.

REVISING THE PAST

The basic causal evolution in orthodox quantum mechanics is strictly forward-in-time. In the relativistic version, a new state is created at each actual instant "Now," and from that new state certain weighted potentialities for possible future events are generated via the Schrödinger equation. An observation associated with the next instant "now" creates the next state by means of a collapse process that acts on the weighted potentialities generated from the prior state.

This strictly orthodox quantum "collapse" produces, however, a certain "effective" retrocausal action. Quantum collapses not only pick out what actually happens from a set of potentialities for what might happen but also eliminate from the "records of the past" (physically stored, say, on computer chips) all traces of the previously existing physical processes that led to the possibilities that were eliminated by nature's choice. Thus after the observation is completed the surviving records of the physical processes that led up to the observation-related collapse event exhibit only those parts of the former past that led to what actually did happen. The other parts of the records of the past disappear without a trace. As Stephen Hawking and Leonard Mlodinow (2010) succinctly put it in their recent book *The Grand Design*, "We create history by our observation, rather than history creating us" (p. 140).

This backward-in-time effect is essential to the understanding of many quantum phenomena, including the famous Delayed Choice experiments first discussed by John Wheeler (1978). It also accounts, as will be explained next, for certain empirical findings that have been interpreted by many scientists and philosophers as showing that the idea we have "free will" is an illusion.

THE TIMING OF THE READINESS POTENTIAL

In certain Libet-type experiments (Libet, 1983), a human subject is instructed to perform, sometime during a future interval, a specified small physical action such as raising a finger. The subject is instructed to note the position of a rapidly moving point on a screen when he or she feels this urge to perform this action. This defines a "time" for the onset of the mental urge, and a marker for the timing of a certain measured electrical activity in the motor cortex. This activity has a positive hump with a maximum about a half-second prior to the "time" of the felt urge.

This result has been used to argue that "free will is an illusion": that your mechanical brain is doing what you feel the core you, your inner mental self, is doing; that your consciousness is a mere by-product of the activity of your brain, not the causally efficacious agent that it *seems* to you to be.

Before any such coordinated bodily action can be performed, a corresponding "template for action" must be created. Such a template is a pattern of neurological activity that will emit a precisely timed sequence of neural signals to the appropriate muscles, which will then respond by causing the specified bodily movements to occur. Let it be presumed, at least for the moment, that the dynamical linkages between mentally felt intentions and associated bodily actions controlled by brain-based templates for action are established by a trial-and-error learning process that begins already in the womb: each of us learns by experience what sort of mental efforts will produce various intended physical behaviors.

The precise time of the to-be-performed action is not specified in the instructions given to the subject in this Libet experiment. Hence the subject's quantum-mechanical brain begins *at various times* to construct an appropriate template for action. The action cannot begin until the full template is in place, and a mental "consent" to act is given (James, 1890/ 1950, Vol. 2, p. 568).

The probability that nature will actualize any single one of these *potential* templates can be small. Hence nature's response will probably be "No" for many of these templates. When the response is "No," the associated physical records of those unrealized potentialities will be annihilated by the negative collapse event.

Some possible template for action will eventually get selected by the subject's ego and then be actualized by nature's positive response. That particular template, and the associated recorded buildup of the readiness potential associated with its construction, will survive the quantum collapses. The surviving record (stored on some external mechanical device) will show the buildup of the readiness potential that precedes by a measurable time interval the subject's will to act (consent), while the records of the buildup of the alternative *un*actualized possibilities will not survive, thereby giving a false impression of backward-in-time causation— namely of the decision-to-act's being made at the beginning of the buildup of the readiness potential, rather than later, at the time of the observer's experienced decision/consent to act. Thus, due to the vanishing of the records of the buildups of the unactualized templates for action, the false impression is created that the decision to act occurred when the brain began to build a *potential* template for action, rather than when the subject's Process-1 free choice initiated the action that led to the actualized-by-nature physical action.

I emphasize here again that it is nature's response that brings into actual being the physical reality that is picked out for possible actualization by the observer's mentally chosen Process-1 probing action.

The tectonic shift that underlies the transition from the classical ontology to the quantum ontology is the conversion of the conception of the *macroscopic* physically described aspects of the putative reality from classically conceived matter to potentialities for the occurrence of actualizing occasions, or events, initiated by Process-1 choices of what properties to inquire about, with these choices being influenced by both the prior potentialities and the core inner self of the observing agent.

The phenomena discussed so far all belong to mainstream science. We now come to the assigned task of discussing whether the anomalous phenomena identified in Chapter 1 above could be accommodated within the framework of the quantum conception of reality described above, and, if so, "how."

SURVIVAL OF BODILY DEATH, REINCARNATION, POSSESSION, AND MEDIUMSHIP

The foundation of the von Neumann theory of reality is his proof that the thinking entity (ego) aspect of each of us is ontologically different from the quantum mechanically described physical universe. The latter includes our bodies and brains, which are related to an ego's brain/body via top-down probing actions, and nature's responses to those probing actions.

When a person dies the special physical structures in the brain to which the person's mind/ego is specially tuned will decay away, and communication via that brain with the physical world will be lost. This thinking entity, this ego, could simply cease to exist. Alternatively, it could conceivably survive, and continue to have a stream of conscious experiences of some sort, as suggested for example by near-death experiences occurring under extreme physiological conditions, but it will then cease to be a factor in the physically described world, unless some alternative mode of its interacting with that physical world is possible. One such possibility is that the detached ego can attach itself to another brain that it is able similarly to influence by means of its probing actions.

One subcategory is reincarnation, in which this other brain is in the process of being created as part of the development of a new biological entity. A second subcategory is possession, in which the detached ego attaches itself to an already formed brain by wholly or partially displacing its current owner. A third subcategory is trance mediumship, in which the detached ego directs its probing actions upon the nervous system of a medium who has voluntarily entered into a receptive state.

In all these cases the detached ego is able to latch onto another brain or nervous system that it can, by means of its probing actions, influence in a way similar to the way that it had influenced its former brain.

The full mathematical machinery of orthodox quantum mechanics can then be retained. The only change would be an elaboration of the rules that fix the details about the capacity of the ego to connect to other brains. The general mathematical formulation could remain intact, with only these details being revised.

This freeing of the ego from its attachment to a unique brain is made logically possible, in orthodox quantum mechanics, by von Neumann's proof of the ego's ontological separateness from the quantum mechanically described atom-based aspects of the psychophysical world, coupled to the fact that the ego's dynamical connection to the physical is not bottom-up, with the physical controlling the mental, but is rather top-down, with the ontologically separate ego probing, and through nature's response influencing, the physical world.

This quantum ontology is basically in line with Descartes' idea that reality is composed of thinking entities and things that occupy space. That is, the classical-physics ontology is expanded from merely the collection of physically described things that occupy space to a psychophysical space that includes our psychologically described egos, a global "nature" that makes choices that are not completely determined by prior space-based physical things, and a space-based structure that serves as a compendium of the prior events, and a representation of the potentialities for future events.

Strictly orthodox quantum mechanics demands that the actions on physical things made by each individual thinking entity be confined to its own unique brain. To accommodate the phenomena listed in the present section heading, that uniqueness requirement is relaxed in order to accommodate the added empirical evidence.

Of course, these listed phenomena, like quantum mechanics itself, focus on a mental aspect of reality that has no place in classical mechanics, and hence they are dismissed by scientists and philosophers who equate science to a science concordant with the principles of classical physics. Such a stance is indefensible now in the twenty-first century.

CLAIRVOYANCE AND MACRO-PK

The nervous systems of observing agents play a central role in orthodox quantum mechanics. The ego normally becomes informed about the physical world via the effects of that world upon its nervous system. And the effects of the ego's queries upon the physical world normally occur through their effects upon its nervous system. The actions in both directions are closely related, and work through the Process-1 choices of what physical properties to inquire about.

While the restriction of the direct physical effects of our mental probing actions to our nervous systems is certainly indicated by von Neumann's words, and by orthodox thinking, there is no logical reason, beyond the empirical evidence, why this limitation is absolutely necessary. It is logically possible that the reason why the nervous system is the particular part of the body that is normally accessed by the ego is simply that the nervous system allows small inputs of certain kinds to produce large bodily outputs of certain useful kinds. But then unusual shifts in the direct object of the Process-1 probing action from the nervous system to other parts of the body might be tied to unusual psychological states. The rarity of those states would cause the resulting phenomena to be categorized as anomalous, without those unusual phenomena being in any way incompatible with the basic general principles.

In keeping with the pragmatic principle that the value of a physical theory lies in its capacity to accommodate "the manifold aspects of our experience," an extension of quantum theory that enlarges the scope of the theory by allowing it to encompass additional scientifically validated data, while retaining its prior successes, is good scientific practice.

From this perspective, a natural way to account, for example, for the phenomena of hypnotic blisters and stigmata would be to assume that the intensely focused mental state of the affected person increases the strength of its inputs into the physical realm to the point of their being able to *directly affect* the pertinent parts of the person's body without acting through his or her nervous system. The nervous system is, after all, made of ordinary matter: it has no magical properties.

If one denies special status to nervous systems then there is no reason beyond strong habit or narrow interest for the questions posed by an ego to be restricted to its own body. According to the present model, the ego scans the world of potentialities mechanically generated by Process 2 in order to identify potential physical properties of special interest to it. Habitually these queries pertain to the observer's own bodily state. But an ego in a highly unusual psychological state might break normal habits and shift focus to possible happenings in more distant regions. Compliant responses by a globally informed nature could then allow that ego to know about and influence distant happenings. Such an extension of orthodox quantum theory could account for clairvoyance and macro-PK.

The scope of the effects of Process-1 probing choices depends on what questions the ego asks and to which nature positively responds. The Process-1 choice from among the Process-2 generated future potentialities, if ruled, as I assume, by sufficient reasons and personal values, would be drawn to potential events rationally related to personal values.

The key point here is that quantum mechanics brings our minds into the causal structure, and a conscious mind can, of course, easily contain mental images of classically conceived spacetime physical properties, both nearby and far away. But conversely, it is, I believe, impossible for a classically conceived reality to rationally contain conscious experiences: classical physical reality was purposely stripped of all consciousness-like properties, thereby rendering it incapable of reaping the benefits of the quantum dynamics to tap into and utilize the long-distance nonlocal features of mind-related quantum dynamics.

The scope of the capacities of us thinking entities to obtain answers to queries about various physically described systems is a matter to be settled empirically. Within the general quantum structure this issue concerns the scope of the queries to which nature responds. That scope can hardly be narrowly restricted by a priori principles. The pertinent principles must be a function of the nature of the empirical facts that need to be explained.

If the ego is indeed able to probe properties of physical systems other than its own nervous system, then the QZE effect would allow various properties of such systems to be manipulated not only in the imagination of the probing agent, but, by virtue of the physical effects of the Process-3 actions, also in the external, physically described world itself. The "generalized" QZE effect would then allow the external physical structure to be dragged about in accordance with a changing idea if in the mind of the agent.

The reports of the phenomena surrounding St. Joseph of Copertino could be accommodated within such a modified form of quantum mechanics, along with the recurrent spontaneous physical activities associated with psychologically troubled adolescents. In the case of St. Joseph it is clear that his mind dwelled intensely on ecstatic ideas, and the physical realities actualized by his intense focus could therefore be unusual. In the case of angry adolescents, their minds also are in highly agitated states. Although many details would need to be developed in order to make a serious proposal, it appears that an extended version of orthodox quantum mechanics modified in the way outlined above, with the focus of the ego's probing actions allowed to lie outside the person's nervous system and physical body, could in principle accommodate these phenomena.

The justification of a physical theory lies both in its utility and in its capacity to quiet the curiosity of minds that cannot rest without a rational understanding of the place of our thoughts, ideas, and feelings in the ongoing unfolding of our experience. Such a comprehension can itself be useful insofar as it guides one's learning of how to hone one's mind in order to bring to pass what one positively values. But what one tries to learn depends on what one believes is possible. Hence a belief about the nature of things can itself be useful insofar as it leads us to learn how to use our minds in ways that can promote what we value.

TRUE PRECOGNITION

Perhaps the most puzzling of all of the targeted anomalies involves seemingly out-of-temporal-order pre-experiences of later very unusual physi-

cal happenings, as described in Chapter 1. The existence of such coordinated pairs of experiences suggests that the future already exists, in some
way, and that some tiny aspect of the completely predetermined future is
occasionally mysteriously accessed ahead of time. But if the future is
really completely predetermined then "free will," as understood here, is
an illusion.

In what way could the future already exist? Laplace, in his famous
exposition of this idea, introduced an "intellect" that stands outside the
physical universe, and which, at any moment, knows the exact physical
state of the universe and the (classical deterministic) physical laws, and
has, moreover, the capacity to compute, on the basis of this knowledge,
the physical state of the universe at all future times. Then the physical
future could be said to exist in this observing and calculating mind, which
exists outside the actual evolving physical universe. Laplace thereby tries
to give some reasonably clear idea of what might be meant by the notion
that if the world were governed by the deterministic laws of classical
mechanics then the future already exists.

This Laplacean explanation requires an existing supermind that stands
outside the evolving physical world that is presumed to exist and to
behave in accordance with the classical worldview.

However, the known quantum laws allow only the *potentialities* for
various possible future happenings to be computable. No rules that determine what will actually happen are given by quantum theory. What actually happens will depend, first of all, upon choices made by the minds of
observers about their probing actions. These choices are not determined—even statistically—by any known, or imagined-to-exist, algo-
rithm. These choices are experienced as coming from an inner mental
realm of thoughts, ideas, feelings, reasons, and consciously felt values.
They are experienced as originating in the "ego" that von Neumann finds
to be ontologically separate from, and not determined by, the atom-based
physical world that it probes. Such probing actions elicit responses from
nature that are conventionally deemed purely random, hence also non-
computable. The famous quantum statistical element enters only in *nature's* choice of response, *not* in the *ego's* choice of question. But, in any
case, the quantum future is not supposed to be computable. Hence Laplace's explanation of how the future might exist does not carry over to
the quantum domain. Indeed, the orthodox quantum framework is fundamentally an expression of the idea that the evolution is strictly forward in

time, and allows our choices to be "free" of any deterministic constraints of the kind that Laplace's classical-physics-based analysis depends upon.

The global character of this phenomenon suggests that the global feature of the orthodox quantum ontology, namely "nature," must be playing a role in the creation of world order that goes beyond the random choices of responses to our probing questions. There are empirical reasons, discussed in the following section, to believe that this is the case. That expansion of the role of "nature" opens the door to a deeper, and potentially extremely useful, conception of the nature of reality.

The work discussed in the following section, unlike "true precognition," is based on results obtained under experimentally controllable conditions. That work indicates that nature's choices are not random, but are more deeply entwined with our lives. On the basis of that conclusion I suggest that the phenomenon of "true precognition" is a consequence of nature's selecting and actualizing, out of the normal temporal order, a few individual psychophysical events, and adjusting the evolving Hilbert space in a way that ensures they will, in due course, come to pass, or have enhanced likelihoods of coming to pass, without greatly disturbing the usual statistical rules. In particular, the occurrence of a few rare out-of-order future events does not logically entail that the entire future is predetermined.

THE PRINCIPLE OF SUFFICIENT REASON VERSUS NATURE'S PURELY STATISTICAL CHOICE: SEMI-ORTHODOX QUANTUM MECHANICS

I have long been troubled by what I regard as an irrational aspect of quantum mechanics, considered as a general theory of reality. A rationally coherent universe should, in my opinion, conform to the "principle of sufficient reason": nothing should happen without a sufficient reason for that particular thing to happen.

The claim that nature's choices are purely "random" contradicts that principle. It asserts that in each individual empirical instance a definite response, "Yes" or "No," just "pops out of the blue," with no reason at all for that response to be what it turns out to be. Such behavior breaches the demand for sufficient reasons. Concordantly, there is now significant empirical evidence that nature's choices are not actually random, but may, like the observers' choices, stem from value-based reasons.

Early in the year 2011, Cornell University Professor Emeritus of Psychology Daryl J. Bem published in the prestigious *Journal of Personality and Social Psychology* an article (Bem, 2011) describing nine different experiments that appear, superficially, to show backward-in-time causation. Bem's nine experiments all have the following general form. First, in each of a series of experimental trials, the subject/participant is presented with some possibilities for actions, and then chooses and performs one of them. These chosen actions are duly recorded. *Later* in each trial, the outputs of some random number generators (RNGs), which are initially physically unconnected to the subject, and his or her choice of action, are introduced into the experiment in a way that ties, in a way specified by the RNGs, the initial choice made by the subject to a later experience of the subject that is expected to have a strong positive (or negative) value in his or her mind, or, alternatively, to a later experience having no strong value. What Bem finds is that the subject's initial choice of action is favored (or disfavored), relative to the probabilities predicted by both orthodox classical and quantum physics, if the subject's subsequent final experience is positive (or negative), as contrasted with neutral. The biasing of the probability of the subject's initial choice would, under these conditions, be naturally and automatically explained in a completely causally forward and local way, if nature's choices of which alternative possibility to choose are biased for (or against) a positive (or negative) subject experience, relative to a neutral experience.

This finding suggests to some scientists that either (1) the believed-to-be dynamically independent RNGs are being influenced in some mysterious and very complex way by the participant's earlier actions, or (2) the participant's earlier actions are being affected in a complex retrocausal (backward-in-time causal) way by the choices made by RNGs. But the simpler direct explanation is that nature's choices are not actually random, but are positively or negatively biased by the positive or negative values in the minds of the observers that are actualized by its (nature's) choices.

There is no rational reason why nature's choices must be "random" (hence irrational) rather than being consequences of sufficient reasons. Given the proposition that nature's choices must have reasons to be what they turn out to be, it is not implausible that the probabilities of these choices should be positively correlated with what living organisms, living in a quantum world, have learned to favor in the guidance of their choices of how to act.

If one examines the logical origins of the orthodox quantum-mechanical rules of probability one finds that they are expressions of the assumption that these choices depend only on physical properties, which conform to certain symmetry properties that physical systems are expected to possess. Thus any reasons for nature's choices that come from mental values that are in principle not fully determined by physical properties should enter as deviations from the orthodox rules.

It must be emphasized that this proposed quantum explanation of Bem's results rests completely on the orthodox idea that the physically described quantum state of the universe represents, even at the macroscopic level, "potentialities" for the occurrence of events that increase our knowledge. Intuitively we all feel, in concordance with the concepts of classical mechanics, that the output of an RNG is definitely one or the other of the two options, and that this choice is made at the time of physical action of the RNG. But the highly non-intuitive effective claim of von Neumann's theory, stemming from his shift of the Heisenberg cut up to the mind–brain interface, is that the immediate effect of the RNG choice is merely to separate the quantum state of the output of the RNG into two wave packets. Within the von Neumann mathematics, this divides the state of the entire universe into two terms, which represent two different "potentialities" for future mental events. The experimental arrangement entails that nature's choice of the final experience of the subject collapses the state of the entire universe to one or the other *of the two branches created by the earlier action of the RNG.* Although the completely orthodox theory demands that nature's choices be "random," the present proposal is to relax that demand in order to account for the empirical results of Bem and others.

This way of comprehending the quantum world may seem to some readers too weird to take seriously. But it is exactly the weirdness that allows all quantum phenomena to make rational good sense, in the way described by von Neumann's mathematics.

Bem's results created a furor in the psychology community, and a number of groups attempted to check Bem's findings. Ninety experiments have so far been carried out, and a meta-analysis of these experiments (Bem, Tressoldi, Rabeyron, & Duggan, 2014) apparently confirms with a high level of confidence that the "retrocausal effects" reported by Bem can be reproduced under experimentally well-controlled conditions.

Evidence for effects of this kind is not confined to Bem-type experiments. Numerous recent experiments (Mossbridge, Tressoldi, & Utts, 2012; Tressoldi, Martinelli, Semenzato, & Cappato, 2011) appear to entail the existence of retrocausal actions that occur directly at the macro-level of perceivable effects. One kind of example pertains to the changed pupil size of a human subject's eye that occurs seconds *before* a randomly timed, shocking stimulus is presented to that subject. The change "predicts" the direction of the post-stimulus reaction of the pupil to that stimulus: the pupil size before application of the stimulus to the subject deviates slightly from a baseline (established by neutral stimuli) in the same direction that it will strongly deviate after the randomly timed, shocking stimulus is applied. Such a macroscopically measurable effect is incompatible with the basic principles of both classical mechanics and orthodox quantum mechanics, but it is a natural consequence of the semi-orthodox quantum mechanics that fully retains the dynamical structure of orthodox quantum mechanics but relaxes the orthodox presumption that nature's choices are governed completely by the standard quantum-mechanical rules of random chance.

In the pupil-dilation experiments, the seemingly retrocausal effect arose from an examination, after the events in question, of the (say, computer-chip) records of the pupil size during the few seconds slightly before the stimulus was applied. But these records lie! They report only the processes that led to the experiences that actually did occur. But if nature's choices of what actually occurs are biased, relative to the orthodox expectations, then the records of the past become biased relative to what existed in the past.

This explanation of the "retrocausal" data is achieved, as with Bem's data, without invoking any actual backward-in-time action, or any dependence of the subject's behavior upon things which that behavior cannot depend upon according to both classical mechanics and orthodox quantum mechanics. No mysterious new kind of causal action into or from the future is invoked. Instead, the orthodox theory is merely made more rational by removing the irrational idea that something definite can be determined by nothing at all.

This semi-orthodox account of these experiments can easily be tested. If, in a Bem experiment exhibiting retrocausal effects with a true RNG, one randomly selects a subset of trials in which a battery of observers actually experience the outcome of the RNG before the associated action of that RNG is injected into the experiment, then in that subset the correlation between the choice made by the subject and the choice made by the RNG is fixed in a way that, according to this theory, cannot be influenced by nature's choice of the subject's final experience. The mere conscious perceptions of the RNG outcomes by the battery of outside observers will, according to the semi-orthodox ontology, already collapse the quantum state of the RNG outcome in a way that eliminates the possibility of the observed "retrocausal" correlations, even though no apparent change is made in the application of the RNG output to the experiment on the subject: the prior conscious perceptions of the RNG outputs will eliminate the empirical retrocausal effect. I have stipulated here a "battery" of observers in order to ensure that a conscious experience of the RNG output actually occurs: a single observer's attention might wander.

The advance from strictly orthodox to semi-orthodox QM is, I believe, needed to give a rationally coherent and relatively simple QM account of the empirically validated "retrocausal" effects. It can also make the quantitative requirements for macro-PK much easier to fulfill. For QZE to do the job—on its own—in, for example, the case of St. Joseph, would require *extremely* rapid rates of probing actions. The reported phenomena would be far easier to achieve if nature lends a helping hand by strongly favoring, in its choices, those outcomes that are concordant with the intensely felt positive personal values of the subject. Indeed, the magnitude of the macro-PK demanded by the St. Joseph case is so great as to make unbelievable its reality without a huge assist from nature's Process-3 choice.

Such a strong involvement of nature's choices in this case opens the door to the possibility of a much expanded role for nature's choices in other phenomena as well. But a mapping out of the limitations and testable ways of making practical use of this potential resource offered by semi-orthodox quantum mechanics needs to be carefully pursued empirically.

CONCLUSIONS

During the last half of the twentieth century several alternative interpretations of quantum theory were propounded that differ from the Copenhagen and orthodox versions by subtracting from original foundational quantum concepts everything mental. The problem with these consciousness-free theories, as with classical theories, is that they are conceptually complete without consciousness, and lack any rational conceptual toehold for bringing the consciously experienced realities back in. Thus they are fundamentally incomplete. On the other hand, the practical utility of scientific theories entails their helping us bring to pass what we positively value; but the deterministic character of these essentially consciousness-free theories eliminates the possibility of our consciously influencing our future in any way. The inclusion of the irrational elements of random chance provides, of course, no help at all.

The orthodox quantum mechanics described in the first part of this chapter explains how we can, by our mental efforts, bring to pass what we consciously value. The elaborated version described in the second part of the chapter describes how that orthodox theory can be modified to accommodate the targeted anomalies, while keeping intact the basically three-part, forward-in-time quantum dynamics that incorporates choices originating in the subjective mental realm. No claim is made here to be presenting a fully developed scientific theory: I have merely indicated a possible direction in which von Neumann's quantum mechanics could be modified to provide a rationally coherent theory of reality that could accommodate the targeted anomalies.

The history of science is marked by abrupt advances in physical theory caused by the need for an adequate theory to accommodate previously unknown regularities—often discovered by dedicated investigators of unusual phenomena. These advances in science have, by making practical use of previously unsuspected regularities, increased the power of human beings to bring about what they consciously value. For example, the understandings of nature created by classical mechanics produced the theoretical underpinnings of the machine-based industrial age, and the subsequent advance to quantum mechanics supported the computer-based information age. If history be a reliable guide to the future, then the advance from strictly orthodox quantum mechanics to the more comprehensive semi-orthodox theory sketched in outline here may provide the science-based conceptual foundations for an age in which we human beings will learn how to make use of the connection of nature's process with our mental states in order to enlarge still further our capacity to bring to pass what we consciously value.

ACKNOWLEDGMENT

Ed Kelly has played a very major and greatly appreciated role in the creation of this chapter.

REFERENCES

Bem, D. J. (2011). Feeling the future: Experimental evidence for anomalous retroactive influences on cognition and affect. *Journal of Personality and Social Psychology, 100*, 407–425. doi:10.1037/a0021524

Bem, D. J., Tressoldi, P. E., Rabeyron, T., & Duggan, M. (2014). Feeling the future: A meta-analysis of 90 experiments on the anomalous anticipation of random future events (April 11, 2014). Manuscript submitted for publication. Available at http://ssrn.com/abstract=2423692 or doi:10.2139/ssrn.2423692

Blair, C., Jr. (1957, February 25). Passing of a great mind. *Life, 42*(8), 89–104.

Bohr, N. (1934). *Atomic Theory and the Description of Nature.* Cambridge: Cambridge University Press.

Bohr, N. (1949). Discussion with Einstein on epistemological problems in atomic physics. In P. A. Schilpp (Ed.), *Albert Einstein: Philosopher-Scientist* (pp. 199–241). Evanston, IL: Library of Living Philosophers.

Crick, F. (1994). *The Astonishing Hypothesis: The Scientific Search for the Soul.* New York: Simon & Schuster.

Hawking, S., & Mlodinow, L. (2010). *The Grand Design.* London: Bantam.

James, W. (1950). *The Principles of Psychology* (Vols. 1–2). New York: Dover. (Original work published 1890)

Kim, J. (2005). *Physicalism, or Something Near Enough.* Princeton, NJ: Princeton University Press.

Koch, C., & Hepp, K. (2006, March 30). Quantum mechanics in the brain. *Nature, 440*, 611–612. doi:10.1038/440611a [My rebuttal: http://www-physics.lbl.gov/~stapp/Koch-Hepp09.doc]

Libet, B., Gleason, C. A., Wright, E. W., & Pearl, D. K. (1983). Time of conscious intention to act in relation to onset of cerebral activity (readiness-potential): The unconscious initiation of a freely voluntary act. *Brain, 106*, 623–642. doi:10.1093/brain/106.3.623

Misra, B., & Sudarshan, E. C. G. (1977). The Zeno's paradox in quantum theory. *Journal of Mathematical Physics, 18*, 756–763. doi:10.1063/1.523304

Mossbridge, J., Tressoldi, P., & Utts, J. (2012). Predictive physiological anticipation preceding seemingly unpredictable stimuli: A meta-analysis. *Frontiers in Psychology, 3*, article 390. doi:10.3389/fpsyg.2012.00390

Schwinger, J. (1951). The theory of quantized fields. I. *Physical Review, 82*, 914–927.

Stapp, H. P. (1977). Are superluminal connections necessary? *Il Nuovo Cimento, 40 B*, 191–205. http://www-physics.lbl.gov/~stapp/NCimento.pdf

Stapp, H. P. (1979). Whiteheadian approach to quantum theory and the generalized Bell's theorem. *Foundations of Physics, 9,* 1–25. http://www-physics.lbl.gov/~stapp/Whitehead-Bell-1979.pdf

Stapp, H. P. (1988). Light as foundation of being. In B. J. Hiley & F. D. Peat (Eds.), *Quantum Implications: Essays in Honour of David Bohm* (pp. 255–266). New York: Routledge.

Stapp, H. P. (2008). Philosophy of mind and the problem of free will in the light of quantum mechanics. http://arXiv.org/abs/0805.0116

Stapp, H. P. (2009). Physicalism versus quantum mechanics. In *Mind, Matter and Quantum Mechanics* (3rd ed., pp. 245–260). Berlin: Springer. http://arXiv.org/abs/0803.1625 or http://www-physics.lbl.gov/~stapp/Physicalism.pdf

Stapp, H. P. (2011). *Mindful Universe: Quantum Mechanics and the Participating Observer* (2nd ed.). Berlin: Springer.

Stapp, H. P. (2012). Quasi-orthodox quantum mechanics and the principle of sufficient reason. http://www-physics.lbl.gov/~stapp/Reason01132012.doc

Stapp, H. P. (2013). Appendix 1: Proof that information must be transferred faster than light. http://www-physics.lbl.gov/~stapp/Appendix-1.doc

Tomonaga, S. (1946). On a relativistically invariant formulation of the quantum theory of wave fields. *Progress of Theoretical Physics, 1,* 27–42.

Tressoldi, P. E., Martinelli, M., Semenzato, L., & Cappato, S. (2011). Let your eyes predict: Prediction accuracy of pupillary responses to random alerting and neutral sounds. *SAGE Open.* doi:10.1177/2158244011420451

Tyndall, J. (1874). *Address Delivered Before the British Association Assembled at Belfast, with Additions.* London: Longmans, Green.

Von Neumann, J. (1955). *Mathematical Foundations of Quantum Mechanics* (R. T. Beyer, Trans.). Princeton, NJ: Princeton University Press. (Original work published 1932)

Wheeler, J. A. (1978). The "past" and the "delayed-choice" double-slit experiment. In A. R. Marlow (Ed.), *Mathematical Foundations of Quantum Theory* (pp. 9–48). New York: Academic Press.

Wigner, E. (1963). The problem of measurement. *American Journal of Physics, 31,* 6–15.

6

MIND–MATTER CORRELATIONS IN DUAL-ASPECT MONISM ACCORDING TO PAULI AND JUNG

Harald Atmanspacher and Wolfgang Fach

With this contribution we outline a conceptual framework for the mind–matter problem that gives rise to a systematic and transparent classification of basic types of mind–matter correlations. We emphasize from the outset that this framework is not a scientific theory—although the argumentation is theoretical in style. The framework we propose provides no mechanism for mind–matter correlations, it does not explain them, and it does not predict their controllable occurrence under particular circumstances. In our opinion, a serious theory of psychophysical phenomena, one capable of providing mechanisms, explanations, and predictions, is not yet anywhere in sight.

The classic starting point for most contemporary discussions of the mind–matter problem and mind–matter relations, respectively, is Descartes' ontologically conceived dualism of the mental (*res cogitans*, thought) and the material (*res extensa*, extended matter). In the history of philosophy, Descartes' position was immediately upgraded, criticized, or replaced by essentially three forms of thought: (1) alternative dualistic approaches (occasionalism, parallelism), (2) essentially monistic approaches (idealism, materialism), and (3) approaches combining (1) and (2) by assuming a monistic domain underlying the mind–matter distinction. An early protagonist of this latter view is Baruch Spinoza.

Spinoza's monism provides an elegant and robust sense in which mind and matter are related to a "unity of essence." It does so by concatenating an ontological monism with an epistemological dualism, yielding an overall worldview in which both philosophy and the sciences can find appropriate places and mutual relations. This framework began to be explicitly exploited in the mid-nineteenth century, by both philosophers and scientists, and today we can recognize two main reactions to Spinozism, called dual-aspect monism[1] and neutral monism.

Unfortunately, there is no authoritative delineation of the two—the many versions of dual-aspect monism and neutral monism that are around today have a tendency to blend into each other in ways that make clear assignments to one or the other problematic. This can be seen in Stubenberg's (2010) excellent overview; see also Silberstein's (2009) taxonomy and Seager's (2009) discussion, among others. Important commonalities and key differences between dual-aspect monism and neutral monism are discussed in Atmanspacher (2012).

In dual-aspect monism, the aspects are not a priori given, but depend on epistemic issues and contexts. Distinctions of aspects are generated by "epistemic splits" of the distinction-free, unseparated underlying domain, and in principle there can be as many aspects as there are contexts. Moreover, for dual-aspect monists this domain is apprehensible only indirectly, by its manifestations in the aspects. Therefore, it is natural for dual-aspect monists to nurture metaphysical conceptions of the underlying domain.

Beyond the well-known historical representatives of dual-aspect monism such as Spinoza, Fechner, Schopenhauer, and others, a number of scientists, notably physicists and psychologists, have explored the dual-aspect route since the mid-twentieth century. An incomplete list: Wolfgang Pauli and Carl Gustav Jung, David Bohm and Basil Hiley, Bernard d'Espagnat, Hans Primas, Max Velmans (for more details see Atmanspacher, 2012). Needless to say, none of their attempts has yet resolved the mind–matter problem in its full scope.

Remarkably, these approaches are, in one way or another, attached to ideas and notions that emerged during the development of quantum theory. In addition to the names just mentioned, quite a number of other physicists have been interested in relating physical processes to mental functions. It is impossible to review all of them in this chapter; hence the reader should consult a review of quantum approaches to consciousness (Atmanspacher, 2011) for more details. In the following we will elaborate on one of them, proposed by Wolfgang Pauli and Carl Gustav Jung from

1932 to 1958, and outline how it may be viable for a better understanding of mind–matter correlations (see Atmanspacher & Primas, 2006, 2009).

A most significant novel feature of the Pauli–Jung conjecture is the suggestion that the dual (mental and material) aspects of the underlying reality should be understood in terms of complementary aspects (Pauli, 1952, p. 164):[2]

> The general problem of the relation between psyche and physis, between inside and outside, can hardly be regarded as solved by the term "psychophysical parallelism" advanced in the last century. Yet, perhaps, modern science has brought us closer to a more satisfying conception of this relationship, as it has established the notion of *complementarity* within physics. It would be most satisfactory if physis and psyche could be conceived as complementary aspects of the same reality.

The notion of complementarity was originally coined by William James (1890, Vol. 1, p. 206) and adopted by some psychologists, for instance referring to the bistable perception of ambiguous stimuli. Bohr (1928) imported it into physics, originally with the purpose of replacing the term wave–particle duality, in his "Como Lecture" in 1927. But his extensive later writings about complementarity make it clear (see Favrholdt, 1999; Kalckar, 1985, 1996) that Bohr's preeminent concern was to extend the idea of complementarity beyond physics. In the same spirit, Pauli (1950) advanced the opinion that the "issue of complementarity within physics naturally leads beyond the narrow field of physics to analogous conditions of human knowledge" (p. 79). Primas (2009) elaborated such a perspective with respect to physical and mental time.

In a letter to Rosenfeld of April 1, 1952 (Meyenn, 1996, p. 593), Pauli writes:

> For the *invisible reality*, of which we have small pieces of evidence in both quantum physics and the psychology of the unconscious, a *symbolic* psychophysical unitary language must *ultimately* be adequate, and this is the distant goal to which I actually aspire. I am quite confident that the final objective is the same, independent of whether one starts from the psyche (ideas) or from physis (matter). Therefore, I consider the old distinction between materialism and idealism as obsolete.

THE PAULI–JUNG CONJECTURE

Pauli and Jung began to think about mind–matter relations fairly soon after they first met in 1932, but the intense interaction that led to their version of dual-aspect monism happened after Pauli's return from Princeton to Zurich in 1946. Their discussions were accompanied by an extensive exchange of ideas that Pauli had with his colleague Fierz at Basel. Fortunately much of this material is today accessible (in German) in von Meyenn's masterful eight-volume edition of Pauli's correspondence.

Although neither Pauli nor Jung nor Fierz were strongly inclined to discuss their ideas with contemporary academic philosophers (aside from only a few exceptions), their discussions had a distinctly philosophical flavor. However, their usage of philosophical concepts and notions was unsystematic: it was typical for them to avail themselves of the history of philosophy as they saw something fit their position or intention. Nevertheless, their comprehensive letters yield valuable information, allowing a fairly detailed reconstruction of their approach in the landscape of philosophical positions.

In the following we will sketch the framework of dual-aspect monism à la Pauli and Jung in four parts: (1) the relation between local realism and holism in (quantum) physics, (2) the relation between consciousness and the unconscious in Jung's psychology, (3) the common, psychophysically neutral ground of both the mental, conscious realm and the physical, local realm, and (4) the relation between these realms as a consequence of or as mediated by their common ground.

Local Realism and Quantum Holism

One of the central problems, if not *the* problem, of quantum mechanics is the process of measurement. Although much progress has been achieved with respect to its understanding since the early days of quantum mechanics, the problem is still not completely solved. However, empirical results and modern formulations of quantum theory allow us to state it in a way that is more precise than ever before. From a conceptual point of view, measurement can be viewed as an intervention decomposing a system constituting an inseparable whole[3] into locally separate parts.

The empirical cornerstone of our understanding of this decomposition involves so-called nonlocal correlations (Aspect, Dalibard, & Roger,

1982; Bell, 1964; Einstein, Podolsky, & Rosen, 1935). They are generic in any system requiring a description in terms of non-commuting observables. These correlations can be measured in suitable experiments and indicate *post festum* that the measured system was in a holistic state before measurement. Conceptually, this means that one can indirectly infer knowledge about an unmeasured state by the result of a controlled intervention into that state due to measurement. At the same time, this controlled intervention entails that the observed system changes its state in a basically uncontrollable way (Bohr, 1935).

It is tempting to say that such nonlocal correlations correlate everything with everything else, thus suggesting a holistic concept of reality through and through. But this would be misleading without precise qualifications. Quantum holism is only one of the two reality concepts that modern quantum theory requires. Equally important is the ("common sense") concept of a local reality which was considered to be *the* reality for centuries of physicists from Newton to Einstein. As Bohr has emphasized over and over, local realism is unavoidable for a proper description of experiments and their results by Boolean (yes–no) propositions.

Today we know that both concepts together are necessary for a comprehensive description of reality, and neither is sufficient.[4] In the framework of algebraic quantum theory, the difference between them can be mathematically formalized and clearly understood by two different state concepts: those of ontic and epistemic states. This distinction, originally suggested by Scheibe (1973, pp. 82–88), has turned out to be attractive and powerful for identifying the differences and similarities of various interpretational schemes in quantum theory. A helpful source for more details in this regard is a comprehensive account of epistemic and ontic quantum realities by Atmanspacher and Primas (2003).

While epistemic states are those states to which empirical access is possible by measurement (and observation in general), ontic states are supposed to characterize the system independent of its observation and our resulting knowledge.[5] One may wonder why it is useful to have an ontic level of description for which empirical (or operational) access is no option at all. However, a most appealing feature at this ontic level is the existence of first principles and universal laws that are unavailable in an epistemic description. From such an ontic level, it is possible to deduce proper epistemic descriptions given enough details—contexts, as it were—about empirically given situations.

The distinction of ontic and epistemic states provides an important clue to understand the distinction between a holistic and a local concept of reality. Ontic states and associated intrinsic properties refer to the holistic concept of reality and are operationally inaccessible, whereas epistemic states and associated contextual properties refer to a local concept of an operationally accessible reality. The process of measurement represents the link between the two. Measurement suppresses the connectedness constituting a holistic reality and generates (approximately) separate local objects constituting a local reality.

Although this is a fairly modern picture, it also has a conservative aspect: quantum theory as of today does not at any place refer to the mental world of human observers, to their cognitive capabilities or psychological condition in general. The standard view in quantum theory is that measurement should be treated in terms of an interaction between an observed system and its environment, including observing devices. For instance, Heisenberg (1936) was very explicit about this, talking about a "cut between the system to be observed and the measuring devices." And Pauli (1957) says: "As Heisenberg has emphasized, quantum mechanics rests on a sharp cut between observer or instrument of observation on one hand and the system observed on the other."

In general, the idea is that any inanimate environment can be understood as a "measuring device," though in a non-intentional manner. No consciousness is necessary for the measurement of a quantum state. On the other hand, as soon as *controlled* experiments are considered, it is clear that issues like the design of an experiment, the choice of observables of interest, or the interpretation of the results of a measurement play crucial roles. They depend on decisions based on the intentions of human observers and are not part of the formalism of quantum theory.

In this context, Pauli speculated in a letter to Fierz of August 10, 1954 (Meyenn, 1999, pp. 742–747):

> It might be that matter, for instance considered from the perspective of life, is not treated "properly" if it is observed as in quantum mechanics, *namely totally neglecting the inner state of the "observer."* . . . The well-known "incompleteness" of quantum mechanics (Einstein) is certainly an existing fact somehow-somewhere, but of course it cannot be removed by reverting to classical field physics (that is only a "neurotic misunderstanding" of Einstein), it has much more to do with *holistic*

relationships between "inside" and "outside" which contemporary science does not contain.

Still today, the mainstream position among physicists is that consciousness is not involved in physical measurements, no matter whether quantum or classical. In his privately distributed manuscript on "modern examples of background physics," Pauli (1948) emphasized that the measurement problem "does not indicate an incompleteness of quantum theory within physics but an incompleteness of physics within the totality of life." Pauli's uneasiness with the status of science in general and physics in particular was not an odd idea but a serious criticism of great relevance. The question is how to turn it into viable research.

Consciousness and the Unconscious

According to Pauli and Jung, the role which measurement plays as a link between local and holistic realities in physics is mirrored by the act in which subjects become consciously aware of "local mental objects," as it were, arising from holistic unconscious contents in psychology.[6] In this sense, which will be discussed in detail below, they postulate a parallel transition from a psychophysically neutral reality to mental and material local realities. This idea is most clearly elaborated in Jung's (1969) supplement to his *On the Nature of the Psyche*.[7] Let us first quote from a letter by Pauli which Jung (1969, para. 439) cites in footnote 130 in this supplement:[8]

> the epistemological situation regarding the concepts of "consciousness" and the "unconscious" seems to offer a close analogy to the situation of "complementarity" in physics, sketched below. On the one hand, the unconscious can only be made accessible in an indirect way by its (ordering) influence on conscious contents, on the other hand every "observation of the unconscious," i.e., every attempt to make unconscious contents conscious, has a *prima facie* uncontrollable reaction back onto these unconscious contents themselves (as is well known, this precludes that the unconscious can be "exhaustively" brought to consciousness). The physicist will *per analogiam* conclude that precisely this uncontrollable backlash of the observing subject onto the unconscious limits the objective character of its reality and, at the same time, provides it with some subjectivity. Although, moreover,

the *position* of the "cut" between consciousness and the unconscious is (to a certain degree) up to the free choice of the "psychological experimenter," the *existence* of this "cut" remains an inevitable necessity. Thus, the "observed system" would, from the viewpoint of psychology, not only consist of physical objects, but rather comprise the unconscious as well, whereas the role of the "observing device" would be ascribed to consciousness. The development of "microphysics" has unmistakably led to a remarkable convergence of its description of nature with that of the new psychology: While the former, due to the fundamental situation known as "complementarity," faces the impossibility to eliminate actions of observers by determinable corrections and must therefore in principle relinquish the objective registration of all physical phenomena, the latter could basically complement the merely subjective psychology of consciousness by postulating the existence of an unconscious of largely objective reality.

This commentary describes Pauli's position in the framework of objective and subjective aspects of the mental, a distinction that he adopted from Jung quite early. Already in a letter to Kronig of August 3, 1934 (Meyenn, 1985, pp. 340–341), he talks about the "autonomous activity of the soul" as "something objectively psychical that cannot and should not be explained by material causes." Hence, the "objective reality" at the end of the quote refers to the holistic reality, while the "subjective" relates to its contextual, epistemic, appearances.

It is important to emphasize that the relation between holistic and local realms in both mental and material domains is conceived as *bidirectional*. Unconscious contents can become conscious, and simultaneously this very transition changes the unconscious left behind. Analogously, physical measurement necessitates a decomposition of the holistic realm, and simultaneously this very measurement changes the state of the system left behind. This picture, already outlined in Pauli's letter to Fierz of October 3, 1951 (Meyenn, 1996, p. 377), represents a genuine *interdependence* between holistic and local domains. It can entail mind–matter correlations via the holistic realm that occur in addition to those correlations that are due to mere dual epistemic "manifestations" of that realm.[9]

In order to give the reader a sense of how Jung (1969, para. 439) embedded the cited Pauli quote in his text, here is the passage in which it appears:

The application of statistical laws to processes of atomic dimensions in physics has a remarkable correspondence in psychology insofar as it pursues the foundations of consciousness to the point where they dim out into the inconceivable and where only effects of *ordering* influences onto conscious contents can be detected [here the above footnote (HA)]. The study of these effects leads to the peculiar fact that they emerge from an unconscious objective reality which, however, at the same time appears to be subjective and conscious. This way, the reality underlying the effects of the unconscious comprises also the observing subject and is therefore of unimaginable constitution. It is in fact both most intimately subjective and most universally true, something that does not apply to conscious contents of personalistic nature. The elusiveness, capriciousness, haziness and uniqueness, with which the layperson connects the conception of the psyche, only applies to consciousness, but not to the absolute unconscious. The efficacious elements of the unconscious, to be defined not quantitatively but only qualitatively, the so-called *archetypes, can therefore not with certainty be designated as psychic.*

". . . can therefore not with certainty be designated as psychic": This peculiarly cautious formulation is due to the shift that Jung's conception with respect to archetypes underwent from early ideas about (biological) hereditary instincts over (psychological) raw feelings and inner images to his final notion of psychophysically neutral, transcendental (or metaphysical) principles. The early 1950s was the time when this move became visible in Jung's publications.[10] Since his mature understanding of archetypes embraces both individual subjective consciousness and the impersonal objective unconscious, Jung invented the term "psychoid" to characterize them as structural principles beyond the conscious psyche alone.

Archetypes and *Unus Mundus*

While the preceding subsections described the way in which Pauli and Jung thought that epistemically accessible physical and mental domains reflect something ontic behind the mind–matter distinction, the present subsection addresses this "background reality" itself. One of its key features is that empirical tools of observation and measurement, as far as they are capable of providing knowledge about it at all, can do this only in an indirect fashion.

From the point of view of physics the background domain of reality refers to the holistic state of a system prior to the transition to a measured state. From the point of view of psychology it refers to the unconscious prior to the transition to a conscious state. Both transitions can be described as transitions from a non-Boolean domain to domains with Boolean classifications based on binary alternatives (see Primas, 2007). In physics these appear as classical states actualized due to measurements; in psychology they appear as actualized distinct mental representations.

The simple but radical idea proposed by Pauli and Jung suggests a background domain of reality from which the mental and the material are supposed to emerge as epistemically distinguishable. Although physics and psychology point to their common basis in different ways, the basis itself is assumed to be of unitary nature: a psychophysically neutral domain that is neither mental nor material and describable by a non-Boolean neutral language. (Needless to say, this "caricature" of a much more complicated picture leaves many details unaddressed here.)

Already in 1948, Pauli expressed his predilection for such a psychophysically neutral domain beneath (or beyond) the mental and the material in a letter to Fierz:[11]

> The ordering and regulating factors must be placed beyond the distinction of "physical" and "psychic"—as Plato's "ideas" share the notion of a concept and of a force of nature (they create actions out of themselves). I am very much in favor of referring to the "ordering" and "regulating" factors in terms of "archetypes"; but then it would be inadmissible to *define* them as contents of the *psyche*. The mentioned inner images ("dominant features of the collective unconscious" after Jung) are rather *psychic* manifestations of the archetypes which, *however*, would *also* have to put forth, create, condition anything lawlike in the behavior of the corporeal world. The laws of this world would then be the *physical manifestations of the archetypes.* . . . *Each* law of nature should then have an inner correspondence and vice versa, even though this is not always directly visible today.

In contrast to the bidirectional relationship between ontic and epistemic domains (see previous subsection), this quote refers to a *unidirectional* manifestation of ontically conceived archetypes in their epistemic aspects. Physical and mental manifestations arise in correlation, and the correlations are due to the joint "ordering factors" of the manifestations.

Now, Jung's psychology hosts quite a selection of archetypes, to which different degrees of unconscious depth can be ascribed (see Roesler, 2010; Young-Eisendrath & Dawson, 1997). Among Jungians there is agreement that the shadow and the anima/animus complex are the first, and therefore least deep-seated, archetypes with whose manifestations individuals typically become acquainted. Candidates for more fundamental archetypes are the self, as the goal of the individuation process, and maybe most basic the archetype of number, expressing qualitative principles like unity, duality, trinity, quaternity, and so forth.

The notion proposed for the ontic, psychophysically neutral domain is the *unus mundus*, the one world, a notion that Jung adopted from the physician and alchemist Gerardus Dorneus (late sixteenth century). In his *Mysterium Coniunctionis* of 1955/1956, Jung (1970, para. 767) writes:

> Undoubtedly the idea of the unus mundus is founded on the assumption that the multiplicity of the empirical world rests on an underlying unity, and not that two or more fundamentally different worlds exist side by side or are mingled with one another. Rather, everything divided and different belongs to one and the same world, which is not the world of sense but a postulate.

Replying to a letter with some quite private excursions by Pauli, Jung relates the *unus mundus* to an inner unity of an individual self with the following remarks (letter to Pauli of December 15, 1956; Meyenn, 2001, p. 800):

> As soon as an individual has managed to unify the opposites within himself, nothing stands in the way of realizing both aspects of the world objectively. The inner psychic dissection becomes replaced by a dissected world view, which is unavoidable because without such discrimination no conscious knowledge would be possible. In reality, however, there is no dissected world: for a unified individual there is one "unus mundus." He must discriminate this one world in order to be capable of conceiving it, but he must not forget that what he discriminates is always the one world, and discrimination is a presupposition of consciousness.

In this sense, making a distinction is a primordial principle of every epistemology, sometimes called an epistemic split.[12] In line with Jung's quote above, an entirely distinction-free state of affairs must indeed be associated with the fundamentally unconscious, to which there is no conscious epistemic access at all.

When the holistic *unus mundus* is split, correlations emerge between the resulting domains. These correlations are remnants, as it were, of the wholeness that is lost due to the distinction made. Splitting the *unus mundus* as the holistic domain into mind and matter, this suggests ubiquitous correlations between mental and material states. The next section will be devoted to this topic.

Mind–Matter Correlations and Synchronicity

Conceiving the mind–matter distinction in terms of an epistemic split of a psychophysically neutral domain implies correlations between mind and matter as a direct and generic consequence. It is important, though, to stress right at the outset that these correlations are not due to direct causal interactions (in the sense of efficient causation as usually looked for in science) between the mental and the material. In a dual-aspect framework of thinking it would be wrong to interpret mind (or mental states) as directly caused by matter (or material states) or vice versa.

Pauli and Jung discussed such correlations extensively in their correspondence between June 1949 and February 1951 when Jung drafted his article on "synchronicity" for the book that he published jointly with Pauli (Jung & Pauli, 1952). In a condensed form, two (or more) seemingly accidental but not necessarily simultaneous events are called synchronistic if the following three conditions are satisfied.

1. Each pair of synchronistic events includes an internally conceived and an externally perceived component.
2. Any presumption of a direct causal relationship between the events is absurd or even inconceivable.
3. The events correspond with one another by a common meaning, often expressed symbolically.

The first criterion makes clear that synchronistic phenomena are *psychophysical* phenomena, intractable when dealing with mind or matter alone. The second criterion repeats the inapplicability of causation in the narrow sense of a conventional cause-and-effect relation. And the third criterion suggests the concept of meaning as a constructive way to characterize mind–matter correlations.

Since synchronistic phenomena are not necessarily temporally "synchronous" (in the sense of "simultaneous"), synchronicity is a somewhat misleading term. For this reason Pauli preferred to speak of "meaningful correspondences" ("Sinn-korrespondenzen") under the influence of an archetypal "acausal ordering." He considered both Jung's synchronicity and the old teleological idea of finality (in the general sense of a process oriented toward a goal) as particular instances of such an acausal ordering which cannot be set up intentionally. In contrast, the mathematical notion of "blind" chance (referring to stochastically accidental events) might be considered as the limiting case of a meaning*less* correspondence.

Similar to their idea of complementary notions of efficient causation and meaningful correspondence, Pauli and Jung discussed a possible complementarity of statistical limit theorems and singular synchronistic events. The upshot of this proposal is that synchronistic phenomena cannot be corroborated by statistical methods as they are usually applied. In a letter to Fierz of June 3, 1952 (Meyenn, 1996, pp. 634–635), Pauli wrote:

> Synchronistic phenomena . . . elude being captured in natural "laws" since they are not reproducible, i.e., unique, and are blurred by the statistics of large numbers. By contrast, "acausalities" in physics are precisely described by statistical laws (of large numbers). — Wanted: a type of natural laws consisting of a "correction of chance fluctuations by meaningful or purposeful coincidences of non-causally connected events."
>
> I would personally prefer to begin with always reproducible acausal dispositions (incl. quantum physics) and try to understand psychophysical correlations as a special case of this general species of correlations.

And in his "Lecture to the Foreign People" of fall 1953 (Atmanspacher, Primas, & Wertenschlag-Birkhäuser, 1995, p. 326), where he sketches some of his ideas about biological evolution, Pauli states his impression that

> *external physical circumstances on the one hand and corresponding adaptive hereditary alterations of genes (mutations) on the other are not connected causally-reproducibly, but occur—correcting the "blind" chance fluctuations of the mutations—meaningfully and pur-*

posefully as inseparable wholes together with the external circum-stances.

According to this hypothesis, which differs from both Darwin's and Lamarck's conception, we encounter the requested *third type* of natural laws, *consisting of corrections of chance fluctuations by mean-ingful or purposeful coincidences of non-causally connected events.*

What Pauli here postulates is a kind of lawful regularity beyond both deterministic and statistical laws, based on the notion of *meaning* and, thus, entirely outside the natural sciences of his time and also, more or less, of today. It remains to be explored how this key issue of meaning can be implemented in an expanded worldview not only comprising, but rather exceeding both psychology and physics. A comprehensive substan-tial account of psychophysical phenomena needs to address them beyond the distinction of the psychological and the physical. This excludes con-sidering them as a simplistic ("additive") composition of these two do-mains.

For the mindset of a psychologist like Jung, the issue of meaning is of primary significance anyway. For a long time, Jung insisted that the concept of synchronicity should be reserved for cases of distinctly numi-nous character, when the experience of meaning takes on existential di-mensions. With this understanding synchronistic correlations would be extremely rare, thus contradicting their supposedly generic nature. Only in later years, Jung (1969, para. 440) opened up toward the possibility that synchronicity might be a notion that should be conceived as ubiqui-tous as indicated above:

As soon as a psychic content transgresses the threshold to conscious-ness, its synchronistic byproducts disappear. Space and time resume their accustomed sway, and consciousness is again isolated in its sub-jectivity. This is one of those cases which can best be captured by the term "complementarity," known from physics. When an unconscious content trespasses into consciousness, its synchronistic manifestation ceases and, conversely, synchronistic phenomena can be elicited by putting a subject into an unconscious state (trance). The same relation of complementarity can be observed in those frequent medical cases in which particular clinical symptoms disappear when their correspond-ing unconscious contents become conscious. We also know that a number of psychosomatic phenomena, otherwise outside the control of volition, can be induced by hypnosis, i.e., by an attenuation of consciousness.

Later, Meier (1975) amplified this idea in an article about psychosomatics from a Jungian perspective.

CHARACTERISTICS OF MIND–MATTER CORRELATIONS

Structural versus Induced Correlations

The development of Pauli's and Jung's views about archetypes and their role in manifesting synchronicities suggests a distinction between two basically different kinds of mind–matter correlations for which we propose the notions of "structural" and "induced" correlations. [13]

Structural correlations refer to the role of archetypes as ordering factors with an exclusively *unidirectional* influence on the material and the mental (Pauli's letter to Fierz of 1948, Meyenn, 1993, pp. 496–497). They arise due to epistemic splits of the *unus mundus*, which manifest themselves as correlations at the level of mental and material aspects. Since these correlations are a straightforward consequence of the basic structure of the model, they do not depend on additional contexts. They must be assumed to be persistent, and insofar as they are persistent, they should be empirically reproducible.

Induced correlations refer to the backreaction that changes of consciousness induce in the unconscious and, consequently, in the physical world as well. [14] (Likewise, measurements of physical systems induce backreactions in the physical ontic reality, which can lead to changes of mental states.) This way, the picture is extended to a *bidirectional* relation (Pauli's letter to Jung of 1954, Jung, 1969, para. 439). In contrast to structural, persistent correlations, induced correlations depend on all kinds of contexts, so they must be expected to occur only occasionally, and to be evasive and not (easily) reproducible.

Pauli's quote from the letter to Fierz of June 3, 1952 (see above) can be seen as an almost seamless fit with this distinction. When Pauli proposes to begin with "always reproducible acausal dispositions," this relates perfectly to the structural mind–matter correlations due to epistemic splits of the *unus mundus*. What Pauli refers to as special cases of psychophysical correlations can then be mapped to the induced correlations superimposing upon those structural, "general species of correlations."

While structural correlations define a baseline of ordinary, robust psychophysical correlations (such as mind–brain correlations or psychosomatic correlations), induced correlations (positive or negative) may be responsible for alterations and deviations (above or below) this baseline (see Jung's quote at the end of the previous subsection). Induced positive correlations, above the baseline, are experienced as unconventional "coincidence" phenomena—similar to "salience" phenomena (see Kapur, 2003; van Os, 2009). Synchronistic events in the sense Jung proposed originally clearly belong to this class. Induced negative correlations, below the baseline, are experienced as unconventional "dissociation" phenomena. In the section "Self, World, and Relations among Them" below, we will relate these features to the phenomenology of exceptional human experiences.

It is important to keep in mind that in both induced and structural correlations there is no direct causal relation from the mental to the physical or vice versa (i.e., no direct "efficient causation"). The problem of a direct "causal interaction" between categorically distinct regimes is thus avoided. Of course, this does not mean that the correlations themselves are causeless: the cause for structural correlations is the epistemic split of the *unus mundus*. The causes for induced correlations are interventions in the conscious mental or local material domain, whose backeffects on the *unus mundus* must be expected to manifest themselves in the complementary domain, respectively.

Intentionality and Meaning

In the characterization of synchronistic events given above, the common meaning of mental and material events figures prominently. However, meaning is a notoriously difficult notion, used differently in different areas and contexts. In a general sense, meaning is a binary relation between a sign and what it designates,[15] or a representation and what it represents. Meaning in this sense is simply a reference relation, in accordance with the philosophical usage of the term "intentionality" coined by Brentano (1874).

What Jung had in mind when he emphasized meaning is different, however. He did clearly aim at meaning as an element of experience, not as a formal relationship. This can be rephrased in the terminology of Metzinger (2003), where intentionality—a reference relation between a representation and its referent—is itself encoded as a (meta-)representation. In Metzinger's parlance this (meta-)representation is called a "phenomenal model of the intentionality relation" (PMIR).

Mental representations have intentional content and they have phenomenal content. While the intentional content explicates their reference, as mentioned above, their phenomenal content refers to "what it is like to" instantiate a representation, in other words: to experience it. So the phenomenal content of a PMIR refers to "what it is like to" experience a particular meaning. Jung's usage of meaning refers to the phenomenal content of PMIRs: the subjectively experienced meaning of a synchronistic event.

In this context we should stress that this kind of meaning, although being subjectively ascribed (by the experiencing subject), is not completely arbitrary. It depends on the situation as a whole, likely including conditions that are not consciously available to the subject. According to Jung, synchronistic events arise due to constellated archetypal activity. This activity limits the range of possibly attributable meanings.

The intentional content of a particular class of PMIRs mediates between internal representations and their external referents.[16] Roughly speaking, the corresponding kinds of intentionality refer from internal mental representations to external material objects. They belong to the ordinary spectrum of structural and persistent mind–matter correlations as indicated in the previous section: the representation of an apple refers to an apple, the representation of a law of nature refers to the events governed by that law (as in the Pauli quote of January 7, 1948—see section "Archetypes and *Unus Mundus*" above).

In typical situations of "ordinary" *structural* mind–matter correlations, this *formal intentionality* is hardly experienced explicitly—subjects usually "know" the corresponding meaning, but are not explicitly aware of its phenomenal quality. This is different for *induced* mind–matter correlations: because of the deviation from the ordinary baseline, *experienced intentionality* is incurred, referring to the phenomenal content of the appropriate PMIR. In this case, the corresponding meaning is distinctly and phenomenally inflicted upon the experiencing subject.

It is plausible to assume that the extent to which contextually induced correlations deviate from the baseline of persistent structural correlations

corresponds with the degree to which the respective PMIR is phenomenally experienced. Small deviations indicate situations of the kind Pauli
suggested to begin with (the generic case, as it were), while large deviations are clear signifiers of what Jung insisted on for truly synchronistic
events: the "numinous" dimension of the experience. The continuum between baseline and extreme deviations would reflect a continuum of degrees of reproducibility.

In his concept of synchronicity, Jung emphasized induced
mind–matter correlations in the sense of meaningful coincidences, i.e.,
positive correlations above the ordinary baseline. The approach presented
here also includes negative correlations below the baseline, whose meaning appears in dissociation events rather than coincidence events. Jungian
synchronicities may be regarded as special cases of induced positive
mind–matter correlations with large deviations above the baseline.

EXCEPTIONAL HUMAN EXPERIENCES

The rich material of extraordinary psychophysiological correlations com-
prehensively reviewed by Kelly (2007) suggests various concrete applications of the typology outlined above. Moreover, a recent statistical analysis of a large body of documented cases of extraordinary human experiences, also called exceptional experiences (EE), provides significant evidence that the Pauli–Jung conjecture matches with existing empirical
material surprisingly well.

Self, World, and Relations among Them

A recently proposed classification of EE (Belz & Fach, 2012; Fach, 2011)
has been based on a few key postulates of Metzinger's (2003) theory of
mental representations. These representations are elements of a *model of
reality* that subjects create, develop, and modify during their lifetime.
Two fundamental components of this model of reality, or two major
representations within it, are the *self-model* and the *world-model*.

The distinction between the two resembles the Cartesian distinction of
res cogitans and *res extensa*, but contrary to Descartes' ontologically
conceived dualism, Metzinger's distinction is explicitly epistemic. It is
evident that self-model and world-model correspond one-to-one with the

dual aspects of the epistemic side of the Pauli–Jung conjecture. However, no psychophysically neutral domain occurs in Metzinger's view.

The world-model contains all representations that a subject has developed about states of the material world, including the subject's own bodily features. As a matter of principle, the referents of these representations are observationally accessible to other individuals as well, so that intersubjective knowledge (sometimes called "objective" or "third-person" knowledge) about them is possible.

The self-model contains all representations that a subject has developed about his or her internal states, such as sensations, cognitions, volitions, affects, motivations, inner images, and so on. Knowledge about these states is private and, as a rule, can only be experienced by that particular subject—it is "subjective" and based on a "first-person" account.

Although world-model and self-model are separate elements within the overall reality-model, their referents are commonly experienced as correlated. For instance, the bodily organs or limbs, referents of representations in a subject's world-model, and bodily sensations, referents of representations in a subject's self-model, are usually experienced in strong and highly predictable mutual relationship.

Nevertheless, a subject can distinguish self and world. Mental states induced by external sensory stimuli differ from states generated by internal processing. This is why, e.g., touching a hot stove, represented in the world-model, can be distinguished from the experienced pain, represented in the self-model. In this sense, (ordinary) subjects are capable of differentiating their inner images, affects, and fantasies from their perception of material events in the external world.

Now, EE typically appear as deviations[17] in the reality-model of a subject, i.e., due to deviant self- and world-representations or links between them (see Belz & Fach, 2012; Fach, 2011). This entails a classification of EE according to four different possibilities based on two pairs of distinguishing features, as depicted in Figure 6.1.

One of the two pairs refers to a deviant experience within either the self-model or the world-model of a subject; the other one refers to the way in which elements of self-model and world-model are merged or separated above or below ordinary baseline correlations. This second pair evidently expresses induced mind–matter correlations. In coincidence phenomena, ordinarily disconnected elements of self and world appear

coincidence phenomena
connection of ordinarily disconnected elements
of self-model and world-model

internal phenomena
deviations in the
self-model

external phenomena
deviations in the
world-model

dissociation phenomena
disconnection of ordinarily connected elements
of self-model and world-model

Figure 6.1.   Fundamental types of exceptional experiences resulting from the conceptual framework of dual-aspect monism.

connected; in dissociation phenomena, ordinarily connected elements of self and world appear disconnected.

It should be underlined that this typology of EE derives naturally from the conceptual framework of dual-aspect thinking, irrespective of the empirical material to be discussed in the following subsection. Let us now explain the four classes of EE in more detail and give some comments concerning their phenomenology.

1. *External phenomena* are perceived in the world-model. Their refer-ents are conceived in the material environment of a subject. This class comprises visual, auditory, tactile, olfactory, and kinetic phe-nomena, the impression of invisible but present agents, inexpli-cable changes to the body, phenomena concerning audio or visual recordings or the location, structure or composition of material objects. For the affected subject, no natural laws, efficient causa-tion, stimulus sources, or otherwise conventional explanations can account for the experienced phenomena.

2. *Internal phenomena* are perceived in the self-model. They include somatic sensations, unusual moods and feelings, thought insertion, inner voices, intriguing inner images. As in class (1), the affected subject is convinced that familiar explanations are suspended, and the experiences appear egodystonic. Since they cannot see conven-tional reasons for the phenomena, they assume that foreign influ-

ences of unknown origin have exerted effects on their consciousness, including bodily experiences.

3. *Dissociation phenomena* are manifested by disconnections of ordinarily connected elements of self and world, i.e., induced negative mind–matter correlations below the persistent ordinary baseline. For instance, subjects are not in full control of their bodies, or experience autonomous behavior not deliberately set into action. Sleep paralysis and various forms of automatized behavior are among the most frequent phenomena in this class.

   Out-of-body experiences are a broad class of dissociation phenomena in which the self-model (together with the bodily sensations usually constituting the basis for its integration with the body-model) dissociates from the body-model, and the mental self is located outside the body.[18]

4. *Coincidence phenomena* refer to experiences of relations between self-model and world-model that are not founded on the regular senses or bodily functions, but instead exhibit connections between ordinarily disconnected elements of self and world. They refer to induced positive mind–matter correlations above the persistent ordinary baseline.

   Typically, these relations are assumed to be non-causal, often experienced as a salient meaningful link between mental and material events, e.g., meaningful coincidences such as Jungian "synchronicities." Spatiotemporal restrictions may appear as inefficacious, as in several kinds of "extrasensory perception."

As mentioned above, the four classes of EE resulting from deviations in a subject's world-model, self-model, and their mutual correlations derive from purely conceptual deliberations, i.e., from a blend of dual-aspect monism à la Pauli and Jung with key notions of contemporary philosophy of mind. In order to assess whether and how these classes are empirically relevant, they need to be compared with empirical data. First steps in this direction are described in the following subsection.

Empirical Classification of EE

An empirical database of EE occurrences has been documented by the counseling department of the Institut für Grenzgebiete der Psychologie und Psychohygiene (IGPP) since 1996 (Belz and Fach, 2012; Fach, 2011). Up to 2006, the database contains 1,465 clients with EE that were described in sufficient detail and quality for accurate factor analyses. For further details of the documentation system and the statistical analyses see Bauer et al. (2012).

It turned out that a six-factor solution yielded the most appropriate basis for differentiation and interpretation. The six factors, ordered by decreasing relative frequency of occurrence, are described in the following. It is important to note that the obtained factors reflect the subjective views of the clients about their experiences. The collected data yield an exclusively phenomenological classification scheme, not a system for clinical diagnosis.

> *Poltergeist and apparitions* (32%) comprise, e.g., unexplained movements or changes, disappearing or appearing objects, sensory impressions without identifiable sources. These phenomena fit class (1) above, the class of external phenomena.
>
> *Extrasensory perception* (25%) refers to experiences of coincidences of events without causal connection, but related by some common meaning. They are reported between the inner, mental state of the affected subject and inner states of others ("telepathy") or external physical events past or present ("clairvoyance") or in the future ("precognition"). They belong to class (4).
>
> *Internal presence and influence* (23%) are characterized by somatic phenomena (energy flux, pain) without medically established explanation, thought insertion, inner voices, and visual impressions exclusively resting on internal perception, falling into class (2).
>
> *External presence and nightmare* (9%) phenomena cover cases in which an invisible entity-like presence, localized externally, is felt by "atmospheric" or even tactile sensations, occasionally accompanied by psychophysical dissociation, e.g., the inability to perform bodily movement (sleep paralysis). They belong to class (3).
>
> *Meaningful coincidences* (6%) classify, different from extrasensory perception, coincidences between "objective" external events (e.g., accidents) among which no causal relation is available or seems plausible. Subjects relate them to one another by attributing salient meaning to them, often in terms of fateful influences or conspiracies (class 4).

Automatism and mediumship (5%) are EE based on psychophysical dissociation which, different from external presence, is often deliberately induced but not controlled. Spontaneous coordinated bodily movements (e.g., automatic writing, channeling) are interpreted as the ability to contact external forces or entities. They fall into class (3).

It is notable that classes (1) and (2) described in the previous subsection are uniquely mapped by the empirical material, while classes (3) and (4) split into two subclasses. These subclasses can be delineated by a slight dominance of external or internal features, respectively, in the irregularly separated or merged psychophysical relations defining them. Figure 6.2 reproduces Figure 6.1 with the empirically determined patterns added.

An extended analysis of clients in the years after 2006 with an improved questionnaire confirms and refines the results achieved so far. An additional study, together with the Psychiatric University Hospital Zurich, based on a sample of 1,578 subjects from ordinary population (rather than advice-seeking clients) was recently published (Fach, Atmanspacher, Landolt, Wyss, & Rössler, 2013). As expected, the average intensity of their reported experiences is rated significantly lower than for IGPP clients. However, the factors extracted from the ordinary population sample as well as their relative frequencies are in perfect agreement with the IGPP sample.

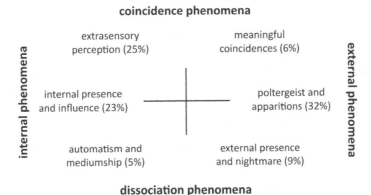

Figure 6.2.   Empirically obtained patterns (factors) of exceptional experiences, embedded within the scheme shown in Figure 6.1; percentages are relative frequencies of patterns documented by the IGPP counseling group.

Beyond Categorial EE

The classification of EE according to the preceding subsection is based on about 97% of all EE reported by IGPP clients. Their common denominator is that all these reports refer to EE in distinctly categorial terms—experiences are described by well-defined notions, mostly of everyday language, that are clearly comprehensible: inner voices express particular statements, precognitive dreams refer to specific events, poltergeist phenomena are described as matters of fact, information by mediums is concretely phrased. (As mentioned before, this characterization of EE as categorial is epistemic and does not entail any ontologically veridical claims about their contents.)

Within the remaining 3%, there are experiences which resist such a categorial characterization or are even incompatible with it. Experiences of this kind are sometimes referred to as "mystical experiences." Stace (1960) extracted some elementary features of them from various mystical traditions (see also Marshall, 2005, and present volume, Chapter 2): unification of opposites, no distinction between mental and physical, no spatial or temporal localization, intense emotion of peace, joy, bliss, blessedness, lucidity or light, awareness beyond ordinary intellectual functions.

Adopting a notion introduced by Gebser (1985), we proposed to characterize some of these types of EE as "acategorial" (Atmanspacher & Fach, 2005). While categorial mental states actualize stable categories, acategorial states are states beyond those categories, e.g., transient states between categorial states. In contrast to non-categorial states, where categories are (still) lacking, acategorial states thus occur against the backdrop of a cognitive architecture with established categories.

Since acategorial states are intrinsically unstable and—under normal circumstances—relax quickly into categorial states, they are not straightforward to experience. Methods for a systematic generation of acategorial states play a central role in the spiritual traditions of Asian cultures. An outstanding example is the Buddhist *Satipaṭṭhāna-Sutta*, lectures on the "foundations of mindfulness" (Nyanaponika, 2001), dating back to the first century BCE. They present detailed instructions for the perception of increasingly subtle objects of phenomenal experience.[19]

Starting with the perception of the body and its autonomous functions, progressive training expands awareness to emotional states and mental processes including those constituting the perceiving subject. This requires that the mental state of the experiencing subject does not adhere to any object of perception—in other words, is not caught in stable categories. In fact, the phenomenology of some clients eluding the typology set out in the previous subsection lets us conjecture that acategoriality characterizes them quite appropriately.[20] Evidently there is a systematic distinction between the categorial EE described previously and acategorial experiences accompanying the spiritual development of individuals.

The difficulties of communicating these experiences in conventional language often result in paradoxical formulations (Bagger, 2007) or lead to metaphorical descriptions in which categorial terms are used to circumscribe them. One way to do this amounts to projections onto physical or psychological entities, e.g., experiences of joy, bliss, and lucidity are typically referred to as experiences of "inner light." Repeating a point made earlier, this should be considered as a genuinely *psychophysical* phenomenon, neither a purely physical (electromagnetic) field within the body, nor a purely psychological image of light.

As discussed above, it is crucial for exceptional experiences to be experiences of meaning. Insofar as meaning is a binary relation between a representation and what it represents, psychophysical phenomena might be conceived as meaningful *relations* between the physical and the psychological. Dual-aspect monism suggests that this relation of meaningfulness arises due to the epistemic split of the mental from the physical: without this split there would be no mental and physical referents which could be related by the meaning.

In this context, let us finally raise the issue of exceptional experiences of what are often described as "subtle bodies" (Poortman, 1978; see also the contributions of Shaw, Biernacki, and Kelly & Whicher in the present volume). As psychophysical phenomena, subtle bodies belong neither to the physical nor to the psychological realm. However, we may speculate that they are not based on relations between these two realms, as we conjecture for psychophysical phenomena, but refer to the psychophysically neutral domain directly, prior to the epistemic split. More systematically speaking, subtle bodies could be patterns of archetypal activity which hold implicit meaning that can be explicated in terms of meaningful psychophysical phenomena.

If this were so, a key difference between the experience of subtle bodies and psychophysical phenomena would be the difference between implicit and explicated meaning. Maybe Pauli's understanding of the "reality of the symbol" (in Jung's sense) comes close to the notion of such implicit, not yet explicated, meaning (letter of Pauli to Fierz of August 12, 1948, Meyenn, 1993, p. 559):

> When the layman says "reality," he usually thinks that he is talking about something evident and well-known; by contrast it seems to me that it is the most important and exceedingly difficult task of our time to work out a new idea of reality. . . . What I have in mind concerning such a new idea of reality is—in provisional terms—the idea of the reality of the symbol.

The very possibility of an apprehension of subtle bodies in the sense proposed above would contradict Jung's fundamental tenet that archetypes per se as formal ordering factors in the psychophysically neutral domain are strictly inaccessible epistemically, and thus empirically (see Kime, 2013, for more discussion). Jung's overly stern neo-Kantian stance does not permit the direct apprehension of anything prior to the mind–matter distinction. The framework of *relative onticity*, mentioned in Note 5 below (see also Atmanspacher & Fach, 2013), offers potential to address this situation in more detail, but we can only indicate this here.

CONCLUSIONS

With the approach conceived in this chapter we propose a link between dual-aspect monism in general, and its particular version due to Pauli and Jung, over contemporary concepts in the philosophy of mind to mind–matter correlations as empirically observed in exceptional human experiences. Our overall message is that dual-aspect monism does naturally accommodate (though not explain) a broad range of phenomena occurring in such exceptional experiences.

A detailed reconstruction of the Pauli–Jung conjecture yields a psychophysically neutral, unitary reality beyond the distinction of the mental and the material. Splitting this *unus mundus* generates two domains as aspects with ubiquitous correlations that are not attributable to direct mutual interactions. Additional correlations may be contextually induced by interventions in the mental or material domain.

In this spirit, we distinguish two types of mind–matter correlation: (1) structural mind–matter correlations that are persistent and reproducible, and (2) induced mind–matter correlations that are occasional and evasive. Persistent, ordinary correlations define a baseline (e.g., mind–brain correlations) from which induced positive or negative correlations may imply deviations above or below the baseline.

From the perspective of contemporary conceptions of intentionality, ordinary mind–matter correlations can be interpreted as reference relations between representations and what they represent, i.e., their meaning. This "formal" intentionality (1) is complemented by contextually induced mind–matter correlations, whose deviation from the ordinary baseline reflects the extent of "experienced" intentionality (2), i.e., phenomenally experienced meaning.

Taking the idea of dual aspects seriously means to conceive of them epistemically, rather than as an ontically given reality. This provides a convenient connection to contemporary philosophy of mind, in particular to ideas of Metzinger, where a subject's model of reality as a whole is composed of two basic elements, the self-model and the world-model. Connections between those models are typical examples of intentionality relations.

Such intentionality relations can be regarded as due to (1) ordinary, structural mind–matter correlations and (2) extraordinary (exceptional) deviations therefrom, due to induced mind–matter correlations. A statistical analysis of extensive empirical material documented by the counseling department of IGPP is in good agreement with this typology. Positive (negative) deviations from baseline correlations refer to coincidence (dissociation) phenomena with connections (disconnections) of ordinarily disconnected (connected) elements of self- and world-model.

The Pauli–Jung conjecture leads straightforwardly to a non-trivial structural framework for mind–matter correlations. Its viable link with contemporary ideas in the philosophy of mind gives rise to a subtle phenomenological typology of exceptional experiences. The derived types are accurately matched by existing empirical material. Although this is a remarkable result in itself, it is only a first step to more detailed studies of the spectrum of psychophysical correlations and their potential basis.

To conclude, the conceptual framework of dual-aspect monism à la Pauli and Jung stipulates that phenomena based on psychophysical correlations are misconstrued if they are described physically (plus some psychological context) or psychologically (plus some physical context). We suggest that genuinely psychophysical phenomena are most properly regarded as relations between the physical and the psychological, not as entities in the physical or psychological realm. This challenging idea may elucidate why the "reality of the symbol," explicated by the binary relation of its meaning, is so essential for psychophysical phenomena.

NOTES

1. Other terms for dual-aspect monism are dual-aspect theory or dual-aspect approach, and frequently "dual" is replaced by "double." It should also be mentioned that the restriction to two aspects is a matter of simplicity rather than canonical. For instance, for Spinoza the number of possible aspects is infinite.

2. This and all other originally German quotations by Pauli and Jung have been translated by HA. All italic emphases are preserved from the originals.

3. The notion of inseparability derives from the fact that, technically speaking, the state ϕ of the system as a whole cannot be represented as a tensor product of the separate states ϕ_1 and ϕ_2 of its parts. A separation of ϕ into states ϕ_1 and ϕ_2 is possible, but this abolishes the former state ϕ of the system as a whole and entails nonlocal correlations between the parts.

4. The core of the well-known Bohr–Einstein discussions in the 1920s and 1930s (Jammer, 1974, Chapters 5 and 6) can be traced down to the belief that only one of the mentioned concepts of reality can be relevant. As far as we know neither Bohr nor Einstein ever explicitly addressed the question of whether different concepts of reality might "simply" have different ranges of relevance.

5. In a more comprehensive picture, the concepts of epistemic and ontic states need to be considered relative to a chosen descriptive framework. This leads to the notion of *relative onticity* introduced by Atmanspacher and Kronz (1999).

6. We use the term "local mental objects" to emphasize the analogy with local material objects, meaning that neither of them are nonlocal in any holistic sense. More concretely, local mental objects should be understood as distinct mental representations or categories endowed with a Boolean (yes–no) structure: a mental state is either in a category or it is not. Such categories can be formally defined, e.g., as attractors in an appropriately defined phase space (Fell, 2004; van Gelder, 1998).

7. The German original was first published as "Der Geist der Psychologie" in 1946, and later revised and expanded (including the supplement) as "Theoretische Überlegungen zum Wesen des Psychischen" in 1954.

8. This letter is contained neither in the published Pauli–Jung correspondence (Meier, 1992) nor in Pauli's correspondence edition by von Meyenn. Since

Jung presents the quotation with the remark that Pauli "was gracious enough to look over the manuscript of my supplement," the letter is likely of 1954.

9. See section entitled "Structural versus Induced Correlations," in particular the context of "induced correlations," for more discussion of this important point.

10. The background of this development is an interesting topic in itself, regarding which we cannot go into detail here. See for instance Roesler (2010), who sketches the conversions and metamorphoses of Jung's ideas about archetypes.

11. Letter from Pauli to Fierz of January 7, 1948, in Meyenn (1993, pp. 496–497). Note that this early account by Pauli of psychophysical neutrality emphasizes the "ordering" influence of archetypes and disregards the backreaction from the conscious onto the unconscious.

12. In somewhat more abstract terms, distinctions can be conceived as symmetry breakings. Symmetries in this parlance are invariances under transformations. For instance the curvature of a circle is invariant under rotations by any arbitrary angle. A circle thus exhibits complete rotational symmetry. Symmetry breakings are a powerful mathematical tool in large parts of theoretical physics, but we do not know better than by pure speculation which symmetries must be ascribed to the *unus mundus*.

13. In an earlier publication (Atmanspacher, 2012), it was suggested that "structural synchronicity" be distinguished from "induced synchronicity." For reasons to be discussed below, this terminology is infelicitous and, thus, has been improved.

14. Jungian psychology describes this in more detail: when a subject becomes aware of some problematic unconscious content, the corresponding unconscious complex may be (partially) dissolved. This affects the archetypal core of the complex, which is supposed to manifest itself in both the subject's psyche and the physical domain.

15. The pioneering approach in this respect due to Peirce (1931–1958) is called semiotics, the "theory of signs." Morris (1938/1955) turned Peirce's ideas into an information-theoretical framework which distinguishes syntactic, semantic, and pragmatic information. In this framework, meaning (the semantic dimension) is encoded in sequences of signs (the syntactic dimension) and becomes operationally accessible by its usage (the pragmatic dimension).

In the theory of complex systems, an interesting connection between pragmatic information and a particular class of complexity measures has been established (Atmanspacher, 2007), which could help relate the notion of meaning to the structure and dynamics of material systems.

16. In the following subsection such internal and external elements will be rephrased as elements of Metzinger's (2003) self-model and world-model.

17. Such deviations are often referred to as "anomalies." We prefer the notion of a deviation because the presented approach leads to particular basic classes of such deviations. This renders their traditional status as unclassifiable "anomalies" inappropriate or at least arguable.

18. An interesting discussion of out-of-body experiences from the perspective of a representational account, including the concept of PMIRs, is due to Metzinger (2005).

19. Poortman (1978) provides a comprehensive compendium of the literature on "subtle bodies" in the first two volumes of his four-volume classic.

20. Compare also the relation between acategorial (as well as non-categorial) states with the topic of "non-conceptual content" recently discussed intensely in the philosophy of mind (see Feil & Atmanspacher, 2010).

REFERENCES

Aspect, A., Dalibard, J., & Roger, G. (1982). Experimental test of Bell's inequalities using time-varying analyzers. *Physical Review Letters, 49*, 1804–1807.
Atmanspacher, H. (2007). A semiotic approach to complex systems. In A. Mehler & R. Köhler (Eds.), *Aspects of Automatic Text Analysis* (pp. 79–91). Berlin: Springer.
Atmanspacher, H. (2011). Quantum approaches to consciousness. In E. N. Zalta (Ed.), *The Stanford Encyclopedia of Philosophy* (Summer 2011 ed.). http://plato.stanford.edu/archives/sum2011/entries/qt-consciousness/
Atmanspacher, H. (2012). Dual-aspect monism à la Pauli and Jung. *Journal of Consciousness Studies, 19*(9–10), 96–120.
Atmanspacher, H., & Fach, W. (2005). Acategoriality as mental instability. *Journal of Mind and Behavior, 26*, 181–206.
Atmanspacher, H., & Fach, W. (2013). Encouraging metaphysics. *Journal of Analytical Psychology, 58*, 254–257. doi:10.1111/1468-5922.12007
Atmanspacher, H., & Kronz, F. (1999). Relative onticity. In H. Atmanspacher, A. Amann, & U. Müller-Herold (Eds.), *On Quanta, Mind and Matter: Hans Primas in Context* (pp. 273–294). Dordrecht, The Netherlands: Kluwer.
Atmanspacher, H., & Primas, H. (2003). Epistemic and ontic quantum realities. In L. Castell & O. Ischebeck (Eds.), *Time, Quantum and Information* (pp. 301–321). Berlin: Springer.
Atmanspacher, H., & Primas, H. (2006). Pauli's ideas on mind and matter in the context of contemporary science. *Journal of Consciousness Studies, 13*(3), 5–50.
Atmanspacher, H., & Primas, H. (Eds.). (2009). *Recasting Reality: Wolfgang Pauli's Philosophical Ideas and Contemporary Science*. Berlin: Springer.
Atmanspacher, H., Primas, H., & Wertenschlag-Birkhäuser, E. (Eds.). (1995). *Der Pauli-Jung-Dialog und seine Bedeutung für die moderne Wissenschaft*. Berlin: Springer.
Bagger, M. (2007). *The Uses of Paradox: Religion, Self-Transformation, and the Absurd*. New York: Columbia University Press.
Bauer, E., Belz, M., Fach, W., Fangmeier, R., Schupp-Ihle, C., & Wiedemer, A. (2012). Counseling at the IGPP—An overview. In W. H. Kramer, E. Bauer, & G. H. Hövelmann (Eds.), *Perspectives of Clinical Parapsychology: An Introductory Reader* (pp. 149–167). Bunnik, The Netherlands: Stichting Het Johan Borgman Fonds.
Bell, J. S. (1964). On the Einstein Podolsky Rosen paradox. *Physics, 1*, 195–200.
Belz, M., & Fach, W. (2012). Theoretical reflections on counseling and therapy for individuals reporting EE [exceptional experiences]. In W. H. Kramer, E. Bauer, & G. H. Hövelmann

(Eds.), *Perspectives of Clinical Parapsychology: An Introductory Reader* (pp. 168–189). Bunnik, The Netherlands: Stichting Het Johan Borgman Fonds.

Bohr, N. (1928). The quantum postulate and the recent development of atomic theory. *Nature (Suppl.), 121*, 580–590.

Bohr, N. (1935). Can quantum-mechanical description of physical reality be considered complete? *Physical Review, 48*, 696–702.

Brentano, F. (1874). *Psychologie vom empirischen Standpunkte.* Leipzig, Germany: Duncker & Humblot.

Einstein, A., Podolsky, B., & Rosen, N. (1935). Can quantum-mechanical description of physical reality be considered complete? *Physical Review, 47*, 777–780.

Enz, C. P., & Meyenn, K. von (Eds.). (1994). *Wolfgang Pauli: Writings on Physics and Philosophy* (R. Schlapp, Trans.). Berlin: Springer.

Fach, W. (2011). Phenomenological aspects of complementarity and entanglement in exceptional human experiences. *Axiomathes, 21*, 233–247. doi:10.1007/s10516-010-9143-7

Fach, W., Atmanspacher, H., Landolt, K., Wyss, T., & Rössler, W. (2013). A comparative study of exceptional experiences of clients seeking advice and of subjects in an ordinary population. *Frontiers in Psychology, 4*, article 65. doi:10.3389/fpsyg.2013.00065

Favrholdt, D. (Ed.). (1999). *Niels Bohr Collected Works: Vol. 10. Complementarity Beyond Physics (1928–1962).* Amsterdam: Elsevier.

Feil, D., & Atmanspacher, H. (2010). Acategorial states in a representational theory of mental processes. *Journal of Consciousness Studies, 17*(5–6), 72–101.

Fell, J. (2004). Identifying neural correlates of consciousness: The state space approach. *Consciousness and Cognition, 13*, 709–729. doi:10.1016/j.concog.2004.07.001

Gebser, J. (1985). *The Ever-Present Origin* (N. Barstad & A. Mickunas, Trans.). Athens: Ohio University Press.

Heisenberg, W. (1936). Prinzipielle Fragen der modernen Physik. In *Neuere Fortschritte in den exakten Wissenschaften* (pp. 91–102). Leipzig, Germany: Franz Deuticke.

James, W. (1890). *The Principles of Psychology* (Vols. 1–2). New York: Henry Holt.

Jammer, M. (1974). *The Philosophy of Quantum Mechanics.* New York: Wiley.

Jung, C. G. (1969). On the nature of the psyche. In H. Read et al. (Eds.), *The Collected Works of C. G. Jung: Vol. 8. The Structure and Dynamics of the Psyche* (2nd ed., pp. 159–234). Princeton, NJ: Princeton University Press.

Jung, C. G. (1970). *Mysterium Coniunctionis.* In H. Read et al. (Eds.), *The Collected Works of C. G. Jung: Vol. 14* (2nd ed.). Princeton, NJ: Princeton University Press.

Jung, C. G., & Pauli, W. (1952). *Naturerklärung und Psyche.* Zurich: Rascher.

Kalckar, J. (Ed.). (1985). *Niels Bohr Collected Works: Vol. 6. Foundations of Quantum Physics I (1926–1932).* Amsterdam: North-Holland Physics Publishing.

Kalckar, J. (Ed.). (1996). *Niels Bohr Collected Works: Vol. 7. Foundations of Quantum Physics II (1933–1958).* Amsterdam: Elsevier Science.

Kapur, S. (2003). Psychosis as a state of aberrant salience: A framework linking biology, phenomenology, and pharmacology in schizophrenia. *American Journal of Psychiatry, 160*, 13–23. doi:10.1176/appi.ajp.160.1.13

Kelly, E. W. (2007). Psychophysiological influence. In E. F. Kelly, E. W. Kelly, A. Crabtree, A. Gauld, M. Grosso, & B. Greyson, *Irreducible Mind: Toward a Psychology for the 21st Century* (pp. 117–239). Lanham, MD: Rowman & Littlefield.

Kime, P. (2013). Regulating the psyche: The essential contribution of Kant. *International Journal of Jungian Studies, 5*, 44–63. doi:10.1080/19409052.2012.698996

Marshall, P. (2005). *Mystical Encounters with the Natural World: Experiences and Explanations.* Oxford: Oxford University Press.

Meier, C. A. (1975). Psychosomatik in Jungscher Sicht. In C. A. Meier (Ed.), *Experiment und Symbol* (pp. 138–156). Olten, Switzerland: Walter.

Meier, C. A. (Ed.). (1992). *Wolfgang Pauli und C. G. Jung: Ein Briefwechsel 1932–1958.* Berlin: Springer.

Metzinger, T. (2003). *Being No One: The Self-Model Theory of Subjectivity.* Cambridge, MA: MIT Press.

Metzinger, T. (2005). Out-of-body experiences as the origin of the concept of a "soul." *Mind and Matter, 3*, 57–84.

Meyenn, K. von (Ed.). (1985). *Wolfgang Pauli. Wissenschaftlicher Briefwechsel, Band II: 1930–1939*. Berlin: Springer.

Meyenn, K. von (Ed.). (1993). *Wolfgang Pauli. Wissenschaftlicher Briefwechsel, Band III: 1940–1949*. Berlin: Springer.

Meyenn, K. von (Ed.). (1996). *Wolfgang Pauli. Wissenschaftlicher Briefwechsel, Band IV, Teil I: 1950–1952*. Berlin: Springer.

Meyenn, K. von (Ed.). (1999). *Wolfgang Pauli. Wissenschaftlicher Briefwechsel, Band IV, Teil II: 1953–1954*. Berlin: Springer.

Meyenn, K. von (Ed.). (2001). *Wolfgang Pauli. Wissenschaftlicher Briefwechsel, Band IV, Teil III: 1955–1956*. Berlin: Springer.

Morris, C. W. (1955). Foundations of the theory of signs. In O. Neurath, R. Carnap, & C. W. Morris (Eds.), *International Encyclopedia of Unified Science* (Vol. 1/2, pp. 77–137). Chicago: University of Chicago Press. (Original work published 1938)

Nyanaponika. (2001). *The Power of Mindfulness*. Kandy: Buddhist Publication Society.

Pauli, W. (1948). Moderne Beispiele zur "Hintergrundsphysik" [Modern examples of "background physics"]. In C. A. Meier (Ed.), *Wolfgang Pauli und C. G. Jung: Ein Briefwechsel 1932–1958* (pp. 176–192), Berlin: Springer, 1992.

Pauli, W. (1950). Die philosophische Bedeutung der Idee der Komplementarität [The philosophical significance of the idea of complementarity]. *Experientia, 6*, 72–81. (English translation in Enz & Meyenn, 1994, pp. 35–42)

Pauli, W. (1952). Der Einfluss archetypischer Vorstellungen auf die Bildung naturwissenschaftlicher Theorien bei Kepler [The influence of archetypal ideas on the scientific theories of Kepler]. In C. G. Jung & W. Pauli, *Naturerklärung und Psyche* (pp. 109–194). Zurich: Rascher. (English translation in Enz & Meyenn, 1994, pp. 219–279)

Pauli, W. (1957). Phänomen und physikalische Realität [Phenomenon and physical reality]. *Dialectica, 11*, 36–48. (English translation in Enz & Meyenn, 1994, pp. 127–135)

Peirce, C. S. (1931–1958). *The Collected Papers of Charles Sanders Peirce* (C. Hartshorne & P. Weiss, Eds., Vols. 1–6, 1931–1935; A. W. Burks, Ed., Vols. 7–8, 1958). Cambridge, MA: Harvard University Press.

Poortman, J. J. (1978). *Vehicles of Consciousness: The Concept of Hylic Pluralism (Ochēma)* (N. D. Smith, Trans., Vols. 1–4). Utrecht: Theosophical Society in the Netherlands.

Primas, H. (2007). Non-Boolean descriptions for mind-matter problems. *Mind and Matter, 5*, 7–44.

Primas, H. (2009). Complementarity of mind and matter. In H. Atmanspacher & H. Primas (Eds.), *Recasting Reality* (pp. 171–209). Berlin: Springer.

Roesler, C. (2010). *Analytische Psychologie heute*. Basel, Switzerland: Karger.

Scheibe, E. (1973). *The Logical Analysis of Quantum Mechanics*. Oxford: Pergamon.

Seager, W. (2009). A new idea of reality: Pauli on the unity of mind and matter. In H. Atmanspacher & H. Primas (Eds.), *Recasting Reality* (pp. 83–97). Berlin: Springer.

Silberstein, M. (2009). Why neutral monism is superior to panpsychism. *Mind and Matter, 7*, 239–248.

Stace, W. T. (1960). *Mysticism and Philosophy*. Philadelphia: Lippincott.

Stubenberg, L. (2010). Neutral monism. In E. N. Zalta (Ed.), *The Stanford Encyclopedia of Philosophy* (Spring 2010 ed.). Retrieved from http://plato.stanford.edu/archives/spr2010/entries/neutral-monism/

van Gelder T. (1998). The dynamical hypothesis in cognitive science [with peer commentary]. *Behavioral and Brain Sciences, 21*, 615–661.

van Os, J. (2009). A salience dysregulation syndrome. *British Journal of Psychiatry, 194*, 101–103. doi:10.1192/bjp.bp.108.054254

Young-Eisendrath, P., & Dawson, T. (Eds.). (1997). *The Cambridge Companion to Jung*. Cambridge: Cambridge University Press.

7

HYPERSPATIAL MODELS OF MATTER AND MIND

Bernard Carr

There can be no doubting the remarkable success of physics in coming to understand the material world from the smallest scales of particle physics (M-theory) to the largest scales of cosmology (the Multiverse). In particular, it has revealed a remarkable unity about the Universe, with everything being made up of a few fundamental particles which interact through four forces that are now thought to be part of a single grand unified interaction. It is even claimed that the end of physics is in sight, in the sense that our knowledge of the fundamental laws and principles governing the Universe is nearly complete and that we are close to obtaining a "Theory of Everything." Of course, this claim has been made before, but more people seem to believe it this time. So at first sight the materialist and reductionist approach of the physical sciences appears to have been triumphant.

Another success of physics has been to explain the development of the dazzling array of increasingly complex structures in the fourteen billion years since the Big Bang. This is encapsulated in the image of the Cosmic Uroborus, shown in Figure 7.1, which depicts the intimate links between the microscopic domains (on the right) and the macroscopic ones (on the left). The point at the top corresponds to the Big Bang; the very large meets the very small here because at larger distances one is looking further back in time, and the Universe was compressed to a point at the Big Bang. The human brain, the culmination of complexity here on Earth, corresponds to a point near the bottom, but this raises a paradox. For one of the apparent attributes of the brain is consciousness, so it is curious that this attribute is mainly neglected by physics. The mainstream view (but not my own) is that consciousness has a purely passive role in the Universe and that minds are just the froth generated by billions of neurons. While the *contents* of consciousness are certainly of interest to science, most physicists assume that the study of consciousness itself is beyond their remit, physics being concerned with a "third-person" rather than "first-person" account of the world.

However, it seems unsatisfactory that the contents of mind (thoughts, memories, dreams, etc.) are neglected by physics. After all, these comprise roughly half our experiences, and even our experiences of the material world (i.e., our ordinary sense perceptions) are ultimately mental. So the claim that physics is close to a Theory of *Everything* seems rather

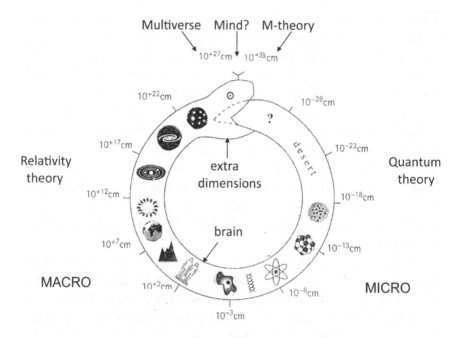

Figure 7.1. The Cosmic Uroborus, showing the hierarchy of scales of structure in the Universe, from the Planck scale of quantum gravitational effects at 10 $^{-33}$ cm to the scale of the observable Universe at 10^{+27} cm. One can regard this as a clock, with the size increasing by a factor of ten for each minute. The structures on the left and right are in the domain of relativity theory and quantum theory respectively, and these theories must be unified at the top. Mind and extra dimensions may play a role here.

hollow. There is a missing jewel in the crown of physics, and it is easy to sympathize with the linguist Noam Chomsky, for whom "physics may well have to expand so as to explain mental occurrences" (Smart, 1978, p. 339). For physics assumes that the world is governed by natural laws, and—given the success of the enterprise so far—it seems plausible that the mental world is also subject to such laws. Physics may have some limits, but we do not know what they are in advance, and the lesson of history is that one should try to push its frontiers as far as possible.

But how feasible is it that physics can accommodate consciousness and mental phenomena? Clearly physics in its *classical* mechanistic form cannot achieve this because there is a basic incompatibility between the localized features of mechanism and the unity of conscious experience (James, 1890). However, the classical picture has now been replaced by a more holistic *quantum* one, and some people have argued that this *can* include consciousness. This view is advocated by Henry Stapp (1993), and he develops it further in Chapter 5 above. However, quantum theory does not *explain* consciousness—it just hints that it plays a role in phys-ics—so some deeper paradigm may be required which incorporates mind explicitly and explains *both* consciousness and quantum theory. Indeed, Roger Penrose (1989) anticipates that "our present picture of physical reality . . . is due for a grand shake-up—even greater, perhaps, than that . . . provided by present-day relativity and quantum mechanics" (p. 371), so maybe the marriage of quantum theory and relativity theory at the top of the Cosmic Uroborus may itself involve mentality in some way.

One argument that physics must expand to accommodate mind (at least for those who accept the data) comes from psychical research. This suggests that there can be a *direct* interaction between mind and the physical world (generically labeled "psi"), as opposed to the *indirect* one which is channeled via the brain (and also not understood). If this is true, then a final theory of physics *must* take account of mind and conscious-ness. But what sort of physics is required and would it be of the kind that mainstream science would recognize as legitimate? Some forms of psi might conceivably be amenable to a reductionist, brain-based explana-tion. However, apart from various technical objections mentioned in Chapter 1 above, such explanations seem unlikely because psi also in-volves other types of phenomena which would appear to be much less brain-based. Such "rogue" phenomena suggest that the physics required is probably not of the usual materialist kind (Kelly et al., 2007).

Unfortunately, the attempt to extend physics to accommodate such phenomena engenders antipathy from both physicists (who are skeptical of the reality of psi) and psychical researchers (who are generally wary of attempts to explain it in physicalistic terms). An important factor in both these antipathies is the status of reductionism (i.e., the notion that the sciences form a hierarchy with physics at the base, thereby providing a "bottom-up" explanation of the world). Physicists see psi as a threat *to* reductionism, while psychical researchers see physicalistic explanations of it as a threat *from* reductionism. However, I believe that this antipathy is misconceived and that a new paradigm—involving a radically different sort of physics (which I term "hyperphysics")—may eventually reconcile psi and physics and throw light on both of them. Quantum effects—such as entanglement, non-locality, and zero-point fluctuations—are often invoked to explain psi, with "observational theory" having many advocates (Walker, 2000). However, this approach is not mainstream, and my own view is that a full theory of psi will require a paradigm shift which goes beyond this.

A key ingredient of the paradigm proposed here—and the main focus of this chapter—is the invocation of extra dimensions beyond the familiar ones of space and time. This notion has a long history but only recently has it taken center stage in modern physics. Physicists no longer adopt the simplistic view that space is 3-dimensional (as posited by Newton) or even 4-dimensional (as posited by Einstein). A unified understanding of the forces which operate in the Universe suggests that there are extra "internal" dimensions which are either wrapped up so small that they cannot be seen or geometrically warped so that normal matter cannot access them. These dimensions are associated with the Planck scale at the top of Figure 7.1.

Although this proposal is supposed to explain certain aspects of the physical world, the key idea of this chapter is that mental experiences may also involve some form of higher-dimensional space and that this space may relate to the one of physics. The argument is most easily understood in the context of ordinary physical perception, where there has been a long-standing philosophical debate over the relationship between phenomenal space (in which percepts reside) and physical space (in which objects reside). The reductionist view is that phenomenal space is just an internal reflection of physical space, with no intrinsic reality. However, the view advocated here is that the phenomenal world (or at least its geometrical aspects) and material world are merely different cross-sections of a 5-dimensional space. I then argue that other types of mental experiences also involve such a space and possibly one of more than five dimensions. The higher-dimensional reality structure (described in more detail below) is termed the "Universal Structure," and it combines aspects of (external) physicality and (internal) mentality. This approach is very much in the spirit of Paul Brunton (1941), who urged that we "must . . . begin to mentalize space and spatialize mind" (p. 218).

This proposal implies that percepts of the physical world are no longer unique in representing an external reality. The idea of higher levels of reality is hardly new. It features prominently in ancient occult traditions and, from a modern perspective, in the work of the many people reviewed in this chapter. What *is* new is the greater mathematical sophistication which can be brought to bear on the proposal from modern physics. Although the higher-dimensional paradigm is still in a fairly primitive form, I regard it as offering the best hope of linking matter and mind in a single mathematical structure. Of course, such speculations are not mainstream, and most of my physics colleagues—even those sympathetic to incorporating mentality into physics—would be uncomfortable with the notion that extra dimensions have any connection with mind. Nor has this idea been widely welcomed by parapsychologists, many of whom are opposed to any physicalistic approach. On the other hand, the idea has at least some prominent supporters in the field. In correspondence cited by John Poynton (2011), Ian Stevenson wrote of becoming "convinced that a further understanding of the existence of two spaces, or perhaps multiple spaces, is necessary for . . . the solution of many problems in parapsychology," while Michael Whiteman professed that "everything hinges for me on the admission of 'other spaces' " (p. 139).

From a philosophical perspective, an important aspect of the Universal Structure is that the usual dichotomy between mind and matter, inner and outer, subject and object, is removed or at least blurred. In particular, the Cartesian split between *res cogitans* and *res extensa* must be shifted in a higher-dimensional paradigm, since many aspects of mind become extensive. This is reminiscent of some of the philosophical traditions described in Chapters 9 and 10 below. This blurring of matter and mind removes the notion of matter as unconscious and mind as conscious. Consciousness must underlie both worlds, so there is merely a distinction between what one might term "inner consciousness" and "outer consciousness."

The plan of the rest of this chapter is as follows. I first give a brief overview of the history of the topic, stressing its interdisciplinary nature. Next I describe my own theory, focusing first on its application to ordinary physical percepts and then extending the discussion to nonphysical ones. The theory was first described some time ago (Carr, 2008) and then presented in popular form (Carr, 2010), but it has evolved considerably, and this is its most up-to-date exposition. The focus on my own theory is not intended to imply that it is better than the others, just that I understand it better. Finally I highlight some general issues raised by the hyperspatial approach and sketch its application to various rogue phenomena.

OVERVIEW OF PREVIOUS HYPERSPATIAL APPROACHES

The space perceived by our ordinary physical senses appears to be 3-dimensional (3D) in the sense that it extends in three mutually perpendicular directions. This means that points can be identified by three coordinates, with the distance between them being given by Pythagoras' theorem. This 3D space provided the arena for Newtonian dynamics and was the basis of classical physics for 250 years. Events can also be assigned a time coordinate, but time is absolute in a Newtonian model, in the sense that it flows at the same rate for everybody, so the time and space coordinates of an event are independent.

The notion that there could be extra dimensions which are not revealed by our physical sensory systems—that ordinary physical reality could be a pale reflection of some deeper, higher-dimensional reality—might be said to go all the way back to the parable of Plato's cave. Observers imprisoned in a cave see only the 2D shadows of objects, projected on a wall by a fire behind them, and so mistake shadows for real objects. This proposal was met with derision by Plato's contemporary Aristotle but provides a powerful metaphor for modern-day arguments that reality may be more than meets the eye. The idea that there could literally be a fourth dimension (in some sense perpendicular to the other three dimensions) seems to have first come from Henry More. His 1671 book *Enchiridion Metaphysicum* associated spirits with the extra dimension, although his contemporary John Wallis, in *A Treatise of Algebra* (1685), dismissed the idea of a geometric extrapolation from three dimensions to a fourth as unimaginable, a "Monster in Nature, and less possible than a *Chimæra* or *Centaure*" (Manning, 1914, p. 3).

In the following few centuries, mathematicians began to consider the implications of a fourth dimension more rigorously. In 1754, Jean d'Alembert considered the possibility that time is a fourth dimension, thereby anticipating Einstein by 150 years. In his 1783 book *Prolegomena to Any Future Metaphysics* Immanuel Kant considered how the handedness of a 3D object in 4D space would depend on which side it is viewed from in the fourth dimension (Rucker, 1984, pp. 38–39). This idea was taken further in 1827 when August Möbius contemplated transforming 3D objects into their mirror image by turning them over in a fourth dimension (Manning, 1914, p. 4). In 1846 Gustav Fechner speculated about the effect of the encounter of a 3D being on 2D "shadow men" (Rucker, 1984, pp. 13, 53). The notion that 3D space could be curved in some higher-dimensional space, so that the separation between points deviates from the Pythagoras expression, was explored by Bernhard Riemann in the 1850s and later by many others. Since then, speculations about higher dimensions have come from a variety of sources and have had a variety of motivations. In this chapter I will describe how it has been prompted by developments in physics, the occult, philosophy, and paraphysics. The discussion is necessarily brief, but there are many hyperspatial approaches, and it is important to understand how they all relate.

Higher Dimensions and Physics

In 1905 Einstein's theory of special relativity showed that space and time measurements are not absolute but depend on the velocity of the observer and transform in such a way that the speed of light is invariant. A few years later, Minkowski interpreted this to mean that space and time are amalgamated into 4-dimensional (4D) "spacetime," with time playing the role of the fourth dimension and material objects corresponding to "worldlines." This means that the 4D distance between two events resembles the Pythagoras formula except that the time part has a negative sign (the time coordinate being "imaginary" in a mathematical sense). As illustrated in Figure 7.2a, with two spatial dimensions suppressed, different observers have different time and space axes, but they all agree on the speed of light since photons travel at 45 degrees. In a 3D representation (with one spatial dimension suppressed), a crucial role is played by the light-cone, as illustrated in Figure 7.2b. We only observe events on our past light-cone, all points on this surface having zero 4D distance from us. While all observers agree that events within the future or past light-cone are in the future or past respectively, they disagree on the order of events in the "elsewhere" region since there is no absolute present.

In 1915 Einstein's theory of general relativity used the ideas introduced by Riemann to show that spacetime is curved by the presence of matter, as though embedded in a space with yet more dimensions. This means that the expression for the interval between two events is no longer given by the Minkowski formula and that the origin of gravity is explained geometrically.

The idea that there could be an extra *spatial* dimension—a fifth physical dimension—was introduced in 1919 by Theodor Kaluza in an attempt to provide a geometrical explanation of electromagnetic interactions analogous to the geometrical explanation of gravitation provided by general relativity. In 1926 Oskar Klein added a further ingredient by suggesting that the fifth dimension is wrapped up on the Planck length of 10^{-33}cm, the smallest scale appearing in Figure 7.1. This is too small to observe, but its existence neatly explains the quantization of the electric charge. Despite the attractions of this idea, it was forgotten by mainstream physics for the next sixty years.

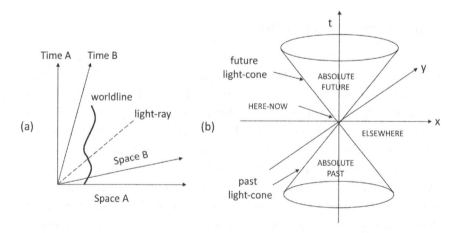

Figure 7.2.   Showing (a) the amalgamation of space and time into 4D spacetime, and (b) the light-cone structure. Some spatial dimensions are not shown.

The situation changed dramatically in the 1980s when it was realized that all interactions between elementary particles can be accounted for by invoking further wrapped-up dimensions. In these modern versions of Kaluza–Klein theory, one distinguishes between the 4D "external" space and the "internal" space which contains the extra dimensions. The number of internal dimensions depends on the model. In "superstring" theory—which became very topical in 1984—the total number of dimensions is 10, so one has a 4D external space and a 6D internal space. There were originally five different versions of superstring theory, but then Ed Witten (1995) suggested that all of these are part of a more embracing 11D picture called *M-theory*. Arkani-Hamed, Dimopoulos, and Dvali (1998) proposed a variant of this model in which some of the extra dimensions are extended rather than compactified. In a later version of this idea, with just one extended dimension, proposed by Lisa Randall and Raman Sundrum (1999), the physical world can be regarded as a 4D "brane" in a 5D "bulk," confinement to the brane being ensured by warpage of the 5D geometry. The sequence of higher-dimensional paradigms is summarized in Figure 7.3.

Higher Dimensions and the Occult

The occult applications of an extra dimension, first posited by More, resurfaced when the astronomer Johann Zöllner invoked a fourth dimension in *Transcendental Physics* (1880) in order to explain some of the spiritualistic phenomena associated with the American medium Henry Slade. For example, Slade's spirits allegedly tied knots in cords whose ends were sealed together, and this should be impossible in ordinary 3D space.

The implications of an extra dimension were explored further in 1884 (by analogy) when Edwin Abbott, a Victorian vicar and schoolmaster, described the effects of a third dimension on the inhabitants of a 2D world in his book *Flatland*. When a sphere suddenly passes through their world, they realize that their 2D plane is just a cross-section of the 3D Spaceland that lies all round them in a direction they never knew existed. Besides being a brilliant satire on Victorian society, the book showed how the intersection of a 3D body with a 2D world would generate anomalies for its inhabitants, reminiscent of spiritualistic phenomena. These are illustrated in Figure 7.4. For example, visitors from the third

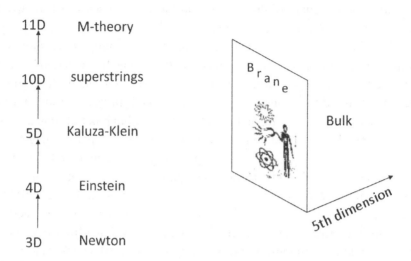

11D   M-theory

10D   superstrings

5D   Kaluza-Klein

4D   Einstein

3D   Newton

Figure 7.3.   **The sequence of higher-dimensional paradigm shifts entailed in the
progressive unification of physics (left). The extra dimensions are usually assumed
to be compactified, but one of them is extended in brane theory (right).**

dimension could inflate a balloon without opening it, and see inside
closed surfaces; objects could appear from and disappear into the extra
dimension, sometimes with reversed parity; and apparently distinct 2D
objects could be part of a single 3D object. So the notion that spiritualistic
and mystical-type phenomena might arise in a 3D world as a result of
interactions from a fourth dimension (as in Zöllner's proposal) seemed
natural.

One of the most ardent early champions of the fourth dimension was
Charles Hinton. He was particularly interested in techniques for visualiz-
ing the fourth dimension. Like Zöllner, he was also interested in the
occult applications of the idea. His 1880 article "What is the Fourth
Dimension?" was subtitled "Ghosts Explained" when reissued, and his
1885 article "Many Dimensions" claimed that minds extend in the fourth
dimension (Hinton, 1980). Although Abbott and Hinton were really pop-
ularizers of ideas developed earlier, they were very influential in generating public interest in the topic. Indeed, the period from 1890 to 1905 was
a golden age for the fourth dimension, and the notion that spirits resided
there became particularly fashionable.

Einstein's theory showed that a fourth dimension really does exist but
that it is very different from the sort of extra spatial dimension invoked

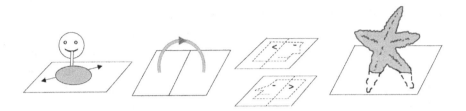

Figure 7.4.   Examples of anomalous effects in Edwin Abbott's *Flatland*.

above and not appropriate for the more exotic purposes envisaged in the pre-relativistic period. Nevertheless, in the following decades there were various attempts by non-physicists to use Minkowski space (or some extension of it) for occult purposes. P. D. Ouspensky associated the fourth dimension with mystical unity as early as 1908 and developed the idea further in subsequent works (Ouspensky, 1931). A book by W. Whately Smith (later Carington) associated survival with Einstein's fourth dimension (Smith, 1920).

There were also proposals to add extra time dimensions into the relativistic picture. In an attempt to explain the passage of ordinary time (t_1) and precognitive dreams, J. W. Dunne (1927) introduced an extra time dimension (t_2). Unfortunately, he then needed a third time (t_3) to describe motion through t_2, etc., so this led to an infinite regress. This idea was discredited by C. D. Broad (1953), who nevertheless introduced his own model with just two times to explain precognition.

Higher Dimensions and the Philosophy of Mind

The link between higher dimensions and mind arose in a more orthodox philosophical context through attempts to understand the relationship between the physical space of objects and the phenomenal space of percepts. That these spaces are ontologically different was first stressed by philosophers like Freddie Ayer (1940) and Bertrand Russell (1948). Indeed, perceptual psychologists now routinely study the geometry of phenomenal space, although not all philosophers accept the validity of this notion (Huemer, 2011).

More radical is the idea that these two spaces could be merged into a single space of more than three dimensions in which sensations of all kinds exist, as first suggested by Broad (1923, pp. 392–393): "[I]t is impossible that sensa should literally occupy places in scientific space, though it may not, of course, be impossible to construct a space-like whole of more than three dimensions, in which sensa of all kinds, and scientific objects, literally have places. If so, I suppose that Scientific Space would be one kind of section of such a quasi-space, and *e.g.*, a visual field would be another kind of section of the same quasi-space." H. H. Price (1953) took a similar view but envisaged these two spaces as causally related parallel universes. He also extended the idea to dreams, arguing that there is an independent dream space, with its own set of images and memories.

The notion that phenomenal space should be afforded equal status to physical space was taken much further by John Smythies (1956), who explored the relationship between these spaces implied by recent developments in neurology and introspectionist psychology. He argued that physical and phenomenal spacetime should be regarded as different cross-sections of a single higher-dimensional space. We experience only phenomenal events but some of these represent physical events, and there is then a causal relationship via the brain, like the causal relationship between events in a TV studio and on a TV screen. These ideas were developed by H. Hart (1965) and H. A. C. Dobbs (1965), and more recently by Smythies himself (1988, 1994, 2003, 2012). The proposal is discussed in more detail later.

Higher Dimensions and Paraphysics

The 1970s saw the birth of paraphysics (the subject which tries to relate parapsychology to physics), and in the 1980s paraphysicists began to consider the possibility of still more dimensions. In particular, a series of papers studied 8D models, in which one complexifies the four coordinates of space and time. This means that there are real and imaginary space and time axes, so that the higher-dimensional separation can be zero even when the 4D separation is not. This model was first proposed in standard relativity, as a way of unifying Einstein's equations for gravity with Maxwell's equations for electromagnetism (Newman, 1973). The paraphysical application of the idea was proposed independently by Targ, May, and Puthoff (1979) and Elizabeth Rauscher (1979). Whiteman (1977) invoked a 6D model, with three real times, claiming that this leads to the Maxwell and Dirac equations. Ceon Ramon and Rauscher (1980) suggested a 12D model, with three complex space and three complex time dimensions, while another particle-physics-motivated 12D model was proposed by Burkhard Heim (1988). All these extensions of relativity theory suppose that points can be contiguous in higher-dimensional spacetime (i.e., with zero higher-dimensional separation) even though they are separated in ordinary spacetime. This contiguity is supposed to explain how events at remote locations or times can be present in consciousness (Schmeidler, 1972).

Perhaps the most mathematically sophisticated attempt to connect matter and consciousness through higher dimensions has come from Saul-Paul Sirag (1993). The key to his approach is group theory: he proposes that there is a hierarchy of consciousness associated with the hierarchy of what mathematicians term "reflection spaces." In particular, an important role is attributed to 7D reflection space, the symmetry group of one of the Platonic solids.

A mathematically simpler approach invokes a single extra spatial dimension (analogous to the Zöllner proposal). In principle, a fifth dimension can take on the same role as that attributed to the fourth dimension in pre-relativistic physics. For example, John Ralphs (1992) claims that this can explain such diverse phenomena as spirit communications, movements of objects through space and time, clairvoyance, and dowsing. The most detailed 5D model of this kind comes from Jim Beichler (1998) and is represented in Figure 7.5a. He assumes that points in spacetime extend into a fifth dimension as what he terms "axial A-lines" and that the existence of material objects reflects the curvature of spacetime in this dimension. For animate objects (and Beichler regards life as more fundamental to psi than consciousness), biochemical reactions are associated with field density patterns along these lines, and nonphysical interactions between them occur via what he terms "lateral A-lines." These extend in both space and time, and provide a signaling mechanism for telepathy, clairvoyance, precognition, and memory. In this picture, the existence of the fifth dimension means that the mind extends beyond the brain, so the 4D body is merely the scaffolding of a more complex 5D structure.

Jean-Pierre Jourdan (2010) invokes a 5D model of this kind to account for the remarkable changes in the perception of the physical world reported in some near-death-experience (NDE) cases. He argues that the brain restricts consciousness to 4D space (resulting in normal perception)

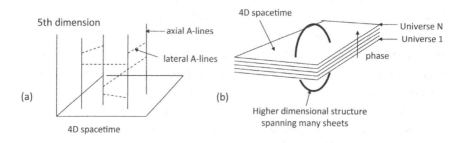

Figure 7.5. Comparing (a) Beichler's model and (b) Swanson's model.

but that NDEs give some "height" in the fifth dimension, with the degree of perceptual anomaly depending on this height. Robert Brumblay (2003) reports similar changes of perception in out-of-body experiences (OBEs), including parity reversal of the nonphysical body (switching of left and right) compared to the physical body.

Several other people have emphasized the possible relevance of higher dimensions to paraphysics. William Tiller (1993) claims the higher dimensions of psi are more supported by experience than the ones associated with particle physics, and his scheme also associates these dimensions with different frequencies (i.e., with higher-dimensional objects having different rates of vibration). Claude Swanson (2003) advocates a similar scheme, his "synchronized universe principle" envisaging parallel universes as sheets in a higher dimension. As illustrated in Figure 7.5b, higher dimensional structures can span many sheets and thereby transfer energy across them. Two "unsynchronized" systems can exist side by side in the same space and time, yet be unaware of each other because of their different frequency and phase.

Christian Hallman (2007a, 2007b, 2008) has also invoked multidimensional models of consciousness. He associates waking sensations with three space dimensions (a cube) and one time dimension (a circle) but dreaming space with an outer cube connected to an inner cube by the fourth dimension of a hypercube. He then extends this proposal to more exotic experiences.

Vernon Neppe and Edward Close (2012) have written extensively about what they call the "Vortex N-dimensional Pluralism paradigm." This features an infinitely extended N-dimensional space with vortices allowing communication across the extra dimensions. The model emphasizes the informational and communication elements associated with consciousness that cannot be translated into space and time. They favor a 9D model, with three dimensions of space, three of time, and three of consciousness. This model has several features in common with my own.

None of these proposals could be regarded as mainstream physics, and they vary in their mathematical sophistication. Also, while all such models are here classified as "paraphysics," the assignment of higher-dimensional speculations into different disciplines is simplistic since a new paradigm inevitably has implications for all fields. Thus Neppe and Close claim their model provides a philosophical-scientific alternative to mind–body theories, linking parapsychology, theology, and philosophy. I would make the same claim for my own model, which is the focus of discussion for the rest of this chapter.

LINKING MATTER AND MIND VIA HIGHER DIMENSIONS

The key question addressed in this section concerns the relationship between the material world, which we encounter in our normal waking state, and the mental world, which we encounter in our memories, dreams, and altered states of consciousness. The usual assumption is that the material world is "external" or "objective" or "public" and constrained by physical laws, whereas the mental world is "internal" or "subjective" or "private" and less lawful. However, one might be suspicious of this dichotomy since even our experience of the material world is ultimately mental. It is certainly important to appreciate that there is a subset of percepts associated with the physical world, so we might term these "physical percepts," but percepts themselves are always mental. This links to a long-standing philosophical controversy about the relationship between our perception of the world and the world itself. Some people have adopted the *direct realist* or *naive realist* view, in which percepts are a direct apprehension of reality, while others have adopted the *indirect realist* or *representative realist* view, in which percepts are just an internalized mapping of reality. However, this controversy originally arose in the context of the 3D Newtonian paradigm, and we will see that it takes on a different form in the 4D relativistic paradigm. It will also be necessary to extend the discussion to include percepts not generated by the physical world, which we term "nonphysical percepts." The resolution of this controversy plays a key role in my own proposal.

Phenomenal Space and 3D Reality Structure

The term "phenomenal space" here refers to the space associated with those percepts which appear to be generated by the physical world via physical sensors (i.e., the only ones associated with an external reality in the standard view). Since we well understand the physical and physiological processes whereby an object emits a signal which is then registered by the sensory system and transformed into a pattern of neuronal firing in the brain, very few people would nowadays support the *direct realist* view that phenomenal space *is* physical space. Also, it is clear that perception is a creative process, with higher-order brain processes filling in gaps or even overriding the raw sensory data. All this ostensibly supports the *representative* view that phenomenal space is just an internal construct of the brain.

The crucial assumption of representative theory is that there is an external reality which reconciles how different observers perceive the world. But what is the nature of this consensual reality? If one were to ask a philosopher of the pre-relativistic age in what sense the physical world is real, he might have replied as follows: there exists a 3D space in which are localized both the sensors through which we observe the world and the physical objects themselves. Each observer has only partial information about that space because of the limitations of his sensory system (his eyes providing him with a projection of the space which is essentially 2D) and the nature of the objects themselves (only their surfaces being visible). However, the crucial point is that, given his location and the direction in which he is looking, one can always predict how he ought to see it. One may say that the physical world is a 3D structure (S_3) which consistently reconciles how everybody within that structure perceives it. This is what is meant by stating that the physical world is real. The situation is depicted in Figure 7.6a, which represents three perceptual fields (P_1, P_2, P_3) by squares and the reality structure (S_3) by a cube. So perception corresponds to what is termed an *aspect map* Π_i from 3D to 2D such that $\Pi_i S_3 = P_i$ for each observer i.

On the other hand, this picture does not provide a complete description because the phenomenal world certainly *seems* to be "outside," and it is

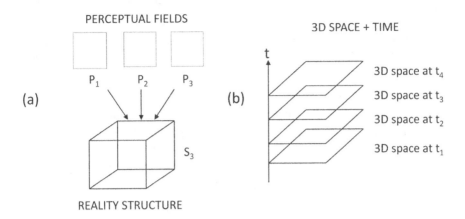

PERCEPTUAL FIELDS

3D SPACE + TIME

P_1 P_2 P_3

(a)

(b)

S_3

t

3D space at t_4

3D space at t_3

3D space at t_2

3D space at t_1

REALITY STRUCTURE

Figure 7.6.   (a) The construction of a 3D reality structure, and (b) the incorpora-tion of time for a 3D Newtonian model.

very improbable that extensive probing of the brain would ever locate the images themselves "inside" (like some sort of filmstrip). This gives rise to the classic mind–body problem (Chalmers, 1996). Indeed, some people have argued that phenomenal space may not be required at all, on the grounds that physical space alone can explain the geometrical aspects of perception (Decock, 2006). More importantly, the above description as-sumes the 3D Newtonian paradigm, whereas we have seen that physicists now adopt a description of the world which involves at least four dimen-sions and possibly many more. This suggests that the "real" world bears very little resemblance to the 3D world we actually experience and that our biological sensory systems reveal only a very limited aspect of real-ity. Indeed, the version of reality assumed by old-fashioned representative theory is itself a representation.

Phenomenal Space and 4D Reality Structure

As a first step to confronting this problem, let us see how the above discussion changes in the 4D paradigm. The construction of S_3 only ap-plies at a particular time. From a Newtonian perspective, time is absolute, so the 3D structures at successive moments can be patched together to incorporate the flow of time, as illustrated in Figure 7.6b. However, this does not give a precise description of the physical world; it is merely an approximation which applies when objects move at much less than the speed of light. A modern-day philosopher, mindful of the implications of special relativity, would argue that the physical world is a 4D structure, denoted by S_4, with the objects and sensors being represented by world-lines. Nevertheless, the notion that the world is real because there is a structure of some dimensionality which reconciles our perceptions of it is the same. Indeed, the prime message of relativity is that one can *only* reconcile how different observers perceive the world if it is 4D.

Figure 7.6a still applies symbolically provided we interpret S and P_i appropriately. To address the latter issue, let us consider the 4D interpretation of perception in more detail. Since an observer's visual field at any moment corresponds to part of his past light-cone, one must distinguish between the *material* object (which is the intersection of the object's worldtube with a spatial hypersurface of constant time) and the *perceived* object (which is the intersection of the worldtube with the brain's past light-cone), as illustrated in Figure 7.7a. The controversy between direct realism and representative theory takes on a different form with this perspective. For since *both* the object and the percept are lower-dimensional sections of a 4D structure, neither is primary and so the standard view of representative theory is superseded. The identification of a percept with some cross-section of a 4D object may seem simplistic, since it excludes secondary aspects (qualia), but for now we are only considering the geometrical aspects.

Of course, perception is generally more complicated than indicated in Figure 7.7a. Not even visual perception is restricted to the past light-cone—it may also involve mirrors, lenses, TV cameras, photographs, etc.—and there are also nonvisual modes (sound and touch) which involve signals that travel much slower than the speed of light. So while the percept is 2D in the 3D model of reality, being just a geometrical projection, it is at least partly 3D in the 4D model because of all the extra information which can propagate from objects to sensors off the light-cone. The distinction between the 3D and 4D models may be summed up as follows:

3D view: 3D object → 2D percept
4D view: 4D structure → 3D object + 3D percept

Physical perception is also dependent upon brain processes and higher-order cognitive functions, but even electrical signals between neurons can

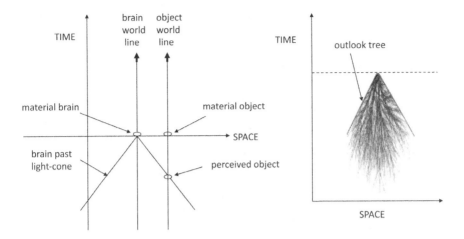

Figure 7.7. (a) Relationship between object and percept in a model which involves observation along past light-cone; (b) more general model of perception, with consciousness at a given time associated with the nexus of signaling worldlines connecting spacetime events to the brain.

be described in terms of (albeit very complicated) worldlines. As illustrated in Figure 7.7b, this suggests that all perception can be represented in terms of spacetime connections of some sort. So perception still corresponds to an aspect map $\Pi_i S_4 = P_i$ but it now goes from 4D to 3D.

With this description it no longer seems natural to locate percepts—and hence consciousness itself—within the brain. Rather one has a sort of *extended mind*, in which conscious experience is associated with the parts of spacetime to which the brain is linked through a causal nexus of signaling worldlines. Perception should be associated with the *entire* 4D process, and the brain is just one end of the chain. This is reminiscent of the "Spacetime Reductive Materialism" model of James Culbertson (1976), in which consciousness is contained within what he terms the "spacetime outlook tree" of the brain.

While this does not resolve the issue of direct versus indirect realism decisively, because any philosophical model of perception could probably be represented in 4D terms, it does obscure the distinction between the two views. Representative theory applies in the sense that 3D perceptual space is distinct from 3D physical space, with some percepts being generated by the part of the spacetime nexus within the brain itself. However, direct realism applies in the sense that physical and perceptual space are merged as part of a 4D reality structure, so percepts need not reside within the head (cf. Decock, 2006).

The Flow of Time and 5D Reality Structure

The 4D description of perception given above is still incomplete because it makes no reference to *experience*. While the 4D reality structure may describe the *contents* of consciousness associated with the physical world, it does not describe consciousness itself and so hardly warrants the description "mental." This leads me to take a more contentious step.

What is missing relates to a long-standing problem on the border of physics and philosophy: how to describe the flow of time. The point is that relativity theory alone does not describe the basic experience of "now" which is such an essential ingredient of our perceptual world. For in the "block" universe of special relativity, past and present and future coexist; the 3D object is just the "constant-time" cross-section of an immobile 4D worldtube, and we come across events as our field of consciousness sweeps through the block. However, nothing within the space-time picture describes this sweeping or identifies the particular moment at which we make our observations. So if I regard my consciousness as crawling along the worldline of my brain, like a bead on a wire, as illustrated in Figure 7.8a, that motion itself cannot be described by relativity theory.

Thus there is a fundamental distinction between physical time (associated with special relativity and the outer world) and mental time (associated with the experience of "now" and the inner world). This point was first emphasized by Arthur Eddington (1920) and Hermann Weyl (1922), and later by numerous others. Indeed the status of the "now" has been the focus of a huge philosophical debate between the *presentists* and the *eternalists* (Savitt, 2014).

The problem of the flow of time also relates to the problem of free will. In a mechanistic universe, a physical object (such as an observer's body) is usually assumed to have a well-defined future worldline. However, one intuitively imagines that at any particular experiential time there are a number of possible future worldlines, as illustrated in Figure 7.8b, with the intervention of consciousness allowing the selection of one of these. The impression of choice may be illusory but that is how it *feels*.

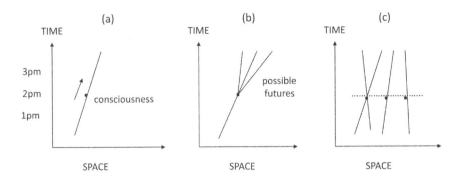

Figure 7.8.   Three problems of consciousness in relativity: (a) the passage of time, (b) the selection of possible futures, and (c) the coordination of time for separated observers.

The middle line in the figure shows the unchanged (mechanistic) future, while the other lines show two alternative (changed) futures.

Another question which arises is how the "beads" of different observers are correlated. If two observers interact (i.e., if their worldlines cross), they must presumably be conscious at the same time (i.e., their "beads" must traverse the intersection point together). However, what about observers whose worldlines do not intersect? Naively identifying contemporaneous beads by taking a constant time slice, as illustrated by the broken line in Figure 7.8c, might appear to be inconsistent with special relativity, since this rejects the notion of simultaneity at different points in space. However, this notion is restored in general relativity because the large-scale isotropy and homogeneity of the Universe singles out a special time direction.

The failure of relativity to describe the process of future becoming past and different possible future worldlines may also relate to quantum theory. This is because the collapse of the wave function to one of a number of possible states (in the Copenhagen interpretation) entails a basic irreversibility. The problem of reconciling relativity theory and quantum mechanics may therefore connect to the problem of understanding consciousness (Penrose, 1992). Note that one also needs some concept of simultaneity at different points in space in quantum mechanics, in order to describe nonlocal effects associated with quantum entanglement.

One way of describing the flow of time, described most cogently by Broad (1953), is to suppose that there is a *second* type of time (t_2), or at least a higher dimension, with respect to which our motion through physical time (t_1) is measured. Physical time is then amalgamated with space into spacetime, while mental time describes how the field of observation moves through spacetime. At any moment in t_2, a physical object will have either a unique future worldline (in a mechanistic model) or a number of possible worldlines (in a quantum model). The intervention of consciousness allows the future worldline to change in the first case or to be selected from in the second case. This is illustrated in Figure 7.9a and is one interpretation of what is termed a "growing block universe." This can also be related to "brane cosmology" (Carr, 2017) and the "many worlds" interpretation of quantum mechanics (Everett, 1957).

The crucial implication of this step is that a unified psychophysical description must involve a 5D reality structure S_5 rather than a 4D one. As illustrated in Figure 7.9b, which is a simplified version of Figure 7.9a, physical spacetime (x,t_1) and phenomenal spacetime (x,t_2) are just different slices of (x,t_1,t_2) space (where x denotes spatial coordinates). Indeed, physical space and phenomenal space are on an equal footing from a 5D perspective. This is a psychophysical model in the sense that it describes the passage of time, which is the basis of all conscious experience. However, to avoid terminological confusion, I will describe S_5 as a "hyperphysical space" and reserve the term "physical space" for S_4 since the latter is the one accessible by physical sensors.

This model might be compared with that of Smythies. In his original model, physical and phenomenal spacetime have a separate set of spatial dimensions but a common time dimension, so he requires seven dimensions. Also his original model makes no connection between the phenomenal spaces of *different* observers, so if there are n observers, he needs 3n+4 dimensions. But the whole point of the present approach is that the different phenomenal spaces are supposed to be different slices of a single 5D space. In fact, his latest model is also 5D and differs from mine only in that he does not identify the fifth dimension with t_2 (Smythies, 2012). While he envisages the phenomenal plane moving through the physical plane, this motion is not itself described by the model because he chooses not to spatialize t_2. His fifth dimension is just an extra space, as illustrated in Figure 7.9c. Obviously the two diagrams look very similar, so our models have almost converged.

These considerations suggest that the problem of the flow of time is intimately related to the problem of the relationship between matter and

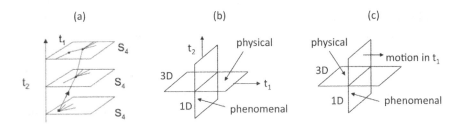

Figure 7.9. (a) How the problem of the flow of time may be resolved by invoking a fifth dimension; (b) represents this as a unified 5D psychophysical space in which phenomenal space and physical space are two different 4D slices; (c) Smythies' model, in which the fifth dimension is spacelike rather than timelike.

mind, so the problems must be solved together. The crucial question is whether the fifth dimension is timelike or spacelike. The introduction of t_2 may seem to be the first step toward Dunne's infinite regress, but t_2 is not introduced to describe the flow of time per se; it is just required to distinguish between mental and physical time.

The 5D model has interesting implications for the nature of memory. The mainstream view is that all memories are stored in the brain, but this is hard to demonstrate since we do not yet understand the process of memory storage. The view encouraged by the 5D model is that memories of physical events reflect the direct access of consciousness to the physical spacetime which contains those events. For if percepts are not inside the head, the same may apply to memories. In this case, the brain need not store the memory itself but only some link to the original spacetime event, so it contains a tag rather than a trace. This accords with Culbertson's model of memory, although the *experience* of memory is associated with S_5 rather than S_4. I return to this issue later.

The Universal Structure and a Space for Nonphysical Percepts

The discussion up to now has only covered those percepts which derive from the physical world. But what about the nonphysical percepts which have no physical counterparts? Some different types of percepts are summarized in Figure 7.10. They are grouped into three classes—normal, paranormal, and transpersonal—and four examples are given of each class. The discussion so far has only covered the first two examples.

Although the breakdown into twelve is somewhat arbitrary, since one could merge or subdivide the phenomena in various ways, the order of the sequence will turn out to be significant. The crucial point is that one needs a model accommodating all three classes.

The controversy between direct realism and representative theory takes on a different significance in the context of nonphysical percepts. One might argue that the percept is now primary and that there is no outside world to be represented. However, there still seems to be a space, Whiteman (1986) stating "in all kinds of nonphysical sensing, objects have extension, position, direction and shape, and are capable of being moved about in that space relative to other objects there" (p. 6). Furthermore, the existence of psi hints that this extended space is collective: clairvoyance and psychokinesis suggest that it *contains* physical space, while telepathy suggests that the nonphysical part is also communal. Transpersonal experiences suggest the existence of even "higher" spaces. So just as S_5 merges physical and phenomenal space for physical percepts, maybe one can envisage some form of merged space for all types of percepts.

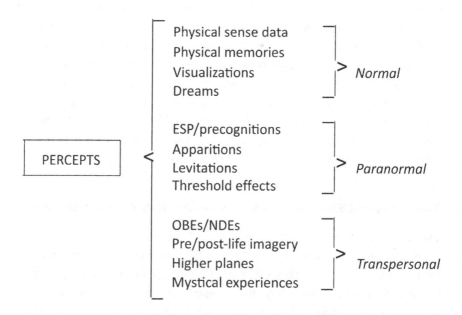

Figure 7.10.   The different types of percept to be accommodated in the Universal Structure.

This possibility motivates an extension of the 5D model of perception in which the reality structure has extra dimensions. The application of the model to specific phenomena is discussed later; here I merely present the idea in a formal way. With the addition of each dimension, the number of "objects" and "sensors" incorporated increases, so one generates a hierarchy of reality structures of increasing dimensionality (S_4, S_5, S_6, . . .). One eventually reaches a maximum dimensionality D, at which point one has extended the reality structure as much as possible. The final one (S_D) is termed the *Universal Structure* and represented symbolically in Figure 7.11 by a hypercube (the 4D analogue of a cube). The lowest member of the hierarchy is taken to be the 4D reality structure of special relativity (S_4) since S_3 since excludes time. The dimensionality of the P_i is unclear, so it is symbolized by a cube.

Any percept which is contained within this reality structure is said to possess "actuality," and in principle all percepts could be included. One can formally regard the extra percepts which are incorporated as one introduces successive dimensions as defining a sequence of "actuality planes" (A_r with $1 < r < D-3$), where the term "plane" is not used in the usual 2D sense but turns out to have geometrical significance. It is implicit here that all perception involves some form of sensor which is itself associated with an actuality plane and cannot receive signals from any higher one. Indeed, there should be a hierarchy of signaling mechanisms: just as a physical sensor on A_1 accesses a 4D outlook tree, so a sensor on A_2 should access a 5D outlook tree, etc.

The precise nature of the extra dimensions is not specified at this point, but our model for S_5 suggests that the extra dimensions are time-like, there being a separate time t_r for each actuality plane. However, there is only one *experiential* time in this model, the different t_r just representing its projections in the different actuality planes. It is as though consciousness perceives the world through a number of windows, each with its own clock. The key point is that there is a hierarchical relationship between the different times, such that the past, present, and potential future of t_r are contained within the present of t_{r+1}.

The interpretation of clairvoyance within the hyperspatial model is that S_5 *contains* physical space. I have also suggested that S_5 contains memories, so this implies a unified model of clairvoyance and memory. Since future worldlines in physical time (t_1) coexist in mental time (t_2), precognition is also allowed but not in the sense of an absolutely prede-

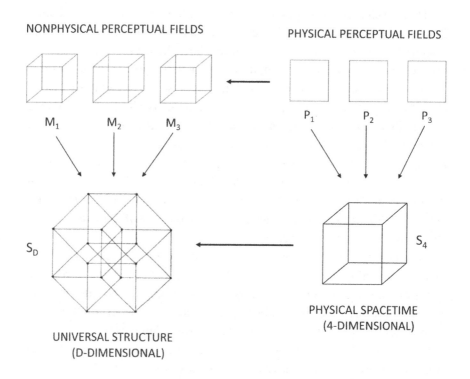

NONPHYSICAL PERCEPTUAL FIELDS   PHYSICAL PERCEPTUAL FIELDS

M_1 M_2 M_3

P_1 P_2 P_3

S_D

S_4

UNIVERSAL STRUCTURE
(D-DIMENSIONAL)

PHYSICAL SPACETIME
(4-DIMENSIONAL)

Figure 7.11. How the notion of a reality structure can be extended to include nonphysical percepts by generalizing from a 4D structure to a higher-dimensional one.

termined future. As illustrated in Figure 7.9a, at any point in t_2 the past in t_1 is uniquely prescribed, but there are many potential futures, and these are successively selected with respect to t_2. So the futures glimpsed in S_5 are alterable, Whiteman (1986) terming this "provisional potentiality." The interpretation of telepathy is that even percepts of nonphysical origin possess some attributes of *externality*. However, it is not clear that this can be described in terms of S_5, and I argue later that at least some psi experiences require a space of higher dimensionality.

The focus of the above discussion has been primarily on the visual sense mode. However, all our experiences of the world must be equivalent in an informational sense, so data obtained through different sensory modes must presumably be compatible. Indeed, one might interpret the Universal Structure as an *informational space*, with D (in some sense) specifying the dimensionality of its information content.

The crucial step in this proposal is the identification of the Universal Structure with the higher-dimensional space of modern physics. In particular, I relate it to the Randall–Sundrum version of M-theory, illustrated in Figure 7.3, in which the physical Universe is regarded as a 4D brane in a higher-dimensional bulk. For if physical objects occupy only a limited part of that higher-dimensional space, it is natural to ask whether anything else exists there. Since the only nonphysical entities which we experience are mental ones, and since it has been argued that all mental experiences have to exist in some sort of space, it seems natural to associate this with the "bulk."

The fact that I adopt the phrases "bulk" and "brane" need not imply commitment to M-theory itself. Indeed, the extra dimensions are usually spacelike rather than timelike in M-theory. Also there is only one extended dimension in the Randall–Sundrum model, although the picture can be generalized to allow more. However, I do require some form of higher-dimensional model, and the term "hyperphysical" is generally used in this context. It should be stressed that the higher actuality planes are not strung out along the fifth dimension (as in Figure 7.5b) in this model; rather they correspond to a hierarchy of branes of increasing dimensionality. So they are packed inside one another like Russian dolls rather than being like slices through a cake. However, the key point is that both percept and object are viewed as the projections of some higher-dimensional structure, so the distinction between matter and mind becomes blurred. For this reason the Universal Structure might be interpreted as a Universal Mind.

The next step is to formulate a theory of how the different elements in the Universal Structure interact with one another. This is a very ambitious task. The Randall–Sundrum picture confines attention to the interaction of objects on the brane, whereas the full theory must also consider the interactions of objects in the bulk. So not only must one provide a model for how objects on A_1 interact (i.e., a complete theory of physics), one must also describe how objects on higher actuality planes interact. This is also necessary if one wants to extend the discussion from the passive aspects of mind involved in perception to more active ones.

The model involves a formulation of what I term "Transcendental Field Theory." The name indicates, firstly, that all the interactions are assumed to proceed via fields and, secondly, that the fields involved are more extensive than the usual physical ones in that they do not only involve space and time. We also assume that all interactions can be interpreted *geometrically*. In the context of objects on the first actuality plane (i.e., physical objects), this interaction corresponds to gravity, which is a manifestation of the fact that spacetime is curved. Thus we can think of A_1 as a 4D sheet within the Universal Structure, with the existence of a physical object being reflected in the fact that it induces curvature of the sheet (cf. Beichler's model). We then extend this idea to higher dimensions, with A_r being associated with an $(r + 2)$-brane in the Universal Structure. Transcendental Field Theory interprets the matter–mind interface as some form of "hyperdimensional" interaction. The details of this are not yet clear, but it does at least offer the conceptual hope of unifying matter and mind within an extension of current physics. The nature of the unification is summarized in Figure 7.12 and its caption.

SOME GENERAL CONSIDERATIONS

The Universal Structure proposal raises many issues which are common to all hyperspatial models. In this section I will highlight some of these issues and then discuss some speculations about the nature of time and subtle matter. However, it must be stressed that all these ideas are very preliminary, providing more questions than answers.

The focus of the above discussion has been on the perceptual aspects of mind, and other aspects would need to be included in a full treatment—for example, cognition, emotion, volition, and dispositional factors. Nor would I anticipate that all such aspects can be described by the model, since some may have no connection to physics at all. So this approach does not aspire to provide a complete theory of mind. Also the above discussion has certainly not resolved the problem of consciousness, although we return to that later.

In any theory purporting to unify matter and mind, the real challenge is to explain the phenomena in the overlap of these domains. In a sense, all the phenomena labeled as "paranormal" in Figure 7.10 come into this category, which is why psychical research plays a key role in bridging these two domains (Carr, 2008). A common feature of these phenomena is that they involve what Michael Grosso terms a "dream bubble" (see below), a fusion of public and private space, in which the ordinary laws

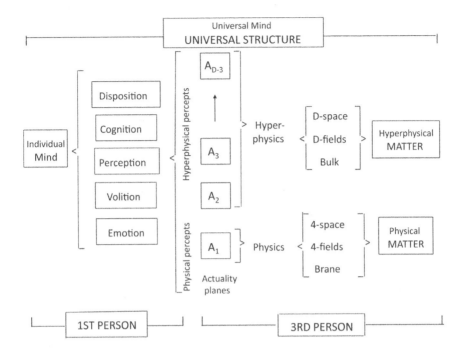

Figure 7.12. This summarizes the relationship between matter and mind in the proposed model. Individual mind has a number of attributes, but we have focused mainly on its perceptual aspects. Both percepts (in the first-person domain) and the objects from which they derive (in the third-person domain) are contained in some higher-dimensional Universal Structure, which comprises a hierarchy of actuality planes {A_i}. Physical objects (i.e., matter) are associated with the lowest plane {A_1}, which corresponds to a 4D brane. Hyperphysical objects (usually classified as mental) are associated with higher actuality planes and these correspond to higher-dimensional branes which interact via higher-dimensional fields. The total dimensionality D is unspecified but determines the number of actuality planes (D−3).

of physics do not apply. The Universal Structure purports to provide this fusion, although the details are not yet fully worked out.

With many rogue phenomena, it can be argued that psi provides an alternative hypothesis to the hyperspatial one. But if psi can itself be interpreted in hyperspatial terms, how can one decide whether psi explains mental space or mental space explains psi? The answer hinges on the nature of psychic perception. In the Universal Structure proposal, all perception is channeled through some form of sensor, but this need not be physical. Indeed, there should be a hierarchy of sensors associated with the hierarchy of actuality planes. To make contact with other chapters in this book, I will refer to these as "subtle" sensors. Presumably this also requires a hierarchy of subtle bodies, a notion familiar in many esoteric traditions.

One important issue is whether we do not observe an extra dimension because it is compactified on too small a scale to be seen (as in the Kaluza–Klein model) or because we are confined to a thin slice of the extra dimension by the warpage of the higher-dimensional geometry (as in the brane model). A related issue is whether the extra dimensions are spacelike or timelike (i.e., whether they have a positive or negative sign in the expression for the distance between points in the higher-dimensional space). Timelike and spacelike dimensions have very different manifestations and could potentially be distinguished by phenomenological reports.

The Specious Present, Personal Identity, and Consciousness

The motion of S_4 through the fifth dimension only permits the animation of spacetime in a *global* sense. It corresponds to a sort of *universal* consciousness but does not explain *individual* consciousness or clarify the distinction between the "first-person" and "third-person" perspectives in Figure 7.12. Another problem is that we have only discussed t_1 and t_2; the roles of the higher times have not yet been considered. Here I make a very speculative proposal which links these two problems.

We first note that the conscious experience of time—and hence the existence of personal identity—only makes sense within certain bounds because we could not be aware of timescales which were too short or too long. The problem on the short timescale is that our physical sensory systems have a finite time resolution and so we cannot observe processes shorter than this. Indeed, it has been suggested that consciousness is associated with a frequency of 40 Hz, corresponding to a time of 0.025 s (Gold, 1999). This minimum timescale of consciousness (τ) is called the *specious present*, a term first introduced by E. Robert Kelly (1882) and taken up by William James (1890). The problem on the long timescale is that our brains do not register changes that are too slow (e.g., on a timescale longer than that associated with short-term memory). So there is a sense in which the conscious flow of time only exists between these upper and lower limits. Of course, we can still *intellectualize* about longer and shorter timescales but we cannot *experience* them.

In the usual waking state, the value of τ is presumably determined by brain processes. However, a striking feature of mental experience is that the specious present appears to change in some circumstances. This applies even in "normal" experiences, is more accentuated in "paranormal" experiences, and is most dramatic in "transpersonal" experiences. This may be partly explained in terms of brain processes, since there is a huge neuroscientific literature on time perception and its variability. On the other hand, in any "filter" theory, one might expect τ to change substantially if consciousness can be decoupled from the brain. This raises the question of whether there could be other levels of consciousness in the Universe, not necessarily associated with brains, operating with a different specious present and perceiving the world through organs sensitive to a different frequency range. Such notions have also been advocated by Josiah Royce (1901) and Henri Bergson (1946).

Variations in the specious present may also relate to psi. Thouless and Wiesner (1947) suggest that the focus of the mind is usually on the brain but that processes termed "psi-gamma" (receptive) and "psi-kappa" (expressive) occasionally operate on the surrounding "penumbra." The above considerations suggest that the penumbra should extend over a timescale τ. Because there is no distinction between past and future within the specious present, this implies that precognition and retrocognition should be possible on timescales below τ, and this may relate to the notion of Consciousness Induced Restoration of Time Symmetry (Bierman, 2010). With the usual brain-based specious present, τ is only a fraction of a second, but this might still suffice to explain the (short timescale) "presentiment" effect (Bierman & Radin, 1997). The penumbra should also have a length scale $c\tau$ (where c is the speed of light), so one might anticipate clairvoyance within a range of around 10,000 km. Longer timescale premonition or wider range clairvoyance would require an increase of the specious present. The model of psychokinesis comes from the quantum side and invokes the transfer of information from the mind to the physical system (Mattuck, 1977). However, the wide spatial range associated with the usual specious present makes PK very weak. One needs to decrease τ to enhance this, so receptive and expressive effects require an increase and decrease in the specious present respectively.

What sort of model could accommodate this concept? Since the specious present is a feature of mental time, which is associated with the fifth dimension in this model, I suggest that the perceptual field of an observer must extend in this dimension by an amount identified with the specious present. Indeed, there should be a hierarchy of specious presents, one for each actuality plane, corresponding to an extension in each time dimension. This proposal has important implications for the nature of personal identity because the fragmentation of Universal Consciousness into individual consciousness presupposes a certain spatial and temporal resolution, which would no longer pertain for a consciousness with a much longer or shorter specious present. Indeed, as one increases the dimensionality, one can envisage a hierarchy of progressively more inclusive selves: supraliminal, subliminal, and beyond (cf. Myers, 1903). This has obvious implications for the survival hypothesis.

Subtle Matter, Subtle Bodies, and Subtle Perception

A crucial issue in the hyperspatial approach, and one potentially amenable to empirical investigation, concerns the nature of subtle matter and how it interacts with ordinary matter. Let us first consider a 5D model, with the extra dimension being spacelike and extended. By definition, physical matter is confined to the first actuality plane A_1, but it will have a small extension in the extra dimension which we term the "confinement scale." One could envisage three different models for subtle matter and these are represented in Figure 7.13: (a) it is 4D but can move in the extra dimension (like another brane in the bulk but not necessarily parallel to the physical one) and may in principle intrude into physical space; (b) it has some extension in the fifth dimension and has a lower dimensional manifestation when it transits physical space (like the intruding sphere in Flatland); (c) it has a *large* extension in the fifth dimension and always overlaps with the brane. Since even physical objects have a thickness in the fifth dimension, the distinction between these cases really depends upon how the extension of subtle matter in the fifth dimension compares to this thickness.

If the fifth dimension is timelike, both physical and subtle matter are associated with 5D worldlines in S_5, just as ordinary matter is associated with a 4D worldline in S_4, so situation (c) applies. However, there is a distinction between the *experienced* dimensionality of an object and the

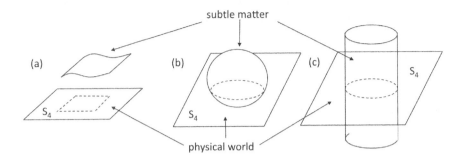

Figure 7.13.   Three models for subtle matter.

dimensionality of the space in which it resides. If there are many timelike extra dimensions, one might argue that subtle matter involves the same space as ordinary matter but operates in a different frequency range (cf. Figure 7.5b). This notion arises in various esoteric traditions, as well as more modern approaches (Swanson, 2003; Tiller, 1993).

By analogy with the physical body, I assume that a subtle body is a form of subtle matter possessing subtle sensors through which consciousness can experience parts of the Universal Structure. A subtle body can *observe* objects on its own or any lower actuality plane but only *affect* objects on its own plane. During normal consciousness, it should be collocated with the physical body and have a specious present determined by the brain, but during altered states of consciousness it may extend further into the fifth dimension, thereby allowing access to a larger domain of space and time. It may also separate from the physical body altogether in some circumstances (e.g., during an OBE). If one can extend this concept to higher actuality planes, there should be a hierarchy of subtle bodies with a hierarchy of specious presents.

So how well does this concept of a subtle body correspond to the traditional description found in religious literature (Samuel & Johnston, 2013)? Loriliai Biernacki's Chapter 10 in the present volume describes the *Tantric* body as a fluctuating hybrid of physical and nonphysical; it is noncorporeal and with greater plasticity than the physical body and with blurred boundaries but still constrained by space and time in the sense that it provides the template to be filled in by the physical body. The subtle body is not explicitly higher dimensional in this description, but its ability to transcend time and see the past and future (pass beyond *kāla*) and to read the thoughts of others (pass beyond *vidyā*) is reminiscent of the S_5 body. Besides this, there is the general conceptual link between matter, mind, and consciousness which underlies both the hyperspatial and Tantric perspectives.

APPLYING HYPERSPATIAL MODELS TO PARTICULAR PHENOMENA

The general theme of this chapter is that incorporating mind into physics requires an extension of the concept of space to higher dimensions. This leads to the notion of a "Universal Structure," which represents a nested hierarchy of reality structures S_r where the index r specifies the dimensionality and goes from 4 to some value D. The previous discussion indicated neither the number of dimensions required for particular phenomena nor the value of D, but this is crucial for determining the mapping between the hierarchy of realities and the full range of normal, paranormal, and transpersonal experiences in Figure 7.10. This section will address these issues by applying the model to all these experiences. I will not attempt to justify the reality of the phenomena or provide a full description of them. My purpose is merely to argue that they all require some form of space which is *communal* in the sense that it can be accessed by other minds. I will focus primarily on my own model, but many of the issues raised apply to other hyperspatial models.

The phenomena will be considered in the order indicated in Figure 7.10, which is also in order of increasing dimensionality according to the present model. That the phenomena can be ordered sequentially like this is not obvious a priori, but at least some of them seem to form hierarchies, as illustrated by the arrowed arcs in Figure 7.14. These form hierarchies in the sense that the phenomena seem to involve a natural progression: the later ones go beyond the earlier ones and so might plausibly entail higher dimensionality. On the right, one has a hierarchy of normal phenomena. These are assumed to derive from the 4D physical world, but I have argued that even ordinary sense perception requires a 5D reality structure. In the middle are the paranormal phenomena, which might be described as "quasi-physical" in the sense that they ostensibly involve an overlap of physical and mental space, thereby forming a bridge between them. There is some ambiguity about the degree of physicality involved with these phenomena, but it seems to decrease as one moves downward. On the left are the transpersonal phenomena. These are progressively remote from the physical world and seem to involve spaces with increasing dimensionality as one moves clockwise.

The details of the classification of phenomena are not essential here; the prime requirement is that one should have a unified model that accommodates *all* of them. Each phenomenon has a hyperphysical aspect, but not necessarily a physical one (i.e., apprehended by the physical sensors). It must be stressed that the division between the phenomena is not sharp, the lines in Figure 7.14 representing the various connections between them. Each of these lines could be discussed at length, but we will not do so here. The large number of them has an "all or nothing" implication: hyperspatial models of mind either work for all the phenomena or for none of them.

Memories

There are different types of memory, but we are discussing only "episodic" memories here; these involve autobiographical events and a subjective sense of time (Tulving, 1972). We argued earlier that memories of physical events reflect the direct access of consciousness to physical spacetime, suggesting that the brain contains a tag rather than a trace. However, the distinction between tags and traces is not clear-cut, since the brain itself is part of the outlook tree and so can *replicate* the spacetime nexus to within the limits of its information capacity (just like a photograph). In this sense, there could be *both* tags and traces, and one would certainly expect the brain to influence the *form* of the memory. However, the crucial point is that memory is in some sense communal in this model: the spacetime nexus persists in t_2 and so might be accessible to nonphysical sensors even when the tags and traces have disappeared for physical sensors in t_1. The evidence for reincarnation memories and alleged mediumistic communications prompted Stevenson (1981) to suggest that memory images may reside in a space which extends beyond the physical one, and this is naturally identified with S_5. However, some memories may transcend the brain's outlook tree altogether if there are nonphysical levels of reality.

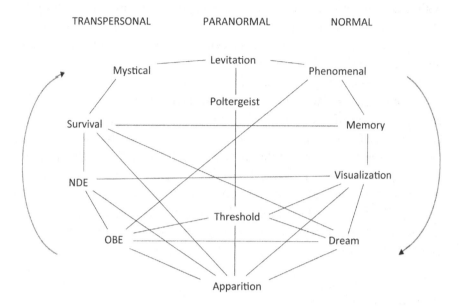

Figure 7.14. The hierarchical relationships and connections between the normal, paranormal, and transpersonal phenomena listed in Figure 7.10. All may be described in hyperphysical terms, but the paranormal ones are quasi-physical. The dimensionality of the associated spaces is not specified here but should increase clockwise.

Visualizations

Visualizations involve what might be termed "imaginal space," and in some circumstances can be very vivid (e.g., eidetic images and hallucinations). This space would not be communal in the mainstream view but the implication of telepathy is that it might be. For if one visualizes something, and another consciousness "sees" it, perhaps it really does exist "somewhere," albeit not in physical space. Visualizations are in some sense intermediate between waking and dreaming percepts, so it is not clear whether they are confined to S_5. Also, consciousness plays an *active* role in visualization, whereas it is relatively passive in ordinary physical perception, so there is a connection with creativity and willful action here. From Figure 7.9a, this suggests some link with S_5. Ordinary perception clearly involves a combination of sensory input, memory, and imagination, which is why all three phenomena are linked in Figure 7.14.

Dreams

A key feature of dreams is that they *seem* to take place in a space which resembles ordinary physical space. Indeed, the spaces are so similar in some circumstances (e.g., in a lucid dream) that it is difficult to tell whether one is awake or dreaming. However, dream space cannot literally be physical space, so this encourages the view that there is an independent dream space, with its own set of images and memories. Price (1965) suggests that we inhabit these two worlds simultaneously and that "a continuous dream-life goes on all through our waking hours, and . . . occasionally we may catch a glimpse of it" (p. 33). This implies that dreams are going on all the time but that consciousness only occasionally accesses them. A. N. Whitehead (1922) expresses a similar view: "The dream-world is nowhere at no time, though it has a dream-time and a dream-space of its own" (p. 5). The mainstream view is that dreams just result from some combination of visualizations and memories. Therefore if memories and visualizations involve S_5, so must dreams. On the other hand, it is not clear that all dream memories relate to the physical world, so dream space may go *beyond* S_5. Just as our physical percepts provide different perspectives of physical reality, so perhaps our dream percepts provide different perspectives of some hyperphysical reality.

Apparitions

The mainstream view is that apparitions are hallucinations with no objective reality. Although they appear to be "outside," they are assumed not to derive from external stimuli. Nevertheless, apparitions sometimes convey veridical information (as with crisis cases), and there are also "collective" cases in which apparitions are viewed from different perspectives, as though in the same space as the observers. There are three possible interpretations of apparitions: (1) They are constructs of the mind but contain psi-mediated information content (Tyrrell, 1943/1953). This implies that a ghost is not "real" in the sense that it has its own consciousness or can be objectively recorded. (2) Apparitions exist in ordinary physical space. Although some ghost photographs may suggest this, their provenance is usually questionable and attempts to detect physical signatures of apparitions with increasingly sophisticated instrumentation have met with little success (Cornell, 2002). (3) Apparitions exist in some nonphysical space.

Even though the visual percept is not produced by ordinary photons, it may still result from the brain's attempt to symbolize something "external." The distinction between (1) and (3) was the basis of the dispute between Frederic Myers and Edmund Gurney, and raises the issue of whether psi explains apparition space or apparition space explains psi. Myers (1903) believed that apparitions involve a "metetherial" space, which he regarded as a sort of collective unconscious, but that they do not affect matter itself, so that supernormal perception is involved. Price (1939) invoked a "psychic ether" which interpenetrates matter and can be molded by the mind, with mental images sometimes splitting off from the originating mind. The current proposal interprets an apparition as a higher-dimensional intrusion and has features in common with both of these models. Of course, there are different types of apparition, and their relationship to the physical world may not always be the same, but it is clear that the "quasi-physical" nature of these phenomena offers an important test of hyperspatial models. Besides the possible link with survival, there is also an ostensible link with dreams, since many apparitions occur just before or after sleep.

Threshold Phenomena

I use this term to cover various quasi-physical phenomena associated with the threshold between sleep and waking, and therefore linked to dream space in Figure 7.14. This includes a variety of effects associated with false awakenings and sleep paralysis, such as the "old hag" phenomenon (Hufford, 1982). I exclude apparitions from this class, although they are clearly connected. Threshold experiences have some characteristics of apparitions, but they are more intense, longer lasting, and involve other sense modes. There might be prima facie evidence that threshold events are physical, since the subjects believe they are awake and may simultaneously be aware of other indisputably physical events. However, there is ambiguity as to whether the effects involved—footsteps, opening doors, creaking bedsprings, etc.—are genuinely physical, in the sense that they would have been captured by a tape recorder or camera. There is clearly an overlap with poltergeist and apparitional phenomena here, since all three share quasi-physical characteristics, and there is also a link with dreams and OBEs.

Poltergeists

Poltergeists necessarily involve physical effects, and these are usually attributed to psychokinesis of human origin. They are clearly related to threshold phenomena, but the degree of physicality is enhanced. There is also a link with apparitions since there is some overlap between ghost and poltergeist cases (Gauld & Cornell, 1979). This suggests that the distinction between interpretations (2) and (3) for apparitions is not clear-cut. Indeed, one might *expect* this in the Universal Structure proposal since hyperphysical space *contains* physical space. This raises important issues about the *relationship* between apparition space and physical space. If an apparition is an intrusion from a higher dimension, can it in some sense become physical or materialize? Raynor Johnson (1953) has proposed that in some circumstances thought-forms might condense enough to reflect light.

Levitations

Could hyperspatial models explain the ecstatic levitations of St. Joseph of Copertino and the dramatic changes observed around him during his raptures (Grosso, 2015)? Besides the gravitational aberration, he appears immune to fire and pain, and even his clothes and the objects which he is holding are unaffected. None of these effects would be possible in normal physical space. In fact, the accounts resemble the space we experience in our dreams, where our bodies are also released from the constraints of ordinary physics. As stressed by Michael Grosso, it is as though we are watching Joseph inside a *dream bubble*, which amalgamates public waking space with private dream space. Indeed, the concept of a dream bubble seems to apply to all the quasi-physical phenomena discussed above. Another striking feature is that Joseph becomes cataleptic during his levitation and has no memory of it afterward. It is as though time has ceased to flow for him altogether, corresponding to a dramatic increase in the specious present within the bubble. Since an extended specious present is associated with a higher dimension in the current proposal, this suggests a hyperspatial model of levitation. Note that levitation involves a link between mystical states and the physical world, so it completes the circle in Figure 7.14. It also sometimes features in poltergeist cases.

OBEs

In an out-of-body experience, the point of consciousness appears to be separated from the physical body and to move around in a space which resembles physical space. Indeed, in this sense an OBE might be regarded as quasi-physical, although it is classified as transpersonal in Figure 7.14. It may also involve the experience of a subtle body, but not always since there are different types of OBE (Whiteman, 1986). The skeptical view is that OBE space is just a mental construct with no intrinsic reality, but the roving consciousness sometimes acquires veridical information about the physical world or causes events there. This leads to the same three types of interpretation as for apparitions: (1) Consciousness is not *really* outside the body, and any effect on the physical world or information obtained from it can be attributed to PK or clairvoyance. (2) OBE space is the *same* as physical space. One way of demonstrating this would be to show that something actually leaves the body—for example, by measuring a weight change or detecting some electromagnetic field disturbance associated with the subtle body (Morris, Harary, Janis, Hartwell, & Roll, 1978). There are also claims that excess light is detected near a target when a remote viewer approaches it (Hubbard, May, & Puthoff, 1986), and that disturbances can be registered on strain gauges (Osis & McCormick, 1980). However, the evidence for such effects is weak, so one faces the same ambiguity as with ghost photographs. On the other hand, we saw earlier that the relationship between phenomenal space and physical space is contentious even for normal perception. (3) OBE space is a *duplicate* of physical space, with nonphysical objects and nonphysical sensors. Furthermore, since one may apparently encounter "higher planes" in an OBE, which are not related to the physical world at all, there may not just be a single OBE space but a hierarchy of them. Whiteman (1986) and Poynton (2001) therefore invoke a "multispace" model. The hyperspatial model advocates a refinement of this interpretation, with physical space and OBE space being envisaged as different aspects of a single higher-dimensional space. The interpretation of OBEs plays a fundamental role in the hyperspatial model. As with apparitions, the issue is whether one invokes psi to explain OBE space or OBE space to explain psi. OBE space also exhibits numerous links with the other types of space: it relates to phenomenal space in that it contains some aspects of the physical world, to dream space in that OBEs often blend into ordinary dreams, to apparition space in that subtle bodies sometimes appear as phantasms, to threshold space in that sleep paralysis sometimes leads to OBEs, and to visualization space in that the content of an OBE is to some extent controllable by imagination.

NDEs

In a near-death experience, consciousness seems to move around in a quasi-physical space, just like the one encountered in an OBE, so NDEs are subject to the same range of interpretations as OBEs. However, various other experiences are involved, and the uniformity of some aspects of these experiences in a variety of different cultures might suggest that NDEs access some higher reality. The 5D hyperspatial model may be supported by the sensory anomalies reported by Jean-Pierre Jourdan (2010). His accounts include: perception of the environment without sensory organs; simultaneous perception of a scene from several viewpoints; transparency of objects and anomalous lighting; 360° vision; disturbed notions of space and time; access to one's personal future; perception of the thoughts of others; access to a universal store of knowledge. Since NDE reports include temporal as well as spatial anomalies, it is not clear whether the extra dimension in Jourdan's model is timelike or spacelike. The last two features suggest that one may need to go beyond the 5D reality structure. Other features also suggest this since NDE space seems to contain OBE space but extend beyond it.

Survival

For proponents of survival, it would be natural to associate NDE space with what we might term "survival space" (i.e., the space in which the "soul" is supposed to reside after death). The view that survival space is the same as physical space is as implausible as the medieval notion that heaven is literally "above" and hell literally "below." If one assumes that NDE space is nonphysical, it would be natural to infer that survival space is also nonphysical. For example, if reincarnation occurs, the soul is presumably located somewhere between incarnations, and the experiences described in some of the traditional religious texts clearly require some form of nonphysical space. In the Buddhist *bardo* ("intermediate state") teachings, this might be associated with dream space (Sogyal Rinpoche, 1993). The possible connection between survival space and mental space has been stressed by Ian Stevenson (1981): if mental images require a space which contains but goes beyond physical space, then the mind is "larger" than the body and so may persist outside it and endure longer than it. Since one's identity is defined by the totality of one's memories, it is also natural to associate memory space with survival space. Stevenson further argues that any memories which persist after death must reside in some sort of container, which he terms a "psychophore," requiring the existence of "mental matter" (Stevenson, 1974). The Universal Structure supports these notions but describes mental matter as "hyperphysical." Of course, if there is a hierarchy of consciousness operating on different levels and with different specious presents, one needs a more complicated model of survival.

Mystical Experiences

The traditional religious view is that mystical experiences involve access to some higher level of reality or perhaps a hierarchy of different levels. This idea also features prominently in the work of Whiteman (1986). Many esoteric traditions invoke such a hierarchy, so it would be interesting to map this onto the hierarchy implied by the Universal Structure. A common feature of mystical experience is a feeling of "unity," and this might be a natural manifestation of the higher-dimensional connection implied by the Universal Structure proposal. Another important feature concerns the nature of time in mystical experience, and this relates to the earlier discussion of the specious present. It is often reported that time is transcended, but an alternative interpretation might be that the specious present is greatly changed. In its most extreme forms, it seems to shrink almost to zero, so that only the present moment exists, or expands almost to infinity, so that one's entire life (or even the history of the entire cosmos) appears to be instantaneous (Marshall, Chapter 2 above). Ed Kelly (personal communication) points out a similarity between the description of mystical experiences produced through the stages of *samādhi* characterized by Patañjali and an early anatomist twisting the focus knob on his microscope: "It's as though the meditator is adjusting the focal length of his hyperphysical sensors and encountering systematically different worlds depending on the settings achieved." These states are described by I. K. Taimni (1961) in *The Science of Yoga*. On the other hand,

Sri Aurobindo associates the *highest* mystical plane with a state of pure consciousness, in which space and time cease to exist altogether, so it is certainly not claimed that all mystical experiences have a hyperphysical description. There are also conceptual links between the hyperphysical approach and some mystical traditions. For example, Ed Kelly and Ian Whicher emphasize in Chapter 9 that the concept of matter (*prakṛti*) in Patañjali's *Yoga Sūtras* covers phenomena which would usually be classed as mental, and they even use the phrase "hierarchy of actualities" to describe the different manifestations (*tattvas*).

CONCLUSION

In this chapter, I have argued that a large class of mental phenomena involves some form of space, although this is not the usual space of classical physics since it involves extra dimensions. The notion of extra dimensions has also been proposed as an explanation of certain aspects of the physical world, so it seems natural to relate these two ideas. They are amalgamated in what I term a "Universal Structure," which can be interpreted as a higher-dimensional psychophysical information space. This space has a hierarchical structure and includes both the physical world at the lowest level and the complete range of mental worlds—from normal to paranormal to transpersonal—at the higher levels. The assumption that mental phenomena require a communal space is tantamount to positing some form of Universal Mind, which is controversial but central to the Universal Structure proposal and to the general theme of this volume. While this approach cannot claim to provide a complete theory of mind, it does demonstrate a unifying link between a wide range of phenomena which are usually regarded as disparate, with each one providing an extra piece in the jigsaw of what might constitute a complete theory. Although some basic questions about the nature of hyperphysical interactions in this model remain unclear, I believe this approach offers the possibility of a paradigm in which matter and mind are merged at a very fundamental level.

ACKNOWLEDGMENT

I thank Ed Kelly and Paul Marshall for their helpful feedback on this chapter and for their great patience in dealing with my numerous revisions.

REFERENCES

[Abbott, E. A.] (1884). *Flatland: A Romance of Many Dimensions*, by A. Square. London: Seeley.

Arkani-Hamed, N., Dimopoulos, S., & Dvali, G. (1998). The hierarchy problem and new dimensions at a millimeter. *Physical Letters B, 429*, 263–272. doi:10.1016/S0370-2693(98)00466-3

Ayer, A. J. (1940). *The Foundations of Empirical Knowledge*. New York: Macmillan.

Beichler, J. E. (1998). Strange facts find a theory: A new dimension for psi. *Yggdrasil: The Journal of Paraphysics, 1*, 567–596.

Bergson, H. (1946). *The Creative Mind* (M. L. Andison, Trans.). New York: Philosophical Library.

Bierman, D. J. (2010). Consciousness induced restoration of time symmetry (CIRTS): A psychophysical theoretical perspective. *Journal of Parapsychology, 74*, 273–299.

Bierman, D. J., & Radin, D. I. (1997). Anomalous anticipatory response on randomized future conditions. *Perceptual and Motor Skills, 84*, 689–690. doi:10.2466/pms.1997.84.2.689

Broad, C. D. (1923). *Scientific Thought*. London: Kegan Paul, Trench, Trubner.

Broad, C. D. (1953). *Religion, Philosophy and Psychical Research*. New York: Harcourt, Brace.

Brumblay, R. J. (2003). Hyperdimensional perspectives in out-of-body and near-death experiences. *Journal of Near-Death Studies, 21*, 201–221.

Brunton, P. (1941). *The Hidden Teaching Beyond Yoga*. New York: E. P. Dutton.

Carr, B. J. (2008). Worlds apart? Can psychical research bridge the gulf between matter and mind? *Proceedings of the Society for Psychical Research, 59*, 1–96.

Carr, B. J. (2010). A proposed new paradigm of matter, mind and spirit. *Network Review, 103*, 3–8.

Carr, B. J. (2017). Black holes, cosmology and the flow of time: Three problems at the limits of science. In K. Chamcham, J. Silk, J. D. Barrow, S. Saunders (Eds.), *The Philosophy of Cosmology* (pp. 40–65). Cambridge: Cambridge University Press.

Chalmers, D. J. (1996). *The Conscious Mind: In Search of a Fundamental Theory*. New York: Oxford University Press.

Cornell, T. (2002). *Investigating the Paranormal*. New York: Helix Press.

Culbertson, J. T. (1976). *Sensations, Memories and the Flow of Time*. Santa Margarita, CA: Cromwell Press.

Decock, L. (2006). A physicalist reinterpretation of "phenomenal" spaces. *Phenomenology and the Cognitive Sciences, 5*, 197–225. doi:10.1007/s11097-005-9006-7

Dobbs, H. A. C. (1951). The relation between the time of psychology and the time of physics. Part I. *British Journal for the Philosophy of Science, 2*, 122–141.

Dobbs, H. A. C. (1965). Time and ESP. *Proceedings of the Society for Psychical Research, 54*, 249–361.

Dunne, J. W. (1927). *An Experiment with Time*. London: A. & C. Black.

Eddington, A. S. (1920). *Space, Time and Gravitation*. Cambridge: Cambridge University Press.

Everett, H., III (1957). "Relative state" formulation of quantum mechanics. *Reviews of Modern Physics, 29*, 454–462. doi:10.1103/RevModPhys.29.454

Gauld, A., & Cornell, A. D. (1979). *Poltergeists*. London: Routledge & Kegan Paul.

Gold. I. (1999). Does 40-Hz oscillation play a role in visual consciousness? *Consciousness and Cognition, 8,* 186–195. doi:10.1006/ccog.1999.0399

Grosso, M. (2015). *The Man Who Could Fly: St. Joseph of Copertino and the Mystery of Levitation*. Lanham, MD: Rowman Littlefield.

Hallman, C. J. (2007a). Part one: A multidimensional model of the dreaming state of consciousness. *Subtle Energies & Energy Medicine, 18*(2), 75–91.

Hallman, C. J. (2007b). Part two: A multidimensional model of the released state of consciousness, *Subtle Energies & Energy Medicine, 18*(3), 89–111.

Hallman, C. J. (2008). Part three: A multidimensional model of the deceased state of consciousness, *Subtle Energies & Energy Medicine, 19*(2), 57–90.

Hart, H. (1965). *Toward a New Philosophical Basis for Parapsychological Phenomena*. New York: Parapsychology Foundation.

Heim, B. (1988). *Postmortale Zustände? Die televariante Area integraler Weltstrukturen* (2nd ed.). Innsbruck, Austria: Resch.

Hinton, C. H. (1980). *Speculations on the Fourth Dimension: Selected Writings of C. H. Hinton* (R. Rucker, Ed.). New York: Dover.

Hubbard, G. S., May, E. C., & Puthoff, H. E. (1986). Possible production of photons during a remote-viewing task: Preliminary results. In D. H. Weiner & D. I. Radin, *Research in Parapsychology 1985* (pp. 66–70). Metuchen, NJ: Scarecrow Press.

Huemer, M. (2011). Sense-data. In E. N. Zalta (Ed.), *The Stanford Encyclopedia of Philosophy* (Spring 2011 ed.). Retrieved from http://plato.stanford.edu/archives/spr2011/entries/sense-data/

Hufford, D. J. (1982). *The Terror That Comes in the Night: An Experience-Centered Study of Supernatural Assault Traditions*. Philadelphia: University of Pennsylvania Press.

James, W. (1890). *The Principles of Psychology* (Vols. 1–2). New York: Henry Holt.

Johnson, R. C. (1953). *The Imprisoned Splendour*. London: Hodder & Stoughton.

Jourdan, J.-P. (2010). *Deadline: Dernière limite*. Paris: Pocket.

Kelly, E. F., Kelly, E. W., Crabtree, A., Gauld, A., Grosso, M., & Greyson, B. (2007). *Irreducible Mind: Toward a Psychology for the 21st Century*. Lanham, MD: Rowman & Littlefield.

[Kelly, E. R.] (1882). *The Alternative: A Study in Psychology*. London: Macmillan.

Manning, H. P. (1914). *Geometry of Four Dimensions*. New York: Macmillan.

Mattuck, R. D. (1977). Random fluctuation theory of psychokinesis: Thermal noise model. In J. D. Morris, W. G. Roll, & R. L. Morris (Eds.), *Research in Parapsychology 1976* (pp. 191–195). Metuchen, NJ: Scarecrow Press.

Morris, R. L., Harary, S. B., Janis, J., Hartwell, J., & Roll, W. G. (1978). Studies of communication during out-of-body experiences. *Journal of the American Society for Psychical Research, 72,* 1–21.

Myers, F. W. H. (1903). *Human Personality and Its Survival of Bodily Death* (Vols. 1–2). London: Longmans, Green. (Available on CTR website, http://www.esalen.org/ctr/scholarly-resources)

Neppe, V. M., & Close, E. R. (2012). *Reality Begins with Consciousness: A Paradigm Shift That Works* [e-book]. Retrieved from http://www.brainvoyage.com

Newman, E. T. (1973). Maxwell's equations and complex Minkowski space. *Journal of Mathematical Physics, 14,* 102–103. doi:10.1063/1.1666160

Osis, K., & McCormick, D. (1980). Kinetic effects at the ostensible location of an out-of-body projection during perceptual testing. *Journal of the American Society for Psychical Research, 74,* 319–329.

Ouspensky, P. D. (1931). *A New Model of the Universe* (R. R. Merton, Trans.). New York: Knopf.

Penrose, R. (1989). *The Emperor's New Mind*. Oxford: Oxford University Press.

Penrose, R. (1992). *The Large, the Small and the Human Mind*. Cambridge: Cambridge University Press.

Poynton, J. C. (1994). Making sense of psi: Whiteman's multilevel ontology. *Journal of the Society for Psychical Research, 59,* 401–412.

Poynton, J. C. (2001). Challenges of out-of-body experience: Does psychical research fully meet them? *Journal of the Society for Psychical Research, 65*, 194–206.

Poynton, J. (2011). Many levels, many worlds and psi: A guide to the work of Michael Whiteman. *Proceedings of the Society for Psychical Research, 59*, 109–139.

Price, H. H. (1939). Haunting and the "psychic ether" hypothesis. *Proceedings of the Society for Psychical Research, 45*, 307–343.

Price, H. H. (1953). Survival and the idea of "another world." *Proceedings of the Society for Psychical Research, 50*, 1–25.

Price, H. H. (1965). Reply to comments by J. R. Smythies on "Survival and the idea of 'another world.'" In J. R. Smythies (Ed.), *Brain and Mind: Modern Concepts of the Nature of Mind* (pp. 31–33). London: Routledge & Kegan Paul.

Ralphs, J. D. (1992). *Exploring the Fourth Dimension: Secrets of the Paranormal*. London: Quantum.

Ramon, C., & Rauscher, E. A. (1980). Superluminal transformations in complex Minkowski spaces. *Foundations of Physics, 10*, 661–669. doi:10.1007/BF00715047

Randall, L., & Sundrum, R. (1999). An alternative to compactification. *Physical Review Letters, 83*, 4690–4693. doi:10.1103/PhysRevLett.83.4690

Rauscher, E. A. (1979). Some physical models potentially applicable to remote perception. In A. Puharich (Ed.), *The Iceland Papers* (pp. 49–93). Amherst, WI: Essentia Research Associates.

Royce, J. (1901). *The World and the Individual* (2nd series). New York: Macmillan.

Rucker, R. (1984). *The Fourth Dimension: A Guided Tour of the Higher Universes*. Boston: Houghton Mifflin.

Russell, B. (1948). *Human Knowledge: Its Scope and Limits*. London: George Allen & Unwin.

Samuel, G., & Johnston, J. (Eds.). (2013). *Religion and the Subtle Body in Asia and the West: Between Mind and Body*. Abingdon, England: Routledge.

Savitt, S. (2014). Being and becoming in modern physics. In E. N. Zalta (Ed.), *The Stanford Encyclopedia of Philosophy* (Summer 2014 ed.). Retrieved from http://plato.stanford.edu/archives/sum2014/entries/spacetime-bebecome/

Schmeidler, G. R. (1972). Respice, adspice, prospice. *Proceedings of the Parapsychological Association, 8*, 117–143.

Sirag, S.-P. (1993). Consciousness: A hyperspace view. In J. Mishlove, *The Roots of Consciousness* (Rev. ed., pp. 327–365). Tulsa, OK: Council Oak Books.

Smart, J. J. C. (1978). The content of physicalism. *Philosophical Quarterly, 28*, 339–341.

Smith, W. W. (1920). *A Theory of the Mechanism of Survival: The Fourth Dimension and Its Applications*. London: Kegan Paul, Trench, Trubner.

Smythies, J. R. (1956). *Analysis of Perception*. London: Routledge & Kegan Paul.

Smythies, J. R. (1988). Minds and higher dimensions. *Journal of the Society for Psychical Research, 55*, 150–156.

Smythies, J. R. (1994). *The Walls of Plato's Cave: The Science and Philosophy of (Brain, Consciousness and Perception)*. Aldershot, England: Avebury.

Smythies, J. R. (2003). Space, time and consciousness. *Journal of Consciousness Studies, 10*(3), 47–56.

Smythies, J. R. (2012). Consciousness and higher dimensions of space. *Journal of Consciousness Studies, 19*(11–12), 224–232.

Sogyal Rinpoche (1993). *The Tibetan Book of Living and Dying*. New York: HarperCollins.

Stapp, H. P. (1993). *Mind, Matter, and Quantum Mechanics*. Berlin: Springer.

Stevenson, I. (1974). Some questions related to cases of the reincarnation type. *Journal of the American Society for Psychical Research, 68*, 395–416.

Stevenson, I. (1981). Can we describe the mind? In W. G. Roll & J. Beloff (Eds.), *Research in Parapsychology 1980* (pp. 130–142). Metuchen, NJ: Scarecrow Press.

Swanson, C. (2003). *The Synchronized Universe: New Science of the Paranormal*. Tucson, AZ: Poseidia Press.

Taimni, I. K. (1961). *The Science of Yoga*. Wheaton, IL: Theosophical Publishing House.

Targ, R., May, E. C., & Puthoff, H. E. (1979). Direct perception of remote geographic locations. In C. T. Tart, H. E. Puthoff, & R. Targ (Eds.), *Mind at Large* (pp. 78–106). New York: Praeger.

Thouless, R. H., & Wiesner, B. P. (1947). The psi process in normal and "paranormal" psychology. *Proceedings of the Society for Psychical Research, 48,* 177–196.

Tiller, W. A. (1993). What are subtle energies? *Journal of Scientific Exploration, 7,* 293–304.

Tulving, E. (1972). Episodic and semantic memory. In E. Tulving & W. Donaldson (Eds.), *Organization of Memory* (pp. 381–403). New York: Academic Press.

Tyrrell, G. N. M. (1953). *Apparitions.* London: Duckworth. (Original work published 1943)

Walker, E. H. (2000). *The Physics of Consciousness: The Quantum Mind and the Meaning of Life.* Cambridge, MA: Perseus.

Weyl, H. (1922). *Space–Time–Matter* (H. L. Brose, Trans). London: Methuen.

Whitehead, A. N. (1922). Uniformity and contingency. *Proceedings of the Aristotelian Society, N.S., 23,* 1–18.

Whiteman, J. H. M. (1967). *Philosophy of Space and Time and the Inner Constitution of Nature: A Phenomenological Study.* London: George Allen & Unwin.

Whiteman, J. H. M. (1977). Parapsychology and physics. In B. B. Wolman (Ed.), *Handbook of Parapsychology* (pp. 730–756). New York: Van Nostrand Reinhold.

Whiteman, J. H. M. (1986). *Old and New Evidence on the Meaning of Life: Vol. 1. An Introduction to Scientific Mysticism.* Gerrards Cross, England: Colin Smythe.

Witten, E. (1995). String theory dynamics in various dimensions. *Nuclear Physics B, 443,* 85–126. doi:10.1016/0550-3213(95)00158-O

Zöllner, J. C. F. (1880). *Transcendental Physics* (C. C. Massey, Trans.). London: W. H. Harrison.

8

PLATONIC *SIDDHAS*

Supernatural Philosophers of Neoplatonism

Gregory Shaw

> Most divine Master . . . a rumor has reached us through your servants
> that when you pray to the gods you levitate from the earth more than
> ten cubits; that your body and clothes change to a beautiful golden hue;
> and when your prayer is ended your body becomes as it was before
> you prayed and you come down to earth and associate with us.
>
> —Eunapius, *The Lives of the Philosophers*[1]

Eunapius' story about Iamblichus in his *Lives of the Philosophers* sheds
light on a philosophic culture with which we are no longer familiar. A
levitating philosopher who mixes scholarly insights with a repertoire of
miraculous acts is entirely unlike philosophy as we know it today. Iamblichus certainly exemplifies this type, but perhaps the best examples come
from later in his lineage, specifically from the school of Pergamum in the
mid-fourth century CE. Blessed with a temperate climate and exquisite
architecture, Pergamum rivaled Athens as a cultural center of the Hellenic
world. There, Aedesius, a student of Iamblichus and the teacher of the
Emperor Julian, established his school after having been coerced by his
students to leave a solitary life in the country. Aedesius was soon joined
in Pergamum by Sosipatra, the wife of Eustathius, who had also been
Iamblichus' student. But Sosipatra had no such lineage. It was said that
she was taught not by men but by divine beings who conferred their
power and knowledge to her while still a child. Eunapius reports that after

attending the lectures of Aedesius, his students went to sit at the feet of Sosipatra whose eloquence and divine presence they positively adored. It was during one of Sosipatra's lectures on the descent of the soul into the body—a standard theme explored by Platonists—that her students witnessed her supernatural power. According to Eunapius,

> In the midst of her bacchic and frenzied flow of speech she became silent, as though her voice had been cut off, and after a short interval she cried: "What is this? My kinsman Philometor riding in a carriage! The carriage has been overturned in a rough place! His legs are in danger! Oh, his servants have dragged him out unharmed, except for cuts on his elbows and hands—not dangerous ones. He is being carried on a stretcher, groaning loudly." This is what she said, and it was so. By this all were convinced that Sosipatra was omnipresent, and, as the philosophers say about the gods, nothing happened without her being there to see. (Wright, 1968, pp. 415–416)[2]

Sosipatra's clairvoyance was not an isolated incident. In another anecdote Eunapius tells us that she clairvoyantly witnessed a ritual performed by her student Maximus and accurately foretold the lives of her own children. Among later Platonists the exercise of supernatural power was not uncommon. Iamblichus, the founder of the theurgic school of Platonism, demonstrated clairvoyance, was reported to levitate, and on one occasion is said to have conjured up two spirits at the baths of Gadara (Wright, 1968, pp. 367–370). Marinus reports that his teacher Proclus received visitations from the goddess Athena, performed miraculous healings, and caused it to rain in Attica (Edwards, 2000, pp. 101–105). Plotinus intuitively realized that Porphyry was contemplating suicide and suggested a vacation to Sicily, an insight probably understandable to contemporary therapists (Porphyry, *Life of Plotinus*, in Armstrong, 1966–1988, Vol. 1, p. 37).[3] Yet at the same time, Plotinus, who has been praised by twentieth-century scholars for his rationalism and freedom from occult interests, clairvoyantly identified a thief, accurately foretold the lives of the children who lived with him, and said that he had once been attacked by a sorcerer whose spell caused his body to be squeezed tight (Armstrong, 1966–1988, Vol. 1, pp. 33–37).

Reports of supernatural occurrences were not unexpected among later Platonists. They formed part of their vision of human nature, one that included the development of psychic powers such as clairvoyance, telepathy, and precognition, supernormal abilities that Yoga traditions describe as *siddhis*. The development of such powers in Yoga is the result of exercises designed to transform the body and mind, and adepts in Yoga who attain these powers are known as *siddhas* (White, 1996, pp. 2, 354n.4). I will argue that *siddhas* existed in the West and were known as theurgists, Platonic adepts who performed divine action: *theios ergon*.[4] Like their South Asian counterparts, Platonic theurgists believed the soul mirrors a hierarchy of cosmic realities and that by nurturing these powers they could transform and perfect their lives. The sixth-century Platonist Hierocles explains that philosophy must include theurgic rites: "Philosophy is united with the art of sacred things since this art is concerned with the purification of the luminous body, *but if you separate philosophical thinking from this art, you will find that it no longer has the same power*" (Hadot, 2004, p. 48; modified, italics added).

Philosophy in the West long ago became an entirely intellectual enterprise separated from the art of sacred things. Philosophy no longer focuses on transforming the soul's affective energies, aligning them to their correspondences in the cosmos or recovering the soul's luminous body. This affective aspect of philosophy, communicated through the physical presence of sages, is no longer recognized today, which is why no one goes to contemporary philosophers for self-transformation. Yet the Platonists maintained—like yogis today—that each soul possesses a subtle body that can be transformed into an *augoeides ochēma*, a luminous vehicle with supernatural powers. Hierocles' sacred art is theurgy, rituals that purify and strengthen the subtle body and allow the soul to share in the life of the gods and their creation—demiurgy. The disciplines of theurgy, like those of Yoga, include attention to diet, exercise, and the care of both physical and subtle bodies. Hierocles explains:

> We must take care of the purity relating to our luminous body (*augoeides*), which the *Oracles* call the subtle vehicle of the soul. *Such purity extends to our food, our drink, and to the entire regimen of our mortal body in which the luminous body resides*, as it breathes life into the inanimate body and maintains its harmony. For, the immaterial body is a kind of life, which engenders life within matter. . . . (Hadot, 2004, p. 37n.133; modified, italics added)

Although the exercise of supernatural powers was part of the repertoire of Platonic philosophers, contemporary scholars ordinarily dismiss such stories as hagiographical exaggerations, the superstitious residue of a credulous culture. In an effort to see Platonic philosophers as our "rational" ancestors, scholars have uprooted their philosophy from the ground of their experience and preserve only a caricature of their tradition. It may be disconcerting to contemporary sensibilities, but supernatural abilities were recognized as an integral part of the later Platonic tradition, and I hope to demonstrate that the exercise of these powers was entirely consistent with Platonic philosophy and is part of our Western heritage. Platonic philosophers who attained perfection were recognized as far more than "intellectuals." They were designated as *theioi*, deified souls, and their exercise of supernatural power was consistent with their metaphysics, ethics, and even their politics.

Throughout this chapter I use the term supernatural rather than "supernormal," the term preferred by F. W. H. Myers and others to refer to anomalous and paranormal events. Myers expressed "grave objections" to the use of "supernatural" to describe paranormal or psychic phenomena because, as he put it, it "assumes that there is something outside nature" that can arbitrarily break its laws (Myers, 1903, Vol. 1, p. xxii). It is, however, the *Christian* supernatural to which Myers objects since it is removed not only from a "fallen" nature but from any kind of shared human participation. As conceived by Neoplatonists, "supernatural" has an entirely different meaning. The term *huperphuēs* (*huper* = above + *phuēs* = natural) was coined by Iamblichus himself and was understood within a Pythagorean and nondual metaphysical context. *Huperphuēs* refers to what is prior to nature and functions as its *archē* or originating principle. As principle of the natural, the "supernatural" is revealed through nature and is contrasted with *para phusin* = "opposed to nature" (Iamblichus, *Myst.* 159.1–3).[5] For a Pythagorean, the supernatural includes numbers, which function as the invisible principles of material reality. For Neoplatonists the natural world is entirely embedded and rooted in the supernatural of which it is the manifestation. I see no justification for avoiding the use of this term in a Neoplatonic context simply because it was misunderstood by Christians. When Myers explains why he objects to "supernatural" it is because of his inherited Christian (mis)understanding of the term. It is time to recover the Neoplatonic supernatural as a valid term that sees nature as the "body" of the supernatural. They are in profound continuity. In fact, there is nothing in nature where the Neoplatonic supernatural is not present, and this is why supernatural events are akin to discovering geometric patterns in the natural world.

Platonic philosophers lived in a world where supernatural principles were continually unfolding in nature, and they imagined themselves as participating in this activity. Their metaphysics reflects this understanding and may help provide a conceptual framework for experiences denied in the current physicalist interpretation of reality. But contemporary scholars have misread the Platonists by anachronistically projecting on them a physicalist worldview that cannot accept, let alone account for, the reality of supernatural experiences.[6] Most scholars accept our contemporary assumption that consciousness is merely an epiphenomenon of the material brain. Supernatural powers that cannot be explained by the materialist model are, therefore, considered impossible. This is why the supernatural powers of the Platonists are either ignored or explained away. Yet it would be another kind of anachronistic mistake simply to adopt the later Platonists' frame of reality as our own. The challenge is to build a bridge between the physicalist worldview in which the supernatural is nonexistent and the anomalous experiences that occur to so many and for which we have no explanation. We live in a profound disconnect between private experience and public discourse, and I believe the later Platonists left a framework, a kind of visionary taxonomy, that might help us bridge this gap, not by denying the discoveries of science or by literalizing anomalous experiences into new forms of orthodoxy but by inviting us into dimensions of experience and reflection that they deeply and intelligently explored. The worldview of the later Platonists may serve *heuristically* as a map of how some of the most brilliant minds in Western history explored a dimension of human experience now lost to us; what F. W. H. Myers referred to as the *subliminal*, William James as *the more*, Carl Jung as the *unconscious*, and what Michael Murphy has characterized as the evolutionary potential of humanity.[7] The Platonists combined acute intellectual and mathematical genius with a profound visionary capacity to engage and understand supernatural experiences.

280 GREGORY SHAW

THE PHILOSOPHIC CONTEXT

> Altars in honor of Plotinus are still warm, and his books are in the
> hands of the educated more so than the dialogues of Plato.
>
> —Eunapius, *The Lives of the Philosophers*[8]

Plotinus (204/205–270 CE) is the founder of Neoplatonism, yet he maintained that he was simply following the teachings of Plato and the ancients such as Pythagoras (*Enn.* V.1.8.10–14). Plotinus' predecessor, Numenius of Apamea (late second century CE), argued that Plato's teachings had been misinterpreted by logicians who failed to grasp the existential and initiatory dimension of his dialogues. Reestablishing the principles of exegesis by applying Plato's metaphysical realities to our psychological states, Numenius reasserted the mystagogic dimension of Plato's philosophy. It is this Platonism, understood as a transformative discipline, that came to be known as Neoplatonism, and although its seeds were planted by Numenius, its growth is indebted almost entirely to the genius of Plotinus. He took the interpretive principles of Numenius and animated them in ways that were stunningly original. The metaphysical realities of Plato: the One and Good, the Demiurge, and the World Soul, were not mere conceptual categories for Plotinus but *personal experiences.* Plotinus led his students and his readers into *states of identification* with these realities. His goal, boldly stated, was "not merely to be sinless but to be god" (*Enn.* I.2.6.3). Plotinus embodied, transmitted, and established this mystagogy and subsequent Platonists followed his lead; thus was born the school of *Neo*platonism that lasted from the early third century to 529 CE when the Academy in Athens was closed by the Christian emperor Justinian.

Although Plotinus claimed only to be an interpreter of Plato and Pythagoras, his innovations had already been recognized by his contemporaries. Longinus said that Plotinus "had an original way of thinking . . . and explained the principles of the Platonists and Pythagoreans more clearly than anyone before him" (Armstrong, 1966–1988, Vol. 1, p. 61). The Platonic dialogues became a vehicle for Plotinus to communicate a spiritual vision perhaps unmatched in the history of thought. His philosophy is marked by dynamism and fluidity, and despite the efforts of many later Platonists and contemporary scholars, Plotinus' thought defies systematization. According to his biographer, Porphyry, Plotinus' teaching always began with questions from students. A text might be read—from Plato, Aristotle, or some more recent philosopher—along with a question, and Plotinus would comment, weaving his insights into the context of the Platonic dialogues. His teaching was simply "a conversation" among students with varied degrees of sophistication. As might be expected, there was often a good bit of confusion—"pointless chatter" as Porphyry put it—and, consistent with his style, Plotinus often did not make the coherence of his arguments explicit (Armstrong, 1966–1988, Vol. 1, p. 11).

What may be gleaned from his *Enneads*, the record of these "conversations" and their extended responses by Plotinus, is as unsystematic today as when they initially occurred, so any presentation of Plotinus' philosophy must be, to some degree, idiosyncratic. Nevertheless, there is a central motif: the human soul is in flux, capable of being lifted to the status of a god or being dragged down to the level of a beast. And this dynamism and movement of the human soul is an expression of a more universal dynamism and flux that is rooted in the One and Good, the source of all reality.

As E. R. Dodds (1973) eloquently explained, for Plotinus "all Being derives from the overspill of a single infinite reservoir of force, a reservoir which is, in Blake's language, not a cistern but a fountain," an infinite upwelling of creative power (p. 130). The source of this fountain is known only through the stream that flows from it. It gives rise to Being and the Platonic Forms, not as static perfections but as dynamic activities. This fontal procession at the level of Forms is personified by Plato's Demiurge, the Maker of the World Soul and physical cosmos. Like the conductor of a cosmic symphony, the Demiurge—identified by Plotinus with Aristotle's Divine Mind (*Nous*)—weaves these fontal streams into a vast Soul that carries them to their sensible expression, the physical world. This defines three levels of reality for Plotinus: (1) The One and Good—the hidden font of Being that is beyond being; (2) Being-Mind-Demiurge—the active principle of intelligence that builds the framework of reality; and (3) the World Soul—the expression of this intelligence as a living cosmos, including our natural world. Schematically, these levels of reality are sketched in Figure 8.1. For Plotinus, human souls are currents of this fountain. In the words of Ralph Waldo Emerson (1883) who read the Neoplatonists deeply, "man is a stream whose source is hidden" (p. 252).

The problem that Plotinus addresses throughout the *Enneads* is existential: What happens when the stream runs dry? What can be done when we become so congealed in the density of physical life that we lose awareness of the divine principles that bring us here? The outflow, or procession of the One, must have a reciprocal inflow or return, and to facilitate the soul's return is the goal of Plotinus' philosophy. He had little interest in puzzling over metaphysics or levels of reality as purely intellectual problems. Properly understood, Plotinus' *Enneads* are therapeutic reflections to lead us out of fixations and back to our infinite and fontal source.

The key to the therapeutic dynamism of the *Enneads* is Plotinus' solution to the problem of how the One becomes Many and subsequently how physical existence participates in the Forms. Instead of following the models outlined by Plato in which participants are described as imitators or parts of the One (or of Forms), Plotinus asserted that the One "gives what it does *not* have" (*Enn.* V.3.15). This begins a revolutionary turn in metaphysics. Plotinus explains: "How then do all things come from the One, which is simple and has in it no diverse variety, or any kind of duality? It is because there is *nothing* in it that all things come from it: in order that being may exist, *the One is not being*, but the generator of being" (*Enn.* V.2.1.3–8; italics added). As cause of multiplicity and being

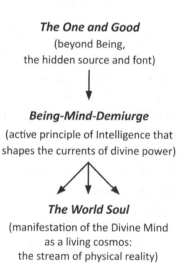

The One and Good
(beyond Being,
the hidden source and font)

Being-Mind-Demiurge
(active principle of Intelligence that
shapes the currents of divine power)

The World Soul
(manifestation of the Divine Mind
as a living cosmos:
the stream of physical reality)

Figure 8.1.   Plotinus' three levels of reality.

the One bestows what it does not possess. Its participants are therefore not imitators or diminished *parts* of the One but *full manifestations* in different orders of reality, and each receives its gift in a unique way. The One, then, remains hidden but is "revealed" as causal generator of all beings. To receive this fontal procession is to reveal what remains hidden in the One, and this mirroring of what is invisible and undivided, this *return* and manifestation of the stream, establishes each grade of reality: the fontal power of the One is revealed as Being-Mind-Demiurge, and the Demiurge is revealed—and mirrored—in the World Soul (Armstrong, 1986, p. 162). Plotinian procession from the One might be imagined as a series of expanding circles, originating from and returning to their source. What occurs at the highest level, when the power of the One establishes the multiplicity of Forms, also happens at the level of the human soul, but our return to higher principles is interrupted by the trauma of birth and embodiment (Plato, *Timaeus* 43). Nevertheless, souls can return to their origin by mirroring the divine source that gives them existence, but since the origin has "no duality" it cannot be discursively known. Plotinus explains:

> But if we do not have it in knowledge, do we have it at all? We have it in such a way that we speak about it, but do not speak it. For we say what it is not, but we do not say what it is: so that we speak about it from what comes after it. But we are not prevented from having it, even if we do not speak it. (*Enn.* V.3.14.3–8)

This is not simply an epistemological observation for Plotinus; it is an existential confession. He continues:

> Is this enough? Can we stop, content with that insight? No. My soul is even more in labor pain. Is she perhaps ripe enough so that she can give birth, having reached the fullness of her labor, in her longing for the One? No. We must call up yet another incantation to find some relief for her pain. Might there be some relief from what we have said already if we sang it over and over again? What spell can we find that has something new in it? (*Enn.* V.3.17.15–21)

Plotinus' philosophical reflections are *incantations* to strip him—and us—of discursive thinking and lead us nakedly into the *activity* of the One. He concludes this passage with the exhortation: "Take away everything!"

We may, then, appreciate Plotinus' *Enneads* as philosophic evocations. Trying to understand the *Enneads* solely as a "metaphysical system"—which many scholars still attempt to do—is to misread and misunderstand Plotinus. His metaphysical discourse was designed to *liberate* readers from discursive metaphysics and lead them to an ineffable presence he describes as the soul's "ancient nature" (*archaia phusis*). In describing the soul's relation to the One, Plotinus uses the image of a choir and its director:

> We are always around it but do not always look to it; it is like a choral dance: in the order of its singing the choir keeps round its conductor but may sometimes turn away, so that he is out of their sight, but when it turns back to him it sings beautifully and is truly with him; so we too are always around him—and if we were not, we should be totally dissolved and no longer exist—but not always turned to him; but when we do look to him, then we are at our goal and at rest and do not sing out of tune as *we truly dance our god-inspired dance around him*. (*Enn.* VI.9.8; italics added)

The technical term Plotinus uses to describe this "god-inspired dance" is contemplation (*theōria*). Plotinian contemplation is not "thinking" as we understand it; it is, rather, turning the soul back to the fontal activity of the One, a turning that is shared by every life that proceeds from the One. In *Ennead* III.8.1, Plotinus recites another incantation about this activity.

> Suppose we said, playing at first before we set out to be serious, that all things aspire to contemplation (*theōria*), and direct their gaze to this end—not only rational but irrational living things, and the power of growth in plants, and the earth which brings them forth—and that all attain to it as far as possible for them in their natural state, but different things contemplate and attain their end in different ways, some truly, and some only having an imitation and image of this true end—could anyone endure so strange a thesis?

Nature itself is drawn toward contemplation. Plants, animals, human beings, and even the earth are all—with more or less intensity—engaged in contemplation of Unity. Later, Plotinus says that the "god-inspired dance" of contemplation is itself *the* creative act, the engine of cosmogenesis (Gatti, 1996, pp. 32–34). "All things," he says, "come from contemplation" (*Enn.* III.8.7). To enter the imagined world of Plotinian contemplation is to enter an immense vortex whose life is permeated by the magnetism of the One at its core. From the Divine Mind and constant rhythms of the stars to the fitful drama of human souls and even the brief life of garden vegetables, all things are drawn to *and* are expressions of the One. The entire cosmos is ordered and sustained by the different intensities and expressions of this magnetism.

When Plotinus describes the cosmos and the soul as erotically charged he invites us, as did Plato, to imagine our own experiences of this magnetism. In the *Symposium* (186a–b; 207a–c), Plato describes the gradations of this experience in terms of our different attractions to the beauty of the One. Like Plotinus, he reminds us that the stars, animals, and even plants are drawn irresistibly by its magnetic power. Both Plato and Plotinus envision an erotic cosmos, a world revealed and sustained by its collective attraction to the One. And our attraction *for* the One is, paradoxically, an expression *of* the One itself in its own ceaseless production of multiplicity. Describing the One as the font of power, Plotinus says:

> If the One did not exist, neither would all things, nor would Divine Mind be the first and universal life. What is above life is cause of life; for the activity of life, which is all things, is not first, but itself flows out, so to speak, as if from a spring. *For think of a spring which has no other origin, but gives the whole of itself to rivers, and is not used up by the rivers but remains itself at rest* . . . or think of the life sap of a huge plant, which moves through the whole of it while its origin remains and is not dispersed over the whole, since it is, as it were, firmly settled in the root. . . . [I]t is a wonder how the multiplicity of life comes from what is not multiple, and yet the multiplicity would not exist if what was not multiple did not exist before it. (*Enn.* III.8.10; italics added)

The common element in these metaphors is that of a unity that permeates multiplicity: the fontal spring and its rivers; the root sap and its branches; the conductor and his choir; and perhaps most simply, the circle, its center, and the radii emanating from it. It is this geometrical image that serves Plotinus as a glyph for his entire metaphysical vision, and its natural image is the sun. Describing how the Divine Mind comes from the One, Plotinus says:

> How did it come to be then? And what are we to think of as surrounding the One in its repose? It must be a radiation from it while it

remains unchanged, like the bright light of the sun which, so to speak, runs round it, springing from it continually while it remains unchanged. (*Enn.* V.1.6)

The Divine Mind reveals the One as sunlight reveals the sun. The Divine Mind, Plotinus says, "springs from the One, and is an outflow and development from it" (*Enn.* VI.8.18.18–21).[9] It is, so to speak, the light in which the One sees itself. But this seeing is not like seeing an object; there is no separation between the seer and what is seen, and it is this very activity of seeing-and-being the One that constitutes the Divine Mind; and this reality, in turn, sees *itself* through the divided light of the World Soul that flows from it just as it flows out of the One. Plotinus' vision is a pulsing and unbroken continuity from center to periphery (Plotinus' identification between knower and known is referred to as the "identity theory of truth"; see Chapter 9 on Patañjali, who shared this view).

The One is the ineffable source of all reality, pouring out like radial lines that remain tethered to their center. Plotinus's multiplicity remains rooted in unity; as he says (*Enn.* III.8.10), "in each and every thing there is some *one* to which you will trace it back" until we reach the originating One which "fills us with wonder." Individual souls are moved by centripetal attraction to this One while its magnetic power simultaneously breathes out to the periphery, creating and sustaining the very lives that are drawn back to it. Plotinus says of the One, "he is, if we may say so, borne to his own interior, as if he were in love with himself" (*Enn.* VI.8.16.12–13). In this light, even the dispersed life of the human soul becomes, for Plotinus, part of the "*inner life* of the One" (Bussanich, 1996, p. 63). Our very attraction to the One is a gift that comes from the One, so all centripetal movements to the source are rooted in the centrifugal movement that pours out of it. Plotinus describes an erotically charged cosmos that is continually created and dissolved by the self-attraction to its source.

In this vision the cosmos is a revelation of the One. Material reality may initially alienate us, but Plotinus believed the cosmos is choreographed by the One (*Enn.* III.6.17.18) according to number (IV.4.35) and proportion (III.3.6). He thus approved of the "wise men of old" (IV.3.11) who built statues and temples to contact the gods. Plotinus also admired the hieroglyphs in Egyptian temples because they "reveal the non-discursiveness of the spiritual world" (V.8.6). The presence of divine power,

Plotinus says, extends into the "nature of stones and herbs with wondrous results" (IV.4.35). Even sense perception is rooted in the Forms (V.3.9). It would seem that developing this choreography into practices that unite souls with divine activity would have been perfectly consistent with Plotinus' principles. It is. And yet the development of such practices by Iamblichus, under the name of theurgy, was judged to be so different from Plotinus' Platonism that later Platonists distinguished themselves as being either theurgists like Iamblichus or philosophers like Plotinus (Athanassiadi, 1999, p. 57). Before exploring the school of Iamblichus as a development of Plotinus's vision we need to ask why it is that Plotinus himself did not develop embodied theurgic practices.

The answer is Gnosticism. As a defender of Platonism, Plotinus saw the Gnostics as a threat. There were Gnostics among his students in Rome, and he had encountered Gnostics in Alexandria so he was familiar with their doctrines. According to Plotinus, Gnostics were anti-cosmic dualists opposed to the unified vision he embraced, and he devoted four entire treatises (*Enn.* III.8; V.8; V.5; II.9) to refuting them. Plotinus specifically criticized their dualism and myth of the fall of Sophia as cause for the creation and embodiment of souls. He also ridiculed their arrogant claims to reach the level of the World Soul as "wishful thinking" (*Enn.* II.9.9.49) and insisted that the soul should coordinate itself with the visible cosmos rather than trying to escape it as the Gnostics encouraged.

Plotinus' positive assessment of the physical cosmos and his intuition that contemplation creates and sustains the cosmos were due, in part, to his effort to refute the Gnostics' dualism and their insistence that the soul's divinization removes it from the cosmos. In response to gnostic views of matter, evil, and the soul, Plotinus presented a positive account of the material world and the soul's capacity for uniting with the One. But Plotinus' encounter with the Gnostics left a defining mark on his understanding of the soul. In *Ennead* IV.8, "On the Descent of the Soul," Plotinus initially explains the soul's existence as reflecting—in its ontological rank—the procession and return of the One. This gives the soul a kind of double life: "Souls, then, become, one might say, amphibious, by necessity living in part in the intelligible world and in part here below" (IV.8.4). This is traditional Platonic teaching, but to answer the question as to *how* the soul lives in the intelligible Plotinus admittedly diverges from his tradition by claiming that "our soul does not altogether come down, but there is *always* something of it in the intelligible" (*Enn.*

IV.8.8.1–4; italics added). As he says elsewhere: "[our] heads remain firmly set in heaven" (*Enn.* IV.3.12). Despite his polemic against the Gnostics, Plotinus seems to have absorbed their distrust of the material world. The essence of the Plotinian soul deigns never to enter a material body, and the evils the soul encounters are caused entirely by matter.

Although Plotinus argues for the divinity of the world against the Gnostics and characterizes matter as an "intelligible Form" and ultimate procession of the One (*Enn.*V.8.7), he also maintains that matter—as the furthest departure from the Good—is evil, "primal and absolute evil" (*Enn.* I.8.3). Consequently, as he outlines in *Ennead* V.8.14, to be deified the soul must *escape* from the evil of matter and withdraw to its unfallen essence. The imagery and terms Plotinus employs to portray the soul's fall into material reality betray the influence of Gnostic descriptions of the fall of Sophia. Plotinus says the soul's inclination to the body is not a true descent but only an illumination (*ellampsis*) of what is below while its essence remains above the material world (*Enn.* I.1.12). Similarly, he says the Gnostic Sophia does not descend into matter "but only illuminates (*ellampsai*) the darkness" (*Enn.* II.9.10). Thus, it appears that Plotinus absorbed the dualist imagery he criticized in the Gnostics.[10] The divinization of soul as recovery of its unfallen condition separated from the evil of the material cosmos seems to conflict with Plotinus' nondualist vision. It may be one of the great ironies of the Platonic tradition that its greatest visionary and the architect of its most profound mystagogy remained, in some sense, outside of the structure that he explained more brilliantly than anyone.

Plotinus had also employed imagery from Greek religion to initiate souls into ineffable states of divinization: he spoke of becoming possessed by gods. In one of his "thought experiments" where the soul visualizes the sphere of the cosmos, Plotinus enjoins us to "invoke the God, the creator of the sphere you now hold, and pray him to enter" (*Enn.* V.8.9). This god, whom Platonists identified as Zeus, enters his sphere whereupon the visionary "must give himself up to what is within and become, instead of one who sees, *an object of vision for another* who contemplates him shining out with thoughts of the kind which come from that world" (*Enn.* V.8.11). In Plotinian mystagogy we do not see the god, *the god sees through us*. It is precisely this experience of entering the activity of a god that is developed by Plotinus' successor, Iamblichus.

Iamblichus (ca. 240–ca. 325 CE) had once been the student of Porphyry and after returning from Rome to his native Syria he initiated students into ritual *practices* that were rooted in the unified vision of Plotinus. After the death of Plotinus, Iamblichus and Porphyry were the leading Platonists of their time. Iamblichus added to Plotinus' vision a Neopythagorean solution to the problem of embodiment, and this put him at odds with his former teacher. Porphyry wrote his *Life of Plotinus* as an implicit critique of Iamblichus and explicitly criticized the practice of theurgy in his *Letter to Anebo* (Saffrey & Segonds, 2012, p. xlv). Yet Iamblichus was not opposed to Plotinus; he adopted his metaphysical vision and—with Neopythagorean adjustments—had made it his own. He was indebted most particularly to Plotinus' understanding that the One "gives what it does not have," for this principle transforms the world into a symbolic landscape where the One is revealed *everywhere*. Iamblichus developed a visionary discipline whereby the traces of Plotinus' One could be entered in theurgic rites, but he objected to two teachings of Plotinus: (1) that sensible matter, as the outermost fringe of divine emanation, is absolute evil; and (2) that the soul never fully descends into this world. Iamblichus criticized these doctrines for the same reason that Plotinus had criticized the Gnostics: they are metaphysically dualist and conflict—Iamblichus claimed—with the teachings of Plato and the ancients.[11] These two doctrines are intrinsically related: if matter is evil the soul should eschew all contact with it and recover its unfallen essence as Plotinus taught. Iamblichus' theory of the completely descended soul, by contrast, is complemented by his view that sensible matter is entirely good.[12] Iamblichus maintained that material objects can be experienced as the outflow of the One if we can learn to perceive it. Plotinus himself had coined the term for this kind of seeing: possessing the "eyes of Lynceus," the Argonaut who saw treasures buried in the earth (*Enn.* V.8.4). It is, again, ironic that it was not Plotinus but his successor, Iamblichus, who used these eyes to develop his theurgic school. Iamblichus exorcised the dualist elements of Plotinus' vision with a Pythagorean interpretation of matter as ultimately rooted in the One. The soul no longer must escape from the evil of matter to unite with the One because the One *is* the material cosmos and is present even in "stones, plants, animals, and human beings" (Iamblichus, *Myst.* 233.9–13). The material objects that were obstacles for Plotinus become icons that unite theurgists with divinity.

PLATONIC THEURGY

> I would be ashamed before the divine Iamblichus if I invented any-
> thing new about these traditions for he was the best interpreter of
> divine realities.
>
> —Damascius, *Problems and Solutions Concerning First Principles* [13]

Iamblichus successfully transformed the philosophic vision of Plotinus
into a living practice applicable to the common man as well as to philosophers. As J. M. P. Lowry put it, Iamblichus "carried the obvious Plotinian
philosophical standpoint to its limits . . . [which is] that philosophy as
intellectual is discursive and as such, *divided*, and so incapable of the
highest possibility—union with the undivided" (Lowry, 1980, p. 21; italics added). Although reason cannot unite the soul with the One, Iamblichus believed the One permeates all reality so its unifying streams can be
entered from virtually any realm of existence, and theurgic rituals that
weave us into the rhythms of nature were ways to enter the choreography
of the One. In Plotinus' terms, by entering this activity "*we truly dance
our god-inspired dance.*" The logic of Plotinus' insight is that philosophy
as a rational exercise must cede to a deeper—undivided—practice exemplified in religious rituals, and by wedding Plotinian reflections to traditional sacrifices and divinational rites Iamblichus transforms Platonism
into a kind of religion. He made "a synthesis of divine philosophy and the
worship of the gods" (Iamblichus, trans. 1991, p. 167). [14]

It is precisely this synthesis that many contemporary scholars have
criticized as a fall into superstition and a loss of rationality. [15] Yet this
critique is more a reflection of the limited view of many post-Enlightenment thinkers about what constitutes philosophy. To use Hierocles' language, theirs is a philosophy without "the art of sacred things," philosophy without transformative *power*. The Neoplatonists were brilliant intellectuals, but they were primarily visionaries, recipients of revelations that
were the root and sap of their metaphysical systems. To try to understand
Neoplatonism by focusing only on their conceptual explanations misses
the visionary element that animates their metaphysics. For these Platonists theurgy deepened and guided rationality to its divine roots: theurgy
was the *culmination* of philosophy, *the embodied realization of Plotinus'
most profound insights*. The preference for "Plotinian rationalism" over
theurgy, therefore, betrays a misunderstanding of Plotinus who warned

against the overvaluation of rational thinking. He seemed to anticipate that his "incantations" would be misread as sophisticated *descriptions* of the noetic world. Those who read Plotinus in this way are, he says,

> like people at religious festivals who by their gluttony stuff themselves with things which it is not lawful for those going in to the gods to take, thinking that these [descriptions] are more obviously real than the vision of the god. . . . (*Enn.* V.5.11)

It is this gluttony that has transformed Plotinus into a "rational" mystic preferred by scholars over the "irrational" Iamblichus. Against this *misreading* of both Platonists, I would argue that it was Plotinus' dualism—not his rationality—that kept him from developing an embodied practice like theurgy.

Iamblichus faced complexities that Plotinus did not need to address. Because the Iamblichean soul is fully embodied, it suffers an alienation not fully explored by Plotinus. According to Iamblichus the embodied soul becomes "self-alienated" (Shaw, 1995, pp. 98–102). Following Plato's *Timaeus*, Iamblichus maintains that the human soul, like the World Soul, is a mean between extremes; it contains divinely numbered proportions (*logoi*) and, with the Demiurge, projects these *logoi* outside itself as it descends into a body. The soul sews itself into the fabric of the material world yet its collaboration with the Demiurge comes at a cost. Although immortal, the soul becomes mortal, alienated from its own divinity and unable to regain its place in the divine hierarchy. Iamblichus presents this condition in stark terms:

> The soul is a mean not only between the divided and the undivided, the remaining and the proceeding, the noetic and the irrational, but also between the uncreated and the created. . . . *Thus, that which is immortal in the soul is filled completely with mortality and no longer remains only immortal.* . . . (Shaw, 1995, pp. 99–100)

Yet the soul can recover its divinity by performing rituals using elements from nature that correspond to the *logoi* projected in the soul's embodiment. The soul's divinization is not realized by withdrawing from the world—as it is with Plotinus—but by including material objects in rituals that unite the soul with the activity of the Demiurge. Theurgists aimed to bring themselves into resonance with this activity by using elements capable of transmitting the power of the gods. Among these elements were stones, plants, animals, and aromatics, less material elements such as prayers and chants, as well as immaterial elements such as visualized images (Shaw, 1995, pp. 162–215). Iamblichus does not provide concrete examples of theurgic rites—no recipes, liturgies, or spells—and because the techniques he alludes to are found in the books of late antique magicians many scholars dismissed Iamblichus as representing a decline in Platonic philosophy. Yet leading Platonists like Proclus and Damascius were also theurgists and followed Iamblichus' modifications to Plotinus' philosophy, namely, that (1) matter, as manifestation of the One, is not evil, and (2) the human soul is fully embodied. The consequence of these doctrines is that (1) the soul returns to the One by ritually appropriating material objects, and (2) the body is no longer an obstacle but becomes an icon through which the soul returns to the One.

This deeper involvement in the material cosmos requires a richer and more diverse metaphysical imagination. The One of Plotinus *excludes* multiplicity. His soteriology is escapist. As Jean Trouillard (1965) put it, Plotinus "returns to the One through a severe negation. . . . He goes to the divinity by night" (pp. 23–25).[16] Iamblichus goes by day. He understands the negation of Plotinus as a cathartic and preliminary step to prepare the soul to enter the *activity* of the One revealed in the generosity of the Demiurge, in stars, animals, plants, and even stones, and finally in theurgic rituals preserved by sacred races (Shaw, 1995, pp. 37–38). The One of Iamblichus *includes* multiplicity. Theurgists understand that all measures that shape the world are *powers* through which the One reveals itself (Shaw, 2005, p. 162n.58). In Plotinian terms, theurgists recognize *how* the One gives what it does not have and they enter its activity: *by dancing their god-inspired dance they become the dance.* Iamblichus *incarnates* the Plotinian vision. Theurgists include all levels of physical and psychic reality in their spiritual practice, an increased complexity that requires a new understanding of the soul.

Plotinus' vision presents an unbroken continuity from the One to sensible matter, but when pressed to address problems of the soul, he employs dualist solutions and the continuity is lost. Iamblichus, faced with the same existential problems, preserves the continuity by using Pythagorean principles. With the Law of Mean Terms, Iamblichus joins the One to the Many and applies it to all oppositions: spirit and matter, eternity and time, soul and body. Iamblichus found precedent for the Law of

Mean Terms in the *Timaeus* (31c) where Plato explains it in cosmogonic and mathematical terms:

> Two things alone cannot be satisfactorily united without a third; for there must be some bond between them drawing them together. And of all bonds the best is that which makes itself and the terms it connects a unity in the fullest sense; and it is of the nature of a continued geometrical proportion (*analogia*) to effect this most perfectly. (Cornford, 1935, p. 44)

In a geometric proportion the first number is to the middle as the middle is to the last (e.g., 2:4::4:8), and the last is to the middle as the middle is to the first (8:4::4:2). The mean thus joins the extremes and at the same time keeps them separate. With this principle Iamblichus solves the problem of how the soul experiences union with the One yet remains embodied. The theurgic symbol, whether it is a stone, hymn, or visualization, becomes *the mean* through which the soul—in a kind of imaginative rapture—joins with and yet remains distinct from the One. The Law of Mean Terms also addresses existential issues since, according to Plato, the soul is the mean of cosmogenesis and weaves unity with multiplicity, allowing the Forms to become embodied. According to Iamblichus, the soul is

> the mean (*meson*) between divisible and indivisible, corporeal and incorporeal beings; [it is] the totality (*plēroma*) of the universal ratios (*logoi*) and that which, after the Forms, serves the work of creation; [it is] that Life which, having proceeded from the Divine Mind (*nous*), has life itself and is the procession of the classes of Real Being as a whole to an inferior status. (Shaw, 1995, p. 71)

Iamblichus believed his definition reflected Plato's account in the *Timaeus* where the World Soul functions as a cosmogonic mean that unites opposites in mathematical proportions (*logoi*). In the case of human souls, however, our cooperation with the Demiurge causes souls to become self-alienated and identify with a single mortal body; to deny this, as Plotinus' doctrine of the undescended soul seems to do, would deny to the soul its demiurgic function. For Iamblichus, the dividedness and mortality of the embodied soul is not an error that could be erased by spiritual insight, for embodiment is the expression of divine activity. To escape from the body and the material world, therefore, would forfeit our participation in cosmogony. For Iamblichus, *mortality and self-alienation constitute the soul's very essence as human.* As Iamblichus put it, "that which is immortal in the soul is filled completely with mortality and no longer remains only immortal" (Shaw, 1995, p. 99). This is something Plotinus could never have said, but Iamblichus found an existential mean to provide continuity even between our mortal and immortal lives.

The existential mediating principle is described by Iamblichus as the *ochēma*, an "etheric body" that exists before and after the soul enters a physical body.[17] The function of the *ochēma* is implicit in Plato, for how else explain the disembodied journey of the "dead" warrior Er to the heavenly world in Book 10 of the *Republic*? While lying on his funeral pyre, Er spent ten days in the transphysical realm to witness souls between their incarnations and, after this revelation, he returned to his body. The question is: what kind of body did Er inhabit in the other world? It is the same question researchers ask of those who have near-death and out-of-body experiences today (Kelly, Greyson, & Kelly, 2007). When the physical body is clinically dead how do we experience anything and in what kind of body? These questions were answered by Iamblichus and later Platonists with the doctrine of the subtle body, the vehicle (*ochēma*) of the soul. It was the belief of all Platonists that the soul preexists its physical body, continues to exist after death, and after a period of time, descends into its next incarnation. According to Iamblichus, the soul's *ochēma* is made from eternal and universal ether through which the soul shares in the generation of the cosmos. This etheric body becomes the organizing vehicle for sense perception and through imagination *joins the soul to its physical body.* Yet, ultimately, this same vehicle, with inspired imagination, leads the soul back to its eternal etheric body.[18] Imagination (*phantasia*) plays a crucial role in this itinerary and, as we will see, Iamblichus distinguished two kinds.

The Platonic sources for the doctrine of the *ochēma* are the *Timaeus* (41e) where the Demiurge places souls in starry vehicles (*ochēmata*) and *Phaedrus* (247b) where the chariots of souls are, again, described as *ochēmata*. Plato refers to a translucent kind of air which he calls ether (*aithēr*) (*Timaeus* 58d), and Aristotle said ether is eternal, heavenly, and the primal body; it moves in a circle like the celestial bodies and is not subject to the changes of terrestrial life (*De Caelo* 270a–b). As regards its physical function, Aristotle (*De Gen. An.* 736b) says that each soul has a pneumatic body, which he likens to the heavenly ether, and this serves as *intermediary* between the immaterial soul and the physical senses. Later Platonists identify this pneumatic and etheric body with the *ochēma*, vehicle of the soul (Finamore, 1985, p. 2). The subtle body also appears prominently in Tantra and Yoga traditions (see Biernacki, this volume, for discussion of the subtle body in Tantra). As will be evident in my discussion of imagination, I follow Mircea Eliade's (1969) interpretation that these esoteric physiologies are "not conceptualizations, but *images* expressing transmundane experiences" (p. 289; italics added). Because Tantra, with its emphasis on ritual and visualization, developed in India in the fourth century CE, Eliade speculated that it was introduced from "the great Western mysteriosophic current," by which he means the teachings of Gnostics and Neoplatonists (pp. 200–202). However one interprets the evidence of chronological priority, the doctrine of an *ochēma* that mediates spirit and matter has no place in a physicalist view of existence. At the same time, the doctrine of a subtle body provides a conceptual framework for understanding anomalous events and out-of-body experiences that cannot be explained in a physicalist model. The question for us is how the *ochēma* functioned for later Platonists.

Augoeides Ochēma: Taking the Shape of the Gods

As intermediary between immortal soul and mortal body it is the *ochēma* through which the soul becomes bound to and released from the body. For Platonists, the cosmos is animated by a universal *ochēma*, etheric and immortal, and the individual soul possesses an *ochēma* that corresponds to its universal counterpart. The existential problem faced by theurgists was identical to that of Plotinus, but they did not—as he did—abandon the body and physical world. Their solution was to integrate the mortal body with its immortal *ochēma*; more precisely, to weave the *ochēma* back into its divine and universal form and thus recover their continuity with the One even while in their bodies. The divine form of the *ochēma* was characterized as radiant and luminous—*augoeides* ("shining form"). For all Neoplatonists, light is the metaphor of divinity, so to recover one's *augoeides* is to become divine. To use a Christian metaphor, theurgy was the art of resurrecting the *ochēma* from its tomb to a glorious body of light.[19]

The sixth-century Platonist, Damascius, describes the descent of the *augoeides* into a body:

> In heaven our *augoeides* is filled with a heavenly radiance that flows
> throughout its depths and strengthens it, making it even more divine.
> But here below, deprived of that radiance, it is dirtied, so to speak, and
> becomes darker and more material. Heedlessly, it falls to the earth, yet
> it remains essentially the same in its identity. (Westerink & Combès,
> 2003, pp. 43–44; my translation)

Damascius compares the vehicle of the soul to something like a balloon,
inflated with divine light before descent, flattened and emptied of light
after embodiment.

> Like a sponge, the soul loses nothing of its being but becomes porous
> and rarified or densely compacted. Just so, the immortal body of the
> soul . . . sometimes is made more spherical and sometimes less; some-
> times it is filled with divine light and sometimes filled with the stains
> of generative acts. . . . (Westerink & Combès, 2003, p. 17; my transla-
> tion).

The "stains of generative acts" are caused by our material appetites and
attachments. The *ochēma* begins its *human* itinerary as a deflated sphere,
identified with mortal impulses and buried in the sarcophagus of the
physical body. Because the *ochēma* joins soul to body and animates it, it
becomes identified with the body. The immortal soul and vehicle become
fused with animal life and sensation; through its *pneumatic ochēma* the
soul is literally "breathed" into the physical world. In this process, the
ochēma becomes dense and its imagination filled with habits of animal
life. Because these impulses trap us in the oppositions of this world, to
recover the vehicle's luminosity theurgists must cleanse the pneumatic
imagination of "the stains of generative acts."

As Damascius explains, the *ochēma* begins its *heavenly* itinerary as
augoeides, a spherical and eternal globe of light coordinated with the
cosmos. For Neoplatonists the sphere symbolizes wholeness and totality.
As a glyph it represents noetic intuition, undivided awareness with no
beginning or end. As Iamblichus said, "whenever the soul is especially
assimilated to the Divine Mind, our vehicle is made spherical and is
moved in a circle" (Iamblichus, trans. 1973, p. 153). The sphere is the
Neoplatonic symbol for Unity that includes multiplicity. In its descent to
the body the soul loses its spherical shape, which is to say, it loses its
divinity. The gods, Iamblichus says, are spheres, "exempt from all contra-

riety and free from every change. . . . The ethereal body of a god is completely liberated from all centripetal or centrifugal movement because it has neither tendency or *because it moves in a circle*" (*Myst.* 202.10–203.1). For theurgists the recovery of their spherical *augoeides* is not an escape from the body but its radical transformation. Through their inspired imagination theurgists enter a sphere; they enter a Unity that contains multiplicity and all contrary movements. This means that each impulse of the soul that ties it to embodied life is given symbolic expression. The very impulses that tear the soul from its universal life are ritually transformed into vehicles that sew it back into Unity. The theurgist honors both sides of this process—the splitting apart and the reuniting—as the diastolic and systolic phases of a divine pulse described by Neoplatonists as procession from and reversion to the One,[20] and in this activity, carefully coordinated in rituals, theurgists recover their *augoeides*. In the paradoxical terms of Iamblichus' psychology, this recovery fulfills the soul's identity as "a mean between the undivided and the divided . . . the noetic and the irrational, and the ungenerated and the generated" (Shaw, 1995, p. 99). Theurgists inhabit both realms. They become the pivot through which the procession of the One separates from *and* reunites with itself. In Heraclitus' terms they become "immortal mortals, mortal immortals." They stretch thinking and imagination into a unified state where oppositions collapse.

In embodiment the *ochēma* is deflated and punctured by the "divisions, collisions, impacts, reactions, and changes" that Iamblichus says are the unavoidable experiences of material life (*Myst.* 217.10–13). To harmonize these oppositions is to transform habits that trap the soul in contraries. To achieve this, Iamblichus encouraged prayer, which he defines as (1) gathering one's mental activities, (2) receiving the gifts of the gods, and (3) entering ineffable union (*Myst.* 237.12–238.5). Iamblichus explains its effect on the subtle body.

> The extended practice of prayer nurtures our intellect, greatly enlarges our receptacle of the gods, reveals to us the life of gods, accustoms our eyes to the brightness of divine light, and gradually perfects our capacity for intimate union with gods. . . . It gently elevates our habits of thought and gives us those of the gods. . . . It increases divine love and inflames the divine presence of the soul; *it cleanses the contrary tendencies of the soul and removes from its ethereal and luminous pneumatic vehicle everything inclined to generation.* . . . It makes those

who pray, if we may express it, companions of the gods. (*Myst.* 238.13–239.10)

For Iamblichus, to bear the light of the gods we must become gods. In theurgic prayer the soul is released from the oppositions of material life: discursive thinking is replaced by *noēsis*. The contrary tendencies of the pneumatic body are unified, which is to say they become spherical like the bodies of gods.

To take this shape—which is to enter unified imaginative activity— the *ochēma*'s receptacle must absorb divine light, a technique that Iamblichus calls *phōtagōgia* ("light-leading"), to unite the soul to a divinity. Iamblichus explains:

> *Phōtagōgia* somehow illuminates with divine light the ethereal and luminous vehicle of the soul (*aitherōdes kai augoeides ochēma*), from which divine visions (*phantasiai theiai*), initiated by the gods, take possession of our imagination. (*Myst.* 132.9–11)

Imagination attaches the soul to a mortal body through sensate images, yet imagination also leads the soul back to its union with the gods in *phōtagōgia*. For Iamblichus, *imagination* is dual: it mirrors sensate phenomena and effects the soul's self-alienation, yet imagination is also the medium for the appearances (*phasmata*) of, and union with, the gods. Iamblichus warns that "divine imaginations" (*theiai phantasiai*) should not be confused with sensate imagination or with images caused by human illness (*Myst.* 160.8–12). This needs to be explained.

To receive the gods and restore our luminous *ochēma*, the imagination must be turned, but the turn is not simply from the outer world to the inner. Noetic images are *not* immaterial "objects" accessible by introspection. The imaginative turn required in theurgy is not toward a different kind of object; *it is a different way of seeing altogether, a different kind of psychic activity*. The divinity of the image is revealed not by "what" one sees but by "the *way* in which one sees" (Hillman, 1997, p. 7). This determines whether our vision engages an imaginal world of noetic and autonomous entities as described by Henry Corbin or engages mere projections of the psyche.[21] The *mundus imaginalis* is not literally an objective "spirit world" nor is it merely subjective. The *imaginal* is a third alternative, a *third place*. For theurgists the imaginal world is rooted in the Divine Mind. It is the *place*, Corbin argues, where the soul enters the *visionary* paradoxes of the One as it simultaneously reveals and veils itself in *images*. Corbin scholar Christian Jambet (1983) says that the *mundus imaginalis* cannot be uprooted from Neoplatonic metaphysics without reducing it to mere imagination (p. 44). The imaginal reveries of Neoplatonic theurgists and Sufis are cosmogonic theophanies rooted in the One and entirely unlike ordinary imagination. These two kinds of imagination may also be compared to Coleridge's distinction between primary imagination, in which one enters God's "eternal act of creation," and mere fancy, the representations of sensate experience.[22] Iamblichus distinguished divine imagination from the merely human in the same way. Since this distinction is based not on whether the image is material or immaterial but rather on our *orientation* to the image, it may be easier to understand his otherwise puzzling description of how we see gods. He says:

> The presence of the gods gives us health of body, virtue of soul, purity of mind and, in a word, elevates all things in us to their proper principles. . . . It brings all things in the soul into proportion with the Divine Mind, makes light shine with noetic harmony, and *reveals the incorporeal as corporeal to the eyes of the soul by means of the eyes of the body.* (*Myst.* 81.10–82.1)

This is remarkably different in tone from Plotinus' exhortation to escape from bodily senses and physical reality (*Enn.* I.6.8). For Iamblichus the physical senses infused with inspired imagination become the portals of theophany. It is similar to the reveries Myers describes when the boundaries of supraliminal and subliminal, subjective and objective, become porous, when one enters the kind of *seeing* described by Wordsworth in *The Prelude*: "An auxiliar light / Came from my mind, which upon the setting sun / Bestowed new splendour" (quoted by Myers, 1903, Vol. 1, p. 111). Far from escaping from the material realm and the senses, the soul uses aesthetic experience as a path to its deification. Wordsworth again captures this sentiment: "In a world of life they live, / By sensible impressions not enthralled, / But by their quickening impulse made more prompt / To hold fit converse with the spiritual world" (Myers, 1903, Vol. 1, p. 111). In theurgic ritual the *ochēma*, purified by daily prayer, is filled with "auxiliar light" and becomes *augoeides*. Theurgists, Iamblichus says, "take on the shape of the gods" (*Myst.* 184.10). Yet the *ochēma* does not lift the soul out of the material realm—as if gods could not be present "down here"—rather, the *ochēma* becomes a vehicle for the appearance of the god *and* the deification of the soul. Physical sensation becomes theophanic. In this aesthetic fusion of the divine and the physical, the gods are seen "by means of the eyes of the body."

This embodied mystagogy was the theurgic development of Plotinus' vision. His "eyes of Lynceus," where all is transparent and the soul sees the Forms in the material world, are the eyes of theurgists seeing through their illuminated etheric vehicle, their *augoeides*. Theurgy is the art of transforming this subtle body, balancing the expansive and contractive impulses of the *ethereal pneuma*, until it recovers its spherical (unified) form. With the eyes of Lynceus, the theurgist possesses a kind of vision not accessible to those caught in the oppositions of material life. Proclus describes this perception as a feature of the *ochēma*:

> The ability to hear daimons is, for some, a hieratic power, for others it is natural, just as for some eyes it is possible to see visions that are invisible to other eyes. For the first vehicle (*proton ochēma*) of souls . . . can hear things inaudible to mortal hearing and see things invisible to mortal sight. (*Commentary on the Republic*, II.167.15–23, Kroll, 1899–1901, my translation)

Theurgists were not so naive as to take these voices and visions literally. The appearances (*phasmata*) of daimons, angels, or gods witnessed in their imagination were considered as both subjective *and* objective. They occupy both fields of perception and are, in a sense, a conflation of Coleridge's primary imagination and fancy. Proclus explains how theurgists understand these apparitions. I quote him at length because his analysis of spiritual visions might apply to spiritual or paranormal experiences today.

> The gods themselves are incorporeal but since those who see them possess bodies, the visions which issue from the gods to worthy recipients possess a certain quality from the gods who send them but also derive something from those who see them. *This is why the gods are seen yet not seen at all.* In fact, those who see the gods witness them *in the luminous (augoeides) garments of their souls.* Since the visions have physical extension and appear in the same kind of atmosphere they are akin to those who see them. However, since these visions emit divine light (*theios phōs*), possess effectiveness, and reveal the powers of the gods through visible symbols, they derive from the gods them-

selves who project them. This is why the ineffable symbols of the gods, expressed through images, are projected sometimes in one form and sometimes in another. . . . Each god is formless even if he is seen with a form. For the form is not in him but comes from him due to the incapacity of the viewer to see the formless without a form. *According to his nature he sees by means of forms.* . . . (*Commentary on the Republic*, I.39.5–17; 39.28–40.5; Kroll, 1899–1901, my translation)

Applied to the contemporary phenomena of near-death experiences (NDEs), Proclus' analysis explains why the NDEs of people in different cultures are described so differently. Indians might describe encounters with Krishna that include features of Hindu belief, while Christians might describe an encounter with Christ. These differences have caused skeptics to dismiss NDEs as nothing more than culturally influenced products of the imagination in the face of death (Kelly, Greyson, & Kelly, 2007). In one sense, Proclus would agree. They are products of the imagination but, significantly, for Proclus, they appear in one's pneumatic/etheric body, and—more significantly—they are rooted in divine realities. Theurgists recognized that incorporeal and ineffable realities can be "seen and grasped" only in images, and the images in which they appear are "according to our nature," that is, they are derived from our culture and personal history. Our images of the ineffable are necessarily shaped by our culture, our personal expectations, and our experiences. The divine can appear to us in no other way. But, again, it is not simply *what* appears that determines the theurgical power of the image; it is the *way* the image appears and this depends on how it is received. According to Iamblichus, the purification of one's *ochēma* determines whether visions exalt the soul or lead it into madness.

A Taxonomy of Apparitions

The capacity to see and hear incorporeal beings is a function of the transformed *ochēma*, and in theurgic divination this requires the experience of ecstasy (*ekstasis*).[23] Following Plato's *Phaedrus* where divine madness is described as superior to human sanity, Iamblichus says the *ekstasis* of theurgists unites them with beings superior to human wisdom. Yet not all ecstasies elevate the soul. Without proper preparation of the *ochēma*, Iamblichus says that ecstasy makes the soul degenerate, confused, and even more alienated from divinity (*Myst.* 158.8–159.4). In late antiquity there were many who claimed to be mediums of the gods, and Iamblichus had earned a reputation for his discernment of incorporeal beings. Eunapius reports that Iamblichus once attended a séance where an Egyptian invoked Apollo and his audience fell into stunned silence when the god became present. "My friends," Iamblichus assured them, "cease to wonder. For this is only the ghost of a gladiator" (Wright, 1968, p. 425). Without proper preparation of the etheric body Iamblichus explained that mediums typically become possessed by inferior spirits pretending to be gods (*Myst*. 91.7–92.7). We no longer value this kind of discernment because physicalist science does not recognize spiritual entities and certainly not the apparition of gods. Yet beneath the veneer of our culture's scientific education there remains a fascination with the paranormal, and the business of mediums and trance channelers is remarkably strong, at least in popular culture. If Iamblichus had the capacity to understand what is happening *imaginatively*, to actually *see* what is being channeled, it might be instructive to study his diagnostic map for transphysical visions in Book II, 3–9, of *On the Mysteries*.

Porphyry had asked what distinguishes the apparitions (*phasmata*) of gods, angels, archangels, daimons, archons, and souls, and Iamblichus begins by explaining his principles of discernment. Employing Aristotle's metaphysical principle that the activity (*energeia*) of an entity reveals the power (*dunamis*) of its essence (*ousia*), Iamblichus reads *phasmata* as active indices of their sources (*Myst*. 70.12–13). We need to remember that Iamblichus' taxonomy of apparitions was only a starting point, not an exhaustive explanation. For, as he reminds Porphyry regarding all theurgy, "it is not enough simply to learn about these things . . . questions that require practical experience for their accurate understanding cannot be explained by words alone" (*Myst*. 114.3; 6.6–7). True knowledge of paranormal events and apparitions is not theoretical; it can only be realized in practice. At best, Iamblichus' taxonomy would provide the seer with guiding principles for engaging and receiving apparitions, but since divination could only be learned by experience, the way in which it was embodied by each theurgist would necessarily have been personal and unique. Because apparitions are seen through the imaginal eyes of the etheric body and since what we see, Proclus reminds us, "is according to our nature," the appearances would be shaped by our personal expectations and capacities. Iamblichus' descriptions of *phasmata* suggest that each entity of the divine hierarchy expresses the luminosity of the gods in diminishing degrees, each apparition revealing a specific expression of divine light and also serving as an index of the soul's receptive capacity.

Iamblichus lists twenty criteria that distinguish epiphanies in terms of uniformity, brilliance, immutability, beauty, speed, size, clarity, stability, and cathartic power among others, and since for Iamblichus god is light, it is a taxonomy of light. For example, if the *size* of an apparition "covers the whole sky, sun and moon, and the earth is no longer able to stand still as the apparition descends," this indicates that a god has descended, but if the light is "more divided" and its size differs with each appearance, the entity is a daimon (*Myst.* 75.12–15; 76.1–3).

In addition to purely descriptive criteria, Iamblichus also distinguishes apparitions according to their effects on the soul. For example:

> At the moment of the epiphany, souls who invoke the gods are lifted above their passions and their own habits are removed in exchange for a vastly better and more perfect activity, and they participate in divine love and experience amazing happiness. (*Myst.* 87.14–18)

In contrast, when daimons appear, they "lead souls down into nature" (*Myst.* 79.9–10; see Shaw, 1995, p. 40).

> When daimons are seen, souls are filled with an urge toward the generated world, a desire for nature and to fulfill the workings of fate, and they receive a power to complete these kinds of activities. (*Myst.* 88.5–8)

Iamblichus' taxonomy includes 120 distinctions of visionary *phasmata*. It is not possible to explore them all, so I will focus on a provocative passage that describes the effects of light on the pneumatic function of the *ochēma*.

> The gods irradiate such subtlety of light that the eyes of the body are not able to receive it. . . . In fact, human beings who behold the divine fire are not able to inhale the subtlety of it and to all appearances they fall into a swoon and are cut off from their natural breath. Archangels radiate a purity not endurable to breathe but not as unbearable as that of the gods. The appearance of angels makes the air tolerable so that it is possible for theurgists to breathe it. (*Myst.* 86.4–13)

This passage may indicate that theurgists fell into trance states in which their breath was cut off, a phenomenon similar to *turīya*, the cataleptic condition of yogis when their breath appears to stop (Eliade, 1969, p. 57). Insofar as breath is an index of the pneumatic body this suggests that theurgists may have practiced breathing techniques to facilitate their visions. For example, in Fragment 130 of the *Chaldean Oracles*, once joined with the god, the soul is instructed to "breathe in the flowering flames that descend from the Father," and Fragment 124 speaks of theurgists "thrust out [of their bodies] by inhaling" (Majercik, 1989, pp. 97–99). The *Mithras Liturgy*, a document from the magical papyri, instructs initiates to coordinate their breath with visualizations: "Draw in breath from the sun's rays, drawing in three times as much as you can, and *you will see yourself lifted up* and ascending to the height so that you seem to be in midair" (Betz, 1986, p. 48). Breath, fire, and the sun were all integrated in theurgic visualizations and suggest some kind of training of the imagination to increase the subtle body's capacity to receive light. Damascius says when the luminous vehicle (*augoeides ochēma*) unites with the sun the soul is deified (Westerink & Combès, 2003, p. 17). Theurgic mysteries appear to have been solar: Iamblichus characterizes the goal of all divination as "ascent to the noetic Fire" (*Myst.* 179.7) and theurgists as "the true *athletes* of the Fire" (*Myst.* 92.10).

It is here that we need to recognize how far we are from the worldview of Platonic theurgists. We live in a culture that denies the existence of a transphysical realm, of transphysical entities, and we no longer believe that imagination has any function other than representing physical objects and certainly not to be coordinated with incandescent breath! No modern, scientifically minded person could take Iamblichus' taxonomy of apparitions seriously, nor, for that matter, would many take seriously Plotinus' ontological taxonomy of the One, Divine Mind, and World Soul. Yet, despite the ridicule and embarrassment enforced by the gatekeepers of our consensus reality, despite Blake's "mind forg'd manacles" that keep us from entering the imagination of Platonic theurgists, there are some who have experiences unrecognized by physicalist science and are looking for answers. Some dive blindly into the spiritual realm and become enthralled by whatever influence draws them in. Iamblichus' description of transphysical entities at least provides a map from which we might begin to explore paranormal experiences even if we have been trained to believe they are *merely* imagination. As Eric Weiss (Chapter 13 below) has argued, if we are *already* immersed in a transphysical world, we are already subject to its influence, and this makes the theurgical taxonomy even more valuable. At the least, Iamblichus offers more than what we have now, and his taxonomy was integrated with a respected philosophic tradition that is the basis of our culture. Yet we have been denied the fullness of our heritage. The later Platonists were far more than speculative thinkers; they were also theurgists. They were adepts who had transcendent experiences and were perceived as divine men and women who possessed supernatural powers.

CONCLUSION

> Rationality for me still remains a powerful means of knowing, but I criticize here the closure of our minds to modes of knowledge, especially visionary knowledge, that bypass the cogito. . . . Vision and intuitive understandings are "reason's prior," and Reason, especially conceptual thinking, we now know, is an imperfect vehicle to express the profundity of visionary thought.
>
> —Gananath Obeyesekere, *The Awakened Ones*[24]

The Neoplatonist philosophers Plotinus and Iamblichus were both rationalists and visionaries. More precisely, they were visionaries who attempted to communicate the transformative power of their visions in the philosophic language of their time: in terms of epistemology, psychology, and cosmology, for which they gave rational accounts. But, as I have suggested above, to study these philosophers simply for their rational accounts is to misunderstand them or to make of them caricatures shaped by our own habits of mind. For, we remain, as Gananath Obeyesekere (2012) eloquently argues, children of the Enlightenment and, as such, we believe that reason is the "only way to knowledge" and view the world through a myopic rationalistic lens (p. 246; see p. 3). This explains why Plotinus has been favored by most scholars; he is more amenable to our own rational habits. Iamblichus, recognizing the risk of reducing visionary experience to rational explanations, explicitly denied that rational thinking can unite the soul with divinity (*Myst*. 96.11–97.7). The visionary experiences of the Neoplatonists, including those of Plotinus, were *not* discovered through rationality; Iamblichus made this plain, and this invited the derision of scholars like E. R. Dodds who characterized *On*

the Mysteries as "philosophically worthless" (1970, p. 538) and "a mani-
festo of irrationalism" (1951, p. 287). Insofar as Iamblichus explicitly
emphasized the priority of visionary experience over rational explanation
he was speaking a foreign tongue, one that sounded "irrational" to Dodds
and to an entire generation of scholars. Obeyesekere's point is that all
religious traditions, all teachings of awakened sages, *originate in experiences that are other than rational.* These visionary experiences can never
be fully articulated rationally, but they give rise to our most profound
philosophic teachings (Obeyesekere, 2012, pp. 4, 246). Because philosophy in the West has lost touch with its visionary roots, the wisdom of the
Neoplatonists has been preserved more by Romantic poets like Blake,
Wordsworth, Shelley, and Coleridge than by philosophers. It needs to be
said plainly: the physicalist worldview in which we live is born of Enlightenment rationalism, and the Cartesian split between mind and matter
has drained the world of what Neoplatonists—in their imaginative capacity—experienced as a living and breathing *soul.*

Despite the voluminous writing of the Neoplatonists and their endless
exegesis of texts, they never lost sight of the fact that the visionary faculty of the soul can never be rationally grasped or explained. As Sara Rappe
(2000) puts it: "Neoplatonists shared the belief that wisdom could not be
expressed or transmitted by rational thought or language" (p. xiii). Yet, it
was this recognition of an ineffable principle underlying their metaphysics—and their thinking—that allowed each Neoplatonic teacher from
Plotinus to Damascius to discover this principle anew and to give it new
formulations in light of their predecessors.[25] The metaphysics of the Neoplatonists provided an elaborate rational framework to ground their visionary experiences, yet it is a metaphysics that always looks past itself,
that vanishes in the face of its origin. Their rationality was *designed* to
transcend itself. Their vision was unitive. It allowed the individual to feel
united with all of reality, to feel inextricably connected to all things
through their participation in the World Soul. Neoplatonists translated
their visionary experiences into a meaningful narrative: (1) the cosmos is
the expression of a divine and generous impulse that pervades all aspects
of existence; (2) each human soul is a participant in this generosity,
consciously or unconsciously; and (3) through a virtuous life, prayer, and
initiation into visionary experience souls can embody the generosity of
the Demiurge even in their mortal life. Later Platonists, following Iambli-

chus, wanted to apply this vision to politics as well, but history was against them.

The Neoplatonists communicated their visionary experiences in such compelling metaphysical formulas that they were later adopted by the dominant religions of the West. In that sense the influence of Neoplatonism on our culture has been significant even if unrecognized. The metaphysics of Plotinus and its application by Iamblichus to ritual practice became the template for Christian theology and its holy sacraments. The lineaments of Neoplatonic metaphysics can also be discerned among the great philosophers of Judaism and Islam. The thinkers and visionaries of the medieval world appropriated the metaphysics of the Neoplatonists in their respective religious domains. Yet Neoplatonism itself differs from these appropriations in a few essential respects. Unlike the Abrahamic traditions, Neoplatonism does not have a Supreme Being. The Neoplatonic One is not a being or even being itself; it is the *source* of being but does not, itself, exist. The One is both utterly inaccessible *and* accessible: it is revealed—in veiled forms—everywhere. Consequently, Neoplatonism is polytheistic. The One appears in a *multitude* of divine forms and to elevate one of them as supreme, as in the monotheistic traditions, would profoundly misrepresent their metaphysics. Perhaps most significantly, there is no revealed or absolute truth for Neoplatonists. While they encourage the practice of mathematics and philosophic reflection, these disciplines are merely provisional and cathartic to prepare the soul to receive what Iamblichus calls its "innate *gnōsis*" of the One (*Myst.* 7.1–13). No discursive formulation of the divine can ever be adequate. The only heresy for Neoplatonism, therefore, is that of believing one can capture the ineffable in a doctrine. There is no true faith, no true doctrine, no dogma, and no catechism. There is nothing to "believe in." Consistent with its polytheism is its pluralism. Neoplatonists maintain that divine and visionary wisdom is necessarily communicated through different traditions and in a variety of forms. Proclus, in his *Theology of Plato* (Book I, Chapter IV), explicitly refers to Orphic hymns, Pythagorean mathematics, Chaldean revelations, and Platonic dialogues, all as sources of divine wisdom (Taylor, 1816/2009, p. 60). Iamblichus maintains that anyone who performs god-given ancestral rites preserves sacred tradition. The only requirement is that the rite embody cosmogonic activity (*Myst.* 249.9–250.5; 259.1–4). The Neoplatonists were unquestionably visionaries *and* intellectuals. Their thinking is visionary and their visions intellectual. They present a *mode of knowledge*, as Obeyesekere puts it, which may be particularly valuable for those of us seeking a meaningful way of reimagining our world.

NOTES

1. Based on Wright (1968, p. 365).
2. Translation draws as well from Dodds (1973, p. 173).
3. Unless otherwise stated, translations of Plotinus are based on Armstrong (1966–1988), modified in places. Subsequent references to the *Enneads* will be abbreviated as "*Enn.*"
4. *Theourgia* derives from the Greek *theios* = divine and *ergon* = action; it was introduced in the second century CE through the transmission of the *Chaldean Oracles*. These texts, referred to by the Platonists as *ta logia* = the oracles, were seen as revelations of Platonic wisdom. Indeed, they believed that some of these oracles were transmitted by the disembodied soul of Plato himself (Majercik, 1989, pp. 1–5).
5. My translations of Iamblichus' *On the Mysteries* (*De mysteriis*) are based, with modifications, on Clarke, Dillon, and Hershbell (2003). References to *On the Mysteries* are abbreviated as *Myst.*, followed by the Parthey enumeration of the text given in Clarke, Dillon, and Hershbell.
6. In addition to disparaging supernatural phenomena among Platonists, contemporary scholars—with few exceptions—have also dismissed another fundamental element of Platonism: the transmigration of souls, i.e., reincarnation. For a correction to this tendency and an examination of the ethical and eschatological aspects of reincarnation in Platonism, see Bussanich (2013).
7. For references to these thinkers and their explorations of paranormal and anomalous experiences, see Kelly et al. (2007).
8. Based on Wright (1968, p. 353).
9. Translation here based on MacKenna (1991).
10. Jean-Marc Narbonne argues that Plotinus' language on the soul's relation to the body (an illumination not a descent) is influenced directly by his engagement with Gnostics, specifically the gnostic treatise *Zostrianos*. Narbonne argues that the Gnostics had appropriated Neopythagorean arithmology to portray creation as a fall caused by the Indefinite Dyad no longer contained by the Limit (*horos*) of the Monad. This is a dualist position that Plotinus counters in his very next treatise "On Number." Plotinus there argues that numbers are the guarantors of measure that encircle the unlimited impulse of matter, and thus hold "*infinite-matter-evil* . . . [as] an enemy bound within the totality of being itself, a rebellious counter-principle, admittedly, yes, but one that remains subordinate to be-

ing" (Narbonne, 2013, p. 424). As noted in Narbonne's language, the portrayal of matter as "enemy" and "rebellious counter-principle" is what later Platonists perceived as a residual dualism in Plotinus.

11. While Plotinus' doctrine of matter as evil remains a topic of significant scholarly debate, the fact is that Iamblichus, Proclus, and the later Platonists disagreed with Plotinus. Their cosmology was more indebted to the Neopythagorean metaphysics promoted by Iamblichus in which sensible matter is seen as the expression of a divine principle: the Indefinite Dyad. For Plotinus the value of the cosmos is diminished in proportion to its degree of sensible expression. This is not the case for Iamblichus or for Proclus. As Iamblichus puts it, the influence of higher principles is "more penetrating" than intermediate principles and therefore the One is *fully present*—and perhaps especially present—in sensible matter (Iamblichus, trans. 1973, p. 236). This provides a rationale for the theurgic use of material objects. Proclus dedicated much of his treatise *On the Existence of Evils* to the refutation of Plotinus' position on matter. As he argues, if matter is evil it becomes an "alternative principle of beings, dissident from the cause of good things, and there will be 'two sources releasing their flow in opposite directions,' one the source of good things, the other of evil things" (Opsomer & Steel, 2003, p. 84). For Proclus matter is necessary for the universe; it is produced by the Good, and the Good cannot produce anything evil. "If, then, matter offers itself to be used in the fabrication of the whole world, and has been produced for the sake of being 'the receptacle of generation and, as it were, a wet-nurse' and 'mother' (*Timaeus* 49a–50d), how can it be said to be evil, and even the primary evil?" (Opsomer & Steel, 2003, p. 81).

12. Given our dualist understanding of Plato and Platonism this may seem hard to understand. Yet Iamblichus (and later Platonists) were quite clear about material reality being good: "It would be far from true to suggest that the material principle is evil. . . . Wouldn't it be senseless to say that the natural receptacle of such a thing [the beauty of numbers] is evil or ugly?" Material reality was entirely good despite the soul's tendencies to excess; matter was the receptacle of the *arithmoi* that shape and inform the world (for sources of quotations, see Shaw, 1995, pp. 28–36).

13. Damascius was the last and arguably the most brilliant leader of the Platonic school before it was closed by Emperor Justinian in 529 CE. See Sara Ahbel-Rappe (2010, p. 391), translation modified.

14. This is Iamblichus' description of Pythagoras, the exemplar of his own ideals.

15. One of the most prominent critics of Iamblichean theurgy was E. R. Dodds, an excellent classical scholar as well as a lifelong student of paranormal phenomena (he was the president of the Society for Psychical Research, 1960–1963). Dodds admitted that Iamblichus influenced the "final shaping of

Neoplatonism" as much as Plotinus yet said he was "immeasurably inferior" to Plotinus because his theurgical writings were, as Dodds dismissively said, "really unspeakable spiritualistic drivellings" (1928, p. 142; 1963, p. xix). Scholars today recognize that Dodds' rationalist biases kept him from recognizing how deeply integrated religious and philosophic language was for Iamblichus and the later Platonists. For a critique of rationalist approaches to understanding theurgy, see Shaw (1985, pp. 1–28) and also Bussanich (2005, pp. 478–494).

16. Translated by Hankey, in Narbonne and Hankey (2006, p. 194).

17. The etheric body is called "astral" because the stars were believed to possess etheric bodies, and thus our etheric body is like the body of stars, astral. The term *astroeides* (starry form) to refer to the subtle body was coined by Proclus in the fifth century CE. For a history of the astral body among Gnostics and Neoplatonists, see "The Astral Body in Neoplatonism" (Dodds, 1963, pp. 313–321).

18. Among Neoplatonists there were differences in their conceptualization of the *ochēma*. Iamblichus said there is only one *ochēma* which is immortal despite its descent into a mortal condition. Proclus held that there are two *ochēmata*: (1) the universal and divine *ochēma*, and (2) a pneumatic *ochēma* made of planetary elements which is not fully immortal. It survives death but dissolves when its sheaths return to their planetary origins.

19. Platonizing Christians like Synesius (fifth century), Bishop of Cyrene, who was the student of the theurgist Hypatia. He imagined the body of resurrection as the shining *pneuma* of the soul, the *augoeides*. For him it was the soul's "first body" (*proton soma*), a purified imaginative *pneuma*. This view was later declared heresy by the Church.

20. Procession (*prohodos*) follows the Plotinian image of emanation from the One, and Reversion (*epistrophē*) when the soul returns to the One by retracing the movement of procession. These cardinal principles of Neoplatonic metaphysics, which I have characterized as its diastolic and systolic phases, are discussed by Dodds (1963) in his translation and commentary of Proclus' *Elements of Theology*, Propositions 25–39.

21. Corbin (1969, *passim*). In terms of Sufi angelology, Corbin describes the theurgic function of these noetic entities. As he puts it: "each sensible thing or species is the 'theurgy' of its Angel"—in Corbin's (1980) description of theurgic practice among Sufis, it is the turning to one's angel that transforms the sensible object into a theurgic symbol (pp. 115–116).

22. In *Bibliographica Literaria*, XIII, Coleridge (1978) writes: "*The primary IMAGINATION I hold to be the living Power and prime Agent of all human Perception, and* as a repetition in the finite mind of the eternal act of creation in the infinite I AM . . . *fancy is indeed no other than a mode of memory emancipated from the order of time and space*" (p. 516, italics added).

23. Neoplatonic divination (*mantikē*) is not the attempt to predict future events. Divination is an essential component of divinization, the soul's elevation to its divine origins (Shaw, 1995, pp. 232–235).

24. Obeyesekere (2012, pp. 3, 246).

25. The Neoplatonic "identity theory of truth" means that "the intellect is its objects" but, as Rappe (2000) points out, "this means that knowing the truth is a state *utterly unlike* that of normal thinking" (p. 27; italics added). *Noēsis* is not rationality; strictly speaking, it is not even rational. In fact, *noēsis* is more amenable to visionary language, to symbols or images that collapse oppositions (e.g., knower and known) into a unity. This is why Iamblichus preferred ritual and symbol over philosophic discourse.

REFERENCES

Ahbel-Rappe, S. (Trans.). (2010). *Damascius' Problems and Solutions Concerning First Principles*. Oxford: Oxford University Press.

Armstrong, A. H. (1986). Platonic mirrors. *Eranos, 55*, 147–182.

Armstrong, A. H. (Trans.). (1966–1988). *Plotinus: Enneads I–VI* (Vols. 1–7). Loeb Classical Library. Cambridge, MA: Harvard University Press.

Athanassiadi, P. (Trans.). (1999). *Damascius: The Philosophical History*. Athens: Apamea Cultural Association.

Betz, H. D. (Ed.). (1986). *The Greek Magical Papyri in Translation*. Chicago: University of Chicago Press.

Bussanich, J. (1996). Plotinus's metaphysics of the One. In L. P. Gerson (Ed.), *The Cambridge Companion to Plotinus* (pp. 38–65). Cambridge: Cambridge University Press.

Bussanich, J. (2005). New editions of Iamblichus: A review essay. *Ancient Philosophy, 25*, 478–494.

Bussanich, J. (2013). Rebirth eschatology in Plato and Plotinus. In V. Adluri (Ed.), *Philosophy and Salvation in Greek Religion* (pp. 243–288). Berlin: de Gruyter.

Clarke, E. C., Dillon, J. M., & Hershbell, J. P. (Trans.). (2003). *Iamblichus: On the Mysteries*. Atlanta, GA: Society of Biblical Literature.

Coleridge, S. T. (1978). *The Portable Coleridge* (I. A. Richards, Ed.). New York: Penguin.

Corbin, H. (1969). *Creative Imagination in the Ṣūfism of Ibn 'Arabī* (R. Manheim, Trans.). Princeton, NJ: Princeton University Press.

Corbin, H. (1980). *Avicenna and the Visionary Recital*. Dallas, TX: Spring Publications.

Cornford, F. M. (Trans.). (1937). *Plato's Cosmology: The* Timaeus *of Plato*. London: Kegan Paul, Trench, Trubner.

Dodds, E. R. (1928). The *Parmenides* of Plato and the origin of the Neoplatonic "One." *Classical Quarterly, 22*, 129–142.

Dodds, E. R. (1951). *The Greeks and the Irrational*. Berkeley and Los Angeles: University of California Press.

Dodds, E. R. (1970). Iamblichus. *Oxford Classical Dictionary* (N. G. L. Hammond & H. H. Scullard, Eds., 2nd ed.). Oxford: Oxford University Press.

Dodds, E. R. (1973). *The Ancient Concept of Progress and other Essays on Greek Literature and Belief*. Oxford: Clarendon Press.

Dodds, E. R. (Trans.). (1963). *Proclus: The Elements of Theology* (2nd ed.). Oxford: Clarendon Press.

Edwards, M. (Trans.). (2000). *Neoplatonic Saints: The Lives of Plotinus and Proclus by their Students*. Liverpool, England: Liverpool University Press.

Eliade, M. (1969). *Yoga: Immortality and Freedom* (W. R. Trask, Trans., 2nd ed.). Princeton, NJ: Princeton University Press.

Emerson, R. W. (1883). *Essays: First and Second Series*. Boston: Houghton Mifflin.

Finamore, J. F. (1985). *Iamblichus and the Theory of the Vehicle of the Soul*. Chico, CA: Scholars Press.

Gatti, M. L. (1996). Plotinus: The Platonic tradition and the foundation of Neoplatonism. In L. P. Gerson (Ed.), *The Cambridge Companion to Plotinus* (pp. 10–37). Cambridge: Cambridge University Press.

Hadot, I. (2004). *Studies on the Neoplatonist Hierocles* (M. Chase, Trans.). Philadelphia: American Philosophical Society.

Hillman, J. (1997). *Archetypal Psychology: A Brief Account* (Rev. ed.). Woodstock, CT: Spring Publications.

Iamblichus (trans. 1973). *Iamblichi Chalcidensis in Platonis Dialogos Commentariorum Fragmenta* (J. M. Dillon, Trans.). Leiden, The Netherlands: Brill.

Iamblichus (trans. 1991). *On the Pythagorean Way of Life* (J. Dillon & J. Hershbell, Trans.). Atlanta, GA: Scholars Press.

Jambet, C. (1983). *La logique des Orientaux: Henry Corbin et la science des formes*. Paris: Éditions du Seuil.

Kelly, E. F., Kelly, E. W., Crabtree, A., Gauld, A., Grosso, M., & Greyson, B. (2007). *Irreducible Mind: Toward a Psychology for the 21st Century*. Lanham, MD: Rowman & Littlefield.

Kelly, E. W., Greyson, B., & Kelly, E. F. (2007). Unusual experiences near death and related phenomena. In E. F. Kelly, E. W. Kelly, A. Crabtree, A. Gauld, M. Grosso, & B. Greyson, *Irreducible Mind: Toward a Psychology for the 21st Century* (pp. 367–421). Lanham, MD: Rowman & Littlefield.

Kroll, G. (Ed.). (1899–1901). *Procli Diadochi in Platonis rem publicam commentarii* (Vols. 1–2). Leipzig, Germany: Teubner.

Lowry, J. M. P. (1980). *The Logical Principles of Proclus' Stoicheiōsis Theologikē as Systematic Ground of the Cosmos*. Amsterdam: Rodopi.

MacKenna, S. (Trans.). (1991). *Plotinus: The Enneads* (Abr. ed.). London: Penguin.

Majercik, R. (1989). *The Chaldean Oracles: Text, Translation, and Commentary*. Leiden, The Netherlands: Brill.

Myers, F. W. H. (1903). *Human Personality and Its Survival of Bodily Death* (Vols. 1–2). London: Longmans, Green. (Available on CTR website, http://www.esalen.org/ctr/scholarly-resources)

Narbonne, J.-M. (2013). The Neopythagorean backdrop to the fall (*sphalma/neusis*) of the soul in Gnosticism and its echo in the Plotinian treatises 33 and 34. In K. Corrigan & T. Rasimus (Eds.), *Gnosticism, Platonism and the Late Ancient World: Essays in Honour of John D. Turner* (pp. 411–425). Leiden, The Netherlands: Brill.

Narbonne, J.-M., & Hankey, W. J. (2006). *Levinas and the Greek Heritage* (pp. 1–96) followed by *One Hundred Years of Neoplatonism in France: A Brief Philosophical History* (pp. 97–248). Leuven, Belgium: Peeters.

Obeyesekere, G. (2012). *The Awakened Ones: Phenomenology of Visionary Experience*. New York: Columbia University Press.

Opsomer, J., & Steel, C. (Trans.). (2003). *Proclus: On the Existence of Evils*. Ithaca, NY: Cornell University Press.

Rappe, S. (2000). *Reading Neoplatonism: Non-Discursive Thinking in the Texts of Plotinus, Proclus, and Damascius*. Cambridge: Cambridge University Press.

Saffrey, H. D., & Segonds, A.-P. (Trans.). (2012). *Porphyre: Lettre à Anébon l'Égyptien*. Paris: Les Belles Lettres.

Shaw, G. (1985). Theurgy: Rituals of unification in the Neoplatonism of Iamblichus. *Traditio, 41*, 1–28.

Shaw, G. (1995). *Theurgy and the Soul: The Neoplatonism of Iamblichus*. University Park: Pennsylvania State University Press.

Shaw, G. (2005). The sphere and the altar of sacrifice. In R. Berchman & J. Finamore (Eds.), *History of Platonism: Plato Redivivus* (pp. 147–161). New Orleans, LA: University Press of the South.

Taylor, T. (Trans.). (2009). *The Theology of Plato by Proclus.* Westbury, England: The Prometheus Trust. (Original work published 1816)

Trouillard, J. (Trans.). (1965). *Proclos: Éléments de Théologie.* Paris: Aubier.

Westerink, L. G. (Ed.), & Combès, J. (Trans.). (2003). *Damascius: Commentaire du Parménide de Platon* (Vol. 4). Paris: Les Belles Lettres.

White, D. G. (1996). *The Alchemical Body: Siddha Traditions in Medieval India.* Chicago: University of Chicago Press.

Wright, W. C. (Trans.). (1968). *Philostratus and Eunapius. Lives of the Sophists.* Loeb Classical Library. Cambridge, MA: Harvard University Press.

9

PATAÑJALI'S *YOGA SŪTRAS* AND THE *SIDDHIS*

Edward F. Kelly and Ian Whicher

Within the Indian philosophical tradition, a large amount of theoretical and practical information related to Yoga was collected, systematized, and condensed into the form of 196 brief aphorisms or "sūtras" by a somewhat mysterious figure named Patañjali, probably around the second or third century CE.[1] This extraordinary work, which together with its various major commentaries is still widely regarded as the most authoritative source available on Yoga philosophy and practice, outlines within its four brief chapters or "books" a sophisticated picture of human psychophysical organization, which in turn provides the theoretical basis for a comprehensive program of self-development. The claimed results of this program, catalogued at considerable length, explicitly include the appearance of both higher states of consciousness and a variety of associated supernormal capacities. Patañjali's system thus directly and systematically addresses the central theoretical concerns of this book. In the present chapter we will briefly sketch his system itself and its foundations in Sāṃkhya metaphysics, assess the state of evidence bearing upon its possible validity, and explore possibilities for further research.

We emphasize here at the outset that our goal is to extract psychological and metaphysical ideas potentially useful for our specific theoretical purposes. This essay is not intended as a work of conventional religious-studies scholarship, and although we have labored to be accurate in all necessary respects, we have avoided being drawn into ongoing academic controversies over various issues of history, fact, or interpretation that we judged irrelevant to our primary concerns. Similarly, in attempting to penetrate the sometimes obscure meanings of particularly important sūtras we have freely relied upon the testimony of advanced practitioners of Yoga as well as that of scholars of religion.

THEORETICAL BACKGROUND

Sāṃkhya and Yoga together form one of three closely connected pairs that collectively constitute the six systems of "orthodox" Hindu philosophy based strictly on the Vedas. They took shape philosophically during roughly the same period (late BCE to early CE) and evolved in interaction both with each other and with other contemporary traditions including Buddhism and Jainism that were undergoing a similar crystallization into formal philosophical positions during this period. Sāṃkhya is more purely philosophical in character than Yoga and provides its metaphysical core, although the two remain distinct in significant ways and are properly regarded as autonomous systems (Feuerstein, 1980; Whicher, 1998). Its classical formulation is the *Sāṃkhya Kārikā* (*SK*) of Īśvarakṛṣṇa, which probably postdates Patañjali's *Yoga Sūtras* (*YS*) but articulates ideas that had long been in circulation (Larson, 1979). Consisting of seventy-three aphorisms (Larson, 1979, Appendix B), the *Kārikā* sketches a profoundly dualistic picture of reality, but one that differs starkly from the Cartesian dualism familiar in the West. Philosopher H. H. Price encapsulates this fundamental contrast as follows:

> [In Sāṃkhya] we find a very sharp dualism between *Purusha* (self or knowing subject) on the one side, and *Prakriti* (usually translated 'matter') on the other. At first sight this reminds us of the equally sharp dualism of Descartes between mind and matter. But on further examination we are astonished to find that the line is not drawn at all where Descartes drew it. Very much of what we are accustomed to call 'mind' is in the Sankhya system regarded as material. Indeed *everything* that we call mental, except only pure awareness, falls on the material side; of course it has then to be added that there are other forms of matter besides those revealed to our ordinary senses. (Dilley, 1995, pp. 27–28)

The term *prakṛti* refers both to the non-conscious primordial ground of the innumerable manifest forms and to those forms themselves. As primordial ground (*mulaprakṛti* or *pradhāna*), it is that out of which the multiplicity of evolutes is brought forth, containing in potential the entire manifest or experienced cosmos in all its levels and categories of being, including the mental. The manifested appearances themselves are conceived as varying combinations and proportions of innumerable qualities or constituents of *prakṛti* that are grouped into three classes—the *guṇas* —the manifestations of which vary in accordance with the categories of things which they cooperatively or synergistically constitute: thus, *sattva* bestows properties such as brightness, lightness, buoyancy, illumination, wisdom, clarity, tranquility, peacefulness, and pleasure; *rajas*, energy, stimulation, activity, restlessness, agitation, attachment, passion, and pain; and *tamas*, darkness, heaviness, dullness, ignorance, fixity, obstruction, resistance, inertia, sloth, and indifference (for more detailed discussions see Bryant, 2009; Dasgupta, 1924/1970; Koelman, 1970; Larson, 1979; Whicher, 1998, 2001).

Puruṣa, the transcendental or true self, is the principle of consciousness or pure consciousness itself, a passive witness or spectator, potentially the knower or seer of all manifestation, itself uncreated and uncreative, unchanging and unchangeable, simple, inactive, free, and separate from *prakṛti* (*SK* 19). Classical Sāṃkhya postulates a plurality of *puruṣas* in order to account for the diversity of embodied beings, without speculating as to their source (*SK* 18).

In the presence of *puruṣa*, the primordial equilibrium of the *guṇas* is disturbed, like that of iron filings exposed to a magnet, and an ontological evolution of *prakṛti* ensues. This process, which is described as taking place for the benefit of the *puruṣa* (*SK* 56–60), transforms its latent potentialities into a hierarchy of actualities comprising twenty-three additional principles, qualities, functions, or "thatnesses" (*tattvas*) of manifest creation. First comes *buddhi* (or *mahat*, in its cosmic expression), usually translated as intellect or will, which includes dispositional and conative aspects but is impersonal or transpersonal in character. *Buddhi* gives rise to *ahaṃkāra*, the I-sense or ego, which in turn produces all remaining objects of potential experience, both internal and external. On its *sattvic* or internal side comes *manas* or mind, conceived essentially as a sensorimotor coordination and relay organ, plus its five sensory capacities or *buddhīndriyas* (capacities for hearing, feeling, seeing, tasting, and smelling), and five action-capacities or *karmendriyas* (drivers of the voice, hands, feet, and organs of excretion and generation). *Buddhi, ahaṃkāra,* and *manas* together make up the "internal organ" or *antaḥkaraṇa*. On its *tamasic* or external side, *ahaṃkāra* produces the entire external world, starting at bottom with five "subtle elements" or *tanmātras* which combine in varying proportions to generate the five gross elements or *mahābhūtas* that make up the objects of everyday waking experience. The *antaḥkaraṇa,* together with its *buddhīndriyas* and *karmendriyas* and a quasi-physical "sheath" formed of *tanmātras* alone, constitutes the *sūkṣma śarīra* or "subtle body," the vehicle of postmortem survival and eventual rebirth. Note that this basic scheme, viewed cosmologically, involves a structural parallelism between the constitution of each embodied individual and the constitution of the world as experienced, a feature which Patañjali will later exploit in his account of the *siddhis* or perfections.

The ordinary embodied individual or *jīva* is characterized by a two-way confusion between *puruṣa* and *prakṛti*. The internal organ—*buddhi, ahaṃkāra,* and *manas*—appears to be consciously intelligent, but that appearance is in fact only "borrowed" from the *puruṣa,* somewhat as the tip of an iron bar inserted into a red-hot fire glows with borrowed heat. The *puruṣa* itself, meanwhile, illuminates and experiences but also mistakenly identifies with the unconscious mechanical workings of its material instrument as reflected especially in the state of the *buddhi,* to which it is most closely allied. The normal condition of the *jīva* is thus analogous to that of a lame man riding on the shoulders of a blind man (*SK* 21), with suffering its inevitable accompaniment. The central aim of classical Sāṃkhya is to eliminate suffering by providing effective intellectual means for proper discernment, discrimination, or disentanglement between *puruṣa* and *prakṛti,* thereby overcoming this two-way misidentification.

Patañjali's system shares the basic soteriological aim of Sāṃkhya and much of its underlying metaphysics, but it also takes a practical psychological turn that emphasizes systematic self-development and progressive control of the wandering mind as the principal means of liberation. Yoga is defined succinctly in the second sūtra of Book I of the *Yoga Sūtras* (*YS* I.2) as inhibition or cessation of the modifications of the mind, but it can also be understood more generally as transcending or overcoming the customary human misidentification with such modifications (Whicher,

1998, Chapters 4 and 5). This is to be achieved, according to *YS* I.12 by a combination of *vairāgya* (detachment) and *abhyāsa* (practice), which Taimni (1961) aptly likens to both releasing the gas pedal and applying the brakes in order to stop an automobile.

In Books II and III, following an incisive analysis of the *kleśas* or afflictions (obstacles or hindrances to quieting the mind), Patañjali sets forth his eight-limbed system of Yogic praxis: *Yama* (restraints) include abstention from counterproductive disturbance-producing activities such as violence, untruthfulness, stealing or misappropriation, lustful incontinence, and acquisitiveness. *Niyama* (observances) include cleanliness or purity, contentment, effortful self-discipline, self-study, and surrender of the ego to a higher power. These first two limbs create a moral foundation for yogic practice and commence the "*sattvification*" (Whicher, 1998) or purification of the internal organ through reduction or elimination of mental and emotional disturbances typical of ordinary life. Limb three is *āsana* or posture, subsequently elaborated into Haṭha Yoga and the myriad forms of Yogic calisthenics that have invaded modern Western culture, but which for Patañjali means only a position that is comfortable and steady, reducing somatic noise and fostering relaxed attention. Limb four is *prāṇāyāma* or control of the flow of vital energies through voluntary regulation of breathing, and especially through cessation of both inspiration and expiration—*kumbhaka*; this is a large and complex subject which Patañjali summarizes in highly compressed terms, clearly expecting it to be well known to his students (*YS* I.34, II.49–53). Limb five, *pratyāhāra*, refers to "withdrawal of the senses," resulting in complete isolation of the mind from the normal demands of the sensory environment.

Book II of the *Yoga Sūtras* ends here, with its description of limbs one to five complete. These together constitute only preliminary or "external" yoga, but it should be clear that we are already into territory unfamiliar from ordinary experience. Limbs six to eight constitute "internal" yoga, the real heart of the subject, and it is significant that Patañjali locates them at the beginning of Book III, the main subject of which is the unusual powers or perfections that are claimed to result from their intense practice. In limb six, *dhāraṇā* (concentration), the mind or attention is deliberately confined to a preselected object, image, or idea, but with allowance for some residual distraction or freedom of movement. Limb seven, *dhyāna* (contemplation or meditation), reflects a higher degree of control in which attention flows uninterruptedly and effortlessly toward the chosen object. In the final limb, *samādhi*, absorption becomes so complete that the sense of self or ego disappears, and the chosen object shines forth in its true character, free from distortions due to residual impurities of the internal organ.

Limbs six to eight together constitute *saṃyama*, Yoga's central technique, and in the remainder of Book III Patañjali goes on to describe how its deepening practice, in application to certain specific objects of attention, yields various kinds of "*siddhis*" or perfections specifically including psi capacities of various sorts. From his more detailed theoretical treatment of the stages of *samādhi* and its results in Books I and IV, it is also apparent that he views these attainments as deeply intertwined with progressive mastery of a hierarchy of altered states of consciousness leading ultimately to the isolation or liberation of *puruṣa* from *prakṛti* in an exalted state of introvertive (contentless or "seedless"—*nirbīja*) mystical experience (see Chapter 2 above; *Irreducible Mind* [henceforth *IM*], Chapter 8; Stace, 1960/1987).

It must be acknowledged immediately that Patañjali's treatment of the *siddhis* is bound to strike scientifically educated modern sensibilities as somewhat strange in multiple respects. Many of the relevant sūtras are extremely cryptic, and they often involve words of very broad or uncertain meaning. Patañjali also does little to explain *siddhis* individually, relying instead on extremely abstract statements about processes common to many or all. Most importantly, perhaps, some of his specific claims seem at first sight quite bizarre (e.g., that *saṃyama* on the moon will yield knowledge of the arrangements of the stars—III.28) and others beyond credibility (e.g., that isolation of *puruṣa* leads to omniscience and omnipotence—III.50).

For many modern scholars, including scholars who otherwise take Patañjali's treatise as a work of high philosophical and historical significance, Book III has clearly constituted something of a conundrum, or even an embarrassment (see e.g., Bryant, 2009, pp. 329–335; Jacobsen, 2012, pp. 12–16; Koelman, 1970, pp. 240–247; Larson, 2008, pp. 27, 28, 74, 124, 132). Much of this discomfort clearly revolves around Patañjali's matter-of-fact acceptance of various psi-type phenomena, which these and many other scholars erroneously presume have been proven impossible by modern science (see Chapter 1 above, and Radin, 2013). Rather than engage with Patañjali's truth claims directly, therefore, most contemporary scholars have been content either to ignore or minimize them, sometimes even suggesting that he was simply acknowledging the prevalence of persisting popular superstitions. Psi researchers, however, have long recognized the potential relevance of Patañjali's system to their own experimental interests, and significant and promising connections have already been found. We next briefly summarize these connections.

SIDDHIS AND PSI RESEARCH:
THE CURRENT STATE OF PLAY

Patañjali catalogues roughly two to three dozen *siddhis* in Book III, depending on how one interprets and counts his examples, and many other such catalogs exist, some far more expansive than his. The important point for our purposes here is that most though not all of his examples clearly fall within the categories of *receptive* and *expressive* psi, with the remainder chiefly involving phenomena of extreme psychophysiological influence. Pertinent examples for receptive psi or ESP include direct knowledge of the past and future (III.16), of the contents of other minds (III.19), and of things happening at a distance (III. 26); for expressive psi or PK, levitation (III. 40); and for extreme psychophysiological influence, immunity to fire (III. 46) (see Chapter 1 above, and *IM*, Chapter 3).

Within their range of overlap, modern psi research and Patañjali's account of the *siddhis* have already proved mutually supportive in important ways. First, modern experimental psi research has definitely confirmed the existence of at least some of the *siddhis*, and field and observational studies confirm the reality of others with varying degrees of confidence (Braud, 2008; Radin, 2013; Rao, 2011). This of course does not warrant automatic acceptance of various other Patañjali claims which at present seem either unintelligible or grandiose, but it certainly invalidates their blanket dismissal in the absence of further investigation.

More importantly for present purposes, elementary Yogic practices themselves, and related practices of various sorts, have also been shown to be at least modestly psi-conducive. In a landmark early paper, Honorton (1977) specifically pointed out that the eight limbs of Yogic practice as outlined by Patañjali can be understood from a conventional signal-processing point of view as a system of progressive psychophysical noise reduction leading to a state characterized by physical relaxation, isolation from the normal sensory environment, and inwardly directed attention, a picture strikingly consistent with the self-descriptions of gifted psi subjects (White, 1964). In that light it seemed likely that procedures which result in such conditions should in general be favorable for receptive psi, and this has indeed proven to be the case, as indicated by an increasing number and variety of experimental studies of psi performance in relation to practices and situations such as progressive muscular relaxation and autogenic training, biofeedback for autonomic quietude, Ganzfeld and dreaming, hypnosis, and various elementary forms of meditation (Braud, 1978, 2008; Honorton, 1977; Radin, 2013; Rao & Palmer, 1987).

These results are definitely encouraging, but it should be clear that in terms of Patañjali's system itself we have so far barely scratched the surface. The central Yogic process of *samyama* certainly involves far more than a movement within the range of ordinary states of consciousness: indeed, as already indicated above, the central thrust of Patañjali's exposition is to describe how the practice of *samyama*, systematically intensified, leads through a hierarchy of increasingly exalted states to the ultimate objective of pure, limitless consciousness—*puruṣa* disentangled from *prakṛti*, the liberated state of isolation or *kaivalya* (Book IV). The emergence of supernormal capacities or *siddhis* is described in matter-of-fact fashion as a by-product of this central movement, their value consisting mainly in providing markers on the developmental path and confirmation of the guiding theoretical scheme.[2]

From a modern scientific point of view, unfortunately, the state of evidence directly pertinent to these more radical claims remains extremely unsatisfactory. Although there are innumerable supportive anecdotes, and field observations of varying impressiveness, there is still little in the way of hard evidence documenting the occurrence of high-grade psi in meditative adepts. This is probably due in part to systematic reluctance on the part of such persons to demonstrate whatever psi abilities they may have. Patañjali remarks in *YS* III.38 to the effect that *siddhis* are powers of the outward-turned mind but obstacles to spiritual progress, and although he himself may have been referring only or mainly to the specific *siddhis* mentioned in the preceding sūtra (Feuerstein, 1980, p. 106), other spokespersons for the meditative traditions have often expressed more generalized cautions or prohibitions of this sort. Skeptics will naturally suspect that this is merely an excuse, and we ourselves do not doubt that this may sometimes be the case, but in our experience with serious meditators it seems far more commonly to be a genuinely held attitude. One can readily appreciate the dangers of paying too much and the wrong kind of attention to these phenomena, but to ignore and denigrate them in a wholesale manner seems equally a mistake in view of their important bearing on the issue of mystical "truth" (see Chapter 2 above, and *IM*, Chapter 8). In the same vein, we deplore the curious tendency of transpersonal psychology to distance itself from psi research, at least in part out of what seems unquestioning compliance with the prevailing negative attitude of the meditative traditions.

Some additional findings supportive of Patañjali's picture have already emerged on the physiological side. For example, there have been striking demonstrations of meditative *pratyāhāra* in connection with some early EEG studies of *samādhi*-like states (Anand, Chhina, & Singh, 1961; Das & Gastaut, 1955), and analogous phenomena are known to occur in mediumship (e.g., Mrs. Piper's immunity to pinpricks and to ammonia held under her nose; Chapter 4 above), in the rapture or "ligature" associated with ecstatic mystical states (Arbman, 1968; Benedict XIV, 1850; Poulain, 1910/1957; see also below), and in extreme sports and combat situations (Murphy & White, 1995). These observations collectively demonstrate that full "withdrawal of the senses," normally impossible for most of us, is an empirical reality. Existing research on meditation has also clearly demonstrated that advanced meditative states are at least sometimes accompanied by nonordinary neurophysiological phenomena (such as gamma-frequency EEG oscillations of high amplitude and wide distribution that are resistant to blocking by external stimuli—e.g., Das & Gastaut, 1955; Lutz, Greischar, Rawlings, Ricard, & Davidson, 2004), although such research remains in its infancy and far more needs to be done to characterize the relevant states both phenomenologically and neurophysiologically. Many of the existing findings, and suggestions for further research, are covered in *Irreducible Mind*, and we have included the relevant pages (pp. 567–573) on Esalen's CTR website as supplemental material for this chapter (see also Rao, 2011).

In sum, although research to date is certainly encouraging as far as it goes, there is currently a near-total lack of evidence *directly* related to the deeper parts of Patañjali's theoretical and practical system, and its claimed connections with psi and the *siddhis*. We strongly encourage any of our readers who are skilled meditative practitioners to consider getting involved in collaborative research with suitably able and open-minded investigators. This need not impact spiritual practice in any material way, and it could greatly facilitate direct investigation both of advanced meditative states themselves and of their putative connections with psi (see also Chapter 4 above). Experiments combining modern techniques of functional neuroimaging with careful phenomenological inquiry and appropriate forms of psi testing in truly accomplished meditators would represent landmark scientific events that could quickly go a long way toward assessing the validity of the underlying conceptual frameworks! Meanwhile, additional analytical leverage on Patañjali's scheme derives from a very different and perhaps surprising quarter, as we will next explain.

INDIRECT CONFIRMATION FROM THE CATHOLIC MYSTICAL TRADITION

Although the linkage reported by Patañjali between the achievement of deep meditative and mystical states and the emergence of strong psi phenomena has barely begun to be explored directly and experimentally, significant further support for such a linkage derives indirectly from comparative study of the meditative and mystical traditions themselves. It is noteworthy first that Patañjali's catalog of *siddhis* is hardly unique: other mystical traditions, including not only Jainism and the various strands of Buddhism but relatively distant and independent ones such as Sufism, Catholicism, and the many forms of shamanism found in preliterate societies, have discovered and catalogued many of the same phenomena in strikingly parallel ways. These parallels have been drawn out in considerable detail by Murphy (1992), who provides what is by far the most systematic attempt up to now to construct a "natural history" of the entire domain.

Of special importance within this massive and scattered literature is the large body of written material regarding the lives and experiences of certain Catholic saints, including the very extensive records of formal Church proceedings leading to their beatification and canonization. In volume and character this material is unique in world religious history, and it contains information substantially convergent with Patañjali's account of *saṃyama* and the *siddhis*. We emphasize here that we hold no brief for Catholicism per se; we wish merely to highlight certain striking parallels to Patañjali's scheme that have emerged under radically different cultural conditions, and with credible evidence supporting them.

There are two main threads to this comparison. The first concerns the enormously rich body of written accounts of mystical contemplation found within the Catholic tradition. Here we call particularly upon the descriptive historian Auguste Poulain (1910/1957), who centers his highly regarded and comprehensive treatment of this subject on the elaborate descriptions of the higher stages of *orison* or contemplative prayer given by St. Teresa of Ávila. Poulain regards Teresa's accounts as covering the entire relevant territory and imposing just the right amount of conceptual order, neither too much nor too little, allowing all other available accounts (from which he provides many useful extracts) to be assimilated to or coordinated with hers. Briefly, beyond the lower stages of ordinary prayer Teresa identifies three higher stages termed the prayer of quiet, prayer of full union, and ecstasy proper, characterized chiefly by increasing and increasingly effortless absorption in the object of contemplation (typically some image or scene, personality, episode, symbol, sacrament, or mystery of the Catholic faith) and a correlatively increasing inhibition or "ligature" of normal sensorimotor and cognitive functions. In keeping with Catholic theology, Poulain generally regards the states as graces granted by God rather than products of individual effort, and he argues that they are in some mysterious way directly causative of the ligature (see his Chapter 14, and Chapter 31, section 5). Underhill (1911/1974) and Arbman (1968) provide essentially equivalent phenomenological descriptions of this mystical ascent.

Externally, the more profound instances of ligature are reflected in publicly observable phenomena such as reductions in heart rate, pulse amplitude, respiration, body temperature, and responsiveness to ordinary or even painful stimuli (Poulain, 1910/1957, Chapter 14; see also Arbman, 1968, pp. 189–238, and Underhill, 1911/1974, pp. 358–363). Internally, there is progressive extinction of ordinary forms of sensation, imagination, and thinking, and an increasing sense of contact with, and influence from, a something more of great power and very different character. The three identified stages of this movement follow a generally upward slope but do not comprise a staircase or ladder; they are heterogeneous in shadings and not sharply distinct. In the highest levels of ecstasy proper the ordinary sense of self is explicitly extinguished, and identification with the object of contemplation becomes complete (Peers, 1951, p.

150).[3] As Underhill (1911/1974) puts it, the two essential marks of deep and genuine mystical experience are the totality or "givenness" of the object of contemplation, coupled with "Self-Mergence" (disappearance of the everyday subject of experience). Thus, the revealed reality is apprehended by way of *participation*, rather than by observation as though from the vantage point of an external observer (pp. 332–333; parenthetically, she explicitly recognizes that these marks appeared to be present in the mystical experiences of Plotinus).

Although more detailed scholarly investigation is certainly warranted and needed, there is a clear parallel here, we submit, to the stages of *saṃyama* as described by Patañjali, and particularly to its culminant stage of selfless absorption or *samādhi*. We are not alone, moreover, in recognizing this parallel: in particular, Arbman (1968, pp. 139–144) specifically makes this comparison in conjunction with his own description of the inner limbs of yoga, noting how deeply Patañjali's picture "agrees with the accounts given by Christian mystics of the ecstatic absorption and its manifestations" (p. 140).

This brings us to the second main thread, which concerns those manifestations themselves. These again have both internal and external aspects. Internally, there are recurring reports of blinding illuminations, sudden expansions or infusions of understanding that transcend ordinary forms of knowing, and all the other aspects of mystical phenomenology described in Chapter 2 above. Externally, and crucially, we again find reports of large-scale psi and related supernormal phenomena. Catholicism, it turns out, has its own catalog of *charisms* or gifts, which partly reflects its own ideological preoccupations such as the crucifixion of Christ and its greater emphasis on grace rather than personal effort in producing such phenomena, but which overlaps strongly with Patañjali's catalog and the various others. What is unique to the Catholic tradition, however, is the large amount of credible evidence supporting the occurrence of these charisms, in varying combinations, in conjunction with the lives of particular saints. For voluminous and well-documented details of the evidence itself we recommend especially Thurston (1952) and Murphy (1992, Chapter 22), but what matters even more for our purposes here is the fact that these charisms are explicitly recognized as occurring more or less invariably in conjunction with mystical ecstasy as characterized by St. Teresa. All of the major commentators including Thurston himself, as well as Poulain, Arbman, and Pope Benedict XIV, agree on this crucial point. For example, ecstasy was a necessary though not sufficient condition for the well-documented levitations of both Teresa herself and St. Joseph of Copertino, and Poulain declares categorically that every known case of stigmata among the saints has been accompanied by ecstatic mystical identification with the wounds of Christ.

We think this large body of evidence, coupled with the evidence summarized in the previous section, strongly suggests that Patañjali is fundamentally on the right track in linking the *siddhis* to these extreme states of absorption. But what is it about such states that could possibly account for this linkage? Here we must attempt, however tentatively, to penetrate further into Patañjali's system.

DEEPENING THE DIALOGUE: MORE ON SĀṂKHYA/YOGA THEORY AND THE *SIDDHIS*

As we begin this effort, we must first say a bit more about the difficulties posed by Patañjali's text. His reliance upon sūtras or aphorisms stems from a period when oral transmission accompanied by direct interaction with a qualified teacher or guru was the standard form of instruction, and always coupled with intense practice. The sūtras themselves are often extremely compressed, and in many places they allude to but do not spell out details of contemporary theory or practice that he could assume to be known and understood by his students. He also uses many Sanskrit words of wide and sometimes uncertain significance that have no direct counterparts in English. The situation is not helped by the fact that subsequent Indian commentators of largely unknown scholarly and/or practical qualifications have often disagreed among themselves and freely imported later or alternative philosophical understandings into their own interpretations of Patañjali's meanings (Feuerstein, 1980; Whicher, 1998). The Sanskrit text has been stable for many centuries, and its more recent transliterations into Roman script equally so, but the available English translations of many individual sūtras, including unfortunately some of the most complex and theoretically important ones, are sometimes stunningly divergent and conflicting, leading Feuerstein (1980), for example, to lament "the general unreliability of the exegetical literature" (p. 86). Despite these genuine difficulties, we believe it is possible to discern the main contours of Patañjali's position as it bears upon the issues at hand.

The situation in regard to explaining the *siddhis* does not at first sight look promising. In his comprehensive text on Indian psychology, for example, Jadunath Sinha (1958/1985) remarks that while nearly all of the Indian schools of thought presume the reality of supernormal phenomena, their treatments are more descriptive than explanatory, simply recording facts of yogic experience, and "no reason is given why these powers are attained and why particular powers are attained as a result of concentration on particular objects" (p. 350). Most modern scholars have declined to engage with the *siddhis* at all, as indicated above, but a number have acknowledged that Patañjali probably included them in his treatise deliberately and might have had good reasons for doing so, and a few, including in particular Bryant (2009), Rao (2011), and Taimni (1961), have gone much further.[4]

Scholar/practitioner Edwin Bryant (2009) is in some ways the most interesting and important of this group. He, like most other contemporary scholars of religion, apparently presumes (while showing no awareness of the relevant scientific literature) that any claims regarding the *siddhis* "fall outside of the realm of empirical science as currently construed, or beyond the boundaries of human reason as understood in the context of post-Enlightenment, rational thought" (p. 329). Nevertheless, pursuing what he calls a "phenomenological" method, and building on the earlier observations of Koelman (1970, pp. 240–247) concerning "unessential results of concentration" (i.e., the *siddhis*), Bryant (2009) specifically sets out to demonstrate that *siddhis* can be understood as expected and necessary consequences of the underlying Sāṃkhya/Yoga metaphysics, while deliberately declining to discuss their possible reality (pp. 329–332). At the other extreme, I. K. Taimni (1961)—who was apparently a scholar/practitioner himself, as well as a Professor of Chemistry at Allahabad and a prominent Theosophist—seems prepared to believe that all of Patañjali's claims are literally true, and seeks mainly to unpack and explain them in terms of Sāṃkhya (and later) metaphysics, using many analogies drawn from modern Western science. Somewhere in the middle is K. R. Rao (2011), an American-trained Professor of both Philosophy and Parapsychology who regards Yoga as formulated by Patañjali as providing a ready-made key to all outstanding problems of contemporary psi and consciousness research.

All three authors work their way sequentially through all of Patañjali's sūtras, with Bryant and Taimni providing the original Sanskrit plus Roman transliterations, English translations, and sometimes extended commentaries. The resulting accounts are worth reading side by side for both agreements and disagreements. Importantly, despite the wide disparity in terms of their general attitudes toward the reality of the *siddhis*, they fundamentally agree in recognizing these as expectable consequences of the general principles of Sāṃkhya/Yoga metaphysics, as summarized especially in *YS* III. 9–15, 45, and 48. The theoretical basis for the receptive-psi or powers-of-knowledge side of this entailment is perhaps best captured by Koelman (1970):

> Yoga considers prakritic Nature as one substantial whole with a quasi-infinite number of immanent self-modifications. Every determination, past, present, or future, is and remains registered in the limitless plasticity of the *guṇas*. These *guṇas* preserve the vestiges of all past evolutive processes, all the present prakritic determinations, and contain in anticipation all the future determinations. On the other hand, knowledge is brought about by a mere reflexion of things prakritic in the mirror of the function-of-consciousness (*buddhi*). If then a prakritic reality can be placed in front of that mirror, all its determinations can become known if the mirror of the function-of-consciousness is absolutely undisturbed by the passionate vibrations of *rajas* and *tamas*, so that the purely reflexive function of *sattvam* may be energized without hindrance. . . . Man's individual body and mind are only superficially and relatively individual substances, fundamentally they are only energizations and self-differentiations of and within prakritic Nature itself, which is the sole genuine substance. Man, therefore, through his prakritic organism, is in communication, is one with prakritic Nature in its universality. On the basis of these doctrines, it seems almost natural that the yogi who attains to perfect concentration (*saṃyama*) can exhaust the entire intelligibility of the object he is focusing his attention on. Not only the superficial arrangement of parts which constitute its relative substantiality, but also the deeper reality of an object, that is, all its potentialities; its whole history and its future development, its relations and its properties will all stand revealed. . . . (pp. 240–241)

Thus, for example, is explained *YS* III.16, which states that knowledge of the past and future of some manifest reality can be obtained by performance of *saṃyama* on its possible transformations (*YS* III.9–15).[5] Similarly, since the sounds emanating from various creatures are expressions of underlying meanings, which are subtle contents of their minds, by performing *saṃyama* on the sounds one can recover the meanings (*YS* III.17).

Bryant (2009), again following Koelman, extends this picture in the direction of expressive psi or powers-of-action:

> [G]ross perceivable matter in essence consists of subtler matter, and this of subtler matter still, etc., all of which in Sāṅkhya is ultimately nothing more than a combination of the three *guṇas*. . . . [T]he *yogī* is held to transcend the limitations of the *kleśas* and the *ahaṅkāra*, which have restricted or localized or, better, individualized a portion of the universal *buddhi* into the personal *buddhi* of the adept, and thereby merge into the cosmic *buddhi*. This means it is now in a position to manipulate the external effects emanating from *buddhi*. Thus by manipulating the substructure one can change the nature of the physical products made of that substructure. (p. 336)

In sum, the core principle underlying the *siddhis* is that by utilizing the process of *saṃyama* to penetrate their own depths and the parallel constitution of the external world, yogis can gain progressive mastery both of *prakṛtic* nature itself and of the higher powers of cognition including psi powers (III.45–49).

Bryant, Rao, and Taimni themselves systematically deploy these concepts to individual analysis of all of the *siddhis* described in Book III, with sometimes inconsistent and not altogether successful but often interesting results. We will not comment on their analyses in detail, nor follow their example, first because there is not enough space in this short chapter to do so, and second because in many cases we would frankly not know what to say. Instead, we will attempt to identify a few specific ways in which Patañjali's conceptual system seems to us potentially capable of helping to explain "rogue" phenomena specifically targeted in Chapter 1.

First and foremost among these are the phenomena of postmortem survival and rebirth. As indicated earlier, Sāṃkhya accounts for these by postulating an inner or "subtle" body—the *sūkṣma śarīra*, consisting of the "internal organ" or *antaḥkaraṇa* (*buddhi*, *ahaṃkāra*, and *manas*) plus the ten generalized capacities for perception and action, clothed in a sheath of *tanmātras*—which is conceptually distinct and functionally separable from the outer, gross, physical body, and which carries impressions, tendencies, and karmic deposits throughout each life and into the next. Note that such an entity could also potentially explain related phenomena, presumably unknown to Patañjali, such as crisis apparitions and NDEs occurring under extreme physiological conditions of deep general anesthesia and/or cardiac arrest (Chapter 1).

But do subtle bodies actually exist? We should first mention that some of Patañjali's commentators, starting with his first great commentator Vyāsa, have sought to dispense with them altogether, and for theoretically interesting reasons. This revolves around the content of a new technical term, *citta*, which Patañjali himself frequently uses, and which for him denotes the entire mental apparatus and is almost but not quite synonymous with the Sāmkhyan internal organ. As discussed particularly by Feuerstein (1980, pp. 58–61) and Whicher (1998, pp. 91–107), this is consistent with Patañjali's practical emphasis on holistic and dynamic properties of mind-in-action, rather than on the static structural or ontological properties emphasized by Sāmkhya, and it enables him to focus on the dynamic interplay between the seer (*puruṣa*) and the seen (*prakṛti*) in producing states of embodied consciousness. Partly in order to explain the possibility of omniscience, Vyāsa and several subsequent commentators argued that *citta* is all-pervasive, and from this they somehow deduced that transmigration must occur in the form of instantaneous transference to a new embodiment at the moment of death. In that case, and in accordance with the views of the Jains and some Buddhist schools, there would be no need for the finite personality to persist in subtle-body form during some interval between death and rebirth, and the concept of a subtle body is thus rendered superfluous (Koelman, 1970, pp. 103–104; Whicher, 1998, pp. 94, 105–107).

Patañjali himself does not specifically endorse or even discuss this picture, which Larson (2008) characterizes as "the simpler and more sophisticated Yoga view" (p. 47), but there seem to be good reasons to reject it. Feuerstein (1980) dismisses the entire issue regarding the "size of the mind" as something of a pseudo-problem, and points out in addition that the notion of an all-pervasive and omniscient *citta* seems to render the concept of *puruṣa* itself superfluous (p. 61). More importantly, from the empirically grounded perspective of this chapter, the hypothesis of instantaneous rebirth is falsified by the fact that the observed median interval between death and rebirth in documented rebirth cases is on the order of sixteen months, with many far longer. Almost 20% of these cases, furthermore, include memories of events occurring during the interim period, and some of these ostensible memories have proven verifiable (see Chapter 1). This is a good example of ways in which modern scientific methods and knowledge can potentially be brought to bear on resolution of ancient theoretical controversies.

There are also internal indications that Patañjali himself retained the subtle-body concept in something close to the classical Sāṃkhya form. Sūtra III.39, for example, alludes to voluntary possession of the physical body of another person, which Bryant (2009, p. 369) specifically analo-gizes to transmigration of the subtle body following physical death. Bryant (pp. 377–378) also interprets sūtra III.44 in parallel fashion as referring to voluntary and genuine (vs. merely imagined) out-of-body experiences, historically a principal source of subtle-body beliefs (McDougall, 1911/1961). Perhaps most significant in this context is sūtra III.18, which states that memory of past lives can be obtained by perfor-mance of *saṃyama* directly upon the impressions or *saṃskāras* pertain-ing to those lives, which are thought to be carried within the subtle body as the vehicle of transmigration but normally inaccessible. Good evidence for the existence of such memories in ordinary adults would strongly support both rebirth and the subtle-body concept, but at present we unfor-tunately have very little such evidence, most of it deriving from a few unusual hypnotic regression and psychedelic cases involving drastically altered states of consciousness. Note also that research of this sort neces-sarily involves the difficult methodological problem of demonstrating that verified "memories" are not in fact due to cryptomnesia—i.e., recall (under special circumstances) of normally learned but subsequently for-gotten material (Stevenson, 1983). There is also of course a large body of popular and scientific literature related to "subtle energies" and the like, but this is very uneven at best and no firm conclusions can presently be drawn (see also Samuel & Johnston, 2013). Probably the best evidence currently available for the possible reality of subtle bodies, ironically, is that pertaining to survival and rebirth generally and to the "quasi-physi-cal" properties of crisis apparitions in particular, as described in Chapter 1.

We will return to the subject of subtle bodies and subtle energies in Chapter 14, but turning now to expressive psi or powers of action, *YS* III.40 states that levitation can be produced by mastery of the "upward current," one of the five main *prāṇic* or "energy" currents thought in Yoga to be circulating in the human body. Presumably this involves intense visualization of the sort mediated by *saṃyama*, and of possible special interest here is the fact that an essential aspect of *saṃyama* is a profound and very particular change in character of the flow of experience. Patañjali pictures all experience (and even the world process itself—*YS* IV.33) as a succession of moments. Under ordinary conditions the momentary contents of consciousness or *pratyayas* come and go haphazardly, driven in large part by impressions, tendencies, and karmic deposits accumulated in subtle levels of the mind or *citta* throughout the course of past experience. But as the yogi gains control of the mind through practice, this changes slowly but systematically, such that unwanted or distracting contents are progressively inhibited or suppressed, and the desired or targeted contents actively enhanced (*YS* III.9–12). In the limit, in states of *samādhi*, these successive momentary contents of consciousness are said to become identical and repeating so rapidly as to be essentially continuous, a condition described as the "*ekāgratā*" *pariṇāma* or transformation (*YS* III.12). Referring to Henry Stapp's model as described in Chapter 5, these would clearly constitute conditions favorable for maximizing the Quantum Zeno Effect, and this could potentially help explain both the occurrence of St. Joseph of Copertino's levitations and their exclusive association with his ecstatic states of consciousness. More generally, it could potentially help explain a wide variety of ASC-associated physical effects including not only other forms of macro-PK but stigmata in Catholic saints, hypnotic blisters, and other physical manifestations of unusually intense imaginal processes (*IM*, Chapter 3).

As described so far, Patañjali's explanations have at least a rough structural similarity to others advanced on largely independent grounds by modern psychical researchers. There are clear parallels in particular with Myers's concept of the Subliminal Self, a deeper but still individual consciousness that is inclusive of the everyday or supraliminal consciousness and has "adits and operations" unique to itself which permit paranormal interactions with the world at large (see Chapters 1 and 4 above). This same basic idea—that is, of descending within the finite personality to connect with external reality at some deeper level beneath that of everyday surface appearances—also recurs in the Pauli–Jung scheme (Chapter 6 above) and in Jahn and Dunne's (2001) "M5" model derived primarily from their work in experimental parapsychology.

But Patañjali goes much further by attributing to each individual and to the surrounding cosmos parallel hierarchical substructures corresponding to stages of the *guṇas* (*YS* II.19, *YS* III.45, 48). As already noted

above, his explanations of *siddhis* often rely upon this ontological parallelism of world and psyche as postulated by the Sāṃkhyan experience-
based metaphysics. Another point in favor of such a metaphysics, parenthetically, is that since mental and physical things or events are conceived
as ultimately composed of the same "stuff" (the *guṇas*), traditional philosophical difficulties (Mundle, 1967) associated with explaining both
telepathy (direct or unmediated perception of the content of other minds)
and clairvoyance (direct or unmediated perception of physically remote
objects or states of affairs) in some theoretically consistent fashion are
potentially circumvented. Note that this sort of picture could also potentially help with phenomena such as "the unreasonable effectiveness of
mathematics" or more generally with veridical intuitions of genius, as
previously discussed in Chapter 7 of *IM* (see especially pp. 484–491), the
basic idea here being that in higher states of consciousness, by virtue of
the parallelism, one can somehow directly access deeper aspects of reality
itself.

This idea is absolutely central to Patañjali's conceptual and practical
system. As Feuerstein (1980) puts it: "the levels of cosmogenetic evolution are simultaneously the levels of psychogenetic involution. Each subsequently 'deeper' layer within the prakṛtic organism becomes a target
for the *yogin*'s conscious involutionary programme, until all levels of
manifestation of the world-ground, and even the world-ground itself, are
completely traversed" (p. 117). Furthermore, there can be no doubt that
Patañjali regards the higher states of consciousness both as more valuable
in their own right, as steps toward liberation, and as systematically associated with greater powers. For example, along with mastery of higher
stages of *samādhi* comes the "dawning" of *prātibha*, a faculty of instantaneous direct perception or insight without the aid of physical senses or the
lower mind (*manas*). This is thought to be an inherent property of *sattva*,
obscured or interfered with by the presence of *tamasic* and *rajasic* impurities of the internal organ, especially the *buddhi*, and hence it is progressively released or unfettered as full *sattvification* is approached, yielding
supernormal perception and ultimately knowledge of everything in
prakṛtic nature (*YS* III.34, 37; see Bryant, 2009, pp. 363–367; Koelman,
1970, pp. 231–233, 246; Taimni, 1961, pp. 334–343). *Prātibha* clearly
has a great deal to do with the real meaning of "intuition" (as contrasted
with the relatively superficial phenomena discussed under the heading of
"unconscious cerebration" by contemporary psychologists and neurosci-

entists—see Chapter 1), and it is echoed, for example, by Myers's concept of an "indwelling general perceptive power," by Schopenhauer's "dream organ," and by mystical *noēsis* as traditionally understood in the West from Plato and the Neoplatonists onward (see Chapters 2, 3, and 8 above).

But just how many such higher states or stages of consciousness are there? This question, unfortunately, is extremely difficult to answer with confidence even in terms of Patañjali's own system, without bringing in the many further complications related to its possible consistency or lack thereof with related cartographies such as those of early Buddhism. Patañjali himself provides only extremely terse descriptions of the lower stages of his hierarchy, and he barely hints at the number and character of the remaining stages. This no doubt has to do at least in part with the fact that the higher stages are increasingly ineffable or resistant to description in ordinary discursive language, and must be directly experienced and then discussed with a suitably qualified teacher in order to be fully understood and integrated. Whatever the reasons, both the original Indian commentators and contemporary Patañjali scholars hold widely divergent opinions as to what he really meant, particularly on the side of *samprajñāta samādhi*—i.e., *samādhi* with a specific object or "seed" (*sabīja*). For example, Koelman, Larson, and Taimni follow the ninth-century commentator Vācaspati Miśra in identifying eight distinct levels of *samprajñāta samādhi,* while Bryant, Dasgupta, Rao, and Whicher find only six, in agreement with the fifteenth-century commentator Vijñānabhikṣu, and Feuerstein, in disagreement with just about everybody else, finds only four. We will not pursue the details of these arguments here, but simply remark that the six-stage solution seems to us to correspond best to conceivable stages of passage backward or inward through the evolutionary sequence of the Sāṃkhyan *tattvas* that constitute the human mind and personality (Whicher, 1998, Chapter 5).

All commentators and scholars agree, however, with the clear statement of Patañjali to the effect that whatever stages do exist are ordered in terms of depth, in some sort of correspondence with progressively more subtle or refined stages of the *guṇas*, all the way down to the level of primordial *prakṛti* (*YS* I.45).[6] There is also agreement about the existence of one still higher state of consciousness—*nirbīja* or seedless *samādhi* (*YS* I.51, III.8, IV.29)—that is, *samādhi* without a specific object of any kind. This corresponds to the ultimate goal of Yoga, in which all modifications of the mind or *citta* have been overcome or transcended, and the seer (*puruṣa*) is established in its own essential, fundamental, and indescribable nature (*YS* I.3, IV.34).[7] Although we will not press the comparison here, the *nirbīja* state also appears to correspond quite closely to Stace's "introvertive" mystical experience (Stace, 1960/1987; see also *IM*, Chapter 8, and Chapter 2 above).[8]

It appears certain that these higher states involve drastic alterations not only in conscious experience but in cognitive function as well. Quite apart from Patañjali's own testimony about their association with attainments of various kinds, including *siddhis*, there is again abundant testimony to this effect from the documented statements of Catholic mystics. Poulain and Arbman, for example, go to considerable lengths to show that much more is involved in the higher stages of prayer than just redistribution of attention among items or skills all existing on the same level. Along with the ligature come infusions of genuinely new and superior faculty, sudden and dramatic expansions and transformations of intellectual capacity. St. Teresa (trans. 1946/2007), in describing her rapturous ecstasies, again speaks for many:

> In a single instant he is taught so many things all at once that, if he were to labour for years on end in trying to fit them all into his imagination and thought, he could not succeed with a thousandth part of them. This is not an intellectual but an imaginary vision, which is seen with the eyes of the soul very much more clearly than we can ordinarily see things with the eyes of the body; and some of the revelations are communicated to it without words. (p. 112)[9]

Many further examples of this sort could easily be supplied. Note here also that the characteristic features of these exalted experiences—their involuntary occurrence ("automatism") and unusual cognitive character ("incommensurability")—are precisely those identified by Myers as core properties of the "subliminal uprushes" of creative genius, a deep correspondence recognized also by Underhill (1911/1974; see also *IM*, Chapters 7 and 8).

In sum, Patañjali's system can provisionally be viewed as a multilevel generalization of Myers's original theory of the Subliminal Self along lines subsequently envisioned by James in connection with his studies of religious experience. Consciousness in its aboriginal nature seems to have vast inherent powers that become progressively contracted or diminished

as it finds expression through successively lower, coarser, or more matter-like layers of the psyche. Taimni (1961) is especially explicit about
this, partly reflecting his Theosophical roots,[10] but for a generally comparable picture founded on a much greater diversity of historical materials see Poortman (1978). This conceptual framework clearly also has
much in common with that of the Neoplatonic philosophers, as described
in the previous chapter, and with others described elsewhere in this book,
and we will return to it in Part III.[11]

There remains one further topic that is fundamental to Patañjali's conceptual system and hence demands comment, but which we approach
with considerable trepidation owing to its difficulty and obscurity. We
refer to a special form of knowing, "knowledge by identity" or "knowing
by being," that is claimed to arise in the course of *saṃyama*. Readers will
recall from our discussion above of the three "inner limbs" of Yoga that
the passage from *dhyāna* into *samādhi* is said to be marked by disappearance of the sense of self or ego as the knowing subject, leaving the object
of attention as the sole occupant of the field of consciousness. Far more is
involved here, however, because this transition, which Feuerstein (1980)
describes as occurring "suddenly and unpredictably" (p. 85), also allows
the object of attention to "shine forth" in a fashion which somehow reveals its own true nature (*YS* III.3). A somewhat fuller hint as to what
may be going on is provided by Patañjali in *YS* I.41, in which he describes
the essential process of *samprajñāta samādhi* metaphorically as one of
samāpatti or gnostic fusion in relation to the perceiving subject (*grāhitṛ*),
the act of perception (*grahaṇa*), and the perceived object (*grāhya*): to the
extent that one's impurities and the resulting uncontrolled modifications
of the mind (*citta-vṛttis*) have been eliminated or subdued, he says, one's
buddhi acts like a transparent jewel that faithfully takes on the color of
any object on which it is placed.[12] As Whicher (1998) puts it, "[T]he
mind and the object in *samādhi* are two different prakṛtic states that at the
moment of the identification appear in the experience of the yogin *as if*
they are the same thing (ontologically) due to the total absorption of the
mind in the object" (p. 217). Similarly, Koelman (1970) describes
samāpatti as "a transcription of the object in the mind . . . a moulding of
the mind's *guṇas* into a prakṛtic likeness of the object" (p. 196).

The concept of knowing by being recurs widely throughout the mystical literature, as indicated in Chapter 2 above. It is inherent, for example,
in the Neoplatonic doctrine of *noēsis* (see previous chapter), and Plotinus

himself declares that for such knowledge to arise, "it is necessary for the knower to be identical with the known and for the intellect to be identical with its object" (*Ennead* V.3.5.22).[13] Within the modern Indian philosophical tradition it plays a major role in the writings of the mystic and sage Sri Aurobindo (1949/2006). Something much like it evidently also underlies Bergson's concept of intuition, by which he means "the kind of intellectual sympathy by which one places oneself within an object in order to coincide with what is unique in it and consequently inexpressible," as contrasted with analysis, which represents it in terms of properties shared with other objects (Dasgupta, 1924/1970, pp. 143–144; Wild, 1938, p. 6). Forman (1999, Chapter 7) likens it—somewhat distantly, perhaps—to the direct, unmediated knowledge we have of our own consciousness, simply by virtue of being alive and conscious.

Taimni (1961) plausibly describes this "fusion" with the object of contemplation as opening up a channel for transfer to the yogin of properties of the object of contemplation, and he characterizes this "axiomatic truth of Yogic philosophy" as the key to many of the perfections described by Patañjali (p. 256). Thus for example *YS* III.24 states that by performing *saṃyama* on desirable human qualities such as friendliness, etc., the yogin can acquire or strengthen those qualities in himself. Similarly, *YS* III.25 asserts that physical qualities such as strength, etc., can be acquired or enhanced by performing *saṃyama* on animals which exemplify those qualities. These phenomena can be viewed as extreme forms of the well-documented effects of autosuggestion (*IM*, Chapter 3), mediated by the sheer intensity of *samādhi* as compared with everyday experience, and note that acquisition of new physical capacities in particular could in principle easily be tested.[14]

But clearly *samāpatti* must involve something other than literal identity. When the yogin performs *saṃyama* on the sun to obtain knowledge of the cosmos, for example (*YS* III.27), no thermonuclear reactions are engendered within. The union must therefore be construed as occurring on some level ontologically prior to that of ordinary manifest reality. Once the sun's "likeness" is properly instantiated in consciousness, that is, its prakṛtic or noumenal background somehow becomes directly accessible, and it can be known in effect from within, from a deeper and more comprehensive ontological perspective that includes but is not restricted to its superficial appearances as conveyed by the senses and lower mind (note the striking similarity here to Neoplatonic theurgy as described in the previous chapter). This process can be repeated, further-more, across the sequence of levels traversed in *samprajñāta samādhi*, and at a certain point in that sequence the knowledge obtained is said to become infallible or "truth-and-right-bearing" (*rtambharā, YS* I.46, 47). Taking this picture to the limit, the *buddhi* of each individual is an ele-ment of the cosmic *buddhi* or *mahat*, which is the all-pervasive first evolute of primordial *prakṛti* and the source of everything else in mani-fest creation; thus, that individual *buddhi* is in principle capable, in com-bination with the light of its associated *puruṣa*, of knowing everything through intuition or *prātibha* (literally, "to-shining"; *YS* III.34). Once again, a *siddhi* that at first sight seems simply bizarre appears to follow from the principles of Sāṃkhya metaphysics (Bryant, 2009, p. 355).

OVERALL ASSESSMENT AND FURTHER HORIZONS

Patañjali's conceptual and practical system clearly has many important strengths. In spirit, his remarkable treatise seems to us more a scientific work than a religious or philosophical one, although it predates this kind of academic dismemberment of its subject matter. Its central doctrines are presented not as authoritarian dogma simply to be believed, but as empiri-cal realities that can be experientially verified through assiduous practice of specified disciplines. Its value as a system of praxis, moreover, is largely independent of its metaphysical background, as argued in particu-lar by Rao (2012).

It also fits well with the central thrust of this book, in that it is explicit-ly a permission/filter theory of the Myers–James type, but extended now in a multilevel way that enables it to make more effective contact with mystical experiences and mystically informed religious philosophies (and see Chapter 2 for discussion of the value and importance of this). The whole system, moreover, is based upon a metaphysics radically different from that of contemporary physicalism, being grounded completely in actual or possible human experience. This difference has not been fully appreciated, we believe, by otherwise excellent modern commentators including Bryant, Koelman, Larson, and even Taimni, all of whom ap-proach Sāṃkhya and Yoga with conventional physicalist presuppositions lurking in the background, and who therefore repeatedly and almost re-flexively assimilate Patañjali's concept of the "subtle" matter underlying appearances to atoms or subatomic particles and so on in the classical-physics sense. Patañjali, however, is operating within an altogether different conceptual framework, as recognized also by Feuerstein (1980, pp. 49–50), and this is precisely the kind of metaphysical "jostling" we are trying to catalyze with this book.

His system also explicitly recognizes and takes into account higher states of consciousness, which we regard as an undeniable and tremendously important reality of human experience, and it provides a provisional cartography of such states that seems at least broadly similar to others such as that of Buddhaghosa's *Visuddhimagga* found elsewhere in the world's mystical traditions. Despite its well-known difficulties, comparative study of these cartographies seems to us a high priority for ongoing scholarly research, along lines already undertaken for example by Bronkhorst (2012), Sarbacker (2005), and Shankman (2008). At the same time, however, we believe that there are limitations to what can realistically be expected from ever more refined and detailed analysis of ancient texts and commentaries. We therefore also strongly advocate a complementary approach based on direct study in living meditative adepts using modern phenomenological and neuroimaging research techniques, and encompassing not only concentrative forms of meditation such as Patañjali's but alternative forms such as the "open monitoring" or mindfulness techniques of Buddhist *vipassanā*. Some of the results already in hand are quite remarkable, and it is certain that far more can potentially be accomplished along these lines (see supplemental material for this chapter).[15]

Another point in favor of Patañjali's system is that it explicitly recognizes the reality of psi phenomena and their deep connections with higher states of consciousness and with normally hidden parts of the world and psyche, and provides an explanatory framework that seems capable of helping us better understand at least some of these challenging phenomena. These properties strongly suggest to us that he is more or less on the right track, theoretically. Taimni (1961) takes a much stronger position, arguing in effect that all of the *siddhis* are real, and that the ability of Patañjali's system to explain them proves that it is correct as it stands (pp. 309–311, 354). Although we are definitely sympathetic to the possibility that the occurrence of psi phenomena and certain other *siddhis* may ultimately *entail* or *require* a metaphysical scheme like that underlying the *Yoga Sūtras*, we find Taimni's claims here to be scientifically premature at best. For one thing, he shows little if any awareness of the relevant scientific literature regarding psi, and his strong convictions about the reality of many *siddhis*, especially the more extreme ones, seem to rest entirely on often repeated but essentially undocumented assertions about the supposed powers and knowledge of unidentified adepts. For another, the real level of explanatory success is not always as clear to us as it apparently is to him. Nevertheless, Taimni's position would have real merit if the facts were as he claims, and the facts seem definitely headed in that general direction. What we most need, clearly, is more and better research.

The prospects for such research seem excellent: Patañjali's system amounts to a generalized transmission or filter model of the Myers–James type, already compatible with a greatly expanded range of empirical phenomena and lending itself to systematic further development and testing in scientifically customary ways. It presents an explicit, elaborate, and testable theoretical statement of relationships between mystical states and supernormal phenomena, one which in principle is surely accessible to deeper empirical investigation.

There are also problems in sight, however, and we will close by quickly pointing out some of these. To begin, Patañjali emphasizes voluntary production of *siddhis* by meditative adepts in conjunction with higher states of consciousness, but psi phenomena also occur at least sporadically under various other conditions, including both experimental conditions and those of everyday life, and it is not clear whether or how these might fit with his system. Of particular interest, perhaps, is his reference in *YS* IV.1 to some sort of psychoactive substance, possibly the fabled "soma" of Vedic times, but unfortunately it is not presently known what that substance was (Bryant, 2009, pp. 406–407).

A much larger issue concerns his means of explaining psi-type *siddhis* that involve access to things or information remote in space or time. As indicated above, Patañjali's commentators, if not Patañjali himself, try to deal with this by conceiving of *citta* as all-pervasive, and enabling the embodied personality to access it in its universality (see Bryant, 2009, pp. 466–467). That move, however, leads as we saw earlier to the false consequence about instantaneous rebirth. Another possibility might be to appeal to the *puruṣa* itself, which is conceived as outside space and time and potentially witnessing all of prakṛtic nature, but this would require some further explanation as to how the *puruṣa*'s knowledge might be selectively reflected into the *buddhi*, or *buddhi* somehow selectively participate in that knowledge. Patañjali does not specifically discuss these matters, but the relationship between *puruṣa* and *buddhi* is the central mystery of his system anyway, and seems rich and complex enough to admit such possibilities.[16]

Closely related to this are some issues in regard to the explanation of *expressive* psi versus *receptive* psi, and more generally how we are to understand phenomena of *activity* and *will* in the embodied person or *jīva* in terms of the Sāṃkhya/Yoga picture, given Sāṃkhya's portrayal of *puruṣa* as a passive and unchanging witness. Patañjali's allegiance to that classical Sāṃkhya doctrine, however, appears less than complete. It is true that he uses a variety of synonyms for the term "puruṣa" that are classified by Feuerstein (1980, pp. 18–19) under the headings of seeing or perceiving, cognizing, otherness, and ownership (or perhaps lordship in the case of *Īśvara*), and only the last of these comes within striking distance of activity and will. The gap that seems to remain caused Koelman (1970, p. 242) in particular to feel puzzled as to the explanation of the physical *siddhis*, and his solution, later built upon by Bryant as described above, seems rather forced, simply postulating that as the yogin progresses in self-control, *prakṛti* somehow "loosens its grip" and permits perfect knowledge to transmute itself into actions.

These theoretical contortions might not have been necessary, however, because upon closer inspection Patañjali seems to have already distanced himself from the supposedly pure passivity of the Sāṃkhyan *puruṣa*. Thus, Whicher (1998) points out that Patañjali also refers to it using words such as *śakti* and *citiśakti*, which connote power and energy, and *YS* II.23 in particular refers explicitly to unfoldment of powers inherent in the *puruṣa* itself (p. 78). This attribution of activity to the *puruṣa* is perhaps present at least in germ even in Sāṃkhya itself, moreover, since in *SK* 17 *puruṣa* is characterized as providing "a supervising power or control," and as somehow directing the "functioning or activity [of *prakṛti*] for the sake of isolation or freedom" (Larson, 1979, p. 261).

Both Whicher (1998, pp. 78–82) and especially Feuerstein (1980, pp. 21–24) are also doubtful of Patañjali's allegiance to the Sāṃkhyan doctrine of plurality of *puruṣas*, regarding it as something foisted upon him by his commentators, especially Vācaspati Miśra. Although the question appears to remain somewhat open, we are inclined to suppose that Patañjali himself had probably abandoned the plurality doctrine as well, and we think he would have been wise in doing so: In the first place, the Sāṃkhyan *puruṣas* are said to be vast in number, all-pervasive, devoid of all positive attributes, and completely isolated, so how and where could they possibly coexist? Even more decisively, perhaps, they appear to be subject to the argument of Stace (1960/1987) regarding the identity of indiscernibles, and hence must necessarily collapse into a singular transcendental Self or Ātman.

The mention of "isolation" brings us to a final point of difference between Yoga and Sāṃkhya, and one of great practical importance. Echoing *YS* I.3, Patañjali's final sūtra, *YS* IV.34, defines *kaivalya* or liberation in terms of cessation of the activity of the *guṇas*, resulting in establishment of the *puruṣa* or seer in its own nature. In line with the radically dualistic Sāṃkhya, many commentators have interpreted this state as one of *ontological* cessation, in which the yogin's material apparatus ceases to operate or disintegrates altogether and his *puruṣa* goes off by itself into some celestial realm. As argued especially by Whicher (1998), however, Yoga need not be, and historically has not been, world-denying in this way. In this more integral view of Yoga, the "cessation" is understood instead as cessation of *misidentification with* the modifications of the mind, freeing the yogin for more effective action in the world. This leads to the concept of the *jīvanmukti*, a liberated individual in the midst of life, and once again we find a striking parallel in the Catholic mystical tradition: when the elimination of egoity that accompanies ecstasy becomes a permanent trait, rather than a temporary state, one has entered the "mystical marriage," the fourth and last of St. Teresa's higher stages of orison, and there can be no doubt that the rare persons who have risen to that level, such as St. John of the Cross and St. Ignatius Loyola, as well as Teresa herself, have been powerful engines of practical worldly accomplishment.

In sum, Patañjali seems to us, and to others such as Prabhavananda (1979), Radhakrishnan (1923/2008), and Rao (2011), to have been moving, or at least capable of moving, away from classical Sāṃkhya and toward what later emerge as full-fledged monistic systems, such as Vedānta in its various forms and nondual Kashmiri Śaivism, which celebrate Yoga as praxis while seeking to improve its metaphysics. The last of these forms the central subject of our following chapter.

NOTES

1. Some editions omit the twenty-second sūtra of Book III, which follows obviously from its predecessor, but our numberings below for subsequent parts of Book III include this sūtra.

2. As parapsychologist William Braud (2008) himself acknowledges, in what can only be described as a massive understatement, "the roles of the last three limbs of yogic praxis have, thus far, not been tested adequately in contemporary psi research" (p. 232).

3. Teresa also identifies a further stage, that of the mystical/spiritual marriage or transformative union, with clear affinities to the Hindu concept of *jīvanmukti* or liberation in life; we will return to this in our concluding section.

4. Other noteworthy modern scholars of Yoga sympathetic to the reality of the *siddhis* include Chapple (2008), Dasgupta (1920/1989, 1924/1970), Eliade (1958, 1975), and Radhakrishnan (2008).

5. The underlying concept here seems strikingly analogous to that of the time-symmetric "Process 2" evolution of the quantum state according to the Schrödinger equation, as described by Henry Stapp in Chapter 5. We do not mean to suggest, of course, that Patañjali anticipated quantum mechanics in mathematical detail!

6. Reflecting his Theosophical and Vedāntic commitments, Taimni (1961) argues that Patañjali's functional stratification of the stages of *samādhi* parallels both the stages of the *guṇas* and the structural classification of *kośas* or sheaths found in the Upanishads. Despite its appealing symmetry, however, this picture is probably too simplistic, and it is summarily though perhaps too hastily dismissed by Feuerstein (1980, pp. 40–41). Theosophical influences are also present in the work of Sri Aurobindo, and through him in that of Eric Weiss (present volume, Chapter 13).

7. Most scholars and commentators have taken the view that the term *asaṃprajñāta* is equivalent to *nirbīja* and refers specifically to the highest type of *samādhi*, but Taimni (1961, pp. 34, 121–124) disputes this on grounds both of its etymology and the fact that these terms are used in systematically different contexts. In this case we think Taimni is correct. He also makes the interesting suggestion that the *asaṃprajñāta* states reflect transitions between *pratyayas* representing the same object of *samādhi* at successively deeper levels of consciousness—"clouds of unknowing," in effect, and perhaps analogous to the "acategorial states" described by Feil and Atmanspacher (2010) in the context of dynamic systems theory.

8. Stace and especially Marshall (2005; see also present volume, Chapter 2) also discuss "extrovertive" mystical experiences in which the natural world remains, but radically transformed in various ways. Interestingly, Vedānta makes a

parallel distinction between *savikalpa* and *nirvikalpa samādhis*, corresponding to experiences of the all-encompassing Brahman *with* qualities (*saguṇa*) and *without* qualities (*nirguṇa*), respectively, and Ramakrishna for example is sometimes described as oscillating between these exalted states (Satprakashananda, 1965, pp. 283–287).

9. Note the striking similarity here, incidentally, with the description by neurosurgeon Eben Alexander (2012) of his coma-induced experiences of what he calls "the Core." "Transcendent" visionary experiences of this sort are common components of deep NDEs (see *IM*, Chapter 6).

10. See for example Taimni, 1961, pp. 32–33, 40–41, 96–97, 113, 123, 143–146, 184, 186, 195, 338–339, 422, and 435–437.

11. A variant of this basic picture more heavily emphasized in the Tantric tradition concerns the system of *cakras* or energy-centers thought to be organized along the longitudinal axis of the body. Patañjali alludes to this system, especially in *YS* III.30–35, but does not discuss or develop it in any detail. Many authors have tried to identify these structures with physiological organs in the body, which is certainly inappropriate, and as in the case of subtle bodies, discussed above, it is unclear at the moment from a scientific point of view whether they actually exist in some more refined or "subtle" physical form, or are purely phenomenal in character. See also Chapter 14.

12. St. John of the Cross uses a strikingly similar figure to describe the transmission of mystical knowledge, treating the soul as a window that must be cleaned in order to permit its passage: "Let us make a comparison. A ray of sunlight is striking a window. . . . If it be wholly pure and clean, the ray of sunlight will transform it and illumine it, in such wise that it will itself seem to be a ray and will give the same light as the ray. Although in reality the window has a nature distinct from the ray itself, however much it may resemble it, yet we may say that that window is a ray of the sun or is light by participation" (Peers, 1951, p. 212).

13. Our thanks to Greg Shaw for this reference (translation by Ahbel-Rappe, 2010, p. 465n.11).

14. Psychoanalyst Nandor Fodor (1963), interestingly, invokes the same concept of identity or "at-oneness" as a possible explanation for phenomena such as stigmata, and proposes that it might also underlie phenomena such as weeping or bleeding statues in which properties seem to flow in the opposite direction.

15. Esalen CTR website, http://www.esalen.org/ctr-archive/bp

16. A variant of this might be to appeal to *Īśvara*, the Lord or God, an element of Patañjali's system that is foreign to Sāṃkhya. In *YS* I.23–26 Patañjali describes *Īśvara* as a special already-liberated *puruṣa*, unafflicted by *kleśas* and *karma,* etc., omniscient, and the teacher of the ancients. Many scholars have viewed this as showing that Yoga is theistic in contrast with Sāṃkhya, but

Sāṃkhya simply does not mention the subject, and Patañjali's inclusion of it probably has to do as much as anything with its value as a component of yoga praxis (Whicher, 1998, pp. 82–87).

REFERENCES

Ahbel-Rappe, S. (Trans.). (2010). *Damascius' Problems and Solutions Concerning First Principles*. Oxford: Oxford University Press.
Alexander, E. (2012). *Proof of Heaven: A Neurosurgeon's Journey into the Afterlife*. New York: Simon & Schuster.
Anand, B. K., Chhina, G. S., & Singh, B. (1961). Some aspects of electroencephalographic studies in yogis. *Electroencephalography and Clinical Neurophysiology, 13*, 452–456.
Arbman, E. (1968). *Ecstasy or Religious Trance: Vol. 2. Essence and Forms of Ecstasy*. Stockholm: Svenska Bokförlaget.
Aurobindo, Sri (2006). *The Life Divine*. Twin Lakes, WI: Lotus Press. (Original U.S. edition published 1949)
Benedict XIV, Pope (1850). *Heroic Virtue: A Portion of the Treatise of Benedict XIV on the Beatification and Canonization of the Servants of God* (Vol. 3). London: Thomas Richardson and Son.
Braud, W. G. (1978). Psi-conducive conditions: Explorations and interpretations. In B. Shapin & L. Coly (Eds.), *Psi and States of Awareness* (pp. 1–41). New York: Parapsychology Foundation.
Braud, W. G. (2008). Patañjali Yoga and *siddhis*: Their relevance to parapsychological theory and research. In K. R. Rao, A. C. Paranjpe, & A. K. Dalal (Eds.), *Handbook of Indian Psychology* (pp. 218–243). New Delhi, India: Cambridge University Press.
Bronkhorst, J. (2012). *Absorption: Human Nature and Buddhist Liberation*. Paris: UniversityMedia.
Bryant, E. F. (2009). *The Yoga Sūtras of Patañjali: A New Edition, Translation, and Commentary*. New York: North Point Press.
Chapple, C. K. (2008). *Yoga and the Luminous: Patañjali's Spiritual Path to Freedom*. Albany: State University of New York Press.
Das, N. N., & Gastaut, H. (1955). Variations de l'activité électrique du cerveau, du coeur et des muscles squelletiques au cours de la meditation et de l'extase yogique. *Electroencephalography and Clinical Neurophysiology*, Suppl. 6, 211–219.
Dasgupta, S. (1970). *Yoga as Philosophy and Religion*. Port Washington, NY: Kennikat Press. (Original work published 1924)
Dasgupta, S. (1989). *A Study of Patanjali* (2nd ed.). Delhi, India: Motilal Banarsidass in association with Indian Council of Philosophical Research. (Original work published 1920)
Dilley, F. B. (Ed.). (1995). *Philosophical Interactions with Parapsychology: The Major Writings of H. H. Price on Parapsychology and Survival*. New York: St. Martin's Press.
Eliade, M. (1958). *Yoga: Immortality and Freedom* (W. R. Trask, Trans.). Princeton, NJ: Princeton University Press.
Eliade, M. (1975). *Patañjali and Yoga* (C. L. Markmann, Trans.). New York: Schocken Books.
Feil, D., & Atmanspacher, H. (2010). Acategorial states in a representational theory of mental processes. *Journal of Consciousness Studies, 17*(5–6), 72–101.
Feuerstein, G. (1980). *The Philosophy of Classical Yoga*. New York: St. Martin's Press.
Fodor, N. (1963). At-oneness: A new phenomenon for parapsychology. *Research Journal of Philosophy and Social Sciences, 1*, 57–64.
Forman, R. K. C. (1999). *Mysticism, Mind, Consciousness*. Albany: State University of New York Press.
Honorton, C. (1977). Psi and internal attention states. In B. B. Wolman (Ed.), *Handbook of Parapsychology* (pp. 435–472). New York: Van Nostrand Reinhold.

Jacobsen, K. A. (Ed.). (2012). *Yoga Powers: Extraordinary Capacities Attained Through Meditation and Concentration*. Leiden, The Netherlands: Koninklijke Brill.

Jahn, R. G., & Dunne, B. J. (2001). A modular model of mind/matter manifestations (M5). *Journal of Scientific Exploration, 15,* 299–329.

Koelman, G. M., S.J. (1970). *Pātañjala Yoga: From Related Ego to Absolute Self.* Poona, India: Papal Athenaeum.

Larson, G. J. (1979). *Classical Sāṃkhya: An Interpretation of its History and Meaning* (Rev. ed.). Delhi, India: Motilal Banarsidass.

Larson, G. J. (2008). Introduction to the philosophy of Yoga. In G. J. Larson & R. S. Bhattacharya (Eds.), *Encyclopedia of Indian Philosophies: Vol. 10. Yoga: India's Philosophy of Meditation* (pp. 21–159). Delhi, India: Motilal Banarsidass.

Lutz, A., Greischar, L. L., Rawlings, N. B., Ricard, M., & Davidson, R. J. (2004). Long-term meditators self-induce high-amplitude gamma synchrony during mental practice. *Proceedings of the National Academy of Sciences USA, 101,* 16369–16373. doi:10.1073/pnas.0407401101

Marshall, P. (2005). *Mystical Encounters with the Natural World: Experiences and Explanations.* Oxford: Oxford University Press.

McDougall, W. (1961). *Body and Mind: A History and a Defense of Animism.* Boston: Beacon. (Original work published 1911)

Mundle, C. W. K. (1967). The explanation of ESP. In J. R. Smythies (Ed.), *Science and ESP* (pp. 197–207). London: Routledge & Kegan Paul.

Murphy, M. (1992). *The Future of the Body: Explorations into the Further Evolution of Human Nature.* New York: Jeremy P. Tarcher/Putnam.

Murphy, M., & White, R. A. (1995). *In the Zone: Transcendent Experience in Sports.* New York: Penguin, Arkana.

Peers, E. A. (1951). *Studies of the Spanish Mystics* (Vol. 1, 2nd ed.). New York: Macmillan.

Poortman, J. J. (1978). *Vehicles of Consciousness: The Concept of Hylic Pluralism (Ochēma)* (N. D. Smith, Trans., Vols. 1–4). Utrecht: Theosophical Society in the Netherlands.

Poulain, A., S. J. (1957). *The Graces of Interior Prayer: A Treatise on Mystical Theology* (L. L. Yorke Smith, Trans.). St. Louis, MO: B. Herder. (Original English translation published 1910)

Prabhavananda, S. (1979). *The Spiritual Heritage of India.* Hollywood, CA: Vedanta Press.

Radhakrishnan, S. (2008). *Indian Philosophy* (2nd ed., Vols. 1–2). New Delhi, India: Oxford University Press. (Original work published 1923)

Radin, D. (2013). *Supernormal: Science, Yoga, and the Evidence for Extraordinary Psychic Abilities.* New York: Random House, Deepak Chopra Books.

Rao, K. R. (2011). *Cognitive Anomalies, Consciousness and Yoga.* New Delhi, India: Matrix Publishers.

Rao, K. R. (2012). Complementarity of Advaita non-dualism and Yoga dualism in Indian psychology. *Journal of Consciousness Studies, 19*(9–10), 121–142.

Rao, K. R., & Palmer, J. (1987). The anomaly called psi: Recent research and criticism. *Behavioral and Brain Sciences, 10,* 539–551. doi:10.1017/S0140525X00054455

Samuel, G., & Johnston, J. (Eds.). (2013). *Religion and the Subtle Body in Asia and the West: Between Mind and Body.* London: Routledge.

Sarbacker, S. R. (2005). *Samādhi: The Numinous and Cessative in Indo-Tibetan Yoga.* Albany: State University of New York Press.

Satprakashananda, Swami (1965). *Methods of Knowledge, Perceptual, Non-Perceptual, and Transcendental, According to Advaita Vedanta.* London: George Allen & Unwin.

Shankman, R. (2008). *The Experience of Samādhi: An In-Depth Exploration of Buddhist Meditation.* Boston: Shambhala.

Sinha, J. (1985). *Indian Psychology: Vol.1 Cognition* (2nd ed.). New Delhi, India: Motilal Banarsidass. (Original work published 1958)

Stace, W. (1987). *Mysticism and Philosophy.* New York: Oxford University Press. (Original work published 1960)

Stevenson, I. (1983). Cryptomnesia and parapsychology. *Journal of the Society for Psychical Research, 52,* 1–30.

Taimni, I. K. (1961). *The Science of Yoga.* Wheaton, IL: Theosophical Publishing House.

Teresa of Avila, St. (trans. 2007). *Interior Castle* (E. A. Peers, Trans.). New York: Dover. (Original translation published 1946)

Thurston, H. (1952). *The Physical Phenomena of Mysticism.* Chicago: Henry Regnery.

Underhill, E. (1974). *Mysticism* (12th ed.). New York: Meridian. (1st ed. published 1911)

Whicher, I. (1998). *The Integrity of the Yoga Darśana: A Reconsideration of Classical Yoga.* Albany: State University of New York Press.

Whicher, I. (2001). *Patañjali's Metaphysical Schematic: Puruṣa and Prakṛti in the Yogasūtra.* Adyar, Chennai, India: Adyar Library and Research Centre.

White, R. A. (1964). A comparison of old and new methods of response to targets in ESP experiments. *Journal of the American Society for Psychical Research, 58,* 21–56.

Wild, K. W. (1938). *Intuition.* Cambridge: Cambridge University Press.

10

CONSCIOUS BODY

Mind and Body in Abhinavagupta's Tantra

Loriliai Biernacki

This chapter proposes to mine the wonderfully rich theorization of the body we find in Indian medieval Tantra toward the goal of mapping a conceptual framework for the relationship between mind and matter, as a way of addressing the kinds of evidence summarized in Chapter 1. With this contribution, I present a model of the body that derives from a Tantric perspective. This model offers a view of body and matter as more than simple physicality, in a blurring of boundaries that intimately weaves body in with what we understand as mind.

Fundamentally, Abhinavagupta's Tantric perspective points toward a panentheistic conception of body and mind. Panentheism is the position that understands the absolute as both immanent and transcendent. This holds whether the idea of the absolute is theorized as a divinity or simply as a principle of cosmology. The "theism" in "panentheism" nods toward ideas of deity; however, as a philosophical position in its own right, it is possible to formulate a panentheistic conception of an absolute as a principle of cosmology and not a deity. In this case, a panentheistic idea of the absolute suggests a capacity of consciousness to function both in terms of embodied human conceptions of consciousness and as an operative principle separate from embodied persons. For instance, a number of Asian traditions which rely on atheistic conceptions of the cosmos demonstrate a panentheistic model (Biernacki & Clayton, 2014). Of course, Abhinavagupta's panentheism from medieval India is located within a

specific historical time, place, and tradition, and as such, relies on a
notion of theism. However, what makes it compelling for us in the twenty-first century are the logical possibilities it presents—quite apart from
its historical location—for rethinking our own assumptions about the relationship between the body and the mind. I suggest that Tantra, and
specifically the writing of the eleventh-century Indian thinker Abhinavagupta, offers a conceptual schema for thinking about consciousness
which integrates mind and body via a third term, namely the idea of the
"subtle body" (*sūkṣma śarīra* in Sanskrit), a kind of quasi-physical yet
nonmaterial body that links the two.

This chapter will take two different approaches. The first part outlines
a Tantric conceptualization of the body as simultaneously material and
nonmaterial, what is known as the "subtle body." The second addresses
the underlying cosmological models that enable the Tantric vision of the
subtle body. There I point to its similarities to and differences from related strands of the Indian religio-philosophic tradition such as Sāṃkhya
and Yoga (as seen in the previous chapter), and nondual Vedānta in its
various forms. I then conclude by comparing the Tantric model to physics-based models of the mind–body connection presented earlier in the
present volume by Henry Stapp, and Harald Atmanspacher and Wolfgang
Fach.

WHAT IS TANTRA?

Tantra is a widespread philosophical and practice-oriented movement that
began to gain traction in India beginning about the fifth century CE. It
grew out of earlier ascetic movements in India such as the Kāpālikas and
Pāśupatas, skull-bearing ascetics who would wander around cremation
grounds (Lorenzen, 1972; Sanderson, 1990). These early movements pro-
gressed into complex sets of ritual practices and cosmology that were to
profoundly influence the practice of religion throughout India, and
throughout Asia, into Tibet and as far as Japan. These practices are based
on the premise that the physical body is capable of transcending its ordinary limitations through aligning it with latent, typically unexpressed, but
nevertheless omnipresent forces.[1]

Of course, like most other Indian traditions, Tantric traditions generally take quite seriously a number of ideas that are anathema to a Western

physicalist position. Specifically for our purposes here, most Tantric thought takes as true (1) the notion of reincarnation, and (2) the idea that humans have a subtle body in addition to a physical body and that the subtle body is capable of acting and affecting material realities apart from the physical body. Along with this is (3) the assertion of a great many disembodied entities.

With regard to the notion of survival of bodily death, I think it is not an accident that the beginnings of Tantra are located among practitioners deeply immersed in the transition of life to death at the cremation ground. The state of the body at the time of death is across many cultures considered an impure taboo state, and Indian religious traditions are no exception to this general attitude toward the body at the time of death. Moreover, across religious traditions this attitude toward the body is underwritten by the idea that the physical body is not the sum total of the person; something survives after the physical body is deprived of life. Of course, our contemporary scientific mainstream strenuously rejects the idea of some sort of consciousness or life present beyond the death of the physical body—and indeed this is a notion we also find in India historically, with the Cārvāka school of philosophy and India's historical atheists (lokāyata).[2]

Tantra offers a bold and creative move toward systematically utilizing and exploring the spaces between bodily instantiations and, with this, the notion of a kind of nonphysical bodied existence, rather than simply marking off the space as taboo. This begins at the origins of Tantra in the first half of the first millennium CE, with the Pāśupatas, ascetics who practiced in cremation grounds and developed rites related to this. By the time we reach the end of the first millennium, Tantric writings display a sophisticated model of the body, including a map of a counterpart to the corporeal body, a nonphysical body known as the sūkṣma śarīra, literally the "subtle body."

We also find a focused attention on nonphysical centers located at precise points in the physical body that interact with the physical body, the cakra system. With this also comes a psychophysical force located within the body, the kuṇḍalinī, which rises through different areas in the physical body and ultimately brings with its motion enlightenment for the person whose kuṇḍalinī is awakened. This psychophysical force is understood as nonmaterial, and yet it is capable of generating material effects, such as a spontaneous whirling motion (ghūrṇita) of the physical body that the meditator feels as the *kuṇḍalinī* rises, apparent hallucinations, and even the capacity to read others' minds. For our purposes here, what is important is the trend in Tantra, not as pronounced elsewhere, toward integrating the physical, material elements of our world with a notion of nonmaterial mentation, an idea of "mind" or "consciousness."[3] In the section below I will address this intermediary term, the subtle body, what it comprises, and how the link between the physical body and the mind operates conceptually and practically.

ABHINAVAGUPTA'S IDEA OF THE SUBTLE BODY

Abhinavagupta lived in Kashmir during the late tenth and early eleventh centuries, and he is considered one of the giants of Indian philosophy, especially well known for his writing on aesthetics. His writings span the gamut from ritual exegesis to cosmology, poetry, aesthetic theory, and philosophy. I focus on this Tantric philosopher in the present chapter because many of the underlying features and principles of cosmology implicit in a good deal of Tantra are made explicit in Abhinavagupta's writings. Moreover, Abhinavagupta is lauded in the tradition as not merely a philosopher, but as *jīvanmukta*, a liberated sage whose writings reflect his own personal spiritual attainments, including his own deep meditative states of *samādhi* (heightened meditation) and the awakened *kuṇḍalinī* in his own embodied experiences.

To begin, Abhinavagupta's understanding of the body offers something more than physical corporeality. The Tantric body is both physical and nonphysical. A hybrid entity, it presents a crossover status containing both what we think of as physical and also what we would think of as consciousness or immaterial being. It is both, body and spirit, and its status continuously fluctuates between the two positions, understood as complementary poles of a single reality. I suggest that this metaphysical ambidexterity of the body derives from his philosophical understanding of the relationship between mind and matter.

I discuss below the underlying philosophical model of this portrait of the body as twofold, as both a corporeal body and an immaterial yet real substance, as subtle body, composed of quasi-spiritual components. Ultimately one of the ramifications of the model is the practical applications of this hybrid body; it enables the use of the immaterial, quasi-spiritual element of the body as a vehicle for attaining supernormal powers. The main text I draw upon for the analysis here is Abhinavagupta's eleventh-century *Detailed Explanation on How to Recognize God* (*Īśvara Pratyabhijñā Vivṛti Vimarśinī*—IPVV).[4]

So what is the body made of? How is it made? Citing an authoritative text of his time, the *Mālinī Vijayottara Tantra*, Abhinavagupta tells us, "The human body, this lump of clay, is said to be governed by what are designated as the primary elements and the Principles (*tattvas*)" (IPVV 353, citing *Mālinī Vijayottara Tantra* 2.42). The primary elements, according to a schema that pervades the ancient Indian world and much of the premodern world[5] are the five elements: water, fire, earth, air, and space. The Principles (*tattvas*) are more particularly connected to Indian philosophical traditions. The Principles derive originally from the early Indian cosmology of Sāṃkhya, where they are twenty-five in number. As described in Chapter 9 above, on Sāṃkhya and Yoga, these Principles include things like the five sense organs, the capacity to smell and hear, the mind which allows us to think, the intellect which affords the capacity of insight, and the ego or I-sense, which allows us to direct our energies toward one task or another. Already in early Indian thought, with Sāṃkhya, beginning about the turn of the first millennium, we see things like "mind" (*manas*) and "ego" (*ahaṃkāra*) located in the category of "body," on the side of matter. This bears repeating—mind and ego for this philosophy are considered matter—lacking sentience. As we saw in the previous chapter, for Sāṃkhya the lower twenty-four *tattvas*, up through *prakṛti*, reference the side of matter. Only *puruṣa*, the twenty-fifth, demonstrates sentiency.[6]

Abhinavagupta expands this list of Principles to thirty-six. He adds to the early Sāṃkhya list a number of other Principles, first a set of limiting factors, numbering six, which we might judge to be fundamentally psychological in nature. In addition he offers a set of five higher Principles. These higher Principles perform two functions in particular. First, they encode a sophisticated articulation of subjectivity and objectivity as both deep structures of consciousness. Second, they demonstrate a temporal unfolding of consciousness through a teleological evolution from pristine awareness to the condition of being object; they mark the objective instantiation of awareness. In fact, one can read the entire set of the thirty-six *tattvas* in Abhinavagupta's system as a kind of teleological blueprint for the evolution of pure spirit into matter.

The six limiting factors consist of the following: (1) *Niyati*, a general-ized order to nature—the limitations of cause and space. It is the power which makes a seed grow into a banyan tree rather than an apple tree. In the medieval Indian context, this ordering principle is close to an idea of fate. (2) *Vidyā*, limited knowledge—the power which makes a person believe that his or her capacities for knowledge are limited. In this con-text, the omniscience of the highest deity, Śiva, is innate in human and other life, but it is clouded over, limited, by the power of *vidyā*. (3) *Kalā*, the limitation of action—like *vidyā*, *kalā* is what obstructs a natural and innate unlimited capacity for action. Here as well, unlimited power is the template, the innate nature of divinity we all share; however, due to *kalā*, our innate power becomes limited. Here *kalā* impedes the development of *siddhis*, supernormal powers. A recognition of one's innate nature, the inborn freedom (*svātantrya*) of consciousness, allows one to transcend the limitations of *kalā*. (4) *Kāla*, time—the power which makes us experi-ence reality as bound by past, present, and future. By identifying with the awareness of consciousness at a level above the Principle (*tattva*) of time, *kāla*, advanced yogis have a capacity to transcend the divisions of time and go into the future or the past. (5) *Rāga*, attachment—*rāga* is an innate sense of desire that pervades beings who identify with an idea of self still bound by duality. (6) *Māyā*, creative capacity to manifest duality—*māyā* is understood in this Tantric context not as illusion, but rather as a crea-tive power of the divine, which causes entities to be bound by duality. *Māyā* generates the idea that something apart from the self exists; *māyā* works to obscure the nondual nature of reality.

These six together work to generate the kind of reality that we find familiar, ordered with the boundaries of space and time, and familiar limitations of awareness and power. Even the sense of time (*kāla*), which for our Western eyes seems so fundamentally separate from the idea of mere body, is for Abhinavagupta an innate property of human subjectiv-ity and figures as part of what makes up our bodies and is ultimately inseparable from our physicality. Thus on a basic level, the boundaries of the body blur somewhat with elements of ourselves that we as Westerners tend to put in the category of "mind," in Descartes' terms, as *res cogitans*.

When the yogi gains self-awareness, recognizing his or her true na-ture, then the six Principles of limitation can be overcome. This is how Abhinavagupta's Tantric system explains most of the anomalous phe-nomena described in Chapter 1. By moving beyond the limitations, one acquires *siddhis*, supernormal capacities that are a fundamental expectation of Indian traditions. I will discuss below the specific impediments, the three *malas* or "stains," that make it difficult to move beyond the six limitations. Here in this Tantric schema is the mechanism by which *siddhis* arise. Thus, by passing beyond *kāla*, the adept can see the future and the past. By passing beyond *vidyā*, the adept can know what others are thinking, and so on. To sum up, the six limitations are familiar, yet, through the process of recognition of the self, one can achieve a state not bound by them and exhibit the kinds of supernormal powers, the *siddhis*, the attainment of which is a primary goal for most Tantric traditions. Thus the six limitations act as a constraining force for what is otherwise a limitless expression of awareness and capacity to act. In this sense they function much like filters, operating in a manner consonant with the "filter" theory outlined earlier in this volume, displaying deep, resonant structural connections with the Myers–James filter approach.

Of the six, *māyā*, the sense of duality, is the most difficult to overcome, as it forms the foundation of the other five limitations. In practical terms, the subtle body is important here, because it functions as a vehicle for the partial release of the limitations, precisely because the subtle body, that component which transmigrates, is less closely bound by the five limitations than the physical body. Yet even though the subtle is not bound so tightly by time, for the subtle body *māyā* remains operational. So Abhinavagupta tells us that the subtle body "is like the physical body, but it does not have limitations in terms of its spatial dimensions" (IPVV 306). It also is not bound by ordinary time as the physical body is.

Above these limitations, not subject to them, are five additional Principles: (1) *śuddhavidyā*, (2) *īśvara tattva*, (3) *sadāśiva tattva*, (4) *śakti tattva*, and (5) *śiva tattva*, with *śiva tattva* as the highest. These five Principles present a map of consciousness as it moves from subject to object, understood as a process that occurs for all sentient entities. A primary subjectivity, an innate "I-ness" (*ahantā*), transforms as it evolves through a process of extending outwardly. This outward extension entails a development and emergence of "thisness" (*idantā*), which ultimately congeals as the object, with its seeming insentience. Thus the two highest *tattvas*, the *śiva tattva* and the *śakti tattva*, demonstrate a position of a plenum of subjectivity. Out of this subjectivity emerges a sense of awareness or knowledge which is the state of *sadāśiva*. There is self-reflection here, turned inwardly. When this knowledge extends outwardly it demonstrates action, which is capacity directed externally, denoted by the *īśvara tattva*. The balance of the two, a measure of inward direction and outward direction evolves into *śuddhavidyā*. This is fundamentally an evolutionary scheme and with this, *śuddhavidyā* is a balanced crystallization of inward directedness and outward directedness, partaking more of a notion of the objective side of reality than the previous four *tattvas*.

The five highest *tattvas* are understood as referencing a state of awareness that is not subject to limitations of mundane time, limited awareness, and the other four limiting factors. Everything below *māyā* is understood to be bound with limitations, but above *māyā*, entities who identify with one of the five *tattvas* are free from the limitations that bind ordinary humans and which in this cosmology bind even some deities (ĪPVV 325). These five map out the transition from the pure subjectivity of consciousness and a pristine sense of "I-ness" (*ahantā*) to a sense of subjectivity that incorporates a sense of object as "that-ness" (*idantā*). "I-ness" or *ahantā* in this context differs from *ahaṁkāra* or "egoity" insofar as *ahaṁkāra* already entails limitations of subjectivity, including the limitations of time, and limited capacity to do and know. *Ahantā*, on the other hand, points to a pervasive, unlimited sense of subjectivity. Here, unlike earlier ascetic models of selfhood, cautioning the restraint of the self, the Tantric approach proposes an embrace and expansion of selfhood as an all-encompassing subjectivity, without boundaries. This contrasts with the general attitude of Indian traditions to the idea of *ahaṁkāra*, egoity, as something to be restrained and ultimately eliminated.

In any case, delving into the nature of these thirty-six Principles is a primary purpose of this section of Abhinavagupta's *Īśvara Pratyabhijñā Vivṛti Vimarśinī*. What Abhinavagupta adds to earlier Sāṃkhya ideas is a richer portrait of subjective identity. In relation to this, the Tantric model proposes that the notion of the highest state, the *śiva tattva*, here always in tandem with the *śakti tattva*, differs from the Vedāntic concept of Brahman precisely because it adds a capacity for action that is not present in the Vedāntic Brahman, which is otherwise conceived of as a transcendent, quietist divinity divorced from the world. This is a natural consequence of the earlier Sāṃkhya demarcation of *puruṣa* or "spirit" as fundamentally separate from *prakṛti* as "matter," "nature," a separation that finds its way into the nondualism of Advaita Vedānta. By contrast, the Tantric model reconceives divinity as inseparable from the world, and here for Abhinavagupta woven into a notion of the complex whole that includes the body.

In thinking of the body, we can also take a different tack: to approach the question of the body from the angle of origin, how a body is made. Abhinavagupta tells us, drawing on a truism of Hindu traditions, "bodies are produced from deeds, actions" (ĪPVV 284). The notion he draws on here is the idea of *karma*, perhaps most famously iterated in the *Yoga Sūtras* (II.13), where Patañjali tells us that our actions, our *karma*, determine our species for our next life—that is, our bodies—along with our life span and pleasant and unpleasant experiences. Far from a model of genetic inheritance driving the form of the body, this ubiquitous Indian notion routinely assumes a link between our mind states, our deeds, and the kind of body we have.

Abhinavagupta, however, fleshes the idea out (pun intended) with much more sophistication. Abhinavagupta understands that the physical body is intimately connected with a deeper template, that of a subtle body that we possess. This subtle body, the *sūkṣma śarīra*, is a very fine body, an outline of a body, a mere template. He tells us, "in fact, this very subtle body is a mere sketch. The gross body is placed upon it, filling it out" (ĪPVV 336).

So our physical bodies fill in what is a somewhat indeterminate template of a body, a very subtle noncorporeal body. This is in keeping with a pervasive principle in Abhinavagupta's cosmology, an appreciation of the homologies between the material and the mental. The form that the physical takes is predicated on a prior, less determinate form. This element of indeterminacy, a kind of fuzzy existence, is an essential feature of the "subtle." The subtle has a greater plasticity, a capacity to take on different forms because the indeterminate nature of subtle existence allows it a greater freedom to express a range of potentialities. As the body becomes less subtle, more gross, it becomes more fixed, less capable of the kind of plasticity that allows for *siddhis*, powers that demonstrate the supernormal capacity of human bodies, for instance, the power to fly or to read others' thoughts (keeping in mind that for an Indian model, another person's thoughts are the workings of *manas*, "mind," which is a form of matter). This Tantric model, we should note, is not so far from a model presented later in the present volume (Weiss, Chapter 13). A great deal of Tantric practice is designed to bring focused attention to the subtle body, with the goal of using the subtle body's greater plasticity to generate or exercise these powers, these *siddhis*.

Cosmologically speaking, the subtle body operates as a kind of template that replicates its own inherent form on the grosser, more physical level of the body with which we are familiar. The subtle body directs the shape the physical body takes. In this way we get a connection between the forms of the physical and the underlying nonphysical forms that offer the outline for the physical body.

So what exactly is this subtle body? As I noted earlier, Abhinavagupta tells us that the subtle body "is like the physical body, but it does not have limitations in terms of its spatial dimensions" (ĪPVV 306). Nor is it bound by the divisions of time into past and present, though it is still connected to time as a category (ĪPVV 306). That is, the notions of time past and present exist but are not binding for the subtle body. So it is not operating in a transcendent timeless space, yet still, it is not strictly bound to linear time. It operates within a framework of time dividing the capacity for awareness. This bears repeating: the subtle body is not a transcendent, time-free entity. This again entails a flexibility in terms of the capacity of the subtle body to access past and future, though in a limited way, since the notion of freedom, *svātantrya*, entails a fundamental openness and newness always available. The subtle body is, moreover, composed of eight components. Dubbed the "City of Eight," the *puryaṣṭaka*, these eight elements include first, the five vital breaths, called *prāṇas*, the inbreath, the outbreath, the upward breath, the downward breath, and the breath which mixes all of these. This makes five of the eight. Next there is the *antaḥkaraṇa*, the inner organ, subdivided into three, the mind, the intellect, and the ego. Finally, two more components make up the eight. These are the two groups of sense organs, the *buddhīndriya*, including the ear for hearing, the nose for smelling, and so on, and the *karmendriya*, the group of organs of action, including the hand, the foot, the sex organ (ĪPVV 334). This description of the subtle body is quite similar to what we see in Sāṃkhya and Yoga, as described in the previous chapter.

Thus we see that the subtle body is much like a physical body. It even contains, as essence or template, if not actually corporeally, hands, feet, and genitalia. In a Western context, if we imagine what might survive death, we tend to use terms tied to notions of "soul." And for Abhinavagupta, as for Sāṃkhya and Yoga, it is the subtle body in fact that survives bodily death and reincarnates life after life. Yet—if we in the twenty-first-century West begin to imagine what "soul" might be, do we often include components such as feet and genitalia?

And yet the mix of breath (the five *prāṇas* here), very subtle feet, hands, and ego, and so on, is somehow not bound by space, and only minimally bound by time. Even if the notion of subtle body operates merely as a sketch, only as a very subtle outline, Abhinavagupta is very clear that this subtle body too is really, without any doubt, unambiguously a body. He tells us:

> The City of Eight does in fact have the nature of a body, because the primary elements, fire, earth, etc., inhere in it. [7] Also, here, in order to remove delusion, [Utpaladeva] uses the word "body" to describe this extremely subtle state, the subtle body, *puryaṣṭaka*, precisely to instigate the reader to voice doubts about the nature of this body and the applicability that the word "body" with its physical implications entails for this subtle existence. (ĪPVV 306)

The idea of a subtle body, a spirit body, with hands and so on, a body with spatially contoured appendages, which is however not confined spatially, was apparently oxymoronic even for the eleventh-century readers of Abhinavagupta, requiring that Abhinavagupta delineate for his audience just exactly what this body is.

Moreover, the body, because it includes the subtle body as well, contains within it a variety of forces residing in various centers of this body, linking the human with the divine in a schema that has become quite popular in the contemporary West as the *cakra* system, a series of "wheels" aligned along the spine of the body that can be activated to instantiate greater mystical or magical powers, all the while embodied in this ordinary material human body. The system of *cakras* and the *kuṇḍalinī* has been immensely popular in Western appropriations associated with the "New Age" movements; however, we should keep in mind that the Indian texts which initially delineate the system offer a great diversity of representations. Abhinavagupta says:

> In this way, *Brahmā* is in the heart; *Viṣṇu* is in the throat; *Rudra* is in the palate. *Īśvara* is in the space between the eyebrows. *Sadāśiva* is upward in the cranial opening at the soft spot on the top of the skull, and *Śakti*, the divine Energy, the second Principle, next to *Śiva*, has the nature of being in no particular abode. These are all the absolute reality

in a sixfold body. The six forms serve as a cause making a ladder in the human body up to the level which is the absolute reality. [Utpaladeva] explains these forms designated by the scriptural texts as the inherent essential nature of each of these places, the heart and so on. (ĪPVV 309)

The physical body is the abode of nonmaterial forces; it entails energies and deities, with particular psychological signatures. Especially the idea of deities as nonmaterial forces is not inappropriate here—Abhinavagupta tends to gloss deities in this text as psychophysical functions, even with a fundamentally panentheistic theology. *Brahmā*, for instance, presents a fundamental creative capacity that humans can demonstrate (ĪPVV 308).[8] And again, what happens on the subtle level, in this case on the level of particular forces like the creative force that is *Brahmā*, is replicated in this mundane lump of flesh we think of as the body. The body functions as the material instantiation of particular forces. So, the creator God *Brahmā* is located in the heart, because the heart is understood by Abhinavagupta as the place in the body where we create ideas, and so on, with different signature functions making a ladder, both physically and metaphysically in the body. These several *cakras* lining up along the spine allow our physical bodies to manifest the energies of various archetypal forces or intentions in the cosmos, and they focally demonstrate the link that enables us to express heightened capacities, for instance, an extraordinary creativity by focusing attention on the *cakra* in the heart.

Even with this, Abhinavagupta's nondual understanding of the nature of mind and body tends toward a reduction of the differences, different signatures of different functional forces, into the essence of all these different forces as an idea of a dense mixture of consciousness and joy (*cidānandaghana*), which he understands as the basic nature of everything, as the *śiva* principle (*tattva*). Abhinavagupta tells us, "the *śiva* principle alone makes up the body (*vapuḥ*) of all entities, of all categories" (ĪPVV 257). This absolute *is* the body, albeit transformed in a way that we will discuss below. The bodies that we see and the noncorporeal bodies that we cannot see both derive from this highest principle, which is, in its essence a body; the Sanskrit here, *vapuḥ*, translates literally as "body."

Abhinavagupta emphasizes this point, in a way that reads the ancient texts of the *Ṛg Veda* against the grain of most of his non-Tantric compatriots. He tells us: "in this way the material appearance of effects which is the world [bodies and stones, etc.] is really just only what makes up the *Puruṣa*, the Person alone. As it is said in Vedic scripture: 'the *Puruṣa* is indeed all this'" (ĪPVV 317).[9] Classically, *puruṣa* is understood as spirit, the element of sentience. Moreover, *puruṣa* in a classical context is always contrasted with, placed in opposition to, *prakṛti* as matter, with *puruṣa* however, as a pristine consciousness, not connected to the components of mind understood as thinking with its psychological additions. Here, however, in a very bold move, Abhinavagupta undermines a millennia-old interpretation of spirit or consciousness, *puruṣa,* as opposition to matter and the body, *prakṛti.* Flipping this on its head, he tells us that the bodies, the stones, and matter that we find here, are really just consciousness; *puruṣa* is indeed the body here. To put it another way, Abhinavagupta tells us that the basic substance of physical matter is a nonmaterial and fundamentally conscious template.

These Tantric texts present the idea that physical bodies are a modality of an all-pervasive conscious essence. The physical body acts as inert matter only because its subtle essence has become fixed into a determinate form. The body's essential nature as consciousness, however, is always available to be accessed by recognizing its primary mode as consciousness. In sum then, what we have here is a hybrid body, a nondualist notion of the body in which the body is understood to be reversible in a flow back and forth between consciousness and matter, a porous body that is both physical and immaterial at the same time.

What causes the shift from matter to consciousness, back and forth, between the body as dense, determinate, insentient on the one hand and as consciousness on the other? It hinges on a perspectival shift between awareness and objectification, a kind of deep grammatology, a grammatical template for consciousness (Biernacki, 2013). When the person participates in the mode of subject, this references the pole of consciousness; when one focuses awareness in a mode of objectification, the side of object, matter becomes predominant. This is where the five highest Principles (*tattvas*) come into play. These five describe the process of the shift from pure subjectivity, *ahantā,* "I-ness" of the highest awareness, as it evolves into the relationality of self and other, subject and object.

In the interests of space, and since I have elsewhere written about it (Biernacki, 2013), I will only limn this here with one quote. Although Abhinavagupta discusses the process at great length, I offer the quote

precisely because it demonstrates that body and consciousness are ultimately reversible and that the attainment of supernormal powers derives
from the shift in perspective—from seeing and experiencing the body as
object to seeing and experiencing the essential subjectivity of the body.

Describing the shift from the state of being object, which Abhinavagupta calls *idantā*, literally *"this-ness,"* to a state of subjectivity, which
Abhinavagupta calls *ahantā* ("I-ness"), he tells us:

> When "This-ness" is in every way destroyed or melted away, one
> exists in the state beyond the Fourth in the pure consciousness of the
> state associated with *śakti* [the second Archetype in descending order],
> as it were along the lines of mercury which is melted with the leavings
> of brass which has come under the control of that [mercury] and ma-
> tured to become completely composed of gold, absorbed into its prop-
> er natural form. Then there is the budding, the beginning of full free-
> dom, even while still existing in the body. In fact, in this way because
> of the attainment of the entirety of extraordinary powers, he obtains a
> body like that of the eternally present god, Sadāśiva. (ĪPVV 348)

Thus, the goal is to let the sense of being object dissolve; what emerges as
a consequence is a naturally inherent sense of subjectivity. In this case,
the object itself, the body here, transforms from inert matter into consciousness and a body capable of extraordinary feats. This alchemical
metaphor suggests that the change hinges not fundamentally on a shift in
the form of matter, but on a recognition of the foundational role that
subjective awareness plays. It is fundamentally a shift in perspective. By
understanding the idea of self as the "I," the subject, rather than object,
the body necessarily transforms to a divine body, just as one can alchemi-
cally transmute mercury into gold. Of course, his very choice of analogy,
alchemical, demonstrates just how far our world view is from this eleventh-century Tantric. Our fundamentally materialist perspective can only
understand the transformation of mercury into gold as mere fancy, even
as here the point he is trying to make entails a shift in hermeneutical
perspective. This type of hermeneutical shift lies at the heart of
Abhinavagupta's philosophy of "recognition" (*pratyabhijñā*). "Recognition," which is a quick attainment of enlightenment (*mokṣa*), is universally accessible precisely because its fundamental requirement is simply a
shift in the lens we use.

How does Abhinavagupta's Tantric perspective compare to other Indian models of the relation between mind and body?

TANTRA IN RELATION TO ADVAITA VEDĀNTA AND SĀṂKHYA/YOGA

In this section I outline the underlying conceptual structure of Advaita Vedānta's and Sāṃkhya's metaphysics in relation to Abhinavagupta's Tantric perspective on the link between consciousness and the body. It is, of course, important to keep in mind that Sāṃkhya, Advaita Vedānta, and Tantra are each complex and varied traditions, a complexity to which this paper will not be able to do justice. The reader is requested to keep in mind that this chapter offers only broad strokes for the sake of setting in relief the significance of Abhinavagupta's model of the relationship between consciousness and the body. What Abhinavagupta's model offers is an explanatory mechanism for the link between consciousness and matter, a conceptual problem that both Advaita Vedānta and Sāṃkhya have difficulty accommodating.

Advaita Vedānta draws from earlier models of consciousness and mind, especially from Sāṃkhya theory, which it attempts to improve upon by positing a nondualism in place of Sāṃkhya's dualistic conception of matter and consciousness. As described in the previous chapter, Sāṃkhya's dualism leans toward a picture in which consciousness is fundamentally severed from physicality and incapable of affecting or being affected by the world of matter. In this respect, Sāṃkhya bears some affinities with our contemporary physicalism, even if unlike contemporary models, consciousness for Sāṃkhya is not determined by matter.[10] Advaita Vedānta proposes to bridge the gap of dualism with an overarching emphasis on consciousness.

One could argue that this model of consciousness, in which consciousness is fundamentally separated from the body and materiality, arises in relation to ascetic traditions, like early forms of Buddhism, Advaita Vedānta, and the Yoga that aligns with Sāṃkhya. And specifically, that it arises as an articulation of the pervasive classical Indian rejection of the physical world, *saṃsāra*, in favor of a triumph of spirit detached from matter.[11] In this Sāṃkhya-influenced ideology, the goal of ascetic meditation was from the classical period onward understood as a withdrawal from the world and the body. Knowledge, with its implications of abstraction from the body, encompasses the idea of the mental. Absolute knowledge in this construction entailed a complete cessation of worldly activity. As we saw in the previous chapter, the epitome of knowledge was figured in the image of the Sāṃkhyan *puruṣa*, omniscient but like a lame person with eyes, all-knowing but completely incapable of affecting the world (Larson, 1969, pp. 265–266). For both early Buddhism and Jainism, the apex of meditative success entailed leaving the world entirely behind,[12] the Buddha and the Jina beyond the reach of us mere mortals left behind, and unable to affect our material situations.[13] On the other hand, insentient nature, *prakṛti*, the prototype and progenitor of the material world, was figured as the blind person, carrying the lame *puruṣa*—*puruṣa* as conscious spirit, with eyes to see and know—on his shoulders. Matter and the world are linked with ideas of body, birth, dying, suffering, and impermanence, and all these are linked to a conception of action. The words *karma* and its cognate, *kriyā*, activity, stand metonymically for the manifestation of the material, objective, externalized world.

Moreover, it is here in the sphere of *kriyā*, the idea of activity, that we find both the operation of *karma* and the operations of cause and effect (ĪPVV 319). By this view, the notion of cause and effect (the bedrock of current, mainstream, classical-physics-based scientific practice) is intrinsically located within the sphere of *kriyā*, the material and objective world. This notion is one that agrees fundamentally with a twenty-first-century materialist epistemology: causes and effects are grounded and measurable within the realm of matter. Our twenty-first-century materialism, however, eliminates the connection of cause and effect with consciousness.[14] We should moreover keep in mind that the Sāṃkhya conception of "matter" is far broader than that of contemporary physicalism: it includes under the rubric of "matter" such factors as *manas*, a capacity for cogitation.

In any case, Sāṃkhya thus proposes an absolute wall between the realms of matter and consciousness. Advaita Vedānta tries to remedy the gap by proposing a monism of reality, *Brahman*, which is the reality *underlying* the measurable differences we see here. While the monism of Advaita Vedānta offers a solution to a problem arising in Sāṃkhya, the problem of dualism as an unbridgeable gap between matter and consciousness (which is, at least if nothing else, aesthetically jarring), this version of monism brings with it its own set of problems. One big problem the Advaita Vedānta model confronts—as a result of retaining the fundamental pristine, unaffected status of the absolute (its modification of the Sāṃkhyan lame *puruṣa*)—is that it must also propose two discrete levels to reality: our familiar one, *vyavahāra*, with its operations of cause and effect, glossed as the realm of *māyā*, illusion, *and* a truly real level. This supreme level is a view from the perspective of the absolute *Brahman, pāramārthika*, which is consciousness, where no real change occurs. This preserves the absolute status, the independence of consciousness from matter, and it also preserves the idea that the absolute really is an overarching principle, not subject to the decay and change that matter undergoes. The problem of change and decay gets shifted in this model to a cipher, the category of *māyā*. Śaṅkara's Advaita Vedānta adds, however, a development to the earlier Sāṃkhya model in that it proposes to locate the difference between *māyā* and consciousness in an act of perception. Not a Cartesian model with two types of stuff, *res extensa* and *res cogitans*, for in Śaṅkara's model the *res extensa* is a mere *trompe l'œil*. It only appears to exist: in reality, like the snake about to bite that is in fact a misperception of a rope in dim light, the *res extensa* is not actually real. Śaṅkara preserves with this a unity of the world: it appears as *māyā*'s illusion, but its frightful and multiple character disappears, rendering its true form as the highest Brahman depending upon our capacity to see.

Māyā thus is the complexity that makes up the world and everything that we see here. *Māyā* is the principle which allows for differentiation. *Māyā* is fundamentally a lens or process that causes us to see things that do not in reality exist, to see a writhing snake where really only a limp rope lies. One important difficulty here is the very counterintuitive position this presents. What we normally experience as real, all the things around us, are not real, and that which is real, the *ātman*, the self, is not something we can easily or ordinarily perceive. Moreover, for medieval Vedāntins like Vijñānabhikṣu, a sixteenth-century commentator on Sāṃkhya, Yoga, and Vedānta, Śaṅkara's ineffable notion of self is a position that is dangerously close to the Buddhist denial of any substantive self at all; Śaṅkara is labeled a crypto-Buddhist, *pracchanna-bauddha*. With this as well, the ideas of body and materiality become fundamentally unimportant for this position. We see here in Advaita Vedānta a reversal of our twenty-first-century materialism. Where our predominant epistemological model today understands consciousness as an epiphenomenon, the Advaita Vedānta position relegates materiality to the role of gratuitous element, itself a mere epiphenomenon.

What differences and developments does Abhinavagupta's Tantric perspective on the relation between body and consciousness offer? Perhaps the most salient shift that Abhinavagupta makes has to do with his employment of the notion of subjectivity. Where Śaṅkara proposes a shift in perception to explain away the duality of consciousness and matter, Abhinavagupta offers a further shift in perception, one not dependent on writing off materiality, but rather one that understands materiality as a continuum of subjectivity. For Abhinavagupta, consciousness and matter function in a continuum. All matter is at base fundamentally of the nature of consciousness; whether this consciousness expresses itself, or whether it appears inert, like the table, depends upon where it locates on the matter–consciousness continuum. This continuum plays out in expressions of subjectivity and objectivity. The position of subjectivity aligns with consciousness; objectivity entails matter. With this reformulation, Abhinavagupta proposes a system that can keep materiality and the body in his understanding of what is real.

In fact, the Tantric use of the body and matter within its schematic of enlightenment is a defining structural difference, from which other differences arise. Rather than understanding enlightenment in terms of an extraction out of the messy world of matter, with its inevitable subjection to flux, Tantra fashions an ideal of enlightenment that incorporates the world here, and concomitant with this, the body as well. Both Sāṃkhya and Advaita Vedānta tend to marginalize the body in the quest for enlightenment. Tantra brings the body back to the center.

This focus on the body plays out on a number of levels, not the least of which is a very sophisticated schematization of the body as not merely physical, but psychophysical, as the subtle body. However, we should note that Tantric traditions, and Abhinavagupta, do not invent the idea of the subtle body. The early *Upaniṣads*, from the seventh century BCE, reference a subtle body, as a collection of sheaths (*kośa*) wrapped one inside the other. In this schema, the outermost or ordinary physical body is the "food-body" (*annamaya kośa*). Inside this is the breath-wind body (*prāṇamaya kośa*), and then the mental body (*manomaya kośa*), covering inside it the body made of discrimination (*vijñānamaya kośa*). The innermost, most subtle body of the five bodies is the body made of bliss or joy (*ānandamaya kośa*) (*Taittirīya Upaniṣad* 2.2–2.5). This understanding of the subtle body as composed of sheaths is picked up also by Advaita Vedānta, in a short set of verses, the *Ātmabodha*, attributed to Śaṅkara (Rangaswami, 2012, p. 13). Sāṃkhya also references a concept of the subtle body. Īśvarakṛṣṇa points to a *liṅga śarīra*, literally a body mark or body sign (*Sāṃkhya Kārikā* 39–42). The word *liṅga* here perhaps suggests the relative imperceptibility of this body; it leaves a trace or mark, but only vaguely articulated. Abhinavagupta's terminology for the subtle body, the *puryaṣṭaka*, is more definitional, pointing to the eight components that make up the subtle body as outlined earlier. Abhinavagupta's term for the subtle body also finds its way elsewhere; Monier-Williams (2008) references it in Kullūka Bhaṭṭa's commentary on Manu's Law Book. What is especially salient about the Tantric incorporation of the body is that not only do Tantric sources elaborate the parameters of the subtle body, it also becomes a fundamental element in the quest for enlightenment.

The focus on the body also plays out in the extensive use of ritual and material objects within Tantric practice, which functions as a mechanistic manipulation of matter and material objects in the service of enlightenment. It also entails the added attention that Tantric traditions pay to the notion of *jīvanmukti*, the idea that a person can attain enlightenment while still in a physical body. Probably most important for our purposes here, the reintroduction of the body and matter within the schema of consciousness and identity affords an explanatory mechanism for the kinds of anomalous phenomena discussed in Chapter 1.[15]

ABHINAVAGUPTA'S SOLUTION AND THE *SIDDHIS*

Abhinavagupta's solution to the problem of consciousness, that is, how to link consciousness with the physical body, also draws on the bifurcation of the mental and the material (though keep in mind, as I mentioned earlier, that a more accurate labeling for his and indeed all of Indian philosophy would be the bifurcation between the *conscious/sentient* and the *material*, since "mind" proper (*manas*) is classified as mere matter). The fault lines for his system's construction of the bifurcation of consciousness and matter fall along the lines of knowledge (*jñāna*) as the marker for consciousness, and activity (*kriyā*) as the marker for the material. This fundamental bifurcation occurs throughout Indian thought.

When Abhinavagupta employs these terms he draws on a long tradition of thought pervasive in classical Indian traditions and throughout Tantric traditions. As Daya Krishna (1991) notes, "The deep division and dichotomy between 'knowledge' and 'action' lie at the heart of India's philosophical thought, and the Yoga-sūtra only confirms it" (p. 206).

I noted earlier that *kriyā* and *karma* are epistemologically related to cause and effect and to the processes of measurement that differentiate and define the nature of the physical world. One method that Abhinavagupta uses to bridge the gap between matter and consciousness is to relocate the concept of causal relations, to propose it as a fundamental property of *consciousness*—rather than having it located solely within the realm of materiality, as we see in Sāṃkhya, in Advaita Vedānta, and in contemporary scientific materialist discourse. That is, consciousness is not fundamentally transcendent or essentially divorced from the object-oriented and material expressions of the world. Rather, it is a logically prior manifestation of materiality. Thus, Abhinavagupta understands causality to be a function of consciousness.

Thus, fundamental to Abhinavagupta's philosophical agenda is a blurring of the boundaries between consciousness (*jñāna*) and materiality (the sphere of *kriyā*). So he says, "It cannot be proved that the relation of cause and effect is grounded within what lacks sentience" (ĪPVV 257). That is, cause and effect, and indeed the very notion of time, of sequence, are not primarily objective realities "out there"; they derive instead from the consciousness of the subject who experiences and creates time and the possibility for cause and effect. Abhinavagupta tells us, "therefore time is an attribute of the subject" (ĪPVV 290).

This might seem a merely psychological truism, but Abhinavagupta here understands it quite literally. Time, sequence, and the corollary of cause and effect are generated out of mind. Similarly, he says, "both knowledge and action are connected with the elements of the physical world" (ĪPVV 257). With this he suggests that mind is directly operative, nonlocally on the level of matter, without the necessary intervention of local material forces or causes. Abhinavagupta arrives at this conclusion as he works toward a philosophy that can coherently reflect how consciousness, *cid*,[16] interacts on the level of matter. Here we ought to keep in mind that Abhinavagupta operates within a worldview that understands causes to be *both* mundane material causes, such as a person's hand moving a pot from a table to the floor, *and* extraordinary, what we might

call supernormal, yogic powers—that is, consciousness can directly intervene without following the ordinary local interventions to move the pot to
the floor.

How can this nonlocal intervention work? For Abhinavagupta the experience of yogins demonstrates that it in fact does work; his job is to
provide a coherent explanation of just why it can work. In a nutshell, the
proposal he offers is that the mental and the material are different expressions of a single impulse, the same force or energy moving in different
directions. That is, nonlocal intervention works along the same lines as
the subtle body does in relation to the physical body. As I note earlier, the
subtle *is* a kind of physicality. Obversely, the material, the physical, is a
kind of mental reality or consciousness. Consequently they are fundamentally convertible into each other. The difference between the two is
that the mental is inward facing (*antarmukhi*) while the material is outward facing (*bahirmukhi*):

> *Māyā*'s creation spreads out, expands into many branches, with the
> Controller still lying within the core. And that creation is twofold still
> when the Energy of the highest Absolute yawns open. When that Ener-
> gy manifests inwardly, naturally it is called the Energy of Knowledge.
> However when it expands in stages with its active awareness gradually
> becoming more firm and fixed, then it manifests externally. This is
> pointed to as the Energy of Activity (*kriyā śakti*). The scripture [*Mālinī
> Vijayottara Tantra* 3.8] states: "When 'this' particular thing is very
> clearly defined as 'this,' in just this way, and clearly differentiated
> from some other thing, and then when one causes it to be known here
> in the world, that is called the Energy of Knowledge (*jñāna-śakti*). 'Let
> this thing be in this way, with this quality'—when again the thing is
> made to manifest externally here with just this quality like that—then
> it is called Activity (*kriyā*)." (ĪPVV 262).

The mental, the process of mind, occurs when energy manifests inwardly.
This inward manifestation is still an unfolding, yet one that is not directed
toward externalization. On the other hand, the material world happens
when that energy is externally directed and becomes fixed and firm as
objective reality. Note here that the action of outward manifestation, the
impetus toward matter entails a loss of the indeterminacy, the fuzziness of
reality that accompanies the impetus toward consciousness. To be an
external object means to become more "firm and fixed." It is conscious-

ness itself, through logical stages, that condenses into a more rigid "thing."

For Abhinavagupta, both of these are actually still forms of a single consciousness, though the internally directed force, the force of the mental is less fixed, less articulated than the externalized form that moves toward externalization as objective material world (*kriyā śakti*). Both exist all the way through. The external world, with this, the idea of *kriyā*, is intrinsic, latent, and yet present in the very heart of subjectivity. At the same time, an internal direction, which is the idea of knowledge and consciousness—or what we might call "mind"—is never entirely absent, even if latent, in even something blatantly objective and insentient as a rock.

These two also map onto ideas of the subjective and objective, which I discussed earlier in conjunction with the transformation from "this-ness" to "I-ness" as the shift from objective to subjective orientation. Abhinavagupta uses just this type of distinction as well to elucidate the bifurcation between *jñāna* and *kriyā*, knowledge and action, and to express the types of discrepancies one must grapple with between subjective and objective representations of reality, that is, from consciousness to materiality, discussed by Kelly and Whicher in the previous chapter.

In regard to the types of anomalous phenomena discussed in Chapter 1 above, these fit easily into the Indian conception of *siddhis*, supernormal powers. What Tantric cosmological schemes offer into the mix, beyond what we see in Sāṃkhya and Yoga, is a conceptual mechanism that incorporates materiality in a way that makes it possible for mentality to have large-scale effects on material circumstances. That is, it is not simply a question of knowing information that cannot be accessed except by extraordinary means, the kind of mind reading, for example, of certain prescribed results of meditation practices, the results of *dharaṇas* that Patañjali points out in Book III, *Vibhūti Pāda*, of his *Yoga Sūtras*. Rather, Abhinavagupta's Tantric cosmology understands that the connections between mind and matter entail the possibility of a direct *mental* transformation of the *material*. As I noted above, Abhinavagupta tells us that what occurs in the material world first takes root in the heart as a stirring, which differentiates what is earlier not differentiated. The process occurs through a sequence: first a lack of differentiation; then there arise the sequences of transformations of this initial energy into intentionality (*iccha*), then knowledge (*jñāna*), and then finally action (*kriyā*) with its incorporation of material results. The material result is, for this system, fundamentally an expected transformation of one form of energy or *śakti* (first as *cit śakti*, consciousness, later into *iccha śakti*, will, and so on), into a denser form, through action (*kriyā śakti*) which becomes matter.

Macro-psychokinetic phenomena are thus not a problem for this system to explain. They require that a particular person's sense of subjectivity be not determinate. That is, there should be not even an unarticulated sense of self as a person with a particular body, particular identity, particular desires (ĪPVV 270, 274, 280), but rather one's subjectivity needs to be aligned with the kind of indeterminate consciousness associated with *cit śakti*. This state of indeterminate consciousness points to a logically prior state of self-awareness characterized by a lack of determinate self-representation. It is in principle accessible to all sentient beings but is usually not accessed by us because we have learned to identify ourselves as stained by three notions: (1) an identification with repercussions of former deeds known as *karma mala*, the stain of karma, (2) an identification with an essential sense of otherness, duality, *māyīya mala*, the stain of *māyā*, and (3) an essential and usually unarticulated conception of the self as inherently limited, *aṇava mala*, the stain of smallness. The first, *karma mala*, is an identification and entanglement with our actions. It ultimately causes us to experience the effects of our deeds at some future point in time, possibly in the current life, or else in a later life. It is the stain of *karma mala* that causes rebirth. Abhinavagupta tells us that soteriological systems like Sāṃkhya work to rid persons of *karma mala* but not of the other two *malas*. *Māyīya mala* causes us to not identify self with the totality of the cosmos. It does not necessarily entail rebirth; various entities can attain a state of freedom from *karma mala*, and thus be not subject to rebirth, but still be bound by a fundamental sense of otherness, duality. *Aṇava mala* is the most difficult of the three to remove. It entails a deeply engrained sense that one is limited. One can be in a state of freedom from rebirth and karma and also free from the duality of seeing something as other but still be bound by a sense of the stain of smallness, *aṇava*. These three stains are the cause of our typical, but not absolute, incapacity to generate macro-PK phenomena. By overriding these three, the natural power of subjectivity can be channeled into a capacity to generate a variety of macro-psychokinetic phenomena, since material forms are just condensed, determinate transformations of mind and consciousness. These phenomena are not considered "miraculous" or

against the laws of nature. Thus a St. Joseph of Copertino, through intense and unadulterated identification with a sense of subjectivity, not
obscured by a sense of limited capacity of action (*kalā*), would be, in this
system, capable of floating to the chapel ceiling.

COMPARISONS WITH PHYSICAL MODELS

At this point I will address structural, metaphysical similarities and differences that Abhinavagupta's model offers to contemporary models. First I
offer comparisons to the model presented by Henry Stapp's semi-orthodox interpretation of quantum theory. Following this I examine
Abhinavagupta's model in relation to Harald Atmanspacher and Wolfgang Fach's dual-aspect monism based on the Pauli–Jung model.[17]

We should note that a number of popular works on physics in the last
few decades have suggested that Eastern philosophies anticipated twentieth-century discoveries such as quantum physics and relativity (Bohm,
1980; Capra, 1975). Frequently, appeals to Indian philosophies rely on
the model of Advaita Vedānta, the nondualist interpretation of the
Upaniṣads, texts of the *Vedas,* Hinduism's holy books.[18] This reliance
may be due in large measure to historical contingency, the confluence of
circumstances involving British colonial politics of the nineteenth and
twentieth centuries and the early self-representations of Indians in the
West. For instance, in terms of structural and metaphorical similarities, it
may be fair to suggest David Bohm's (1980) schematic explanation of
quantum phenomena as an example following the model of Advaita
Vedānta. Apart from historical links, such as his conversations with the
Indian mystic Jiddu Krishnamurti (Bohm & Krishnamurti, 1999), his
conception of the fundamental noncollapse of the quantum wave, where
the wave function presents an underlying, ever-present reality, and where
the wave function is the "guide" for the particles (Bohm, 1980; Stapp,
2014, Chapter 6), echoes the relationship that Advaita Vedānta presents
between the underlying reality, *Brahman*, in relation to the particular
individuations that make up the differences we see here. Graphically, for
instance, in a popular Indian metaphor that draws on the image of the
"wave," the ocean is the absolute Brahman, and the individual waves rise
out of this indistinguishable mass beneath.

I should stress again that this chapter does not suggest that we might be able to compare contemporary physics to medieval India. This kind of comparative analysis presumes an already implicit suggestion of a universal or anachronistic essentialism that I think is not merited here. Rather I offer only structural, metaphysical analogies, useful for thinking about the kinds of maps we make. I do not think that medieval Indian cosmological models might have anticipated the discoveries of contemporary physics. Nothing that I find in Abhinavagupta's writing, his status as *jīvanmukta* or enlightened sage notwithstanding, suggests that his philosophical understanding omnisciently presaged twenty-first-century quantum theory. Moreover, as I read him, his openness to the possibilities of additional, uncharted Principles (*tattvas*), suggests from his own perspective the opposite of a static view of an unchanging, pristine reality knowable to the mind of an enlightened sage (ĪPVV 293). Rather he embraces the possibilities of newness, new discoveries. This feature of his personality is in fact reflected in the laudatory title he was given: "Abhinava" meaning "ever new." With this I suggest only the idea that we might compare relational metaphors of self in juxtaposition to the world. Explicitly articulating the metaphors and homologies employed across these disparate disciplines offers a way of opening up other routes for mapping the relationship between mind and body.[19]

Stapp's "Semi-Orthodox" Interpretation of Quantum Theory

At this point we move on to address Henry Stapp's model of the mind–matter connection based on his modifications of Orthodox Quantum Theory presented in Chapter 5—here in terms of its comparative relationship to Indian models of mind–matter relations, including Advaita Vedānta, Sāṃkhya, and Abhinavagupta's Tantra, as a way of tracing out the underlying conceptual propositions. To address the apparent paradoxes of quantum mechanics, Stapp's underlying conceptual model differs fundamentally from earlier models such as David Bohm's, which proposed nondualist cosmologies, in Bohm's case a model in accordance with the Indian nondualist Advaita Vedānta. Rather, Stapp's model shares some structural similarities with the atheistic Sāṃkhya, and some individual features associated with Abhinavagupta's panentheistic conception of mind–matter relations, in addition to features shared with panentheistic qualified nondualism of systems like

Rāmānuja's. But Stapp's model also does not fit these perfectly, and leaves open space for a third agency, apart from matter and mind.[20]

As we saw in his chapter, Henry Stapp's use of quantum theory proposes that mind is an operative feature within the physical world, and that our mental intentions do in fact have consequences on the level of physical matter through a quantum intervention, specifically through what he designates, following Heisenberg, the Process 1, the free choice of the observer, and in relation to the operations of Process 3, the associated choice on the part of nature. His theory, based on the mathematics and physics of quantum theory, suggests both that our mental experiences are not epiphenomenal and describes a possible mechanism for connecting the mental to the physical. This connection occurs through the quantum interactions on the atomic level within neurons following a model of simple harmonic oscillations, for precisely how the mind can influence the physical realm. Stapp also proposes that Process 3 in von Neumann's delineation of quantum phenomena—where nature's choice, the choice of a "yes" or "no" that collapses the smeared-out continuum of possibilities into a particular response—is not entirely random.[21] "Nature" via Process 3, as Stapp points out in Chapter 5, displays an agentive function in his model, ultimately determining the outcome of any particular event. With Nature's predisposition to favor the emotional life of the mental probing by a consciousness, by von Neumann's "abstract ego," it may make sense to correlate Stapp's model with a version of dualist Vedānta, which we see associated with some of the bhakti traditions, and also to the type of qualified nondualism that we find in Rāmānuja's panentheistic theology.[22]

However, the fundamental reliance of these traditions on a theological notion of God makes this ultimately problematic for Stapp's model. Stapp is careful to minimize the similarities between his notion of nature and the idea of all-powerful deity, for nature merely gives "yes–no" responses. In any case, the suggestion that nature has a "choice" makes it difficult to avoid a notion of agency attributed to something beyond both the individual and the "predetermined" laws of physics. By implication, Stapp's model perforce relies on some notion of extra-human agency, even if he hesitates to explore the ramifications of a cosmology that incorporates this extra agency as indicative of intentionality, whether deity or teleology or something else. This makes Stapp's model amenable in some respects, if not entirely, to both a model with a limited view of deity and to a Sāṃkhya view like Īśvarakṛṣṇa's, which offers something of a personification of nature (*prakṛti*), with the implications of agency, even as nature is denied sentience. That Stapp affords agency to nature as a separate entity from mental consciousness, von Neumann's "abstract ego," means that Stapp's model does not correlate well with an Advaita Vedānta model.

The kinds of critique that Stapp presents against Bohm's interpretation of quantum physics, not surprisingly, also rule out correlations with an Advaita Vedānta description of the relationship between consciousness and matter. Stapp (2014) notes specifically that Bohm's physics in itself "says nothing about our minds" and in this respect is incomplete and no different from classical physics (Chapter 6). Stapp recognizes that Bohm went on to develop ideas that do find a place for consciousness, by positing "an infinite tower of observing systems," but he finds these ideas very complex compared with the simplicity of Bohm's original hidden-variable physics and they merely serve to transfer the mystery of consciousness elsewhere. In contrast, Stapp's selection of the "orthodox" quantum position that incorporates "measurement" works to avoid a notion of an underlying universal substratum, Bohm's noncollapsing wave, which is a feature of Bohm's model that shares a conceptual similarity with Advaita Vedānta.

In contrast, Stapp's embrace of the part played by the consciousness of the individual observer, the experimenter's "free choices" along with the intervention of a third agency that brings about wave-function collapse, instead approximates to some extent a panentheistic conceptual model, and in some respects the panentheism of Abhinavagupta's conceptual scheme. I should point out that here Stapp's stress on the role of the individual consciousness in the quantum process has a corollary response in an Indian context—while the nonduality of Śaṅkara's *advaita* is attractive insofar as it contains a way of subsuming the totality, it becomes difficult for it to explain the effects of individual karmas, that is, the "free choices" that individuals make and their consequences. In an Indian context, this becomes a very weighty problem, given the central and ubiquitous importance of the notion of karma across all Indian philosophy. So much so, that Śaṅkara's nonduality necessarily resorts to a two-tiered system, the "real reality" (*pāramārthika*), which is nondifferentiated, and on the other hand, "what things look like here" (*vyavahāra*), in order to regain ideas of the individuality and the consequences of karma for the operations of the system.

Thus, it is not so surprising to see the focal, predominant role that nature plays in both Stapp's and Sāṃkhya's systems (here with Sāṃkhya's *prakṛti* typically translated as "Nature"). And like Sāṃkhya, nature in Stapp's system is somewhat vague, a functional property rather than an entity and a totalizing feature; in Stapp's (2014) assessment, "all aspects of nature, including our own mental aspects, must be interacting parts of one mental whole" (Chapter 3). However, unlike Sāṃkhya, which irreconcilably separates materiality from consciousness, Stapp asserts that consciousness does interact with and influences materiality. Here Stapp's model draws closer to Abhinavagupta's conception of consciousness. Stapp understands the influence of the consciousness to arise through its capacity for "free choices" via a sustained set of questions that any one particular agent—Stapp's (von Neumann's) "abstract egos"—put to nature (Stapp, 2014).

This emphasis on "free choice" is one Stapp shares with Abhinavagupta. For Abhinavagupta freedom (*svātantrya*) is a key component of his system; its function is to afford a capacity for cause and effect within the transcendent, as we saw earlier. For this reason, Abhinavagupta's system has been frequently characterized as a dynamic nondualism, because transcendent divinity in this system is not cut off from the world of mere materiality as it is in both Sāṃkhya and Advaita Vedānta. In this respect, Stapp's use of free choice, as a means of linking individual mentality with material effects functions in a similar fashion to Abhinavagupta's use of freedom (*svātantrya*), as a way of linking consciousness with materiality, linking the poles of transcendence and immanence.

For Abhinavagupta, the idea of freedom is constitutive of consciousness. As Stapp notes, fundamental to quantum theory is the notion of a lack of a predetermined future; our choices are truly free, and like in Abhinavagupta's system, consciousness participates in enacting how the future unfolds in a nonmechanistic and hence unpredictable manner. Stapp's (2014) system, as he notes, entails a shift from a materialist-based conception of reality to a knowledge-based conception.

Moreover, for both Abhinavagupta and Stapp, it is precisely this freedom affecting materiality that demonstrates the link between consciousness and matter; however, in Stapp's system this occurs through the intermediating link of nature (that is, Process 3), responding to individual human agency. For Stapp, this is demonstrated via the Quantum Zeno Effect:[23] a rapid succession of questions put forth will statistically alter the outcome, through nature's predisposition to favor the mental probing, beyond an expected random quantum selection of the outcome. In the spirit of Abhinavagupta, we could say this occurs because the inherent freedom is a consequence of the dynamic, moving, changing nature of transcendent consciousness. Consciousness is inextricably involved in the realm of *kriyā*, activity—in the realm of matter. This is exactly what affords consciousness its freedom, its dynamic capacity to choose to make the world different, by consciousness alone. This of course is in essence "spooky action at a distance," and a concept that is fundamental to an Indian conception of *siddhis*, the supernormal powers of the yogī.

We might note here also that Stapp's use of the Quantum Zeno Effect connects to a broader construal of agency within an Indian context. The mental focus, in Stapp's case the sustained rapid probing of a particular question, the watchdog's sustained glances toward the burglar at the gate, sounds remarkably like the kinds of activity entailed in certain forms of pan-Indian meditative practices. As Stapp (2014) tells us, "This result means, roughly speaking, that increasing the repetition rate of the probing action tends to keep the physical state corresponding to the answer 'Yes' in place longer" (Chapter 4). Practices we see in an Indian context, for instance, the meditative use of visualizations, body scannings of *vipassanā*, and especially *mantras*, entail a repetitious probing activity. In particular, *mantras*—verbal formulas repeated mentally over and over hundreds of thousands of times to acquire supernormal powers—look a lot like the sustained repetition of the Quantum Zeno Effect that Stapp discusses, and they operate precisely by sustained repetition to acquire a capacity to directly influence the material world through the focus of consciousness alone, without material interventions.

Atmanspacher and Fach's Dual-Aspect Monism

In one respect the model presented in this volume by Harald Atman-spacher and Wolfgang Fach appears to share characteristics with an Advaita Vedānta view. Specifically, the dual-aspect monism that they propose is underwritten by an ontological substratum, as we see also in Advaita Vedānta. Additionally, Atmanspacher and Fach's model compares to Śaṅkara's in that both hinge upon a category differential, a shift between levels of organizational principle in the distinctions they make— which is precisely how they both can accommodate an underlying monism in relation to a plural everyday world. The underlying monism is ontological and the everyday appearance is epistemological, thus encapsulating both in a way that avoids contradiction. Advaita Vedānta, with its emphasis on duality as a function of a shift in perception, operates similarly with an ontological monism and an epistemic dualism. Yet Advaita Vedānta also differs from Atmanspacher and Fach's model insofar as their dual-aspect monism contains three terms, the underlying ontic substratum, which they call the *unus mundus* (following Jung), plus its two correlated epistemic manifestations, mental reality on the one hand and material reality on the other. Śaṅkara, on the other hand, conceives of two categories, the absolute reality, which is the ontological basis, and enfolded epistemologically within it, material reality as *māyā*, fundamentally a riddle, incomprehensible (*anirvacanīya*). With this, *māyā* is fundamentally unreal, operative in relation to materiality, but a distraction from our real goal of transcendence of the physical. [24]

Moreover, Atmanspacher and Fach's dual-aspect monism proposes that ontic states, located in the *unus mundus*, are not directly accessible. This would be problematic for Indian traditions generally. The question is what does "accessible" mean? Within Indian mystical traditions, even beginning with the *Upaniṣads*, ontic states could be accessed, just not through ordinary conscious states and the usual apparatus of language. Thus the sage Yājñavalkya, when questioned about the nature of the absolute, replies apophatically, *neti, neti*, "not thus, not thus" (*Bṛhadāraṇyaka Upaniṣad*, e.g., 3.9.26 and 4.5.15, in Olivelle, 1996, pp. 51, 71). With this he indicates to his hearers that nothing that one can point to can capture the reality of the absolute. Yet, the difficulty is primarily a difficulty of language. In the context of the *Upaniṣad*, Yājñavalkya is debating with other brahmins about the nature of the self. The king Janaka, who sponsored the debate, has offered the winner a thousand cows, with gold coins attached to their horns. Yājñavalkya himself claims the cows with gold coins precisely because he has accessed the state of the absolute. He says in no uncertain terms in the debate he has with the brahmin Śākalya, "I know that self" (*Bṛhadāraṇyaka Upaniṣad* 3.9.10–17, in Olivelle, 1996, pp. 47–49), and challenges his opponent Śākalya with the warning that his head will explode if he does not know the principle of the self. Indeed Śākalya's head explodes, and robbers take his bones, the text tells us. What we can take away from this is the assertion that the ontic level *can* in fact be directly accessed, for example, in mystical states of consciousness. Paul Marshall's Chapter 2 in the present volume addresses this amply. The claim of *mokṣa, nirvāṇa*, enlightenment and knowledge, if it is not mere book knowledge, is precisely a direct access to the ontic state of reality.[25]

As for the relation of Atmanspacher and Fach's theory to Abhinavagupta's, the latter on the surface also presents itself as a type of dual-aspect monism. However, ultimately the nondual impetus of Abhinavagupta's theory depends upon a fundamental convertibility between mind and matter, a feature not present in Advaita Vedānta, nor actually similar to the dual-aspect monism that Atmanspacher and Fach present. This shows up tangibly in their differing perspectives on the subtle body. As Atmanspacher and Fach note in Chapter 6:

> As psychophysical phenomena, subtle bodies belong neither to the physical nor to the psychological realm. However, we may speculate they are not based on relations between these two realms, as we conjecture for psychophysical phenomena, but refer to the psychophysically neutral domain directly, prior to the epistemic split.

Atmanspacher and Fach present the possibility of the subtle body as a direct expression of the inaccessible, holistic substratum, the *unus mundus*, which undergirds both the physical and the psychical. The idea of the "subtle body" in this case offers difficulties for Jung's model because, as they point out, the "subtle body" is in this interpretation theoretically not accessible. They write, "The very possibility of an apprehension of subtle bodies in the sense proposed above would contradict Jung's fundamental tenet that archetypes per se as formal ordering factors in the psychophysically neutral domain are strictly inaccessible epistemically, and thus empirically." This stipulation in Jung's model is based on the complementarity of quantum physics, with a mutually exclusive relationship between measurement, with its empirical determination, and the holistic indeterminate state before measurement. Thus, the "subtle body," participating in both the holistic fusion of the *unus mundus and* the determinate state of body, as matter measured out, is theoretically, definitionally, an unworkable concept. However, this goes directly counter to what we find within Indian traditions. The idea of a "subtle body" is a staple feature, prevalent across religious lines. Atmanspacher and Fach's development and elaboration of the Pauli–Jung model thus has difficulty integrating this ubiquitous feature of Indian traditions.

As they elaborate on Jung and Pauli, Atmanspacher and Fach also propose an analogy for the subject–object divide with the complementarity of quantum physics, where the subject and object find a psychophysically neutral origin within the "ontic," the holistic underlying substratum. Atmanspacher and Fach's expansion of the Pauli–Jung model here helpfully adds to the schema of subjective and objective insofar as it presents the possibilities for an "objective" appraisal of the subjective, phenomenological stratum of subjectivity, with, as Pauli notes, "the physical manifestations of the archetypes" (cited in Chapter 6 above). This he tells us is an *objective* iteration of a fundamentally *subjective* state. Here it appears that Pauli's location of the "cut" low on the chain, so that the recording device falls on the side of consciousness, affords the possibility of generating an "objective" status for the seemingly intangible Jungian archetypes. Though, we should keep in mind that it becomes objectively accessible only when it loses its holistic, ontic state in the process of measurement and the concomitant delineation into object.

It may be that locating the "cut" between the subjective and the objective as Pauli conceives it to include the mechanical recording device on the side of the subjective in part generates the difficulty with the idea of a subtle body. As I noted earlier, within Indian traditions we see the opposite classification, from Sāṃkhya onward, where the idea of mind (*manas*) is already classified as materiality, evolving out of primordial Nature (*prakṛti, pradhāna*). Much less a recording device. The classification of mind and ego as matter naturally lends itself to a conception of a subtle body. Locating the cut so much lower on the continuum of matter and consciousness leaves less space for a subtle body. Thus, both the location of the "cut" between subjective and objective and the axiomatic inaccessibility of the ontic contribute to difficulties with the idea of the subtle body.

In one respect Atmanspacher and Fach's position does resemble Abhinavagupta's. The indeterminacy of the holistic ontic state of the underlying substratum evokes the indeterminacy at the heart of consciousness in Abhinavagupta's model. Abhinavagupta points out that the essence of subjectivity, what he calls "I-ness," *ahantā*, shifts from pristine subjectivity, through an emanationist unfolding to increasing degrees of objectivity-oriented consciousness. As it does so, it necessarily entails a loss of its unified state in its shift into distinct, divergent objects. Abhinavagupta says, "At the stage of stirring in the heart it becomes something which has duality, distinctions. First, before this it is consciousness without distinctions and then it has differences" (ĪPVV 260–61), and also, "in the first moment of creation it is conceived as only simply a mere cloudy indistinct outline of a picture, resembling the indistinct, fuzzy heap of entities which are the objects appearing to our inner sense organs [mind, intellect, and ego]" (ĪPVV 264). However, for Abhinavagupta, unlike Sāṃkhya, and Atmanspacher and Fach's development of the Pauli–Jung model, the process represents a continuum, marked by precise definitional shifts no doubt, but still a continuum rather than an irreversible state change.

CONCLUSIONS

In summary, Abhinavagupta's Tantric model of the relation between consciousness and matter also offers additional explanatory mechanisms to earlier Indian explanations of material-based anomalous phenomena, such as the macro-psychokinetic phenomena described in Chapter 1, since it explicitly attends to and works into its model of consciousness an incorporation of the body, and a concomitant materiality. It is probably fundamentally this addition of the body and matter as inseparably linked within a nondual framework that affords this Tantric model explanatory possibilities beyond what we find in Sāṃkhya/Yoga dualism and in Advaita Vedānta's nondualist idealism. The implicit panentheism of this Tantric nondualism also facilitates the linkage between consciousness and materiality.

In relation to the physics-based models of Stapp and of Atmanspacher and Fach, no single Indian tradition fits either of their views completely. Stapp's use of a third agency tends to distance his model from Abhinavagupta's Tantric model; however, the concept of freedom and a notion of nonmechanistically determined outcomes offer important points of contact that bring these two conceptual positions closer. Atmanspacher and Fach's conception of the mutually exclusive complementarity of the holistic substratum and the immanent reality poses some difficulties for

Indian models generally. However, in contrast to Stapp's model, it offers some similarities to an Advaita Vedānta model.

NOTES

1. One can tap into these forces especially through exploring the energies present in the cremation ground, in the transition from life into death, and for later Tantra through the intensity of sexual encounters enacted ritually.

2. Some forms of early Buddhism, such as Theravāda, might also be understood to subscribe to a similar formulation of this idea.

3. This happens frequently through the mediating figure of a goddess. For historically contingent reasons, goddesses were cosmologically associated with matter, the material world. However, by virtue of being gods, they simultaneously partake of the notion of transcendence. Moreover, Tantra as a whole offers precisely a philosophy that works to integrate matter with spirit.

4. This voluminous text has yet to be translated from Sanskrit into English. All translations here are my own. The text is a commentary on his predecessor Utpaladeva's *Verses on Recognizing God* (*Īśvara Pratyabhijñā Kārikā*).

5. In ancient Greece, for instance, these show up as four elements, with occasionally the fifth as aether as a correlate to *ākāśa*, space in the Indian conception. They also appear in the medieval alchemy of western European.

6. We should note that some early forms of Sāṃkhya align *prakṛti* as *avyakta*, the "unmanifest," with sentient *puruṣa*.

7. Via the connection of the subtle elements to the sense organs.

8. Abhinavagupta writes: "'And the waking state' is associated with *Brahmā*. [Utpaladeva] says, 'because he is born out of the lotus' in the heart, *Brahmā* is called 'the One seated on a lotus.' . . . In this gloss that Utpaladeva gives for *Brahmā*, through connecting *Brahmā* with the heart lotus, he indicates that not only does *Brahmā* exist in the first moment when existence becomes manifest, so far as this goes, but also he reaches into the state of dreams and also in memory." Here Abhinavagupta alludes to the idea that creation also occurs in these two places as well, and the function of memory and dream come from the heart.

9. The quote is from *Ṛg Veda, Puruṣa Sūktam*, 10.90.2.

10. The Nyāya school too, as Daya Krishna (1991, p. 4) notes, would fall into this position of epiphenomenalism. We should note also that this comparison needs to be qualified insofar as the consciousness that Sāṃkhya proposes is an independent, preexisting ontological reality, whereas contemporary physicalism has an ineffectual consciousness derived from brain processes. In this case for Sāṃkhya mentality is determined by matter, but consciousness is not.

11. Parallels with contemporary physicalism, insofar as this position is its mirror opposite, here may not be entirely inappropriate.

12. *Nirvāṇa* for Buddhism, *kaivalya* for Jainism.

13. This is aesthetically portrayed in early Buddhist art as a complete eschewal of portraits of the Buddha. We see instead only images of footprints in early Buddhism: the Buddha who has thus gone (literally, *tathāgata*) only offers the path via footprints; he is not available to hear our prayers.

14. By contrast, Abhinavagupta's model incorporates cause and effect, as *kriyā*, into the sphere of consciousness.

15. Note here the parallels with the theurgic developments of later Neoplatonism, as described by Shaw in Chapter 8.

16. Here the divine consciousness of Śiva; at this "evolutionary" stage of consciousness, consciousness is understood to be at a stage prior to embodiment.

17. While Bernard Carr's (Chapter 7) speculation on string theory evocatively suggests the vibratory power of mantra within Tantric speculation, and in particular Abhinavagupta's understanding of *spanda*, a key concept in Abhinavagupta's understanding of the universe as undergirded by vibrational essence, a comparison seems not pertinent, since the similarities appear to be not conceptually driven, but instead a merely adventitious surface similarity.

18. In any case, *Vedānta*, the source set of texts called the *Upaniṣads*, are much more fluid in their philosophical position, spanning nondualist and dualist interpretations. The form of Advaita Vedānta that has become popular and representative to Western eyes today has been especially associated with a particular interpretation of these nearly 3,000-year-old texts. While the *Upaniṣads* date to about the eighth or ninth century BCE, the popular interpretation of the texts was put forth around the eighth century CE by the Indian philosopher and renunciant Śaṅkara. The ascetic monastic order he started, with four heads, the Indian "popes," has been a somewhat influential political institution that has also played into the Western image of the quintessential Indian philosophy as Advaita Vedānta.

19. Along these lines, see Lakoff and Johnson (1980), and Lakoff (1987).

20. It is precisely in the use of the third term that Stapp demonstrates resonances with Rāmānuja's "qualified nondualism," which incorporates the idea of god, a supreme person that gives efficacy to the actions of the individual's desires. However Stapp's notion of this third category remains comparatively impersonal in contrast to the idea of god in Rāmānuja's thought. See also Freschi (in press) on Rāmānuja and Vedānta Deśika.

21. Stapp draws on the findings of recent experiments by Cornell psychologist Daryl Bem to propose that mind influences matter also through our emotional stances, and elsewhere Stapp (2009) draws on neurological research that links electromagnetic oscillation frequencies to support the interaction between the

brain and consciousness. Stapp suggests, particularly in his analysis of the Bem experiments on the basis of empirical evidence, that nature has a predisposition to support our subjective positive emotions (present volume, Chapter 5).

22. A good analysis of this panentheistic conception may be found in Clooney (2014).

23. The Quantum Zeno Effect is a fundamental mathematical property of quantum mechanics that entails that a sufficiently rapid sequence of observations has the capacity to affect the behavior of the directly observed system, which in the orthodox theory is the brain of the observer. These observations, these "mental probing actions," originate in the mind of the observer, but can influence a physically described system. Thanks to Henry Stapp for this definition.

24. This, of course, is in tandem with the obvious differences in soteriological perspective.

25. There are here also some suggestive analogies to "the One" of Plotinus. See Shaw, present volume.

REFERENCES

Abhinavagupta (1987). *Īśvara Pratyabhijñā Vivṛti Vimarśinī* (Madhusudan Kaul Shāstrī, Ed., Vols. 1–3). Delhi, India: Akay Reprints.

Atmanspacher, H. (2011). Quantum approaches to consciousness. In E. N. Zalta (Ed.), *The Stanford Encyclopedia of Philosophy* (Summer 2011 ed.). Retrieved from http://plato.stanford.edu/archives/sum2011/entries/qt-consciousness/

Biernacki, L. (2013). Abhinavagupta's theogrammatical topography of the One and the Many. In C. Boesel & S. W. Ariarajah (Eds.), *Divine Multiplicity: Trinities, Diversities, and the Nature of Relation* (pp. 85–105). New York: Fordham University Press.

Biernacki, L., & Clayton, P. (Eds.). (2014). *Panentheism across the World's Traditions*. New York: Oxford University Press.

Bohm, D. (1980). *Wholeness and the Implicate Order*. London: Routledge & Kegan Paul.

Bohm, D., & Krishnamurti, J. (1999). *The Limits of Thought: Discussions Between J. Krishnamurti and David Bohm*. New York: Routledge.

Capra, F. (1975). *The Tao of Physics: An Exploration of the Parallels Between Modern Physics and Eastern Mysticism*. Berkeley, CA: Shambhala.

Chalmers, D. J. (1996). *The Conscious Mind: In Search of a Fundamental Theory*. New York: Oxford University Press.

Clooney, F. X. (2014). The drama of panentheism in Shatakopan's *Tiruvaymoli*. In L. Biernacki & P. Clayton (Eds.), *Panentheism across the World's Traditions* (pp. 123–141). New York: Oxford University Press.

Freschi, E. (in press). Are the limbs of God's body free? Yes, if He wants so—Free will in and before Veṅkaṭanātha. In S. Sellmer & M. Schmücker (Eds.), *Fate, Freedom and Prognostication in Indian Traditions*. Vienna: VÖAW.

Krishna, D. (1991). *Indian Philosophy: A Counter Perspective*. Delhi, India: Oxford University Press.

Lakoff, G. (1987). *Women, Fire, and Dangerous Things: What Categories Reveal About the Mind*. Chicago: University of Chicago Press.

Lakoff, G., & Johnson, M. (1980). *Metaphors We Live By*. Chicago: University of Chicago Press.

Larson, G. (1969). *Classical Sāṃkhya: An Interpretation of Its History and Meaning.* Delhi, India: Motilal Banarsidass.

Lorenzen, D. N. (1972). *The Kāpālikas and Kālāmukhas: Two Lost Śaivite Sects.* Berkeley, CA: University of California Press.

Monier-Williams, M. (2008). *Sanskrit-English Dictionary* (2008 version). Cologne Digital Sanskrit Dictionaries. Retrieved from http://www.sanskrit-lexicon.uni-koeln.de/download.html.

Olivelle, P. (Trans.). (1996). *Upaniṣads.* New York: Oxford University Press.

Patañjali. (2012). *Yoga Sūtras.* Göttingen Register of Electronic Texts in Indian Languages (GRETIL). Retrieved from http://gretil.sub.uni-goettingen.de/gretil/1_sanskr/6_sastra/3_phil/yoga/patyog_u.htm

Rangaswami, S. (Ed.). (2012). *The Roots of Vedānta: Selections from Śaṅkara's Writings.* New Delhi, India: Penguin.

Sanderson, A. (1990). Śaivism and the Tantric traditions. In F. Hardy (Ed.), *The World's Religions: The Religions of Asia* (pp. 128–172). London: Routledge.

Stapp, H. P. (2009). Physicalism versus quantum mechanics. In *Mind, Matter and Quantum Mechanics* (3rd ed., pp. 245–260). Berlin: Springer. http://arXiv.org/abs/0803.1625 or http://www-physics.lbl.gov/~stapp/Physicalism.pdf

Stapp, H. P. (2014). *On the Nature of Things: Human Presence in the World of Atoms.* Manuscript submitted for publication.

11

WHY WE ARE CONSCIOUS OF SO LITTLE

A Neo-Leibnizian Approach

Paul Marshall

For thinkers such as William James, Frederic Myers, and Henri Bergson, the question is not why psychical and mystical expansions of consciousness occur at all but why they occur so infrequently. If consciousness has a very great range of potential contents, why is it ordinarily so limited? The answer according to James and other proponents of filter theory is that consciousness, as we ordinarily know it, is kept in check by biological and psychological processes that feed it with percepts and memories of only immediate relevance, shielding it from distracting or disturbing material. Too much information can be a bad thing, for the everyday functioning of the individual and the long-term survival of the species. But when previously excluded contents make an appearance, by accident or design, nonordinary experiences occur.

Filter theory offers a neat explanatory approach but requires elaboration. In particular, two basic components need attention. First, there is the *filter* or selection mechanism that regulates consciousness, determining which contents will be "supraliminal," above the threshold of awareness (see especially Chapters 3 and 4 above). Second, there is the *reservoir* from which contents are selected for presentation or representation in supraliminal consciousness. The reservoir may itself contain forms of consciousness, but because these lie below the threshold of everyday awareness they are called "subliminal" or "subconscious." Theorists can look to cognitive and depth psychologies for insights into the shallower

regions of the subconscious, but to fathom its deeper nature, it is necessary to turn to metaphysics. Of particular interest are the monist forms of
mind–matter philosophy—idealist, dual-aspect, neutral—that challenge
materialism by taking consciousness, mind, perception, experience, or
feeling to be characteristic of the world at large. These philosophies may
help shed light on the farther reaches of the subconscious, beyond individual minds, and on the supernormal phenomena it appears to support.

An outstanding example in this regard is the metaphysics of Gottfried
Wilhelm Leibniz (1646–1716), an early critic of the materialist understanding of nature that Descartes had enshrined in his dualism. Leibniz's
mature metaphysics, the "monadology," has often been classified as a
form of idealism, a hazy category into which significantly different philosophies are placed, metaphysical and epistemological, exemplified respectively by Berkeley's immaterialism and Kant's transcendental idealism. According to the former, the world consists of minds and their ideas,
of percipients and their percepts ("to be is to perceive or be perceived"),
while the latter merely asserts that we know the mind-conditioned appearances of things, not the things themselves, whatever they may be. It is
often a matter of debate whether a particular philosophy constitutes idealism, and the question has arisen whether pre-Cartesian systems of
thought, such as those of Plato and Plotinus, can rightly be called idealism (e.g., Burnyeat, 1982; Bussanich, 1994). It has also been a matter of
debate whether non-Western philosophies commonly labeled idealist,
such as Advaita Vedānta and the Buddhist Yogācāra, qualify as such,
and, if so, what kinds of idealism they are (e.g., Trivedi, 2005). The
Pratyabhijñā philosophy of nondual Kashmir Śaivism, elaborated by
Abhinavagupta (see Biernacki, previous chapter), has often been called
idealist, a "realistic idealism" (Pandey, 1963) because the reality of the
world, grounded in the ultimate consciousness, is strongly affirmed, in
contrast to Advaita Vedānta, for which the world is "neither real nor
unreal" (sadasadvilakṣaṇa).

Leibniz's idealist credentials have been increasingly disputed: it is
debated whether the monadology preserves his earlier, Aristotelian
understanding of fundamental entities as organisms that unite soul and
body ("substantial form" and matter) or transforms it within an idealist
framework (see Hartz & Wilson, 2005). In the common, idealist reading,
Leibniz's monadology reduces material bodies to perceptual contents, or
more precisely to percipients' percepts of other percipients, and so qual-

ifies as metaphysical idealism if this is the view that material bodies have no existence external to consciousness, mind, or the mind-like. Leibniz supposed that the world consists of numerous, indivisible, transforming units. These "monads" are not the atoms of the materialists but complete perceptions of the universe organized from centers. In fact, the universe has concrete existence only as it is realized in the perceptions of monads. We ourselves are monads, and as monads we have complete perceptions of the universe, although largely confused ones. To the question "Why are we conscious of so little?" Leibniz would reply that it is because most of our perceptions are indistinct, too faint or "minute" to be discriminated individually, and so below the threshold of awareness.

Even if the idealist interpretation of Leibniz's monadology is incorrect or one-sided, it can still be used as a basis for theory construction. A metaphysics that takes complete, subconscious perception of the universe to be intrinsic to individuals looks as though it might find useful employment in a filter theory of supernormal perception. After introducing the monadology, I follow in the footsteps of Oxford philosopher H. H. Price, who suggested that it provides a framework for understanding psi perceptions. However, if the monadology is to account for psi, it probably requires a major adjustment, a modification demanded even more strongly by mystical experience, and so I go beyond Leibniz here and offer a *neo*-Leibnizian approach to the supernormal. Attention will also be given to postmortem survival. Monads are indestructible, but the question arises whether their indestructibility guarantees continuation of personal identity.

It might be judged excessive to resort to a metaphysics as exotic as Leibniz's, one that Bertrand Russell (1900) thought "a kind of fantastic fairy tale" when he first encountered it (p. vii). Clement Mundle's (1971) comment, directed at Bergsonian explanations of psi, could equally well be applied to Leibnizian ones: "It seems extravagant . . . to explain the sporadic exercise of ESP by a few people, by supposing that we are all potentially omniscient!" (p. 205). But exotic philosophy may be exactly what is needed, not just to make sense of psi, but of mystical experience too, and above all to resolve the problem of bringing mind and matter into relation, a central concern for Leibniz and his contemporaries in the wake of Descartes, and a pressing issue once again in our own day. Moreover, it is striking that two fundamental developments in modern physics have a "monadological" feel, the special theory of relativity and quantum physics, which suggests that the monadology may be no mere historical curiosity. Russell (1927) came to the opinion that Leibniz's system contains "hints for a metaphysic compatible with modern physics and with psychology" but requires serious modification (p. 159). Among his contemporaries, Russell was not alone in this view, and several thinkers of the time put forward philosophies indebted to the monadology, including H. Wildon Carr, James Ward, Dietrich Mahnke, and Russell himself. An outstanding example is A. N. Whitehead, whose panexperientialist process philosophy (see Weiss, Chapter 13 below) constitutes a major transformation and modernization of Leibnizian metaphysics (Basile, 2009), and arguably can be considered a form of idealism too.[1] While modification and updating are undoubtedly required, given developments in physics, biology, philosophy, and theology since the late seventeenth century, there is, I think, reason to stay closer to the Leibnizian original than some of its updaters have thought necessary, at least on certain matters, such as the all-inclusiveness of monads. The modification I shall suggest here preserves their cosmic wholeness but frees them from the inherent perceptual indistinctness that sets firm limits on their conscious experience.

A WORLD OF PERCEPTIONS

In Leibniz's mature metaphysics, the world consists of a plurality of simple substances, the monads (*monas*, "unit," "unity"). Monads are termed "substances" because they are independent beings, existing in their own right, and they are "simple" because they are not composite, not compounded of separable parts. These indivisible beings are the ultimate atoms of nature, the fundamental units on which matter and composite structures are based. However, unlike the atoms of the materialists, monads have inner complexity, each expressing the entire universe from a sequence of points of view as it changes from state to state. In expressing the universe, a monad is a unity, representing together all the other monads, and so a monad is a representation of the many in the one. The representational content of the monad is its *perception* while the tendency of perceptions to shift from state to state is its *appetition*, a striving and unfolding toward more distinct perception and knowledge. Active and representational, monads are "living mirrors" of the universe. Uncompounded and indivisible, they cannot be created or destroyed by natural means, but their perceptual states are unities characterized by multiplicity and transformation, for they express the universe, a universe that exists only as the contents of these changing perceptual states.[2] Expressive of the entire universe, monads are complete in themselves, in content and activity, developing from within but in mutual accord because they represent one another and express the selfsame universe. However, they are not entirely self-subsistent, for they have a common origin in God and are sustained through their transformations by the divine power, comparable to the way a thinker produces thoughts. One might say that in creating and sustaining the universe, God thinks it from multiple perspectives, and each of these autonomous but mutually accommodated, parallel trains of thought is a monad.

Monads are identical insofar as they express the same universe, but for a plurality of monads to exist there must be a "principle of individuation." Their individuality is partly derived from the unique spatial and temporal sequence of points of view from which they express the universe. Each monad has a unique "path" of development, but it should not be supposed that the monads themselves are positioned *in* space or undergo change *in* time. Rather, the point of view is a center internal to the monadic perception, a center from which the perceptual universe is organized, and space and time are derivative of the perception and appetition of monads. Moreover, a monad carries within itself something of all its past and future states, and also the past and future states of all the other monads.

Monads are distinguishable in another way. Their perceptions differ in distinctness, depending on the types of bodies they represent themselves as having. The default state of monads is perceptual confusion, for they consist of a universe of innumerable, minute perceptions. However, their bodies can organize and amplify perceptions to some extent and so confer a degree of perceptual distinctness. The more sophisticated the body, the greater the distinctness achievable. Monads can therefore be classified according to the types of bodies they have and the associated level of distinctness. The most primitive monads have very basic bodies and therefore no conscious perception. Although these insensible "simple monads" are living beings endowed with perception and appetition, they give the appearance of being inert matter. In fact, *matter consists of representations of groups of simple monads in the indistinct perceptions of other monads.* One might say that physics, which describes the behavior of simple monads, is the psychology of very confused, passive minds.

Matter, however, is not completely passive because it reduces to mind or the mind-like. If matter were mere Cartesian extended substance it would be completely inactive, for its only property would be extension, but being perceptual and appetitive it is inherently active. Some monads are more active than others: the more distinct a monad's perception, the more it is an actor than a reactor in the system of monads. Monads are active in relation to one another in respect of the degree to which they are the reasons for changes in one another (*Monadology* §§49–50). There is no direct interaction *between* monads ("transeunt" causation), no transfer of properties or contents, for they are self-contained wholes, but since they express the same universe they are accommodated to one another. What we call interaction or causation is, at this level, mutual accommodation or "pre-established harmony" in Leibniz's terminology. However, there is causation *within* a monad ("immanent" causation), and this activity does involve other monads indirectly for they represent one another and are mutually accommodated from the beginning through their common source. So while there is no direct, "physical" action between monads, it is perhaps nonetheless valid to claim that they do in fact *interact causally*, in a manner that is indirect or "ideal," as Puryear (2010) has argued.

Leibniz's philosophy of matter is a kind of panexperientialism, a "panperceptualism" in which the units of nature are cosmic perceptions. It is also a kind of panpsychism if it is allowed that the monads, if not in many instances fully developed minds, are at least mind-like by having perception and appetition, the precursors of the sensation and self-consciousness and the desire and volition of more advanced monads. Unlike many forms of panexperientialism, monadology is not beset by the "combination problem" (Seager, 1995), the difficulty that attends the idea that primitive units of experience combine into more complex experiences. Monadology has no such problematic compounding because perceptions are always complete wholes, expressive of the universe in its totality (Marshall, 2005, pp. 244–245). There is no bottom-up amalgamation of experiences into more complex ones. Rather, monadology is a top-down approach that begins with total experience but obscures it in some way. The principle of limitation in Leibniz's system is matter, which in the idealist reading boils down to confused perception and the passivity it entails. Leibniz sometimes calls this limiting factor the *materia prima* of the monad, the primary matter or "primitive passive force" that imposes limits on the monad's inherently active nature as a soul or "entelechy."

If the mind-like nature of monads is admitted, then the metaphysics also qualifies as idealism, a panpsychic idealism, for the world and its elementary units are understood in terms of mind or something akin to mind. Like space and time, matter is not a "substance," an existent in its own right, but is derivative of the perceptual constitution of the world. The form of idealism is therefore not eliminative, for it has a place for matter, which like space and time, is a "well-founded phenomenon." Rather, the idealism is reductive: the existence of matter is affirmed, but it is explained in terms of that which is more basic, the mind or the mind-like. An attraction of Leibniz's metaphysics is its genuine attempt to grapple with the nature of matter. Philosophies that regard consciousness, mind, or experience as a basic reality may fail to address matter adequately, either hastily disposing of it or uncritically taking over materialist assumptions. By contrast, Leibniz gave matter its due while reappraising it in drastic fashion.

More sophisticated monads have bodies with sense organs and therefore a less confused form of perception, *sensation*. These more advanced bodies confer sentience, memory, and a crude, associative kind of reasoning, and their "central" or "dominant" monads are termed "animal souls." Bodies themselves are composed of monads, or rather of representations of monads and their own bodies, and so there is a tiered arrangement of monads and bodies that proceeds to ever smaller scales. Nowadays, the arrangement would most likely be understood to proceed through the organs to cells and their organelles, and more speculatively to molecular, atomic, and subatomic levels. However, it is necessary to distinguish between an organism, which is unified by a central monad, and a mere aggregate or collection of organisms, and it is open to discussion whether the various units of matter identified by contemporary science correspond to organisms or aggregates.

Human bodies bring yet greater sophistication, conferring true rationality, reflective consciousness (*apperception*), and greater potential for activity. The central monads of these bodies are termed "minds," "rational souls," and "spirits." They have access to abstract ideas and truths grounded in God, and so are directly expressive not only of the universe, as all monads are, but of God too. According to Leibniz, human embodiment is not the most advanced condition, as there are many superior rational beings, including angelic and demonic spirits, with yet clearer perceptions and superior knowledge, indeed an intuitive knowing comparable to the divine a priori knowledge. However, none of these created beings are supernatural, for like all other monads, they are units in the system of nature, expressive of the universe, embodied, and subject to continuous transformation.

PSI PHENOMENA AND LATENT OMNISCIENCE

With some relevant features of the monadology set out, let us now consider how they can be applied to psi phenomena, following the example of H. H. Price (1899–1984), Wykeham Professor of Logic at the University of Oxford. Although inclined toward a non-Cartesian form of interactionist dualism, Price (1960) thought that of all the great classical philosophers Leibniz was the one whose ideas are "most suggestive for the psychical researcher" (p. 78). This is because Leibniz's metaphysics makes paranormal cognitions normal, a natural feature of the way things are, and gives a fundamental place to the subconscious, an essential part of filter theory. Price claims that Leibniz was the first modern philosopher to recognize subconscious mental activity, and the subconscious in question was not just a personal affair but a universe of subconscious knowledge. Leibniz gave us "the strange and exciting idea of latent omniscience," omniscience because the monad knows "all the empirical facts," and latent because much of the knowledge is subconscious (Price, 1960, p. 79). Price explains that in Leibniz's philosophy latent omniscience is "the inherent possession of every mind," knowledge we have possessed since we were created.

But Price is too cautious to take onboard the ideas so expressed and would rather tone down the language by saying that the monadic mind is subconsciously "in touch with" the world rather than has knowledge of it. In making this qualification, Price does not depart radically from Leibniz, who takes perception rather than intellection to be the essential nature of the monad, although Leibniz does refer to the monad knowing everything "confusedly" (*Principles of Nature and Grace* §132; Woolhouse & Francks, 1998, p. 64). Monads are omnipercipient, but their omniscience is highly qualified. For Leibniz, only God is truly omniscient.

Price had raised Leibnizian metaphysics in "Some Philosophical Questions about Telepathy and Clairvoyance," delivered to the Jowett Society in May 1940. Here he begins by asserting that philosophical interest in psychical research is justified, for there is good evidence for telepathy, clairvoyance, and precognition, and the phenomena challenge common understandings of mind, time, and causality. Price raises two explanations of telepathy and clairvoyance. According to the *radiation hypothesis*, physical radiation passes from brain to brain (telepathy) or from object to brain (clairvoyance), while the *direct acquaintance hypothesis* maintains that one mind has immediate knowledge of another mind (telepathy) or of a spatially distant object or event (clairvoyance). Neither explanation impresses Price. The radiation hypothesis cannot account for psi perceptions over great distances or through formidable obstacles, and, by analogy with wireless telegraphy, it requires that information be coded prior to transmission and decoded on reception. Against the direct acquaintance hypothesis, Price (1940) points out that psi cognitions are often "partly right and partly wrong" or symbolic in character, whereas direct acquaintance should give entirely accurate, undisguised knowledge (p. 372). To account for the errors and symbolism, there must be an intermediary process of "reproduction" or "representation," and so acquaintance is not direct.

Price (1960) was later to incorporate this important observation into a two-stage model of paranormal cognition: in the *contact stage*, access to normally subconscious material occurs, while in the *emergence stage* the accessed material appears in consciousness, often in disguised or substituted form, as if it has been censored (p. 80). In fact, Price's observation that paranormal cognition often emerges with inaccuracies and disguises suggests that three stages can be usefully distinguished, with a *modification stage* interposed between contact and emergence (Figure 11.1). Errors, disguises, and imagery, which could be personal, cultural, or archetypal, are introduced here, and further selection may take place.

Another criticism of the direct acquaintance hypothesis was made by C. D. Broad (1953). Broad doubts that clairvoyants have direct access to things, for their reports of clairvoyant perception do not describe the entities we would expect from our scientific knowledge of matter. For instance, a clairvoyant sees a playing card in a form comparable to how it would appear in normal vision, not as a "swarm of very small colourless electric charges in very rapid rhythmic motion" (p. 44). So if direct appre-

1. CONTACT   2. MODIFICATION   3. EMERGENCE

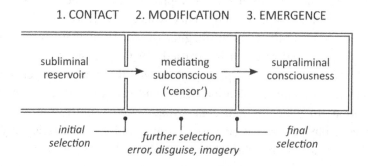

Figure 11.1.   Stages of mediated paranormal cognition. (© Paul Marshall, 2005, p. 240, Fig. 8.1 (modified), from Ch. 8, _Mystical Encounters with the Natural World: Experiences and Explanations._ By permission of Oxford University Press.)

hension takes place, it must be subconscious, in "a part of the mind" that is "cut off" from "ordinary waking experience," with the subconscious direct apprehension then "translated" into the familiar clairvoyant perceptions (p. 45). This can be called the _subconscious direct acquaintance hypothesis_, a hypothesis I shall adopt here. Our minds have an ordinarily subconscious dimension that is in direct contact with the world. In psi perceptions, this dimension is still subconscious to us, but it feeds consciousness with contents sourced from its direct acquaintance with the world, although in modified form. Hence, psi perceptions, while not themselves direct, depend on subconscious direct acquaintance.

Price effectively arrives at such a hypothesis when his discussion leads him to Leibnizian metaphysics. To explain telepathy, he raises the idea of a "common unconscious" that links minds causally. Minds are not isolated substances, as in the standard Cartesian view, but have direct causal relations with one another. The idea of a common unconscious leads straight to filter theory. Price (1940) suggests that we may be asking the wrong kind of question when we ask how psi perceptions are possible: "Perhaps the right question to ask, anyhow at the beginning, is not 'Why does Telepathy occur sometimes?' but rather 'Why doesn't it occur all the time?'" (pp. 374–375). The shift in perspective, explains Price, is equivalent to Bergson's remark about memory: we should ask "Why do we remember so little?" rather than "Why do we remember at all?" (p. 375). Just as it would be incapacitating to remember everything all at once, so too telepathy would be paralyzing if it were not largely shut out.

The filter has utilitarian and protective functions, and its origin is evolutionary, promoting the survival of the species.

Price turns his attention to clairvoyance but finds it more theoretically challenging because it is difficult to conceive of a causal connection between material objects and minds in the way that a common unconscious can be invoked to link minds telepathically. Clairvoyance suggests that there is not just "unconscious contact" with other minds but with the world in general. At this point Price brings into play Leibnizian metaphysics to explain how unconscious contact with the world is possible. He is aware that the introduction of speculative metaphysics may be shocking to his Oxford audience, particularly to its positivist members, but he feels that recourse to speculative metaphysics is necessary. Price explains that his preference is to look for a solution in Leibniz's *Monadology* and in the Leibniz-inspired parts of Russell's *Our Knowledge of the External World* (1914), but he acknowledges that other systems of metaphysics might be useful too, including Berkeley's idealism. Some metaphysical systems, observes Price, furnish conceptual frameworks into which supernormal cognitions can be readily fitted, whereas our customary frameworks, ultimately Cartesian in origin, cannot provide an explanation. The Leibnizian scheme not only provides a framework for clairvoyance and telepathy but does so in a manner compatible with the "theory of repression" (i.e., filter theory). Monads have complete perceptions, but the perceptions are largely subconscious for all but the most developed monads:

> Every monad has clairvoyant and telepathic powers, not occasionally and exceptionally, but always, as part of its essential nature. Every monad represents the entire Universe from its own point of view (Clairvoyance) and the perceptions of each are correlated with the perceptions of all the rest (Telepathy). In fact, what Leibniz calls "perception" is always both clairvoyant and telepathic. Moreover, he tells us that this perception is to a greater or lesser degree unconscious. (Price, 1940, pp. 382–383)

Price goes on to explore Russell's (1914, pp. 94–101) version of monadology, extending it to include memory as well as perception at every point of view, in order to account for hauntings and psychometry in terms of "place-memory." He also raises the idea that clairvoyance works by means of telepathic contact with the "perspectives" of Russell's theory or the monads of Leibnizian cosmology. If I am at one place and have a clairvoyant vision of an event at another place from a point of view at that other place, then perhaps I am telepathically attuned to a perspective or monad at that other place (Price, 1940, p. 384).

In "Paranormal Cognition and Symbolism" (1960), Price once again suggested that Leibnizian metaphysics, or more likely some adaptation of it, can elucidate unconscious contact, and he pointed out that according to the metaphysics we do not *come into contact* with the subconscious contents but are *always in contact* with them. He also returned to the idea that clairvoyance in a monadological universe is essentially telepathy. Matter-to-mind cognition (clairvoyance) is mind-to-mind cognition (telepathy) because material objects are really "a collection of minds or mind-like entities" (p. 78). While it is probably true to say that clairvoyance would reduce to telepathy in Berkeley's idealism, the same is not so clear in Leibniz's metaphysics. In Berkeley's system, minds receive their ideas, including their perceptions, from the mind of God, and the same will hold true if the system is applied to clairvoyant perceptions. As Mundle (1971) put it, "In a successful clairvoyance experiment, the subject would be getting information about and from certain ideas in God's mind, for on Berkeley's account, the concealed target objects *consist* of God's ideas" (p. 206). But in a Leibnizian universe, perception of objects, clairvoyantly or otherwise, does not consist of "reading" the contents of a mind distinct from one's own, but of perceiving contents of one's own self-contained but inclusive mind or mind-like nature. Whether perception of the contents of one's own greater mind is better called "telepathy" or "clairvoyance" I leave open, and perhaps it does not matter very much. What we can say is that all kinds of psi perceptions derive from the fact that monads are perceptual in nature, express the entire universe, and represent one another.

Price (1960) views retrocognition and precognition as just "dimensions" of telepathy and clairvoyance (p. 79), and so does not pay special attention to them. He no doubt appreciated that paranormal cognitions of the past and future are conceivable within a Leibnizian framework because each state of a monad has temporal depth to it. The present state of a monad is full of the past and "big with the future," a future that is enfolded but which will be unfolded in due course (*Principles of Nature and Grace*, §13; Woolhouse & Francks, 1998, p. 264). Leibniz himself referred to this characteristic of monads, along with the "perfect interconnection between things," when he explained to a correspondent that genuine occurrences of prophecy would be consistent with his hypothesis of pre-established harmony (Cook, 1998, p. 122). A monad's precognition will be cognition of its *own* future states, but since its own states express the entire universe all future events are potentially cognizable. The same is true of retrocognition: the past states of a monad are implicit in its present state, and so all past happenings are open to a monad that has very distinct perceptions.

Price does not attend to the monadic origin of psychokinetic effects. However, it is easy to imagine how the phenomena could be approached in a manner consistent with his treatment of the psi cognitions. One can begin by pointing out that in idealist metaphysics psychokinesis is likely to be treated as a form of telepathy. Because matter reduces to mind, "mind-over-matter" is effectively "mind-over-mind," and so psychokinesis is *telepathic action*. Being omnipercipient, the monads that are the basis of material bodies have subconscious perceptions of the thoughts, emotions, and volitions of higher-level monads. It can be supposed that if the mental states of these higher-level monads become particularly clear, concentrated, or prominent, the monads on which material bodies are based will conform to them through mutual accommodation. The question arises whether such monadic "action by conformity" bears any relation to the "action by identity" that I raised in Chapter 2. According to the action-by-identity thesis, one's field of activity expands through unification with an object or idea. One can act on something because one has become it. Now a monad is by its very nature united with its objects, for it is all things, a many-in-one, although it is usually unaware of its inclusivity. However, if a monad becomes more conscious, it will be more aware of its unity and more active too, for the monad's level of consciousness determines the degree to which it can be a reason for changes in other monads. There are, then, grounds for supposing that entry into a unitive state, insofar as it involves a heightening of consciousness, increases the capacity to act.

But the typically limited scope of a monad's self-directed activity is no bad thing. In filter theory, the limitation will be viewed as protective of the monadic organism, other creatures, the environment, and indeed the universe in general, for unlimited capacity to act would be even more hazardous than unlimited consciousness, except for individuals who are extraordinarily mature, self-controlled, and free of ego. Too much power is even more dangerous than too much knowledge. The filter, then, works to limit activity as well as consciousness. But what is the filter in Leibnizian metaphysics and in what sense does it regulate activity and consciousness? It is open to discussion whether the philosophy, as it stands, qualifies as filter theory. The philosophy does posit a cosmic "reservoir" of perception that supports ordinary perception, but the perceptual process involves no restriction of consciousness by "reducing valves," for the reservoir consists of highly confused perceptions. There is no need to "eliminate" or "repress" these perceptions because, being so indistinct, they are out of awareness. On the other hand, there is a kind of selection in operation, performed by the *body* a monad represents itself as having (*Monadology* §§61–62). By being where it is and having the sensory apparatus it does, the monad's body receives motions that come to it from the rest of the represented universe and provides distinct perception or "sensation." Because the motions that impinge on the monad's body are the ones most relevant to its situation, a utilitarian kind of selection occurs. So there is some justification for thinking that the metaphysics has a "filter" or "selection" component, in addition to the "subliminal reservoir" it clearly does have.

The monad's body also regulates the self-directed activity open to its central monad. While all monads are constantly engaged in universal activity, their perceptual confusion and limited consciousness means that their self-originated actions are very limited, restricted to what can be performed mechanically through their bodies of monads. The more advanced the body, the less confused the perception, and so the greater the potential for action. Advanced bodies provide monads with heightened perceptions and consciousness, and so enable their central monads to be reasons for changes in other monads. The organismic body makes conscious activity possible but also sets limits insofar as it supports only limited consciousness.

The above discussion has hopefully shown that Leibnizian metaphysics is applicable in a broad way to the classic psi phenomena, for the philosophy supports the idea that subconscious contact with the entire world is not only possible but the normal state of affairs. The universe exists as one's perceptual contents, and so subconscious contact with it is normal and uninterrupted. However, there is a worrying detail that requires attention, one that suggests the metaphysics needs modification if it is to provide an adequate framework for psi. As it stands, the philosophy accounts for the contact stage, but it is not clear how it might explain the emergence stage. For psi perception to occur, there must be a way in which ordinarily indistinct perceptions become more distinct and therefore conscious. In Leibniz's system, distinct perceptions follow from the operation of the body's sensory system. However, there is reason to think that psi perceptions, given their reach and immunity from obstruction, are *not* dependent on stimulation of the bodily senses and so arise in a different manner from ordinary perceptions—hence their popular designation as "extrasensory perception." Thus, while Leibnizian monadology gives us subliminal contact with an entire universe of contents, its resort to the body and sense organs as the means by which perceptions are made distinct implies that little beyond the familiar range could ever become conscious to us. To account for psi, it may be necessary to modify the monadology in a fundamental way, a modification called for even more strongly by mystical expansions of consciousness.

MYSTICAL EXPERIENCE AND INVERTED MONADS

Within standard Leibnizian monadology there is no reason to think that a monad, associated with the body it has, can attain to perceptions significantly more distinct than usual, other than through technologies that assist the bodily senses, such as microscopes and telescopes. Yet according to mystics, significantly deeper experiences of the world do occur, and the more expansive ones are prone to arise through *withdrawal* from the senses, in inward contemplation, sleep, and near-death "unconsciousness," as noted in Chapter 2. It seems that by turning away from the senses, one can attain to exceptionally clear perceptions of the universe, a most unexpected outcome from a Leibnizian standpoint but one that will be no surprise to mystics. Plotinus records that many times he was lifted out of his body to the vision of intellectual beauty (*Ennead* IV.8.1), the ascent to the apex of the soul revealing a universe of very clear perception or "intellection" (*noēsis*), for the soul at this level is mind, a unity of intellect and its intelligible universe. The intellections there are clear perceptions, unlike the perceptions here, which are dim intellections (*Ennead* VI.7.7). Thus Plotinus, like Leibniz, has a concept of subconscious perception, but unlike the Leibnizian confused subconscious, the Plotinian one is a very clear superconscious.

The idea that we are, in our depths, a universe of intellection suggests a modification to Leibnizian monadology that makes it better able to account for psi and mystical experiences, and which brings it closer to the mystical sources upon which the metaphysics partly drew. Leibniz brought precision and systematization to scientific, philosophical, and mystical ideas current in his day, including Platonic and Neoplatonic ones, unifying them into a remarkably logical and coherent system. Leibniz's monadic universe is comparable in some respects to Plotinus' intelligible universe, although there are certainly major differences. Leibnizian monadology turns the exalted Plotinian intelligible cosmos into the reality we ordinarily know, the natural world, transforming the interreflecting Plotinian intellects into the mutually representative monads and the atoms of nature. Leibniz brings the Neoplatonic heaven fully down to earth but in the process turns the vivid perceptions there into highly confused ones. Although sympathetic toward mysticism, Leibniz was neither a mystic nor an outright mystical thinker, and his thought is a step away from the mystical sources.

When modern philosophers have attempted to modify and update Leibniz's monadology, they have often removed it further from those sources, limiting the monads by depriving them of their cosmic wholeness and fitting them with windows and doors to let things in and out, but I suggest that we reverse the trend: not only grant the monads their completeness and qualified autonomy but let them have fully distinct perceptions too. This is to invert the standard perceptual composition of the Leibnizian monad, which consists of some relatively distinct perception supported by a cosmic sea of very indistinct perception. In contrast, the neo-Leibnizian monad proposed here consists of an island of relatively indistinct perception in a cosmic sea of perfectly distinct perception, a sea of intellection. In the modified scheme, all monads have perfectly distinct subliminal perceptions of the universe. These intellections can be called "noumenal" to distinguish them from the phenomenal experiences of ordinary, limited consciousness, for they are intellectual intuitions of the universe as it exists in a monadic mind. At a subliminal level, all monads are now minds, and following the Plotinian example, they are minds in which knower, knowing, and known are united. Here everything is known directly through knowledge by identity (Marshall, Chapter 2; see also Shaw, Chapter 8, and Kelly & Whicher, Chapter 9). It is now accurate to say that the monads are omniscient, although subliminally so, at a level of consciousness difficult to access but perhaps vaguely felt in aesthetic experiences and less developed mystical experiences, and more fully in deeper mystical experiences. Presumably the mystic's sense of "coming home," of returning to a familiar but forgotten condition, derives from the fact that the reality disclosed is not other than oneself. It is one's own deeper, monadic nature, and may even feel like one's "true" or "higher" self. By making Leibnizian monads a little more like Plotinian intellects, we can understand them to be selves, to have an intrinsic apperception or self-consciousness at their universal level, a self-awareness that is also a social awareness because a monad represents all other selves within itself.

If mystical experiences really do give access to our monadic interiors, they provide clues about the character of monads beyond the knowing and unity that is to be expected of them as intellects that are a many-in-one. For example, the evidence suggests that monadic intellections have a luminous quality, that love has a profound role to play in the communal unity of monads, and that their states are temporally inclusive. Leibniz gave his monads temporal depth, making them full of the past and pregnant with the future. Some mystical experiences suggest that the temporal range of perception is truly inclusive, each state of a monad being an "eternal moment," expressive of the universe in its full temporal as well as spatial extent. Modern physics can be understood to point in the same direction, for the idea of a "present state of the universe" has been made problematic by relativistic physics, and there are grounds for supposing that all events coexist in a spacetime whole. Each state of a monad will be such a whole, organized from a unique point of view. As such, a monadic state is "permanent" in the sense that it does not evaporate out of existence to be replaced by the next in sequence. Rather, the many states of a monad coexist. For all their felt transience, our everyday experiences are eternal too because they are parts of permanent monadic states.

While it can be debated whether classical Leibnizian monadology is, strictly speaking, a form of idealism and panpsychism, the modified version is certainly idealist and panpsychic: all monads, not just the more sophisticated ones, are minds, and these minds are the units of nature. But while all monads are now perfect minds at the subliminal level, they can still be categorized according to the quality of their *supraliminal* perceptions and associated cognitions, and so Leibniz's natural history of monadic organisms and his understanding of their relative activity and passivity remain largely intact. Simple monads, with very basic surrounding structures or "bodies," have highly indistinct phenomenal perceptions and nothing in the way of body-based mental activity, and so are largely passive reactors in the system of mutual accommodation. Sensitive souls are those with specialized organs that bring greater phenomenal distinctness and encourage basic mental activities, and therefore some self-originated activity. Rational souls have well-developed bodies that support yet more advanced mental functioning as well as creative activity. But unlike Leibnizian monads, all types of neo-Leibnizian monads have in common perfectly distinct subliminal intellections, and so even the most outwardly dull ones are universes of intelligence, light, and life.

The inversion of the monad's zones of perceptual confusion and distinctness has further repercussions, but here I shall address one topic of special importance, the theory of sense perception and its relation to filter theory. In Leibniz's theory, the more distinct perceptions result from a summation of numerous minute perceptions (*petites perceptions*), an idea that Leibniz liked to illustrate by reference to the noise of the sea, made by the beating of numerous waves. Leibniz supposed that if we are to hear the noise we must hear the sound made by each wave, even though we are not consciously aware of each sound. Sensations in general are like this, summations of all the minute perceptions through the medium of the body. Summation brings distinctness but with a degree of confusion, for the result lacks detail. But in the revised metaphysics, the monad's perceptual universe consists not of a mass of indistinct perceptions but of perfectly distinct perception or intellection. It is therefore necessary to consider more closely the way in which sense percepts arise. I have suggested elsewhere that the traditional "representative theory of perception" (also called "indirect realism" and "representative realism"), although long out of fashion among philosophers, can provide a suitable framework if brought into line with the idealism of the metaphysics (Marshall, 2001, 2005).

Traditional representative realism is set within a dualist understanding of mind and matter: the objects displayed in sense experience are typically regarded as inner *mental representations* of objects that exist externally in the *material world*. But in the revised monadology, the external world is not the material universe of dualism and materialism but the internal cosmic contents of a monad's intellection. It follows that the objects displayed in sense experience are mental representations of objects that are themselves mental, objects that exist as contents of the monad's cosmic intellection. Take, for example, sense perception of a tree. According to standard representative realism, perceptions of a tree are indirect: we perceive the external tree indirectly through direct acquaintance with our sensory representations of it, with our sense-data. Exactly how the representations arise is not too clear, but neuroscientists explain that visual perception proceeds as follows. Electromagnetic waves/particles ("light") from the sun or another source fall on the surface of the tree. Some of the reflected radiation is picked up by the eyes and focused onto the retinas to produce images there. Electrical impulses pass along the optic nerves from the light-sensitive retinal cells to the brain, where they are subject to processing, and mental images of the external tree are produced, drawing on the signals from both eyes to give a combined image. The creation of the mental image in the above account is, of course, the great mystery in standard representative realism, the transition from material brain processes to experience being at the heart of the mind–body problem.

The concept of "mental representation" is objectionable to materialists, for they reduce the mental to the material or eliminate it altogether. Rejecting the dualism inherent in standard representative realism, they can either dismiss the representative approach outright or reconceive it in materialist terms, reducing mental representations to material brain-states. Sense perception, then, is the representation of external material objects in material brain-states. For idealists, however, the concept of mental representation should be entirely acceptable, and the dualism of standard representative realism can be overcome by reframing the theory in idealist terms. There will, then, be no unbridgeable gap between mental representations and the world that supports them, for the universe itself exists as the contents of mind. Consider Zoë, who on her lunch breaks likes to escape from the office to a nearby park, where she admires the trees (Figure 11.2).

Like other human beings, Zoë is a rational soul or spirit, a living mirror of the universe and its creative source, and somewhat godlike herself, omniscient, immortal, and creative to a degree, even though she and the majority of her coworkers do not realize it. Zoë's monadic mind has the entire universe as its contents, including her human body, sense organs, and brain, as well as her sense perceptions and associated human mind. The tree, which exists in fully distinct detail in Zoë's monadic

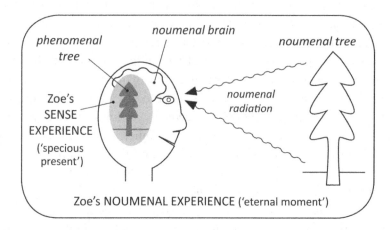

Figure 11.2.   **An idealist version of representative realism, applied to a neo-Leib-nizian monad (the phenomenal field of experience is shown as a tinted patch—not to scale). (© Paul Marshall, 2005, p. 264, Fig. 8.4 (modified), from Ch. 8,** *Mystical Encounters with the Natural World: Experiences and Explanations.* **By permission of Oxford University Press.)**

intellections, reflects radiation, some of which is picked up by Zoë's eyes. The complex processing in Zoë's brain gives rise to sense representations of the tree in what could be called her "phenomenal field of experience" or "phenomenal display."

Note that the display has no separate observer: Zoë's phenomenal field is just a special part of her overall noumenal or monadic field of experience, that is to say, a small part of her great monadic mind, a part that depends on and is conditioned by her nervous system. Where is this phenomenal display situated? One option is to locate sense-data in a "phenomenal space" distinct from everyday space (e.g., Smythies, 2003, pp. 50–51; see Carr, present volume, Chapter 7), but there is an alternative better suited to the present theory. Let's suppose that sense-data are located "in the head," in some brain structure. As a content of her cosmic field of experience, Zoë's brain is experiential, and so it is acceptable to suppose that sensory and other phenomenal experiences, such as dreams, can be located there. The suggestion is equivalent to Bertrand Russell's (1927) idea that percepts are parts of the percipient's brain, or as he wittily and somewhat confusingly put it, "what the physiologist sees when he looks at a brain is part of his own brain, not part of the brain he is examining" (p. 383). When the physiologist inspects a brain in a lab, he perceives it indirectly through direct acquaintance with his sense-data, and these sense-data are parts of his own brain. The idea that percepts are parts of the percipient's brain is a position that monists can take, unlike the dualists who put experience in a separate ontological realm. Monists keep mind and matter together in various ways, and Russell, in making his suggestion, was adopting a neutral monist approach in which a neutral "stuff" is primitive, and mind and matter are derivative. Materialists can also take percepts to be "in the head," as in the mind–brain identity theories that reduce mental events to material brain states (e.g., Smart, 1959). It is also a position that idealists can adopt if they reduce matter to mental contents, as I do here.

Russell (1927) pointed out that if our percepts are parts of our brains they should tell us something about the stuff out of which our brains and the rest of the world are made (p. 382).[3] Our percepts indicate that this world stuff has felt characteristics or "qualia," such as the colors of our visual experiences. Matter, it would seem, has qualia. It follows that the materialist form of monism is untenable, for the stuff of materialism has by definition no such felt qualities. The stuff of neutral monism does have felt qualities, which is why Russell could justifiably locate percepts in the percipient's brain. However, the supposedly neutral stuff is not really neutral with respect to the mental and the material, for its experiential character makes it much more like the former than the latter. In practice, neutral monism tends to be closer to idealism than materialism.

Our phenomenal experiences, as parts of our brains, may give us some insight into the stuff of the world, notably its experiential qualities, but we should not expect them to be a very reliable guide, for they are the outcome of much processing. Thus, while Zoë's noumenal percepts show the tree as it is, distinct in every detail down to its finest structures, her phenomenal percepts represent just the radiation-emitting surfaces of the tree that face her eyes, and in a very confused way, as a blur of colors with very little definition. The mystical evidence suggests too that there is a difference in temporal quality: the noumenal perception has an eternal, inclusive quality to it, encompassing past, present, and future states, while the phenomenal perception has a transient quality and represents the tree over just a few states, for the perception is dependent on radiation received by Zoë's eyes from the tree. Each state of Zoë's noumenal experience is an "eternal moment" that contains all space and time, while each moment of her phenomenal experience is a "specious present" that draws on the past for its perceptual contents.[4]

Phenomenal experiences may be situated in the brain in the ordinary course of events, but this is not to say that they are permanently located there. Several traditions describe subtle vehicles or bodies that are detachable from the gross body (see, for instance, Chapters 8, 9, and 10 above). If the phenomenal display is located in such a detachable body, then it is conceivable that phenomenal experiences persist when the subtle body leaves the gross body, fed by the subtle body's own organs of perception, if it has such, or by imaginal perception, a power of the imagination informed by intellect. I raise this possibility because of those experiences, out-of-body, near-death, and mystical, in which one seems to exit the body and have perceptions of the environment.

The above account of perception modifies standard representative realism by transforming the material world of dualism and materialism into a mental world, into the cosmic, intellective contents of the monads. Although the representative theory has been made idealist, it is still a form of realism in the sense that it upholds the reality of objects external to human minds, although in a universe now internal to monadic minds. In terms of filter theory, the "subliminal reservoir" is the entire universe as it exists in the perfectly distinct intellections of a monad, and the "filter" consists, at least in part (see below), of the sense organs and neuropsychological processing that introduce a phenomenal zone into the noumenal field of experience. Again, it can be asked how it is that we are ordinarily conscious of so little. Although we are fully conscious of everything in the universe at a subliminal level, we are conscious of very little at the supraliminal level because the phenomenal field of experience is very narrow. In higher organisms, it is dependent for its contents on stimulation of sense organs and processing in the nervous system, and is therefore limited in its spatial and temporal scope, and in the detail that can be represented. Thus the "principle of limitation" in this version of monadology is the formation, within cosmic intellections, of experiences that are highly limited in perceptual range and quality. But rather than view the limitation as a regrettable departure from wholeness and clarity, we can regard it as creative and progressive. Finite beings and their experiences give content, complexity, and a particular beauty to the world, and their evolution leads to personhood and the compassion and understanding that life as a vulnerable, dependent creature can foster.

The various kinds of perception can now be summarized as follows:

sense perception—direct acquaintance with sense-data in the brain
psi perception—subconscious direct acquaintance with the world
mystical perception—direct acquaintance with the world (deeper cases only)

For understanding psi, the revised monadology may be an improvement on classical monadology, but a full understanding is still some way off. It remains to be explained how the revised monad's perfect intellections become translated into psi perceptions, that is, how contact proceeds to modification and emergence (Figure 11.1). Our monadic minds know everything distinctly, but how is some of the knowing selected and translated into psi perceptions? One step toward a more complete understanding might be a suggestion I made in Chapter 2: Mind at Large has an inbuilt discriminative capacity of its own, which singles out specific items for incorporation into ordinary consciousness. There are, then, two kinds of selection at work. Sense representations depend on selection performed by one's sense organs and human mind/brain, while psi representations depend on selection initially performed by a discriminative capacity of one's monadic mind. Clearly, the matter needs further attention, and one area to consider is the role of imagination as an intermediary between monadic intellect and the human mind, operative in the mediating subconscious.

As for mystical experiences of the natural world, they can now be explained as follows (see also Marshall, 2005, p. 267). In the less developed ones, the phenomenal field of sense-data changes somewhat, losing the sharply dualistic self–other conceptual structuring ordinarily imposed on it and so gaining a unitive quality. As experience deepens, the phenomenal field or "specious present" changes further: experience becomes more open to and interfused with the noumenal reality of which it is a part. Thus experience becomes luminous and vibrant, and there is the knowingness, altered time-experience, diminution of ego, and so forth. As experience deepens further, the phenomenal field and associated cognition recedes, and the monadic mind and its qualities and capabilities come to the fore, including perhaps the hypothesized discriminative capacity that can home in on details. The monadic mind comes to dominate, inseparable from its cosmic object, resplendent with intellection, light, temporal inclusiveness, multiplicity-in-unity, and love. However, it seems that mystical experience can go deeper still, bringing contact with the source of the monadic mind, indeed the ground reality of all the monads, which is God or the mind of God in Leibniz's system, but which could be understood in other ways, as the Plotinian One or some other ultimate that is able to support a world of interlinked cosmic minds. It should also be added that the symbolic imagination undoubtedly plays a role in some mystical experiences, including cosmic visionary ones. But enough has been said about the imagination in the present volume to make clear that it can be much more than mere fancy.

Admittedly, the above account requires a rather exotic metaphysical commitment, but it has the advantage of encompassing a range of experiences from mild nondual perceptions of the immediate environment to cosmic expansions of consciousness and beyond. Moreover, based as it is on idealist metaphysics of a panpsychic variety, it has a place for intuitions of the inner life or consciousness of things, the discovery that nature is alive with minds, souls, centers of experience. [5]

POSTMORTEM SURVIVAL AND REINCARNATION

Zoë will grow old, her eyesight fade, and her body fall apart beyond repair, and one day, like all human beings, she will breathe no more. Is this the end? For all intents and purposes, monads are indestructible, a feature of Leibnizian metaphysics that is rich with possibilities if brought to bear on the question of postmortem survival. Drawing on a venerable Platonic argument for the immortality of the soul, Leibniz explains that monads, as simple substances without parts, can neither be created nor destroyed by natural means, that is, from within the system of nature. They are not composites that can be put together or taken apart bit by bit, and so are not subject to growth or decay. In a more original move, Leibniz says that monadic indestructibility follows from the inner, perceptual nature of monads, for they are expressive of the universe as a whole, a reality that endures for a very long time. Were monads to express just bits and pieces of the universe they could be very ephemeral indeed, but as cosmic wholes they endure at least as long as the universe endures, and so are essentially imperishable. In Leibniz's Christian theistic system, with its finite, linear time, monads unfold from the creation to the end time, but other scenarios can be envisaged to fit different cosmological, soteriological, and eschatological schemes. For instance, if mona-dology were transplanted into some Indian religious contexts, monads would be understood to exist from beginningless time, transmigrate through innumerable deaths and rebirths, and perhaps reach a liberative conclusion of some kind.

Although monads are extremely robust by virtue of their indivisibility and cosmic expressiveness, their perceptual contents are subject to con-tinuous transformation, including the composite bodies that monads per-ceive themselves as having. The most dramatic transformation, of course, occurs at death, when the body seems to fall apart completely, but Leib-niz supposed that a monad is never entirely divested of its body, so there is neither complete birth nor death, just "unfolding and growth" and "enfolding and diminution" of the body (*Monadology* §73; Woolhouse & Francks, 1998, p. 278). A monad is tied to the body with which it was initially associated at the Creation, which means that a monad cannot change the species of its body, and so progress up the ladder of nature is very limited. Drawing on microscopical observations and preformationist theory of his time, Leibniz supposed that monads are created with tiny, seedlike or "spermatic" bodies that eventually grow into full-sized bod-ies. At death, the macroscopic bodies decay, reverting to the spermatic bodies or "animalcules." In the case of subrational monads, these are liable to grow again into full-sized bodies, and the cycle of decay and growth can continue indefinitely. This cyclical process might look like transmigration, but Leibniz emphasized that it is *metamorphosis*: there is no complete change of body, just decay and regrowth. In his *New Essays on Human Understanding*, completed in 1704, Leibniz (trans. 1996) ac-cepted the theoretical possibility of transmigration, even across species "in the Brahmin or Pythagorean manner," if the transmigrating soul were to retain a rarefied body and shed only its coarse body (pp. 233–234). But his belief that nature proceeds in small steps rather than leaps (the "Prin-ciple of Continuity") inclined him to reject the abrupt change that trans-migration to a new coarse body would entail.

Leibniz was fairly unadventurous in his account of the postmortem fate of human souls, for he exempted the bodies of rational souls from the repeated cycles of growth and decay through which subrational beings can go, and he shied away from doctrines of transmigration in the air at the time, derived from the ancient Pythagorean and Platonic sources, and the teachings of the Lurianic Kabbalah, a sixteenth-century mystical development in Judaism (Coudert, 1995). Francis Mercury van Helmont, who helped bring the latter to the attention of Christian scholars, including Leibniz, had a theory of transmigration in which humans pass through several human incarnations, and van Helmont's friend Lady Anne Conway even allowed interspecies *transmutation* (an exemplary horse might become a man, and an unvirtuous man a brute or a devil). But Leibniz entertained no such transmigrations or transmutations for human beings, whose bodies revert at death to their animalcules and remain so until the Last Judgment, their monadic souls entering a long period of dormancy until the final awakening because the animalcule is a primitive body that furnishes less distinct perceptions.

Here again Leibniz's system invites modification in light of the evidence, for certain phenomena that arise as death approaches, such as terminal lucidity and near-death experience, suggest that dying can be attended by a sharpening and expansion of consciousness, rather than a dulling and contraction. The revised monad described above, with its inverted constitution, is in accord with such sharpening and expansion because it has a subliminal consciousness of great clarity and inclusiveness. With the unraveling of ordinary consciousness near or at death, this noumenal background will begin to make itself known. Leibniz's somewhat arbitrary view that repeated metamorphosis or transmigration applies only to subrational monads is also undermined by the evidence, for "cases of the reincarnation type" (Kelly, Chapter 1 above) suggest that human beings are subject to some kind of "life-to-life" progression, at the very least sporadically but perhaps as a general rule, whether understood as Leibnizian cycles of metamorphosis or more conventionally as transmigration from body to body.

That life should continue after death is to be expected in a monadological world. The destruction of the body and its brain is just the disintegration of a composite structure *within* experience, experience that continues unabated and in which new bodily structures, sense perceptions, and associated minds will emerge in due course. As an uncompounded, indiscerptible whole, the monad is untroubled by death, and its individuality and uniqueness as a substance are uncompromised. Moreover, in the revised monadology presented here, there is reason to suppose that the monad, as a being of perfect intellection, constitutes an apperceiving self. There would, then, be a higher dimension of self that passes unperturbed through the vicissitudes of life and death to which the limited, personal self is subject.

But is there any way in which the personal self can be said to survive death? All monads are imperishable, but can the more advanced ones, such as the souls of human beings, be deemed *immortal*, if immortality is taken to mean the continuation of personal identity beyond death (Brown, 1998, pp. 576–577)? What, if anything, is left of human personality, of memories, traits, and habits? The indestructible monad formerly known as Zoë survives, but is there anything left of Zoë as a distinct personality and a moral agent responsible for her actions? Leibniz (trans. 1996) supposes that there is, for a monad is full of the past and so retains perceptions of its past existence: "It retains impressions of everything which has previously happened to it, and it even has presentiments of everything that will happen to it" (p. 239). The "continuity and interconnection" of perceptions ensures the continuation of personal identity (p. 239). Ordinarily these perceptions are too minute to come into awareness, but some day they might (presumably at the Last Judgment), and memories too are recoverable, for they are perceptions of past events carried over into the present. Leibniz concludes that if transmigration of the soul from coarse human body to body does take place, as his friend van Helmont had believed, then "the same individual would exist throughout," and a sufficiently acute mind would be able to discern the past existences (pp. 239–240). Furthermore, the monadic soul would continue to express its past when it migrates to a new coarse body, which would feel the effects and show "real marks of the continuance of the individual." Traces of past lives would be found in the present mind and body. Although Leibniz was not convinced that transmigration occurs, he appreciated that it would preserve personal identity in a monadological system, for perceptions and memories from previous lives would be carried over into the current one. The same can be said of transmigration in the revised monadology introduced above, although the clarity of the monad's subliminal intellections means that knowledge of previous lives would be more accessible. Moreover, in the revised monadology there is now the possibility of a continuing, background self-presence, a greater dimension of self that stands behind the cycles of transmigration, a vantage point from which all the little lives and their meanings are discernible.

THE PHYSICS OF EXPERIENCE

Monadology builds on the innocuous observation that the world is experienced from points of view—there is no "view from nowhere," no perspective-free perception. But elevated and universalized into a metaphysical claim about the nature and organization of the world, it can seem very odd indeed, "a kind of fantastic fairy tale" as Russell put it. Applied to such contested phenomena as psi, mystical experience, and postmortem survival, monadology is likely to appear even more fantastic. It is therefore encouraging to find that two major developments in early twentieth-century physics, the relativistic and quantum theories, both hint at a universe organized along monadological lines.

In 1905 Einstein put forward his "special theory of relativity," as it was later to be called. The theory sets forth two basic postulates, the Relativity Principle and the Light Postulate. The former states that the same laws of physics will be valid in all observational frames of reference in which the laws of mechanics hold good ("inertial frames"), while the latter asserts that the velocity of light is the same in all these frames. From the standpoint of classical physics, the Light Postulate is highly counterintuitive. Whether stationary or moving apart relative to one another, observers will measure the velocity of light c to be the same, about 186,282 miles per second. In classical physics, the observer's relative state of motion has an impact on velocities measured, but in special relativity the measured velocity of light is invariant, independent of the observer's state of motion. Given the invariance, counterintuitive results follow, including *length contraction* and *time dilation*. Simply put, if you and I are moving relative to each other, I will measure your rulers to contract and your clocks to run slow, and you will measure my rulers to contract and my clocks to run slow. These and other surprising effects have been confirmed by experiment.

It is important to note that Einstein's theory deals with measurements, not with the physical actualities that lie behind the measurements. In Einstein's own terminology, the special theory as originally formulated was a "theory of principle," not a "constructive theory" (e.g., Brown, 2005). It gives a mathematical description of the phenomena of motion and allows them to be predicted, but it does not provide deep insight into them. At the time that Einstein formulated his special theory, there was a constructive theory that could account for the various effects and furnish some understanding of them, namely the deformation theory of George FitzGerald and Hendrik Lorentz. According to this theory, measuring devices are deformed as they pass through a stationary luminiferous ether, the medium through which it was supposed light waves propagate. As a result of these deformations, observers in relative motion measure the velocity of light to be the same, even though it is only in the stationary ether frame that light really travels at its velocity c. By contrast, special relativity dispensed with talk of the ether and took it as a given that light has velocity c in all the measurement frames.

Experimentally, the special theory and the deformation theory are indistinguishable because they are mathematically equivalent and make the same predictions, but the deformation theory had the advantage of making peculiar effects such as length contraction and time dilation comprehensible within a classical Newtonian framework of absolute space and time, whereas Einstein's approach had great simplicity and economy, being undisturbed by the complexities and uncertainties that surrounded the nature of ether and matter. The deformation theory was exposed in this respect, with its undetectable ether and hypothetical ether–matter interactions, even more so as quantum effects were coming to be recognized, complicating the picture of radiation and matter even further. With Einstein's "theory of principle" approach, physicists could get on with measurement and prediction without worrying about behind-the-scenes mechanism and ontology. A comparable but better known and more flagrant evasion of deep explanation was to prevail for many years in the field of quantum physics.

Principle theories are unsatisfying because they provide little or no insight, and Einstein himself considered the special theory of relativity unsatisfactory in this regard. The special theory gained some explanatory depth when it was claimed that it leads to a new, non-Newtonian understanding of space and time in which the two are inextricably joined, and that it is in this unified, four-dimensional spacetime world that relativistic effects are based. In 1908, the mathematician Hermann Minkowski introduced such a unified concept of space and time, and the special theory, couched in terms of absolute Minkowski spacetime, can be interpreted as going beyond its "theory of principle" status to something more like an explanatory "constructive theory" and even ontology. However, it is open to debate whether the Minkowski approach goes deep enough, and indeed whether its understanding of spacetime as an "absolute world" behind the relativity of distance and time measurements is anything more than a mathematical abstraction (Marshall, 2006, pp. 218–219).

It is here that monadology may show its worth, supplying an ontology that dispenses with the absoluteness of spacetime and which finds the ultimate basis of relativistic effects in a plurality of monadic representations of the world. The special theory of relativity can be repositioned as a fully constructive theory, one that makes statements about the deep construction of the world. This would mean that for observers in relative motion the velocity of light is not *just measured* to be the same but *really is* the same. But how can this be? It is possible if observers each possess their own versions of the universe, as monads do. Observers, whether scientists with instruments or fully automated measuring devices, are to be understood as monadic perceptual perspectives. Each basic unit of nature expresses its own version of the universe, organized from its own sequence of viewpoints. Because monads express the same universe, they transform in exactly the same way and so are described by the same laws of physics (Relativity Principle). Similarly, in each monadic version of the universe, light radiation propagates in the same way and has the same velocity (Light Postulate). We are stationed at the perceptual centers of our own versions of the universe, centers relative to which the transformations called "light radiation" propagate at the same velocity. As suggested above, each state of a monad is in fact a spatiotemporal whole, an entire spacetime version of the universe, structured from a unique point of view, and so there is a multiplicity of relative spacetimes, not one absolute spacetime. Expressed in terms of the largely abandoned ether approach, it could be said that there is no longer one absolute stationary luminiferous ether but a multiplicity of relative stationary ethers, each centered on one observer, through which electromagnetic changes propagate at velocity c. But in monadology, the "stationary ether" of each monad is simply the monad's cosmic field of perception organized from its points of view.

Relativistic effects, then, can be understood to follow from the organization of the universe as a plurality of mutually accommodated monadic versions. Quantum phenomena can also be understood to stem from the nature and accommodation of monads, if not so straightforwardly. Although monads in their inner constitutions are continuous fields of experience, they confer upon the world a fundamental discontinuity or "granularity" because they are discrete perceptions. The representation of monads within a monad means that this discreteness will be present within monads too, represented within the monad's perceptual continuum. Furthermore, the atomism of the monadology is holistic. Leibniz believed all matter to be interconnected mechanically because the universe is a plenum, and so an action here will have an effect there, whatever the separation (*Monadology* §61). However, it can be supposed that monadic atoms support a deeper kind of interconnection, one that follows from each fundamental particle being a perception of the entire universe. As representations of monads, particles would carry everything past, present, and future locally, including their own future states, and as active, purposive units directed toward ends ("final causation") they are no mere passive slaves of the past ("efficient causation"). Moreover, all particles are mutually accommodated, and the laws of mechanics that describe their behavior will reflect the universe-wide harmonization.

It is possible to see here resonances with features of quantum physics, such as nonlocality, holism, and discontinuity. Quantum physics, with its "spooky action at a distance," may have uncovered effects that stem from the mutual accommodation of monads, from their inherently active nature and appetition directed toward ends, and perhaps even from their perception of future states. It is interesting that some explanations of quantum physics do give a role to causes or relations that extend from the future, all events being understood to coexist in the spacetime universe.[6] Moreover, it is possible that monadology, with its union of the discontinuous and the continuous, can bring together quantum physics with its microphysical discontinuities and general relativity with its large-scale spacetime continuum. But are the parallels with quantum physics more than superficial? The challenge is to show in detail how the metaphysics meshes with the physics, and that is no easy task. For one thing, it is necessary to show how monads, as the realities on which matter is founded, are related to the fundamental particles of contemporary physics. I have suggested elsewhere that the concept of extra, hidden dimensions, which in the 1980s and 1990s took center stage in attempts to achieve a unified physical picture of the world, may provide a route to forging a connection. My recourse to dimensions here differs significantly from that of many theorists who invoke extra dimensions to explain paranormal phenomena (see Carr, present volume), for it is set within a monadological framework. This is not the place to go into details, but the basic idea proceeds as follows (Marshall, 2006). If matter consists of representations of groups of monads, and the perceptions of those monads are *fully* represented within a monad, then the material microstructure of the monad will incorporate the full dimensionality of the represented monads. For example, if a monadic state were a four-dimensional spacetime universe, then its full representation in the microstructure of another monad would introduce a set of four spacetime dimensions into that monad. Because monads are mutually representative, there will be an endless repetition of microstructure within microstructure, nested sets of spacetime dimensions without end. The particles and forces of modern physics are to be understood in terms of these embedded dimensions in a manner comparable to the way in which extra dimensions have been invoked by physicists in recent years, reducing forces to spacetime geometry, a geometrification of nature that takes its inspiration from Einstein's treatment of gravitational force in the general theory of relativity.

CONCLUSION

I have suggested that Leibnizian monadology, if suitably modified, can shed light on psychical and mystical perceptions. It may prove helpful too for understanding psi actions, which in an idealist world consist of "mind over mind," and which in a monadological world perhaps derive specifically from mutual accommodation. I say "perhaps" because I feel less confident in deriving psi actions from monadology than I do psi and mystical perceptions. Expanded perceptions follow fairly straightforwardly from the perceptual nature of monads, but paranormal action calls for a more detailed and careful consideration of causation and mutual accommodation than I have attempted here. Postmortem survival poses no difficulties, for monads are extremely robust, and perceptions of the past support continuation of personal identity, whether across reincarnations or in some alternative afterlife scenario. The counterintuitive effects unearthed by twentieth-century physics seem to fit well with the intersubjective, holistic world of the monads, which is perhaps a sign that the philosophy is on the right track. It may be through further advances in physics that monadology will receive decisive corroboration or contradiction.

There are other phenomena too, not discussed here, that could be approached from a monadological direction, such as meaningful coincidences between inner states and outer events (Atmanspacher & Fach, present volume). Jung sometimes mentioned Leibnizian pre-established harmony in his discussions of synchronicity (e.g., 1969, pp. 498–501), and it would be worth exploring whether his synchronistic "acausal connecting principle" can be understood in terms of the mutual accommodation of minds. In an idealist framework, the outer world is as much mind as the inner one, and mind–matter connections will be mind–mind ones. Monadology may also have a bearing on the phenomena of automatisms and secondary centers of consciousness (Kelly, present volume, Chapter 1), for it places multiple, hierarchically organized streams of perception throughout brain and body. The central monad of an organism is far from alone in its body, which is packed, so to speak, with other monads, and the question arises whether normal mental processing, never mind secondary personalities, depends on the activities of multiple centers of consciousness. Monadology can also contribute to spiritual understandings of evolution, for monads are just the kind of entity that over long ages could build an evolutionary tree of life and climb up it toward some fulfillment, driven at first obscurely by appetition, then by desire and conscious intent as monadic organisms grow in complexity.

Monadology blurs the boundaries between the normal and the supernormal. It reenchants a disenchanted world yet at the same time normalizes the supernormal. From the standpoint of monadology, it would be extraordinary indeed if there were no psychical and mystical perceptions, and if death were truly the end. But *why* is it that we are usually conscious of so little? For all the ignorance and suffering it entails, limitation of consciousness serves valuable purposes, creative, protective, developmental, evolutionary, personalizing. There is beauty too in the finite—shadowy, delicate, transitory, never quite graspable, but special nonetheless—and love and understanding ripen there in the fullness of time. *How* is it that we are conscious of so little? As a consequence, it would seem, of incomplete perceptions that develop within complete ones and take on a life and mind of their own.

NOTES

1. Leibnizian monadology and Whiteheadian process metaphysics have idealism in common if it is conceded that the basic experiential units they postu-

late ("monads" and "actual occasions" respectively), although not endowed with consciousness in the majority of instances, are *mind-like*, being of the nature of perceiving, striving subjects, and so appropriately placed in the category of mind. Early twentieth-century experientialists critical of absolute idealism were apt to treat experience as neutral with respect to mind and matter and so espouse "neutral monism," a label often applied to Whitehead's metaphysics. Basile (2009) rejects the classification of Whitehead's metaphysics as neutral monism or dual-aspect theory, stating that it "is really a form of panpsychistic idealism that straightforwardly identifies the ultimate constituents of reality with mind-like, wholly experiential entities" (p. 10).

2. Monads, like Whitehead's actual occasions, are in process, but there is ostensibly a major difference between the Leibnizian and Whiteheadian understandings of becoming, which stems from the distinction between "substance" and "event" ontologies. Whitehead put great weight on the distinction, his metaphysics deriving in part from a critique of the traditional philosophical concept of substance that Leibniz's metaphysics inherited with some modification. As a substance, a monad is thought of as a "being" or "continuant" that endures through change. By contrast, actual occasions are "happenings" or "events" that arise and perish. In place of one enduring individual there is a series of transitory individuals. However, it is debatable whether substance and event ontologies are as different as sometimes claimed (see Sprigge, 2006, pp. 416–417).

3. See Lockwood (1989, pp. 159–160).

4. On the specious present, see my Chapter 2 above. Bernard Carr (Chapter 7) makes use of the concept. It is sometimes thought to be a feature of Whitehead's philosophy of actual occasions—but see Sprigge (2006, pp. 437–440).

5. For criticism of this approach, see Perovich (2011), who raises panpsychic metaphysics to explain mystical perceptions in which nature is transfigured and living presences intuited there. Perovich appreciates the value of the specious present for interpreting the "timeless" quality reported by mystics, and in this connection he draws on idealist philosopher Josiah Royce, but the metaphysics he presents is not sufficiently elaborated to account fully for unitive expansions of consciousness, including the experience of living presences in nature that particularly concerns him. To explain unitive experiences, Perovich (2011) adopts the concept of "subsumption," raised by Tim Bayne and David Chalmers in regard to the unity of ordinary consciousness, and applies it to mystical experience: "nature mysticism consists in the subsumption of experiences that in the first instance are the experiences associated with other bodies" (p. 14). However, in the absence of a more developed metaphysics, it is not clear how such subsumption would work. Nature may be full of living presences, but we would not be able to intuit their subjectivity unless our minds have access to those pres-

ences and their interiority. Neo-Leibnizian monads have such access by virtue of their inherent perceptual inclusiveness.

6. These approaches can differ significantly: e.g., Cramer's (1986) transactional interpretation, Hadley's general relativistic theory (Chown, 2001, pp. 62–71), and Silberstein, Stuckey, and Cifone's (2007) relational blockworld interpretation.

REFERENCES

Basile, P. (2009). *Leibniz, Whitehead and the Metaphysics of Causation*. Basingstoke, England: Palgrave Macmillan.

Broad, C. D. (1953). *Religion, Philosophy and Psychical Research*. London: Routledge & Kegan Paul.

Brown, H. R. (2005). *Physical Relativity: Space–Time Structure from a Dynamical Perspective*. Oxford: Clarendon Press.

Brown, S. (1998). Soul, body and natural immortality. *The Monist, 81*, 573–590.

Burnyeat, M. F. (1982). Idealism and Greek philosophy: What Descartes saw and Berkeley missed. *The Philosophical Review, 91*, 3–40. doi:10.2307/2184667

Bussanich, J. (1994). Realism and idealism in Plotinus. *Hermathena, 157*, 21–42.

Chown, M. (2001). *The Universe Next Door*. London: Headline.

Cook, D. J. (1998). Leibniz on enthusiasm. In A. P. Coudert, R. H. Popkin, & G. M. Weiner (Eds.), *Leibniz, Mysticism and Religion* (pp. 107–135). Dordrecht, The Netherlands: Kluwer.

Coudert, A. P. (1995). *Leibniz and the Kabbalah*. Dordrecht, The Netherlands: Kluwer.

Cramer, J. G. (1986). The transactional interpretation of quantum mechanics. *Review of Modern Physics, 58*, 647–687. doi:10.1103/RevModPhys.58.647

Hartz, G. A., & Wilson, C. (2005). Ideas and animals: The hard problem of Leibnizian metaphysics. *Studia Leibnitiana, 37*, 1–19.

Jung, C. G. (1969). Synchronicity: An acausal connecting principle. In H. Read et al. (Eds.), *The Collected Works of C. G. Jung: Vol. 8. The Structure and Dynamics of the Psyche* (2nd ed., pp. 417–531). London: Routledge & Kegan Paul.

Leibniz, G. W. (trans. 1996). *New Essays on Human Understanding* (P. Remnant & J. Bennett, Trans.). Cambridge: Cambridge University Press.

Lockwood, M. (1989). *Mind, Brain, and the Quantum: The Compound "I."* Oxford: Blackwell.

Marshall, P. (2001). Transforming the world into experience: An idealist experiment. *Journal of Consciousness Studies, 8*(1), 59–76. Available at http://www.esalen.org/ctr-archive/bp

Marshall, P. (2005). *Mystical Encounters with the Natural World: Experiences and Explanations*. Oxford: Oxford University Press.

Marshall, P. (2006). *The Living Mirror: Images of Reality in Science and Mysticism* (Rev. ed.). London: Samphire Press.

Mundle, C. W. K. (1971). The explanation of ESP. In J. R. Smythies (Ed.), *Science and ESP* (pp. 197–207). London: Routledge & Kegan Paul.

Pandey, K. C. (1963). *Abhinavagupta: An Historical and Philosophical Study* (2nd ed.). Varanasi, India: Chowkhamba Sanskrit Series Office.

Perovich, A. N. (2011). Taking nature mysticism seriously: Marshall and the metaphysics of the self. *Religious Studies, 47*, 165–183. doi:10.1017/S0034412510000211

Price, H. H. (1940). Some philosophical questions about telepathy and clairvoyance. *Philosophy, 15*, 363–385.

Price, H. H. (1960). Paranormal cognition and symbolism. In L. C. Knights & B. Cottle (Eds.), *Metaphor and Symbol* (pp. 78–94). London: Butterworths Scientific Publications.

Puryear, S. (2010). Monadic interaction. *British Journal for the History of Philosophy, 18*, 763–796. doi:10.1080/09608788.2010.524756

Russell, B. (1900). *A Critical Exposition of the Philosophy of Leibniz*. Cambridge: Cambridge University Press.

Russell, B. (1914). *Our Knowledge of the External World*. London: George Allen & Unwin.

Russell, B. (1927). *The Analysis of Matter*. London: Kegan Paul, Trench, Trübner.

Seager, W. (1995). Consciousness, information and panpsychism. *Journal of Consciousness Studies, 2*(3), 272–288.

Silberstein, M., Stuckey, W. M., & Cifone, M. (2007). An argument for 4D block world from a geometric interpretation of nonrelativistic quantum mechanics. In V. Petkov (Ed.), *Relativity and the Dimensionality of the World* (pp. 197–216). Dordrecht, The Netherlands: Springer.

Smart, J. J. C. (1959). Sensations and brain processes. *The Philosophical Review, 68*, 141–156.

Smythies, J. (2003). Space, time and consciousness. *Journal of Consciousness Studies, 10*(3), 47–56.

Sprigge, T. L. S. (2006). *The God of Metaphysics*. Oxford: Clarendon Press.

Trivedi, S. (2005). Idealism and Yogacara Buddhism. *Asian Philosophy, 15*, 231–246. doi:10.1080/09552360500285219

Woolhouse, R. S., & Francks, R. (Trans.). (1998). *G. W. Leibniz: Philosophical Texts*. Oxford: Oxford University Press.

12

CONTINUITY OF MIND

A Peircean Vision

Adam Crabtree

Charles Sanders Peirce (1839–1914) was a philosopher, scientist, expert in the construction of scientific instruments, logician, mathematician, and originator of semiotics. More revered internationally than locally in his day, Peirce has been the subject of growing interest in recent decades. In his attempts to create a scientifically based philosophy, he made significant sorties in the areas of concern of this book. To make intelligible his particular contribution to this field, I would like to give a brief exposition of relevant parts of his philosophical system. Regrettably, there are certain important ideas in Peirce's philosophy (especially his experiential categories of Firstness, Secondness, and Thirdness) that I will not be able to explore in this short chapter. For those I refer the reader to *An Introduction to C. S. Peirce* by Robert Corrington (1993).

PEIRCE'S PHILOSOPHY

Background

Peirce's philosophical writings insist again and again that any workable metaphysics must be based on empirical evidence. He once remarked that if more philosophers came from experimental laboratories rather than, as they often do, from theological seminaries, we would be further ahead in our inquiries.

Peirce's friend William James had high regard for his philosophical ideas, and it is well known that James explicitly credited Peirce with the principles that formed the foundations of pragmatism. There were other ideas used by James that were first formulated by Peirce. One of these was James's musing that one could think of the laws of nature as consisting in habits formed over many eons of time, rather than rules imposed on the world by an unknown power. The idea of natural laws as habits was in fact a centerpiece of Peirce's cosmology. Even more significant influences of Peirce on James's ideas are found in the area of empiricism. Late in his philosophical development, James significantly revised his ideas, introducing his notion of "radical empiricism" (James, 1912), which asserts that experience includes both particulars and relations between those particulars. Peirce had developed this doctrine decades earlier and described himself as a "radical empiricist" (CP 7.616).[1]

Peirce went one step further in this direction, asserting that all things and their relations are perceived in a world that is a "profusion of signs," where all we ever experience are those signs and the complex of relations that they represent. Peirce was the inventor of semiotics, the formal study of signs and sign processes, and his pioneering work influenced such theoreticians as Ferdinand de Saussure and Umberto Eco. His understanding of the role of signs, not only in human life but in the world at large, was highly original and closely tied in with his metaphysics. He developed a unified theory of reality which gives cosmic significance to human behavior (Sherrif, 1994, pp. 18–19). Peirce's core philosophical concept is that the world is in its very essence meaningful, a tapestry of signs that constitutes and makes intelligible every existing thing, and that the activity of signs is at the heart of evolution (CP 4.55).

Abduction

If the world is intelligible, what is the process by which we get to know it? Specifically, Peirce wonders how we can make judgments about things of which we have no direct experience and through those judgments add something new to our knowledge. How is it, he asks, that, given exposure to a certain set of facts, we can form correct theories about the way nature must be to produce those facts. He points out that with any complex set of facts the odds against coming up with the correct explanatory theory are astronomical, so that it should not be possible to discover it in twenty or thirty thousand years of trial and error (CP 5.591). Yet the remarkable fact is that we usually arrive at a workable theory on the first few tries. He expressed the process this way:

> The surprising fact, C, is observed;
> But if A were true, C would be a matter of course,
> Hence, there is reason to suspect that A is true. (CP 5.189)

A is a hypothesis, a *guess* about the nature of the reality underpinning the fact, one that can be tested by observing further facts. But why is it that both in ordinary life situations and in scientific investigations, we quickly arrive at hypotheses that are so close to the truth? Peirce called this guessing *abduction*, which, he said, consists in "examining a mass of facts and in allowing these facts to suggest a theory" (CP 8.209). According to Peirce, neither deduction nor induction originates any fundamentally new knowledge in science; only abduction can do that: "every single item of scientific theory which stands established today has been due to Abduction" (CP 5.172).

Abduction involves the *play of musement* in which ideas are associated in a new synthesis. Peirce advises the scientific investigator to develop this state as a means ready at hand to help him move beyond the merely given to what might constitute a solution to the question posed by the facts encountered. For Peirce musement is a state of mind which entails being, as it were, abstracted from time, a kind of space between past and future. In musement the mind slips out of gear and in that state is not trying to accomplish some particular purpose, but is unconditionally contemplating a free flow of ideas. It is *pure play*, which opens itself to a continuum of possibilities (CP 6.452–466; see Ibri, 2006, pp. 91–92).

Why does Peirce suggest such an approach in the development of hypotheses and theories? Peirce holds it an undeniable truth that "man's mind must have been attuned to the truth of things in order to discover what he has discovered" (CP 6.476). He is not alone in this view, for "Galileo appeals to *il lume naturale* [natural light] at the most critical stages of his reasoning. Kepler, Gilbert, and Harvey—not to speak of Copernicus—substantially rely upon an inward power . . . supplying an essential factor to the influences carrying their minds to the truth" (CP 1.80).

Peirce said, "Man seems to himself to have some glimmer of co-understanding with God, or with Nature," and "really penetrates in some measure the ideas that govern creation" (CP 8.212). He believed that this power is an innate gift given to human beings, comparable to instincts occurring in lower animals:

> Our faculty of guessing corresponds to a bird's musical and aeronautic powers; that is, it is to us, as those are to them, the loftiest of our merely instinctive powers. I suppose that if one were sure of being able to discriminate between the intimations of this instinct and the self-flatteries of personal desire, one would always trust to the former. For I should not rate high either the wisdom or the courage of a fledgling bird, if, when the proper time had come, the little agnostic should hesitate long to take his leap from the nest on account of doubts about the theory of aerodynamics. (CP 7.48)

It is from this background that Peirce developed his notion of pragmatism. For him, Pragmatism means that if a conception is true it must have palpable consequences, "either in the shape of conduct to be recommended, or in that of experiences to be expected" (CP 5.2). Peirce said, "[T]he question of Pragmatism is the question of Abduction" (CP 5.197):

> What, then, is the end of an explanatory hypothesis? Its end is, through subjection to the test of experiment, to lead to the avoidance of all surprise and to the establishment of a habit of positive expectation that shall not be disappointed. Any hypothesis, therefore, may be admissible, in the absence of any special reasons to the contrary, provided it be capable of experimental verification, and only insofar as it is capable of such verification. This is approximately the doctrine of pragmatism. (CP 5.197)

We are able to deal with the world around us by forming beliefs about what it is like. Beliefs are opinions on which we are prepared to act. We want to "avoid all surprise," that is, possess beliefs that let us accurately anticipate what will actually happen when we take action. If a belief fails and things happen that we are not expecting—if we are surprised—we are thrown into a state of doubt. We then try to establish a new belief, one that produces expectations that will stand the test of reality.

Here pragmatism and abduction travel the same road. Whether in science or in life, we are sometimes "surprised" by a fact we encounter.

The old belief, the old explanatory hypothesis, has let us down and must be discarded. It has lost all of its pragmatic value. We are now in a state of doubt. We can only find rest when we have a new, more reliable belief to replace the failed one.

Synechism

How did it come about that we have this instinct for right guessing and what serves as the basis for the doctrine of pragmatism? He says that our instinctive nose for the truth has its grounding in his synechistic philosophy, his philosophy of *continuity*. Peirce says that all of reality is one continuum. He notes that "If all things are continuous, the universe must be undergoing a continuous growth from non-existence to existence" (CP 1.175). Everything evolves from a common origin and enjoys an unbroken continuity with everything else. This means that a thought and a stone are on one continuum, and as such affect each other constantly. That continuum is *mind* as it has evolved into this particular universe. For Peirce there is no mind–body problem. All that exists is mind evolving, and therefore everything lies on the same continuum. This is Peirce's doctrine of *synechism*. Peirce's view is radical:

> Once you have embraced the principle of continuity no kind of explanation of things will satisfy you except that they *grew*. The infallibilist naturally thinks that everything always was substantially as it is now. Laws at any rate being absolute could not grow. They either always were, or they sprang instantaneously into being by a sudden fiat like the drill of a company of soldiers. This makes the laws of nature absolutely blind and inexplicable. Their why and wherefore can't be asked. . . . The fallibilist won't do this. (CP 1.175)

And Peirce is a fallibilist. For him, by the principle of synechism, laws simply cannot be absolute, and any determination of physical laws and constants by experimental observation will of necessity be prone to error and imprecision (see Reynolds, 2002, pp. 17–18).

The implications of the doctrine of synechism for Peirce's evolutionary metaphysics are vast, far more than we can trace here. But let me for a moment go back to where we started to try to understand why we "guess" quite accurately about the underlying nature of things.

Since we are part of the same continuum as the things we are trying to explain, we are directly connected to them and thereby have the instinctive means to say something true about them. The utter continuity of the universe, the recognition that between matter and thoughts, for instance, there is unbroken continuity (matter being merely mind hidebound by habit, as we shall see), leads to the fact that the logic of the human mind is what characterizes the logic of the universe as a whole. The reality of continuity says that all is connected, that these connections spread back in time and spread across space in the present, and will spread further into the future. This will become clearer through an examination of what Peirce calls "the law of mind."

The Law of Mind

Peirce's central notion of "The Law of Mind" has profound implications for our discussion of survival and related phenomena. He presented his understanding of this conception in an article, "The Law of Mind," in *The Monist* in 1892. He states the law in this way:

> Logical analysis applied to mental phenomena shows that there is but one law of mind, namely, that ideas tend to spread continuously and to affect certain others which stand to them in a peculiar relation of affectability. In this spreading they lose intensity, and especially the power of affecting others, but gain generality and become welded with other ideas. (CP 6.104)

Peirce drew out the implications of the *continuum* (ideas spread "continuously") for our understanding of mind. He stated his starting position:

> I have begun by showing that *tychism* [evolutionary theory based on the notion of "pure chance"] must give birth to an evolutionary cosmology, in which all the regularities of nature and of mind are regarded as products of growth, and to a Schelling-fashioned idealism which holds matter to be mere specialized and partially deadened mind. (CP 6.102)

He is here referring to something he had written in *The Monist* in 1891: "The one intelligible theory of the universe is that of objective idealism, that matter is effete mind, inveterate habits becoming physical laws" (CP 6.25). By calling his philosophy *objective idealism*, he indicates that the only thing that can be called real is what appears in experience, but what appears in experience is what it is regardless of that experience: this is a *realism*, one that indicates that, although everything is mind, reality is independent of our thoughts and that our experiences are objectively determined.

So, Peirce conceived of physical laws as ingrained habits exhibited by matter, and, in turn, he thought of matter as mind that has become sodden with habit (Reynolds, 2002, pp. 52). He says that he must "regard matter as mind whose habits have become fixed so as to lose the powers of forming them and losing them" (CP 6.101), that "if habit be a primary property of mind, it must be equally so of matter, as a kind of mind" (CP 6.269).

Later in his "Law of Mind," Peirce makes this observation:

> Consistently with the doctrine laid down in the beginning of this paper, I am bound to maintain that an idea can only be affected by an idea in continuous connection with it. By anything but an idea, it cannot be affected at all. This obliges me to say, as I do say, on other grounds, that what we call matter is not completely dead, but is merely mind hide-bound with habits. It still retains the element of diversification; and in that diversification there is life. (CP 6.158)

Here Peirce maintains that although matter is heavily habitualized, it does retain something of Freedom/Chance/Spontaneity—though a very small amount of it.

Later in the article, Peirce examined the notion of *habit* in detail. He defined habit in terms of the law of mind: habit is that specialization of the law of mind whereby a general idea gains the power of exciting reactions. A past idea brings about a tendency for a future idea to occur, and this is precisely what habit consists in: the tendency to make certain future events happen. In this sense, the mind is not subject to "law" in any absolute sense: "It only experiences gentle forces which merely render it more likely to act in a given way than it otherwise would be" (CP 6.148). These "gentle forces" are what Peirce means by the presence of *final causes* in the evolution of the universe. Final causes are determined by mind in all its forms, with the greatest freedom to choose exercised in human beings. For Peirce there is no specific overall telos governing the universe. Rather, a thing evolves through a myriad of teloi that continually change, each new moment setting a new telos for action. This is what Peirce means by "developmental teleology." Teleology, understood in this way, is the only thing that can make sense of evolution.

So for Peirce:

> [G]eneral ideas are not mere words, nor do they consist in this, that certain concrete facts will every time happen under certain descriptions of conditions; but they are just as much, or rather far more, living realities than the feelings themselves out of which they are concreted. And to say that mental phenomena are governed by law does not mean merely that they are describable by a general formula; but that there is a living idea, a conscious continuum of feeling, which pervades them, and to which they are docile. (CP 6.152)

According to Peirce, the beginning and evolution of the universe happen according to the Law of Mind. The universe arises first of all from feeling. Things within the universe affect each other and evolve exactly as ideas do, because the universe is in its basic essence mind. Whether it is mind found in forms that evince a notable amount of Freedom/Chance/Spontaneity, such as living things, and especially human beings, or found in more habitualized forms with a much reduced capacity for spontaneity, such as rocks and thermostats, it is still mind.

Personality

Needless to say, personality is a crucial topic for issues relating to survival, but for Peirce it is also crucial for understanding paranormal phenomena more generally. Peirce's idea of personality flows directly from the preceding discussion of the Law of Mind. He calls personality "a particular phenomenon which is remarkably prominent in our own consciousness," and is "some kind of coördination or connection of ideas" (CP 6.155). He points out that in the previous discussion it was discovered that a connection between ideas is a general idea and that a general idea is a living feeling. For Peirce the person is a unified living feeling, bringing all of its elements together through mutual relations: "All that is necessary . . . to the existence of a person is that the feelings out of which he or she is constructed should be in close enough connection to influence one another" (CP 6.270).

For Peirce, personality is a general idea and, like any general idea, cannot be apprehended in an instant, but must be lived in time. Also, no finite time can actually embrace it in all its fullness. "Yet," says Peirce, "in each infinitesimal interval it is present and living, though specially colored by the immediate feelings of that moment" (CP 6.155).

But there is more to it than that, says Peirce, for insofar as personality is a coordination of ideas, it manifests a *teleological harmony of ideas*. The teleology here is more than the mere purposive conscious pursuit of a premeditated end:

> [I]t is a developmental teleology. This is personal character. A general idea, living and conscious now, it is already determinative of acts in the future to an extent to which it is not now conscious. This reference to the future is an essential element of personality. Were the ends of a person already explicit, there would be no room for development, for growth, for life; and consequently there would be no personality. The mere carrying out of predetermined purposes is mechanical. (CP 6.156–157)

For personality to be teleological it must possess the power to act. Peirce identifies that power with the "I": "the leading part of the meaning which we express by 'I' is the idea of an unrestrained cause of some future events" (MS 668, 16–17, in Colapietro, 1989, p. 112). This makes the "I" a creative spring of efficacious exertions. This is crucial for Peirce. He wrote, "it is plain that intelligence does not consist in feeling in a certain way, but in acting in a certain way. . . . How we feel is no matter; the question is what we shall do. But that feeling which is subservient to action and to the intelligence of action is correspondingly important; and all inward life is more or less so subservient" (CP 6.286). Peirce seems to be indirectly referring to the "I" in this passage:

> [E]ach personality is based upon a "bundle of habits," as the saying is that a man is a bundle of habits. But a bundle of habits would not have the unity of self-consciousness. That *unity* must be given as a centre for the habits. The brain shows no central cell. The unity of consciousness is therefore not of physiological origin. It can only be metaphysical. (CP 6.228–229)

Peirce poses the question: how does one person recognize the personality of *another*? He responds that it happens more or less the same way a person becomes aware of his own personality: *through direct perception*, that is, "that second personality itself, enters within the field of direct consciousness of the first person, and is as immediately perceived as his ego, though less strongly. At the same time, the opposition between the two persons is perceived, so that the externality of the second is recognized" (CP 6.160).

Peirce goes on to say that a genuinely evolutionary philosophy, which makes the principle of growth a primordial element of the universe, actually requires the idea of a *personal* creator. This creator is the great personality, the great coordinator and connector of ideas. Peirce makes this bold statement:

> A difficulty which confronts the synechistic philosophy is this. In considering personality, that philosophy is forced to accept the doctrine of a personal God; but in considering communication, it cannot but admit that if there is a personal God, we must have a direct perception of that person and indeed be in personal communication with him. Now, if that be the case, the question arises how it is possible that the existence of this being should ever have been doubted by anybody. The only answer that I can at present make is that facts that stand before our face and eyes and stare us in the face are far from being, in all cases, the ones most easily discerned. (CP 6.162)

Personality and Others

According to Peirce's doctrine of synechism, self and other are inextricably involved with each other. The synechist must not say, "I am altogether myself, and not at all you" (CP 7.571). Nevertheless, although for Peirce a central feature of the self is its connections to other selves and the divine self, still he made a point to preserve the notion that the self is in some significant way autonomous. For Peirce, human self-consciousness is the achievement of an incarnate consciousness; that is, the human body with its unique capacities plays an indispensable role (Colapietro, 1989, p. 69). The child is able to become conscious of itself not only through sensing things and desiring them, but also through refined capacities for acting and for communicating. For these things, the body is indispensible. In the process of communicating with others, the growing child finds out that what others say is the best evidence for what is real, "so much so, that testimony is even a stronger mark of fact than *the facts themselves*, or rather than what must now be thought of as the *appearances* themselves" (CP 5.233).

To the child, testimony about the nature of the world comes largely from adults and has a certain authority. That testimony may conflict with the child's personal take on things, and that fact, along with his own growing fund of experience, brings home the possibility that he can be mistaken in his perceptions. When his further experience confirms the falsity of his previous ideas, "he becomes aware of ignorance, and it is necessary to suppose a self in which this ignorance can inhere" (CP 5.233). So it is that "testimony gives the first dawning of self-consciousness" (CP 5.233). The child also comes to know that what he feels or wants may not be shared by others (he wants to pick up the spider, but his mother says "no"). The child becomes aware that these feelings are unique to him, part of a private world. The speech and actions of others reveal that they too have their own private worlds. All these realizations bring home the fact of error (they can be right and I wrong), and error can only be explained by supposing a self that is fallible (CP 5.233). The experience of the testimony of others, the possibility of error, and the discovery of privacy, all reinforce the idea that the individual self is constituted by its relations to others and is distinguishable but not separate from others. Peirce said that to be a self is to be a possible member of some such community (CP 5.402n.2). Peirce held that the self must also be a center of purpose and power, and although the self is defined by its relations to others, it is also something in itself—as James (1890) said in *Principles*, "a sort of innermost centre within the circle, of sanctuary within the citadel" (Vol. 1, p. 297). This center of power and purpose is the "I."

Remember that for Peirce an open-ended future is an essential element of the individual personality (CP 6.157), and such a future involves the possibility of pursuing purposes different from those presently pursued. The self's evolving identity too is constituted by its association with other selves. In opposition to the early ideas of James about the self (who considered it essentially separated from other selves) and self-consciousness, Peirce says the synechist must deny the view that says that the self is an absolute rather than relative being. Colapietro (1989) explains Peirce's notion of the creation of community precisely in these terms:

> The synechistic approach to the individual self denies any absolute breach between self and other. It does so to such an extent that selves in communion with one another form in some way and to some extent, a self of a higher order. That is, genuine community is never a mere collection of individual selves; it is always a living union of integrated selves. This union of selves that constitutes a community is analogous to the coordination of ideas that constitutes a personality; indeed, the community is in some measure a person. (p. 78)

For James (1890) in his earlier writings, the self is in absolute isolation from other selves, and in taking this position he creates an irreducible pluralism (Vol. 1, p. 221). For Peirce, the self is defined in terms of continuity. While James made the distance between two minds the most absolute breach in nature, Peirce held that distance to be easily crossed. In response to James's view of the self of the *Principles*, Peirce asked him, "Is not the direct contrary nearer observed facts? You think there *must* be such isolation, because you confound thoughts with feeling-qualities; but all observation is against you. There are some small particulars that a man can keep to himself. He exaggerates them and his personality sadly" (CP 8.81). This reflects Peirce's general difficulty with James's pluralistic approach, confessing in a letter to him that "pluralism . . . does not satisfy either my head or my heart" (CP 8.262). It should be noted, however, that, although this was true of James in the 1890s, he moderated his ideas in his later writings, giving greater emphasis to human interconnections.

Self and Signs

Embodiment is necessary for having a self. The self is a *sign*; it derives from relations and produces new relations. Peirce also saw evidence of the action of signs outside a nervous system and even outside a biological organism: "It appears in the work of bees, of crystals, and throughout the purely physical world; and one can no more deny that it is really there, than that the colors, the shapes, etc., of objects are really there" (CP 4.551). Nevertheless, in humans the action of signs reaches its greatest fecundity:

> Human instinct is no whit less miraculous than that of the bird, the beaver, or the ant. Only, instead of being directed to bodily motions . . . or to the construction of dwellings, or to the organization of

communities, its theatre is the plastic inner world, and its products are the marvellous conceptions of which the greatest are the ideas of number, time, and space. (MS 318, 44, quoted in Colapietro, 1989, p. 85)

A person as an individual is a continuity of reactions, and, as an entity, an enduring network of interpenetrating habits, so Peirce's exposition of the self as a semiotic process does not contradict his belief in the self as an enduring agency.

For Peirce, a person also has *inwardness*, the capacity to withdraw from the public world with its public signs to a private world, a secret world with its private signs. For Peirce the private world is important to the development of our thoughts, but nonetheless "one of these two worlds, the Inner World, exerts a comparatively slight compulsion upon us . . . while the other world, the Outer World, is full of irresistible compulsions for us, and we cannot modify it in the least, except by one peculiar kind of effort, muscular effort, and but very slightly even in that way" (CP 5.474).

Peirce summed up his vision of the human person in this way:

> Two things here are all-important to assure oneself of and to remember. The first is that a person is not absolutely an individual. His thoughts are what he is "saying to himself," that is, is saying to that other self that is just coming into life in the flow of time. When one reasons, it is that critical self that one is trying to persuade; and all thought whatsoever is a sign, and is mostly of the nature of language. The second thing to remember is that the man's circle of society (however widely or narrowly this phrase may be understood), is a sort of loosely compacted person, in some respects of higher rank than the person of an individual organism. It is these two things alone that render it possible for you—but only in an abstract, and in a Pickwickian sense—to distinguish between absolute truth and what you do not doubt. (CP 5.421)

For Peirce, thinking involves two roles, what he called the *critical self*, representing the habits of the person, and the *innovative self*, representing a challenge to these habits. The former is both a summation of the past and an orientation toward the future. Peirce called this network of interwoven habits at various points "soul," "real self," and "true self" (Colapietro, 1989, pp. 93–96). The habits that constitute the critical self are the final product of the self's interpretive efforts. The innovative self introduces Freedom/Chance/Spontaneity in the form of thought into the soul's unfolding. This gives the human personality the power of self-control.

Mind

Peirce complained that psychologists failed to distinguish between mind and consciousness. He believed that mind is present in (and constitutes) all of reality, while consciousness is found only in higher animals. According to the law of continuity, the continuous spread of feeling produces general ideas. So habit-taking and continuity are more or less the equivalent of "mind," "intelligence," or "reason," bringing about the spread of feeling through signs.

Peirce says personality is a special kind of mind, one whose parts are coordinating in a particular way, possessing interrelated capacities of self-consciousness, self-criticism, and self-control, and exhibiting the abilities to feel, act, and learn.

If personality is one type of mind, what is mind in general for Peirce? There are two aspects of mind in general. One is that it is characterized by *feeling*: "A feeling is a state of mind having its own living quality, independent of any other state of mind" (CP 6.18). The other is the fact that it involves final causation:

> Mind has its universal mode of action, namely, by final causation. The microscopist looks to see whether the motions of a little creature show any purpose. If so, there is mind there. (CP 1.269)

> The psychologists say that consciousness is the essential attribute of mind; and that purpose is only a special modification. I hold that purpose, or rather, final causation, of which purpose is the conscious modification, is the essential subject of psychologists' own studies; and that consciousness is a special, and not a universal, accompaniment of mind. (CP 7.366)

Peirce saw final causality operating in three realms: (1) in matter (habitualized mind) detached from any biological organism, (2) in biological organisms, and (3) in societies, ranging from the family to the public, and in our indefinite posterity (CP 1.267). Peirce believed that the facts of evolution indicate a finality at work in nature. Since operating by final causation is a mark of mind, Peirce held that our observations of nature as evincing final causes confirm that nature is mind. He said that according to the principle of continuity,

> matter would be nothing but mind that had such indurated habits as to cause it to act with a peculiarly high degree of mechanical regularity or routine. Supposing this to be the case, the reaction between matter and mind would be of no essentially different kind from the action between parts of mind that are in continuous union, and would thus come directly under the great law of mental association . . . of which the laws of matter are regarded as mere special results. (CP 6.277)

PEIRCE ON PARANORMAL PHENOMENA AND SURVIVAL

Peirce got involved with issues relating to the paranormal at various points in the development of his philosophical system. He was not impressed by the tendency of the British Society for Psychical Research (SPR) to invoke telepathy as its explanation for various paranormal phenomena. Not that Peirce doubted the reality of telepathic communication—quite the contrary. He was prepared to accept all facts of experience no matter how odd, and even if an explanation for those facts was not immediately forthcoming. For that reason he was prepared to accept the phenomena of psychical research and survival on the basis of the evidence. He had no problem admitting that direct communications between persons without the benefit of sense experience (telepathy) could occur. Peirce did not reject telepathy as a phenomenon, but *as an explanatory principle*. He was particularly bothered by the approach of Edmund Gurney who, he believed, was all too ready to call upon telepathy for that purpose. As a means of explanation, Peirce judged telepathy to be inadequate because, in his opinion, no one seemed able to give an accounting of why telepathy itself existed; so explanation of certain complex paranormal phenomena by telepathy would amount to explaining the obscure by the equally obscure. Any worthwhile explanation would have to go deeper and uncover the metaphysical foundations that accommodate these facts. Peirce believed that he had an *explanation*, not only for person-to-person extrasensory communication, but for all the established phenomena of psychical research.

The phenomena of the paranormal encounter no resistance from Peirce's philosophy. For him, the discussion of these phenomena does not center around such philosophical issues as the possibility of mind affecting matter, but the empirical standing ascribed to the phenomena. If there is good evidence that the phenomena exist (and Peirce did not doubt that), then he is ready and eager to utilize abduction in searching for a theory.

For Peirce there is no real knowledge that is not scientific. All knowledge must proceed from the given facts, and all increase of knowledge consists in the theories we devise to explain those facts. As far as he is concerned, the world is fundamentally explainable, for the world, as a manifestation of mind, operates from the same logical structure that resides in the human mind. The road of inquiry of the human community must not be blocked, he says, and we cannot declare that there are impenetrable mysteries that we must exempt from our rational investigations. Such an approach is unacceptable for dealing with a universe that is mind evolving.

In this framework, study of the paranormal is and must be science, and the phenomena of the paranormal, if shown to exist, must be explainable in the long run. I say in the long run, because the penetration of the darkness of the unknown does not happen easily or all at once. Because of this, scientific knowledge can only really make headway if it is a community undertaking. Peirce identifies a community of inquirers who proceed gradually in the direction of the truth, operating through trial and error, gradually correcting those inevitable errors that occur along the way and moving forward bit by bit. This community of inquiry exists in time. It stretches back into untold ages from the first attempts to deliberately apply reason to discovery, and in every age reaches out in space to all inquirers in every location and every culture.

Peirce saw psychical research as part of this process of inquiry, and although he felt progress thus far had been scant, he was encouraging to those who seriously applied themselves to the task. His criticisms of Gurney, examining his work in such detail and with such care, did not come from a spirit of dismissal of his efforts, but from a feeling of wanting the community of inquirers to succeed at producing ways of explaining paranormal phenomena that are adequate to the task.

If, as far as Peirce is concerned, psychical research is and must be a science, then there must be viable explanations for the established phenomena. Telepathy, clairvoyance, psychokinesis in all its forms, must in the end be intelligible and susceptible of scientific explanation. And this explanation must do justice to the facts—all the facts—and not force them into theories that are not adequate to the phenomena. Not only that, they must also be explained in terms that are philosophically sound, which for Peirce meant they must be considered as taking place in a *continuous* universe which is, at bottom, mind.

An Alternative Explanation

Here is a summary of Peirce's approach to the paranormal. Paranormal abilities are natural capacities, existing everywhere in nature. They are based on the continuity of all things. This posits that everything is connected on one continuum, and everything has access to everything else. This access provides the basis for communication beyond the senses and producing movement without contact.

To those who today continue what psychical research began, Peirce's approach might be attractive. He certainly agreed with Myers that the inquiry is fully and fundamentally scientific. He also agreed that the phenomena must never be ruled out on any kind of a priori ground. He also insisted that the only true theories are those that can be tested by experience. He believed that if there is no way to put a theory to the test, to devise experiments (in the broadest sense) that can verify the theory through predictable results, then that theory is a waste of time, for it does not lead us any further along the road of inquiry into truth.

Peirce offered, for the consideration of psychical researchers, an alternative explanatory principle for rogue phenomena related to perception (telepathic and clairvoyant type). He developed his theory in an article, "Man's Glassy Essence," written for *The Monist* in 1892, appearing just three months after his article on "The Law of Mind." It is a theory that uses his basic conceptions of continuity, habit, and the law of mind, and he approaches the problem through a discussion of personality.

Peirce believed that theories of origin of the universe should be verifiable through observation of the world as it is today. Psychical research had given evidence of extraordinary forms of perception and communications between persons. He said that as far as he was concerned, this type of phenomenon was not only *compatible* with his vision of the origin and evolution of the world, but, on the basis of his assumptions, should actually be *expected* to occur. To give some idea of how Peirce developed his theory in the 1892 article, I will have to back up a few steps.

The bulk of the ideas developed in "Man's Glassy Essence" were inspired by Peirce's close study of protoplasm. He found this a most fruitful area of investigation because he believed that the presence of mind can be confirmed anywhere we can observe the operation of final causes, and, in his opinion, the behavior of protoplasm clearly reveals teleological actions which can be easily observed. For Peirce there was no question that *feeling* is operative in protoplasm, and in this sense interiority and consciousness, and that "it not only feels, but exercises all the functions of mind" (CP 6.255). Now the presence of feeling cannot, says Peirce, be derived from the three laws of mechanics, and "it can never be explained unless we admit that physical events are but degraded or undeveloped forms of psychical events" (CP 6.264). Wherever Chance/Freedom/Spontaneity are found, there, and in the same proportion, will be found feeling. In evolution, wherever we find diversification, chance must be operative; wherever we find uniformity or regularity, habit must be operative. So that when we view a thing from the outside, considering its relations of action and reaction with other things, it appears as matter, whereas viewed from the inside in its immediate character as feeling, it appears as consciousness (CP 6.268).

In reading Peirce's writings, it becomes evident that for him the central problem with telepathy is not that mind-to-mind communication is impossible, or that it is (as he thought) rare. Rather it is that the explanation of such phenomena conceives of this communication as occurring between two radically separated persons, isolated from each other and the broader community. If one is going to make sense of mind-to-mind communication, it must be in terms of a philosophy that recognizes the fundamental principle that human beings exist in a continuum (manifesting as a web of interconnections) with one another and that this fact explains—and even requires—that some such mind-to-mind communication should exist.

Writing in 1905, Peirce declared:

> The myriad strange stories [in spiritualistic lore] prove nothing. . . . If you have already admitted the general proposition of Spiritualism, you will naturally be inclined to use it to explain some of these stories. If, on the other hand, your judgment is that general experience is emphatically opposed to that proposition, these stories will assuredly not shake that judgment. Meantime, those who are engaged in psychical research should receive every encouragement. They may have reached little or

no result, so far; perhaps will not till they dismiss the phantom of telepathy from their minds. But scientific men, working in something like scientific ways, must ultimately reach scientific results. Psychology is destined to be the most important experimental research of the twentieth century; fifty years hence its wonders may be expected to occupy popular imagination as wonders of electricity do now. (CP 6.586–587)

Spiritualism and Survival of Death

Peirce had a straightforward notion of the nature of survival: "By the doctrine of a future life, I understand the proposition that after death we shall retain or recover our individual consciousness, feeling, volition, memory, and, in short (barring an unhappy contingency), all our mental powers unimpaired" (CP 6.548). He noted that the direct positive evidence of survival comes from miracles, spiritualistic marvels, and apparitions.

Writing about psychical research (as he knew it), Peirce in 1887 had occasion to comment on descriptions of communications from the departed. He said that even if the ghost stories that we have all heard added up to a confirmation of the reality of spiritual manifestations, it is impossible to ignore the apparent characteristics of spirits. They exhibit but a remnant of mind, he wrote, with a stupidity that makes them more like lower animals than human beings. He stated that if he did believe in them, he would have to conclude that the soul was not always immediately extinguished at the death of the body, but was reduced to a "pitiable shade, a mere ghost, as we say, of its former self." He continued:

I fancy that, were I suddenly to find myself liberated from all the trials and responsibilities of this life, my probation over, and my destiny put beyond marring or making, I should feel as I do when I find myself on an ocean steamer, and know that for ten days no business can turn up, and nothing can happen. I should regard the situation as a stupendous frolic, should be at the summit of gayety, and should only be too glad to leave the vale of tears behind. Instead of that, these starveling souls come mooning back to their former haunts, to cry over spilled milk. (CP 6.550)

One cannot escape the conclusion that Peirce was not acquainted with the more impressive and significant phenomena of spiritualism, but was relying mainly on fictional and imaginative accounts (some of which he explicitly cites). Even granted this, Peirce still showed a consistent respect for that movement. So we find Peirce writing in 1903:

> Suppose, for example, it is a question between accepting Telepathy or Spiritualism. The former I dare say is the preferable working hypothesis because it can be more readily subjected to experimental investigation. But as long as there is no reason for believing it except phenomena that Spiritualism is equally competent to explain, I think Spiritualism is much the more likely to be approximately true, as being the more anthropomorphic and natural idea; and in like manner, as between an old-fashioned God and a modern patent Absolute, recommend me to the anthropomorphic conception if it is a question of which is the more likely to be about the truth. (CP 5.47n.)

And elsewhere, speaking of the theory of telepathy, he said, "I felt that I would far sooner believe in spiritualism. For according to this latter theory, we *all* pass into another life; nor would this experience common to us all be much more wonderful than the development that we all undergo when the child becomes a grown person" (CP 7.602).

Around 1905, Peirce wrote a fascinating treatise on "Logic and Spiritualism." He noted that by and large spiritualists had little time for scientists. Speaking as a scientist, he wrote, "We may as well acknowledge it, [scientific men] are, as such, mere specialists. . . .We are blind to our own blindness; but the world seems to declare us simply incapable of rising from narrowness and specialism to take broad view of any facts whatsoever" (CP 6.560). In this connection, he sings the praises of common sense, saying that it is a far more valuable reservoir of truth than the aggregate of man's special experience. Common sense improves, corrects itself over time, but it does not attain infallibility (CP 6.571–574). When common sense looks at the feat of the medium Slade, who was able to produce a knot in Zöllner's loop of string sealed at the ends, it believes the most likely explanation is trickery, although Peirce believed that Zöllner's suggestion that a fourth dimension of space was involved cannot be absolutely ruled out (CP 6.575). Peirce counsels caution when investigating the phenomena of spiritualism, suggesting four things to keep in mind: (1) all men are liars, (2) the existence of hypnotism, imagination, and hysteria, (3) we may receive and act upon indications of which we are quite unconscious, and (4) a certain number of coincidences will occur by chance (CP 6.586). This cautiousness should not, however, be taken as an indication that Peirce was rejecting of spiritualistic phenomena, but that he was recommending great care and caution in dealing with such experiences.

One further point: as we have seen, Peirce accepted the reality of apparitions, but considered them "shades," mere remnants of the formerly living person. We must be mindful that he dealt with them in the context of his discussion of spiritualism, and did not provide a philosophical account of them. This subject is for him quite separate from the issue of survival of death. This reveals a certain ambiguity in his thinking about the matter, for he seems to accept some phenomena of spiritualism and reject others, while conjecturing that spiritualism may not be that far from the true view of things.

Telepathy

In 1905 Peirce wrote: "Hypnotism I question not, nor double and triple personality" (CP 6.559). After this confession of his willingness to accept the possibility of the unusual, he expressed his skepticism about telepathy and added, "Not that telepathy is absurd, or that its nature is impossible, but in the coarse form it has been imagined, impracticable as voyage to planet Mars" (CP 6.559).

In regard to the discussion of telepathy by psychical researchers, Peirce found himself dissatisfied with what he read of it in the publications of the SPR. He was critical on two scores: (1) the questionableness of using telepathy as an overall explanatory idea, and (2) what he believed to be the wrong-headed way investigators used observations and statistics. He carried on a dialogue with Gurney about these matters, an exchange that ended with Gurney's death in 1888 (see Gurney, 1887a, 1887b; Peirce, 1887a, 1887b; see also Myers, 1887; the whole dialogue can be found in Peirce, 2000, pp. 73–154).

Stephen Braude has published a detailed discussion of Peirce on telepathy (Braude, 1998), including an analysis of the Peirce–Gurney dialogue. He says that Peirce's problems with telepathy are somewhat superficial. Braude presents reasons why, even if the reality of telepathy is accepted, there are great methodological difficulties in conducting experiments that isolate the phenomena due specifically to telepathy. Braude also examines Peirce's views on psychokinesis, survival, and miracles, leaving us with some idea of the complexity of his attitude toward these phenomena and the sometimes seemingly contradictory nature of his remarks.

In his discussion of communication in "The Law of Mind," Peirce asked the question of whether his philosophy was favorable to telepathy. He said that at first sight it might seem unfavorable. "Yet," he continued, "there may be other modes of continuous connection between minds than those of time and space" (CP 6.159). Elsewhere (CP 7.597–688) he said he did not feel enthusiastic about telepathy as an explanatory principle because it seems to refer to such a rare phenomenon—few people ever experience it. Obviously, Peirce was ill-informed about the paucity of data, and he failed to take into account the fact that telepathy might be very active in human life without being easily detected. However, in other places he seems to draw back from the view that telepathy, which he described as the action of one mind on another by means fundamentally different from those of everyday experience, is a rare phenomenon. In an article in *The Nation* in 1897, Peirce acknowledged that recent experiments in telepathy had been conducted "with a measure of good sense." Here Peirce (1978) wrote:

> The results of the best of these experiments have usually afforded what appear to be indications, though extremely slight ones, of some tendency to something like telepathy. Now it was precisely such very slight phenomena, occurring with a certain frequency, that were wanting a dozen years ago to bridge the chasm between the ordinary course of nature and the apparently supernatural. (p. 143)

I believe that in Peirce's writings we must distinguish between telepathy as an explanatory principle and telepathy as an empirical fact. He did not rule out the possibility of telepathy as a fact. In 1896 he wrote, "At present, while the existence of telepathy cannot be said to be established, all scientific men are obliged by observed facts to admit that it presents at least a very serious problem requiring respectful treatment" (CP 1.115). Nevertheless, he certainly did find using telepathy as an explanatory principle for other paranormal phenomena objectionable and considered his synechistic explanation to be superior.

In addition, phenomena of clairvoyance find a friendly reception in Peirce's philosophy. For Peirce, reality is a profusion of signs, and all communication, all experience, is semiotic. There is nothing in Peirce that indicates that all the signs that we process must be experienced consciously. In fact, he insists that most are not. Neither does he say that all signs manifest to us in sense experience. This leaves open the door for the possibility that we can both receive and process unconsciously signs that are received through nonsensory channels. Some of this extrasensory semiotic processing would derive from connections with other persons, through a community network of relations. For Peirce, we do not have to be physically in the presence of someone to be semiotically in touch with that person. He says that this communication occurs with our "neighbors," but our neighbor "is one whom we live near, not locally perhaps, but in life and feeling" (CP 6.289). It would be through this kind of communication that events unavailable to the senses could nevertheless become known to the clairvoyant.

Psychokinesis

Again and again Peirce demonstrated his openness to investigating paranormal phenomena and his refusal to reject the possibility out of hand. His view that all of reality is a manifestation of mind permitted him to say, "Every fact has a physical side; perhaps every fact has a psychical side. Its physical aspect—as a mere motion—is due exclusively to physical causes; its psychical aspect—as a deed—is due exclusively to psychical causes. This remains true, though you accept every doctrine of telepathy, table-turning, or what you will" (CP 1.265). It is this view of the constitution of reality that formed the outlines of a Peircean theory of the paranormal.

Peirce was a mere boy of thirteen when, in 1852, the table-moving craze, spawned by Spiritualism, swept across North America and Europe (see Crabtree, 1993, pp. 236–265). This phenomenon consisted in a cooperative group experience originally aimed at communicating with spirits of the departed. People would typically sit around a table, hands flat on the surface or held just above it, with little fingers touching those of one's neighbors. Questions would be posed and answers obtained through knocks produced by a raising and lowering of a table leg, seemingly of its own accord, or through simple knocking sounds emanating from the wood of the table itself. These knocks would be translated alphabetically, so that answers could be spelled out. Public interest in the phenomenon lasted for several decades, so Peirce had a chance to experiment with it as a grown man. He wrote:

> In the days of table-turning we used to be commanded to sit quite away from the table, and "*with all our might*" to will that the table should move; and since the whole weight of our outstretched arms soon made our finger-tips unconsciously numb (for things are not apt to be consciously unconscious; and there were other concurring physiological effects that we did not suspect), while we were possessed of no other "might" over the table than through our muscles, we used to be speedily rewarded, by a direct consciousness of willing that the table move, accompanied by the vision of its wondrous obedience. (CP 1.331)

Elsewhere, Peirce wrote:

> If I can turn a table by the force of my will, this will simply establish the fact that something between me and the table acts just as a stick with which I should poke the table would act. It would be a physical connection purely and simply, however interesting it might be to a psychologist. But on the other hand, as my hand obeys, in a general way, my commands, clutching what I tell it to clutch, . . . so the table-turning experiment would, I suppose, show that I could give similar general orders to the untouched table. That would be purely psychical, or final, causation, in which particulars are disregarded. Meantime, one may note that the table certainly *will* turn, if I really and truly *will* that it shall without being too meticulous about ways and means. (CP 1.265)

This seems to be as far as Peirce went in developing a theory to explain table-moving as a species of what today we call psychokinesis (the unmediated influence of a living being on the physical world).

Finally, at this point it should be clear that in Peirce's scheme of things, phenomena of paranormal psychophysical effects are as unproblematic as those of paranormal communications.

Precognition

It is hard to see how precognition could be incorporated into Peirce's philosophy. For him the world has been evolving from time immemorial, moving forward by means of a developmental teleology, by which individuals are at one moment choosing their future in view of a specific goal, and at the next moment, having moved forward under the influence of that goal, set themselves a new goal. They do not move forward under some preconceived detailed plan given from above. There is an intention that they should reach their greatest possible realization (evolutionary love), and there is the gentle attraction of a distant goal of the supreme good, but that does not amount to a plan that can somehow be known beforehand. For Peirce, even God does not know the specific future of the universe or any individual.

Developmental teleology is based on free choice. However, most of the evolutionary increments of change are overpowered by the inertia of habit. Although no one can know beforehand for certain what choice will be made, it would be possible to make good guesses in terms of the habits in place. But of course this is not what is meant by precognition.

Subtle Bodies

The subject of subtle bodies and the role they may play in the production of paranormal phenomena and survival of death emerges at several points in this book. If subtle bodies do exist, it would probably be possible to account for them in terms of a Peircean view of reality.

For Peirce, all that exists is embodied. Embodiment consists in habituatedness. The most mobile embodiment is that with the least habituation. "Matter" is the most habituated thing we know of. Although it is "hidebound with habit," it never comes to the point of being totally habituated and totally predictable. There is always at least some very small degree of chance or freedom at work everywhere. This picture derives from Peirce's notion that "natural laws [of physics]" are simply habits—fallible and subject to irregularities. Bodies are not "matter" as commonly understood; rather they are highly habituated mind. So there are no "degrees" of matter in the Newtonian sense, with some matter being of finer or less coarse constitution than others. Rather there are degrees of habituation. Our bodies, for instance, insofar as they are physical are highly

habituated mind. Also, Peirce claims that "the organism is only an instrument of thought" (CP 5.315). But since thought is essentially a process of
semiosis, the kind of instrument that the organism provides is that of an
expressive medium. We need a body to function semiotically. The human
being is not "shut up in a box of flesh and blood" (CP 7.591). The body is
not something *in which* the self is located, but the medium *through which*
the self expresses itself (Colapietro, 1989, p. 39). But this notion of body
can and must be universalized, taken beyond the mere physical organism
of the human self. Since all of reality is mind, all of reality is embodied,
for everything shows some degree of habituation (some degree of being
matter-like). The physical aspect is the most highly habituated aspect of
the human person. But one would expect there to be degrees of habituation, beginning with the physical and moving by degrees to less and less
habituation. These would correspond to what is meant by "subtle bodies."
What those lesser degrees of habituation might look like, we cannot
know. But if the human person is to survive and remain in contact with a
broader, semiotic world, some kinds of bodily semiotic expression must
remain possible after death.

A Synechistic Framework for Human Survival of Death

In his paper "Immortality in the Light of Synechism," Peirce begins with:

> The word *synechism* is the English form of the Greek συνεχισμός,
> from συνεχής, continuous. For two centuries we have been affixing -ist
> and -ism to words, in order to note sects which exalt the importance of
> those elements which the stem-words signify. Thus, *materialism* is the
> doctrine that matter is everything, *idealism* the doctrine that ideas are
> everything, *dualism* the philosophy which splits everything in two. In
> like manner, I have proposed to make *synechism* mean the tendency to
> regard everything as continuous. (CP 7.565)

Within this framework, Peirce gives us an intriguing description of spiritual consciousness, and opens the door for the survival of a spiritual
aspect that has an individual identity. Elsewhere Peirce described the
evolution of this consciousness from the primordial Nothing to an eternal
reality. In the present treatises he claims that, at death, this consciousness
would not simply disappear as an individual by merging with the one
great consciousness, but would retain an identity. He envisioned a panen-

theistic universe in which that identity nonetheless involves an identification with the divine:

> A Brahmanical hymn begins as follows: "I am that pure and infinite Self, who am bliss, eternal, manifest, all-pervading, who am the substrate of all that owns name and form." This expresses more than humiliation,—the utter swallowing up of the poor individual self in the Spirit of prayer. All communication from mind to mind is through continuity of being. A man is capable of having assigned to him a *rôle* in the drama of creation, and so far as he loses himself in that *rôle*,— *no* matter how humble it may be,—so far he identifies himself with its Author. (CP 7.572)

Peirce says further that:

> Synechism refuses to believe that when death comes, even the carnal consciousness ceases quickly. . . . But, further, synechism recognizes that the carnal consciousness is but a small part of the man. There is, in the second place, the social consciousness, by which a man's spirit is embodied in others, and which continues to live and breathe and have its being very much longer than superficial observers think. . . . Nor is this, by any means, all. A man is capable of a spiritual consciousness, which constitutes him one of the eternal verities, which is embodied in the universe as a whole. This as an archetypal idea can never fail; and in the world to come is destined to a special spiritual embodiment. (CP 7.574–576)

He concludes: "I have said enough, I think, to show that, though synechism is not religion, but, on the contrary, is a purely scientific philosophy, yet should it become generally accepted, as I confidently anticipate, it may play a part in the onement of religion and Science" (CP 7.578).

EVOLUTION AND GOD

The overarching vision that arises from Peirce's evolutionary philosophy could best be described as a form of "evolutionary panentheism," which holds that God is in the process of evolving in this universe and that human beings participate in the coming into being of God. This doctrine was perhaps best formulated in the writings of Friedrich Schelling

(1775–1854), who wrote that evolution is the process by which *Deus implicitus* (implicit God) becomes *Deus explicitus* (explicit God). It should come as no surprise that Peirce acknowledged Schelling's influence on his ideas. In a letter to William James in 1894, Peirce wrote:

> Your papa, for one, believed in creation, and so did the authors of all the religions. But my views are probably influenced by Schelling,—by all stages of Schelling, but especially by the *Philosophie der Natur*. I consider Schelling as enormous; and one thing I admire about him is his freedom from the trammels of system, and his holding himself uncommitted to any previous utterance. In that, he is like a scientific man. If you were to call my philosophy Schellingism transformed in the light of modern physics, I should not take it hard. (Perry, 1935, Vol. 2, pp. 415–416)

Evolutionary panentheism is entailed in Peirce's synechism, which holds that all communication from mind to mind is through continuity of being, and that our relations to other finite selves and to the divine self are constitutive of our identity. Peirce gives the divine a central position in this evolutionary vision of reality, yet he seems to labor to form a clear picture of God's place in the evolutionary process:

> The hypothesis of God is a peculiar one, in that it supposes an infinitely incomprehensible object, although every hypothesis, as such, supposes its object to be truly conceived in the hypothesis. This leaves the hypothesis but one way of understanding itself; namely, as vague yet as true so far as it is definite, and as continually tending to define itself more and more, and without limit. The hypothesis, being thus itself inevitably subject to the law of growth, appears in its vagueness to represent God as so, albeit this is directly contradicted in the hypothesis from its very first phase. But this apparent attribution of growth to God, since it is ineradicable from the hypothesis, cannot, according to the hypothesis, be flatly false. Its implications concerning the Universes will be maintained in the hypothesis, while its implications concerning God will be partly disavowed, and yet held to be less false than their denial would be. Thus the hypothesis will lead to our thinking of features of each Universe as purposed; and this will stand or fall with the hypothesis. Yet a purpose essentially involves growth, and so cannot be attributed to God. Still it will, according to the hypothesis, be less false to speak so than to represent God as purposeless. (CP 6.466)

Here Peirce struggles with the relationship between *Deus implicitus* and *Deus explicitus*. He takes the stand that God *both* evolves (grows) *and* is unchanging. To have purposes is to be unfinished. God is coming into being through a developmental teleology, that is, by means of purposes formed on the fly by a universe which is evolving toward an infinitely distant terminus. So God as evolving evinces purposes. Yet this purposeful God is also that which lies beyond all change, and this God, as originator of the evolving universe, is somehow beyond it and its evolutionary growth. In this formulation Peirce leaves us with a disturbing and perhaps unresolvable tension. Nevertheless, his philosophy offers the modern mind tools and perspectives that may enable the present version of humanity's community of inquirers to move us further down the path of understanding.

In Peirce's scheme of things, God's love is the driver of the evolutionary process. He takes over the Christian notion of *agape*, transforms it into a metaphysical principle, and calls it evolutionary love. He traces how he reached this position in his treatise "Evolutionary Love": "Philosophy, when just escaping from its golden pupa-skin, mythology, proclaimed the great evolutionary agency of the universe to be Love" (CP 6.287). The Greek word for "love" in those early times was *eros*, the love described in Plato. But *agape* is not just another name for *eros*. *Eros* regards the love object as valuable and desires to be enriched by that value. *Agape* on the other hand is given by grace, not merit, and the love object is not loved to enrich the lover. *Agape* is "the ardent impulse to fulfill another's highest impulse" (CP 6.289), the desire that the love object flourish in its evolution and develop itself to the utmost.

An attitude of "evolutionary love" toward oneself plays a crucial role in personal growth and evolution:

> Everybody can see that the statement of St. John [about love] is the formula of an evolutionary philosophy, which teaches that growth comes only from love, from—I will not say self-*sacrifice*, but from the ardent impulse to fulfill another's highest impulse. Suppose, for example, that I have an idea that interests me. It is my creation. It is my creature . . . it is a little person. I love it; and I will sink myself in perfecting it. It is not by dealing out cold justice to the circle of my ideas that I can make them grow. . . . (CP 6.289)

An evolving being moves forward on the crest of this love, but has its own crucial role to play. It makes choices among the many possibilities that life's circumstances place before it. The goal it tries to achieve in any particular action is a limited one and will be replaced at the next moment by another. This is what Peirce calls developmental teleology. In this way it makes its contribution to the evolution of God, but the ultimate outcome is not known and cannot be predicted. All that can be said about it is that the guiding and inspiring energy of this process is God as the *summum bonum*, and that the final shape of things will be the ultimate manifestation of the *summum bonum* that is possible in this world. In this process the evolutionary love showered on the evolving being is not coercion, but supportive inspiration.

Peirce's vision of evolutionary love in a context of evolutionary panentheism influenced many philosophers who came after him. Preeminent among them is Alfred North Whitehead with his "process philosophy." Whitehead's approach to evolutionary panentheism was further elaborated by Charles Hartshorne and David Ray Griffin. In the next chapter, Eric Weiss makes process philosophy the starting point for the development of his theory of "Transphysical Worlds."

NOTE

1. In line with the conventions of Peirce scholarship, citations in the form CP *v.p* are used here to refer to Peirce's writings as they are set out in *The Collected Papers of Charles Sanders Peirce* (Peirce, 1931–1958), *v* indicating the volume number, and *p* the paragraph number.

REFERENCES

Braude, S. E. (1998). Peirce on the paranormal. *Transactions of the Charles S. Peirce Society, 34,* 203–224.
Colapietro, V. M. (1989). *Peirce's Approach to the Self: A Semiotic Perspective on Human Subjectivity.* Albany: State University of New York Press.
Corrington, R. S. (1993). *An Introduction to C. S. Peirce: Philosopher, Semiotician, and Ecstatic Naturalist.* Lanham, MD: Rowman & Littlefield.
Crabtree, A. (1993). *From Mesmer to Freud: Magnetic Sleep and the Roots of Psychological Healing.* New Haven, CT: Yale University Press.
Gurney, E. (1887a). Remarks on Professor Peirce's paper. *Proceedings of the American Society for Psychical Research, 1,* 157–180.

Gurney, E. (1887b). Remarks on Mr. Peirce's Rejoinder. *Proceedings of the American Society for Psychical Research, 1*, 286–300.

Ibri, I. A. (2006). The heuristic exclusivity of abduction in Peirce's philosophy. In R. Fabbrichesi & S. Marietti (Eds.), *Semiotics and Philosophy in Charles Sanders Peirce* (pp. 89–111). Newcastle, England: Cambridge Scholars Publishing.

James, W. (1890). *The Principles of Psychology* (Vols. 1–2). New York: Henry Holt.

James, W. (1912). A world of pure experience. In *Essays in Radical Empiricism* (pp. 39–91). New York: Longmans, Green.

Myers, F. W. H. (1887). Postscript to Mr. Gurney's reply to Professor Peirce. *Proceedings of the American Society for Psychical Research, 1*, 300–301.

Peirce, C. S. (1887a). Criticisms on "Phantasms of the Living." *Proceedings of the American Society for Psychical Research, 1*, 150–157.

Peirce, C. S. (1887b). Mr. Peirce's rejoinder. *Proceedings of the American Society for Psychical Research, 1*, 180–215.

Peirce, C. S. (1931–1958). *The Collected Papers of Charles Sanders Peirce* (C. Hartshorne & P. Weiss, Eds., Vols. 1–6, 1931–1935; A. W. Burks, Ed., Vols. 7–8, 1958). Cambridge, MA: Harvard University Press.

Peirce, C. S. (1978). *Charles Sanders Peirce: Contributions to* The Nation, *Part 2: 1894–1900* (K. L. Ketner & J. E. Cook, Eds.). Lubbock: Texas Tech University Press.

Peirce, C. S. (2000). *Writings of Charles S. Peirce: A Chronological Edition, Volume 6: 1886–1890* (N. Houser, General Ed.). Bloomington: Indiana University Press.

Perry, R. B. (1935). *The Thought and Character of William James* (Vols. 1–2). Boston: Little, Brown.

Reynolds, A. (2002). *Peirce's Scientific Metaphysics: The Philosophy of Chance, Law, and Evolution*. Nashville, TN: Vanderbilt University Press.

Sherrif, J. K. (1994). *Charles Peirce's Guess at the Riddle: Ground for Human Significance*. Bloomington: Indiana University Press.

13

MIND BEYOND BODY

Transphysical Process Metaphysics

Eric M. Weiss

Chapter 1 of this book calls attention to *Irreducible Mind*, to its assemblage of empirical data supporting the existence of parapsychological phenomena, and to its demonstration of the inability of conventional mainstream physicalist understanding to explain either these phenomena, or the mind/brain connection more generally. That chapter ends with a call for a more adequate explanation than those provided by mainstream thinking. This chapter is a response to that call.

I offer here a summary of some ideas that I presented more elaborately in my book, *The Long Trajectory: The Metaphysics of Reincarnation and Life After Death*. In Part I of that book, I consider parapsychological phenomena in the light of the ideas of Transphysical Process Metaphysics, which is a type of process philosophy that I have developed out of a revision of the ideas of Alfred North Whitehead. These ideas start from everyday experiences and scientific knowledge. In accounting for everyday experience and science from a view rather like Whitehead's, I develop conceptual resources which allow a coherent accounting for parapsychological phenomena as well. In Part II of that book, I start from a broader perspective suggested by Sri Aurobindo, and develop a theory that places everyday phenomena and parapsychological phenomena in a context which also allows for an explanation of mysticism and precognition. The theory developed in Part II is entirely consistent with, but more general than, the theory presented in this chapter. The theory I am presenting here starts from an analysis of everyday experience, whereas the theory developed in Part II begins with consideration of an Absolute factor in existence that transcends time and space. It seems to me that without such an Absolute factor, we cannot do full justice to either mysticism or precognition, but the consideration of an Absolute factor is so far outside of normal scientific discourse that I will not raise these issues here. Readers interested in the broader theory can find it outlined in Part II of *The Long Trajectory* (Weiss, 2012).

THE PARAPSYCHOLOGICAL VIEW OF THE WORLD

I propose to begin my response to the need for an explanation of parapsychological phenomena by asking a question: "What must the universe be like in order to support the functioning of these phenomena?" I will divide parapsychological phenomena into four functional groups (receptive functions, causal functions, independence functions, and the reincarnation function) and see what they say about the world in which they occur.

Receptive Functions: Empathy, Telepathy, and Other Functions

For the purposes of this chapter, I will define "empathy" as the direct knowledge by one being of the feeling state of another being—unmediated by sensory cues. Telepathy is the direct knowledge by one being of the thoughts and the meanings of another, unmediated by sensory cues. If empathy and telepathy are actual phenomena, then it must be the case that living beings have a way of directly communicating feelings and thoughts among themselves that bypasses all presently known physical processes.

Other receptive functions give us the knowledge of events (other than that experienced through empathy and telepathy) taking place outside of any possibility of sensory transmission. This includes phenomena such as clairvoyance (remote viewing) and clairaudience. The existence of these functions shows that our reliance on sensory input is not absolute, and that human beings[1] have direct access to knowledge about the world that, again, is not transmitted through the sensory channels.

According to the conventional worldview in place today, human beings cannot have direct knowledge of the feelings and thoughts of others.

This follows from the prevailing assumption that the world consists of substantial objects existing in an objective, container-like spacetime, that our bodies are such objects, and that our experience results from processes taking place inside our separated bodies. In the context of these assumptions, we can only regard ourselves as utterly isolated from each other, each in the solitude of our own bodies, relating to each other only indirectly through sensations provided by our sense organs and nervous systems. If this view is correct, then empathy, telepathy, and other parapsychological receptive functions cannot be possible. This worldview must be abandoned if we are to find a way of genuinely accounting for the paranormal perceptive functions we are here discussing.

Causal Functions: Psychokinesis (PK)

Psychokinesis is the ability of a personality to influence the movements of physical and biological objects without using bodily effort. It implies that mental decisions have causal impacts in the world. PK is also implicated in those phenomena discussed in Chapter 1 under the heading of "extreme psychophysiological influence." While PK is often treated as particularly mysterious, the question of PK cannot be separated from the question of how it is that we can induce our own bodies to behave according to our wishes. Even that is an operation of "mind over matter." From this point of view, PK—far from being exceptional or extraordinary—is involved in every bodily action that we take.

It is broadly held that mind is either everything (idealism), purely insignificant and epiphenomenal (materialism), or else a mysterious entity, entirely other than matter, but somehow functioning parallel to it (dualism). There is a large literature debating these approaches to the critical problem of the relationship between the mind and the body. None of these approaches enables us to formulate a way of understanding that is adequate to the demands of science, everyday life, and parapsychology. In the approach that I am advocating in this chapter, idealism, materialism, and dualism are all rejected in favor of a process-oriented, Whiteheadian, panexperientialist view. In this I am entirely in agreement with David Ray Griffin, who has also explored the application of Whitehead's ideas to all of these domains (and to parapsychology in particular in Griffin, 1997). Later in this chapter I will expand on this process-oriented approach and on how my ideas take a somewhat different direction than Griffin's.

Independence Functions: Dreams, Lucid Dreams, Out-of-Body Experiences, and the Survival of Bodily Death

All of these functions seem to me to point to the ability of a personality to function independently of its waking body. Consider the following sequence:

- I begin sitting at my desk and trying to work on some obligatory paperwork.
- I get bored and begin to daydream. My mind is now "a million miles away."
- I fall asleep and begin to dream.
- My dream might start out as an experience of a world very much like the waking world, or it could be a more normal type of dream in which the reality is quite different from waking life. Also, I might awaken within my dream so that my dream becomes lucid— i.e., I find myself in the dream with my waking mentality intact, so that I remember having been awake, anticipate reawakening, and can think about the dream world around me in a critical way.

All that is necessary in order for me to access my "dream body" is for me to withdraw attention from the world disclosed by my bodily senses without losing continuity of awareness and memory. This refocusing of the attention might be brought about in various other ways, as in the extreme conditions triggering near-death experiences (NDEs). In any case, I am suggesting that any shift from normal waking consciousness to some extrasomatic experience can be understood as a refocusing of the attention.

In my normal waking state, I am focused on the data of the five senses and my responses to them. I call the world disclosed by our five bodily senses the "waking world." The waking world comprises both the world of our everyday experience, and the physical world which is abstracted from it.[2] I call the worlds that we experience in dreaming, lucid dreaming, and life after death the "transphysical worlds." Transphysical worlds are worlds that are fully actual but which cannot be found anywhere in the physical world as defined by physics.

When I daydream, I let go of the waking world and find myself on the edge of the dream world which is transphysical. Then I cross over into a full dream. Finally, if my attention is properly tuned, I may find myself lucid in the dream world. Since all of these experiences can come about merely by shifts of my attention, it seems plausible that I am already having experiences in a dream world even while I am awake. Only the vividness of my sensory experiences and the training of my mind to a way of thinking that is closely adapted to waking life keep me from noticing this other range of my experience.

This, of course, is a very different way of understanding these experiences from that which is characteristic of our modern, scientifically informed common sense. In that mode of thought, we imagine dreams as being caused by electrochemical activity in the sleeping brain. But the experiences we have in all of those dream-like states seem to take place in a world quite other than the one that we inhabit in our normal waking state. Note that in this context, I use the word "world" to designate a system of entities causally interacting within some spatiotemporal set of relations.[3] The word "entity," as used anywhere in this essay, refers to individualized events, or sequences of events. "Entities" is rather like "things," but it is a broader category, including all physical objects (living or nonliving) as well as "transphysical things" (the objects we experience in dreams and other altered states of consciousness that are not embodied in physical matter). My dreams include, for example, dream cities which I visit again and again (but which are nowhere in the waking world), and various other physically disembodied beings with whom I interact. It seems to me that if we are to take dreaming and lucid dreaming seriously, we should acknowledge the actuality of the environments in which these activities take place. These environments are transphysical worlds. Of course, the laws governing these worlds are not the same as the laws governing the world of waking life. In these transphysical worlds, we can be at more than one place at a time, we can instantly change location based on our moods and thoughts, and, in general, the behaviors of all entities in these worlds are much more flexible and much more responsive to our feelings and intentions than are the various entities inhabiting the physical world disclosed in waking consciousness.

The idea of transphysical worlds is one which Griffin does not consider. In his careful consideration of out-of-body experiences (OBEs), Griffin (1997) is very supportive of the idea that the personality really does function extrasomatically, and that this extrasomatic functioning may indeed be possible after the death of the waking body (pp. 229–268). He makes, however, a clear-cut distinction between those experiences in which the dreamer functions in a world very much like the waking world (as, for example, when people under anesthetics nonetheless witness the events of their surgery), and the "transcendental aspects" of these experiences in which we encounter scenes and persons not in the waking world (such as the lights and tunnels often characteristic of NDEs, or the strange scenes that populate our nighttime dreams).

Griffin (1997) is willing to entertain seriously the idea that the personality can function out of its body in a world quite like the waking world, but rather than taking the "transcendental" aspects of OBE experiences at face value, he explains them away as "a creative synthesis of nonsensory, archetypal, cultural, and individual elements" (p. 262). I, on the other hand, consider these transcendental aspects of NDEs and OBEs to be pointers to the existence of objective, nonphysical, but still actual worlds. We will consider later in this chapter how it is that these worlds fit into process philosophy.

This vision of the world opens the possibility of a cosmological shift that could dwarf the Copernican revolution. The Copernican revolution opened into a vision of the Earth as a small planet, revolving around an average star in one of the billions of galaxies making up the physical world. This new cosmological vision would make the entire physical world into a small part of a much vaster world—the dream world (also called the "vital" or "astral" world)—which spans everything imaginable, including worlds vastly different from our physical world and, probably, countless other physical worlds as well. This involves a total reversal of perspective. Where our modern thought has tended to see physical matter as the ultimate reality, and tried to interpret dreams and other extrasomatic experiences as the result of the functioning of physical matter, in this new mode of thought we could regard our common memories of extrasomatic experiences as confused glimpses of a much larger, much less constrained, and entirely real world—the vital world. In this case, the entire waking world can be seen as a very rigid and highly constrained dream, as a limitation of the vital world in which the laws under which entities operate are very restrictive. For example, in dreams I can fly, buildings can be immense in a way that is impossible in the physical world, space can be ordered in mysterious ways (e.g., in dreams we can sometimes be in two places at the same time), and so forth. None of these things are possible when we are working through the physical world and the physical senses. In this model, the astral world is itself contextualized by a still more richly and flexibly organized "mental world." Note, however, that the various transphysical worlds constitute a continuum, and the division of this continuum into individual worlds such as the "vital" and "mental" is as somewhat arbitrary as the ascription of just seven colors to the spectrum of visible light (see Weiss, 2012, Part II).

The idea of transphysical worlds runs counter to the currently prevailing doctrine of materialism and is consistently ignored or derided in mainstream academic discussions. But it should be pointed out that our civilization, which has denied the existence of these worlds for the past three hundred years or so, is the only civilization in all of history to have done so (Poortman, 1978).

If the transphysical worlds are, indeed, part of the actual world, then why isn't that obvious? There are many ways to answer this question, but in this chapter I just want to point to the remarkable extent to which our experience of the world is a socially sanctioned construct. We have created an environment in which we are trained from an early age to dismiss the transphysical dimension of our experience as "mere imagination." The personal experiences that we have in which we are shamed into ignoring whole aspects of our experience are traumatic and lead to strongly defensive behaviors—we mock others who are espousing what we have been trained to repress. This general repression is reflected in our dominant ideas, and even in our language, to the point where the existence of nonphysical worlds has become almost impossible to imagine. These prejudices prevent us from acknowledging the pervasive influence of transphysical realities in waking life.

One of the underlying motives for my work is to produce a language appropriate both to waking experience and to transphysical experience and, in this way, to encourage continuity of consciousness—i.e., the ability to remain lucid as we focus our attention in one world or another, and to retain our memories when we focus back in the waking world—and make the relevance of the transphysical worlds to the waking world much more obvious.

Now the question is: "What happens to my dream body, my vital body, if my waking body dies?" There seems to be a transitional period in which it stays very close to the waking world (this is the part of the death experience that is covered by Griffin's explanation), and I suggest that it then continues to survive *in a transphysical body in a transphysical world*. To make this fully intelligible, I will have to discuss the mind/brain connection more fully, which I will do shortly.

The Reincarnation Function

Reincarnation is the ability of a living personality to survive the death of one physical body and to continue its existence in another physical body at another time and place. Chapter 1 of the present volume refers to the broad body of evidence which supports the existence of reincarnation. There are many different theories of reincarnation, and I suspect that reincarnation is such a complex phenomenon that many of these different theories are simultaneously true (Weiss, 2012, Chapter 11). Some of them involve the persistence of personality through a sequence of lifetimes without a soul, while other theories of reincarnation involve a soul—an immortal entity that takes on various personalities as its incarnations in this world.

Whether or not we accept the soul theory (I lean toward it strongly), the fact of reincarnation requires that the actual world is one in which strong causal connections can be established between deceased personalities and current personalities, such that one can be said to be a reincarnation of the other.

To sum up, in the parapsychological view of the world, our knowledge is not exclusively dependent on the senses, mind has causal influence directly in nature, our personality can function independently of its physical body, and we can reincarnate.

THE MODERN WORLDVIEW OF SCIENTIFICALLY INFORMED COMMON SENSE AND THE PARAPSYCHOLOGICAL VIEW OF THE WORLD

Given this brief examination of the parapsychological view of the world, we are now in a position to contrast it clearly with the vision of the world of reductive materialism.

The prevailing modern worldview in which we have been educated sees our feelings and thoughts as entirely private because we are cut off from all direct participation in the experiences of others by being trapped inside our bodies, behind our senses. It sees a world in which the personality—if it has effects on the world at all—does so only through its waking body. It sees a world exclusively constituted of insentient (or dead) matter/energy/events, one in which all complex phenomena are mere arrangements of those dead entities and so are entirely devoid of meaning. It sees a world in which the personality is entirely lost with the death of its body, and in which both survival of bodily death and reincarnation are inconceivable.

In the parapsychological view of the world, people—and indeed all living beings—are linked in webs of empathy and telepathy. If this is true, then we must undertake a revisioning of psychology, history, and sociology. If humans are united in world-spanning (indeed, universe-spanning) webs of empathy and telepathy, any attempt to account for the evolution of human collectives solely in terms of factors such as geography and economics, which are entirely physical, or merely features of the waking world, is doomed to failure. In order to understand collective human action, we must take into account the *transphysical dimension of the waking world.* (The "transphysical worlds" are worlds, like dream worlds, in which the laws of physics are loosened and modified. The "transphysical dimension of the waking world" refers to the ongoing occurrence of empathy, telepathy, and other parapsychological functions that take place in the waking world itself.) This also implies that isolated individuality is a social fiction. By this I mean that we have trained ourselves to interpret any "inner" phenomena—such as feelings, thoughts, and intuitions—as purely private, failing to notice how much of this apparently "inner" activity is a direct causal expression of the thoughts and feelings of those around us in the waking world and in the transphysical worlds in which the waking world is embedded.

This lack of privacy is confirmed by the data on forms of parapsychological receptivity such as remote viewing, suggesting that even our outer activities in the waking world are not as private as we typically imagine.

I have already discussed my belief that commitment to the data of parapsychology is a commitment to a doctrine of transphysical worlds. Such a commitment amounts to a rejection of the physical reductionism of conventional science. Rather than imagining that experiences are ultimately based in the activities of the physical world (the part of our waking experience that can be apprehended through the application of scientific ideas and methods), we can imagine that the entire waking world is, itself, just a limitation on the much more flexible and powerful actions of transphysical worlds.

The two worldviews involved here—the worldview of scientific common sense on the one hand, and the parapsychological worldview on the other—are very, very different.

Parapsychological phenomena present a fundamental challenge to the commonly accepted view of our time. They take us beyond the realm of the measurable (without denying the validity of it) into a new, vaster, still logical, but quite reenchanted universe of experience. There are a number of core assumptions underlying the modern worldview that have to be challenged to reach this new way of thinking, and a new metaphysical approach needs to be articulated. In an attempt to answer this challenge, I have developed a philosophy that I call "Transphysical Process Metaphysics" (TPM). I will now present a very brief introduction to that new way of thought.

OVERCOMING MIND/BODY DUALISM

Preliminary Definitions

Before entering into this discussion, I would like to clarify the way in which I am using the terms "consciousness," "feeling," "meaning," "mind," and "body."

- "Consciousness" is that factor of existence by virtue of which there is feeling, meaning, and decision.

- "Feeling," in this sense, is just the experience of being causally affected. We sometimes imagine that causality is something that takes place outside of consciousness, whereas feeling is conscious. But in this context, "to be causally affected" and "to feel" are synonymous. This will be further explicated in what follows.
- "Meaning" is notoriously difficult to define but for the purposes of this essay, I will use the word to refer to experience of the world in relation to the aims of consciousness and, in general, a way of seeing the world against a background of unrealized possibilities.
- "Mind" is the modality of consciousness that surveys possibilities and chooses among them. The decision, by mind, to affirm one possibility among several *actualizes* a definite fact for the future.
- "Body" is that part of our own past with which we are most intimate. In an important sense, our bodies are just the mass of past facts out of which we arise. However, that region of the past which I call "my body" (1) has been intimately affected by my own consciousness, and (2) is that through which I transform the past into the orderly appearance that it takes from my perspective.

It is impossible to speak about parapsychological phenomena in abstraction from the presence of an actively participating consciousness. It is only in the presence of consciousness that the world can be considered meaningful, and the perception of parapsychological phenomena often rests on their meaning. For example, suppose I am sitting in front of a random number generator and "willing" it to deviate from the statistical norm. If it does so, as it often does (Jahn & Dunne, 1987), then it is only in relation to the intention of my consciousness that the deviation becomes meaningful. It is the consciousness which knows things that it cannot perceive through the senses. It is the consciousness that causes detectable changes in the behaviors of inorganic systems outside of it. It is the consciousness that has, and in waking life reports, experiences of transphysical worlds.

Mind/Body Dualism

I have found in Whitehead's process philosophy the conceptual tools necessary for resolving the mind/body dualism. Whitehead's extraordinary breakthrough in the mind/body problem is based on his idea of "actual occasions." Without entering into the many fascinating and complex details that are necessary to explicate this idea fully, let me present it in a very simple way.

Quantum physicists have accustomed us to the idea that the "outer world" consists, ultimately, not of enduring substances, but rather of short-lived dynamic events. We can, for example, imagine that a rock is a very large number of subatomic events taking place very rapidly and organizing themselves into a stable, repetitive pattern.

There is also a psychological tradition which treats conscious personality as a sequence of individual "drops of experience." The experiential basis of this idea can be easily observed. Notice any object in your environment—I am looking at a pen on my desk. The experience of noticing the pen happens to me all at once. First, I didn't notice it; then I did. So the pen comes to me in a drop of experience. I could then try to deconstruct the experience of the pen analytically or retroactively. Then I might notice its top, its cylindrical body, its pointy writing end, but each of those is also a drop of experience that comes all at once. So we can plausibly describe our experience as being composed of closely interrelated drops of experience, each with its own distinctness, each flowing smoothly into subsequent drops.

Whitehead's fundamental assumption is this: *There is only one type of event.* The events that we experience as having constituted our own past are of the same ontological type as the events that constitute our own stream of experience.

This idea is very different from the ideas of scientifically informed common sense which tell us that there are two types of events: those that take place outside of us are "objective," while our inner experience is merely "subjective." It is this assumption, in fact, that creates the mind/body problem in the first place. But suppose that we, ourselves, are in each moment of our existence a perfectly valid example of what it is to be actual. My awareness in each moment is an event, and in each such event I experience myself as being causally affected by the past, elaborating a set of possibilities, and then choosing which of those possibilities I will actualize.

Each of us thus, in any moment of our experience, is an actual occasion of experience, and every event constituting our past was also an actual occasion of experience. In light of this principle, we can say that the events of which the outer world is composed and the "drops of experience" of which we are composed are strictly analogous—each is an experience of the past, an elaboration of possibilities for the future, and a present choice among them. This means that every event that happens in the actual world is, like us, a drop of experience; and every drop of experience is, after it has completed its process of becoming, a causally effective event in the past universe. Given this, we can study our own experience and generalize from that to the nature of all the events constituting the universe.[4, 5, 6]

Let us then look at the nature of our moment-to-moment existence and see what we find there that can be generalized to describe all other events as well. At each moment we go through a process in which we take in the world around us as its causes bring us into being, we form a coherent perception of how the world appears to us, we elaborate a matrix of possibilities for action, and then we decide among them, acting in a determinate way, and thus presenting facts to succeeding moments. Whitehead calls this process "concrescence."

Let us say that I am giving a lecture in a classroom. At each moment, I take in my own thoughts from the immediate past, the general environment of the classroom, the reactions I am sensing from my students, and so forth. I interpret that into a coherent picture of my situation, and out of that I elaborate a set of possibilities. For example, I might continue the sentence I am speaking or interrupt it. I might get up out of my chair and pace, or I might continue to sit still. I make all of the relevant decisions, and then I become an actuality for my students to take in. My students, of course, are going through the same process, and they decide whether or not to stay in the classroom, whether or not to ask questions, and so forth. On our current assumption, all of the events constituting the universe feel their pasts, interpret those pasts into a coherent appearance, elaborate the possibilities afforded by the situation as it appears, and then decide which of those possibilities to actualize. When I experience the definiteness of the past, I am feeling the feelings and decisions of past actual occasions. My experience of the world is my feeling of past feelings.

Note that when we regard the universe in this way, consciousness (in its mental modality) is seen as *the fundamental agency of actualization*. Actualization is a process of selection among a set of possibilities leaving only one, and that one is thereby actualized. Nothing becomes actual and definite without the decisive participation of mind. Mind, therefore, is not some mysterious something other than matter, but rather is built into matter as that factor which renders it definite and thus actual.

If I look more deeply into a single drop of my own experience, I can see that it is composed of many smaller drops of experience, such as a visual drop of experience that is busy synthesizing a visual picture for me, an auditory drop of experience that is synthesizing an auditory image, a heart consciousness that is feeling and interpreting my emotional environment, and so on. Each of these drops, in turn, is composed of still smaller drops of experience: cellular drops of experience, molecular drops of experience, and so on all the way down to subatomic drops of experience. This idea, while it may sound startling, is by no means original to me. Versions of the idea can be found in William James (who coined the term "drops of experience"),[7] Alfred North Whitehead (my principal inspiration here), Pierre Teilhard de Chardin, Sri Aurobindo, Ken Wilber, and others.

The smaller drops of experience which constitute my experience in any given moment are called "prehensions." Thus a "concrescence" (the process of forming a new actual occasion) is a concrescence of prehensions. We will discuss prehensions more fully in a later section.

One objection to this analysis needs to be mentioned here. The continuity of our experience, the fact that one moment flows into the next so smoothly that we have no sense of a gap between them, is sometimes taken as an argument against an interpretation of experience in terms of actual occasions. The continuity of experience cannot be denied. Whitehead, while analyzing experience into discrete drops, also acknowledges the way in which one drop of experience flows seamlessly into the next. Henri Bergson, a contemporary of Whitehead's, also analyzed experience, but his analysis, unlike Whitehead's, puts most of its emphasis on the continuity, rather than the discontinuities, in experience. On the other hand, even Bergson acknowledges that experience has a rhythmic structure, so that the continuity that he posits is divided into pulses. Whitehead, starting from an emphasis on discontinuity, also accounts for continuity. Bergson, starting from continuity, also acknowledges the discontinuities in experience. Thus it seems reasonable that continuity and discontinuity are two complementary ideas, both of which are required for the elucidation of experience. In this essay, I am taking the Whiteheadian position—which places greater emphasis on the aspect of discontinuity—

because it is easier to reconcile Whitehead's thought with modern (classical) and postmodern (relativity and quantum theory) scientific thought.

Our commonsense point of view, of course, is dominated by our perception of enduring objects. Any event ontology needs to account in a very clear way for the emergence of enduring objects in the field of experience. Whitehead (1929/1978) accomplishes this with the idea of "societies" of actual occasions (p. 34). A "society" is a group ("nexus") of actual occasions so arranged that they enforce a continuity of form on the group of occasions that succeeds them. A spoon, for example, is a society of occasions, and those occasions, by enforcing rigid conformity on one another, guarantee the ongoing existence of the spoon they constitute. An atom, too, is a society of subatomic occasions, and these occasions perpetuate the form which makes that atom distinct. A "personally ordered society" is a society in which *individual* occasions are arranged serially, like beads on a string, For example, we can imagine the group of occasions constituting my stream of experience as a stream of individual occasions, each of which accepts the imprint of the immediate past occasion in such a way that the characteristics making me what I am endure through time. Thus, as a personally ordered society of actual occasions, I can consider myself to be an enduring object.

The proper description of enduring objects requires both a notion of continuity and a notion of discontinuity. Consider our normal waking consciousness. From one point of view, our experience is divided into drops by the decisions that choose among possibilities and thus introduce decisive boundaries between moments. But from another point of view, it seems continuous as each occasion pours its own experience into subsequent occasions. It was pointed out earlier that Whitehead accounts for the discontinuity by his notion of discrete drops of experience, and he accounts for the continuity by the way in which drops of experience flow into one another. In a society with "personal order," this flow is channeled with particular smoothness and completeness between a succession of singular drops, one in each moment.

The full explication of this idea is beyond the scope of this introductory discussion, but one interesting feature of these personally ordered societies is that they do not, like physical objects, need to trace continuous trajectories in spacetime. A particular personally ordered society can leave off at one location in spacetime and then recommence elsewhere with varying degrees of continuity of memory and purpose at another location entirely. This hypothesized feature of personalities, should it be accepted, provides conceptual resources that can be used effectively in the explanation of personality survival and reincarnation.

At the end of this analysis, we are left with a universe composed of actual occasions, or causally effective drops of experience, each of which takes in its past world, interprets it, elaborates a matrix of probabilities, and then decides among them. This might be thought of as a philosophical generalization of quantum theory, which makes it plausible for us to see even a moment of our own ongoing consciousness as a quantum event.[8]

Now, if we assert that all events, from subatomic events to the events constituting our own streams of experience, are actual occasions, then it is clear that there are many differences among actual occasions. In particular, we think of all actual occasions as characterized by "grades." Low-grade actual occasions are the occasions making up the physical world—subatomic occasions and the occasions presiding over atoms.[9] I am making the assumption, for now, that molecules are not individual actual occasions, but rather associations of occasions. Then the actual occasions presiding over cells, organs, and so forth are medium-grade actual occasions. Plants, like molecules, may be more or less democratic associations of such medium-grade occasions. Animals, which clearly possess central personalities, are presided over by high-grade actual occasions, such as those that preside over humans, but not quite as complex.

This mode of interpretation understands the world as a vast hierarchy of living occasions, permeated by creativity, spontaneity, life, and intelligence.

Up to this point, what I have been presenting is well in accord with Whitehead's ideas, and also with those of Griffin. One of the ways in which Transphysical Process Metaphysics differs from Whitehead's ideas is in its understanding of grades. Whitehead, in accordance with the generally reductionistic thinking of his time, tends to think of actual occasions as very, very brief in their duration. There may be many actual occasions constituting a single subatomic event, many subatomic events constituting an atom, and so forth. TPM envisions the duration of an actual occasion as being proportional to its grade. This is an idea which differs from the ideas of Whitehead, though Griffin (2007) and I are in agreement on this point (p. 182). While Whitehead, to my knowledge, does not discuss the relationship of grade and duration, this notion follows very naturally from a consideration of the nature of actual occasions. Each actual occasion is a process (a "concrescence") that actualizes (in the form of an event) certain possibilities, and those actualized possibilities become the character of that event. It takes time to actualize a possibility. The mystery of quantum mechanics is, in part, due to its notion that there is a minimum quantum of action, and that every quantum of action endures for a finite amount of time. It seems natural to suppose that the realization of a more complex character requires a longer duration. So, for example, an atom is a cycling system of subatomic events. An atom cannot be actualized in any duration shorter than the cycle of subatomic occasions which gives it its character. An atom, then, has a longer cycle time than a subatomic particle.

A single event in the stream of a human individual might last, say, some tenth of a second. During that relatively long period, there might be millions of cellular actual occasions, billions of atomic actual occasions, trillions of subatomic occasions, and so forth. TPM also holds that the lower-grade occasions are bound into the higher-grade actual occasions by a "mechanism" involving final causes. This is spelled out below in the section on causality.

Another way that Transphysical Process Metaphysics differs from a more standard Whiteheadian approach is in the ontological status of actual occasions of different grades. While Whitehead suggests that higher-grade occasions are ontologically dependent on societies of lower-grade occasions, in TPM, on the other hand, societies of higher-grade actual occasions can exist on their own, entirely in the absence of lower-grade occasions with which they may, however, interact. Thus there can be a transphysical world constituted by medium-grade actualities (the vital or astral world), and a world constituted solely by higher-grade occasions (the mental world).

Griffin (1997) provides part of the metaphysical justification for the idea of transphysical worlds. He argues that the creative power of occasions is proportional to their grade, so that a human personality, for example, has much more creative power than a single cell (pp. 146–148). Griffin uses this idea to justify the notion that human personalities may be the only personalities to survive bodily death. But I would like to point to another implication of this idea. Actual occasions of low grade at a particular moment create the conditions under which other actual occasions of low grade can arise in a subsequent moment. Thus the physical world is a society of low-grade occasions that endure. It is generally assumed that all higher-grade occasions can function only if they are in significant causal relations to the many lower-grade occasions constituting their bodies. But Griffin has already suggested that high-grade occasions can continue to endure even after the death of their bodies. Thus higher-grade occasions can exist independently from the bodies with which they are associated in waking life. I want to take this one step further by pointing out (1) that even medium-grade occasions such as those presiding over cells may survive the death of their bodies, and (2) that such high-grade occasions existing apart from physical bodies can interact with each other to form worlds of experience that are in no way dependent on low-grade occasions, and which may include entities that can be found nowhere in the waking world. Also, given that such worlds would be more creatively powerful than the physical world, it may be plausible to think that such transphysical worlds preexist the physical world, and that the physical world emerges out of those transphysical worlds by a process of self-limitation. I explore this idea more fully in the second part of *The Long Trajectory* (Weiss, 2012).

A human being is a complex society of occasions involving actual occasions of all three major grades. TPM holds that occasions of medium and high grade *are not part of the physical world at all*. Thus those medium-grade occasions that, for example, preside over our cells are living occasions, belonging to the vital world, and are not detectable by scientific instruments (Weiss, 2012, especially Chapter 10).[10]

The idea of actual occasions, which are both mental and physical (causal), allows us to resolve the mind/body problem and to articulate the nature of transphysical worlds,[11] thus setting the stage for an understanding of parapsychological phenomena.

EXPANDING THE IDEA OF CAUSALITY

I call the scientific ideas that preceded relativity and quantum theory "modern science" or "conventional science" as opposed to the "postmodern" science of our day. The modern idea of causality is quite narrow. The paradigm example used in defining modern causality is the collision of two billiard balls. There is some sort of direct physical contact through which there is a transmission of forces. When science changed its metaphysical position so that it recognized the existence of fields, this notion of contact was expanded to include interactions among fields, or between fields and particles or events. But the basic idea of causality exhibits the same essential features: (1) causality involves the interaction between an immediately past event and a current event, and (2) the nature of the forces transferred during this contact is such that it is subject to mathematical analysis. This type of causality, "efficient causality," is at the center of modern scientific thought.

Because modern science analyzes the world in terms of entirely insentient, self-existent, mutually external entities, the only causal interaction it envisages among them is one of mathematical regularity among results of experiments. But if we interpret the world in terms of actual occasions, each of which is sentient to some (however minimal) extent, then efficient cause takes on, as we have seen, an entirely new aspect. Efficient cause is now *the transmission of experience from occasion to occasion*. The paradigm example of efficient causation here is not that of an interaction among billiard balls, but rather that of the interaction between the actual occasion of experience that you were a split second ago and the actual occasion of experience that you are right now. The last actual occasion flows into the current occasion virtually seamlessly. It pours into you with all of its emotions, its interpretations, its thoughts, and its purposes. I say "virtually seamlessly" because the current moment of experience is separated from the past moment of experience by virtue of the binding decisions that were made in the last moment that can no longer be changed in this moment. We can, thus, look at the flow of experience either as a series of drops that flow continuously into one another, or as a continuum that is divided into pulses by the decisions that it makes as it functions.[12]

This way of looking at efficient causation has a number of advantages over the way we look at causation in terms of modern scientific common sense. First of all, it reintegrates mind into nature in a most profound way. As I suggested above, all of the individual characteristics that give actual entities their particular character are the results of more or less conscious *decisions*. Just as, for example, the decisions that I am making at this moment cause these particular words to be written, thus causally affecting you as you read them, so each subatomic event chooses which probabilities it will actualize, each plant and animal chooses how it will respond to the environment in which it finds itself, each human chooses how to behave. All of these decisions are what gives this world its interesting character. Consciousness thus, as *the agency of actualization*, is intimately involved in the process of the actual world. [13]

Secondly, as discussed above, in Transphysical Process Metaphysics we understand efficient cause as a flow of experience. This enables an entirely new way of understanding the perceptual process. For instance, if we accept this point of view, we will view each cell in the perceptual apparatus of the human body as an actual occasion, and it is, thus, an experience of its entire past world. It functions under the influence of the dominant personality, in a manner which I will shortly outline, to focus its attention on some particular feature of its past world. Consider, for example, a cell in the retina. It might focus its conscious attention on a certain edge or a certain patch of color. It then passes that whole experience on to subsequent occasions in the nervous system. Notice that what is passed on from cell to cell in the nervous system is not just electrical energy, but an actual experience of the past world with some features particularly emphasized. The electrochemical activity studied by cognitive scientists is an abstract aspect [14] of what is actually taking place in the nervous system. That electrochemical activity is not the most important part of the intercellular interactions in the nervous system: rather it is the measurable, physical part of a process which is actually the transmission of experience. Now, when some cell in the nervous system takes in experiences from several other cells, it can integrate them into a whole picture, since each experience that it receives is an experience of the entire world with some feature highlighted. This could constitute a solution to what cognitive scientists sometimes call "the binding problem"—or the problem of how the various elements of experience are assembled, in each moment, into one unified experience of the whole of the past.

Since the experiences that are passed from cell to cell are whole experiences, they include within them emotions and thoughts. This is rather clear within our bodies, where the discomfort of even a few cells (say those involved in a hangnail) are shared empathically by the other cells in the body. This is also at work in interhuman interactions, where we are able to feel each other's feelings and, in some cases, pick up each other's thoughts. It is impossible to explain these empathic and telepathic phenomena in terms of mere physical causes, but if we assume that the world is composed of actual occasions of various grades, then we can understand empathy as a direct transmission of experience (efficient cause)

among medium-grade occasions, and telepathy as a transmission of experience (efficient cause) among high-grade occasions. Further, while it is
impossible to explain empathy and telepathy in terms of interactions
among dead, insentient atoms making up a human body, it is easy to
account for the limited causal interactions among low-grade, inorganic
actual occasions as simplifications or limitations on the normal functioning of higher-grade occasions. High-grade occasions are naturally
telepathic. In medium-grade occasions, this telepathy is limited to a communication of images and feelings. In low-grade occasions, it is limited to
a mere communication of sensa. If we start with the idea of insentient
atoms, we can never account for empathy and telepathy, but if we start
with high-grade occasions in which telepathy is normative, we can understand lower-grade occasions as higher-grade occasions that are operating
under restrictions. That is, in lower-grade occasions, the capacity to elaborate an interpretation of the past, to lay out a matrix of possibilities, and
to decide among them does not function as fully as it does in higher-grade
occasions.[15]

Finally, this doctrine of causation, because it sees causal transmission
as a flow of experience, equates "being caused by something" with "feeling something." As was said earlier, to be affected by an efficient cause is
to feel the impact of that cause directly. We know that if the evolution of
the universe had been different, then we would not be who and what we
are. In fact, in an important sense, we are a causal outcome of the entire
past functioning of our universe. Since efficient causality is the felt transmission of experience, and since we are efficiently caused by the entirety
of our causal past, in each moment of experience we begin with a *feeling*
of *everything* that is having any causal effect on us.[16] We are not *fully
aware* of all of the details of the past because, as it forms itself, each
actual occasion interprets the world in accordance with its aims and interests, and many details are suppressed. Under the right conditions—conditions involving particular intentions and an adequate concentration of
attention—these detailed experiences can be brought into consciousness,
which can explain our experience of clairvoyance and clairaudience.

Modern science's treatment of causation is limited by the fact that it
only explicitly considers efficient causes in its analyses. But there are
other types of causal process. Aristotle identified four types of causation,
which he called material, efficient, formal, and final causation. I have just
been discussing the way Transphysical Process Metaphysics expands the

category of efficient causation, but it also includes the rest of Aristotle's causes.

When Aristotle began to analyze the existence of simple natural objects, what he found was all of the characteristics that he could name. For example, examining a white stone, he found whiteness, hardness, heaviness, solidity, and so on. But it was also clear to him that there was something in the stone that was more than just the sum of its characteristics. Rather, the stone had its own individuality, and that individuality in some way served as a ground in which the various characteristics could inhere, and which held them together in their characteristic pattern. That mysterious something Aristotle called "Substance." Since Substance is the substrate of forms, it is itself formless. It merely serves the function of holding the various characters together and of individualizing the object that they define.

Whitehead replaces Aristotle's category of Substance with what he calls "Creativity." Creativity is the process which continually gives rise to actual occasions. Whitehead (1929/1978) defines Creativity as the process by means of which the "many become one, and are increased by one" (p. 21). The many, in this case, are the actual occasions of the past. The formation of a new actual occasion brings all of those many into the unity of a new, coherent occasion of experience. That new occasion of experience transmits its experience into the future, where it is incorporated into new actual occasions. This is what Whitehead calls "the creative advance." Note that Creativity, like Substance, explains how it is that characters come together into the unity of individual things; only here, rather than being thought of spatially, as a kind of mobile substrate, it is thought of *temporally*, as a process. The replacement of Substance by process is a huge philosophical move, with great historical and philosophical implications which are, however, beyond the scope of this short chapter (Lucas, 1989). Science, as long as it assumes the existence of Substance, employs an essentially Aristotelian notion of the material cause. Process metaphysics replaces *substance* as material cause with *process* as material cause.

For Aristotle, *formal cause* was the pattern or template for the character of an object. In the case of an artificial object, such as a house, Aristotle would identify the blueprint as the formal cause. For a natural being, like a living organism, Aristotle would identify the formal cause with the efficient cause and the final cause (soon to be discussed), so that the organism was imagined as the functioning of the forms in substance for the purpose of realizing the formed organism. Although many scientists would deny this, modern science operates with a very strong sense of formal cause. Formal causes in science are natural laws. Natural laws are the causes which dictate the forms assumed by objects. But in science, formal causes are restricted to mathematical relations. All other forms (color, sound, consciousness, love, meaning) are supposed to be derived from the interactions of insentient entities, taking place according to mathematically expressible formal causes.

Transphysical Process Metaphysics completely transforms the idea of formal causation by stating that the formal cause of an emerging actual occasion is the field of possibilities that is opened up for it by its situation. To understand this idea, we can start with an analogy from quantum physics. An event, as it forms, must elaborate a probability matrix, which is to say that it elaborates the various possibilities that are open to it, given its own character and the situation in which it finds itself. Then, a decision is made that "collapses the wave function," and the event becomes a causal actuality for subsequent events. The probability matrix, as an elaboration of all the forms that might characterize this emerging event, is its formal cause. I can also use a moment of human experience as an example here. In each moment, I take in my past, discern a set of possibilities for my next action, and then choose among them. The set of elaborated possibilities is the formal cause for the coming together of a new actual occasion. By understanding formal causation in this way, TPM is able to take seriously the quantum of freedom that each occasion exercises as it becomes actual.[17] Each occasion *freely chooses* which possibilities (among those which the past has made available) will characterize it for its future. That is why the problem of determinism does not arise in this context.

Finally, Transphysical Process Metaphysics thoroughly rehabilitates Aristotle's notion of *final* cause. The final cause is "the reason why." In classical times, it was taken for granted that nothing happened unless there was a reason for it. For Aristotle, the reason why could be either the intentions of a human being (in the case of the creation of an artificial object), or else what Aristotle imagined as the drive of form toward actualization in natural things. In TPM, as well as in Whiteheadian process metaphysics, the final cause is restricted only to the intentions of actual entities. The idea here is that each individual actual occasion begins its process of formation with an aim or a purpose.

Each actual occasion starts with a general aim that is twofold. First, each actual occasion aims at unifying the multiple occasions of the past into the unity of a single, novel experience. Second, each actual occasion aims at maximizing value in itself and in its relevant future. This is certainly something that we can recognize in our own moments of existence, in each of which we strive to maximize value in the present (to make the moment interesting, pleasurable, intense, or satisfying in some other way) and in the subsequent moments of experience that we anticipate as outcomes of our current moment (to prepare the grounds for greater value in the future). These general aims are further conditioned by the environment in which an actual occasion is functioning, and this further conditioning establishes the particular values which will be maximized by a given occasion. These more specific aims can be broken down into the following:

- A cosmic aim, the aim at evolution that characterizes our cosmos as a whole.[18]
- A social aim, which reflects the aims of the larger societies to which we belong. In the case of a human being, these social aims will be determined by the Earth as a whole, by the aim of our species, by the aims of our culture, our nation, our local civic society, our family and so on.
- A personal aim, which is the aim of the smallest society to which we belong—the personally ordered society of occasions making up our own personalities. This aim is the only one over which we have significant control. The values given to me by the larger societies to which I belong may or may not be consistent with each other. This gives me the possibility of choosing, to some extent, the values for which I decide in a given moment. Also, in usual cases, I may discern and pursue values not yet envisioned within the context of those societies. These value choices will be transmitted to the subsequent occasions in my stream of experience, and thus, over time, will come to determine my individual character.

Each moment of my waking experience is, as we have seen, composed of many smaller drops of experience, and these smaller drops of experience belong to the actual occasions making up my waking body. But how are these individual occasions bound into the unity of a single body? The answer is that all of the occasions of my body receive a significant part of their aim from the high-grade actual occasions that make up my personality. Consider the occasions that constitute my visual sense. We can easily identify in our experience the occasions that govern our eyes. Clearly these occasions function in a way that enables me to see the world. For example, when I want to see what is to my right, I suggest to my eyes that they move in the appropriate direction, and they do so. But these occasions also retain a significant degree of freedom from my intentions. This can easily be observed if I tell my eyes *not* to blink. They will follow that suggestion and remain open only for a short time, and then they will overrule me and blink in spite of my intentions. The actual occasions making up my visual apparatus are each a full actual occasion, with its own freedom of choice, and yet they generally function as an expression of my aim at seeing. In this sense, the unity of the body is a unity of aim.

How is it that the occasions of my body come to be an expression of my aim, whereas the occasions constituting the rest of the world do not? First of all, an actual occasion A can influence the aims of another occasion B only when B begins its process of becoming while A is in *its* process of becoming. For example, the duration of the medium-grade actual occasion presiding over a single biological cell is much longer than the durations of the constituent macromolecules. Thus many macromolecules begin their process of becoming during the becoming of the cell itself, and so it is possible for the cell-occasion to impose its aims on the aims of the macromolecular occasions that constitute its body.

However, a cell does not impose its aims on *all* of the occasions which come into being during its own concrescence. Rather it imposes its aims on those with which it is most intimate. This notion of "intimacy" needs further definition. Remember that each actual occasion contains—and feels—all of the occasions in its past. But it feels those past occasions more or less abstractly. For example, say I go into a restaurant to order an iced tea. I may know the person who serves me very abstractly as "the waiter." But, in that same situation, I might also know that person more concretely, and more intimately, as a friend or a lover. While there are many factors governing intimacy among occasions, one important factor is focused attention. The more fully I focus my attention on another occasion (or on another enduring entity), the more intimate I come to be with it. Clearly there is a special intimacy between the dominant occasions of my personality and the occasions that constitute "my body." We can easily observe this as our attention is, while we are awake, almost entirely occupied by our bodies and the data that it provides us about the rest of the world.

In Transphysical Process Metaphysics, if an occasion A is in unison of becoming with another occasion B, and if B is of lower grade than A, then A will be able to imprint some of its aims on B. We then say that B is a prehension belonging to A, and that A is "embodied" in B.[19] This explanation, which is unique to TPM, gives us a new way to understand how we are related to our own bodies (Weiss, 2012, especially Chapters 7 and 8).

This notion of final causes operating among occasions not only can explain the unity of complex organisms, but also can help to explain phenomena such as psychokinesis (PK), which can be understood as an extension of the way the presiding personality influences its own body. It affects the constituent occasions of its body by imposing its aims on them, so that they tend to make decisions which serve those aims. In the case of PK, the presiding personality of a human body achieves, through intense focus on a society of inorganic occasions outside of its body, an intimacy with those occasions which enables it to impose its aims on them. In that way it can, in effect, make them part of its body, and they, under the guidance of higher-grade aims, can then make decisions regarding their own trajectories which are very different from the ones they normally make. The importance of this explanation is that it (1) envisions PK as an extension of the process through which we operate our own waking bodies, and (2) gives us a way of understanding PK that does not rest on efficient causes alone, but rather focuses our attention on the factors that allow us to feel intimate not only with our own bodies but also with the rest of the world around us.

Transphysical Process Metaphysics gives us, thus, an expanded idea of causality: consciousness plays a causal role as the agency of actualization; efficient causes are a flow of experience from occasion to occasion; an individual formal cause is intrinsic to each actual occasion; final causes have an important role in the unfolding of the actual world.

REFORMULATING THE MODERN IDEA OF SPACETIME

The conventional scientific mind—operating under the still pervasive influence of Sir Isaac Newton—pictures space as a substantial,[20] infinitely extended container. This container is imagined (like infinite, 3D graph paper) as an array of tessellated empty cubes, each existent at an instant.[21] It pictures time as a line on which an infinite array of such instantaneous substantial, empty spaces crowd together, one after another.

There are many difficulties with this idea of space and time, but it will not be necessary to enter into a critique of those ideas here since, in science, that image has already been exploded by Einstein's Special Theory of Relativity. In Newton's system, the measurable distance between objects is purely a function of their various positions in some absolute space (or, in practice, a function of their relative positions). According to the Theory of Relativity, the distances between entities are not only a function of their position in space, but also are a function of their *velocity*. Given two objects, passing through a given point of space, but traveling on different trajectories, each will measure the distance between themselves and some third object differently. The effect of this is that spacetime, as a whole, can no longer be visualized, but only mathematically analyzed. An acceptance of the Theory of Relativity forces us to abandon the notion of space as a substantial, extended nothingness occupied by objects.[22]

What is needed to replace the old Newtonian understanding of spacetime? The first sign of a shift in thinking about spacetime was articulated (to my knowledge) by Leibniz, who proposed that spacetime is not a container but rather *a relationship among individual entities.* Leibniz has a beautiful argument for this view of spacetime which is grounded in the doctrine of the "identity of indiscernibles." This doctrine says that if we are considering what we take to be two entities, but we can find nothing whatsoever that distinguishes them one from the other, then we are actually considering one and the same thing. Applying this principle to the notion of space as an infinitely extended substantial nothingness, we could represent space to ourselves as an infinite array of points. The problem with this way of imagining space is that, in the infinite extended emptiness, there is nothing whatsoever to distinguish any point from any other point. Unless we establish some point to act as a point of reference, all of the points are absolutely identical, and thus collapse, in our understanding, into a single point. If we take the doctrine of the identity of indiscernibles into account, the imagination of an infinitely extended array of points becomes entirely indistinguishable from the imagination of a single point. Thus space, as extension, can only be a relationship among individually existing entities of some form or another. So, space is not extended nothingness, but rather a pattern of relationship among entities (Leclerc, 1972). I have presented this argument in terms of space, but it can easily be generalized to Einsteinian space-*time*.

Once we comprehend space as a form of relationship, we become able to imagine spacetimes other than the Cartesian/Newtonian spacetime so dear to scientifically informed common sense. The mathematics of these different spaces has been gradually worked out in the science of geometry since the recognition of non-Euclidean geometries at the beginning of the nineteenth century (Kline, 1980).

Without going into details that transcend the scope of this paper, I have developed a way of understanding the spacetime geometries of the transphysical worlds in terms of meta-geometry and network topology as different forms of relationships among actual entities.

In the modern world, spacetime is defined largely in terms of the mathematical structures of geometry. Spacetime, as envisioned by science, is a set of mathematical relations among physical entities. In Newton's science, for example, space is a 3D grid, and time is a line, while in Einsteinian thought, spacetime is a 4D continuum. These are both mathematical descriptions. In order to demonstrate the continuity of the transphysical worlds with the physical world as understood by science, it is necessary to demonstrate that the transphysical worlds have geometries of their own. Without an understanding of the geometry of transphysical worlds, there would be no way to demonstrate their continuity with the world as defined by physics. While I do not claim to have worked out all of the details of transphysical geometry, I have established its plausibility and made some suggestions as to how further investigation of this subject can proceed (Weiss, 2012, especially Chapter 9).

There is one result of these investigations, however, which I would like to mention here. As we know, physics expresses its knowledge of the world by systems of equations that reveal invariant relations among numbers that are generated by experiments. Experimentation, as the operation that turns observations into numbers, is at the very foundation of all physical theory. But as Whitehead (1929/1978, especially Part IV, Chapter 5) has demonstrated, measurement is only possible if two conditions can be met. First, rulers have to retain their size, and clocks must maintain their even periodicity, as they are moved through spacetime. Second, measurement is only possible in the context of a metrical geometry—i.e., a geometry in which parallel lines are defined.

Earlier, we spoke of the division of actual occasions into grades—low-grade occasions making up the physical world, medium-grade occasions presiding over cells and primitive biological organisms, and mental-grade occasions presiding over mental beings (more evolved animals and humans). Transphysical Process Metaphysics also suggests that while low-grade occasions constitute the physical world studied by physics, medium-grade occasions constitute a world of their own—the vital world—and high-grade occasions constitute the mental world. Neither the vital world nor the mental world is dependent on low-grade, physical occasions. Since beings in the transphysical worlds are all occasions of medium or high grade, which means that transphysical beings are constantly transforming just as living things and thinking things do, there are—in those worlds—no reliable rulers and clocks. We could not, for example, use our heartbeat as a clock because its rhythm is determined by a vast number of factors and is, therefore, quite irregular. Nor could we use a snake as a ruler. Also, there are many spacetimes in which parallel lines are not defined, and thus measurement, in the classical sense, is not possible.

We can, by a rethinking of the categories of entity, space, time, and causality, demonstrate the objectivity of transphysical worlds, but that same rethinking reveals that classical measurement is not possible in those worlds, thus challenging us to invent a new kind of scientific research in that context.

HOW TRANSPHYSICAL PROCESS METAPHYSICS DIFFERS FROM WHITEHEAD'S AND GRIFFIN'S PROCESS METAPHYSICS

I have mentioned earlier in this chapter several ways in which Transphysical Process Metaphysics differs from the thinking of Whitehead and Griffin. In this section, I would like to summarize those differences.

First, in Whitehead's scheme (and in Griffin's), the ultimate actualities are actual occasions, and each actual occasion can be divided into its component "prehensions." For example, I am experiencing a drop of experience, and that drop of experience can be decomposed into the smaller drops of experience of which it is constituted. For Whitehead, an actual occasion on the one hand and its component prehensions on the other are of a different ontological type. Occasions of experience are fully actual, whereas their prehensions (which have their aims determined by the actual occasion to which they belong) have no separate actuality. In TPM, on the other hand, the prehensions of an actual occasion are actual occasions in their own right. One actual occasion serves as a prehension to an actual occasion of higher grade to the extent that that higher grade occasion sets its aims. This difference, which thoroughly revises Whitehead's doctrine of causation by allowing actual occasions of higher-grade to contribute its aims to a lower-grade concrescence with which it is in unison of becoming, allows TPM to articulate the way in which higher-grade actual occasions become "embodied" in systems of lower-grade occasions.

Second, Transphysical Process Metaphysics draws out the significance of Whitehead's ideas of space and time in a way that I have not seen elsewhere. Transphysical Process Metaphysics clarifies the important sense in which actual occasions are not *in* spacetime but rather *are* basic units of spacetime themselves. This drawing out of Whitehead's ideas allows us to consider the geometrical nature of the spacetimes in which transphysical worlds unfold.

Third, Transphysical Process Metaphysics purges Whitehead's metaphysics of some lingering reductionism. Whitehead envisions the order of our universe (or what he would call our "cosmic epoch") as fundamentally constituted by subatomic events (or, perhaps, events that are even smaller), and he implies that all more complex forms of order, and the higher-grade occasions that come with them, are somehow dependent on those low-grade events. Griffin recognizes that certain high-grade occasions—notably the occasions constituting the dominant stream of experience in a human—may survive the death of the body. TPM goes further by suggesting, by contrast, that all medium- and high-grade occasions (living and thinking entities) never do exist in the waking, physical world. Rather, they exist in transphysical worlds, from which they become "embodied" in societies of low-grade occasions, and in which they continue to exist after the death of their physical bodies. Societies of higher-grade occasions exist in complete independence from any lower-grade occasions and can, thus, constitute transphysical worlds.

Fourth, Whitehead's and Griffin's theology specifies God as a special sort of actual occasion which is, itself, a creature of Creativity, and is neither creative nor omnipotent. TPM replaces this with a different theology in which God is an omnipotent creator, and in which there are many aspects and levels to our experience of that ultimate factor. This view is more congenial to the varieties of mystical experience. This view also allows Transphysical Process Metaphysics to deal with precognition. It suggests a Divine or "Supermental" time consciousness in which three temporal modes exist side by side. First, the Divine can experience the creation of a Universe as taking place all at once as a single event. Second, it can survey the universe so created by tracing its temporal grain. Then, third, it can experience its own creative act as following the temporal grain event by event. Our own experience is in this third mode, but the first and second modes provide the possibility for access to the entirety of the past and the future. This broader theology derives from India and has been expressed in the works of Sri Aurobindo. It has not been discussed in this introductory essay but is more deeply explored in Part II of *The Long Trajectory* (Weiss, 2012).

These differences expand the explanatory power of Whitehead's scheme in a way that better suits it to the explanation of parapsychological and mystical phenomena.

SUMMARY AND CONCLUSIONS

The world as described by scientifically informed common sense is a rather desolate place. In this description, all that is truly actual is accessed by operations of measurement, and all causal relations can be described by mathematical equations. Because matter is held to have no characteristics other than those that can be mathematically expressed, it is held to be entirely dead and insentient. Matter has no reason to exist, it has neither aim nor motive, it has no feelings. It just simply is, with no value for itself.

Consciousness, in the world as described by scientifically informed common sense, is an utter mystery, often held to be illusory or epiphenomenal. In fact the richness of purposes, feelings, and thoughts that populate our waking lives seems to rise out of dead matter by a miracle that cannot be explained. Furthermore, when consciousness is acknowledged, it is taken for granted that consciousness is a product of the brain, and thus is trapped in its body, gaining access to the world only through the narrow gates of the bodily senses. Empathy and telepathy are either reduced to subtle interpretations of sensory data or else dismissed out of hand. Since all the information about actuality that is available is limited to the bodily senses, ESP is simply unthinkable. Because consciousness is utterly dependent on matter, psychokinesis cannot be explained. Dreams are understood as the product of neural activity in the sleeping brain; lucid dreams and out-of-body experiences are just weird dreams; survival of bodily death is impossible because the entire reality of the personality is in the physical body, and there is no place for deceased personalities to exist. Reincarnation is unthinkable in a worldview in which personality reduces to organized matter, and death is the disorganization of the matter making up the body.

But all the evidence of waking life and all the evidence of parapsychology teach us that we don't live in the world described by these views. Instead, we live in a world where people actually feel each other's feelings, and telepathically sense the thoughts and meanings of other beings sharing the world with us. Human beings can, under the proper conditions, bring into the focus of conscious awareness, any detail of the past out of which they emerge. Dreams, lucid dreams, out-of-body experiences, and life after death are all different ways of accessing the transphysical worlds which surround and contextualize the physical world. Reincarnation is possible, even (as the Buddhists suggest) without the introduction of a soul hypothesis, which posits the existence of some entity that transcends both the physical and the transphysical worlds, an entity which nevertheless retains, in some measure, the experiences of a sequence of personalities and which is the true reincarnating entity.

Clearly, our scientifically informed common sense is just too narrow and too abstract to do justice to the world in which we actually exist.

To make the world in which we actually do exist plausible, we need to rethink the world of scientifically informed common sense from the ground up. Transphysical Process Metaphysics is a new approach that gives us a more satisfying way of thinking about the terms "finite entity" (thing), time, space, and causality.

In this new approach to actuality, we no longer think of the world in terms of substantial entities like atoms but rather in terms of actual occasions of experience. These occasions come into being by a process which experiences the past, interprets it, elaborates possibilities for its becoming, and then chooses among them to become actual and a causal influence on its future. Causal interactions among these occasions are much more complex than causal interactions among the entities stipulated by conventional physicists. First of all, efficient causes are, for the entity being affected by them, feelings. So each actual occasion feels the entirety of its past and can, under suitable circumstances, draw any part of that past into the focus of conscious attention: this provides a basis for the reality of the various receptive functions in parapsychology.

Secondly, efficient causes—which in this framework are understood as transmissions of experience—naturally include both empathy and telepathy. Also, the behaviors of actual occasions are profoundly influenced by aims and purposes which can be shared among occasions in a way that binds organisms into a unity. This approach can be used as a starting point for an effective account of PK.

Dreams, lucid dreams, out-of-body experiences, and survival of bodily death are, in this new context, seen as a continuum. Since we already exist in transphysical bodies, all we need to do to access them is to withdraw our attention from the data that are coming in from the waking body. We all do this whenever we daydream or dream, but we need to learn to bring attention to this process and to master it consciously. While all past cultures have acknowledged transphysical realities (in their own language, of course), our modern culture does not, and this makes it particularly difficult to master these skills at this time. Also, we need to learn the skill of focusing our thoughtful mode of waking consciousness while we are functioning in the transphysical worlds, so we can perceive them as objective in the way that we now perceive the waking world as objective.

Since we are already occupying transphysical bodies, the survival of bodily death becomes an entirely plausible hypothesis. Also, because I, with Whitehead and Griffin, have redefined the personality as a personally ordered society of actual occasions—a society in which one occasion follows another like beads on a string—and because a personally ordered society of this sort can continue across gaps in time and space, reincarnation becomes entirely plausible as well. The worldview of scientifically informed common sense is too abstract and too poor in its descriptions to do justice to consciousness itself, let alone to parapsychological phenomena. In my articulation of Transphysical Process Metaphysics, I have tried to entirely rethink the categories of finite entity, time, space, and causality in order to create a language in which we can effectively think about the facts of everyday life, the results secured by modern and postmodern physics, and the data of parapsychology.

NOTES

1. In this chapter, I will be primarily concerned with human beings. I believe that all finite beings share in these parapsychological abilities to various degrees, but a consideration of this would unnecessarily complicate the discussion here.

2. To explore the idea of the physical world (the world as disclosed by science) as an abstraction from the world of everyday experience, see Whitehead (1920/1964, 1922, 1925/1982). See also Weiss (2003, 2012).

3. As we will see in a later section, Transphysical Process Metaphysics thinks of spacetime not as a container (actual occasions are the containers in this point of view), but rather as a pattern of relationships among actual occasions. Each society of actual occasions must be bound by a single spacetime relationship.

4. It may sound strange, to those of us educated in the modern world, to imagine consciousness attributed to anything other than ourselves. I have justified this assumption in some depth in Weiss (2012). For the purposes of this chapter, this can be taken as a hypothesis. It is possible to account for all scientific results on the basis of this assumption, and it makes the world make sense.

5. More detailed expositions of many of the key concepts referenced in this essay are available on the Esalen CTR website at http://www.esalen.org/ctr-archive/bp in the form of three long excerpts from Weiss (2012). These will be referred to as Supplements 1, 2, and 3.

6. See http://www.esalen.org/ctr-archive/bp , Supplement 1.

7. James (1909/1971, Chapter 6).

8. While we can regard Transphysical Process Metaphysics as a generalization of quantum theory, it involves an interpretation of quantum theory in which every event is seen as precipitating its own actualization. For other versions of this idea, see Whitehead (1920/1964) and Weiss (2003, 2012). For attempts to reconcile this with the complexities of quantum theory, see Epperson (2004), Malin (2001), and Shimony (1965).

9. See http://www.esalen.org/ctr-archive/bp, Supplement 2.

10. See http://www.esalen.org/ctr-archive/bp, Supplement 3.

11. See http://www.esalen.org/ctr-archive/bp, Supplement 1.

12. See http://www.esalen.org/ctr-archive/bp, Supplement 1.

13. See http://www.esalen.org/ctr-archive/bp, Supplement 1.

14. From the perspective suggested by Transphysical Process Metaphysics, each moment of each neuron is an "actual occasion" and, as such, is an experience of the entire past universe. What is passed from cell to cell is just that experience itself. So the electrical activity that scientists observe in the nervous system is just that part of the transmission of experience that can be scientifically measured. Since the electrical activity is just that part of the transmission of experience that can be scientifically measured, it is an "abstract representation" of the whole event.

15. See http://www.esalen.org/ctr-archive/bp, Supplement 3.

16. Whitehead calls this "perception in the mode of causal efficacy," and he contrasts it with sensory experience, which he calls "perception in the mode of presentational immediacy." See Whitehead (1929/1978, pp. 157–167). We also have relations with contemporary occasions through quantum nonlocality, but that consideration is outside the scope of this discussion.

17. Transphysical Process Metaphysics proposes to interpret Quantum Theory in such a way that each event is seen as choosing among its own probable outcomes. From this point of view, even a subatomic occasion is structured, in its essential features though not its details, like a moment of human experience. For an elaboration of such a theory, see Epperson (2004).

18. It is through the assumption of a cosmic aim that Transphysical Process Metaphysics accounts for the salient features of the evolutionary advance. The assumption is entirely plausible within the context of Transphysical Process Metaphysics, but may be considered as simply a hypothesis by readers of this chapter.

19. See http://www.esalen.org/ctr-archive/bp, Supplement 3.

20. Space is imagined as substantial insofar as it needs nothing other than itself to exist. Thus it is imagined that space would continue to exist even if there were no finite entities occupying it. Later in this essay I will outline why the notion of space as a substantial container is untenable.

21. In classical physics, the real world is defined as a configuration of matter at an instant, and an instant is a cut through linear time with no temporal duration at all. It is like a "snapshot" of the world. In the world of quantum physics, and in the world of process metaphysics, each real entity requires a finite duration of time in order to express fully its own characteristics, and reality at an instant is a mere abstraction.

22. For an excellent, non-technical explication of the Theory of Relativity, see Čapek (1961, Part II).

REFERENCES

Čapek, M. (1961). *The Philosophical Impact of Contemporary Physics.* Princeton, NJ: Van Nostrand.
Epperson, M. (2004). *Quantum Mechanics and the Philosophy of Alfred North Whitehead.* New York: Fordham University Press.
Griffin, D. R. (1997). *Parapsychology, Philosophy, and Spirituality: A Postmodern Exploration.* Albany: State University of New York Press.
Griffin, D. R. (2007). *Whitehead's Radically Different Postmodern Philosophy: An Argument for Its Contemporary Relevance.* Albany: State University of New York Press.
Jahn, R. G., & Dunne, B. J. (1987). *Margins of Reality: The Role of Consciousness in the Physical World.* San Diego, CA: Harcourt Brace Jovanovich.
James, W. (1971). *A Pluralistic Universe.* In *Essays in Radical Empiricism and a Pluralistic Universe* (pp. 121–284). New York: E. P. Dutton. (Original work published 1909)
Kline, M. (1980). *Mathematics: The Loss of Certainty.* Oxford: Oxford University Press.
Leclerc, I. (1972). *The Nature of Physical Existence.* London: George Allen & Unwin.
Lucas, G. R., Jr. (1989). *The Rehabilitation of Whitehead: An Analytic and Historical Assessment of Process Philosophy.* Albany: State University of New York Press.
Malin, S. (2001). *Nature Loves to Hide: Quantum Physics and the Nature of Reality, a Western Perspective.* New York: Oxford University Press.
Poortman, J. J. (1978). *Vehicles of Consciousness: The Concept of Hylic Pluralism (Ochēma)* (N. D. Smith, Trans., Vols. 1–4). Utrecht: Theosophical Society in the Netherlands.
Shimony, A. (1965). Quantum physics and the philosophy of Whitehead. In M. Black (Ed.), *Philosophy in America* (pp. 240–261). London: George Allen & Unwin.
Weiss, E. M. (2003). *The Doctrine of the Subtle Worlds: Sri Aurobindo's Cosmology, Modern Science, and the Metaphysics of Alfred North Whitehead* (Doctoral dissertation). ProQuest Dissertations and Theses database. (UMI No. 3078797)
Weiss, E. M. (2012). *The Long Trajectory: The Metaphysics of Reincarnation and Life After Death.* Bloomington, IN: iUniverse.
Whitehead, A. N. (1922). *The Principle of Relativity, with Applications to Physical Science.* Cambridge: Cambridge University Press.
Whitehead, A. N. (1964). *Concept of Nature.* Cambridge: Cambridge University Press. (Original work published 1920)
Whitehead, A. N. (1978). *Process and Reality: An Essay in Cosmology* (D. R. Griffin & D. W. Sherburne, Eds., Corr. ed.). New York: The Free Press. (Original work published 1929)
Whitehead, A. N. (1982). *An Enquiry Concerning the Principles of Natural Knowledge* (2nd ed.). New York: Dover. (Original work published 1925)

III

Putting the Pieces Together

14

TOWARD A WORLDVIEW GROUNDED IN SCIENCE *AND* SPIRITUALITY

Edward F. Kelly

> We may safely predict that it will be the timidity of our hypotheses, and not their extravagance, which will provoke the derision of posterity.
>
> —H. H. Price, "Haunting and the 'Psychic Ether' Hypothesis"[1]

Let us begin by briefly recalling the context from which this book emerged.[2] Despite many magnificent and undeniable successes, current mainstream neuroscience, psychology, and philosophy of mind are incapable of accommodating various well-evidenced mental and psychophysiological phenomena of the sorts catalogued in Chapter 1 above, *Irreducible Mind*, and many other places. Conventional *production* models of brain/mind relations, according to which everything in mind and consciousness is generated by physiological events and processes occurring in the brain, are inadequate and must be rejected. Their philosophical companion and foundation, the ontological doctrine of classical physicalism, is also too narrow and must give way to some richer form of metaphysics. Science itself, however, is inherently more adaptable and must *not* be rejected; rather, it can and must develop further, along lines more adequate to the full range of our subject matter. In the inspiring words of Francis Bacon (1620/1960), once again, "[T]he world is not to be narrowed till it will go into the understanding . . . but the understanding to be expanded and opened till it can take in the image of the world as it is in fact" (p. 276).

Contemporary science has already initiated the needed expansion it-self, perhaps most dramatically in connection with the advent of quantum theory. Quantum theory has resulted in a seismic shift in the foundations of physics, and despite ongoing controversies about its proper interpreta-tion, it has undermined the received classical physicalist conception of the ultimate nature of Reality, brought the mystery of consciousness back into the foreground, and opened up new theoretical possibilities of nu-merous sorts while simultaneously preserving all that was good in the classical formulations (Atmanspacher, 2011; Rosenblum & Kuttner, 2011; Stapp, 2007).

Our own work is offered in a similarly revolutionary yet conservative spirit. Our central contention is that a more thoroughgoing and synoptic scientific empiricism, unencumbered by theory-driven physicalist pre-conceptions about the nature of the world and our human psyches, leads inexorably into expanded psychological and philosophical territory tradi-tionally occupied by the world's religions. This need not reflexively en-gender terror or outrage in well-educated modern persons, however, for in the prescient words of William James (1909/1971): "Let empiricism once become associated with religion, as hitherto, through some strange misunderstanding, it has been associated with irreligion, and I believe that a new era of religion as well as of philosophy will be ready to begin" (p. 270). By "empiricism," of course, James meant not only collection of a broader range of data but development of whatever new conceptual and theoretical resources might be required for its explanation.

That sort of innovation is what we are attempting to help catalyze with this book. We are at an early stage of what seems certain to be a long and difficult process, the detailed outcomes of which must remain for now largely unknown. Nevertheless, with these qualifications and the limita-tions of our current project firmly in mind, and encouraged by philoso-pher H. H. Price's call in the chapter epigraph for bold theorizing in response to the unique empirical and logical properties of our targeted phenomena, we will now go on in the remainder of this chapter to sketch as best we presently can the main contours of this "undiscovered country of the mind," insofar as they are presently recognizable to us.

INTO THE MORE

The central commonality and driving metaphor of the conceptual frameworks presented in Part II, and the key shift away from production models, opening up new horizons of human possibility, involve their recognition of a tremendous *something*, what William James in *The Varieties of Religious Experience* called "the more," underlying the physical and mental dimensions of everyday experience.

Even on the physical side, appearances are deceiving, and ordinary perception fails to disclose the real nature of things. The classical theory of matter was invented to explain these appearances, but it has proven inadequate at a fundamental level. What lies below the phenomenological surface of the external world as we routinely experience it is not the conventional solid bits of self-existent and locally interacting material stuff that we were told about many years ago in high school but something far more subtle and complex, still largely unknown (Chapters 5 to 7).

Our everyday mental worlds also emerge in relation to some sort of vast but largely hidden background or substrate. Such a picture is widely accepted among contemporary psychologists and neuroscientists, but what has *not* yet been widely recognized is that this hidden background involves far more than the large-scale, fast, and parallel operations of the brain. "Unconscious cerebration" of that sort mainly provides automatic and efficient regulation of vital bodily functions plus sensorimotor coupling to the local environment, or in Myers's terms an "infrared" extension of the spectrum of everyday conscious experience. But there is also an "ultraviolet" extension—the more interesting but less studied part of "the more"—consisting of levels of psychic organization characterized by increasing scope, precision, speed, and complexity of mental operations, and by capacities for supernormal phenomena such as psi and mystical experience that outstrip the explanatory resources of physicalism.[3] These "deeper" (or "more inward" or "higher") levels are normally hidden, probably within all of us, but can definitely be accessed under an increasing variety of recognized circumstances both deliberate and spontaneous (see *IM*, plus Chapters 1 to 4 above).

The conceptual frameworks presented in Part II, deriving from areas as diverse as modern physics (both quantum theory and relativity), mystically informed religious philosophies, and Western psychology and metaphysics, variously describe aspects of this hidden background of the everyday consciousness and/or its experienced world in terms of a Myers–James Subliminal Self; the quantum state of the universe and responses on the part of nature to our human questioning; the Pauli–Jung conception of an underlying ontic reality, the *unus mundus*, which amounts to a metaphysical interpretation of Jung's concept of the collective unconscious in its later "psychoid" form; higher-dimensional subspaces or actuality planes in a "bulk" vs. "brane"; the Plotinian hypostases of the One, the Intellect (*Nous*) and its Intelligible World, and the World Soul; the primordial matter (*prakṛti*) and/or consciousness (*Śiva, Brahman*) of Indian philosophical traditions; the depths of inverted Leibnizian monads; Peirce's synechism with its continuum of mind; or transphysical worlds built upon Whiteheadian process metaphysics. All involve in some form Bergson's (1913) basic notion of "a consciousness overflowing the organism," and all in their varying but complementary ways represent possible pathways toward reconciliation of science and spirituality.

At the *psychological* level, the presented frameworks all fit naturally under the umbrella of "permission" or "filter" models as sketched in our Introduction and in Chapters 3 and 4, with the possible exception of the Pauli–Jung dual-aspect monism of Chapter 6, which takes a somewhat different although conceptually related form. In beginning our effort to draw these threads together, we wish first to propose what we regard as a richer metaphor and modestly improved terminology for psychological models of this general sort.[4] Specifically, we suggest designating this class of models more generally as "ROSTA" models, incorporating the central common notion of Resonant Opening to Subliminal and Transpersonal Assets.

The acronym itself is reasonably word-like and memorable, has no obviously irrelevant or misleading connotations, and is not too easily parodied. More importantly, its expansion more accurately captures the underlying concept, and in a form which engenders no "homunculus" problems of the sort pointed out in *IM* (pp. 606–607). The "Resonance" aspect has to do with getting the brain into an unusual state or condition of some relevant sort, as discussed in particular in Chapter 4, and by tuning ourselves in such ways we create "Openings" to higher or deeper or more inward parts of the psyche—i.e., to "the more." "Subliminal" encompasses all forms of a dynamic psychological unconscious including in particular that of Myers. Myers's model itself already includes a "Transpersonal" element or aspect (the Subliminal Self, which for him is the vehicle of survival), and these transpersonal or "spiritual" aspects more generally constitute the main target of this book. By "Assets" we mean both information and capacities of various relevant or appropriate sorts that originate within those regions and would otherwise not be available to the everyday conscious ego or supraliminal self.[5]

At the moment we are thinking of ROSTA models in mainly psychological and scientific terms, and we are confident that in this respect they can be developed significantly further, along lines already indicated in Chapter 4 and elsewhere in the book. However, particularly because of their transpersonal aspects (as well as the unsolved problems at the heart of the mind, as summarized in Chapter 1), they will also require some sort of nonphysicalist ontology to accompany and support them, and it is much less clear as yet what form that expanded ontology should take. Metaphysical aspects will enter the discussion increasingly as we proceed, but first there are several narrower scientific issues in relation to ROSTA models that we must quickly get out of the way.

THE GENERAL SCIENTIFIC STATUS OF ROSTA MODELS

We begin by summarizing our view as to the theoretical and empirical viability of ROSTA-type models vis-à-vis conventional production models. What ultimately emerges will presumably be determined in large part by the customary criteria for "good" scientific theories, such as predictive power, testability, empirical fecundity, aesthetic appeal, pragmatic utility, conceptual clarity, consistency, and economy, and so forth as described for example by Chalmers (1976/1994), Dawson and Conduit (2011), Marshall (2005, pp. 11–17), and numerous others. Of course in the present book we are dealing primarily with general conceptual frameworks or philosophical/metaphysical worldviews rather than well-developed scientific theories, so that elaborate comparisons are premature, but in general terms it seems to us now, as it did earlier to William James (see Chapter 4), that ROSTA models are more or less on par with conventional production models in most such respects, and in some respects actually superior. In particular, all of the conceptual frameworks presented in Part II already go beyond current physicalist conceptions by explicitly accommodating in some fashion an expanded range of well-evidenced empirical phenomena including at least some of the phenomena targeted in Chapter 1.

More importantly, they all attempt to show how we can potentially explain or make sense of such phenomena by entertaining alternative conceptions as to the general nature of Reality in light of which it would become natural for them to occur.[6] This may appear to some to violate the criterion of parsimony—William of Ockham's infamous "razor"—by making the world appear more complicated than that imagined by contemporary physicalists, but we regard these complications as theoretically necessary and hence scientifically justifiable. Our views here echo those of philosopher Thomas Nagel (2012):

> Major scientific advances often require the creation of new concepts, postulating unobservable elements of reality that are needed to explain how natural regularities that initially appear accidental are in fact necessary. The evidence for the existence of such things is precisely that if they existed, they would explain what is otherwise incomprehensible.
>
> Certainly the mind-body problem is difficult enough that we should be suspicious of attempts to solve it with the concepts and methods developed to account for very different kinds of things. Instead, we should expect theoretical progress in this area to require a major conceptual revolution at least as radical as relativity theory, the introduction of electromagnetic fields into physics—or the original scientific revolution itself, which, because of its built-in restrictions, can't result in a "theory of everything," but must be seen as a stage on the way to a more general form of understanding. (p. 42)

That "more general form of understanding" is what we are groping toward in this chapter.

One further theory-evaluation criterion has been thought by some to be of special and generic concern in regard to ROSTA-type models—specifically, *falsifiability*, which of course is closely tied to *prediction*. The view that falsifiability is *the* crucial demarcation criterion for scientific theories is associated especially with philosopher of science Karl Popper (1968), and he introduced it in the context of his attack upon the psychodynamic theories of Adler and Freud, which can be viewed as impoverished ROSTA models devoid of transpersonal aspects. His basic point against theories of this type was that by postulating unverifiable unconscious thoughts and motives of various sorts they could potentially "explain" any possible empirical outcome, and for that reason were essentially unfalsifiable and hence unscientific.[7] If ROSTA models are similarly incapable of generating potentially falsifiable predictions, on this view, they too must fail to qualify as properly scientific.

Several things should immediately be said in response to this concern. First, philosophers of science now generally reject Popper's arguments for universal primacy of falsification over confirmation. Falsifiability is desirable, yes, but it is often difficult to achieve, due both to the general fallibility of empirical observations and to the ever-present possibility of ad hoc modifications of a given theory designed to insulate it from potential falsification. Furthermore, falsification certainly has *not* played a dominant role in historically documented scientific practice (Chalmers, 1976/1994; Feyerabend, 1975/2010). Scientific theories in general cannot be conclusively proved or disproved, but instead typically bootstrap themselves by progressively accumulating weights of evidence congruent or incongruent with them in varying degrees. The most significant scientific advances in fact derive from *confirmation* of bold conjectures and *falsification* of cautious ones (Chalmers, 1976/1994, pp. 54–55).

Consider in this light NDEs occurring under extreme physiological conditions such as deep general anesthesia and/or cardiac arrest. These are totally unexpected from the conventional point of view, but they definitely do occur (Chapter 1) and in so doing they exert both kinds of effects at once in favor of the ROSTA perspective: On the one hand, that is, conventional physicalist models make a clear but cautious prediction that no experience of any kind should be possible under these conditions, and this prediction is falsified by the experiences that do in fact occur. From the ROSTA perspective, meanwhile, the possibility of such experiences can certainly be anticipated, if not strictly "predicted" as if by some sort of deductive logic (as Myers in fact did—see *IM*, p. 367), and this "bold conjecture" is confirmed.

Myers's model and ROSTA models in general also lead to the expectation that supernormal phenomena will emerge in proportion to the "abeyance of the supraliminal," as for example in dreams and hypnagogic states, and these conjectures have similarly been confirmed (Chapter 4). In addition, the entire class of ROSTA models is falsifiable in a generalized sense, inasmuch as they would become superfluous and in effect falsified in practice should some expanded form of physicalism prove able to accommodate our targeted phenomena. Particular forms or aspects of ROSTA models may also prove directly falsifiable, as in the case of the instantaneous rebirth implied by certain strands of Yoga philosophy, which as we saw in Chapter 9 is falsified by the empirically observed distribution of time intervals between death and rebirth in cases of the reincarnation type.

In sum, we do not see the falsifiability issue as posing special problems for ROSTA models in general.

Another commonly voiced a priori objection to ROSTA models concerns a supposed selection or "magic filter" problem arising in their application to receptive psi (ESP in its various forms). "Targets" might in principle be virtually anywhere in space and/or time, so how out of this essentially infinite amount of potentially relevant information do percipients find their way to what they actually need and exclude everything else? Would not the amount of information to be selected from or "filtered" overwhelm the information-processing capacities of the brain, which can barely cope even with the relatively modest demands of everyday life in our strictly local environments?

This objection, however, *presumes* the conventional physicalist understanding of brain/mind relations! In the context of ROSTA models, selectivity can be accomplished by something in addition to, or other than, the unaided brain. Their general move, to be explored in more detail below, is to invoke "the more" itself—that is, to conceive of higher or deeper or more inward strata of the psyche as having direct access to larger tracts of Reality, or to contain information deposited within them by some other agency which has such access, such as other minds or a higher mind with which it in some sense merges or overlaps. In either case, the needed information is already "within," but in making its way toward supraliminal consciousness may be corrupted or suppressed through interactions with intervening strata. This basic picture goes back in particular to Myers and James, plus Tyrrell (1947). What will ultimately become more important here concerns our efforts to supplement this basic *psychological* model with some sort of appropriate *metaphysics* to support and rationalize it (see also Chapter 2 above, and Marshall, 2005, Chapter 8).

PREVIOUS THEORIES OF PSI

Before proceeding further we wish to say a little about the general drift of previous scientific theorizing about psi, and to characterize the main way in which our own approach differs from this. General readers may wish to skip to the take-home message of the final paragraph of this section on a first reading.[8]

It has been widely recognized that the absence of some sort of credible theory or conceptual framework in terms of which psi makes sense and does not conflict with other parts of our understanding of nature is at present the greatest obstacle to its acceptance by mainstream science. Contrary to widespread misimpressions, however, there have already been many attempts to produce such theories—see for example Braude (2002), Carr (2008), Radin (2006, Chapter 13), and Stokes (1987) for more comprehensive overviews. Given that the phenomena are inherently *psychophysical*, typically appearing to have both psychological and physical aspects, both psychological and physical explanations of various kinds have been proposed.

On the psychological side, the most significant have involved psychodynamic models of the ROSTA sort, which we will be developing in greater theoretical detail below. Parenthetically, however, an important recent contribution to this lineage is the "First Sight" model of Carpenter (2012), which updates and generalizes the experimentally fertile "psi-mediated instrumental response" (PMIR) model of Stanford (1990), and which demonstrates clearly that psi-derived information is treated much like other forms of input that are also subliminally acquired but by conventional physical means. Although excellent as far as it goes, this model is not helpful for our more far-reaching theoretical purposes, most importantly because it simply presumes the availability of psi-derived information at some unconscious level of a brain/mind system which otherwise is conceived in conventional terms.

There have also been many *physics*-based models which sought to explain how various psi-type processes might actually work. These typically began with ideas drawn from conventional/classical physical science: on the receptive psi or ESP side, for example, it was natural to propose possible explanations based on signal-transmission ideas and analogies with ordinary perception. Thus for example "telepathy" was initially imagined, perhaps in response to the then nascent technology of radio, to be a matter of sending some sort of electromagnetic signal through space from one brain to another.[9]

Such models have all proven inadequate, however, for a variety of well-known reasons. For example, no effective means of physical shielding has ever been identified, and although the existing research leaves extremely low frequencies (including those of human EEG, which does actually exist in space outside the skull) as a remaining possibility, these frequencies have very limited information-carrying capacity. Furthermore, there have been no plausible suggestions as to how the relevant mental content might be encoded by such a "source" and selectively and reliably decoded by the intended "receiver."

Further problems became apparent in relation to receptive psi involving physical (clairvoyance) targets such as the geometric-symbol ("Zener") cards originally used by J. B. Rhine and his associates. How for example can such objects be imagined to produce any sort of useful signal, and how could anything analogous to an ordinary perceptual process distinguish cards located in the middle of a deck, or oriented sideways with respect to the subject? Other factors that strongly influence ordinary perception such as the subject's physical distance from the target, symbol size, and stimulus contrast, also have little or no effect. Worse yet, the targets need not even have been chosen at the time the responses are made, as in precognition studies of various kinds.

Other versions of signal-transmission theory have been proposed which postulate exotic special-purpose particles or waves capable of carrying the needed information through space and/or time, but most of these have been untestable mathematical or physical fantasies, and the more exotic the supposed carriers the harder to conceive anything in the body or brain which could selectively receive and decode them (Beloff, 1980; Stokes, 1987).

On the expressive psi or PK side, F. W. H. Myers (1903) quickly recognized that the recently advanced concept of a Maxwell's Demon—a hypothetical tiny being who could direct things at the atomic or molecular level without violating conservation laws, essentially by injection of information into physical systems—could potentially explain phenomena as diverse as object movements accompanied by cool breezes, luminous appearances of various kinds, and the production of unusual odors (Vol. 2, pp. 529–543).

Physicist Jean Burns (2012) has recently been developing a similar approach based on informational ordering of quantum fluctuations within the limits imposed by the uncertainty principle, apparently independently of Myers and in much more quantitative detail, and her work is just one expression of a more general recent trend. Specifically, a number of contemporary investigators steeped in the relevant physical sciences, including a number of the contributors to this volume, share a deep sense that the world revealed by quantum theory is hospitable to psi in a way that its classical predecessor certainly was not, and that this is somehow connected with *complementarity* and *non-local entanglement* as basic and experimentally verified features of that theory (Radin, 2006). There is considerably less agreement, however, as to how these connections might actually work. We will next briefly describe the two main ways in which quantum-theoretic principles have previously been applied to theorizing about psi.

First are the so-called Observational Theories (OTs), mathematically formulated in somewhat varying forms by a number of different investigators starting in the 1970s. These are tied more or less directly to the special properties of the measurement situation as viewed in Copenhagen-style quantum theory (see Chapter 5 above), and they have focused primarily on experimental psi tasks involving inherently random processes—for example, PK studies using dice and random event generators (REGs) of various kinds, and forced-choice ESP tasks using suitably randomized Zener cards and the like. Their fundamental idea is that the statistically uncertain outcomes of such experiments are not settled until a conscious and motivated observer, normally the experimental subject, receives feedback, and that such observers can inject information which slightly biases the collapse of the wave function in directions they prefer. This picture leads to some surprising expectations that have been experimentally confirmed, such as the possibility of apparently retroactive PK success on pre-recorded targets, and effects attributable to persons who simply check the results.[10] It also purports to solve the selectivity or magic-filter problem in ESP in a novel way, postulating that the information received *now* corresponds to feedback which will be presented *later*, and which becomes available to the subject by way of retroactive PK on that subject's own brain conceived as a kind of REG which controls or at least influences the flow of mentation.[11] From this perspective all forms of psi thus seem potentially reducible to a single PK-like process (Hout-kooper, 2002). [12]

The OTs have already generated a considerable amount of experimental work. They continue to undergo further development and testing, and they are certainly worthwhile scientific accomplishments. Nevertheless, we strongly doubt their generality. Leaving aside all the difficulties involved in pinning down what really constitutes "an observer" and "observation," they fail in the first place to account for cases of ESP success with only partial feedback, such as feedback of overall results rather than trial-by-trial results, or with no feedback whatsoever. More pointedly, they have had nothing useful to say about psychological conditions conducive to psi success, and they seem inherently limited to the sorts of weak psi effects typically seen in the specific experimental settings they target.

In fact, they fail even to cope with the richness of the phenomena occurring in some of those experimental settings themselves: in free-response protocols such as the Ganzfeld, for example, subjects are typically put into a mildly altered state using relaxation and sensory deprivation techniques, and encouraged to provide rich, running reports of imagery or mentation potentially related to a complex remote target such as a randomly selected art print, video clip, or geographic location. In these settings, the flow of psi-derived information occurs initially in the form of the reports accompanying the Ganzfeld procedure; only secondarily, and in our opinion quite artificially, does the entire session get turned into a single forced-choice trial by requesting subjects to rank these reports blindly against the actual target and three or more randomly selected decoys. The OTs focus primarily on the slight biasing of the final forced-choice hit probabilities, but the real information is in the reports themselves; furthermore, those reports can be successfully matched against the possible targets by persons *other than* the original subjects.

The second stream arose mainly in connection with the introduction by Atmanspacher, Römer, and Walach (2002) of "weak" or "generalized" forms of quantum theory which aspire to realize the clear expectations on the part of Bohr, Pauli, and other founders that the core ideas of quantum theory would be found applicable to wider areas of human experience. Starting with an axiomatic formulation of standard quantum theory, Atmanspacher and colleagues showed that certain axioms which apply strictly only in physics contexts could be progressively relaxed or eliminated, yielding a hierarchy of models that carry the central QM notions of *complementarity* and *entanglement* into increasingly general contexts at the cost of decreasing quantitative precision. This demonstration has already opened up a wide spectrum of applications, ranging from relatively rigorous experimental applications to topics in cognitive psychology, such as bistable perception, decision processes, learning, and semantic networks, using models relatively close to the standard theory (Atmanspacher, 2011, section 4.7), to what can perhaps best be described as largely metaphorical excursions into much broader matters more relevant to our purposes here, including in particular psi phenomena, using models of more generalized sort (Walach, Schmidt, & Jonas, 2011).

Without going into the detail that would be needed for a full treatment, these latter applications seem to us to falter in two main respects: First, they inherit the problems of the OTs with respect to fuzziness in key concepts such as "observers" and "observation," and add to these an excessive elasticity in the identification and characterization both of "systems" in general, and of systems expected to be subject to complementarity and entanglement effects (and the form of those effects) in particular. Secondly, and again like most other previous physics-based theorizing about psi, they suffer from the narrowness of their empirical base, which consists primarily of experimental studies using unselected or mildly selected subjects. Under these circumstances, experimenters are at least as likely as the persons nominally identified as "subjects" to be the sources of any observed psi effects, especially if they are highly motivated, and this leads to the current preoccupation with experimenter effects and with supposedly capricious and elusive properties of psi that we believe are probably specific to those experimental settings (Hansen, 2001; Kennedy, 2003).

Most importantly, in our view, the widespread inclination of contemporary theoreticians to ignore or reject quasi-experimental and field observations entails a failure to take into account more dramatic phenomena that characteristically occur only in the midst of real human lives, but which place correspondingly severe empirical constraints on theory building (see also Tyrrell, 1947). For example, St. Joseph of Copertino's levitations, and phenomena suggestive of postmortem survival such as verified past-life memories and NDEs occurring under extreme physiological conditions (Chapter 1), appear beyond the reach of all of the physics-based theories briefly canvassed in this section.

Our driving intuition here is that frameworks capable of accommodating the more extreme phenomena will in general accommodate the simpler or lesser ones. Thus, rather than starting with a model that tries to explain psi phenomena alone, or perhaps even some subset of these, and then trying to generalize it, our basic strategy from the beginning has been to seek some more comprehensive kind of conceptual framework or model that can potentially make sense not only of the full range of psi phenomena but of other related things as well, including in particular mystical experiences and higher states of consciousness, along with the unexplained everyday phenomena at the heart of the mind, as described in Chapter 1. The emerging physics-based theories canvassed in Chapters 5 to 7 all strive for this kind of generality, and are prepared to stretch the boundaries of present-day relativity and/or quantum theory in order to achieve it. It remains possible, of course, that different categories of phenomena will turn out to require different sorts of explanations, and persons with predilections different from ours are certainly free to pursue their own preferred approaches. Since no one knows at this point what approach(es) will ultimately work best, all should be given the opportunity to prove themselves. In that spirit, we will now continue to develop our own approach, starting with several other large and difficult topics that remain in play, all needing much further work.

SUBTLE BODIES AND SUBTLE ENERGIES

Notions of these sorts are endemic to the world's spiritual traditions, and as shown for example in the chapters above on Neoplatonism, Sāṃkhya/ Yoga, and the Kashmiri Śaivism of Abhinavagupta, they have routinely been invoked to explain supernormal phenomena of various kinds including psi and postmortem survival. It is also the case that persons who have experienced vivid OBEs or NDEs, including highly educated modern persons, typically find it virtually impossible to resist the conviction that they have literally vacated their ordinary bodies and yet continued to function as fully conscious or even hyperconscious agents, usually in some sort of embodied form. These intense experiences in fact often lead to expectations of postmortem survival, accompanied by profound reduction in any preexisting fears of death.

But do subtle bodies really exist as "physical" entities of some clearly specifiable sort? Their explanatory potential and phenomenological persuasiveness are not sufficient to answer this question in the affirmative, and, although we have already briefly touched upon it in Chapter 9, we must now deal with it more fully and generally, inasmuch as it represents a possible watershed in our theory-construction efforts. Useful background for this discussion is provided by the work of Poortman (1978), whose four-volume treatise, although still far from complete at his death, constitutes the most systematic attempt known to us to survey the worldwide history of the subject. Also relevant here is the fact that Poortman's principal mentor was the distinguished Dutch philosopher and psychologist Gerardus Heymans, often described as the William James of Holland, who was a champion of "psychic monism." Both of these scholars, parenthetically, fully accepted the reality of psi. Poortman's studies ultimately led him to break with Heymans and join the Theosophists in embracing a doctrine of "hylic [material] pluralism" that postulates one or more types of subtle matter in addition to ordinary matter—but was this really warranted?

There is no obvious or compelling a priori reason why there can be nothing "in between" consciousness and matter, or between the subjective and the objective, as these terms are ordinarily understood. Metaphysicians as far removed from each other as Abhinavagupta and Peirce specifically postulated continuous gradations in between, and as Myers (1886) himself remarked, "it is no longer safe to assume any sharply-defined distinction of mind and matter. . . . [O]ur notions of mind and matter must pass through many a phase as yet unimagined" (pp. 178–179). Furthermore, the recent discoveries regarding "dark" matter and energy, previously unrecognized constituents of the universe which together represent something like 96% of its physical contents, suggest that there might be room for such possibilities within physics, and at minimum should encourage humility as to the limits of current knowledge.[13]

Subtle bodies need not violate any current physical principles, and in fact room is specifically reserved in the hyperdimensional framework of Chapter 7 for a hierarchy of subtle bodies analogous to that found in Kashmiri Śaivism (Chapter 10). The direct evidence for such things, however, remains equivocal. A useful reference point here is the scholarly work by Samuel and Johnston (2013), which first surveys subtle-body and subtle-energy concepts and practices originating especially in South Asian religions, Neoplatonism, and Sufism, and then traces their penetration of the modern West and their proliferation into innumerable schools of self-development, martial arts, and healing. In its final chapter Geoffrey Samuel, himself a scholar of Tibetan religion who also trained in physics, tries to interpret these experiences and practices in a nonreductive way that honors their value while remaining steadfastly within the framework of current physicalist psychology and neuroscience. Specifically, he suggests, perhaps such practices secure their demonstrated health benefits, and other genuine benefits of various sorts, simply by enabling us to recognize and control aspects of *ordinary* bodily processes and mental activity of which we are normally not fully aware. In effect this treatment of subtle-body concepts attempts to split the difference between summary dismissal based on naive reductive physicalism and complete acceptance based on naive New-Age realism. Although useful as far as it goes, it essentially bypasses the more difficult task of evaluating evidence specifically relevant to the ontological issues at hand.

We ourselves have already rejected physicalism, of course, but this in itself does not entail acceptance of subtle bodies and subtle energies as traditionally conceived. The general state of *evidence* can perhaps best be described as intriguing but scientifically unsatisfactory. There is of course a vast amount of popular and semi-scientific literature on these subjects, and Googling on the relevant terms will typically produce literally millions of hits, but few of these lead to anything of real scientific substance. Much the same, unfortunately, is true of the large and extremely uneven "scientific" literatures dealing with topics such as auras, *cakras* and meridians, *kuṇḍalinī*, spirit photographs, and Kirlian photography (including its recent descendant, gas discharge visualization or GDV), all of which are routinely invoked in support of subtle-energy and subtle-body concepts.[14]

The most substantial supporting evidence currently available in fact comes from psychical research: this includes, for example, crisis apparitions with their quasi-physical properties, especially collective and reciprocal cases as described in Chapter 1, a few existing OBE experiments using detectors of various kinds at the target site (see *IM*, Chapter 6), and the work of Ian Stevenson on cases of the reincarnation type. Stevenson himself thought that the subset of his cases involving birthmarks and/or birth defects corresponding to fatal wounds inflicted on the previous personality implied the existence of some sort of physical carrier, in effect a "body" of *some* sort, to mediate these connections. Recognizing the similarity of his notion to traditional concepts of the subtle body, but wishing to avoid their surplus religious and occult connotations, he introduced the term "psychophore" instead (Stevenson, 1997, Vol. 2, pp. 2083–2089).

The jury remains out, in our opinion, on the *physical* reality of subtle bodies and subtle energies. The situation is further confused by the fact that new information is constantly emerging in regard to unexpected bio-electromagnetic phenomena, such as pulsed magnetic fields and emission of light in the visible range, which can possibly be explained by conventional physical principles operating in unusual ways within the human body (Oschman, 2000). The boundaries between "normal" and "subtle," that is, are constantly being redrawn.

More decisive evidence is certainly needed, but enough has already been accomplished to show that all of the relevant subjects are definitely accessible to further research. Much work is currently being directed to development of novel forms of instrumentation that purportedly enable reliable detection and measurement of subtle-energy and/or subtle-body phenomena, and these efforts, if successful, will support extension of conventional third-person or "objective" scientific methods into this new arena. Pending or even absent such developments, moreover, much of scientific value could be accomplished simply through more systematic deployment of available first-person methodologies: far more could easily be done than has been done so far, for example, in terms of assessing intersubjective agreement among detailed and careful phenomenological descriptions—obtained from multiple observers under conditions free of contamination by demand characteristics, social-influence processes, doctrinal compliance, and the like—of auras, *cakras*, meditative lights, and numerous related experiential phenomena.

Meanwhile, it seems evident that if subtle bodies of some meaningfully "physical" sort do *not* exist, ontologies such as that of Sāṃkhya/Yoga, or more generally *all* of those advanced under the umbrella of hylic pluralism by Poortman, must necessarily either collapse altogether or merge somehow with one of the other positions identified below.

Our hesitation here, we emphasize, concerns only the correct *interpretation* of the relevant experiences and not the experiences themselves. We have always been impressed by the fact, noted also by Geoffrey Samuel, that the traditions which embrace subtle-body doctrines are suspiciously diverse in what they report regarding crucial matters such as the number and character of "bodies," "sheaths," *cakras,* and the like, which seems inconsistent with the view that independent skilled observers are reporting on a single, common reality of some sort. Perhaps what we are seeing instead, as suggested in several previous chapters, is a spectrum of imaginative experiences, characteristically accompanied by a sense of embodiment in some form, among which our everyday sense of physical embodiment happens to be the most stable and communally shared. That is, it may ultimately make more theoretical sense to question the conventionally understood physicality of the *ordinary* body than to introduce new species of matter with mysterious properties (see also *IM*, pp. 630–638).

THE IMAGINAL

A topic deeply entangled with that of subtle bodies, but if anything even less well researched at present, concerns human capacities for imaginal activity of a kind that greatly outstrips ordinary waking types of imagination or fancy. These capacities often express themselves under special circumstances involving extreme emotion, trauma, trance, or other altered states, and they reveal imagination as potentially far more than a mere spinner of fancies, indeed a potent *reality-discovering* and perhaps even *reality-creating* form of mental activity. [15]

Anyone who routinely experiences vivid dreams, or has experimented with psychedelics, can hardly fail to suspect that we all harbor creative assets of this sort, inaccessible from the ordinary conscious state. Moreover, there exists a long and illustrious intellectual and cultural tradition, sketched in Chapter 3 above, which explicitly holds such views: Beginning with Plato, for example, for whom the everyday world was a mere shadow of the real world of the Forms, that lineage extends through Plotinus and the later Neoplatonists with their visionary theurgy (Chapter 8 above), to Marsilio Ficino and other Renaissance figures, and to Carl Jung with his archetypes and collective unconscious, especially in the later "psychoid" form as conceived with the help of physicist Wolfgang Pauli (Chapter 6). It also includes Romantic poets and thinkers such as Blake, Coleridge, and Wordsworth (Abrams, 1971), with whom F. W. H. Myers was intimately familiar; William James's godfather Ralph Waldo Emerson and the American transcendentalists; the great German idealist philosophers of the nineteenth century, including Schopenhauer with his concept of a "dream organ" by means of which we can contact ultimate reality (Chapter 3); and concepts of creative imagination associated with Iranian mysticism (see Corbin, 1969/1997, and its remarkable preface by the literary theorist Harold Bloom).[16]

A central impulse of this entire lineage is to identify and characterize whatever it is that underlies the involuntary and incommensurable inspirations or "subliminal uprushes" of genius, as described briefly in Chapters 1 and 3 above and more fully in Chapter 7 of *IM*. Cognate notions have also been invoked by Paul Marshall in Chapters 2 and 11 above, as a feature of the "mediating subconscious" that introduces archetypal and cultural symbols as well as errors and disguises, by Bernard Carr in Chapter 7 with his concept of "actuality planes" associated with higher states of consciousness, and by Eric Weiss in Chapter 13 in connection with his model of "transphysical worlds."

Mainstream psychological theory and research, unfortunately, have made little contact with this enormous and humanly vital subject. There is some interesting but decades-old psychoanalytic work on "primary process" thinking as exemplified for example in the art of the insane, and on "regression in service of the ego" as central to the creative process, plus some early work on the impact of psychedelics such as LSD and psilocybin on creative thinking, but those approaches subsequently fell from favor, and the contemporary cognitive science of imagination seems to us conceptually impoverished, deliberately confining itself to the shallows of the subject (Chapter 4 above; see also Brann, 1991, and *IM*, Chapter 7).

Some of the most interesting and relevant work in fact again derives from psychical research and associated fields of study. For example, well-documented phenomena of extreme psychophysical influence, such as stigmata, hypnotic blisters, and skin writing, demonstrate that the body itself is to some degree plastic, and that sufficiently intense and focused conscious imagery can somehow alter it *directly*—i.e., in ways that go beyond the reach of the physiological output mechanisms available to the unaided brain (Chapter 1 above; *IM*, Chapter 3). A related example comes from the strange case of Ted Serios, who when sufficiently inebriated was able to impress mental images directly onto Polaroid film. Importantly, these sometimes included images of local external objects that were easily recognizable as such, but which incorporated *distortions* that could not be reproduced optically (Eisenbud, 1967).

This leads directly into the larger arena of macro-PK, in which consensually verifiable alterations of the observable environment occur, again typically in the presence of an unusual person experiencing some sort of unusual or extreme state (Braude, 1986). Poltergeist phenomena for example fall into this category, and can perhaps be viewed as imaginal productions in the sense that they are physical symbols or expressions of the extreme emotional states that apparently catalyze them. The levitations and associated phenomena of St. Joseph of Copertino, maximally challenging for theoreticians, also seem to us most plausibly interpreted as similar sorts of plastic modifications of the local consensus reality that are induced somehow by his ecstatic states—i.e., anomalous "psychophysical correlations" in the sense of Chapter 6—rather than as resulting from application of conventional physical "forces" mobilized somehow by ordering of quantum fluctuations and the like. Ordinary consensus reality itself may thus ultimately be experiential or ideal in character—as argued explicitly by Henry Stapp in the context of quantum theory (Chapter 5), and from related points of view throughout the remainder of Part II—rather than "physical" in the conventional classical sense. Note that "subtle" or "astral" bodies and crisis apparitions could also potentially be interpreted as imaginal productions of this sort (Braude, 1986, pp. 212–213).

Related phenomena that are currently less well documented but potentially amenable to further investigation include the "thought-forms" or "tulpas" of Tibetan lore (David-Neel, 1937) and bilocation among the Catholic saints (Thurston, 1952). For an example of how such phenomena could be objectively studied see Schatzman (1980), who had his eidetiker patient position her externalized images between herself and repetitive visual stimuli such as a reversing checkerboard, resulting in attenuation of the electrical responses normally evoked in her brain by those stimuli. Her "apparitions" were also apparently witnessed by others on at least a few occasions, although not reliably.

In sum, we clearly need a richer and more comprehensive theory of human imagination (and see also *IM*, Chapter 7). At the moment our popular and scientific culture mainly offers a stark black-and-white contrast between what's "real"—i.e., classically physical, and hence accessible to our senses—and what's merely imagined or imaginary and hence unreal. *But not everything imagined is necessarily imaginary.*

THE EVOLUTION OF CONSCIOUSNESS: GENERAL CONSIDERATIONS

Relying primarily on empirical arguments of the sort set forth in detail in *IM* and summarized in Chapter 1 above, we have already explicitly rejected the conventional mainstream production model of brain/mind relations, according to which mind and consciousness somehow emerge *synchronically*, at a particular moment in time, from physiological processes occurring in brains. There remains however the question of *diachronic* emergence—i.e., how conscious mentality of increasing richness and complexity has emerged across time in conjunction with biological evolution. Nobody versed in the relevant contemporary science can rationally doubt that this coevolution occurs; the question again concerns how best to interpret and explain it.

The currently dominant position, exemplified in works such as Clayton and Davies (2006) and Thompson (2007), clings to the promissory-materialist view that we will eventually become able to explain how consciousness itself emerges in terms of the increasing complexity of the material biological structures that become available during the course of evolution (however in detail that evolution happens). This seems to us nothing other than the conventional production model viewed from a different angle, and for the same sorts of reasons doomed to failure. This conclusion applies equally, we believe, to emergence in the course of individual human development.

Interest has been increasing, however, in various forms of *panpsychism* or *panexperientialism* among both philosophers (including Peirce, Whitehead, and other process thinkers such as Charles Hartshorne and David Ray Griffin, plus Thomas Nagel, David Skrbina, William Seager, and Galen Strawson) and scientists (including the recently reformed Christof Koch, Giulio Tononi, and T. X. Barber in his later years). In the currently favored atomistic or bottom-up forms, such theories postulate that some sort of rudimentary "awareness" or capacity for experience is a primitive of nature associated even with low-level material structures. Simply *there*, at or near the bottom of things in some proto-form from the very beginning, it somehow evolves into more complex forms over time in conjunction with its increasingly complex material accompaniments. [17]

There are serious problems with atomistic emergentisms of this sort, the most difficult of which is to explain precisely how this composition or "combination" process works. The importance of the issue can readily be appreciated from an acrimonious exchange between philosophers John Searle and David Chalmers, recorded in Searle (1997). Chalmers had mused at some length about the possible mental life of thermostats, but Searle ridicules these speculations on grounds that thermostats lack the kind of biological organization that he thinks we know to be necessary for *any* form of conscious experience. This sort of attempted *reductio ad absurdum* has been common in response to panpsychist theorizing, but as emphasized especially by Griffin (1998, Chapter 9) it ignores a long tradition, extending from Leibniz to Peirce, Whitehead, Hartshorne, and Griffin himself (and Eric Weiss in the previous chapter), which attempts to distinguish systematically between mere "aggregates" (such as rocks and thermostats) and "compounds" or "organisms" (such as earthworms and ourselves). Clearly, to the degree that these distinctions can be grounded in an adequate understanding of the process of composition, the *reductio* can be circumvented. Existing philosophic attempts to accomplish this, however, including Griffin's, seem to us primarily descriptive—that is, essentially restating the original observations of mind/matter correlation in a different and not particularly helpful language—rather than genuinely explanatory. Furthermore, although quantum theory encompasses modes of composition that have no analogue in classical physics, and can undoubtedly explain the emergence in more complex systems of *some* novel properties not possessed by their constituents (as discussed for example by Seager & Allen-Hermanson, 2013), we see little reason to hope that consciousness itself could be such a property. [18]

These issues are undergoing active investigation in various quarters, and it remains to be seen how far the purely bottom-up forms of panpsychism can get. Meanwhile, an alternative top-down interpretation of the coevolution of mind and matter, also broadly panpsychist, is that the increasingly complex material structures generated in the course of evolution permit increasingly full expression of powers that are inherent in some sort of antecedently existing and relatively tremendous consciousness situated at the source of all manifestation. This picture of course connects closely with traditional mystically informed philosophies such as those set forth in Chapters 8 to 10, which were deliberately formulated in light of unusual states of consciousness ranging beyond everyday supraliminal consciousness toward the highest forms of extrovertive and introvertive mystical experience. We believe that this is the more promising theoretical direction; furthermore, an ideal historical context for developing it further in the remainder of this chapter was provided by William James, who demonstrated in his most mature work that Myers's basic model extends naturally in the overall direction suggested by these traditions. We will next briefly recapitulate that evolution.

Among the supplemental materials for this chapter we have included the final section from the last of Myers's nine enormous papers on the Subliminal Self, in which he presents his conceptual scheme in a pictorial form that also incorporates all the varied kinds of challenging data unearthed by himself and his psychical-research colleagues up to that time (Myers, 1895). We encourage readers to study this short but illuminating document before proceeding further here, taking particular note of the role played in it by a "World Soul" of some sort. What exactly Myers meant by that expression is anything but clear (see Gauld, 1968, pp. 305–312, and the Epilogue in Myers, 1903, Vol. 2), but it almost certainly derives from the metaphysics of Plotinus—"the eagle soaring above the tomb of Plato" (Myers, 1903, Vol. 1, p. 120)—with whose works Myers was intimately familiar, and whom he regarded as a paragon of human genius.

James of course was thoroughly conversant with Myers's model, and he deliberately and approvingly applied it to his own later work on religious experience and metaphysics. That influence was already apparent in the 1897 Ingersoll lecture, noted in Chapters 3 and 4 above, where he suggested that the mental reality behind the brain might conceivably take forms ranging from a finite mind or personality to some sort of World Soul or mother-sea of consciousness. Subsequently, in the *Varieties*, James was explicit as to how Myers's model enabled him to provide pragmatically useful and theoretically unified explanations for all the major forms of religious experience—including mystical experience, "the vital chapter from which the other chapters get their light." In his Conclusions, however, he was careful to add that these explanations mainly involved incursions into supraliminal conscious life from what he calls the "hither side" of Myers's subliminal consciousness, which is in some sense adjacent to or continuous with it, while what might lie on the "farther side" of that larger spiritual realm—the "more"—remains largely unknown (James, 1902, pp. 507–519; these magnificent concluding pages have also been included in the supplemental materials for this chapter). How shall we conceive the nature and organization of that larger something within?

In *A Pluralistic Universe*, James (1909/1971) delivered on a promise first made in his postscript to the *Varieties*, setting forth in general terms his sense of the right sort of answer—specifically, a "pluralistic panpsychism" along lines originally suggested by the polymath scientist and mystic Gustav Fechner, to whose metaphysics he devotes an entire chapter. The facts of ordinary psychology, together with those of psychopathology, psychical research, and mystical experience, established for James a "decidedly *formidable* probability" in favor of such a view: "[T]he drift of all the evidence we have seems to me to sweep us very strongly towards the belief in some form of superhuman life with which we may, unknown to ourselves, be co-conscious" (p. 268, italics in the original).

Fechner himself, relying upon a profusion of intensely concrete analogies sensitive to both similarities and differences between the things he was comparing, had constructed a speculative metaphysics (his "daylight view") according to which vaster orders of mind accompany vaster orders of bodies, from the earth itself to the solar system, to whole galaxies, and ultimately to the universe as a whole, which for him constituted the body of a highest-order, unimaginably powerful, all-encompassing mind. James greatly admired this "thick" and experience-driven approach to metaphysics, and encouraged by Fechner (and by Bergson, who helped him overcome certain "logical scruples" which had prevented him from moving in this direction sooner), he goes on to picture our co-conscious life as having a complex internal structure of its own, taking the form of a hierarchy of progressively more comprehensive *integrations* of the consciousnesses appearing at lower levels.

We emphasize here that James's concept of integration involves far more than mere *summation*. Again following Fechner, James (1909/1971) likens it to what we find in our own everyday experience: just as the meaning of a sentence is something above and beyond a summation of the meanings of its constituent words, our mind is not the bare sum of our sights plus our sounds plus our pains, but in adding these terms together also finds relations among them and weaves them into schemes and forms and objects of which no one sense in its separate estate knows anything. . . . It is as if the total universe of inner life had a sort of grain or direction, a sort of valvular structure permitting knowledge to flow in one way only, so that the wider might always have the narrower under observation, but never the narrower the wider. (p. 202)

The evidence Myers had assembled in support of his theory of the Subliminal Self played a major role in convincing James that this phenomenon of "compounding of consciousness" is an empirical reality. He also recognized that in combination with evidence from the worldwide history of mysticism it held the key to arriving at a more satisfying kind of metaphysics than the various forms of absolute idealism which prevailed at that time. In general terms, referring again to Myers's 1895 diagram and pursuing James's lead, one can now readily imagine one or more additional dotted circles of larger diameter interpolated between the farther side of the Subliminal Self and the "World Soul," and foresee the possibility of linking these somehow with the higher states of consciousness disclosed by the world's mystical traditions.[19]

A strong sympathy to the mystical pervaded Myers's thinking as well, but this rarely found overt expression in his *scientific* writings. His central aim there was rather to provide empirical justification for distinguishing between two levels of *personal* individuation—the "supraliminal self," corresponding to the ego or everyday personality, and the deeper and more comprehensive "Subliminal Self," corresponding to a true Self or Individuality.[20] The Subliminal Self of course is what Myers believed survives bodily death, and in the 1895 paper he initially advanced a characterization of mystical states that seems to terminate his own conception of "the more" at this same level: "True ecstasy I regard as a condition where the centre of consciousness changes from the supraliminal to the subliminal self, and realises the transcendental environment in place of the material" (pp. 567–568).

As we have already seen, Myers's final diagram in that same paper incorporates a somewhat mysterious reference to a Plotinian "World Soul" situated at a level still higher and more inclusive than that of the Subliminal Self. But in the system of Plotinus even that level is ontologically derivative from Intellect and the One (Chapter 8), and of course a central historical tendency of the Indian philosophical tradition, as sketched in Chapters 9 and 10, is to identify the deepest level of the individual human self with a universal self or source of all—*Brahman* or *Śiva*. Myers's own contemporary Edward Carpenter (1912), who himself had experienced high mystical states, seems like all the great mystics including Plotinus to strain toward that ultimate level:

> Of all the hard facts of Science . . . I know of none more solid and fundamental than the fact that if you inhibit thought (and persevere) you come at length to a region of consciousness below or behind thought, and different from ordinary thought in its nature and character—a consciousness of quasi-universal quality and a realisation of an altogether vaster self than that to which we are accustomed. (p. 79)

But how far up have the mystics reached, really? How far up does James's hierarchy extend, and what lies at the top?

EMPIRICAL INTERLUDE: SOME EVIDENCE SUGGESTIVE OF HIGHER-LEVEL MIND

James saw Myers's argument for the Subliminal Self as a kind of "existence proof" for the compounding of consciousness, justifying his direct leap with Fechner into the central metaphysical issue of their time and ours. We will return to that subject shortly, but we would be remiss if we did not first briefly pause to take note of some additional *empirical* indications, relatively tentative but definitely meriting further investigation, of possible levels of psychic integration situated above (and below) that of individual human beings. Here we will simply identify a number of reported phenomena of relevant types, without attempting to document or discuss them in any detail, in hopes that others may be encouraged to look into these with the greater care and thoroughness that they deserve and will certainly require.[21]

First are some cases in which unusual forms of subliminal collaboration seemed to be required for production of artistic effects. One of these concerns James Merrill and his partner David Jackson, who jointly produced one of the masterpieces of twentieth-century poetry, *The Changing Light at Sandover*, using a Ouija board operated with an inverted coffee cup (see *IM*, pp. 446–447). The flow of writing produced in this way seemed to outstrip in quality what either man could accomplish on his own, and it ceased the instant either took his finger off the cup. Similar types of creative partnership can be found in the collaboration of William Butler Yeats with his wife Georgie, and in many legendary accounts of telepathic and psychokinetic interactions during famous jazz-group improvisation sessions.

Related phenomena have often been reported by psychical researchers. From her monumental studies of crisis apparitions, for example, Eleanor Sidgwick (1962) concluded that the canonical type or norm of telepathic interaction consists not of some sort of signal *transmission* between isolated minds, but of a kind of *diffusion* of information between minds that are partially united at some deep level, thinking and feeling together behind the scenes (pp. 419–423). G. N. M. Tyrrell (1953) advanced similar ideas in attempting to account for the intricate cross-observer coordination of reported experience in cases of collective and reciprocal apparitions. Similarly, starting from his studies of the survival evidence, Gardner Murphy (1945) proposed a "field" theory of human personality, according to which we are not as individualized as we normally seem to ourselves to be, but operate continuously in the context of a shared background, an interpersonal network or "group mind," with influences occasionally leaking in both directions.[22] Authors such as A. R. G. Owen and Kenneth Batcheldor have also written extensively about apparent group-level subliminal cooperative dynamics in the production of macro-PK effects.

Psychic functioning in general seems often to imply or require some sort of overlap of minds, or even a "big mind" or "mind at large" that sees and thinks and feels beyond the ordinary limitations of time and space, and which can directly make things happen in the physical world (Stokes, 1987). Something of this sort may also conceivably underlie at least some of the many known cases of simultaneous invention, even after allowance for relevant cultural and situational factors (Ogburn & Thomas, 1922). Jung's collective unconscious was postulated specifically to explain the recurrent appearance, throughout history and across widely divergent cultural settings, of "archetypal" motifs and symbols, and although he initially conceived it in strictly biological terms as associated with the human nervous system, a cumulative product of biological evolution, it later assumed a "psychoid" form associated with the ontological substratum of the Pauli–Jung model—the *unus mundus*. Similarly, the Plotinian

Nous or Intellect, like the cosmic *buddhi* or *mahat* of Sāṃkhya, can be viewed as a kind of collective mind in which individual minds participate.

Another relevant phenomenon involves super-complicated or large-scale synchronicities which appear to exceed the capacity of any single identifiable human agent to produce, and which thus suggest the involvement of some larger or more powerful agent in nature that takes an interest in the outcome (Beitman, 2014; Greyson, 2010). Perhaps the most extreme of all such "coincidences" involves the simultaneous setting of various basic physical constants to the very precise values they need to have in order for life even to be possible on earth—the "Anthropic Principle."

Conceptual difficulties arise here analogous to those underlying the interminable survival vs. superpsi debates in psychical research (see *IM*, pp. 595–599): in particular, how could we determine with confidence where the boundary lies between psi-like synchronicities attributable to single human agents and synchronicities that require more complex forms of explanation, and how could we be sure that a higher-level "agent" or "group mind" actually exists, perhaps with its own center of perspective or "I-sense"? We note in passing that synchronicities provided one of the principal motivations for the Pauli–Jung model of Chapter 6, and also that the "quasi-orthodox" interpretation of quantum theory introduced by Henry Stapp in Chapter 5 (especially his proposed modification of the role of von Neumann's "Process 3") provides another possible way of explaining such phenomena—i.e., by thinking of complex synchronicities as responses on the part of nature to intense emotional needs or desires of the participants. Of course we would then also have to explain why so many seemingly equally deserving needs and desires *fail* to produce such responses.

The same approach might extend to some fairly well-documented "mass phenomena," such as the Marian visions at Lourdes, Zeitoun, and Medjugorje, and the worldwide 1995 Hindu Ganesh milk miracle, all of which were protracted or recurring and hence accessible to investigation. It also seems potentially capable of explaining the notorious "goal-directedness" of psi—for example the apparent indifference of micro-PK to seeming complexities such as the number, character, and spatial or temporal location of the REGs which control the display presented to the subject (Schmidt & Pantas, 1972).

We should also note in passing that similar issues about possible group-mind aspects have arisen in connection with phenomena such as "swarm intelligence," as exemplified in the astonishing murmurations of starlings, schooling of fish, and the like. Serious efforts are underway to explain these observed behaviors mechanistically as "subjectless processes" mediated entirely by local interactions among individual members, but to our knowledge these have so far met with only limited success.

It is also worth noting in this connection that there is an increasing amount of direct evidence for what might be termed the "protomentality" that observers such as Peirce believed could be recognized in lower species, extending down through the animal kingdom and even to creatures without nervous systems such as one-celled organisms of various kinds, and perhaps even plants. Recent work on plants using time-lapse photography, for example, shows them behaving in ways much like those that lead us to attribute conscious intelligence to mammals, but on a longer time-scale—perhaps a different "specious present" in the sense of Chapter 7 above? Further work along these lines seems to us potentially capable both of providing further evidence against conventional brain-based production theories of mind and of directly exploring how far down in nature conscious mentality may actually penetrate. We emphasize, however, that such views remain for the moment highly speculative, and that much more work will need to be done before any firm conclusions can be drawn.

Most of the poorly understood phenomena scouted in this empirical interlude, as well as the broader issues central to this chapter, fit naturally within a framework set forth by William James (1909/1986) himself in his last published essay, and we can do no better in ending this section than to quote in full this magnificent final statement as how things looked to him:

> Out of my experience, such as it is (and it is limited enough) one fixed conclusion dogmatically emerges, and that is this, that we with our lives are like islands in the sea, or like trees in the forest. The maple and the pine may whisper to each other with their leaves, and Conanicut and Newport hear each other's fog-horns. But the trees also commingle their roots in the darkness underground, and the islands also hang together through the ocean's bottom. Just so there is a continuum of cosmic consciousness, against which our individuality builds but accidental fences, and into which our several minds plunge as into a

mother-sea or reservoir. Our 'normal' consciousness is circumscribed for adaptation to our external earthly environment, but the fence is weak in spots, and fitful influences from beyond leak in, showing the otherwise unverifiable common connexion. Not only psychic research, but metaphysical philosophy and speculative biology are led in their own ways to look with favor on some such 'panpsychic' view of the universe as this. Assuming this common reservoir of consciousness to exist, this bank upon which we all draw, and in which so many of earth's memories must in some way be stored, or mediums would not get at them as they do, the question is, What is its own structure? What is its inner topography? This question, first squarely formulated by Myers, deserves to be called 'Myers's problem' by scientific men hereafter. What are the conditions of individuation or insulation in this mother-sea? To what tracts, to what active systems functioning separately in it, do personalities correspond? Are individual 'spirits' constituted there? How numerous, and of how many hierarchic orders may these then be? How permanent? How transient? And how confluent with one another may they become?

What again, are the relations between the cosmic consciousness and matter? Are there subtler forms of matter which upon occasion may enter into functional connexion with the individuations in the psychic sea, and then, and then only, show themselves?—So that our ordinary human experience, on its material as well as on its mental side, would appear to be only an extract from the larger psycho-physical world? (pp. 374–375)

The agenda outlined in this summary remains as relevant today, in our opinion, as when James first advanced it. In any case, we will now begin to revisit, with considerable trepidation, the central metaphysical issue that James was attempting to address in *A Pluralistic Universe*.

PLURALISTIC PANPSYCHISM VS. ABSOLUTE IDEALISM: JAMES AND BRADLEY

As early as the *Varieties* James had noted that mystical experiences generally express "a pretty distinct theoretic drift" toward *some* sort of idealist metaphysics, and by the time of *A Pluralistic Universe* he was developing such a metaphysics himself. Above we sketched his approach to pluralistic panpsychism, which amounts essentially to a metaphysical generalization of his detailed and penetrating psychological analyses of human experience and the stream of consciousness. Passing beyond his earlier dualistic outlook, James pictures the only reality we know or can know as consisting entirely of innumerable streams or pulses of experience. Each moment of experience expresses an aboriginal form of manyness in oneness, with multiple elements or aspects of awareness individually present and yet integrated into some sort of higher unity. Similarly, as empirically demonstrated by Myers, the everyday or supraliminal consciousness is simultaneously both itself and part of a higher or more comprehensive consciousness, the Subliminal Self (see *IM*, Chapters 2 and 9).

Encouraged by Myers, Fechner, and Bergson, as described above, James now postulates the existence of still higher-order integrations, expressions of an ongoing, evolving process, the current highest stage of which is a tremendous conscious reality of some sort corresponding to the common person's notion of God. But James's is a finite, incomplete, and imperfect God that falls short of *total* integration and thus has some sort of external environment of its own. This allows, in James's view, both for the possibility of evil that does not originate within God himself, and for the possibility of its eradication over time through the ethically grounded efforts of human beings equipped with free will. That highest-level reality might also be in some respects like us, for example in ignoring, forgetting, or failing to notice things going on at lower levels, thus affording a desirable sort of "intimacy." For all these reasons James prefers his pluralistic doctrine to its main contemporary rival, absolute idealism as conceived by philosophic colleagues such as Royce and Bradley. Their doctrine just cannot be right, James (1909/1971) thinks: its "thin," abstract, timeless, static, all-encompassing and already perfect One—"the unintelligible pantheistic monster" (p. 271)—seems to him an abominable and alien fiction remote from real experience, the pernicious result of abstract intellectualizing unconstrained by empirical data.

James originally expressed these views in the context of his 1909 Hibbert lectures at Oxford, where the powerful nineteenth-century idealist current was beginning to weaken but still ran strong. Explicitly declining even to discuss other existing alternatives such as the already nascent materialist picture and traditional scholastic or "monarchical" theisms, both of which he clearly regarded as untenable, he contrasts his pluralistic panpsychism with Oxford-style absolute idealism as the two principal candidates for what we humans most urgently need—an essentially spiritual view of Reality that is not in conflict with science. Describing the aesthetic and ethical aversions indicated above (with which we strongly sympathize) as merely "sentimental" objections, James (1909/1971) goes on to attack the absolutists' position at its philosophical core. On their view the world is not a vast collection of variably interrelated facts but one all-inclusive fact which exists by virtue of being the known of an all-thinker. The absolute and the world are identical in content and "compenetrate and soak each other up without residuum" (p. 139). The absolutists believe they can prove that the world *must* ultimately be this way: "The great claim of the philosophy of the absolute is that the absolute is no hypothesis, but a presupposition implicated in all thinking, and needing only a little effort of analysis to be seen as a logical necessity" (pp. 146–147). But James proceeds to examine this central philosophical claim more closely, providing fairly detailed technical dissections of the arguments of absolutists such as Lotze, Royce, Bradley, and Hegel, and finds it *not* in fact coercive. The absolute is not proven, he concludes, but merely a possibility, a *hypothesis* as to the ultimate nature of Reality, on par with his own and subject to the same sorts of empirical constraints.

The most exhaustive and rigorous evaluation known to us of the arguments on both sides of this debate is that provided by philosopher Timothy Sprigge (1983, 1993, 2006), who describes himself as having spent his entire career attempting to decide between the views of F. H. Bradley and those of the person he regards as Bradley's most effective critic—William James. We highly recommend this work to readers interested in pursuing the voluminous and intricate details of the respective positions in greater depth. Sprigge himself ends up siding mostly with Bradley, and in his 1983 defense of absolute idealism he specifically points out its close kinship with what he considers to be the idealist monism of Advaita Vedānta, a philosophy touched upon in Chapter 10 above.[23] For several reasons, however, we think his decision in favor of Bradley was premature. First, whereas he shares with Bradley a presupposition that abstract reasoning is capable of leading on its own to a full and correct grasp of the ultimate nature of Reality, we share with James a deep distrust of that presupposition. We are reminded here of the case of Thomas Aquinas, who had already produced several volumes of the *Summa Theologica* when he had a mystical experience so profound that he ceased writing altogether and declared his previous efforts "nothing but straw . . . compared to what I have seen and what has been revealed to me" (Pieper, 1965, pp. 38–41), thus exemplifying the relative valuation of gnostic experience vs. reason within the world's mystical traditions. Perhaps more to the point, despite the fact that Sprigge (1993) proclaims the core logic of Bradley's monism *"inexorable"* (p. 581), few others have found it so. Unaided theoretical reason has never yet banished differences of opinion on such profound matters, and it probably never will.

Both Sprigge and Bradley also seem to us less interested than they should be, and certainly far less so than James, in relevant empirical data, including in particular the data of psychical research. Sprigge (1993), perhaps having absorbed an initially negative attitude toward psychical research directly from Bradley, greatly underestimates its role and force in shaping James's thought. Indeed, he seems in that book to find James's deep involvement with such work somewhere between puzzling and embarrassing, and his summary description of that involvement (p. 251) is mostly misleading and inaccurate. Even in his last book, Sprigge (2006) shows surprisingly little awareness of the existing empirical evidence for postmortem survival (p. 527) and rebirth (p. 520), despite having acknowledged by now its potential relevance to his philosophic concerns. Even more poignantly, perhaps, he laments the fact that none of his idealist predecessors paid sufficient attention to the literature of mystical experience, while neglecting to acknowledge that he is guilty of the same omission (pp. 541–542).

Sprigge (1993) was understandably most concerned with *differences* between James and Bradley, but he also makes clear that they have a great deal in common, and in this respect he may actually have understated the case. The deep resemblance of Bradley's views both to James's and to views expressed in Chapters 11, 12, and 13 above is highlighted in the concluding comments of Candlish and Basile (2013):

> [A] Leibnizian strand pervades Bradley's philosophy, one which finds expression in his doctrine of finite centres of experience. On this view, the Absolute articulates itself in a plurality of lesser sentient wholes, unified psychic individuals of the nature of the human soul. Bradley thus comes close to holding something very like a theory of monads, yet this is incorporated within the general framework of his monistic metaphysics. Interestingly, the doctrine of the Absolute can be seen as a solution to the problem of monadic interaction; like Leibniz's monads, Bradley's finite centres are incapable of a direct sharing of con-

tent . . . and of causal interaction; however, they are coordinated to one
another in that they are all partial manifestations of the same overarching Reality.

Candlish and Basile go on to point out that later British metaphysicians
including Whitehead drew principally upon Leibniz rather than Kant and
Hegel, and of course Whitehead (1938/1968) himself credits James, "that
lovable genius," as his immediate precursor (p. 3). It should also be
evident that the postulated "coordination" could in principle account for
many apparent psi-like phenomena in a manner similar to that suggested
by Henry Stapp in Chapter 5.

Despite these deep similarities between James and Bradley, significant
differences remain, the most critical of which for our purposes here are
their respective attitudes toward *time* and *free will*. For Bradley, the rationalist, what is ultimately real is the eternal Absolute, to which all
experience past, present, and future is simultaneously present. The idea
that time is real and the future genuinely open therefore seems an illusion,
along with that of genuinely free will. For James, the empiricist, lived
experience in the world of temporal becoming is the ultimate reality, and
purposeful actions of his human players are both needed and not fully
determined. [24] Our "sentiments" once again gravitate toward the Jamesian
side, but as we will next explain, additional *empirical* considerations
come into play here that may ultimately prove more decisive.

THEORETICAL INTERLUDE: PRECOGNITION, FREE WILL, AND TIME

For James and Whitehead, as well as for contemporary orthodox quantum
theory (Chapter 5), the future is unformed, yet to take shape, undeter-
mined, or "open" (apart from its conditioning by whatever exists *now* in
the form of objective tendencies of various kinds), and we humans help to
determine what subsequently happens through exercise of our genuine
capacities for voluntary action—our free will. [25]

This humanly appealing picture appears to be challenged, however, by
empirical phenomena such as "true precognition" (Chapter 1) and the
eternal or outside-of-time aspects of deep mystical experiences (Chapter
2), for these converge with metaphysical systems like Bradley's in sug-

gesting that the future in some sense already exists, and this in turn seems at least naively to put the possibility of free will in doubt.

Here we will attempt to sketch in very compressed form our provisional sense of a possible pathway through these extremely difficult and intertwined issues, about which so much has already been written, anchoring our discussion to precognition because of its relatively clear-cut empirical character.[26]

Of particular importance in this connection is the work of philosopher David Ray Griffin (1993, 1997, 1998). Griffin is one of the chief modern advocates of Whitehead's process metaphysics, and in addition he takes psi phenomena including postmortem survival and rebirth very seriously, viewing them as potentially explainable by, and supportive of, this metaphysics.

There is one glaring exception however: "true precognition" Griffin regards as strictly *impossible*. For him a cause cannot follow its effects in time, period, and this is an analytic truth rooted in our most basic scientific ideas about time and efficient causation. The precognitive dream that I had last night cannot be caused by a corresponding future event simply because that future event does not yet exist, and hence cannot serve in that capacity. Furthermore, as argued particularly by his fellow philosopher Stephen Braude (1986), the concept of *retrocausation*, which both regard as necessarily implicated in the possibility of true precognition, proves on closer examination to be anything but a simple mirror image of the ordinary concept of forward-in-time causation, and ultimately unsustainable (pp. 256–277).

What then about the evidence for precognition? Well, what we really have, on Griffin's view, is only evidence of "apparent" precognition, and this *must* be explainable in other ways. Griffin (1993) goes on to marshal no less than thirteen alternative possibilities that he regards as collectively capable, singly or in variable combinations, of explaining away *all* of the evidence we have.[27]

We do not doubt that much of the ostensible evidence for true precognition is potentially subject to alternative explanations of these sorts, but much remains, in our opinion, that cannot be dismissed in this way, as detailed especially in the supplemental materials for Chapter 1. Despite Griffin's somewhat desperate and theory-driven efforts to deny it, true precognition seems to be a real empirical phenomenon. But what does this imply in regard to free will?

Current mainstream scientific opinion of course holds that there is no reason to have this discussion, because free will is already known to be an illusion, as shown for example by Wegner (2002) and Harris (2012). The substantially overlapping arguments in these (and other) books, however, seem to us deeply flawed. To begin, both rely heavily on an antiquated concept of determinism inherited from classical physics: thus Wegner's (2002) book opens by quoting the famous depiction by Laplace in 1814 of the clockwork universe, as if that were the scientifically proper view of things, and Harris simply declares, also incorrectly, that "we *know* that determinism, in every sense relevant to human behavior, is true" (p. 16, italics added).

Both also argue in effect that either we consciously author all of our actions voluntarily or we author none of them, and since there have been many experimental demonstrations of actions or behaviors that are not consciously authored, there can be no free will. This argument, however, is unsound: everyone by now acknowledges that much of our ongoing behavior is determined in part or even in whole by genetic, developmental, neurophysiological and/or psychological factors of various kinds of which we are typically unaware. The crucial question is not whether *all* actions are truly voluntary, which is certainly not the case, but whether *any* are.

Such a capacity would most readily become evident, of course, in situations where persons initiate and sustain actions that are contrary to all identifiable factors of such sorts, and possibly even contrary to their own survival. From this point of view the widely cited experiments of Benjamin Libet are simply irrelevant; they utilize an impoverished experimental model of voluntary action, and in any case their results have been interpreted in a variety of mutually inconsistent ways. For further details, see the review of Wegner's book by Kelly (2003). We also recommend here the argument of Griffin (1998) that free will constitutes one of the essential elements of what he terms "hard-core common sense"—principles that we must inevitably presuppose in practice for the proper regulation of our lives, denial of which results in performative contradictions (pp. 16–45). Note that this principled argument goes well beyond the usual sort of casual appeal to garden-variety "common sense" as justification for whatever we would like to be the case.

Currently available arguments both for and against free will are not compelling, in our opinion, but for present purposes we will assume its reality as a probable contributor to at least some ongoing behavior, and return to the question of possible implications for free will of true precognition.

Readers may recall from Chapter 1 and its supplemental material that Myers (1895) had found some cases in which timely "intervention" appeared to have forestalled the occurrence of precognized evils of some sort (see for example the case of the falling coachman, who died in the precognitive dream but not in actuality). Myers himself interpreted such cases as demonstrating both the reality of free will and its capacity to alter the future, but this conclusion was certainly premature. The key landmark here is a valuable paper by Louisa Rhine (1955), for which she scoured both her own large case collection and much of the older literature in search of possible examples of successful intervention. Even the three best cases she was able to find (not including Myers's coachman case, incidentally) could potentially be explained alternatively by assuming that only part of the original experience was a direct, psi-mediated, and literally correct perception of the future event, while the crucial remainder, the averted part, might have been supplied consciously or unconsciously by the percipient, as commonly happens in cases of approximately contemporaneous telepathy or clairvoyance (p. 30).[28]

More and better cases are certainly needed, but meanwhile we will now go on to sketch an alternative way of thinking about free will in relation to precognition, one that takes true precognition as an "ultra-revolutionary" phenomenon in precisely the way that Griffin and Braude had hoped to avoid by successfully dismissing it in the context of conventional ideas about causation and time.

Specifically, we consider it possible that the future could be *determinate*—existing, and hence potentially accessible to precognition—and yet not *determined*, in the sense that it is not an inevitable, causal consequence of what preceded it, with no place for free will. Such pictures go back through Thomas Aquinas at least to Boethius in the early sixth century CE, and a version of it is in fact developed in some detail by Sprigge (2006, pp. 491–496) in the context of his form of absolute idealism. The basic idea is that from the point of view of an eternal absolute, standing as it were outside of time, past and future would look essentially the same in terms of free will. That is, what we experience phenomenally as a world progressively unfolding in time would be experienced simultaneously or noumenally by that larger consciousness, with free will contributing equally to all of its parts.

The key point here is that James probably did not have to fear that all forms of an absolute are necessarily hostile to free will. A picture such as Sprigge's not only circumvents the real theoretical problems associated with retrocausation conceived in conventional terms (Braude, 1986), but potentially also secures (admittedly in more counterintuitive fashion) what James himself most wanted—the possibility of amelioration of evil through the ethically guided actions of human agents equipped with free will.[29]

In terms of precognition itself, the basic picture emerging here is that information about the future is potentially available at some higher or highest level of Jamesian "integration," and can express itself in the usual ways via automatism or subliminal uprush, possibly in distorted or disguised form, in supraliminal waking or dreaming consciousness. Multiple levels could conceivably be involved, as for example in the hyperdimensional model of Chapter 7, where higher consciousnesses with expanded "specious presents" may be associated with higher "actuality planes" of the Universal Structure. The common occurrence in conjunction with NDEs of rapid or instantaneous "life reviews" (which sometimes also include life "previews"—Bruce Greyson, personal communication) seems potentially consistent with a picture of this sort.

If this section has accomplished nothing else, we hope it has made clear the potentially decisive theoretical importance of precognition, while exposing some of the uncertainties that remain. The evidence for true precognition cannot be cavalierly dismissed, but its theoretical implications are profoundly puzzling and difficult to assimilate. It would be hard to overstate the desirability of more and better documentation of cases of this sort, and especially of the rich spontaneous precognitions that sometimes accompany deep near-death and mystical experiences.

BEYOND CLASSICAL THEISM AND PANTHEISM: PANENTHEISM AS TERTIUM QUID

The debate between William James and the absolute idealists forms just one particularly relevant chapter in the much larger historical contest between *classical theism* and *pantheism*. Both come in many related forms, and each sometimes contains elements more characteristic of the other, but in general the theistic positions posit some sort of highest being or personal God who created the world that we inhabit and know, but who remains ontologically and perhaps functionally separate from it, whereas pantheisms equate divinity ontologically with nature or the experienced world itself. The Abrahamic faiths are of course the principal world-historical exemplars of classical theism, while Bradley and Sprigge exemplify modern philosophical pantheism, deriving from Spinoza, and James falls somewhere in between.

Here we call upon a landmark work by Hartshorne and Reese (1953/2000), which systematically samples the history of serious and disciplined thought about the central religious questions as to the existence and character of God. Drawing upon selections from some fifty major thinkers, both Eastern and Western and from ancient to modern times, they construct what amounts to a systematic exposition and defense of *panentheism*—a third point of view, or tertium quid—which attempts to overcome the historical polarization between classical theism and pantheism, and which for them represents the culmination of millennia of philosophical theology.

Panentheism's supreme being paradoxically absorbs into itself, or into separate aspects of itself, the various ultimate polarities that previous theisms and pantheisms have projected onto their conceptions of God in a more one-sided manner—polarities such as eternal vs. temporal, being vs. becoming, spiritual vs. corporeal, simple vs. compound, necessary vs. contingent, absolute vs. relative, potential vs. actual, and one vs. many. The panentheistic God is characterized by five defining properties: it is conceived as both eternal *and* temporal, conscious, knowing of the world, and world-inclusive (see the powerful Introduction by Charles Hartshorne for details). God fills the world, as in pantheism, but there is also something left over, as in theism. God thus is to the world roughly as we are to our bodies, and note here the striking metaphysical parallel to the move that Myers made in psychology—his own tertium quid—by conceptualizing the psyche as stratified in depth, with the deeper part, the Subliminal Self, more inclusive. Hartshorne and Reese's (1953/2000) extensive treatments of Fechner and James are also highly relevant to our purposes here, demonstrating clearly that Fechner was not the "lazy absolutist" that James thought him to be but rather a budding panentheist, and that James himself, whom they classify as a "limited panentheist," could have ar-

rived at a full-fledged panentheism much like Whitehead's had only he
exercised his own basic principles a little more vigorously (for the details
of these marvelous selections and commentaries, see pp. 243–257 for
Fechner, and pp. 335–352 for James).

Panentheism itself is not a single, unified, fully articulated doctrine,
but a family of related doctrines occupying two principal historical
branches—classical or static forms, and modern or dynamic forms explicitly tied to the concept of evolution. It seems to be gaining traction in
theological circles (Clayton & Peacocke, 2004; Cooper, 2006), and the
recent book by Biernacki and Clayton (2014) shows clearly that all of the
world's major faiths already contain significant panentheistic themes or
elements.[30]

Particularly in its modern evolutionary forms it also appears more
compatible with *science* than any previous theological position, as argued
in particular by Clayton and Peacocke (2004), and it is this aspect that we
wish to emphasize here. With all due respect, we think these authors have
considerably understated the case: whereas their driving impulse seems to
be to reconcile antecedently held theological views with conventional
physicalist science, or something very close to it, our approach is anchored in an expanded vision of science itself, and the more comprehensive empiricism advanced in *IM* and throughout this book carries us much
closer both scientifically and philosophically, we submit, to convergence
with a full-fledged evolutionary panentheism.

The conceptual frameworks canvassed in Part II connect with this
generic panentheistic vision, and with each other, at numerous points.[31]
Most of us have long been attracted to the nondual views of mystical
philosophers such as Plotinus, Śaṅkara, and Abhinavagupta, which share
the fundamental experience-driven recognition of a tremendous consciousness at the source of all manifestation. The Neoplatonism described
in Chapter 8 constitutes the very fountainhead of classical panentheism in
the West, as shown especially by Cooper (2006), and as indicated in
Chapters 9 and 10 a central movement of the Indian philosophical tradition, building upon the Vedic *mahāvākyas* or great sayings with their
identification of *ātman* and *Brahman*, passes from the dualism of classical Sāṃkhya through Advaita Vedānta to the more explicit panentheism
of Abhinavagupta and later figures such as Sri Aurobindo and Radhakrishnan.

Alfred North Whitehead was *the* foundational figure of modern panentheism according to Hartshorne and Reese, and he drew heavily on Plato, Leibniz, and the late work of William James for his inspiration. In his version of a pluralistic panpsychism or panexperientialism, an experiential aspect is present even in the ground-level bits, but the evolutionary emergence is guided throughout by influences flowing downward from God at the highest level—an approach, that is, which is neither purely bottom-up nor purely top-down, but "top-down from the bottom up."

The monadological model advanced by Paul Marshall in Chapter 11 derives directly from Leibniz and naturally shares important features with the Whiteheadian picture and Weiss's adaptation of it. For both, the world is experiential through and through, and "matter" must ultimately be understood in terms of experience. Both reject conventional physicalist atomism and mechanism and view the basic units of nature instead as experiential, active, constantly evolving or becoming, extensively interconnected, and coordinated (Leibniz) or influenced in a top-down manner by God. Both distinguish compounds or organisms from aggregates by virtue of the presence in the former of higher-level unifying centers (Leibniz's dominant monads or Whitehead's presiding occasions), both use their postulated forms of interconnectedness to explain receptive psi, and both conceive of expressive psi or PK as a kind of "mind over mind," there being no such thing as matter as classically conceived. The inverted Leibnizian monadic model also fits well with the central thrust of evolutionary panentheism, in that its subliminally omniscient monads evolve ever more sophisticated organismic bodies and minds, thus opening up the possibility of conscious integration of their inherent subliminal nature with the evolving supraliminal mind or self.

There are important differences, however, as well. Each "windowless" neo-Leibnizian monad fully represents the cosmic whole within itself, including all other monads and all of spacetime, both past and future, whereas standard Whiteheadian actual occasions relate more "externally" to other occasions through the process of selective "prehension," and only to occasions that lie in their past. Receptive psi and the factors which limit it are thus conceptualized in somewhat different ways: in the original Whiteheadian picture each occasion is potentially connected to every other occasion in its past light-cone, and the final experiential outcome or "concrescence" reflects a combination of positive (incorporative) and negative (eliminative) prehensions—a sort of filtering process. In Paul

Marshall's "inverted" monadic model with its subliminally omniscient monads, by contrast, all the needed information is already within, but (as in Myers's model) errors and disguises creep in as it makes its way to the surface.

Charles Sanders Peirce (Chapter 12) is for us an important transitional figure. Grounded in science, like Whitehead, he insists on the need for metaphysics to be based upon empirical evidence and accepts the reality of supernormal phenomena. He emphasizes the continuity of mind, like Leibniz, and portrays matter as habit-sodden mind, possessing only the barest residue of freedom and spontaneity. His Law of Mind assures connectivity among related ideas, forms the basis of personality while breaking down its apparent isolation from others, and opens a path to transpersonal community and higher forms of mind. He sees the universe as progressively unfolding in accordance with a principle of evolutionary love, cooperatively shaped by us and a necessary highest being of some unfathomable sort that is somehow simultaneously eternal and unchangeable yet engaged in a process of becoming, expressing itself temporally in the profusion of manifest forms in nature. He would surely endorse the opinion of Hartshorne and Reese (1953/2000, pp. 258–269), who classify him explicitly as a modern panentheist.

In Chapter 13 and his associated book, Eric Weiss builds upon Whitehead's basic panentheistic vision, drawing in addition upon the work of the modern mystic and philosopher Sri Aurobindo, to show how it can potentially accommodate many of our targeted supernormal phenomena including not only mystical states but all forms of psi including precognition. Eric overcomes Griffin's problems with precognition by allowing actual occasions to access the future, mediated by a supreme consciousness which is aware of all temporal manifestations at once, like Sprigge's absolute. The conditions in our normal existence which block or permit such access remain to be determined, but at least it becomes possible in principle, and this brings Eric's model into closer correspondence with the monadological model of Chapter 11, while retaining the strengths of Whitehead's original formulation.

The physics-based models of Chapters 5, 6, and 7 also appear broadly consistent with a panentheistic outlook. Henry Stapp's quasi-orthodox interpretation of quantum theory, for example, with its conception of humans as causally effective agents equipped with free will, and of nature at large as responding to our needs and values in accordance with the principle of sufficient reason, echoes William James in striving for a sense of global order in an evolving Universe to which we meaningfully contribute. Henry does not specifically address the mystical in reaching these views, but there is room for it in the model. He creates a place for the mind or psyche without attempting to describe its structure in any detail, but it can surely have whatever structure independent evidence suggests or requires it to have, including the sort of multilevel and mystically grounded structure argued for by Myers and James. Also important here is his demonstration that this model is potentially capable of explaining many if not all psi phenomena; indeed, we surmise that this feature could ultimately help to establish his as the preferred interpretation of quantum theory.

Building upon the pantheistic metaphysics of Spinoza, and perhaps rationalizing the psychophysical parallelism of Leibniz, the dual-aspect Pauli–Jung model of the mind/brain connection presented by Harald Atmanspacher and Wolfgang Fach in Chapter 6 portrays our mental and physical aspects as epistemic and resulting from decomposition of an underlying holistic ontic domain, rather than emerging by means of composition from some sort of dual-aspect or neutral-monist atomic bits in a single-level ontology. It is an atypical dual-aspect monism in that a third term—the *unus mundus*—both generates and mediates between the two derivatives, but this third term with its cosmic reach also operates in a top-down manner analogous to that of Henry Stapp's "nature" or panentheism's supreme being, and is the crucial factor in the production of anomalous psychophysical correlations. This model also specifically makes room for the mystical with its conception of "acategorial states" (see also Atmanspacher & Fach, 2005), although that aspect of the framework remains to be developed in greater psychophysiological detail, and as shown in Chapter 10 above it has definite affinities with nondual Vedānta and David Bohm's (1980) interpretation of quantum theory. Most importantly for present purposes, Jung scholar Roderick Main (2013, and personal communications) has recognized independently that Jung's analytic psychology implicitly advances a panentheistic metaphysics to undergird his synoptic empiricism.

The "hyperdimensional" model of Bernard Carr (Chapter 7), growing out of relativity and string theory rather than quantum theory, postulates a "Universal Structure," interpretable as a higher-dimensional psychophysical information space, which gives rise to a hierarchical structure of projections to lower-dimensional actualities including the physical world at the lowest level and the complete range of mental worlds at the higher levels. Like Abhinavagupta, Peirce, and Paul Marshall, Bernard blurs or dissolves the usual dichotomies between mind and matter, subjective vs. objective, and internal vs. external. There are also striking similarities between his notion of higher "actuality planes" and Eric Weiss's model of "transphysical worlds," although Bernard unlike Eric regards metrical aspects as crucial throughout. Most importantly, perhaps, and in parallel with James's later elaboration of Myers's model as described above, Bernard's hierarchy of subspaces can also be viewed as a hierarchy of conscious "selves," associated with progressively expanded "specious presents" and leading to what amounts to a universal mind or consciousness at the level of the entire structure.

The physics-based frameworks of Chapters 5 and 7 seem at first sight to have little in common, and this is not surprising given that they arise from theories of the micro domain (quantum theory) and the macro domain (relativity theory) respectively. However, it is widely recognized that any "final" theory of physics will have to amalgamate these domains in some way, and it is conceivable that consciousness may enter physics through this amalgamation. Therefore the two approaches are not necessarily incompatible, and they may turn out to be complementary. It seems significant in this respect, and reminiscent of the role of *Brahman/ātman* or *Śiva* or the One in traditional mystically informed philosophies, that the physics-based models of Chapters 5 to 7 all assign responsibility for some forms of psi to a holistic aspect of reality where everything needed is available—nature, the *unus mundus*, or the Universal Structure.

As we have seen, both the individual models of Part II and the panentheistic vision generically provide room for most or all of the supernormal phenomena catalogued in Chapter 1, and in substantially common ways. This certainly seems promising, but many gaps and details will need to get filled in before we have anything resembling fully developed scientific theories. As we attempt to move in this direction, two general issues will need to be kept in mind.

First, it is not sufficient simply to indicate in general terms how it is that these phenomena can happen—how the world is constructed in such a way as to permit them to happen. We must also explain the specific forms that they take, and why it is that they are typically so rare and fugitive. A theory that can explain any possible happening, without limitations, is empirically vacuous. "Prehension," for example, may in principle connect everything to everything, but explanation of what actually happens must ultimately descend into the details of the positive and negative prehensions or filtering which produce that specific result. Similarly, Henry Stapp's proposed expansion of the role of "nature" through von Neumann's Process 3 is simultaneously exhilarating and terrifying: exhilarating, because it opens up a path toward possible explanations for many things that otherwise look very hard to explain; terrifying, because it does so, at least so far, with essentially no constraints. Lurking in the background here also is the perennial problem of theodicy, that is, of explaining why it is that a supposedly benign agency of such immense power would be unable or unwilling to prevent or cure the manifest and pervasive evils of our contemporary world.

Second, we will need to defuse the charge that in moving toward panentheism we are simply being metaphysically self-indulgent, building into the system from the beginning what we want to get out of it in the end. The general form of many of the proposed explanations of supernormal phenomena, for example, is to say that a more comprehensive and capable mind or consciousness explains them. Thus the "measly trickle" of everyday consciousness with its unified character, qualitative feels, and subjective point of view is simply a pale and contracted reflection, possibly through multiple stages, of properties postulated to be inherent in the tremendous consciousness at the source of all manifestation. The best way to counter such objections, we submit, is to show through further research that the powers of consciousness do in fact expand, as predicted by the ROSTA perspective, in the context of higher states. Such research will simultaneously address the complementary issue, also generic to that perspective, that we need to know more than we presently do about the nature of the "limiting factors" that produce the normal contraction.

To recapitulate: some form of idealistic evolutionary panentheism has emerged as our central theoretical tendency, driven both by advances in philosophical theology and by the expanded empiricism advocated in *IM* and throughout this book. Such views have been out of favor for a long time, to be sure. However, they have never been disproven or shown to be fatally flawed in some way, but rather were simply brushed aside by the rising tide of twentieth-century physicalism and its accompanying technological triumphs. But now classical physicalism has encountered its own limits, and something radically different must take its place.

As we have struggled throughout the Sursem project to achieve a sense of what that "something" might be—an approximately correct picture of the general character of Reality—we have now advanced two primary claims: First—and we have regarded this as axiomatic from the beginning—serious metaphysical thinking or theorizing cannot hope to succeed unless it builds upon an adequate empirical foundation, one that includes the rogue phenomena targeted in *IM* and summarized in Chapter 1—especially psi phenomena and mystical experience with their deep interconnections, postmortem survival, and genius in its highest expressions. Second—and this comprises the main conclusion of the present chapter and our book as a whole—we now claim in addition that a rich and worldwide history of efforts toward *abduction* from that sort of broadened empirical foundation points inescapably in the direction of a panentheistic metaphysics of the sort emerging here.[32]

Although our views are converging they have by no means fully converged, and many details and differences of opinion remain to be sorted out, both among ourselves and with respect to the broader picture of modern panentheism as described for example by Clayton and Peacocke (2004) and Cooper (2006). And this is not a bad thing! We have no need or wish to attempt some sort of premature theoretical closure. Conceptual frameworks or theories are essentially stories we make up in order to make subjects of interest intelligible to ourselves in useful ways, conceptual tools that both provide and take away, reveal and conceal, satisfy and frustrate, always unfinished or incomplete and never capable of encompassing Reality in its ultimately mysterious totality. The specific frameworks canvassed here present many illuminating commonalities and complementarities. There is certainly no guaranteed winner among them, but all seem headed in the general direction of modern evolutionary panentheism, and we firmly share the sense, articulated by James in a letter to Leuba, that "*thither lies truth*" (see *IM*, p. 502). We emphasize here that like James we are referring only to a sense of direction, a gradient, and not to a fixed terminus or omega point of some sort.

What we have arrived at so far amounts only to a kind of loose-limbed metaphysical vision, one that not only permits but encourages all of the current theoretical diversity to flourish, and one that we hope will stimulate further discussion and inquiry. To bring it into sharper focus will certainly require further progress on many fronts, both theoretical and empirical, but in keeping with the general orientation of this book we wish to emphasize the latter: although many theoretical issues remain that cannot be resolved on the basis of currently available information, we know how to go about obtaining additional empirical evidence of various relevant sorts, and we see no insuperable obstacles to doing so. We turn next to that.

FURTHER HORIZONS IN RESEARCH AND APPLICATIONS

Mystical experiences, especially the deeper kinds, clearly hold a vital key to further theoretical progress: they cannot be viewed naively and universally as simple photographs of reality, for they are typically conditioned in varying ways and degrees by our multilayered psychic apparatus.[33] But they are not mere subjective hallucinations either, and the deeper ones in particular enable us to encounter or at least glimpse normally hidden properties of the world *as it actually is* (Chapter 2 above).[34] Psi phenomena of all forms, moreover, appear deeply and inescapably intertwined with such experiences, as indicated in Chapter 2 and throughout this book.

Further research on mystical experience, and on the known means of systematically facilitating it—in particular, deep meditation and the major psychedelics—therefore seems of the highest priority, scientifically speaking, affording numerous opportunities for genuinely ground-breaking research. Direct approaches to research on mystical experience should include, in addition to further work on identified historical cases and the associated texts and descriptions, more intensive study of *contemporary* cases, which would afford new possibilities for more penetrating investigation of its causes, consequences, and phenomenological properties. Detailed and penetrating *phenomenological* reports could have important theoretical implications, as illustrated provisionally by the NDE reports of Jourdan (2011), which appear potentially consistent with Bernard Carr's hyperdimensional approach, and by testimony like that of the mystic Thomas Traherne, which seems possibly consistent with Paul Marshall's (2005, p. 260) monadological scheme (although in this latter case, like many other historical cases involving existing documents of one or another sort, the genuine phenomenological content is not easily disentangled from possible doctrinal infusions). We appeal again for more systematic research effort on these core topics, which in principle will expose the structure and topography of "the more" to a fuller and more accurate mapping (thus addressing "the problem of Myers"), and which to us represent the most promising empirical vehicles in sight for further theoretical progress.

Work of the proposed sorts also has potentially enormous *practical* implications for human development and the effective use of human potentials. Transformative practices of numerous types have existed for many thousands of years, emerging under vastly divergent cultural and physical circumstances, and although the practices that have so far appeared must be effective to some degree—or they would not have remained in play—there is no reason to suppose that any one tradition has succeeded in *optimizing* them. There could be many opportunities for technological advance, as already indicated by the discussion in Chapter 4 of psychobiological approaches to understanding and manipulating the resonant-access or permission/filtering properties of the brain. Possibilities already within probable reach include, for example, development of novel biofeedback regimes to support the early stages of meditation practice, and development of a new generation of psychedelics which provides relatively reliable and gentle access to "the more" in a dose-dependent manner. Further work on the psychological and physiological foundations of ROSTA models should result in making the relevant subliminal and transpersonal capacities more widely available both for research *and* for more effective application in human lives, as long foreseen by our colleague Michael Murphy (1992). Psychologists, neuroscientists, philosophers, scholars of religion, and advanced practitioners of all sorts, including scholar-practitioners, can work together productively on these matters, without prior commitment to the metaphysical views advanced here, and they should![35]

CODA

In the Preface and Introduction to this book we expressed our shared conviction, contrary to the recent spate of anti-religious polemics, that *meaningful* reconciliation of science and religion, arguably the two most powerful forces in human history, constitutes the most humanly urgent and potentially consequential task of the present era. We agree with physicist Wolfgang Pauli, who spoke of the attempt to achieve an expanded worldview that embraces both "rational understanding and the mystical experience of unity" as the central "mythos" of our present age (Heisenberg, 1974, p. 38). Furthermore, we believe that to be truly meaningful this "reconciliation" of science and religion must necessarily go beyond uneasy coexistence from within hermetically isolated magisteria to a creative synthesis, taking the form of an enlarged conception of the nature of Reality that is both spiritually satisfying and compatible with science. It seems to us certain that such a synthesis will necessarily involve some sort of mutual transformation of existing forms of religion and science, requiring change on both sides. *Both* science *and* religion, we believe, must evolve.

In this chapter we have sought to identify a viable pathway toward such an enlarged conception, building upon materials assembled earlier in the book. Reverting again to our Lewis and Clark metaphor, we view the emerging science summarized in Chapter 1, the diverse conceptual frameworks surveyed in Part II, and recent work in philosophical theology as complementary scouting expeditions which seem to be converging toward a substantially shared picture of the overall shape and character of the undiscovered country of the mind.

At the core of this emerging common vision stands the conviction expressed by William James in his most mature work, and shared by us, that a tremendous conscious reality of some sort lies at the heart of the world, that we are intimately linked with that reality in the depths of our individual being, and that the universe as a whole is in some sense slowly waking up to itself, partly in conjunction with our conscious human choices and efforts. As Myers (1903) himself put it in the climactic final sentences of his posthumously published masterwork, "That which lies at the root of each of us lies at the root of the Cosmos too. Our struggle is the struggle of the Universe itself; and the very Godhead finds fulfilment through our upward-striving souls" (Vol. 2, p. 277).

This generic panentheist vision remains far from complete at present, but we know how to make further progress, and we feel confident that *something* along these lines will ultimately emerge as a significantly improved scientific *and* metaphysical description of the world we inhabit, a description that enables us for the first time to make real sense of phenomena ranging from psi and mystical experiences to the difficult prob-

lems at the heart of the mind—including consciousness itself, the supreme mystery.

Meanwhile, what matters most here in human terms is the seismic
shift in worldview that this vision entails (and here see also Sprigge,
2006, Chapter 10). Again paraphrasing James, *the world pictured by
panentheism is not just the same old physicalist world with an altered
expression, but a world whose constitution is fundamentally different in
ways that matter to us human beings.*

The vision tentatively arrived at here provides an antidote to the prevailing postmodern disenchantment of the world and demeaning of human possibilities. It not only more accurately and fully describes our
human condition but engenders hope and encourages human flourishing.
It provides reasons for us to believe that freedom is real, that our human
choices matter, and that we have barely scratched the surface of our
human potentials. It also addresses the urgent need for a greater sense of
worldwide community and interdependence, a sustainable *ethos*, by demonstrating that under the surface we and the world are much more extensively interconnected than previously realized. We strongly suspect that
our individual and collective human fates in these exceptionally dangerous and difficult times—indeed, the fate of our precious planet and *all* of
its passengers—may ultimately hinge upon wider recognition and more
effective utilization of the higher states of being that are potentially available to us but largely ignored or even actively suppressed by our postmodern civilization with its strange combination of self-aggrandizing in-
dividualism and fundamentalist tribalisms.

Finally, and again with a certain amount of trepidation, we must say at
least a few words about our sense of the implications of this emerging
vision for traditional religious beliefs. Although Sursem's members all
take seriously the possibility that a tremendous conscious *something* lies
at the heart of Reality, we ourselves do not collectively advocate or
accept the more detailed truth-claims of any existing faith. We surmise
that persons who came to this book with such commitments in place, and
who remain reluctant to abandon them, might at least find their spiritual
lives enriched by taking more seriously the panentheistic currents already
present in their faiths of choice (Biernacki & Clayton, 2014). We certainly do not envision creation of some new meta-faith with its own sacred
books, clergy, and communities! In the end all of us, Sursem members
and readers alike, must decide individually how to integrate the data and

arguments presented here into our ongoing lives. The one thing we should all regard as unacceptable is unyielding and aggressive fundamentalism, whether of the religious or the scientific sort.

Nobody has thought more about the humanly vital matters touched upon in this brief coda than our colleague Mike Murphy, and we turn next to him for concluding reflections.

NOTES

1. Price (1939, p. 341).

2. Although I am nominally the sole author of this chapter, I have had much help from other members of our Sursem group, and in attempting to express as best I can our collective theoretical tendencies I will usually speak in the first person plural. This does not absolve me, however, of responsibility for the defects that remain.

3. A striking parallel to Myers's distinction between "infrared" and "ultraviolet" regions beyond ordinary consciousness can be found in the modern Indian Tantric mystical philosopher Sri Aurobindo, who speaks of the "inconscient" and the "superconscient," respectively. Interestingly, Aurobindo overlapped with Myers at Cambridge and was apparently quite familiar with the early work of the Society for Psychical Research (Kripal, 2012, pp. 486–492).

4. See also the terminological remarks at the beginning of Chapter 4 regarding limitations of the more common "transmission," "permission," and "filter" metaphors.

5. See Crabtree (2014) for discussion of hypnosis in very similar terms. We should also add here that similar "opening" processes may conceivably occur at higher levels of "the more," depending on the character and complexity of its own internal organization. Also, in emphasizing supernormal cognitive capacities and information we do not mean to suggest or imply that *everything* emerging from the subliminal region is thereby automatically good or helpful in some way. Following Myers and James, we conceive the more as containing "a rubbish-heap as well as a treasure-house" (Myers, 1903, Vol. 1, p. 72), and having both "dissolutive" and "evolutive" aspects. "Seraph and snake" abide together in that region (James, 1902, p. 426), and what emerges therefrom must be tested or verified, as in the case of the subliminal uprushes or inspirations of genius (*IM*, Chapter 7).

6. This is essentially the process of "abduction," as originally conceived by Charles Sanders Peirce (Chapter 12). Note also that we are alluding here to "explanation" in a sense appropriate to psychology, *not* the sort of explanation in

terms of deduction from covering laws that figured prominently in early philosophy of the *physical* sciences. What form(s) "explanation" should take in the *human* sciences remains a topic of intense discussion.

7. It seems to be mostly forgotten these days that William James (1890) had argued at length and for similar reasons against the notion of "unconscious mental states" (Vol. 1, pp. 162–175), which he regarded as "the sovereign means for believing what one likes in psychology, and of turning what might become a science into a tumbling-ground for whimsies" (p. 163). Indeed, it was considerations of this sort that led him to embrace Myers's very different theory of a wider consciousness with contents potentially accessible to verification.

8. We thank our electrical engineering colleague Ross Dunseath for help with this section.

9. It is of some historical interest that the principal early pioneer of human EEG research, Hans Berger, was strongly motivated by a spontaneous psi interaction with his sister, which he surmised could potentially be explained by transmission of EEG signals through space (Millett, 2001).

10. Steven Braude (2002) has argued that the OTs are vitiated from the outset by vicious causal loops, but his objections do not appear to take into account the apparently retrocausal effects of wave-function collapse that comprise one of the genuinely strange features of orthodox quantum theory, as described in Chapter 5.

11. A different approach to the selectivity problem arises in connection with David Bohm's (1980) interpretation of quantum theory. According to "holographic" or "holonomic" models of this sort there is no need for anything to travel anywhere, since all of manifest reality is encoded in the smallest bit of the underlying implicate order. Leaving aside technical issues in regard to Bohm's theory, such models have nothing to say about expressive psi, and in the context of receptive psi they do not so much *solve* the selectivity problem as *relocate* it to memory "traces" of an atypical sort. Problems generic to trace theories are discussed in Braude (2002) and *IM*, Chapter 4.

12. Of course some would prefer that the reduction go in the opposite direction. For example, physicist Ed May has argued that apparent PK success in REG experiments might alternatively be explained in terms of precognition, if subjects can somehow become aware that favorable sequences are about to be generated by an REG and initiate trials or runs accordingly (May, Utts, & Spottiswoode, 1995).

13. Physicist Gerhard Wassermann (1993) in fact postulated, based upon then emerging developments in string theory, that ordinary physical bodies have duplicates comprised of extremely light "Shadow Matter," and showed that this could potentially account for most if not all known psi phenomena. His theory, essentially a modern physics-based form of subtle-body theory, failed to gain

traction due to lack of independent evidence for the specific type of shadow matter it requires.

14. Note incidentally that the traditional doctrine according to which a latent subtle energy (*kuṇḍalinī*) rises in parallel to the spinal column through an ordered series of subtle-body centers or plexuses (*cakras*), progressively releasing supernormal abilities and ultimately the highest mystical experiences, amounts to a multistage opening process of the sort anticipated in Note 5 above. See also Marshall (2011).

15. Special thanks to Jeff Kripal for help with this section.

16. Henri Corbin is probably the person most responsible for bringing the term "imaginal" (and the associated concept of a *mundus imaginalis* or imaginal world of myth and symbol that mediates between everyday physical reality and the spiritual world) into scholarly prominence in the modern study of religion, and his work can be traced in part back to Myers. Myers's concept of creative imagination as a "mythopoeic" stratum of the subliminal was picked up by the Swiss psychologist Théodore Flournoy, who deployed it in his studies of the medium Hélène Smith (see *IM*, pp. 448–450, for descriptions of this case and the even better one of Patience Worth), and Flournoy himself was a principal mentor of Carl Jung, who in turn deeply influenced Corbin. All four took seriously the basic concept of higher forms of imagination with increased access to supernormal capacities.

17. See Whitehead (1938/1968, Part III) and *IM*, pp. 633–638. It also seems relevant here that mystical experiences are frequently described as revealing by direct perception that all of nature—including even inanimate objects—is in some way pulsing or boiling with conscious life.

18. See also William James's (1890) arguments against "mind-dust" theories in *The Principles* (Vol. 1, Chapter 6). There is also a question in regard to atomistic/emergentist varieties of panpsychist theorizing whether in principle consciousness can go "all the way down" to the lowest-level physical constituents, or whether that move is blocked by the requirement in quantum theory for entities such as electrons to be strictly indistinguishable.

19. Parenthetically, implications of James's late work for the study of mystical experience have been explored in an excellent book by our Sursem colleague G. William (Bill) Barnard (1997).

20. Jung makes a structurally equivalent distinction between ego and Self. Jung's Self, however, lies within the collective unconscious, which later became the *unus mundus* (Chapter 6), and unlike the Myers–James Subliminal Self it is inherently dark, unconscious, and inaccessible except by way of its symbolic products. Allegiance to this conception caused Jung to describe mystical experiences consistently, and in flagrant contradiction with the first-person reports, as a dimming or darkening of everyday consciousness as it becomes flooded or over-

whelmed by unconscious contents. See also *IM*, pp. 555–558, and Kakar (1994) who argues that Jung's preexisting theoretical commitments rendered him unable to come fully to grips with the Indian mystical/philosophical tradition. Related issues are discussed in Chapter 10 above.

21. Thanks to our colleague Michael Grosso for help with this section.

22. It may also be recalled from Chapter 12 that Charles Sanders Peirce conceived of personality as a "coordination of ideas," a cohesive network of relations operating under the influence of a unified developmental teleology and possessing both individual and collective characteristics, with the collective often assuming the greater importance. Thus he was led to postulate the existence of group minds at various levels, the existence of which he apparently thought could be verified experimentally. Unfortunately, he does not seem to have described in any detail how this might be done. See also the related views of psychologist Raymond Cattell in Hartshorne and Reese (1953/2000, pp. 385–394).

23. We cannot resist noting here the irony that Sprigge was routinely faulted during his lifetime for being at odds with mainstream science, while it now appears that his views are in fact *more* in line than conventional physicalism with emerging developments in physics! Idealism in some form may in fact provide a better metaphysical grounding for science than does physicalism; as Paul Marshall (2005) remarks, "Physics was the route by which mind was excluded from conceptions of the world at large, and physics may be the route by which mind finds its way back in" (p. 278). See also Chapter 5.

24. James, for whom effortful attention is the essential phenomenon of will, rejects the sort of "soft" determinism or compatibilism supported by Bradley and other absolutists. We also feel sure that he would not have been tempted to appeal to the randomness associated with quantum theory as a means of saving free will. Sprigge (1993) greatly overstates the role of chance in James's thinking about free will (p. 577).

25. The process philosopher Charles Hartshorne recognized that the concept of a sharp boundary between the settled past and an open future was threatened by the special theory of relativity (Hartshorne & Reese, 1953/2000, p. 11), but as explained in Chapter 5 a generalized "now" has reappeared in relativistic quantum field theory (RQFT).

26. Special thanks to Bob Rosenberg, Paul Marshall, and Jeff Kripal for help with this difficult section.

27. One kind of counter-explanation particularly emphasized by Braude (1986) seeks to interpret ostensibly precognized events as causally produced through PK on the part of their "precognizers." Note that Henry Stapp's extension of orthodox quantum theory (Chapter 5) attempts to deal with precognition

in a somewhat similar way, but in his case by allowing nature itself to steer the quantum state of the universe toward agreement with the experience.

28. It remains the case, however, that precognition is unique in that precognitions, unlike present- and past-directed psi, could conceivably feed causally into the events precognized and alter them somehow. Whether any such cases actually exist remains at present unclear.

29. Lurking here is a more general issue, which we cannot pursue here, concerning the less-than-ultimate character of space and time as ordinarily experienced, and the inadequacies of previous mechanical-physical models such as Newton's 3-dimensional space and Einstein's 4-dimensional block universe with consciousness crawling though it, vs. idealist conceptions according to which time and space are not independently preexisting fixed "containers" for events, but constructs we necessarily invent in our embodied condition (perhaps involuntarily or automatically, per Kant) to prevent everything from happening all at once in the same place. Sprigge (2006) makes some interesting remarks about these issues, including the relatively greater difficulties he finds in dealing with *space* in panpsychist terms (pp. 440–448).

30. The book by Cooper (2006) provides an excellent historical survey of panentheism, but in the end he rejects it due to his a priori commitment to a traditional Christian theology based on the view of its scripture as "divinely inspired, infallibly true, and authoritative in all that it teaches" (p. 320). Sprigge also does not accept it, but he does not explicitly reject it either; rather, he seems to regard it as a variant of his basic idealist position. See Sprigge (1997, 2006).

31. Thanks to all of our Part II authors for help with the following comparisons.

32. See also Shear (1994) for a similar argument. Related views have recently been advanced by psychologists Max Velmans (2009) and Donald Hoffman (2008), who arrive at them independently and without explicit reliance upon rogue phenomena such as psi and mystical experiences. Jahn and Dunne (2011), for whom laboratory psi research is the starting point, also end up embracing a ROSTA-like viewpoint, but their "source of reality" seems to be a kind of sea of information in which we all are embedded, while consciousness itself is conceived as arising separately, and in the conventional way, from neurophysiological processes occurring within individual, isolated brains (p. 292). We should also point out here that should "subtle matter" prove to exist, our generic panentheism would probably take the form of some sort of synthesis or fusion of the "gamma" and "delta" standpoints of Poortman (1978).

33. See Paul Marshall's article "Mystical Experience and Metaphysics," Esalen Center for Theory & Research, http://www.esalen.org/ctr-archive/bp

34. Interestingly, our scientific members are much more inclined than our humanistic scholars to suppose that the world really *is some way* that we can potentially find out about, at least at a given historical moment.

35. What we also need, of course, is something like a division of the National Institutes of Health specifically devoted to research on mystical and transpersonal experiences, complete with its own fund-raising postage stamp like that of the National Cancer Institute. It provides a sad commentary on the state of modern civilization that the entire worldwide history of psychical research has been funded by something like the cost of one or two trailing-edge military jet fighters.

REFERENCES

Abrams, M. H. (1971). *Natural Supernaturalism: Tradition and Revolution in Romantic Literature*. New York: Norton.

Atmanspacher, H. (2011). Quantum approaches to consciousness. In E. N. Zalta (Ed.), *The Stanford Encyclopedia of Philosophy* (Summer 2011 ed.). Retrieved from http://plato.stanford.edu/archives/sum2011/entries/qt-consciousness/

Atmanspacher, H., & Fach, W. (2005). Acategoriality as mental instability. *Journal of Mind and Behavior, 26*, 181–206.

Atmanspacher, H., Römer, H., & Walach, H. (2002). Weak quantum theory: Complementarity and entanglement in physics and beyond. *Foundations of Physics, 32*, 379–406. doi:10.1023/A:1014809312397

Bacon, F. (1960). *The New Organon and Related Writings* (F. H. Anderson, Ed.). New York: Liberal Arts Press. (Original work published 1620)

Barnard, G. W. (1997). *Exploring Unseen Worlds: William James and the Philosophy of Mysticism*. Albany: State University of New York Press.

Beitman, B. (2014). *Connecting with Coincidence: Synchronicity in Practice*. Manuscript in preparation.

Beloff, J. (1980). Could there be a physical explanation for psi? *Journal of the Society for Psychical Research, 50*, 263–272.

Bergson, H. (1913). Presidential address (H. W. Carr, Trans.). *Proceedings of the Society for Psychical Research, 27*, 157–175.

Biernacki, L., & Clayton, P. (Eds.). (2014). *Panentheism across the World's Traditions*. New York: Oxford University Press.

Bohm, D. (1980). *Wholeness and the Implicate Order*. London: Routledge & Kegan Paul.

Brann, E. T. H. (1991). *The World of the Imagination: Sum and Substance*. Lanham, MD: Rowman & Littlefield.

Braude, S. E. (1986). *The Limits of Influence: Psychokinesis and the Philosophy of Science*. London: Routledge & Kegan Paul.

Braude, S. E. (2002). *ESP and Psychokinesis: A Philosophical Examination* (Rev. ed.). Parkland, FL: Brown Walker Press.

Burns, J. E. (2012). The action of consciousness and the uncertainty principle. *Journal of Nonlocality, 1*(1). Retrieved from http://journals.sfu.ca/jnonlocality/index.php/jnonlocality/article/view/9

Candlish, S., & Basile, P. (2013). Francis Herbert Bradley. In E. N. Zalta (Ed.), *The Stanford Encyclopedia of Philosophy* (Spring 2013 ed.). Retrieved from http://plato.stanford.edu/archives/spr2013/entries/bradley/

Carpenter, E. (1912). *The Drama of Love and Death: A Study of Human Evolution and Transfiguration*. London: George Allen.

Carpenter, J. C. (2012). *First Sight: ESP and Parapsychology in Everyday Life*. Lanham, MD: Rowman & Littlefield.

Carr, B. J. (2008). Worlds apart? Can psychical research bridge the gulf between matter and mind? *Proceedings of the Society for Psychical Research, 59*, 1–96.

Chalmers, A. F. (1994). *What Is This Thing Called Science?* (2nd ed.). Indianapolis: Hackett. (Original work published 1976)

Clayton, P., & Davies, P. (Eds.). (2006). *The Re-Emergence of Emergence: The Emergentist Hypothesis from Science to Religion*. New York: Oxford University Press.

Clayton, P., & Peacocke, A. (Eds.). (2004). *In Whom We Live and Move and Have Our Being*. Grand Rapids, MI: William B. Eerdmans.

Cooper, J. W. (2006). *Panentheism: The Other God of the Philosophers*. Grand Rapids, MI: Baker Academic.

Corbin, H. (1997). *Alone with the Alone: Creative Imagination in the Sūfism of Ibn 'Arabī* (R. Manheim, Trans.). Princeton, NJ: Princeton University Press. (Original work published 1969)

Crabtree, A. (2014). *Memoir of a Trance Therapist: Hypnosis and the Evocation of Human Potentials*. Victoria, British Columbia, Canada: Friesen Press.

David-Neel, A. (1937). *Magic and Mystery in Tibet*. New York: Crown Publishers.

Dawson, J. L., & Conduit, R. (2011). The substrate that dreams are made on: An evaluation of current neurobiological theories of dreaming. In D. Cvetkovic & I. Cosic (Eds.), *States of Consciousness: Experimental Insights into Meditation, Waking, Sleep and Dreams* (pp. 133–156). Berlin: Springer.

Eisenbud, J. (1967). *The World of Ted Serios*. New York: Morrow.

Feyerabend, P. (2010). *Against Method* (4th ed.). London: Verso. (Original work published 1975)

Gauld, A. (1968). *The Founders of Psychical Research*. London: Routledge & Kegan Paul.

Greyson, B. (2010). [Review of the book *Signs: A New Approach to Coincidence, Synchronicity, Guidance, Life Purpose, and God's Plan*, by Robert Perry]. *Journal of Near-Death Studies, 28*, 163–177.

Griffin, D. R. (1993). Parapsychology and philosophy: A Whiteheadian postmodern perspective. *Journal of the American Society for Psychical Research, 87*, 217–288.

Griffin, D. R. (1997). *Parapsychology, Philosophy, and Spirituality: A Postmodern Exploration*. Albany: State University of New York Press.

Griffin, D. R. (1998). *Unsnarling the World-Knot: Consciousness, Freedom, and the Mind–Body Problem*. Berkeley and Los Angeles: University of California Press.

Hansen, G. P. (2001). *The Trickster and the Paranormal*. Philadelphia: Xlibris.

Harris, S. (2012). *Free Will*. New York: Free Press.

Hartshorne, C., & Reese, W. L. (Eds.). (2000). *Philosophers Speak of God*. Amherst, NY: Humanity Books. (Original work published 1953)

Heisenberg, W. (1974). *Across the Frontiers* (P. Heath, Trans.). New York: Harper & Row.

Hoffman, D. D. (2008). Conscious realism and the mind–body problem. *Mind and Matter, 6*, 87–121.

Houtkooper, J. M. (2002). Arguing for an observational theory of paranormal phenomena. *Journal of Scientific Exploration, 16*, 171–185.

Jahn, R. G., & Dunne, B. J. (2011). *Consciousness and the Source of Reality: The PEAR Odyssey*. Princeton, NJ: ICRL Press.

James, W. (1890). *The Principles of Psychology* (Vols. 1–2). New York: Henry Holt.

James, W. (1902). *The Varieties of Religious Experience: A Study in Human Nature*. New York: Longmans, Green.

James, W. (1971). *A Pluralistic Universe*. In *Essays in Radical Empiricism and A Pluralistic Universe* (pp. 121–284). New York: E. P. Dutton. (Original work published 1909)

James, W. (1986). The confidences of a "psychical researcher." In F. H. Burkhardt (Ed.), *Essays in Psychical Research* (pp. 361–375). Cambridge, MA: Harvard University Press. (Original work published 1909)

Jourdan, J.-P. (2011). Near death experiences and the 5th dimensional spatio-temporal perspective. *Journal of Cosmology, 14*, 4743–4762.

Kakar, S. (1994). Encounters of the psychological kind: Freud, Jung, and India. In L. B. Boyer, R. M. Boyer, & H. F. Stein (Eds.), *The Psychoanalytic Study of Society: Vol. 19. Essays in Honor of George A. De Vos* (pp. 263–272). Hillsdale, NJ: The Analytic Press.

Kelly, E. F. (2003). [Review of the book *The Illusion of Conscious Will*, by Daniel M. Wegner]. *Journal of Scientific Exploration, 17*, 166–171.

Kennedy, J. E. (2003). The capricious, actively evasive, unsustainable nature of psi: A summary and hypotheses. *Journal of Parapsychology, 67*, 53–74.

Kripal, J. J. (2012). The evolving *siddhis*: Yoga and Tantra in the human potential movement and beyond. In K. A. Jacobsen (Ed.), *Yoga Powers: Extraordinary Capacities Attained through Meditation and Contemplation* (pp. 479–508). Leiden, The Netherlands: Koninklijke Brill.

Main, R. (2013). Secular *and* religious: The intrinsic doubleness of analytical psychology and the hegemony of naturalism in the social sciences. *Journal of Analytical Psychology, 58*, 366–386. doi:10.1111/1468-5922.12019

Marshall, P. (2005). *Mystical Encounters with the Natural World: Experiences and Explanations*. Oxford: Oxford University Press.

Marshall, P. (2011). The psychical and the mystical: Boundaries, connections, common origins. *Journal of the Society for Psychical Research, 75*, 1–13.

May, E. C., Utts, J. M., & Spottiswoode, S. J. P. (1995). Decision augmentation theory: Toward a model of anomalous mental phenomena. *Journal of Parapsychology, 59*, 195–220.

Millett, D. (2001). Hans Berger: From psychic energy to the EEG. *Perspectives in Biology and Medicine, 44*, 522–542. doi:10.1353/pbm.2001.0070

Murphy, G. (1945). *Three Papers on the Survival Problem*. New York: American Society for Psychical Research.

Murphy, M. (1992). *The Future of the Body: Explorations into the Further Evolution of Human Nature*. New York: Jeremy P. Tarcher/Putnam.

Myers, F. W. H. (1886). On telepathic hypnotism, and its relation to other forms of hypnotic suggestion. *Proceedings of the Society for Psychical Research, 4*, 127–188.

Myers, F. W. H. (1895). The subliminal self. Chapter 9: The relation of supernormal phenomena to time;—Precognition. *Proceedings of the Society for Psychical Research, 11*, 408–593.

Myers, F. W. H. (1903). *Human Personality and Its Survival of Bodily Death* (Vols. 1–2). London: Longmans, Green. (Available on CTR website, http://www.esalen.org/ctr/scholarly-resources)

Nagel, T. (2012). *Mind and Cosmos: Why the Materialist Neo-Darwinian Conception of Nature Is Almost Certainly False*. New York: Oxford University Press.

Ogburn, W. F., & Thomas, D. (1922). Are inventions inevitable? A note on social evolution. *Political Science Quarterly, 37*, 83–98.

Oschman, J. L. (2000). *Energy Medicine: The Scientific Basis*. Edinburgh: Churchill Livingstone.

Pieper, J. (1965). *The Silence of St. Thomas: Three Essays* (J. Murray & D. O'Connor, Trans.). Chicago: Henry Regnery.

Poortman, J. J. (1978). *Vehicles of Consciousness: The Concept of Hylic Pluralism (Ochēma)* (N. D. Smith, Trans., Vols. 1–4). Utrecht: Theosophical Society in the Netherlands.

Popper, K. (1968). *The Logic of Scientific Discovery* (2nd ed.). London: Hutchinson.

Price, H. H. (1939). Haunting and the "psychic ether" hypothesis. *Proceedings of the Society for Psychical Research, 45*, 307–343.

Radin, D. (2006). *Entangled Minds: Extrasensory Experiences in a Quantum Reality*. New York: Simon & Schuster.

Rhine, L. E. (1955). Precognition and intervention. *Journal of Parapsychology, 19*, 1–34.

Rosenblum, B., & Kuttner, F. (2011). *Quantum Enigma: Physics Encounters Consciousness* (2nd ed.). New York: Oxford University Press.

Samuel, G., & Johnston, J. (Eds.). (2013). *Religion and the Subtle Body in Asia and the West: Between Mind and Body*. London: Routledge.

Schatzman, M. (1980). *The Story of Ruth*. New York: Putnam.

Schmidt, H., & Pantas, L. (1972). Psi tests with internally different machines. *Journal of Parapsychology, 36*, 222–232.

Seager, W., & Allen-Hermanson, S. (2013). Panpsychism. In E. N. Zalta (Ed.), *The Stanford Encyclopedia of Philosophy* (Fall 2013 ed.). Retrieved from http://plato.stanford.edu/archives/fall2013/entries/panpsychism/

Searle, J. R. (1997). *The Mystery of Consciousness*. New York: New York Review of Books.

Shear, J. (1994). On mystical experiences as support for the perennial philosophy. *Journal of the American Academy of Religion, 62*, 319–342.

Sidgwick, E. M. (1962). *Phantasms of the Living*. New Hyde Park, NY: University Books.

Sprigge, T. L. S. (1983). *The Vindication of Absolute Idealism*. Edinburgh: Edinburgh University Press.

Sprigge, T. L. S. (1993). *James and Bradley: American Truth and British Reality*. Chicago: Open Court.

Sprigge, T. L. S. (1997). Pantheism. *The Monist, 80*, 191–217.

Sprigge, T. L. S. (2006). *The God of Metaphysics: Being a Study of the Metaphysics and Religious Doctrines of Spinoza, Hegel, Kierkegaard, T. H. Green, Bernard Bosanquet, Josiah Royce, A. N. Whitehead, Charles Hartshorne, and Concluding with a Defence of Pantheistic Idealism*. Oxford: Clarendon Press.

Stanford, R. G. (1990). An experimentally testable model for spontaneous psi events: A review of related evidence and concepts from parapsychology and other sciences. In S. Krippner (Ed.), *Advances in Parapsychological Research 6* (pp. 54–167). Jefferson, NC: McFarland.

Stapp, H. P. (2007). *Mindful Universe: Quantum Mechanics and the Participating Observer*. Berlin: Springer.

Stevenson, I. (1997). *Reincarnation and Biology: A Contribution to the Etiology of Birthmarks and Birth Defects* (Vols. 1–2). Westport, CT: Praeger.

Stokes, D. M. (1987). Theoretical parapsychology. In S. Krippner (Ed.), *Advances in Parapsychological Research 5* (pp. 77–189). Jefferson, NC: McFarland.

Thompson, E. (2007). *Mind in Life: Biology, Phenomenology, and the Sciences of Mind*. Cambridge, MA: Belknap Press.

Thurston, H. (1952). *The Physical Phenomena of Mysticism*. Chicago: Henry Regnery.

Tyrrell, G. N. M. (1947). The "modus operandi" of paranormal cognition. *Proceedings of the Society for Psychical Research, 48*, 65–120.

Tyrrell, G. N. M. (1953). *Apparitions* (Rev. ed.). London: Society for Psychical Research. (Original work published 1943)

Velmans, M. (2009). *Understanding Consciousness* (2nd ed.). Hove, England: Routledge.

Walach, H., Schmidt, S., & Jonas, W. B. (Eds.). (2011). *Neuroscience, Consciousness and Spirituality*. Dordrecht: Springer.

Wassermann, G. D. (1993). *Shadow Matter and Psychic Phenomena: A Scientific Investigation into Psychic Phenomena and Possible Survival of the Human Personality After Bodily Death*. Oxford: Mandrake.

Wegner, D. M. (2002). *The Illusion of Conscious Will*. Cambridge, MA: MIT Press.

Whitehead, A. N. (1968). *Modes of Thought*. New York: The Free Press. (Original work published 1938)

15

THE EMERGENCE OF EVOLUTIONARY PANENTHEISM

Michael Murphy

PART I

Through that which to others seems a mere dead mass, my eye beholds this eternal life and movement in every vein of sensible and spiritual Nature, and sees this life rising in ever-increasing growth, and ever purifying itself to a more spiritual expression. The universe is to me no longer what it was before—the ever-recurring circle, the eternally-repeated play, the monster swallowing itself up only to bring itself forth again;—it has become transfigured before me, and now bears the one stamp of spiritual life—a constant progress towards higher perfection in a line that runs out into the Infinite.

—J. G. Fichte, *The Vocation of Man*[1]

I posit God as both the first and the last, as the Alpha and Omega, as the unevolved, *Deus implicitus*, and the fully evolved, *Deus explicitus*.

—F. W. J. Schelling, *Denkmal der Schrift von den göttlichen Dingen*[2]

God is God only insofar as he knows Himself: this self-knowledge is, further, a self-consciousness in man and man's knowledge of God, which becomes man's self-knowledge in God.

—G. W. F. Hegel, *Philosophy of Spirit*[3]

If it be true that Spirit is involved in Matter and apparent Nature is secret God, then the manifestation of the divine in himself and the

realisation of God within and without are the highest and most legitimate aim possible to man upon earth.

—Sri Aurobindo, *The Life Divine*[4]

In the early eighteenth century, Isaac Newton, the most famous scientist
of his day, supported the claim of Archbishop James Ussher, the Anglican Primate of All Ireland, that by various means it could be calculated
that the world was created by God on Sunday, October 23, 4004 BCE.
Newton's assent to this proposition may surprise us, but he wasn't alone
among prominent thinkers in believing that the earth was just a few
thousand years old.

Within decades, though, this foreshortened perspective became increasingly untenable for thinking people. Astronomy, geology, biology,
and other fields began to show that the history of our planet and the
universe stretched back not for thousands but for millions of years. This
recognition of our world's great age, which by 1800 had been accepted by
scientists and philosophers as diverse as Jean-Baptiste Lamarck and Immanuel Kant, constitutes one of history's swiftest and most fundamental
alterations of worldview among intellectual elites.

With this, there emerged a growing realization that sentient creatures
had developed on earth over an immense stretch of time. Evidence for
this had grown enormously since the early 1600s, giving rise to theories
of life's development which, as the eminent historian of ideas Arthur
Lovejoy (1936) put it, could "in a broad sense, be called evolutionistic"
(p. 268). Although such theories had elements that seem naive or even
outlandish today, they were based on irrefutable evidence that increasingly complex forms of life had emerged on our planet since the distant past.

And in conjunction with these discoveries, there came an increasing
belief in social advance. The growth of science and technology, the advent of constitutional democracy, and the burgeoning prosperity of America and Western Europe prompted many to celebrate the idea of general
human progress. In the mid-nineteenth century, this belief, that humankind was capable of widespread development, was reinforced by the
eventual acceptance of evolution as a fact by scientists around the world.
After Charles Darwin's publication of *On the Origin of Species* in 1859,
more and more people came to see that life on earth had developed for
eons and might continue to develop for many more.

With the dawning of this evolutionary perspective, many thinkers began to reframe philosophy's most fundamental and enduring questions: What is the relation of this (ancient and evolving) world to God? What is humankind's role in its further advance? And since the earth has given rise to increasingly complex and conscious creatures, can human nature itself evolve? In the 1790s and early 1800s, a compelling response to these and related questions emerged among philosophers such as Fichte, Schelling, and Hegel which, briefly, can be stated as follows: while remaining transcendent to all created things, the divine spirit manifested itself through the birth of the physical world, so that the process that followed—the often meandering but seemingly inexorable emergence of new forms of existence from matter to life to humankind—is the unfolding of hidden divinity. What is implicit is gradually made explicit, as the "slumbering spirit" within all things progressively reveals itself. In Schelling's famous phrase, the *deus implicitus*, in the long course of time, becomes the *deus explicitus*. Or in the words of the philosopher Sri Aurobindo (2005), "apparent nature is secret God" (p. 6).

Lovejoy (1936) called this shift of worldview "the temporalizing of the Chain of Being," through which the manifest world with all its hierarchies was conceived "not as the inventory but as the program of nature" (p. 244). The vision of this "temporalization"—let us call it evolutionary panentheism (the term *panentheism*, in distinction to *pantheism*, refers to the doctrine that the divine is both immanent in and transcendent to the universe)—has been given different names and elaborated in different ways by the philosophers Fichte, Schelling, and Hegel; by Henry James, Sr., the father of Henry and William James; by the philosopher Charles Sanders Peirce; by Frederic Myers, the great pioneer of psychical research; and by well-known twentieth-century thinkers such as Henri Bergson, Pierre Teilhard de Chardin, Paul Tillich, Alfred North Whitehead, Charles Hartshorne, and Sri Aurobindo.[5]

Here I would like to propose that the worldview represented by thinkers such as these constitutes an emerging canon of sorts which, although it lives today on the margins of academic, scientific, and religious opinion, is giving rise to a vision that will eventually capture the world's imagination. The essential set of ideas that make up this still-developing body of thought has fundamental implications for philosophy, psychology, religion, and everyday life. Some examples follow.

It provides us with a unifying account of our evolving world's relation to the deepest source of things, an account that makes sense of our spiritual yearnings and desire for ultimate meaning. For if it is indeed the case that the entire universe presses to manifest its latent divinity, then we must share that impetus, which is evident in our desire for the illuminations, self-existent delight, self-surpassing love, and sense of eternal freedom and identity we experience in our highest moments. And it does this in a way that neither reductive materialism nor ascetic denials of the world's emerging Godhead can. It tells us that the universe has an aspiring heart, that human nature is primed for self-surpassing, and that our will to grow is supported by the world's insistent (although often meandering) drive toward a greater existence.

It helps explain our world's inexhaustible creativity. If the entire universe is a play, revelation, or unfolding of divinity, creativity must be accessible to us all. Novel organizations of energy and matter, new creatures and consciousness have emerged on earth in countless ways, and it can even be said that when life arose from matter, and mind from life, evolution itself evolved. The recognition of novelty permeating and reshaping the world contradicts the Solomonic doctrine that "there never was nor ever will be anything new under the sun" (Ecclesiastes 1:9). From its inception, the universe has been in the habit-breaking (as well as habit-making) business in its relentless self-surpassing.

The best things we experience often seem to be given rather than earned, spontaneously revealed rather than produced by laborious effort (although contemplative, artistic, athletic, or other practices usually set the stage for them). This sense of grace in human affairs, which is shared by people in every land, is more understandable if we hold that life's highest goods were involved in the world from its start, waiting for the right conditions to make their appearance. This understanding can alert us to the richness, ubiquity, and complexity of grace and help us account for the joyous, knowing response we feel—in our mind, our heart, and our flesh—when it comes to us. *The greater life that is latent in us instinctively knows and embraces those incursions of that greater life from without.*

And with this support for belief in grace, evolutionary panentheism undercuts doctrines of human alienation that are embedded in many faiths. If we view ourselves to be one with the cosmos in our beginnings and essential aims, we will be less inclined to war and world-weariness than we are if we take the world to be hostile or illusory.

It gives us a compelling reason for the resonance between human volition, imagination, cognition, emotion, and physiological processes through which psychosomatic transformations (as well as the influence of mind over inanimate matter evident in psychokinesis) appear to be mediated. Our cells, feelings, and thoughts resonate with one another because they share the same omnipresent reality, responsive to the same indwelling spirit. Mind and matter, consciousness and flesh, inform each other because they have evolved from (and within) the same ever-present origin. Recognizing this, evolutionary panentheism helps us account for the transformative effect that awareness of our essential divinity can exert on all our parts, the synergetic effectiveness of practices that embrace the whole person, the contagious inspirations of groups that are joined in creative endeavor, and prayer's power to join our spiritual longings with the greater life that awaits us.

It gives us a theoretical basis for understanding why human attributes such as perception, cognition, volition, and love can rise to self-surpassing levels. If we are secretly allied with the source and impetus of this evolving universe, we must to some degree share its all-encompassing powers of transformation. We can actualize capacities beyond our present existence because that is our basic predisposition.

Thus it opens the world before us, broadening our conceptions of further advance without requiring us to accept unwarranted religious or metaphysical truth claims. If we harbor a secret divinity that presses to manifest on earth, there's no telling how far our transformations might reach. We don't know the limits of mind and will. The flesh itself might reveal the glories of spirit. Evolutionary panentheism implies possibilities for humankind beyond those that science and religion have yet given us.

No philosophy or worldview by itself can eliminate evil in our world today, but this one gives us advantages over reductive materialism, "postmodern" relativism, and religious fundamentalisms in the relief of suffering on this planet. By orienting us to our essential divinity, it helps open us to our greatest sources of inspiration, the healing powers of grace, the unitive awareness that helps heal conflict, and the greater adventures of spirit we most deeply seek. And in doing all this, it can remain open and elastic enough to accommodate discoveries about our further reaches, including our postmortem existence. It may well provide a conceptual

gathering place for the global village from which to launch an unprecedented exploration of the greater life that awaits us.

PART II

> Nature herself ascends gradually in the determinate series of her crea-
> tions. In rude matter she is a simple existence; in organized matter she
> returns within herself to internal activity,—in the plant to produce
> form, in the animal motion;—in man, as her highest masterpiece, she
> turns inward that she may perceive and contemplate herself,—in him
> she, as it were, doubles herself, and, from being mere existence, be-
> comes existence and consciousness in one.
>
> —J. G. Fichte, *The Vocation of Man*[6]

> And I have felt
> A presence that disturbs me with the joy
> Of elevated thoughts; a sense sublime
> Of something far more deeply interfused,
> Whose dwelling is the light of setting suns,
> And the round ocean and the living air,
> And the blue sky, and in the mind of man;
> A motion and a spirit, that impels
> All thinking things, all objects of all thought,
> And rolls through all things.
>
> —William Wordsworth, "Tintern Abbey"[7]

Evolutionary panentheism, as I'm framing it here, emerged in the thinking of Fichte, Schelling, and Hegel. But the worldview it comprises is
developing still and had countless predecessors. In Part IV below I will
speculate about its future possibilities but here will note some of the
naturalists, philosophers, mystics, and visionaries who anticipated its various features. These forerunners can be seen to make up two streams of
thought, one in the developing science of post-Renaissance Europe, the
other in those schools of visionary speculation variously characterized as
Neoplatonic, Hermetic, Kabbalistic, or Pietistic. I will start with the first.

Humans had gathered knowledge of the inorganic world, sentient
creatures, and human nature since prehistoric times, but such discovery
greatly accelerated during the seventeenth and eighteenth centuries. With

the advent of modern science, an increasingly organized community emerged in Europe and around the world in which countless new ways were found to observe the heavens, the fossil record, animal life, and the complexities of human nature. As this worldwide enterprise grew, it revealed a long development on earth of increasingly complex life forms that eventually gave rise to humankind. Nature, it seemed, had a long and stupendous story to tell. Life appeared to be going somewhere, step by step, in spite of meanders, cataclysms, and the annihilations of entire species. By the mid-eighteenth century, countless naturalists viewed this process as a fact. That all living things had originated in a small number, or perhaps a single pair of original ancestors, was proposed by Pierre-Louis Maupertuis, the president of the Berlin Academy of Sciences, in 1745, and by Denis Diderot, the famous editor of the *Encyclopédie*, in 1749.[8]

But differing theories emerged to account for this epic story. In 1669, for example, the Dutch insectologist Jan Swammerdam proposed in his *Historia insectorum generalis* that among insects the female "semen" already contained a preexisting adult form, and he generalized his theory to embrace other animals, including the human race (Richards, 2002, pp. 211–212). After an English reviewer of Swammerdam's book described this process of embryological change as "a gradual and natural Evolution and Growth of the parts" (pp. 211–212), the term *evolution* was attached to a theory of preformation that eventually moved from embryological to species change. In this view, a miniature version of a creature's form, or "homunculus," was enclosed in the egg or sperm. But subsequent discoveries challenged this idea, and a rival set of theories, to which the term *epigenesis* was given, held that the embryo began as a formless mass that grew into a definite structure. Although eminent naturalists such as Albrecht von Haller and Charles Bonnet refined their own preformationist views in the light of empirical discovery, their theories eventually gave way to the increasing evidence for epigenesis. And other theories of species development were found wanting as discoveries multiplied in the biological sciences, among them proposals that certain "archetypes" shaped the development of life forms and the Lamarckian doctrine that acquired characteristics are passed genetically from one generation to the next.

But although various theories of organic development rose and fell as discoveries in geology, biology, and other fields multiplied, the evolution of sentient creatures on earth grew more and more evident, leading naturalists and philosophers to seek overarching principles, patterns, or forces to account for it. Physician and physiologist Johann Friedrich Blumenbach, for example, proposed:

> There exists in all living creatures, from men to maggots and from cedar trees to mold, a particular inborn, lifelong active drive [*Trieb*]. This drive initially bestows on creatures their form, then preserves it, and, if they become injured, where possible restores their form. . . . It shows itself to be one of the first causes of all generation, nutrition, and reproduction. . . . I give it the name *Bildungstrieb* (*nisus formativus*). (Cited in Richards, 2002, pp. 218–219)

Blumenbach extended his theory to embrace the origination of species as well as individual organisms, attributing the *Bildungstrieb*'s effects to the "great changeability in nature," which resulted from the "most beneficent and wise direction of the Creator" (Richards, 2002, p. 222). These ideas resonated with many thinkers of the day, among them Johann Gottfried Herder, a widely educated man of letters, who constructed a vast, naturalized version of the cosmic advance from nebulae and planets to life on earth and human history. "Could we but penetrate to those first periods of creation," he wrote, "we would see how one kingdom of nature was built upon another; what a progression of advancing forces would be displayed in every development!" (p. 223). The entire world, in Herder's cosmology, advanced with deliberate intent toward the perfection of human nature. "The purpose of our present existence," he proclaimed, "is directed to the formation of humanity [*Bildung der Humanität*], and all the lower necessities of the earth only serve and lead to this end" (p. 223). Schelling would adopt ideas close to Blumenbach's and Herder's in his *Naturphilosophie* and dynamic evolutionism.

In the 1790s, such visions of world development were gaining increasing support from discoveries in various fields of science. But the evolutionary panentheism that emerged in Fichte, Schelling, and Hegel was influenced too, directly or indirectly, by a long line of religious mystics and visionaries who believed that the divine is progressively unfolding on earth. Although these forerunners framed their visions in different ways, they agreed that cosmic history was impelled by God's inexorable desire to manifest in the physical world. In the late twelfth century, for example, Joachim of Fiore, a Calabrian monk, saw history as reflecting three stages of the Christian Trinity's manifestation, an Age of the Father, an Age of the Son, and an Age of the Holy Spirit, each of which advanced humankind's freedom and nearness to God. This progression would result in the triumph of spirit over the flesh, contemplation over worldly preoccupations. In history's third and culminating age, organized religion would end. The Church would "wither away," replaced by individualistic forms of worship and a worldwide spread of religious joy (Magee, 2001, pp. 236–240).

Some four hundred years later, Jacob Boehme developed a similar vision. A native of Görlitz on the borders of Bohemia, he was a shoemaker who in 1600 had a vision of the world's fundamental essence: "The gate was opened unto me, so that in one quarter of an hour I saw and knew more than if I had been many years together at a University. . . . For I saw and knew the Being of all beings . . . the birth or eternal generation of the Holy Trinity; the descent and origin of this world" (cited in Magee, 2001, p. 36).

Through such vision, Boehme saw that God "others Himself" by creating this world so that he can progressively incarnate himself through a history that reaches consummation in Christ. In this consummation, God's desire for self-revelation is fulfilled through humankind's knowledge of him through his son. But Boehme's worldview was often clothed in obscure language. In Hegel's words, "Böhme's great mind is confined in the hard knotty oak of the senses—in the gnarled concretion of ordinary conception—and is not able to arrive at a free presentation of the Idea" (Magee, 2001, p. 49). Nevertheless, his vision of God and the world resembles (and anticipates) Fichte's vision of "eternal life emerging in every vein of sensible nature," Schelling's "slumbering spirit," and Hegel's dialectical advance of the *Geist*. In the words of Boehme scholar David Walsh, "Böhme is the herald of the self-actualizing evolutionary God" (Magee, 2001, p. 39).

But Boehme was not alone in this. Several thinkers of the seventeenth and eighteenth centuries saw the divine emerging in world history. Friedrich Oetinger, a theologian and naturalist, claimed that "God is an eternal desire for self-revelation" who emerges "from Himself and returns to Himself" (Magee, 2001, p. 65). "Embodiment is the goal of God's work" (*Leiblichkeit ist das Ende der Werke Gottes*), and spirit (*Geist*) comes to its fullest actualization through corporeality (*Geistleiblichkeit*) (p. 66). We can apprehend this basic fact of existence, Oetinger believed, through a *sensus communis*, an "unmediated cognition" of things-as-a-whole that reveals their fundamental identity with God (p. 67). This capacity lies at our "very center," beyond the separative consciousness we usually inhabit. The *sensus communis,* as Oetinger framed it, resembles the higher faculty, or "intuitive thinking," by which we see things in a supraintellectual light, which would be described (in various ways and with different terms) by Fichte, Schelling, and Hegel. Like them and evolutionary panentheists such as Bergson, Teilhard, and Sri Aurobindo, Oetinger saw a higher consciousness emerging in humankind through which we can progressively perceive and embody our latent divinity.

Reading visionaries such as Joachim, Boehme, and Oetinger, it becomes evident that evolutionary panentheism had been dawning for several centuries before its advent in the 1790s. But with Fichte, Schelling, and Hegel, it found an enduring place in the canon of Western philosophy, largely because it was more acceptable to post-Enlightenment thought than esoteric visions such as Joachim's and Boehme's. And its central tenets have been developed in various ways during the last two centuries. Hegel, for example, like Boehme and Oetinger, viewed human life as a progressive embodiment of God, but added a rich history of its emergence by identifying successive forms of consciousness (*Gestalten des Bewusstseins*) that transcend and integrate (*aufheben*) the ones that precede them. Jean Gebser (1985) extended a panentheistic vision of human development back to the Stone Age, drawing on historical and anthropological discoveries not available to Hegel. Philosopher Ken Wilber (1995) has shown ways to integrate the findings of dynamic psychiatry, developmental psychology, general systems theory, and other fields into an overview of the divine unfoldment. And Sri Aurobindo, the greatest practicing contemplative among the thinkers I've noted, outlined an elaborate psychology of our further development, a phenomenology of supernormal consciousness, and an "integral yoga" to transform all our faculties as instruments of the divinity we harbor (Heehs, 2008). Many thinkers besides these—too many to enumerate here—have added something new to this lineage-in-the-making, partly because they could draw upon knowledge not available to their forerunners and largely because they could learn from the various moral, psychological, and basic conceptual shortcomings—some of them grievous—of its various iterations.

One reason that evolutionary panentheism has attracted thinkers such as these, even though they've come from different cultures with disparate philosophic commitments, is that it is based on just a few fundamental principles, among them, first, that evolution is a fact (although its discovery has given rise to various theories about it); second, that our universe arises from and is constituted by a world-transcending supernature, call it the One, God, Brahman, the Absolute, Buddha-Nature, Allah, *Geist*, or the Dao; and third, that humans have a fundamental affinity or identity with that supernature, which can be known through immediate experience either spontaneously or by means of transformative practice. Because this worldview is so basic and so broad and because it can be embraced without superstitions, dogmas, or metaphysical abstractions that one cannot accept, it has been adopted, implicitly or explicitly, by countless men and women who have recognized its power to illuminate our human nature and destiny. However, its development has had a complex, meandering, often faltering history and remains on the margins of intellectual opinion today. While gathering support from wide-ranging scholarly studies of the wisdom traditions, depth psychology, and other disciplines that are giving us ever-greater understanding of our subliminal depths, its acceptance has been impeded by the reductive materialism that has accompanied the advance of mainstream science as well as by rancorous disagreements among its primary exponents and dramatic failures of social movements it has informed (among them Hegelian doctrines of inevitable human advance appropriated by tyrannies of the Left and Right). And perhaps most importantly, it has lacked sufficient anchoring in the transformative practices that are necessary to actualize its promise.

For more than two centuries now, evolutionary panentheism has been obscured in the fog of paradigm wars that have raged among scientists and philosophers even as discoveries from many fields have increasingly lent it support. It has, in short, sailed a zigzag course into powerful headwinds but with significant tailwinds. The story of its journey, I believe, will eventually be described with scholarly depth and find a generally accepted place in the history of ideas, but however it comes to be viewed by historians, it will continue to be framed in various ways—and given different names—as it is adopted by people with different backgrounds and temperaments. Since that is the case, perhaps it is better to call it a "basic vision" or "worldview" rather than a "philosophy" as that term is typically understood today by professional philosophers. And we need to distinguish it as well from most versions of panentheism that have existed since ancient times. The vision of a divinity that is both immanent in and transcendent to worldly things has animated spiritual life for millennia but has taken a dynamic and historic turn, I propose, since around 1800, a turn that embraces the facts of evolution as they've been revealed by modern science. Such an embrace brings new coherence and meaning— and a deeper basis in empirically grounded fact—to our understanding of humankind's greater possibilities. Unlike most past versions of panentheism, it sees the entire world as an evolutionary disclosure of the divine, as "slumbering Spirit" pressing insistently through the world's long meandering course toward a greater existence on earth, and in this it views supernormal capacities that appear in the course of spiritual practice not as hindrances to higher life but as emerging attributes of our latent supernature.

To repeat, though it carries enormous promise and has been potentially enriched by discoveries of many kinds, this worldview does not command an allegiance as widespread today as the reductive materialism, postmodern relativism, and religious fundamentalisms prevalent in our universities, religions, and opinion elites. Indeed, among historians and laypeople alike, it does not have a commonly accepted name. It remains on the margins of contemporary thought and only grows by fits and starts. Though it will, I believe, capture a wider following one day, orienting us to the greater life that awaits us, it remains largely invisible to most thought leaders. As it emerges from the mists of modern opinion, we might call it a "stealth worldview," appearing as if on a fuzzy screen, pixel by pixel for those with eyes to perceive it. Here I will briefly describe some of the ways in which it has developed since 1800 and in doing so will argue that its emergence is made possible by certain human advances, such as the advent of science, that appear to be irreversible.

PART III

Science has spread to every continent, influencing each nation's agriculture, industry, and cultural practices. It has stimulated new lines of critical thought, leading more and more people toward fact-based rather than faith-based inquiries related to our deepest concerns. It increasingly informs athletic, therapeutic, contemplative, and other practices to liberate body and soul. It has a pervasive (though not universal) influence among the world's leading thinkers. And without it, we wouldn't continue to discover the often astonishing facts of cosmic, biological, and human evolution. Those facts and the stupendous story they reveal have confirmed the intuition of pre-Darwinian thinkers such as Fichte, Schelling, and Hegel that human development is rooted in the world's general advance. As our understanding of the world has grown, science has expanded our awareness of the world's age far beyond the belief that it was created in 4004 BCE, showing that it has developed for billions of years. And we've also learned that cosmic evolution had a definite start, in a colossal explosion from a tiny seed, followed by an instantaneous and stupendously rapid expansion that continues still, with a future that stretches beyond our mind's reach. This picture of our universe is more detailed and empirically grounded than those held by the pioneers of evolutionary panentheism, adding powerful support to their view that evolution is a fact and that it becomes conscious of itself in us.

But the evolution story is not limited to discoveries in the physical and biological sciences, which cannot by themselves reveal human nature's further reaches and transformative capacities. For these, we need psychology, anthropology, comparative religious studies, and other fields that reveal the great scale and depth of our latent supernature. Through a multidisciplinary, synoptic empiricism that embraces subjective reports, observable behaviors, and bodily processes, we are learning more than ever before about humankind's possibilities for extraordinary life.[9] Research on meditation, imagery practice, somatics, and other transformative disciplines; discoveries about our bodily functioning (including the brain's neuroplasticity); growing acquaintance with the varieties of mystical experience; and our increasing access to the lore of shamanism and the wisdom traditions have given us more publicly available information than humankind has ever possessed about our capacities for creative transformation. Data from these and other fields show that men and women since the Stone Age have experienced grace-laden energies, illuminations, and ecstasies that give credence to beliefs such as Schelling's that we harbor a *deus implicitus*. Evolutionary panentheism gives us a compelling—and for me, the best—context within which to understand such experience.

Today, the collection of such data forms a natural history of sorts, not of fossils or living creatures as in paleontology and biology, but of extraordinary human capacities. A few thinkers, moreover, have made attempts to classify these. William James, Frederic Myers, Herbert Thurston, Marghanita Laski, Abraham Maslow, and others have proposed tax-onomies of supernormal capacities, and I have continued this work by gathering some ten thousand studies of them in fields ranging from sport to shamanism (Murphy, 1992). Working with this material, it is possible to identify supernormal expressions of perceptual, kinesthetic, move-ment, cognitive, and communication abilities, love, volition, imagination, memory, sense of self, bodily structures, and other attributes we've inher-ited from our primate ancestors. Viewed in their entirety, these still-developing capacities reveal a continuous advance across the separate domains of the world's often meandering evolution. The fact that the progress they exhibit has been produced through different means—in animals by mutation and natural selection, for example, and in humans through transformative practices—suggests that evolution has a telos of sorts, a creative tendency toward greater life on earth that works through the different evolutionary processes operating in the inorganic, animal, and human domains (Murphy, 1992, pp. 24–35, 171–200). This overarch-ing pattern of development, which connects the earliest forms of life to our highest moments, is consonant with a vision that sees a *deus implicit-us* emerging to become the *deus explicitus*. The worldwide gathering of knowledge upon which such insight rests—in its scale, richness, and growing exactitude—is something new in human history. Taken as a whole, it suggests that humankind harbors possibilities greater than most people have guessed, and it has helped to inspire a worldwide adoption of transformative disciplines.

Thus science today promises to extend its reach into regions of human transformative experience that have been limited by the dogmas and superstitions of earlier times. It still meets resistance in this, some of it fierce, from established religions, New Age cults, common attachments to familiar social practices, and the reductive materialism of many scien-tists. But the habits of data gathering and critical inquiry that it nurtures, with their power to reveal once-hidden facts of body and soul, drive it ever further into the undiscovered countries of our latent supernature. In doing this, it is giving rise to newly sophisticated research methods for the exploration of consciousness in its further reaches, paranormal phe-nomena, postmortem survival, and bodily changes that support ecstatic states and superordinary functioning.

For example, sport psychology, somatics, and medical science now provide newly efficient ways to increase fitness, health, and longevity, in addition to sensitivity, coordination, strength, and balance to facilitate peak performance. Psychology has given rise to new insights and methods that can increase awareness of self and others, broaden our behavioral repertoires, foster emotional intelligence, and facilitate family, organizational, and ethnic understanding. And once esoteric scriptures—Tibetan, Chinese, Indian, Jewish, Muslim, and Christian—are available at Internet sites, libraries, and bookstores worldwide. Countless men and women today, including leaders of long-established religious traditions, are affected by the worldwide spread of such teachings. Father Pedro Arrupe, the much-esteemed Jesuit leader, for example, practiced meditation in the lotus position, and when he was questioned about it by fellow Catholics, he said that he found God while doing so in ways he did not while kneeling in prayer (Bishop, 2007, p. 200). The two practices, he said, complement each other.

Whether we know it or not, most of us are to some degree influenced like Arrupe by cultural practices other than ours, which can bring recognitions that we have more latent capacities than we had once realized. In addition, many of us are learning that spiritual experiences and moral inspirations don't require the acceptance of superstitions and dogmas that may be associated with them. Continuing the call for such discrimination by thinkers of the eighteenth-century Enlightenment, sociologists, cultural anthropologists, and religious scholars have with increasing exactitude described this social dynamic, this winnowing of exalted experiences from the limiting beliefs that may accompany them, and have thus contributed to a growing sophistication about unwarranted truth claims, moral bullying, high-minded cruelties, and other liabilities of traditional religious practice.[10] And such cross-cultural learning has also been strengthened by analytic philosophy, general semantics, cognitive psychology, and the cultural criticism of philosophers such as Michel Foucault and Jacques Derrida, all of which can help free us from crippling habits of thought and the everyday limitations imposed by our immediate culture.

But for countless men and women today, this expansion of consciousness calls for a conceptual framework, a worldview, a basic vision to connect the many complexities it reveals. Because the opportunities for greater life emerging in the global village today bring both new challenges and new joys, both new problems and new spiritual openings, many of us seek a guiding philosophy with which to pursue them and are thus led to some version of evolutionary panentheism. However, attraction to this worldview does not require that we reject every philosophic or religious allegiance we hold. Its basic simplicity and breadth make it compatible with various religious traditions. Faithful Protestants and Roman Catholics, for example, can find such vision in Paul Tillich and Pierre Teilhard de Chardin, Indian aspirants in Sri Aurobindo, believing Jews in Abraham Kook, faithful Buddhists in the Dalai Lama's evolutionary thought. Arguably, this adaptability allows it to operate as a progressive influence in the world's religious communities by leading some believers beyond the limitations their faith entails.

Given this complexity of spiritual practice and belief, it's hard to say how many people now embrace the emerging worldview I'm describing. Nevertheless, we know with certainty that many men and women today share an unprecedented availability of insights and disciplines that inform their spiritual pursuits. Many are battle-tested in the paradigm wars, having experienced suspect gurus, destructive cults, flawed practices, and failed enthusiasms of various kinds while being graced by illuminations beyond those they've experienced in the cultures they were born to. Their belief in the divine immanence draws upon an embrace of science as well as religion and a broadly empirical approach to their respective disciplines. In this, their faith is increasingly fact-based, more so than it was for earlier generations. Many say their worldview is "spiritual," not "religious," and share an ever-broadening common ground in the foothills of contemplative experience.

The physical, biological, and human sciences have contributed profoundly to these developments, through both their discoveries and the empirical spirit they've stimulated among thinking people worldwide. But there is a complexity here. With these gifts, science has also erected barriers to explorations of our latent supernature. The reductive materialism it has given rise to has generally rejected the study of paranormal phenomena and the truth claims of mystical practice. Studies of telepathy, clairvoyance, and psychokinesis; research on "reincarnation-type" memories, mediumship, and postmortem survival; and related inquiries are out of fashion today (and hard to fund) in academia and professional science associations. And such resistance isn't new. It was already growing in the nineteenth century, when Frederic Myers, Edmund Gurney, and other scholars founded Great Britain's Society for Psychical Research to promote the disciplined study of supernormal experience and the possibility of life after death. Eminent philosophers and scientists joined this effort in succeeding decades, but their efforts were eventually engulfed by the now prevalent reductionism of neuroscience and psychology. Today such reductionism rules the human sciences.

For this reason, among others, evolutionary panentheism lives now on the margins of intellectual life. Although it is more empirically grounded and richly articulated than it was in 1800, it remains largely unrecognized—and sometimes actively resisted or suppressed—by countless thought leaders and laypeople alike. But perhaps this invisibility will turn out to have an adaptive advantage. Just as new species typically evolve on the margins of their original habitats, which allows them to develop without being reabsorbed by their ancestral populations, cultural advances often begin on the peripheries of established social orders, where there is room to experiment and learn from trial and error. This is the case, I believe, with the emerging vision I'm describing, which is taking shape out of sight of most opinion elites while fostering practices and institutions that have begun to embody it.

PART IV

Having briefly described the emergence of evolutionary panentheism, I want to propose that it gives us a special vantage point from which to predict further human advances. For example, its increasing acceptance will almost certainly give rise to newly imaginative visions of the greater life we harbor. Indeed, that's been happening for more than two centuries. Henri Bergson (1935), who was awarded a Nobel Prize in literature for his philosophic writing, famously called the universe "a machine for the making of gods" and deemed mystics to be at evolution's cutting edge (p. 275). Jean Gebser (1985) believed that an emergent "integral" consciousness will comprehend life on our planet with new richness and depth (pp. 277–281). Pierre Teilhard de Chardin (1959) saw a "noosphere" coalescing on earth that will progressively unify the human race and converge to an "omega point" through which the spirit of Christ will irradiate life on our planet (pp. 180–184, 257–260). And Sri Aurobindo, one of India's foremost independence leaders and a richly educated intellectual and realized mystic, proclaimed the emergence of "Supermind," a level of exis-

tence in which the divine is realized in its primordial ecstasy, transforming mind and flesh in the light of God (Heehs, 2008, pp. 374–375).

Such visions herald a philosophic boldness and breadth that will accompany discoveries that reveal human nature's further reaches. But the
truths they embody will not, I believe, find their primary expression
through intellectually abstract, overburdened, muscle-bound metaphysics
that provide descriptions of the cosmos and human life too thin and
constrictive for thinking people today who have been influenced by ideas
and practices from around the globe. Going forward, I believe, empirical
disclosures of our latent supernature will take precedence over speculative philosophy, while suggestive art and language will be more persua-
sive than logic in spreading the worldview I'm describing. In *The Future
of the Body*, I listed a wide range of extraordinary human attributes described in fantasy literature, movies, science fiction, and other artworks
(Murphy, 1992, pp. 211–213); and the historian of religions Jeffrey Kripal (2011) has explored this subject at length in his book *Mutants and
Mystics*. Such visions aren't new, of course. From its inception, evolutionary panentheism, however named, has influenced and found powerful
expression among poets such as William Wordsworth, Samuel Taylor
Coleridge, William Blake, William Butler Yeats, Friedrich Hölderlin,
Novalis, Victor Hugo, and Walt Whitman; philosophers such as Ralph
Waldo Emerson and Alfred North Whitehead; historians such as Thomas
Carlyle; and naturalists such as Henry David Thoreau.

This emerging vision of heaven and earth, this stealth worldview, has
unfolded in many ways since 1800. And we can guess that its emergence
will accelerate. It is, I believe, like a coiled spring waiting for release
from its compression. Just as Albert Einstein, Niels Bohr, and their colleagues did not immediately see that their theories would lead to the atom
bomb, the discovery of black holes, and the mysteries of quantum entanglement, we cannot see everything that evolutionary panentheism entails.
But we can guess that as the evidence supporting it grows in the light of
the knowledge that science and transformative practice bring, it will command an increasing allegiance. In this, it will resemble scientific theory,
which catalyzes empirical discovery while being reshaped and strengthened by it.

Many activities will drive this coevolution of vision and practice,
among them comparative studies of extraordinary human capacities.
These, however, will not be limited to academia. Sri Aurobindo's *Record*

of Yoga, for example, which contains a wide-ranging, richly detailed, self-critical account of illuminations and powers that appeared in his yoga, heralds such accounts now appearing among spiritual explorers both inside and outside universities and research centers (Heehs, 2008, pp. 242–245). According to several sociological studies and public-opinion polls, more and more people are becoming amateur comparativists, as it were, comparing practices from different traditions without formal studies of culture or spiritual life.[11] With the perspective evolutionary panentheism gives us, supernormal faculties such as those that these seekers are experiencing today can be seen as budding capacities of our emerging supernature rather than hindrances to our further development as many religious traditions have deemed them. If our world is embraced as an arena of divine disclosure rather than *māyā*, or illusion, as certain Hindu and Buddhist philosophies assert, or as essentially a vale of suffering from which spiritual life will release us, then such capacities may well become central to our further advance.

And for this reason, I believe the spread of evolutionary panentheism will further the integral development of human life. Countless seekers experience benefits such as Father Arrupe did from once foreign insights and practices, and considerable scientific research has demonstrated the synergies produced through the joining of once separate disciplines (Murphy, 1992, pp. 541–586). We've learned, for example, that physical fitness can improve the results of one's meditation practice, and that meditation can, in turn, strengthen athletic performance. Likewise, psychotherapy can help clarify and energize many kinds of transformative disciplines. Such discoveries will encourage a many-sided approach to transformative practice, one that embraces body, mind, heart, and soul. That perspective is fundamental to Sri Aurobindo's Integral Yoga, Ken Wilber's integral epistemology, the Integral Transformative Practice I've developed with George Leonard, and many other ways of growth (Leonard & Murphy, 1995).

And as interest in such practices spreads, it is likely to stimulate research on phenomena that to date have eluded mainstream science, among them the "subtle energies" (*prāṇa* in Sanskrit, *pneuma* in Greek, *ki* in Japanese, *chi* in Chinese) that have long been evident in the lore of transformative practice (Murphy, 1992, pp. 451–457). These are deliberately employed in the martial arts and have been dramatized in action movies. They inform Eastern architecture and landscape design through the art of *feng shui*. And they are evident in the halos of medieval and Renaissance European art, the luminosities of Roman Catholic sanctity, the radiance of the Sufis' Man of Light, the "boiling *num*" of Kalahari Bushmen, and the "magical heat" of Siberian shamanism (pp. 201–210, 505–508). But they haven't been studied with significant depth by modern researchers, in large part because they aren't perceived with regularity and because they have not been recorded with certainty by physical instruments. Yet their existence has been testified to for millennia by shamans, yogis, and monastic contemplatives, and in recent times by artists, athletes, and laypeople alike.[12] Given this indubitable fact, we can predict that ways will be found through which science can study them. Even if they can't be detected with today's physical devices, their frequent occurrence can be increasingly documented through systematic collection of subjective reports.

We can also predict that other once esoteric manifestations of transformative practice will be studied more intensively in the years to come. These will inevitably include the *vibhūtis* and *siddhis* of Hindu-Buddhist yogas; the "charisms" of Roman Catholicism; the "adornments" of Sufi mysticism; the extraordinary powers of shamanism; and other supernormal phenomena now described and compared by religious scholars. Translations of Sanskrit, Pali, Tibetan, Chinese, Japanese, and other religious texts continue to multiply, broadening our access to descriptions of such experiences, among them radical transformations of the flesh such as the physical elasticities (or "elongations"), incorruptibility, and luminosities of Roman Catholic sanctity; the radiant eyes and skin noted in Tibetan lore of the "rainbow body"; and accounts of bodily "shapeshifting" to be found in shamanism, Daoist texts, and accounts of Asian martial artists (Murphy, 1992, pp. 464–477, 511–517). This long-standing witness to human nature's capacity for dramatic transformation is supported by the ever-increasing demonstration of the brain's neuroplasticity and the growing recognition of our capacity to renew any part of our body through exercise and strong mental intention (Schwartz & Begley, 2002).

It is also highly likely that sports will continue to appropriate such research. Athletes often use mental training derived from yoga and the martial arts in conjunction with advances in fitness training discovered by medical science; and Olympic committees as well as national sports federations have incorporated such discoveries in their training regimens, for both profit and enjoyment.[13] Today we see a worldwide proliferation of sports, both old and new, that push the edges of human capacity, with an attendant acceleration of record breaking in all age groups. The dramatic appeal of this self-surpassing activity will only increase, I believe, if sport is imbued with a worldview that embraces the wide range of supernormal phenomena it evokes.

The arts, too, will further the ideas and practices I've described. Architecture, landscaping, and town planning already anticipate this with their growing appreciation of design's effects upon mood, consciousness, and behavior. Novel writing possesses more means of expression than ever before with which to express the surprise, complexities, and scale of higher powers. And cinema is ripe for such change, not only because its worldwide audience constantly seeks excitement and inspiration, but also because it has developed new technical means with which to dramatize phenomena that are usually invisible to us. For millennia, humans have turned to dark spaces in which they can enter new depths of the soul, whether in caves such as those at Lascaux or in the enclosures that housed the Eleusinian Mysteries. Pioneering film editor Walter Murch (2001) argues that movie houses can have a similar effect, which comes into play with special force in films such as *2001: A Space Odyssey*. In the future, more films of such scale and depth may appear in response to a culture that seeks new adventures of consciousness.

And these many ideas and activities will inevitably give rise to supportive social structures. That is the case because every great human advance has required institutions to support it. The Academy, the Lyceum, and the Stoa nurtured philosophy in ancient Greece. Indian ashrams and Christian monasteries have fed contemplative life for three millennia. The modern university arose among churchmen of the late Middle Ages who sought freedom from Church dogma for scientific inquiry and humanistic studies. Silicon Valley incubates the largest, most innovative teams of engineers the world has ever seen. "Growth centers" such as the Esalen Institute were organized to further the exploration of human potentialities without the inhibitions of mainstream religion and academia. If the vision and practices I'm outlining here continue to spread, institutions to nurture them will be invented.

These many advances, I believe, will have an increasingly cumulative effect, leading more and more people into undiscovered countries of body and soul. To repeat, such explorations could accelerate in the decades to come, inspiring breakthroughs we do not foresee. In the long history of our universe, evolution has often accelerated, breaking long-established laws while giving birth to new forms of existence. Could that happen again, on earth, *among us*? Given the advances I've noted and the increasingly liberated sensibility emerging around the world today, it is conceivable that humankind now approaches another rebirth. To quote playwright Christopher Fry (1951), "Affairs are now soul size. The enterprise is exploration into God, where no nation's foot has ever trodden yet" (p. 48).

NOTES

1. Fichte (1800/1889, p. 476).

2. This is a poetic paraphrase of a statement by F. W. J. Schelling (*Denkmal der Schrift von den göttlichen Dingen*, 1812) that was quoted by Arthur O. Lovejoy (1936): "I posit God as the first and the last, as the Alpha and the Omega; but as Alpha he is not what he is as Omega, and in so far as he is only the one—God 'in an eminent sense'—he can not be the other God, in the same sense, or, in strictness, be called God. For in that case, let it be expressly said, the unevolved God, *Deus implicitus*, would already be what, as Omega, the *Deus explicitus* is" (p. 323).

3. Quoted in Magee (2001, p. 226).

4. Aurobindo (2005, p. 6).

5. For further background on panentheistic philosophers, see Hartshorne and Reese (1953/2000).

6. Fichte (1800/1889, p. 340).

7. Wordsworth (1798/1988, p. 160).

8. On mid-eighteenth-century evolutionary theories, see Bowler (1989, pp. 50–89).

9. In 1992 I published a thoroughly researched study of the cross-cultural evidence from past and present that supports the contention that several normal human capacities often display supernormal expressions and possibilities—see Murphy (1992).

10. This trend dates to William James's groundbreaking study of religious experience at the dawn of the twentieth century—see James (1902).

11. For background on this comparative trend, see Fuller (2001, pp. 153–174).

12. For evidence of such experiences by artists and lay people, see Kripal (2011).

13. See Association for Applied Sport Psychology, http://www. appliedsportpsych.org

REFERENCES

Aurobindo, Sri (2005). *The Life Divine.* In *The Complete Works of Sri Aurobindo* (Vols. 21 & 22). Pondicherry, India: Sri Aurobindo Ashram.

Bergson, H. (1935). *The Two Sources of Morality and Religion* (R. A. Audra & C. Brereton, Trans.). London: Macmillan.

Bishop, G. (2007). *Pedro Arrupe SJ* (Rev. ed.). Leominster, England: Gracewing.

Bowler, P. J. (1989). *Evolution: The History of an Idea* (Rev. ed.). Berkeley and Los Angeles: University of California Press.

Fichte, J. G. (1889). *The Vocation of Man.* In W. Smith (Trans.), *The Popular Works of Johann Gottlieb Fichte* (4th ed., Vol. 1, pp. 319–478). London: Trübner. (Original work published 1800)

Fry, C. (1951). *A Sleep of Prisoners: A Play.* London: Oxford University Press.

Fuller, R. C. (2001). *Spiritual, but Not Religious: Understanding Unchurched America.* New York: Oxford University Press.

Gebser, J. (1985). *The Ever-Present Origin* (N. Barstad & A. Mickunas, Trans.). Athens: Ohio University Press.

Hartshorne, C., & Reese, W. L. (Eds.). (2000). *Philosophers Speak of God.* Amherst, NY: Humanity Books. (Original work published 1953)

Heehs, P. (2008). *The Lives of Sri Aurobindo.* New York: Columbia University Press.

Hegel, G. W. F. (1967). *The Phenomenology of Mind* (J. B. Baillie, Trans.). New York: Harper Torchbooks. (Original work published 1807)

James, W. (1902). *The Varieties of Religious Experience: A Study in Human Nature.* New York: Longmans, Green.

Kripal, J. J. (2011). *Mutants and Mystics: Science Fiction, Superhero Comics, and the Paranormal.* Chicago: University of Chicago Press.

Leonard, G., & Murphy, M. (1995). *The Life We Are Given: A Long-Term Program for Realizing the Potential of Body, Mind, Heart, and Soul.* New York: Tarcher/Putnam.

Lovejoy, A. O. (1936). *The Great Chain of Being: A Study of the History of an Idea.* Cambridge, MA: Harvard University Press.

Magee, G. A. (2001). *Hegel and the Hermetic Tradition.* Ithaca, NY: Cornell University Press.

Murch, W. (2001). *In the Blink of an Eye: A Perspective on Film Editing* (2nd ed.). Los Angeles: Silman-James Press.

Murphy, M. (1992). *The Future of the Body: Explorations into the Further Evolution of Human Nature.* New York: Penguin Putnam.

Richards, R. J. (2002). *The Romantic Conception of Life: Science and Philosophy in the Age of Goethe.* Chicago: University of Chicago Press.

Schelling, F. W. J. (1978). *System of Transcendental Idealism* (P. Heath, Trans.). Charlottesville: University Press of Virginia. (Original work published 1800)

Schwartz, J. M., & Begley, S. (2002). *The Mind and the Brain: Neuroplasticity and the Power of Mental Force.* New York: HarperCollins.

Teilhard de Chardin, P. (1959). *The Phenomenon of Man* (B. Wall, Trans.). New York: Harper & Row.

Wilber, K. (1995). *Sex, Ecology, Spirituality: The Spirit of Evolution.* Boston: Shambhala.

Wordsworth, W. (1988). Lines composed a few miles above Tintern Abbey. In Joseph DeRoche (Ed.), *The Heath Introduction to Poetry* (3rd ed.). Lexington, MA: D. C. Heath. (Original work published 1798)

INDEX

ABOUT THE EDITORS AND CONTRIBUTORS

Harald Atmanspacher has been an associate fellow at Collegium Helveticum in Zurich since 2007. He received a PhD in physics at Munich University in 1986 and worked as a research scientist at the Max Planck Institute for Extraterrestrial Physics at Garching until 1998. He then served as head of the theory group at the Institute for Frontier Areas of Psychology and Mental Health in Freiburg until 2013. He is the current president of the Society for Mind–Matter Research and editor-in-chief of the interdisciplinary journal *Mind and Matter*. His areas of research are the theory of complex systems, conceptual and theoretical aspects of (algebraic) quantum theory, and mind–matter relations from interdisciplinary perspectives.

Loriliai Biernacki is Associate Professor in the Department of Religious Studies at the University of Colorado at Boulder. She studied at Princeton University and received her PhD in Religious Studies from the University of Pennsylvania. Dr. Biernacki's research interests include Hinduism, ethics, gender, and the interface between religion and science. Her first book, *Renowned Goddess of Desire: Women, Sex, and Speech in Tantra* (2007), won the Kayden Award in 2008. She is coeditor of *Panentheism across the World's Traditions* (2014). She is currently working on a study on the eleventh-century Indian philosopher Abhinavagupta in relation to wonder, the new materialisms, and ideas of the body and the body–mind interface.

Bernard Carr is Professor of Mathematics and Astronomy at Queen Mary, University of London. He studied for his doctorate under Stephen Hawking at the Institute of Astronomy in Cambridge and the California Institute of Technology. He was elected to a Fellowship at Trinity College, Cambridge, in 1976, took up a Senior Research Fellowship at the Institute of Astronomy in 1980, and moved to Queen Mary in 1985. He has also held visiting professorships at Kyoto University and Tokyo University and is a frequent visitor to institutes in America and Canada. His professional area of research is cosmology and relativistic astrophysics, and includes such topics as the early universe, black holes, dark matter, and the anthropic principle. His recent books are *Universe or Multiverse?* (2007) and *Quantum Black Holes* (2014). He has a long-standing interest in the relationship between science and religion, and especially in psychical research, which he sees as forming a bridge between them. He is Chairman of the Scientific and Medical Network and a former President of the Society for Psychical Research.

Adam Crabtree has been a practicing psychotherapist for forty years, specializing in dissociative identity disorder and the dissociative disorders in general. He has written books in the area of the history of animal magnetism and hypnotism, as well as the history of psychodynamic psychology. Two of his books are *Animal Magnetism, Early Hypnotism, and Psychical Research, 1766–1925: An Annotated Bibliography* (1988) and *From Mesmer to Freud: Magnetic Sleep and the Roots of Psychological Healing* (1993). He has a book in press: *Memoir of a Trance Therapist: Hypnosis and the Evocation of Human Potentials.* He has a special interest in the philosophies of William James and Charles Sanders Peirce. He lives in Toronto and is on the faculty of the Centre for Training in Psychotherapy and the LingYu International Psychology Centre. He is an associate of the Esalen Center for Theory and Research.

Wolfgang Fach is a psychologist and certified psychotherapist. Since 1999 he has worked as a counselor for individuals reporting exceptional experiences and as a research scientist at the Institute for Frontier Areas of Psychology and Mental Health. His research fields are the phenomenology and mental representation of exceptional experiences, with particular emphasis on the role of complementarity within the philosophical framework of dual-aspect monism

Michael Grosso, presently an independent scholar, received his PhD in philosophy from Columbia University where he also studied classical Greek. He has taught humanities and philosophy at Marymount Manhattan College, City University of New York, and City University of New Jersey. He is actively affiliated with the Division of Perceptual Studies at the University of Virginia and on the Board of Directors of the American Philosophical Practitioner's Association, and is a past editor of the Journal for that Association. His published books include *The Final Choice* (1985), *Frontiers of the Soul* (1992), *The Millennium Myth* (1995), *Soulmaking* (1997), *Experiencing the Next World Now* (2004), *Irreducible Mind* (2007, coauthor), and *The Man Who Could Fly: St. Joseph of Copertino and the Mystery of Levitation* (2015).

Edward F. Kelly is currently a Research Professor in the Division of Perceptual Studies (DOPS) at the University of Virginia. He received his PhD in psycholinguistics and cognitive science from Harvard in 1971, and spent the next fifteen-plus years working mainly in parapsychology, initially at J. B. Rhine's Institute for Parapsychology, then for ten years through the Department of Electrical Engineering at Duke, and finally through a private research institute in Chapel Hill. Between 1988 and 2002 he worked with a large neuroscience group at UNC-Chapel Hill, mainly carrying out EEG and fMRI studies of human somatosensory cortical adaptation to natural tactile stimuli. He returned full-time to psychical research in 2002, serving first as lead author of *Irreducible Mind* (2007), and has now returned to his central long-term research interest—application of modern functional neuroimaging methods to intensive psychophysiological studies of psi and ASCs in exceptional subjects (http://cedarcreekinst.org).

Paul Marshall is an independent researcher with interests in mysticism, philosophy and psychology of religion, science–religion relations, and consciousness studies. He read Natural Sciences at the University of Cambridge and received his PhD in Religious Studies from Lancaster University. Dr. Marshall is author of two books, *The Living Mirror: Images of Reality in Science and Mysticism* (1992), and *Mystical Encoun-*

ters with the Natural World: Experiences and Explanations (2005). At present he is completing a third book, in which he looks again at mystical experience and its significance for understanding the relationship between self and world, and explores evolutionary spirituality in a universe based on Leibniz's metaphysics.

Michael Murphy is cofounder and Chairman Emeritus of Esalen Institute, and now serves as director of its Center for Theory and Research (CTR). He is the author of four novels and several non-fiction works: *In the Zone* (1995), an anthology of extraordinary sports experiences, coauthored with Rhea White; *The Life We Are Given* (1995), a book about transformative practice, coauthored with George Leonard; *The Physical and Psychological Effects of Meditation* (1988), coauthored with Steve Donovan; *God and the Evolving Universe* (2002), coauthored with James Redfield and Sylvia Timbers; and *The Future of the Body* (1992), a large-scale study of human capacities for transformation. In the 1980s he helped organize Esalen's pioneering Soviet-American Exchange Program, which became a premiere vehicle for citizen-to-citizen relations between Russians and Americans, and in recent years he has helped foster the program of long-term integral transformative practices (ITP) he founded with George Leonard.

David E. Presti is a neurobiologist and cognitive scientist at the University of California in Berkeley, where he has taught in the Molecular and Cell Biology, Cognitive Science, and Psychology programs for more than twenty years. For more than a decade (1990–2000) he also worked in the clinical treatment of addiction and of post-traumatic-stress disorder (PTSD) at the Department of Veterans Affairs Medical Center in San Francisco. His areas of expertise include the chemistry of the human nervous system, the effect of drugs on the brain and mind, and the neuroscience of consciousness. He has doctorates in molecular biology and biophysics from the California Institute of Technology and in clinical psychology from the University of Oregon. Since 2004, he has been teaching neuroscience to Tibetan monastics in India, part of a dialogue between science and religion initiated by the Dalai Lama.

Gregory Shaw is Professor of Religious Studies at Stonehill College, Massachusetts. He received his PhD in Religious Studies from UC Santa

Barbara in 1987. He is the author of *Theurgy and the Soul: The Neoplatonism of Iamblichus* (1995, 2014) and a number of articles on the later Neoplatonists and on Iamblichus in particular. He is currently working on a manuscript that explores the embodied aspects of later Platonic philosophy and its similarity to the tantric traditions of South Asia. The theurgical Platonism of Iamblichus presents a radically nondual vision that defined the Platonic tradition from the late third to the sixth century CE. It was an embodied Platonism very much at odds with the dualism that has been identified with Platonic philosophy.

Henry P. Stapp received his PhD working under Nobel Laureates Emilio Segrè and Owen Chamberlain. His thesis work is the basis of our current understanding of the low-energy properties of the nucleon–nucleon system. He has worked closely with the founders of quantum mechanics Werner Heisenberg and Wolfgang Pauli, and with John Wheeler, and less closely with David Bohm. He has written extensively in journals, compendiums, and edited books about the foundations of quantum mechanics, and about the issue of faster-than-light transfers of information arising from the works of A. Einstein and John Bell, and about the basic issue of free choices, which are forbidden by classical mechanics but are a key element of quantum mechanics. He is the author of three books on these topics: *Mind, Matter, and Quantum Mechanics* (1993); *Mindful Universe: Quantum Mechanics and the Participating Observer* (2007); and *On the Nature of Things: Human Presence in the World of Atoms* (forthcoming).

Eric M. Weiss, MFT, received his PhD in Philosophy, Cosmology, and Consciousness from the California Institute of Integral Studies in 2003. His dissertation was entitled "The Doctrine of the Subtle Worlds: Sri Aurobindo's Cosmology, Modern Science, and the Metaphysics of Alfred North Whitehead." Prior to that, Dr. Weiss studied and taught Tibetan Buddhist practices for seven years under the direction of Chögyam Trungpa, Rinpoche. He has been on the faculty of CIIS and the Sophia Center at Holy Names University. He is also a distinguished scholar at the Esalen Center for Theory and Research, where he is engaged in the study of reincarnation and the survival of bodily death by the personality. He has recently published a book entitled *The Long Trajectory: The Metaphysics of Reincarnation and Life After Death* (2012).

Ian Whicher is a Canadian and earned his PhD from the University of Cambridge. A long-time Yoga practitioner, Dr. Whicher is a Professor and Head of the Department of Religion at the University of Manitoba in Winnipeg, Canada. He specializes in approaches to spiritual liberation in India and the Yoga tradition, and is the author of several books and articles including *The Integrity of the Yoga Darśana* (1998), and coeditor of *Yoga: The Indian Tradition* (2003). Dr. Whicher is currently writing a book on *The Yoga of Intelligence* and is frequently invited to speak at conferences, public venues, and workshops throughout the world.

Made in the USA
Monee, IL
09 December 2023

48624581R00351